W9-AUG-132

Aging in Contemporary Canada

neena chappell university of victoria

ellen gee simon fraser university

lynn mcdonald university of toronto

michael stones lakehead university

Prentice
Hall

Toronto

We thank our families and friends for their love and support.

National Library of Canada Cataloguing in Publication

Main entry under title:

Aging in contemporary Canada / Neena Chappell... [et al.].

Includes bibliographical references and index.

ISBN 0-13-093752-5

1. Aging—Canada. 2. Gerontology—Canada. I. Chappell, Neena L.

HQ1064.C2A375 2003 305.26'0971 C2002-902262-2

Copyright © 2003 Pearson Education Canada Inc., Toronto, Ontario

All Rights Reserved. This publication is protected by copyright, and permission should be obtained from the publisher prior to any prohibited reproduction, storage in a retrieval system, or transmission in any form or by any means, electronic, mechanical, photocopying, recording, or likewise. For information regarding permission, write to the Permissions Department.

Statistics Canada information is used with the permission of the Minister of Industry, as Minister responsible for Statistics Canada. Information on the availability of the wide range of data from Statistics Canada can be obtained from Statistic Canada's Regional Offices, its World Wide Web site at www.statcan.ca, and its toll-free access number 1-800-263-1136.

Chapter opener photo credits:

Chapter 1, David Young-Wolff / Getty Images; Chapter 2, Steve Smith / Getty Images; Chapter 3, CP (Fred Chartrand); Chapter 4, Ian Shaw / Getty Images; Chapter 5, CP (Whitehorse Star – Chuck Tobin); Chapter 6, Comstock Royalty Free; Chapter 7, Steve Meltzer / First Light.ca; Chapter 8, Kerri Picket / Getty Images; Chapter 9, Comstock Royalty Free; Chapter 10, Photodisc / Getty Images; Chapter 11, Comstock Royalty Free; Chapter 12, Comstock Royalty Free; Chapter 13, Piecework Productions / Getty Images; Chapter 14, Adam Hinton / Getty Images; Chapter 15, Bruce Ayres / Getty Images; Chapter 16, Jerry Gay / Getty Images.

ISBN 0-13-093752-5

Vice President, Editorial Director: Michael J. Young
Senior Acquisitions Editor: Jessica Mosher
Marketing Manager: Judith Allen
Signing Representative: Katherine McWhirter
Developmental Editor: John Polanszky
Production Editor: Cheryl Jackson
Copy Editor: Rohini Herbert
Proofreader: Laurel Sparrow
Permissions Manager: Susan Wallace-Cox
Photo Researcher: Christina Beamish
Production Manager: Wendy Moran
Page Layout: Carolyn E. Sebestyen
Art Director: Mary Opper
Cover Design: Jennifer Federico
Cover Image: Raechel Running/Firstlight.ca

3 4 5 DPC 06 05 04

Printed and bound in Canada

Contents

PART V POLICY

Preface

Aging in Contemporary Canada is written from a social psychological perspective by authors who specialize in sociology and psychology. Instead of taking a biological or physiological perspective, it focuses on individuals and their social worlds. The book has been organized into five parts, outlined below.

Part I: Introduction to Gerontology

Chapters 1 to 3 provide students with an overview and explanation of what gerontology is, how we theorize about aging, and how we measure aging so that it can be studied. A description of the aging of the population in Canada and elsewhere is discussed in Chapter 1. Various definitions of aging, including the construction of age 65 as the entry point for old age, are examined. Chapter 2 explains the theoretical foundations of gerontology, and how thinking within the field has evolved over time. Research and the research process are the focus of Chapter 3. The key principles of the scientific method are reviewed, and a number of quantitative and qualitative methodologies are discussed.

Part II: Commonality and Diversity

In Part II, the focus of the text shifts to the commonalities and diversity found in later life, with an emphasis on gender, ethno-cultural communities, and attitudes. Chapter 4 examines the gendered life course, looking at how many gender differences begin early in life and continue throughout the life course. Cultural diversity within the context of aging, and the importance of race and ethnicity to an understanding of aging are the central themes of Chapter 5. This leads to a discussion of attitudes and aging in Chapter 6. Attitudes toward violence, abuse, and sexuality are highlighted, revealing how many societal stereotypes are inconsistent with the realities of aging.

Part III: Health and Well Being

Physical, mental, cognitive, and overall health aspects of aging are covered in Part III. The physical aspects of aging are discussed in Chapter 7, examining athletes as a means of understanding age changes in physical aspects of the body. Chapter 8 deals with mental well being and mental disorder within the population aged 65 and over. The focus is on happiness, which seems to vary little over the life course. Chapter 9 looks at aging and cognition, establishing that not all memory changes associated with aging are negative. The discussion then turns to personality, with a focus on aspects of personality that are stable throughout our lives, compared with those that change. Chapter 10 provides a general exploration of health, distinguishing between health and illness: Health includes both physiological well being and overall well being, while sickness includes both disease and illness.

Part IV: Social Institutions

Part IV looks at some major social institutions—the family, the workplace, and social support networks—and the effects these have on the process of aging. Chapter 11 discusses families and aging, including the changes that are evident in contemporary family structures. Chapter 12 focuses on work and retirement, including a discussion of the flexible nature of retirement at the beginning of the twenty-first century. Chapter 13 examines social support and caregiving, its importance for well being and quality of life, and its critical role for seniors as their health declines.

Part V: Policy

The final section of this book examines three areas that have special relevance for policies that affect us as we age: pensions and economic security, health care, and end-of-life issues. Chapter 14 looks at the development of the pension system in Canada, what it looks like today, and what direction the future may hold. Because socio-economic status is a major correlate of one's health in old age, economic security takes on special importance. Chapter 15 discusses the Canadian health care system and health care policy, including current attempts at health reform. Chapter 16 concludes the text with a focus on end-of-life issues, a tremendously important topic that has not received very much attention from researchers to date. During this period in our history, most Canadians can expect to live well past age 65, to have a prolonged dying process prior to death, and to leave behind loved ones who must cope with their absence.

Our hope is that *Aging in Contemporary Canada* conveys an accurate picture of the most current knowledge available about aging from a social psychological perspective, and that this will stimulate students' interest in aging. Every effort has been made to include the most current demographic and census data available at the time of writing. Each chapter also offers Learning Objectives, a Chapter Summary, a list of Key Terms, and Study Questions. These features are designed to help students develop a deeper and more critical understanding of the topics covered. We have also included numerous boxes throughout the text that feature articles, stories, or information that help bring to life and more fully illustrate many of the most important issues related to aging. The relevance of aging, both personally and societally, will not wane, so it is important to understand all aspects of it to ensure quality of life and care throughout the aging process.

Acknowledgments

We would all like to thank the staff at Pearson Education Canada for their professional assistance. They have been helpful without being intrusive. They have kept us on appropriate timelines without being unrealistic. And they have been responsive to our needs and demands.

We would also like to thank the staff at the University of Victoria's Centre on Aging for assistance at every step of the long process of getting a book together. In particular, Lindsay Cassie and Tracey Hanton's skills and hard work ensured this book came to fruition.

Neena Chappell: I would like to thank Michael and Kristen Barnes for their supportive acceptance of my many work commitments, including the undertaking of this book and for their living proof of the social perspective. As well, many friends and colleagues challenge my thinking and support my endeavours.

Ellen Gee: Thanks to Jeanne Persoon for secretarial assistance and Gloria Gutman for help with proofreading. I am grateful for the support of my husband, Gordie, my daughter, Adrienne, and my mother, Margaret Thomas.

Lynn McDonald: Thanks to Joanne Daciuk, Julie Dergal and Ron Jockheck for research assistance and the Faculties of Social Work at the University of Toronto and Calgary for their support. I would also like to acknowledge my family for their continual encouragement.

Mike Stones: I would like to thank my wife, Lee, for supporting and putting up with me during the long hours spent writing this book. To my research collaborator, Al Kozma, recently retired from Memorial University. We, the three of us, made a great team and together learned a lot about aging. To Sister Angela Fowler, Dr. Len Foley, Dick McNiven, Nettie Russell, and Dr. Gracie Sparkes, who showed me how to age well.

Introduction

Aging is an important issue in contemporary society in terms of both our own selves and the people who are significant in our lives. We all age. We age physiologically, socially, psychologically, and emotionally. We change over time. The experience of aging—how we age—varies over time and from society to society. At the turn of the twentieth century in Canada, we could expect to die much younger than at the turn of the twenty-first century. Currently in Canada, virtually everyone, barring accidental death or death due to violence, can expect to live a long life—well into their sixties, seventies, eighties or beyond. This is historically unique—never before has this been true for society as a whole. Now, in industrialized societies, reaching at least age 65 (see Chapter 1 for a detailed discussion of the demographics and definitions of old age) has become the norm. Some developing countries are rapidly approaching this position as well. Those who are currently elderly in Canadian society are the first cohort to have achieved this distinction, where the vast majority of their peers reach old age. This means that middle-aged adults, by and large, have parents who are still alive and children who know their grandparents. More and more young children know their *great* grandparents. When children today look ahead, they can expect to live well into old age. What sort of meaning will this profound change have on society as a whole?

For Canadians, the aging of individuals and of the population is occurring within a culture that metaphorically searches for the fountain of youth, values youth, and associates vitality with youth. Despite the increase in the group of individuals who are now elderly, agist stereotypes and attitudes prevail. The reasons for this are speculative. As an individualistic and capitalistic society, Canada places emphasis on individuals who are visibly contributing to the economy. Unlike more collectivist societies in which, historically, seniors are valued, respected, and considered wise, Canada's seniors are viewed as no longer productive because they are, by and large, retired. Within Canada, traditional Aboriginal societies tend to value elders more than mainstream society; similarly, immigrant groups originating in non-Western societies tend to place a higher value on older people than does the host society.

The outward or visible signs of biological aging are undeniable. Long before the age of 65, the body shows signs of aging: grey hair, baldness, wrinkles, decreasing agility, etc. As Australian sociologist Turner (1995) points out, we age socially largely because of the body's visible aging. Phenomenologically, the inner self, or the subjective self (variously referred to as the spirit, the internal, the soul), remains useful, evolves, grows, and becomes wiser as we age. There is a disjuncture between the inner self and the external self. Modern Western society sees the physiological body, the external, and generalizes to the internal, producing what Turner refers to as the **paradox of aging**—a visibly deteriorated outer body coexisting in most cases with a vibrant, mature, and wise inner self. Biological aging is seen negatively as deterioration. The difficulty for seniors is that biological, visible change is then assumed to be associated with decline in the subjective sense of the inner self. Aging within Western society, then, is often a search to try to at least prevent, if not reverse, deterioration of the body with much less attention paid to the nurturing of one's subjective self. The huge growth in cosmetic surgery attests to our preoccupation with fighting the visible signs of aging.

Aging has relevance for social institutions, from the family, to the educational system, to the social system including retirement, health care, recreation, etc. Families look different today than they did before: They are less likely to lose young people to death, and more generations are alive at the same time. Retirement, instituted just over 100 years ago in Germany, is now undergoing important changes including much greater flexibility in its timing and form (part-time, full-time, contract work, etc). As we hear in the news daily, our health care system is under attack as increasingly unaffordable. While this is popularly attributed to the aging of the population, there is good reason to believe that the aging of the population itself will make only minor demands (one to two percent per year) when the baby boom generation enters old age. Nevertheless, declining health is an important matter as we age, and all Canadians want a health care system that is appropriate to meet their needs. As the awareness grows that health includes more than sickness and treatment, interest in alternative forms of health care (including recreation and healthy lifestyles) is burgeoning. Overall, the relationship between social institutions, population, and individual aging is reciprocal. That is, the aging of the population affects society's institutions, but these institutions also affect the experience of aging.

While academics often identify trends, and therefore focus on commonalities, it is important to understand that there is tremendous diversity in the aging experience. There are important differences by gender, for example. Not only do women live longer than men, but the aging experience is also very different for women. For example, older women are far more likely to live alone, be poor, and be institutionalized in later life. Similarly, aging varies, depending on whether or not you are a member of a minority ethno-cultural group and, if so, of which group. Furthermore, aging differs depending on whether you are a member of that ethno-cultural group within Canada or in your homeland. For example, aging as an elderly Chinese woman in Canada is different from aging as an elderly Chinese woman in Shanghai.

There are also differences depending on whether a person is rich or poor. Despite the existence of universal health care in Canada (covering physician services and hospital care), older persons with money can afford to hire other types of assistance as well. They can afford better housing, and they can afford luxuries such as spending time in warmer climates if they desire. Also, socio-economic status is a strong correlate of health: Those who are poor experience worse health in old age. There are also variations in terms of where a person lives within Canada. Aging in rural areas is distinct from aging in urban areas: Aging in the harsh winters of Winnipeg is different from aging in the Niagara peninsula or Victoria.

The aging experience also varies depending on one's social embeddedness—some seniors are surrounded by family and friends with strong social ties, whereas others live a more isolated (although not necessarily lonely) existence, interacting with a few close friends within a smaller social circle. While seniors share much with one another by virtue of their age, there is also tremendous diversity within this age group that spans over three decades (that is, from the age of 65 to over 95).

Aging at both personal and societal levels is constantly evolving. In recent years, increased globalization has had a significant impact on Canadian society. Numerous technological advances, such as the Internet, and economic initiatives, such as the adoption of the North American Free Trade Agreement (NAFTA), have had a profound effect upon Canadian social policy. The long-term impact of these changes is still uncertain. For example, one viewpoint suggests that the "technological imperative," rather than the needs of the people, is increasingly what drives health care. A contrasting perspective believes that technology allows for improved health that would otherwise not be possible. The rapid changes taking place in societies worldwide also often mean that seniors can be perceived as obsolete. However, there is tremendous diversity among seniors in computer use, computer ownership, and use of the Internet. Since they are primarily not members of the paid labour force, seniors have fewer demands on them to learn this new technology. Some are interested in learning these new skills and can afford to, while others cannot.

Globalization also brings with it increased diversity, including ethnic diversity. Canada has become increasingly heterogeneous in its ethnic composition, especially over the last 20 years. In part, this is due to the increasing global mobility of labour. The movement of refugees—often displaced by globalization and related instabilities—plays a role as well. Increasing ethnic diversity has numerous consequences. It means that we have the opportunity to learn more directly about other cultural perspectives. It also means that social services need to become more sensitive to cultural differences and more accessible to persons not fluent in an official language. This has direct and immediate implications for health and social services for elders.

A major issue for gerontology is that many policy changes (such as changes to the Canadian welfare state) are driven by global economic needs, but seniors, by and large, are not active members of the labour force. Consequently, their needs tend not to be taken into account. There has also been a politicization of aging at both the societal and individual levels. Individuals have become much more aware of the institutions that affect them within society, and of the reasons why politicians make the policies and policy changes they do. Similarly, at the societal level, population aging has been used as a reason for social reform. We have heard that the pension system has to be re-organized or the baby boomers will bankrupt the system when they are old. Almost identical words are used in discussions of the health care system. As we will see, these issues are far more complicated than these simplistic charges would suggest.

The issue of aging ultimately encompasses all of the diversity and variability of human society itself. The complex interaction of psychological, sociological, economic and political factors is what makes the study of the aging individual in a social context so fascinating. As Canadian society evolves and changes, meeting the many new challenges of the twenty-first century, so too does our understanding of and approach to aging. One can only hope that with every new question raised, a greater appreciation of elderly persons and of old age as an integral part of society is achieved.

Population Aging

In this chapter, you will learn about:

- A number of different ways population aging can be measured.
- Statistics on the aging of the Canadian population since the end of the 19th century, and its variation over time.
- The major cause of population aging (which is declining fertility, rather than declining mortality).
- Epidemiological transition theory and its concern with changes in the causes of death as mortality declines.
- The major causes of death among elderly Canadians.

- "Compression of morbidity," a debated topic that posits that more and more people will live in a healthy state until just before their death.
- Gender differentials in life expectancy.
- The place of immigrants among the senior population in Canada.
- Provincial variation in age structures.
- Migration among seniors.
- Apocalyptic demography, which refers to the view that demographic change— in this case, population aging—can have highly negative consequences for a society.

Introduction

Demography (a subfield within sociology and economics) studies the characteristics of population and the dynamics of population change. One important aspect of a population is its age structure (sometimes also called age composition). The Canadian age structure is getting older; indeed, if this were not so, it is unlikely that books such as this would be written or that you would be taking a course in gerontology, which is the study of aging and the aged. While the demographic fact of population aging is central to gerontology, very few gerontologists are demographers. Typically, gerontologists take the demographics of aging for granted—or, at best, treat it as a backdrop to or justification for the phenomena that they study—and others do research on demographic change per se. While this division of labour works quite well, it is, nevertheless, important for beginning students of gerontology to have a basic understanding of the demography of aging.

In this chapter, we first look at the extent to which aging has occurred and is expected to occur in the Canadian population, and how Canada compares with other countries. We then turn our attention to the demographic processes that lead to population aging. This is followed by a discussion of the characteristics of the aged population in Canada. Next, we examine causes of death in relation to lowering mortality. The chapter ends with a discussion of apocalyptic demography—the exaggeration of the consequences of population change in general and population aging in particular.

Assessing Population Aging

Assessing the degree to which a population is aged or aging depends upon the measurement that is used. Thus, a brief examination of three measures of population aging follows. [1]

Percentage Aged 65+

The most common measure of population aging is the percentage of the population that is aged 65 years and over. (See Box 1.1 for a discussion of age 65 years as the entry point for old age.) By rule of thumb, a population in which at least 10 percent of the population is aged 65 years and over is deemed to be old. Canada is, therefore, considered to have an old population because 12.3 percent of our population was aged 65 years and over in 1998 (Statistics Canada, 1999a).

The percentage of the population that is aged 65 years and over is a simple and easily understood indicator of population aging—as the percentage increases, the population is aging. However, it does have limitations. It implies that populations with the same percentage aged 65 years and over have identical age structures, but that is not necessarily the case. As pointed out by McDaniel (1986), the populations may have very different proportions of children, youth, and working-

---

Box 1.1 Why Is Age 65 Years the Entry Point for Old Age?

There is no logical reason why age 65 years is now considered to mark the commencement of old age. This age marker has been socially constructed, and it could just as easily be any other age. In order to understand this social construction, a little history is helpful. In the late 1800s, Otto Von Bismarck, on the basis of advice from actuarial consultants, chose 65 years as the age at which his military personnel would be eligible to receive pension benefits. This decision was based on two factors. First, Bismarck believed that the promise of a pension would increase the loyalty and productivity of his employees. Second, making the age of pension eligibility 65 years would not be costly to Bismarck's coffers since the mortality levels of the time meant that most of his employees would likely die before that age or shortly after! After this initial demarcation of the entry point for old age, the age of 65 years gradually became the norm, institutionalized first in a number of private pension plans and later in government pensions and other policies. It is noteworthy that the social construction of age 65 years as the starting point of old age had nothing to do with the characteristics of people and everything to do with meeting the needs of employers, both as a benefit to retain employees and as a way to be rid of older and more highly paid workers. Given increases in life expectancy and improvements in health, there is no reason why age 65 years will continue to be the socially defined entry point to old age. Canadian demographers Denton and Spencer (in press) foresee that age 70 years will gradually come to replace age 65 years.

---

age adults. This measure also homogenizes the aged, implying that all persons aged 65 years are the same; however, there are tremendous differences, on average, between people aged 65 years or so and those aged 90 years and over, for example. In recognition of this, Neugarten (1974) made the following categorization of the senior population: the young-old (aged 65 to 74 years), the middle-old (aged 75 to 84 years), the old-old (aged 85 to 89 years) and the frail-old (aged 90 years and over). These distinctions, which are commonly used by gerontologists, help de-homogenize seniors, but it must be remembered that a considerable amount of variation across people exists even within these more age-delimited categories. For example, people aged 75 years range from the very rich to the very poor, from the hale and hearty to the frail, from those living alone to those living in multigenerational households, from the fluent in English or French to recent immigrants with no facility with an official language, and so on.

Median Age

Another single measure of population aging is the **median age of the population**. The median age is the age at which one-half of the population is older and one-half is younger. As the median age increases, the population is considered to be aging. In Canada, the median age is now 36.8 years (Statistics Canada, 2000). Usually, demographers consider a population with a median age of 30 years to be "old"; therefore, by this measure as well, the Canadian population falls into the old category. However, the relationship between the two measures—median age and the percentage of the population aged 65 years and over—is far from perfect. As discussed by McDaniel (1986), the rankings of populations by the two measures can differ; for example, a population that ranks the oldest by one of these measures will not necessarily rank the oldest by another measure.

Dependency Ratios

A number of age **dependency ratios** can be used to assess population age structure. All dependency ratios share in their attempt to measure the relative proportion of persons of "dependent" ages within a population and in viewing dependent age groups as a social burden. Regarding this last point, dependency ratios are sometimes called "dependency burden"; this is less common now than in the past, but this shift does not reflect a fundamental perceptual change. Rather, it merely signals an increased sensitivity to the use of pejorative terminology when referring to groups of people.

The most frequently used dependency ratios take the total population in the "working ages" of 15 (or 18) to 64 years, that is, the age range in which most people find paid employment, as the nondependent ages. Using the total population aged 15 (or 18) years as the denominator, three dependency ratios are calculated: an **aged dependency ratio**, a **youth dependency ratio**, and a **total dependency ratio**. The aged dependency ratio is the number of persons aged 65 years and over as a ratio of the number of persons aged 15 to 64 (or 18 to 64) years. In 2000, the aged dependency ratio in Canada was 183; that is, there were 183 elders for every 1,000 persons aged 15 to 64 years. The youth dependency ratio is the number of persons aged 0 to 15 (or 0 to 18) years relative to the population aged 15 to 64 (or 18 to 64) years. In 2000, the youth dependency ratio in Canada was 279; that is, there were 279 children aged 0 to 14 years for every 1,000 persons aged 15 to 64 years. The aged dependency ratio and the youth dependency ratio can be combined to form the total dependency ratio—the total dependent population (the old and the young) relative to the population considered to be nondependent. In 2000, the total dependency ratio in Canada was 462 (183 + 279) persons for every 1,000 persons in the nondependent ages.

A second type of dependency ratio uses the population aged 15 (or 18) years that is in the paid labour force as the denominator and again involves the calculation of aged, youth, and total dependency ratios. Since the denominator is smaller (i.e., not everyone aged 15 to 64 years is in the paid labour force), each of the three dependency ratios (aged, youth, and total) is larger.

Another type of dependency ratio is the ratio of the number of persons aged 65 years and over to those aged less than 15 years. In 2000, in Canada, this ratio was 656 (i.e., there were 656 elders for every 1,000 children aged below 15 years). As an overall measure of population aging, this ratio is superior to the others mentioned above. As we will see in a later section of this chapter, fertility (the number of children born) and mortality (deaths in a population) are key demographic processes in population aging. This ratio captures the persons closest to fertility (the young) and mortality (the old) and, thus, is a better measure of population "age" than the previous dependency ratios.

Yet another type of dependency ratio is the **familial old-age dependency ratio** (Kart & Kinney, 2001). It is the ratio of the number of elderly parents (population aged 65 to 84 years) to the children who would support them (population aged 45 to 54 years). This ratio is taken as a proxy for the dependency burden of middle-aged children, although it is recognized that not all persons aged 65 to 84 years need support from their children or have children, and that not all children are able or willing to provide support to elderly parents. The familial old-age dependency ratio in Canada was 787 in 2000; that is, there were 787 older parents for every 1,000 persons in the ages likely to be their children. All dependency ratios contain a problematic assumption regarding older people, that is, that they are all economically dependent. This assumption ignores a number of realities, such as that some older people are members of the paid labour force; many older people pay taxes and contribute to the general economy in that way; and many older people are engaged in unpaid labour (as volunteers, as caregivers to spouses and/or grandchildren, for example), which contributes much to the Canadian economy. Dependency ratios also carry difficult-to-justify assumptions regarding other age groups. For example, not all people of working age are economically independent; the work of homemakers is not considered when the dependency ratio is calculated on the basis of the paid labour force; children can contribute in a variety of ways to the family economy. The fundamental problem, then, is the making of a simplistic equivalence between age and economic productivity. Another criticism of dependency ratios is their narrow conceptualization of economic usefulness as tied only to paid labour.

Canada's Aging Population

We now look at how the Canadian population has aged over the last 150 years and how it is expected to age in the coming decades. Figure 1.1 presents data on the percentage of the population aged 65 years and over from 1881 to 2036.[2] It can be observed that our population has been aging continuously over the entire period; in other words, population aging is not new. However, certain time periods have experienced more rapid aging than others. Clearly, the decades to come will experience a large increase in the proportion of the population aged 65 years and over. This increase is a direct result of the aging of the baby boomers—the large cohort of persons born between 1946 and 1962—who will begin entering traditionally defined old age (i.e., age 65 years) in 2011. Between then and 2027—when the youngest baby boomers turn age 65 years—the ranks of the older population will grow substantially. The effect of the baby boom on the percentage of the population aged 65 years and over will gradually dissipate; by 2050, even most of the youngest boomers will be dead.

It is also important to note that the senior population is itself aging; that is, there is an increasing number and percentage of persons who are aged 80 years and over. In 2000, there were approximately 910,000 Canadians aged 80 years and over, making up 3 percent of the total population. In 1981, the comparable percentage was 2.4 percent, and in 1961, it was 1.4 percent. In fact, the population aged 80 years and over is proportionately the fastest growing age segment in Canada.

Canadian Population Aging in Comparative Perspective

Approximately 7 percent of the world's population is aged 65 years and over, with a sharp division between more developed and less developed nations. The youngest populations occur in Africa; the oldest populations are in Europe. With 12 percent of our population aged 65 years and over, the Canadian population is, comparatively speaking, quite old. However, many European nations are substantially older than Canada. For example, Sweden, Belgium, Italy, and Greece all have 17 percent of their populations aged 65 years and over; and the figure is 16 percent in France, Germany, Spain, and the United Kingdom (Population Reference Bureau, 2001) (Table 1.1). In

Figure 1.1   PROPORTION OF PEOPLE AGED 65 YEARS AND OVER IN THE TOTAL POPULATION, CANADA, 1881-2036

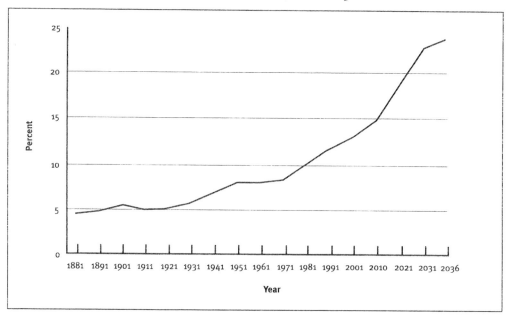

Source: Desjardins, Bernard. 1993. Population Ageing and the Elderly. Ottawa: Statistics Canada Catalogue No. 91-533E, page 13.

Table 1.1   PERCENTAGE OF POPULATION AGED 65 YEARS AND OVER,
BY REGION: CIRCA 2001

REGION	PERCENTAGE
World	7
More Developed Countries	14
Less Developed Countries	5
Africa	3
Asia	6
Europe	14
Latin America (and Caribbean)	5
North America	13

Source: Population Reference Bureau (2001).

contrast, the percentage aged 65 years and over is as low as 2 percent in Niger and Uganda in Africa and Bhutan in South Central Asia.

So far, we have been considering relative proportions only; absolute numbers are also important to take into account. The number of older persons in the continent with the greatest proportion of old people, Europe (including Russia) totals approximately 102 million; in Asia, the 6 percent figure translates into approximately 221 million elderly persons. India alone, with only 4 percent of its population aged 65 years and over, contains about 44.1 million elders—almost 10 million more people than the total population of Canada (Population Reference Bureau, 2001). Thus, the developed and developing worlds face different age structure issues. In the North, we are dealing with a relatively high proportion of the seniors, compared with other age groups; in the South (or the Third World), the issue is one of a large and growing number of older persons, although they do not constitute a large fraction of the overall population. To the degree that elderly people require special resources (and only some do), the North faces a relatively smaller proportion of working-age people to support them. Southern countries, in contrast, are concerned about the sheer numbers of older persons who do or might need support.

What Causes Populations To Age?

The Important Role of Fertility

Why is it that developed countries, such as Canada, have an age structure that is so much older than that in developing countries? The answer may surprise you: the main factor accounting for population aging is declining fertility, as established by noted American demographer Ansley Coale (1956) nearly 50 years ago. As fertility declines, the number and proportion of children in a population decline. As that occurs, the proportion of older people increases, by default. In "youthful" Africa, the total fertility rate (the average number of children born to a woman by the end of her childbearing years) is 5.3; in "old" Europe, the comparable figure is 1.4 (the Canadian total fertility rate is 1.5) (Population Reference Bureau, 2001).

The reason why Canada (as well as the United States) has a younger population than most European countries is because we had a large and long baby boom after World War II, as noted above. The immediate effect of this boom was to increase the proportion of children and then young adults in our population, that is, to "young" our population. However, because the baby boom was followed by declining—and now low—fertility rates, its ultimate consequence has been only to delay population aging.

Although declining fertility is key to population aging, gerontologists have not devoted much attention to it as a research topic (although family size and number of children is studied by gerontologists in another guise—in relation to aging families and social support, as shown in Chapters 11 and 12). Fertility levels and trends have been, and remain, the purview of demographers, who have identified a number of factors that acted as important causes of fertility decline in the West—for example, urbanization and the declining value and increased costs of children in cities; the decline of the family wage and the consequent increase in women's labour force participation; increasing levels of education, particularly for women; the women's movement; increasingly available and effective means to control reproduction (e.g., Balakrishnan, Lapierre-Adamcyk, & Krotki, 1993; Ford & Nault 1996; Matthews, 1999). Apart from academic specialization, one reason why gerontologists have not studied fertility is that fertility becomes less predictive of population aging as mortality becomes lower. As discussed by Friedlander and Kinov-Malul (1980), after a population reaches a life expectancy at birth of 70 years, almost all young people survive; thus, any further declines in mortality are concentrated at older ages. These declines translate into relatively more growth in the older age groups and, therefore, population aging.

Population Pyramids

It is common to represent age structures graphically by what are termed **population pyramids**; these illustrate the proportion of males and females in each age group (usually five-year age groups up to the older ages, where there is aggregation due to small numbers) in a population. There are three "ideal types" of pyramids: (1) expansive pyramids, which have a broad base (and look most like pyramids), reflecting a high proportion of children in the population, the result of high past and present fertility levels; (2) constrictive pyramids—where the base is somewhat narrower than the middle, and which occurs when fertility has been rapidly declining: and (3) stationary pyramids, which have a narrow base and approximately equal percentages of people in each age group, tapering off at older ages and which are the result of a lengthy period of low fertility. Figure 1.2 presents Canadian population pyramids for selected years from 1881 to 2036. We can see that in 1881, the Canadian age structure was expansive, reflecting high fertility that had not yet begun to decline; decreases in fertility are evident in the 1921 pyramid, as the base of the pyramid is narrowing; continuing constriction is interrupted by the baby boom, the beginnings of which can be observed in the 1951 pyramid; in 1991, the pyramid has taken on the classic characteristics of the constrictive type as a result of the significant decline in fertility that commenced in the mid-1960s; and the future pyramids in 2011 and 2036 increasingly take on the stationary shape.

Mortality Decline

While declines in fertility are the major cause of population aging, decreases in mortality (deaths) are important as well. This is more intuitive; because we associate population aging with more older people, we automatically equate population aging with higher life expectancy (the flip side of lower mortality). **Life expectancy** refers to the number of years that persons in a given country/population can expect to live. Conceptually, life expectancy is virtually identical to longevity; the difference between them lies in measurement issues. Life expectancy is calculated in a very strict way, using what is termed life table analysis (see Box 1.2); longevity is not associated with any particular statistical technique. Both life expectancy and longevity are distinct from life span, which refers to the number of years that humans could live under ideal conditions.[3]

Table 1.2 shows trends in life expectancy at birth and at age 65 years for the period from 1921 (when Canada began a national system of death registration) to 1996. We can see that life expectancy increased steadily over the course of the 20th century. The major gains in life expectancy at birth were made in the earlier part of the period. For example; from 1921 to 1961, life expectancy at birth increased 10 years for males and nearly 14 years for females. Over this same period, life expectancy at age 65 years increased a mere 0.6 years for men and 2.5 years for women. However, after 1961, life expectancy at age 65 years increased dramatically. These trends indicate that young Canadians were the first to benefit from mortality reductions; it was only later that longevity in later life increased appreciably. This is the typical experience of the developed countries.

It is not known whether life expectancy will continue to increase as we move through the 21st century, and, indeed, this is a subject of a fair amount of debate. Part of the debate concerns the length of the human life span. Some (e.g., Fries, 1983; National Institute on Aging, 1996) argue that Western populations are approaching a biologically fixed maximum or finite life span—probably in the

Figure 1.2 AGE PYRAMIDS, CANADA, 1881–2036

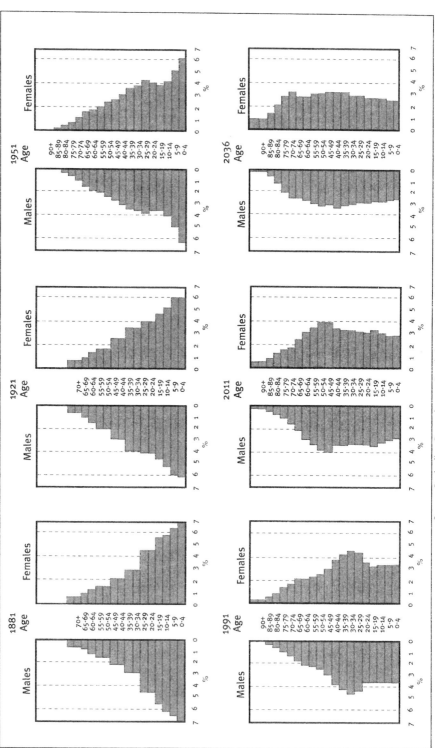

Source: Desjardins, Bernard. 1993. Population Ageing and the Elderly. Ottawa: Statistics Canada Catalogue No. 91-533E, page 18.

Box 1.2 Measuring Life Expectancy

Life expectancy is a summary measure of mortality in a population. Statistics on life expectancy are derived from a mathematical model known as a life table. Life tables create a hypothetical cohort (or group) of 100,000 persons (usually of males and females separately) and subject it to the age-gender-specific mortality rates (the number of deaths per 1,000 or 10,000 or 100,000 persons of a given age and gender) observed in a given population. In doing this, we can trace how, say, the 100,000 hypothetical persons (called a synthetic cohort) would shrink in numbers due to deaths as they age. The average age at which these persons are likely to have died is the life expectancy at birth. Life tables also provide data on life expectancy at other ages; the most commonly used statistic other than life expectancy at birth is life expectancy at age 65 years, that is, the number of remaining years of life that persons aged 65 years can expect to live.

   Life expectancy statistics are very useful as summary measures of mortality, and they have an intuitive appeal that other measures of mortality, such as rates, lack. However, it is important to interpret data on life expectancy correctly. If it is reported that life expectancy at birth in a given population is 75 years in 2000, this does not mean that all members of the population can expect to live to the age of 75 years. Rather, it means that babies born in that population in 2000 would have a life expectancy at birth of 75 years, if they live their lives subject to the age-specific mortality rates of the entire population in 2000. This is not likely; as they age, age-specific mortality rates will almost certainly change in some ways. Also, older people in that population will have lived their lives up to the year 2000 under a different set of age-specific mortality rates. Thus, it is important to be aware of the hypothetical nature of life expectancy statistics.

Table 1.2   LIFE EXPECTANCY AT BIRTH AND AT AGE 65 YEARS, MALES AND FEMALES: CANADA, 1921–1997

	MALES		FEMALES	
	At Birth	At Age 65	At Birth	At Age 65
1921	58.8	13.0	60.6	13.6
1931	60.0	13.0	62.1	13.7
1941	63.0	12.8	64.6	13.4
1951	66.4	13.3	70.9	15.0
1961	68.4	13.6	74.3	16.1
1971	69.4	13.8	76.5	17.6
1981	71.9	14.6	79.1	18.9
1991	74.3	15.6	80.8	19.8
1997	75.8	16.3	81.4	20.1

Source: Moore and Rosenberg (1997), p. 12; Bélanger et al. (2001), Table A9.

range of 85 to 100 years. Others suggest that the human life span can be extended by many more years—due to advances in molecular medicine (Schwartz, 1998) or dietary improvements (Walford, 1983), for example. Another position is more intermediate—that there is no rigid limit to the human life span and unforeseen biomedical technological breakthroughs could gradually increase life span.

A considerable amount of research, based on the foundational assumption of a finite human life span, has focused on the concept of dependency-free life expectancy (also called dependence-free life expectancy, healthy life expectancy, active life expectancy, disability-free life expectancy, and functional life expectancy). These varying terms refer to the number of years that people in a given population can expect to live in (reasonably) good health, with no or only minor disabling health conditions. Much of the research on dependency-free life expectancy tests, in varying ways, the validity of the **compression of morbidity** hypothesis, originally formulated by Fries (1983). This hypothesis states that at least among Western populations, more and more people are able to postpone the age of onset of chronic disability; hence, the period of time between onset of becoming seriously ill or disabled and dying is shortening or compressing (Fries, 1983). The general idea is that we are moving to a situation in which we will all live hale and hearty lives until a very old age and then die quickly. While some research finds support for the compression of morbidity hypothesis (Hayward, Crimmins, & Saito, 1998), more does not (e.g., Crimmins, 1990; Ford, Haug, Roy, Jones, & Folmar, 1992; Verbrugge, 1984). Canadian research by Roos, Havens, and Black (1993) finds no evidence of morbidity compression in Manitoba. As discussed in Chapter 15, the biomedical model dominant in the Canadian health care system does not provide the most appropriate care, given the chronic conditions people suffer from.

In addition to finding no evidence of morbidity compression, research on dependency-free life expectancy in Canada reveals an important gender difference (Martel & Bélanger, 2000). While, at age 65 years, women can expect to live about four years longer than men, their expectation of dependency-free years of life is less than one year more than that of men. In other words, older women will spend proportionately more of the remaining years of their lives (32.4 percent) in poor health than will men (21.1 percent). Gender differences in health in later life are discussed more extensively in Chapter 10.

The Role of Immigration

It is commonly thought that one way to cope with population aging is to try to avoid it by "younging" the population through increased immigration. The reasoning is that because immigrants tend to be young, their numbers will counteract population aging. However, immigration plays a relatively small role in population aging, especially at the national level. Canada's Chief Statistician, Ivan Fellegi (1988), has estimated that Canada would have to allow in more than

600,000 immigrants per year in order for immigration to have a measurable impact on our age structure. The Canadian government sets its annual immigration targets in the neighbourhood of 200,000 to 225,000 (and has failed to meet these targets in recent years). An approximate tripling of the number of immigrants who enter Canada annually does not seem likely, given additional costs for immigrant services such as ESL or FSL and public opinion that is less than enthusiastic about current levels of immigration, let alone increased levels. In the wake of the terrorist attacks in September 2001 on the World Trade Center in New York and the Pentagon in Washington, D.C., it is likely that immigration will become even more limited.

Summary

Canada's aging population is due to the combined effect of declining fertility and declining mortality, with international migration playing a fairly minor role. Historically, fertility has been the major determinant of our age structure. In the absence of another baby boom—which no one is predicting—and in the face of low fertility, mortality will take on increasing importance in determining our age structure.

Causes of Death

As a population undergoes mortality reduction, and becomes older, the causes of death—and relatedly, the ages of death—change.[4] The epidemiological transition deals with changes in the causes of death that accompany declines in mortality (and consequent increases in life expectancy) (Omran, 1971). Gerontologists are particularly interested in causes of death, since in modern societies, such as Canada, deaths are concentrated at old ages.

Epidemiological Transition Theory

According to **epidemiological transition theory**—which is less a theory than it is a description of the relationship between mortality decline and changes in the relative importance of different causes of death in the West—a society or a population goes through three mortality stages in its transition to a modern pattern. The first stage—the Age of Pestilence and Famine—is characterized by high death rates that vacillate in response to epidemics, famines, and war. It should be noted that epidemics and famines tend to go hand in hand, since malnourished people are particularly susceptible to infectious diseases. In the second stage, the Age of Receding Pandemics, death rates start to decline steadily, and the proportion of deaths due to infectious diseases decreases as a result of the improved nutrition and sanitation and medical advances that accompany socioeconomic development. Eventually, the third stage is reached—the Age of Degenerative and

(Hu)man-Made Diseases—in which death rates are low (life expectancy at birth is over 70 years) and the chief takers-of-life are chronic diseases associated with aging, such as cardiovascular disease and cancer. It is implicitly assumed that infectious and parasitic diseases become less and less important and that mortality levels and causes of death in the less developed countries will eventually come to mirror those in the West.

Omran's (1971) epidemiological transition model[5] generally reflects the situation for countries in the West, at least for the period from the Agricultural Revolution until the late 20th century. Prior to the Agricultural Revolution, it is highly likely that malnutrition (starving to death) was a more important killer than infectious diseases (Barrett, Kazawa, McDade, & Armelagos, 1998; McKeown, 1988). Once agriculture predominated, the denser settlement pattern of humans, as well as closer proximity to animals and animal waste, contributed to the spread of infectious diseases. One of the most spectacular examples of epidemic-caused loss of life in the West was the Black Death (the Plague) that hit hardest in the middle of the 14th century but which continued to recur for more than three centuries. By the eve of the Industrial Revolution, the plague had virtually disappeared in Europe, as a result of changes in shipping, housing, sanitary practices, and so on, that affected the way that rats, fleas, and humans interacted (McNeill, 1976). Other types of infectious diseases (such as cholera, influenza, smallpox, and pneumonia) remained important killers and were eventually conquered through improved nutrition, hygiene, and public health measures, and knowledge thereof. Medical advances played a small role, although the smallpox vaccine was important (McKeown, 1976), until well into the 20th century.

For the data that we have available for Canada, the epidemiological transition model is appropriate. The large increases in life expectancy at birth for 1921 to 1961, seen in Table 1.2, are the result of our control over infectious diseases that are important takers-of-life of infants, young children, and young women of childbearing ages. As Canadian society came to control these infectious diseases, mortality at young ages declined, and life expectancy at birth increased. Over the latter part of the 20th century, deaths became concentrated at older ages, and the causes of death shifted to chronic, degenerative diseases.

The epidemiological transition model applies less well to the developing world. Western mortality decline, with the changing configuration of causes of death associated with it, was fuelled by socioeconomic development. In contrast, in Third World countries, there is a much smaller relationship between mortality and economic development. In the post-World War II decade of the 1950s, mortality declines in many Third World countries were substantial. In those cold-war years, public health measures and death-reducing technologies were imported by the West (largely the United States) to many less developed countries, at least in part as an attempt to woo nonaligned countries towards the West and away from the Soviet Union. As a result, deaths due to infectious diseases fell dramatically, often in the absence of any significant economic development or modernization.

However, probably the biggest challenge to epidemiological transition theory comes from the emergence of new infectious diseases and the re-emergence of old ones in the latter part of the 20th century. This has led to debate about epidemiological transition theory's end stage. Is the third stage the final one? A number of fourth stages have been proposed, the most popular being the Age of Delayed Degenerative Diseases (Olshansky & Ault, 1986), corresponding to declines in death rates due to cardiovascular disease experienced in Western countries through the 1970s and 1980s. This stage conforms with the expectations of the compression of morbidity hypothesis discussed above. But now, a radically different fifth stage is being proposed in light of increasing death rates due to viruses and bacteria (Olshansky et al., 1997). Indeed, Barrett et al. (1998) view the trend of increasing mortality due to infectious diseases as characterizing a new epidemiological transition altogether. However, Murray and Lopez (1996), taking both death and disability into account, argue that noncommunicable diseases will take on increasing importance in the "global burden of disease."

The emergence of new infectious and parasitic diseases (e.g., acquired immune deficiency syndrome/human immunodeficiency virus [AIDS/HIV], legionnaires' disease, Lyme disease), the re-emergence of diseases (e.g., smallpox, malaria) that we thought had been conquered, and the evolution of antibiotic-resistant strains of bacteria have led to a re-appraisal of the possible future role of microbes in mortality. While it does not seem likely that infectious and parasitic diseases will overtake degenerative and chronic diseases as killers, it is difficult to predict the relative importance of the two major categories of death causation in the future. Much appears to depend on how successful we will be in controlling HIV/AIDS—which is estimated to have taken anywhere between 1.9 million and 3.6 million lives worldwide in 1999 alone. (Given the depression of the immune system that comes with AIDS, it is possible that even the high estimate is low; some persons with AIDS might be mistakenly counted as dying from another infectious disease to which they are vulnerable.)

Major Causes of Death among Elderly Canadians

As predicted by epidemiological transition theory, most deaths in Canada occur in old age and are the result of chronic, degenerative diseases. Circulatory diseases (which include heart disease and stroke as major categories) are the most important killer, increasingly so with advancing age. See Table 1.3. For example, among men aged 70 to 74 years, cardiovascular diseases account for 38 percent of total deaths; among men aged 90 years and over, they account for 44 percent. Malignant neoplasms (cancers) are the second most important cause of death among older Canadian men overall and are the leading cause among young-old men aged 65 to 69 years. Respiratory diseases are the next most important cause of death. This category includes both chronic degenerative diseases, such as emphysema and chronic bronchitis, as well as infectious diseases, such as influenza

Table 1.3 CAUSES OF DEATH (PER 100,000) BY AGE AND GENDER—
POPULATION AGED 65 YEARS AND OVER. CANADA: 1997

MEN	65–69	70–74	75–79	80–84	85–89	90+
All Causes	2,324	3,591	5,804	9,596	1,5138	25,236
Diseases of the Circulatory System	771	1,348	2,309	4,021	6,646	11,212
Ischemic heart disease	512	835	1,392	2,278	3,470	5,545
Cerebrovascular disease	99	206	402	801	1,424	2,262
Malignant Neoplasms	868	1,269	1,720	2,292	2,831	3,354
Lung cancer	321	443	533	603	644	506
Prostate cancer	61	134	266	449	686	1,059
Respiratory Diseases	156	335	662	1,298	3,533	4,527
Accidents and Adverse Affects	70	32	125	228	396	742
Accidental falls	10	18	44	118	257	553
Suicide	20	21	22	31	32	41
WOMEN	65-69	70-74	75-79	80-84	85-89	90+
All Causes	1,224	1,990	3,371	6,001	10,457	20,928
Diseases of the Circulatory System	346	676	1,336	2,670	5,061	10,441
Ischemic heart disease	187	378	718	1,352	2,419	4,777
Cerebrovascular disease	70	127	301	648	1,314	2,549
Malignant Neoplasms	545	741	973	1,227	1,486	1,685
Lung cancer	151	190	205	212	174	144
Breast cancer	92	113	146	172	233	313
Respiratory Diseases	87	161	315	622	1,129	2,590
Accidents and Adverse Affects	26	47	66	147	282	703
Accidental falls	7	18	31	96	233	619
Suicide	4	6	4	4	4	7

Source: Adapted from Statistics Canada, "Mortality-Summary List of Causes, 1997," Catalogue No. 84F0209, July 1999.

and pneumonia. The latter may afflict the frail-old who are suffering from chronic illness(es) as well. In such cases, the seemingly tidy distinction between infectious and degenerative diseases becomes quite blurry.

Elderly women have lower mortality rates for all causes of death than have elderly men, reflecting their higher life expectancy. However, women's mortality advantage decreases with age; at ages 65 to 69 years, women's overall mortality rate is about one-half that of men but at ages 90 years and over, the difference is only approximately 20 percent. There are some exceptions to this general pattern, however. The death rate for cerebrovascular disease (stroke) is higher for women than for men in the oldest age category. Also, the gender ratio in mortality due to respiratory diseases tends to stay high, and not narrow, with increasing age. In addition, death rates due to suicide—although not a common cause of death—are much higher for older men, generally about five times higher than for older women.

Differentials in Population Aging

So far, we have been referring to the older/aged population as if it were homogeneous. However, this is not the case; the elderly Canadian population is very diverse. In this section, we examine some dimensions of this diversity, with a focus on gender, ethnocultural variables, and place of residence.

Gender

It is sometimes said that "aging is a women's issue." This is because elderly women outnumber elderly men by a substantial margin, one that increases with advancing age. In 1998, there were 2.1 million Canadian women aged 65 years and over, compared with 1.6 million men; therefore, women make up about 58 percent of the total senior population (Statistics Canada, 1999b). However, among the Canadian population aged 85 years and over, women make up nearly 70 percent of the total. The reason for the numerical dominance of women in old age is gender differences in mortality and life expectancy. As we saw in Table 1.2, at age 65 years, women can expect to live about four years longer than men, and Table 1.3 indicates that women have lower death rates for most causes of death.

Gender and Mortality.

Why is it that female life expectancy is so much higher than that of males? At least in some part, the gender difference in mortality is biologically based. It is universally found that more male than female babies are born. While the magnitude of the gender ratio at birth (the number of male births per 100 female births) varies somewhat, it is almost always in the range of 103 to 107. There is some debate about why male births exceed female births, in part centred on the issue of gender differentials in the number of conceptions. Overall, the research evidence suggests that more males are conceived but that the male fetus is biologically weaker. However, that conclusion must be tempered with the fact that it is extremely difficult to obtain accurate data about fetal mortality in the first few months of pregnancy.

While there is uncertainty about the gender mortality differentials in the early gestational period, data for the first year of life are very clear. In virtually all places and times, infant mortality rates are higher for males than for females. Quite a bit of evidence points to biological factors playing a role in the higher mortality of infant males. Despite their higher birth weights (a factor associated with infant survival), male babies are more likely to suffer from congenital abnormalities that lead to death and to have immune deficiencies associated with X chromosome-linked genetic defects and with exposure to testosterone prenatally and in early infancy. This latter factor may also contribute to greater activity levels among male babies that are associated with higher mortality due to accidents (Waldron, 1998).

Other biologically based factors contributing to gender differentials in mortality include the protective effect of women's XX chromosome structure against heart disease, especially at ages under 55 years (Waldron, 1985), and a propensity to violence in men that can have lethal consequences (Boyd, 2000). The degree to which men are more violence-prone than are women and the reasons for it are, however, hotly debated, and it cannot be categorically stated if and how biology may be implicated.

While biological factors can explain part of the gender differentials in mortality, these differentials vary too much by time and place to be accounted for by biology to any great extent. What other factors are involved? One way to approach an answer to this question is to look at trends in the size of the gender differential in life expectancy over the course of the 20th century. In the middle of the 20th century, the average gender differential in life expectancy at birth (favouring females) in the more developed countries was approximately five years (United Nations, 2000); in Canada, it was 4.5 years (Table 1.2). At the beginning of the 20th century, the difference is estimated to have been two to three years (United Nations Secretariat, 1988). Trends in mortality favoured women in the more developed countries from at least the beginning of the 20th century to the early1980s. Mortality trends in different age groups contributed differentially to this overall trend of widening of the gender gap in mortality. Nearly two-thirds of the widening can be attributed to mortality among persons aged 65 years and over. In other words, death rates for older women declined more quickly than did death rates for older men. An additional one-quarter of the increase resulted from mortality trends among persons aged 55 to 64 years, for whom, as well, female death rates declined more than did male death rates. Very little of the increase was due to mortality among children aged one to 14 years (less than 3 percent). In contrast, trends in infant mortality operated in opposite fashion, to narrow the gender differential in mortality. High male infant mortality was overcome to a considerable degree so that eventually, for the most part, only the genetically caused higher susceptibility to death of male infants remained (United Nations, 1988).

Differential trends in various causes of death contributed to the widening of the gender mortality differential. By far the most important cause of death in this widening is diseases of the circulatory system. While there is variation from country to country, overall, the fact that male deaths due to circulatory disease declined less than did female deaths is responsible for approximately three years of the widening gap. Of the different kinds of circulatory diseases, trends in ischemic heart disease played the biggest role in this three-year widening, with men's death rate increasing over most of the 20th century, while women's death rates were stable or declined. Rheumatic heart disease and stroke (for which women and men have more equal risks of death) have decreased in importance as takers-of-life. Thus, the composition of the circulatory disease category—with an increasing prevalence of ischemic heart disease—played a role in widening the gender mortality differential.

The second most important cause of death in explaining the widening gender differential in mortality is malignant neoplasms. At the turn of the 20th century, female mortality rates from cancer (especially breast cancer and cancers of the female genital organs) tended to be higher than male cancer mortality rates. However, over the course of the 20th century, increasing rates of male mortality due to respiratory (e.g., lung) cancers served to widen the male–female mortality difference. In the United States, for the period from 1900 to the early 1980s, shifts in the trends and pattern of cancer mortality accounted for more than one-third of the widening gender mortality differential; in other Western countries, such as England/Wales and Australia, the contribution made by malignant neoplasms to widening the gender mortality ratio was even greater (United Nations, 1988).

Other causes of death are much less important contributors to the widening gender mortality differential. For example, declines in maternal mortality, although very substantial, have had only a small effect; as well, trends in accident mortality and suicide have not played a big role. In contrast, declines in infectious and parasitic diseases—for which males in the West tended to have higher mortality than did females—had an opposite effect, that is, to narrow the gender gap in mortality.

The increase in respiratory cancer among men and the slower decreases in circulatory system mortality among men have been attributed to smoking differences, in large part. Over the earlier years of the 20th century, men—much more so than women—took up cigarette smoking, the effects of which show up in mortality statistics among older age groups, given that cigarettes are slow killers (Retherford, 1975).

In the last 20 or so years, the gap between male and female mortality rates has narrowed somewhat. As we can see in Table 1.2, the biggest difference between male and female life expectancies at birth occurred in 1981, when it was 7.2 years; since then, the difference has become smaller such that by 1997, it was 5.6 years. The female advantage in life expectancy at age 65 years has similarly decreased, from 4.3 years in 1981 to 3.8 years in 1997. It is still the case, though, that the male mortality rate is higher than the female mortality rate for every major cause of death. The major factor accounting for the narrowing of the gender gap in mortality rates is that men have been experiencing greater declines in deaths due to circulatory diseases than have women (Gilbert & Bélanger, 2001). Trends in cancer, particularly respiratory cancer, account for some of the decrease in the gender mortality ratio; women's lung cancer rates have increased substantially, reflecting, in large part, the later adoption of smoking by women (Wright, 1997).

If the gender differential in mortality rates is to be reduced, the preferable route is to decrease male mortality rates, not increase female mortality rates! Smoking cessation is clearly required in order to achieve this. Also, research has shown that the gender gap in mortality rates is much smaller among the educated and economically advantaged segments of the population (Rogers, Humer, & Nam, 2000). This suggests that mortality rate is, to a large extent, determined by social and economic factors and that improvements in male mortality rates are attainable.

Women and Aging.

The general longevity advantage of women has important social and individual implications. For example, as will be seen in later chapters, it means that women are more likely to become widowed; live alone and/or be institutionalized; be grandparents for a longer time; be poor in old age, since in part, any savings have to be spread over more (possibly inflationary) years; and deal with the physical difficulties of extreme old age without age peers able to provide support or assistance. Yet, older women have shown their resilience, in part nurtured through the more intense and long-lasting personal relationships that women maintain over the course of their lives (Gee & Kimball, 1987). Also, it should be kept in mind that the men who do live very long lives, especially the few who do not remarry, may face social isolation because there are very few other older men for companionship and due to attenuated family ties, as women are more likely to be the "kin-keepers" (Rosenthal, 1983) who keep family ties activated.

Ethnocultural Variations

Canada's senior population has the highest percentage of foreign-born or immigrant persons; whereas 17 percent of the total Canadian population is foreign born, 27 percent of Canadians aged 65 years and over (or approximately 982,000 persons), in 1996, were born outside Canada. Most foreign-born seniors have lived in Canada for a long time; for example, approximately 61 percent immigrated to Canada before 1961. During that period of time, Canadian immigration policy discriminated on the basis of ethnicity/race; hence, the majority immigrated from Europe (71 percent) and other Western countries. Thus, the majority of today's foreign-born seniors are of a Western cultural background and have home languages that are relatively similar to Canada's official languages; in 1996, only 6 percent were members of visible minority groups. This is in marked contrast to the younger foreign-born population in Canada; among persons born outside Canada aged under 65 years, 35 percent were born in Asia and another nearly 12 percent were born in Africa or the Caribbean. This reflects the fact that the current leading sender countries to Canada are the People's Republic of China, India, the Philippines, Hong Kong, and Pakistan (Citizenship and Immigration Canada, 1999). In other words, the seniors of the future will be much more ethnically diverse than today's seniors.

However, it is important not to discount minority older immigrants because their numbers are small. Every year, approximately 6,000 elders immigrate to Canada; most are of non-European origins, and most are family-class immigrants. As sponsored immigrants, they do not have economic resources and are not eligible for any Canadian public pension until after 10 years of residence. Also, many lack the ability to communicate in either English or French. They represent a particularly vulnerable segment of the Canadian aged population, as do First Nations seniors, who make up a small percentage (3.5 percent) of the total First Nations population. This is due to higher fertility and higher mortality levels among First Nations people. However, a rapid aging of the First Nations population is expected; a doubling of the percentage aged 65 years and over (to 7 percent) is expected by 2016. Since registered First Nations seniors are more likely than nonseniors to live on reserves, their proportionate growth will affect locations that are not equipped to serve the aged and are, for the most part, impoverished.[6]

Place of Residence and Migration

With percentages of persons aged 65 years and over at 15 percent, Manitoba and Saskatchewan are Canada's "oldest" provinces. At the other end of the spectrum is Alberta, which has only 10 percent of its population in the 65 years and over age group. Fertility differentials across provinces are very small; therefore, the usually strong effect of fertility is not responsible for provincial variation in population age structure. Neither are provincial mortality differentials particularly large. Rather, migration plays the most important role. However, it is not migration of seniors that accounts for this pattern; rather, it is the migration patterns of younger persons that is responsible. The "have-not" provinces of Manitoba and Saskatchewan are "old" because of high levels of emigration of younger people; the "have" province of Alberta has received large numbers of young immigrants in recent years. This illustrates that while (the current level of) migration does not play an important role in affecting our national age structure, it can and does affect the age structure of smaller areas/populations. However, in absolute numbers, the majority of elderly people live in the most populous provinces, in Ontario (1.5 million), Quebec (1 million) and British Columbia (0.5 million) (Statistics Canada, 1999b).

Older Canadians are about as likely (76 percent) as nonseniors (79 percent) to live in an urban area. It has been found that the 24 percent of Canadian elders who live in rural areas face unique problems (Joseph & Martin Matthews, 1994).

While they are well integrated into family and nonfamily support systems as are urban elders, these supports are not as reliable, for example, children live farther away, they have fewer personal visits, and they have fewer younger neighbours who can provide practical assistance. Transportation is a major concern for rural elders; they have less access to adequate transportation but more need for it, given the geographic dispersion of people, facilities, and services in rural areas. Also, it has been observed that rural Canada has sufficient institutional facilities for frail elders; what is lacking are services for seniors who need only limited formal help to live independently in the community (Joseph & Martin Matthews, 1994). However, with such factors as hospital closures in the latter half of the 1990s, it may well be that the quality of life of frailer rural seniors is declining.

The foreign-born and Canadian-born seniors have substantial differences in the sizes of the places in which they live. Among the Canadian born, approximately one-quarter live in one of Canada's three largest cities (Toronto, Montreal, and Vancouver), and nearly one-half live in places smaller than a city. However, about 40 percent of elders born in Europe and approximately 70 percent of seniors born in Asia live in one of the big three cities; and among the Chinese born, the figure is 75 percent. Conversely, very small percentages of Asian-born elders live in smaller places (Gee, 1996). Other things being equal, then, the foreign born, and especially those born in Asia, are in an advantageous position with regard to accessing services if they become frail. However, things are never equal, and we must remember that many Asian-born elders face language barriers in service access and delivery.

Canadian cities vary quite widely in age structure. Victoria is Canada's "oldest" city, with 18.2 percent of its population aged 65 years and over. Second is the St.Catharine's–Niagara metropolitan area, at 15.9 percent. In contrast, Calgary and Oshawa have approximately 9 percent of their populations in the elderly age group. As with provincial variations in age structure, migration accounts for these differences. A combination of the migration of both nonseniors and seniors is at work.

Litwak and Longino (1987) provide a three-fold typology of senior migration. The first type shows up in the high percentages of seniors in Victoria and the Niagara area—this is amenity-oriented migration, often associated with retirement, which is mostly undertaken by young senior married couples with higher than average income. The second type occurs at older ages and is precipitated by increased difficulty in performing daily tasks, such as shopping, housework, and preparing meals. The elders move to be closer to family members who are able to provide assistance. Since difficulty in performing daily tasks is exacerbated by the death of a spouse, widows are most likely to be involved in this type of move. The third type occurs at still older ages and involves a move to an institutional setting. More than one-third of the population aged 85 years and over reside in institutions, with a high proportion being widows. While we do not know a lot about the transition process to institutionalized living, it appears that a sizable proportion of seniors who live in institutions are there mostly because of the lack of adequate supports in the community (Moore & Rosenberg, 1994; Shapiro & Tate, 1985).

Older Canadians are less likely to move than are younger individuals; in a five-year period, about one-half of persons aged 20 to 59 years change their place of residence at least once, but less than one-quarter of those aged 60 years and over do (Che-Alford & Stevenson, 1998). When elderly individuals do move, it tends not to be far; in 1995, only 10 percent moved more than 200 kilometres. Canadian data support the age-related model of senior migration proposed by Litwak and Longino (1987). That is, the older the mover, the more likely the reason for the move is related to being closer to family and to declining health (Che-Alford & Stevenson, 1998). Canadian data also indicate that moves to smaller homes with special features (e.g., bathroom adaptations, street-level entrance, extra handrails, lifts) are common, posing challenges for the housing industry as the population continues to age (Che-Alford & Stevenson, 1998).

One unique aspect of Canadian elder migration is the "snowbird phenomenon". **Snowbirds** are elderly Canadians who move, on a seasonal basis, to southern states in the United States, such as Florida and Arizona. We are not sure of the numbers of Canadian seniors who engage in snowbird migration to spend the winters in a warmer climate, but it has been estimated that as many as 250,000 older Canadians are annual "snowbirds" to Florida alone (Mullins & Tucker, 1988). The duration of stays in the southern states varies, but rarely exceeds six months, probably as this would result in loss of Canadian health care benefits. These older "migrants" rarely make a permanent move to the United States, but other permanent movers may be a factor in recruiting snowbirds. For example, Longino et al. (1991) report that nearly 20 percent of Canadian senior snowbirds to Florida have a relative there, and 70 percent have friends who are permanent residents of the state. Research shows that Canadian snowbird migration is selective in nature; that is, the type of older persons who are most like to engage in this seasonal migration are relatively young, married, of higher levels of income and education, and in relatively good health (Longino & Marshall, 1990; Tucker, Marshal, Longino, & Mullins, 1988). Canadian snowbirds have been found to be somewhat healthier, with fewer chronic conditions, than their American counterparts, who, of course, do not make international moves (Martin, Hopps, Marshall, & Daciuk, 1992).

Nevertheless, many Canadian snowbirds have some medical conditions that require monitoring and attention. Marshall, Longino, Tucker, and Mullins (1989), in a study based on a sample of anglophone Canadian snowbirds in Florida, report that snowbirds have a strong preference for the Canadian health care system and engage in strategic behaviours concerning their health while in the United States. For example, most snowbirds take out special health insurance to cover any difference between Canadian health care reimbursements and costs they may incur in Florida if they have a health emergency; many make a visit to their physician before leaving Canada and stock up on prescription medications; and many make special arrangements to return to Canada in the event of a medical crisis. As a result, Canadian snowbirds do not strain the American health care system. On the other hand, they do not significantly lower health care costs in Canada.

Apocalyptic Demography

While one should not discount the social importance of population aging, it is important not to overemphasize it, either. The term **apocalyptic demography** (sometimes also called voodoo demography) is used to characterize the over-simplified notion that a demographic trend—in our case population aging—has catastrophic consequences for a society (Gee, 2000). (An earlier version of apocalyptic demography occurred in the 1960s and 1970s, when it was felt by some Western researchers and the public in the West that high fertility in many Third World countries would lead to such overpopulation that starvation would mean the end of such countries as India. An example is Paul Ehrlich's widely read book *The Population Bomb*.) When apocalyptic demography exists, a complex issue—in Ehrlich's case, Third World economic development—is cast in simplistic terms as a demographic problem. In the case of apocalyptic demography applied to population aging, the complexity of aging is reduced to a one-sided negative view that our society cannot afford increasing numbers and percentages of older people. Apocalyptic demography is prominently seen in mass media.

According to Gee (2000), apocalyptic demography consists of five inter-related themes: (1) One prominent theme is that aging is a social problem. Rather than celebrating the control over unwanted births and early deaths that population aging represents, it is viewed as negative, as a problem that somehow needs fixing. (2) A second theme is the homogenization of older people—in particular, all old people are stereotyped as comfortably well off, for example, as rich golfers and cruise-ship travellers, as "greedy geezers" (Binstock, 1994). (3) The third theme is age blaming. That is, seniors are blamed for overusing social programs and, consequently, for government debt/deficits. (4) Fourth is the theme of intergenerational injustice. Specifically, this entails the idea that older people are getting more than their fair share of societal resources and the related prediction that this will lead to severe intergenerational conflict/clashes. (5) A fifth theme is the intertwining of population aging and social policy; aging has become the "guiding paradigm" of the Canadian welfare state (McDaniel, 1987). So, for example, social policy reform is guided by the idea that deep cuts have to be made to accommodate the increasing numbers and percentages of seniors in our population. If we believe that seniors will bankrupt our society through their demands on the public health care and pension systems, it is a simple step to move towards a dismantling of the old age welfare state—and the whole welfare state, for that matter—in order to counteract the societal burden of an aging population. Evidence of this can already be seen in attempts to privatize pensions as much as possible (e.g., the Senior's Benefit, a plan that would have seen the elimination of Old Age Security, the Guaranteed Income Supplement (for low-income seniors), and age and pension tax credits, and their replacement with a single benefit based on household income and subject to a large clawback to households with an annual income starting at under $26,000, (proposed in the late 1990s and failed to materialize, at least so far), and in the reductions in health care spending (and associated privatization) that have been posed as inevitable due to population aging.

The fourth theme—intergenerational injustice—is very important and is manifested in what is termed the **intergenerational equity debate**. On the one (and more popular) side are those who argue that the aged are getting more than they deserve from the public purse (i.e., our society is organized such that there is generational inequity that favours the old). Along with some academic research/writing—such as Samuel Preston's (1984) "Presidential Address to the Population Association of America" and the work of economists (such as Kotlikoff, 1993) on what is called generational accounting-an American political movement (AGE, Americans for Generational Equity, funded for the most part by large corporations and conservative foundations, e.g., Longman, 1987) has become quite influential, as well as media that have promulgated this theme. Although the intergenerational inequity movement/perspective originated in the United States, it has found its way to Canada. We hear it with respect to pensions, such as the Canada Pension Plan (CPP), in which it is argued that today's younger people are paying much more to finance the pensions of seniors than they will ever receive when they themselves retire. An even stronger version is that the CPP will no longer exist when today's young people are old; that it will have been completely "used up" by earlier generations of "greedy geezer" seniors.

On the other side of the debate is the intergenerational interdependence perspective (Williamson & Watts-Roy, 1999). The proponents of this side emphasize that the generations are, and should continue to be, interdependent. They make the important point that transfers across generations are both public and private (e.g., McDaniel, 1997); it is partial and biasing to focus only on public transfers, as is done by those who view intergenerational relations as unfair to the young. Older persons help younger ones in many ways—within the family setting, they assist with child care and provide cash gifts/loans to grown-up children to help with a down payment on a home, for example. Indeed, it has been estimated by Kronebusch and Schlesinger (1994) that over the course of their lives, parents give 50 percent more to their children than they receive. Outside the family, elders engage in volunteer activities and give to charities that benefit younger people. However, these private transfers are not counted by those who only look at the costs of elderly persons with regard to pensions and health care (however, to be fair, it is not easy to obtain hard data about these essentially private activities). Proponents of intergenerational interdependence also point out that cuts to pensions and health care to older persons (deemed necessary by intergenerational equity advocates) will adversely affect the children of older persons, who will have to "pick up the slack" out of their own wallets (Williamson & Watts-Roy, 1999). It is also important to note that our society is stratified in many ways other than by age (e.g., gender, social class, ethnicity/race), and any attempts to dismantle old-age benefits—to promote generational equity—would negatively affect some groups of older people more than others and, thus, generate further inequities.

General Criticisms of Apocalyptic Demography

Is aging a social problem—the most basic postulate of apocalyptic demography? Much of the conclusion that aging is a social problem is based on looking at aged dependency ratios, and the extrapolation that the number/percentage of older people (considered to be dependants) is increasing too much. However, it is important to look at youth and total dependency ratios as well, and not fixate on the aged dependency ratio only. This is so because the youth and aged dependency ratios have counterbalancing effects on the total dependency ratio. Canada provides a particularly good example of these counterbalancing effects. In 1951, the total dependency ratio in Canada was 0.83 (that is, there were 83 dependants—old and young people—for every 100 persons in the working ages). In 2041, it is expected to be 0.82. This basically unchanged situation is caused by a large increase in the aged dependency ratio (from 0.14 to 0.46) accompanied by a large decrease in the youth dependency ratio (from 0.69 to 0.36). It is also interesting to note that now (2001)—at the approximate midpoint between 1951 and 2041—the overall dependency ratio is at a historical low point (0.62) (Denton, Feaver, & Spencer, 1998). This knowledge makes it difficult to accept the "everyday" view that many of the social problems of the day are due to changes in the Canadian age structure, in population aging in particular. Also, research shows that economic productivity is an important part of the equation; Canada will be able to afford an aging population with little difficulty as long as we experience at least moderate levels of economic growth (Denton & Spencer, 1999; Fellegi, 1988). Canada would be better off looking at ways to improve our economic productivity than worrying about increases in the proportion of the population that is aged and consequently cutting social programs.

Are the aged "greedy geezers" using more than their fair share of government monies? It is true that the largest portion of the social envelope goes to seniors, in the form of public pensions and health care. However, the majority of older Canadians are far from wealthy, and nearly one-half of old women without a spouse (mostly widows) live in poverty. As McDonald (1997) points out, poor elders are invisible—unlike the seniors we do see on cruises and so on. Also, research in both the United States and Canada reveals that age makes virtually no difference in public support for old-age social programs (Hamil-Luker, 2001; Northcott, 1994). A related question is: Are the aged to blame for increasing costs in government spending and, consequently, government debt/deficit? A considerable amount of research, much of it conducted by Robert Evans and his colleagues at the University of British Columbia, shows that population aging itself will account for only a small part of future health care costs and will require little, if any, increase in public expenditures for health care (e.g., Barer, Evans, & Hertzman, 1995; Evans et al., 2001).

Using administrative data from the province of British Columbia for the period from the mid-1970s to the late 1990s, Evans, McGrail, Morgan, Barer, and Hertzman (2001) report that acute care hospital use rates fell dramatically, the result of declines in age-specific use rates (i.e., declines at all ages); the use of physician services increased substantially, resulting from rises in age-specific use rates that are associated with increases in the number of physicians per capita and in billings per physician (especially among specialists); and per capita expenditures on prescription drugs rose far faster (over the period since 1985, the only data available) than would be projected on the basis of changes in the age structure, even if one focuses on the elderly population alone. What, then, has led to increased health costs (that are so often assumed to be the result of an aging population)? An important component is rapidly rising costs for pharmaceuticals, the result of a combination of inflation and shifts in prescribing more expensive medications without scientific evidence of therapeutic benefit. The pharmaceutical industry is an important cost driver; one publication dedicated to this issue is cleverly titled *Tales from the Other Drug Wars* (Barer, McGrail, Cardiff, Wood, & Green, 2000). Other factors include cost increases present in the pricing and rate of uptake of new technologies and an oversupply of physicians (Evans et al., 2001). Thus, while it makes "sense" that an aging population leads to increased health care costs, the evidence—at least in terms of hospital use, physician use, and pharmaceuticals—strongly negates the importance of age structure in affecting health care costs.

When Canada, and other Western countries, ran into trouble with government debt/deficit, it was widely attributed to increased spending on social programs, and the target of this supposed overspending was the seniors. A number of Canadian economists have shown that the debt/deficit are not due to overspending on social programs (e.g., Fortin, 1996; Osberg & Fortin, 1996; Rosenbluth, 1996), pointing the finger instead at Canadian monetary policy and especially the Bank of Canada (which, it can be added, operates outside the democratic process). In particular, the Bank's decision in the late 1980s to reduce inflation led to increased interest rates, which, in turn, contributed significantly to Canada's growing debt. Fortin (1996) shows that anti-inflationary measures were the most important cause of our increased government debt.

It should be evident that the "hard, dry facts" on population aging are deceiving. Population aging is an intensely political issue; apocalyptic demography is playing an important role in shaping the future of a Canadian welfare state that will be "leaner and meaner." As such, it is being used by those who favour a neoliberal (that is, pro-free market and anti-welfare state) social agenda. Three books have recently been published—*Demography is Not Destiny* (National Academy on an Aging Society, 1999) in the United States; *The Imaginary Time Bomb: Why an*

Ageing Population is Not a Social Problem (Mullan, 2000) in the United Kingdom; and *The Overselling of Population Aging: Apocalyptic Demography, Intergenerational Challenges, and Social Policy* (Gee & Gutman, 2000) in Canada—which all have the theme and aim of debunking apocalyptic demography. Together, they may—along with the research of Canadian health economists, such as Robert Evans and Morris Barer—begin to put some dents in the view that population aging necessarily has dire social and economic consequences.

CHAPTER SUMMARY

In this chapter, we have seen that the demography of aging encompasses a wide variety of topics—from a presentation of "dry facts" to a discussion of the intertwining of population aging and politics.

Key ideas to remember from this chapter include:

- The Canadian population has been aging since the beginning of the 20th century and will continue to age for many decades to come, with a rapid aging expected when the "baby boom" generation arrives at ages 65 years and over. The main driving force behind population aging is decreases in fertility; since Canadian fertility decline lagged behind that of Europe and because of our very large baby boom after World War II, the Canadian population is somewhat younger than those in many other parts of the Western world.

- There are many ways to measure population aging, and none is perfect. However, relying on aged dependency ratios to measure population aging contains a number of problems, including assumptions about dependency. It is important to examine changes in total dependency ratios and youth dependency ratios along with aged dependency ratios. When we do, we see the counterbalancing effects of a decreasing youth population and an increasing aged population. At the present time in Canada, we are at a historical low point in overall dependency, and our future total dependency in the years when the baby boomers are old will not be higher than it was in the middle of the 20th century.

- Life expectancy increased substantially over the course of the 20th century, with the major gains in life expectancy at birth made in the earlier part of the period. Young Canadians were the first to benefit from mortality reductions; it was only later that longevity in later life increased appreciably, a trend that is typical of developed countries.

- The compression of morbidity hypothesis states that more and more people are able to postpone the age of onset of chronic disability; hence, the period of time between onset of becoming seriously ill or disabled and dying is shortening or compressing. The general idea is that we are moving to a situation in which we, at least in Western countries, will live in a healthy state until a very old age and then die quickly.

- Epidemiologic transition theory deals with the relationship between mortality decline, on the one hand, and changes in the relative importance of different causes of death, on the other. As mortality declines, the changes in causes of death shift from infectious diseases to chronic diseases; this occurs in three stages. The theory holds quite well for Western countries, such as Canada, but is not as applicable to countries of the Third World. However, the theory is now being challenged by the emergence of new and the re-emergence of old, infectious diseases, beginning in the latter part of the 20th century.

- As predicted by epidemiologic transition theory, most deaths in Canada occur in old age and are the result of chronic, degenerative diseases. In order of importance, the major causes of death are: circulatory diseases (which include heart disease and stroke as major categories); cancer; respiratory diseases (including both chronic degenerative diseases, such as emphysema and chronic bronchitis, as well as infectious diseases, such as influenza and pneumonia).

- Older women have lower mortality rates for virtually all causes of death than older men, reflecting their higher life expectancy.

- Women's life expectancy at birth improved more than men's throughout most of the 20th century in Canada. At the turn of the 20th century, women could expect to live two more years than men. By approximately 1980, that difference had grown to 7.2 years. Although biological differences account for the greater longevity of females to some extent, social factors are responsible for this large increase in the gender gap in mortality over the 80-year period. In Canada, the mortality of older women (i.e., aged 55 years and over) decreased much more rapidly than that of older men. This was due mostly to substantial declines in circulatory diseases among women; for men, on the other hand, rates declined much more slowly and, in the case of heart disease, rose. Another factor was trends in cancer mortality—which decreased for women, but increased for men, especially respiratory cancers. These trends have been attributed to men's greater likelihood of smoking during this period. Since the early 1980s, the gender gap in mortality has narrowed—from 7.2 years to 5.6 years in Canada. This is due to more rapid declines in deaths due to circulatory diseases among men, along with increases in cancer deaths, especially lung cancer, among women. Again, the overall trend is attributed to smoking, which women have taken up more than men in the last few decades.

- Canada's senior population is diverse in age (from 65 to 100+ years) and gender. As well, more than one-quarter of Canada's senior population is foreign born (which is much higher than for the nonaged population). Most foreign-born seniors are of European origins and have lived in Canada for a long time, with 61 percent immigrating before 1961. However, Canada is now receiving approximately 6,000 older immigrants annually; most are of non-European origins and most are family-class immigrants with few economic resources and no eligibility for any public pension.

- Manitoba and Saskatchewan are Canada's "oldest" provinces. At the other end of the spectrum is Alberta, which has only 10 percent of its population in the 65 years and over age group. These differences are largely due to migration—particularly of nonseniors.

- Canadian elders tend to move less, and less far, than do younger people. However, some young-old, married, and reasonably well-off seniors are part of the snowbird phenomenon—spending up to six months per year in southern U.S. states, such as Florida and Arizona.
- Apocalyptic demography represents an exaggeration of the negative effects of population aging. One of its five themes is that of intergenerational inequity—the view that older persons create an unfair (to younger people) drain on social programs. The research evidence does not support an apocalyptic view of population aging.

KEY TERMS

Median age of the population, (p. 3)

Dependency ratios, (p. 4)

Aged dependency ratio, (p. 4)

Youth dependency ratio, (p. 4)

Total dependency ratio, (p. 4)

Familial old-age dependency ratio, (p. 5)

Population pyramids, (p. 8)

Life expectancy, (p. 9)

Compression of morbidity, (p. 12)

Epidemiological transition theory, (p. 13)

Snowbirds, (p. 23)

Apocalyptic demography, (p. 24)

Intergenerational equity debate, (p. 25)

STUDY QUESTIONS

1. Find out how "old" your province is compared with the Canadian average. What accounts for its relative age? (For example, if your province is younger than the Canadian average, why is this the case?)

2. Provide a critique of dependency ratios. What are their strengths, their weaknesses?

3. Why do Canadian women live longer than Canadian men? What are some of the social consequences of this longevity differential?

4. Evaluate epidemiological transition theory. Does it hold equally well for the West and the non-West? Do you think it will continue to be valid in Canada?

5. Do you think population aging is a crisis for Canadian society? Why, or why not?

SUGGESTED READINGS

Desjardins, B. (1993). *Population ageing and the elderly*. Ottawa: Statistics Canada Catalogue No. 91-533E.

Gee, E.M. & Gutman, G.M. (Eds.) (2000). *The overselling of population aging: Apocalyptic demography, intergenerational challenges, and social policy*. Toronto: Oxford University Press.

Moore, E.G., & Rosenberg, M.W., with McGuinness, D. (1997). *Growing old in Canada: Demographic and geographic perspectives.* Toronto: Statistics Canada and ITP Nelson.

Murray, C.J.L. & Lopez, A.D. (1996). *The global burden of disease: A comprehensive assessment of mortality and disability from diseases, injuries, and risk factors in 1990 and projected to 2020.* Boston: Harvard School of Public Health, on behalf of the World Health Organization and the World Bank.

Williamson, J.B., Watts-Roy, D.M., & Kingson, E.R. (Eds.). (1999). *The generational equity debate.* New York: Columbia University Press.

ENDNOTES

1. Other less frequently used measures of population aging are presented by McDaniel (1986).

2. Projections about the future age structure are not certain. They depend on assumptions made about future levels of fertility, mortality, and migration. In particular, if our fertility rates were to undergo another boom, our future age structure would be younger than projected.

3. The term "life span" is used differently by researchers in varying disciplines. In demography, the concept of life span means, as above, the maximum number of years that members of a given species can live. For example, parrots and elephants have a longer life span than people, whereas cats and dogs have a shorter life span. In psychology, on the other hand, life span takes on a very different meaning—it refers to developmental changes over the course of a (human) life.

4. The relationship between fertility decline and mortality decline is complex, in terms of direction of causation and timing. It is sufficient here to point out that at least in the case of the West, the fertility declines that led to population aging occurred quite close in time to mortality declines.

5. The epidemiological transition theory or model has its roots in demography, not gerontology, and, therefore, is not covered in Chapter 2.

6. The data in this section, unless otherwise specified, are from Statistics Canada (1999b).

Social Theory in Gerontology

Learning Objectives

In this chapter, you will learn about:

- What theory is and how it is different from some related concepts.
- Barriers to theoretical development within social gerontology.
- Why theory is important.
- The challenges of level of analysis and assumptions about the individual–society relationship.

- Some details about the major theories within social gerontology.
- Life course theory.
- Some very recent theoretical perspectives that are challenging some core assumptions of gerontology.

Introduction

This chapter provides an introduction to the major theories of social gerontology, the majority of which have their origins in the United States over the last 50 years. While gerontological theory is not in crisis per se, two "camps" on the status of theory can be identified. One group is highly dissatisfied with the state of theory; a representative feeling is expressed in the following well-known quotation: "Gerontology is rich in data but poor in theory." (Birren & Bengtson, 1988: ix). This statement is made in the face of a large number of theoretical perspectives within social gerontology, many of which will be outlined in this chapter.

A second, and much larger, group consists of gerontologists who seem not to be concerned about theory and theoretical issues and, thus, are not worried about the general state of social gerontology theory. As Bengtson, Rice, and Johnson (1999: 3) state: "Many researchers in gerontology seem to have abandoned any attempt at building theory." In general terms, we can say that social gerontology is not without theory but that much of that theory has not developed over the years, in part because a substantial number of researchers have not made the theory or the theoretical underpinnings of their studies explicit. For example, a recent study by Bengtson, Burgess, and Parrott (1997) reports that an examination of eight leading gerontology journals found that 72 percent of articles did not mention any type of theory in relation to the findings. Similarly, Chappell and Penning (2001) characterize sociological gerontology in Canada as empirical, often without explicit theoretical content or direction.

This characterization of theory is very much "married" to research. As pointed out by prominent American sociologist Robert Merton (1968), theory and research are two sides of the same coin—or at least should be. Scientific knowledge progresses when theory informs/directs research and, in turn, research findings play an important role in theory development. Therefore, the separate study of theory (in Chapter 2) and research methods (in Chapter 3) in this text is somewhat artificial and does not reflect the real way that scientists proceed in their work—moving back and forth between theoretical and methodological issues and concerns. It is, however, standard practice to separate the two interrelated processes of theory and research in textbooks, in part because each topic contains much material. But, it is important to keep in mind when reading Chapters 2 and 3 that the subject matters of both chapters intersect in the actual practice of knowledge building.

The chapter begins with an examination of what theory is. In the process, theory is distinguished from a number of related concepts, such as paradigm and fact. Given the dissatisfaction about gerontological theory—at least among a small but vocal group of gerontologists—we then turn to a discussion of some factors that account for lack of theoretical development. Third is a discussion of why theory is important. Then, we look at two issues that gerontological theory building faces: (1) the level of analysis issue; and (2) the tension between differing assumptions about the relationship between individuals and society. These two issues form the basis for a way of organizing different social gerontological theories. The last part of the chapter examines in more detail some key social gerontological theories. You will see that gerontology is not short on theories; rather, it is the application of theory in real-life research that is problematic.

The Nature of Theory

In everyday life, we use the term "theory" quite loosely, often to refer to a guess or a hunch we have about something. For example, you will hear people say things like: "My theory is that old people vote more conservatively than young people do." Besides the fact that this statement is not true (older people's votes are distributed in much the same way as younger people's [Binstock, 1997]), it is not a "theory" in the way that scientists mean the term. Within science, theory has a specific meaning; Bengtson et al. (1999:5) define **theory** as "the construction of explicit explanations in accounting for empirical findings." The most important part of this definition is *explanation*—what theories do is explain something. And they do not explain just anything. They explain things that have been or can be empirically observed; that is, data-based findings (from any number of sources—interviews, administrative data, textual materials, laboratory trials, and so on). In the above "theory" about voting, there is no explanation. Neither is there empirical (data-based) confirmation that older people vote differently from younger people. Even if data confirm a relationship between age and voting choice, there is still no explanation.

Some explanatory schemes are called theoretical perspectives, rather than theories. **Theoretical perspectives** are not as tightly organized as theories, offering more loosely linked explanations. Usually, theoretical perspectives are more descriptive and less explanatory than theories. However, in practice, the distinction between theory and theoretical perspective is quite blurry. While noting the distinction is useful to avoid confusion, for our purposes, the two terms mean basically the same thing.

Facts and paradigms are related to theory, but need to be distinguished from it. **Facts** are empirically established findings; they form the building blocks of theories. Facts are not "cut and dried" with an essential meaning of their own; rather, *facts take on the meaning that theory gives them.* For example, let us take a fact (to avoid confusion) from Chapter 1—women outlive men by a substantial margin, at least in Western societies. If we apply a biological theory to this fact, we might conclude that women have a physiologically and genetically superior constitution that enables them to live longer than men. This would provide an explanation based on physiology and genetics, in other words. If, on the other hand, we apply a sociological theory to this fact, we might provide an explanation based on social norms that both protect and constrain women (e.g., not engaging in physically hazardous work or leisure pursuits defined as "masculine"; not drinking in excess because this is not "ladylike" behaviour). Therefore a fact—here, that women outlive men—is not neutral. It takes on different meanings, depending upon the theory applied to it.

Facts that are confirmed, especially repeatedly, form **empirical generalizations**. Empirical generalizations can be linked together descriptively to form **models**. For example, the relationship between gender and longevity can be linked to levels of social and economic development. Models are not theories (although sometimes the terms "model" and "theory" are used interchangeably), since they offer descriptions (and sometimes quite complex and sophisticated ones) but not explanations. In the above example, we still do not know *why* women outlive men to a greater degree in the more developed countries.

Another important concept is paradigm. **Paradigms** are the world views that underlie theories. They contain assumptions that are so deep that we may not even be aware of them. The following exercise is sometimes given to students to illustrate the power of paradigms. They are asked to write down an answer to the question: What three words do you least want to hear when you are making love? After everyone has finished writing down their three-word answers (which they do by themselves, without consulting each other), the students are asked to read out their answers. Typically, the answers are something like: "Is that it?"; "Who are you?"; "What's your name?"; or "I gotta go." These answers are wrong (in the sense that they are not what is asked for.) The right answer is given in endnote 1 of this chapter.[1] When you read it, you will probably chuckle (and, indeed, much humour is based on poking holes in the taken-for-granted). With some thought, you will see what assumptions you brought with you to the answer. One is the assumption that only two people are involved in the scenario. A deeper assumption is an adherence to the rule of monogamy. Researchers are people, and just like everyone else, they carry deeply held and, often, unconscious assumptions about the world and how it operates—a paradigm. Their paradigms influence their choice of theory, and this is to be expected. However, their paradigms and all their assumptions may be hidden from them; then they go about their research not realizing (or caring, perhaps) that they are viewing "facts" through a lens that is consistent with the way they think things should be, rather than the way they actually are. When this happens, some facts (which do not fit with their paradigms) go unnoticed, and other facts may be given an interpretation/explanation that is comfortable, rather than useful or valid. These comments are not meant to be a criticism of any particular scholars. Uncovering deep-seated assumptions can be extremely difficult.

Thomas Kuhn (1962) first introduced the term paradigm in one of the most widely read books on the history of science. Kuhn argued that most of the time, researchers do "normal science," in which a given paradigm is shared. However, every so often, there is a shift in paradigm; Kuhn calls this a scientific revolution. After a while, the new paradigm takes hold, and normal science takes place again (although a different kind of normal science, since the paradigm is different)—

until another shift in paradigm (or revolution) occurs. According to Kuhn, during the phases of normal science, much of what is done by researchers is tidying-up work, rather than innovative and creative work. If that is true, it may be that the lack of theoretical development in social gerontology signals a paradigm shift in the making.

To sum up this section, theories are explanations of empirical findings. They can be distinguished from facts—the building blocks of theories; empirical generalizations—regularities in facts and fact-based relationships; and models—descriptions of how empirical generalizations may be related together. If facts are the building blocks of theories, then paradigms are their umbrellas. Paradigms contain untested and often unrealized assumptions about the world and are influential in determining which theories are favoured by researchers.

Barriers to Theory Development in Social Gerontology

Given the overlapping connection between theory and research in the scientific enterprise, you may be wondering why research in gerontology has been criticized for its lack of theoretical attention and development. One reason is that a considerable amount of research in gerontology has been driven by immediate problems and the need to solve them. While this is a laudable goal, it contains some dangers—perhaps the most important one is that the assumptions of the gerontologist(s) are likely not unearthed or evaluated. Some of these assumptions—if we can ascertain them-may be just simply wrong, leading to wrong or partial findings and the implementation of solutions that are not likely to be successful. For example, if a researcher is charged with finding a way to reduce loneliness among a group of elderly people, he or she may assume that contact with children (or pets) will solve the problem—with no theoretical direction. He or she may interview only those elders who seem enthusiastic about the idea of interacting with children or pets.

A program is implemented, and the elders are exposed to, say, biweekly visits with young children or pets. However, the program fails; the elders do not interact much with the children or pets and do not feel less lonely, and some even feel more lonely. What could have gone wrong? In this hypothetical example, the elders might have felt sad and even more lonely because the presence of the visiting children reminded them that they were not able to see their own grandchildren (who perhaps live a long way away); the visiting pets reminded the elders of their own past pets and/or that they could no longer keep their own pets; and, in some cases, the visiting pets were not the kinds of animals that they liked, for example, big dogs rather than cats. In other words, this researcher might have assumed that any young children and any pets would alleviate loneliness, without any guidance from a theory pointing to, for example, the importance of symbolic meanings.

Another stumbling block to gerontological theorizing—which applies to other scientific disciplines as well—is the general failure of earlier "grand theories" to meet expectations. (Bengtson et al., 1999). In the earlier part of the 20th century, **grand theories** (that is, broad and general theories that focused on establishing universal principles) emerged in many disciplines, accompanied by optimism and confidence that science (both theory and methods) could understand and "fix" virtually all problems. Within gerontology, grand theories include disengagement theory, activity theory, and modernization theory (which will be discussed in more detail later in this chapter). Grand theories, in their generality, proved not to be adequate for solving all problems, especially specific applied problems. This resulted in a turning away from most aspects of these theories (and perhaps a case of throwing out the baby with the bathwater). At the same time, gerontologists began to specialize in subareas, without attention to creating theories about aging or old age per se. The resulting scientific norms that developed (sustained by gatekeepers, such as journal editors, and the emergence of increasingly specialized journals) focused on the reporting of (often numerical or quantitative) findings and a lack of emphasis on theory.

Bengtson et al. (1999) identify a third factor involved in the devaluing of theory; the relatively recent emergence of the "postmodern turn" in the social sciences (Derrida, 1978; Foucault, 1972; Habermas, 1972; Lyotard, 1984; Rorty, 1991)—a line of intellectual exposition emanating from Western European philosophy, art, and science. It is, perhaps, not a coincidence that Western Europe gave birth to postmodernism, given its connection to colonial guilt. Reaching gerontology later than some other disciplines, such as sociology and anthropology, the postmodern intellectual discourse represents a significant challenge to theory, as well as to the whole scientific enterprise. The postmodern challenge rests on a number of interrelated propositions. One is that science itself and, therefore, the knowledge that it claims are hierarchical—belonging to the privileged classes only. The second, and related, is the idea that scientific knowledge excludes the voices of the marginalized (the colonized and the minorities, including women, of the West); voices that are just as valid as those of so-called scientific authority. Third, reason itself—the basis of science, research, and theory—is attacked, as a holdover from the Western Enlightenment era. This translates into a rejection of scientific knowledge claims, since all knowledge is relative. Fourth, the relativity of all knowledge—scientific and nonscientific—lies in the fact that it is socially constructed, in both time and space.

At its extreme, postmodernism is anti-theoretical. For example, Bauman (1987: 3) tells us "to live without explanation." An example within social gerontology is Hazan (1994), who discredits any attempts to understand, or theorize about, old age. Marshall (1996), however, feels that less radical forms of postmodernism have had a liberating effect on gerontological theory. On one level, this is probably true; theorists have become more sensitive to the voices of people, especially marginalized and previously silenced people. Also, we have begun to pay more attention to the subjective elements of knowledge and to be more concerned about processes of domination in social life and less focused on the pursuit of "objective" knowledge. However, on another level, one can argue that postmodernism has had a stultifying effect on theory development within gerontology (and other social sciences). In an ironic twist, this anti-imperialist movement in intellectual discourse has taken on its own imperial power. That is, at least to some degree, researchers who do not hold to the tenets of postmodernism have been silenced. Rather than propose "old-fashioned" theoretical statements or propositions, they have retreated from theory altogether. While postmodernism proposes that no universal truths exist, in practice, postmodernist discourse has taken on the quality of a universal truth. The overall dilemma for gerontological theory (and other social theory) is that on the one hand, postmodernism eschews theory and, on the other hand, more mainstream theories are viewed as inadequate. The end result is that theory development is "in neutral."

The Importance of Theory

The above barriers to gerontological theory building matter only because theory matters. Bengtson et al. (1999) identify four ways in which theory is important.

1. *Theories integrate knowledge.* Theories summarize empirical findings and empirical relationships by incorporating them in a parsimonious way. In other words, theory synthesizes existing knowledge—without such synthesis, we would have a mass of findings that would not seem to be related and would not mean very much.
2. *Theories offer explanations.* While it is useful for findings to be synthesized, theory goes beyond synthesis to provide an understanding of how and why phenomena are related together. These explanations are provided in a way that they can be tested. If subsequent research does not support the theory, or supports it only in part, the theory will be abandoned or modified.
3. *Theories provide predictions.* A good theory will provide predictions that will lead to future discoveries and the furthering of knowledge.
4. *Theories can offer interventions to improve our lives.* This is not a defining characteristic of theory in the way that explanation is, but it can happen that the knowledge gained through the development of theory and its testing can be used to help alleviate social problems. In other words, theory has practical applications. It is not the case that theory exists in an abstract vacuum that is unrelated to applied concerns. Indeed, the opposite is the case; good theory leads to good practice.

The practice of science (and hence, the development of knowledge) depends on an ongoing weaving of research and theory. Each depends on the other; each is useless alone. Not every gerontologist would agree with all the four points listed above, as noted by Bengtson et al. (1999). For example, some focus more on theory as a way to explicate themes of meaning (rather than explanation) (e.g., Lynott & Lynott, 1996); others may view theory more in terms of highlighting diversity, rather than identifying empirical generalizations or regularities (e.g., Hendricks, 1997). However, most would agree that theory is an indispensable element in knowledge development. However, it is important to note that theories are, at best, partial explanations. Theories can provide a good explanation about that part of the social world upon which they cast their lenses.

Organizing Theories in Social Gerontology

The subject matter of gerontology is very large in scope. Bengtson et al. (1999) identify the three major foci of social gerontology as: (1) the aged; (2) aging as a process; and (3) age as a dimension of social structure. The aged and the aging process deal with individuals and their experiences, and hence are at the **micro-level of analysis**; theories attempting to explain individuals are micro-level theories. Age as an aspect of the social structure, in contrast, focuses on the **macro-level of analysis**; theories that deal with this dimension of aging are macro-level theories. While the micro–macro distinction is important, in reality, individuals and the societies in which they live are intimately and intricately interrelated. Can we really understand older and aging individuals without taking into account the broader social context in which they are embedded? Can we understand the social structure of age without, at the same time, looking at individuals and how they deal with that wider structure? Some social theorists, such as Anthony Giddens (1984), argue that the distinction between the individual and society, between micro- and macro-levels, is fallacious and unhelpful to the advancement of social scientific knowledge. Be that as it may, social gerontological theories often focus on either the micro- or the macro-level of analysis, reflecting what Marshall (1996: 14) characterizes as "a longstanding tension within social gerontology between the social psychological and the social structural levels of analysis." However, some theories, such as the life course perspective (discussed later in this chapter) attempt to bridge and link the micro- and macro-levels.

A recent article on the "state of the art" in social gerontological theory decries what is termed a trend toward "microfication" (Hagestad & Dannefer, 2001). "Microfication" involves an increasing tendency to focus on the characteristics of individuals and of micro (face-to-face) interaction, and to neglect macro-level phenomena, such as social institutions, social cohesion, social conflict, and norms and values. Hagestad and Dannefer (2001: 5) state that, with only some exceptions, "few systematic attempts to develop a general approach for conceptualizing age beyond the individual level can be found." They attribute this state of affairs to three factors: (1) the general "mood" of social science theory at the present time, with its emphasis on individual agency; (2) a tendency to "medicalize" old age, viewing it as a problem that individuals face; and (3) research funding agencies, which tend to view aging as an individual problem.

Second, social gerontological theories differ as to the assumptions made about the relationship between the individual and society—the distinction between normative and interpretative theorizing (Marshall, 1996). And, the differing assumptions have methodological consequences. Normative theories assume that individual behaviour is determined by social norms (rules); people learn, through socialization, the norms of their society and generally abide by them. Methodologically, normative theories favour the scientific method, and the use of deduction (that is, the testing of hypotheses deduced from theoretical propositions). In contrast, interpretative theories assume that people are creative in their use and construction of rules and do not automatically abide by them. On the methods front, interpretative theories are not tied to deduction and are more often associated with inductive techniques (that is, the building of theory from the "ground up" [that is, from observations of the real world], rather than theory testing). The distinction between normative and interpretative approaches is very similar to the distinction between consensus and conflict theoretical stances. Within sociology, major consensus theorists include Emile Durkheim and Talcott Parsons, while Karl Marx is the leading conflict theorist.

On the basis of these two axes—level of analysis and assumptions about the individual–society relationship—Marshall (1996) proposes a nine-cell classification of theories within social gerontology. His classification scheme is adapted here, for the placing of 11 theories that we will look at in more detail.[2] It should be noted that some of these theories have their origins in other disciplines—for example, social exchange is a theory from sociology; political economy perspectives existed in sociology, political science, and economics before being adopted by gerontologists. Others are the offshoots of theories from outside gerontology—for example, age stratification theory and disengagement theory have roots in structural functionalism. The only theory that social gerontology can (probably) claim as its own is the life course perspective, although one of its leading proponents, Glen Elder, argues that it has antecedents in structural functionalism and symbolic interactionism (Elder, 1992; Elder & Caspi, 1990).

Theories within Social Gerontology

We now turn to examine each of the 11 theories that appear in Table 2.1. We start with the earliest social gerontological theories. After that, we will look at more recent theories, with an emphasis on life course theory. We conclude with an examination of the most recent (or emergent) theories.

Early Theories

All the early theories in social gerontology focused on individuals and particularly on how individuals can best adjust to aging, that is, increase their satisfaction with life.

Table 2.1   CLASSIFICATION SCHEME FOR SELECTED SOCIAL GERONTOLOGICAL THEORIES

Individual/Society Relationship

Level of Analysis	NORMATIVE	BRIDGING	INTERPRETIVE
MACRO	Modernization		Economy Political
LINKING	Disengagement Age stratification	Life course Feminist	Critical
MICRO	Role Activity	Social exchange	Continuity

Source: Adapted from Marshall, V.W. 1996. The state of theory in aging and the social sciences. In R.H. Binstock & L.K. George, (Eds.). *Handbook of aging and the Social Sciences* (4th ed.), page 13.

Role Theory.

Cottrell (1942) was one of the first to propose a social theory of aging, when he applied role theory to the adjustment of aged individuals, in the mid-20th century. His conceptualizaton of role reflected the dominant structural–functional paradigm in American social science at the time. Roles were viewed as a set of highly structured expectations for role incumbents. **Role theory** focuses on role changes that individuals experience with aging, which were classified as being of two types. One type of role change is role loss, for example, the relinquishing of roles typical of adulthood, such as work roles. The other type of role change is role substitution, for example, the retiree role replaces the worker role. The problem, however, that older individuals face is that role loss is more likely and more frequent than role replacement. Individuals must adjust to a situation in which they have fewer roles and a reduced likelihood of gaining new ones. Together, the reduced roles and the inability to find new ones can lead to loss of self-identity and lowering of self-esteem. Research in this theoretical tradition focuses on how people can maintain life satisfaction despite the loss of roles. Some findings are: persons who self-identify as old are more likely to be unhappy than those who continue to self-identify as middle-aged; and men and women who adopt personality characteristics and role behaviours of the other gender (i.e., are more androgynous) are more satisfied in later life (Kart & Kinney, 2001).

Role continues to be an important concept in social gerontology, but it is now defined less normatively and deterministically. Role theory itself is no longer a dominant theory in social gerontology, but the concept of role remains important. We will see that it is used in many of the more contemporary theories, such as age stratification theory and the life course perspective.

Activity Theory.

Like role theory, activity theory is a micro-level theory focusing on the individual and his/her adjustment to old age. **Activity theory** holds that aging brings with it problems for individuals (i.e., decreases in life satisfaction) that can be alleviated by engaging in activities. Activity theory is sometimes characterized as the *implicit theory of aging,* meaning that it is implicitly held (and not actually stated) in a considerable amount of social gerontological research (Kart & Kinney, 2001). This theory is based on the proposition that older people—although they may face health declines—continue to have the psychological and social needs of earlier life. Activity theory posits that individuals who are able to meet their social and psychological needs through maintaining the activity level of middle life—through taking on new roles, friends, and activities—will be the most adjusted and satisfied with life. Some empirical research partially supports activity theory; in general, it has been found that older individuals who engage in a lot of informal, social activities (e.g., visiting with friends) are more satisfied than those who do not, but involvement in formal activities (e.g., participating in clubs, political parties, and so on) may (Aquino, Russell, Cutrona, & Altmaier, 1996; Caro & Bass, 1997) or may not (Lemon, Bengtson, & Peterson, 1972; Longino & Kart, 1982) enhance life satisfaction. However, overall, empirical support for activity theory has been mixed, and a number of criticisms have been voiced against it, leading researchers to advance their ideas.

One, activity theory assumes that taking on any kind of activity can substitute for the activities of the past. This view does not take into consideration the meanings that different people attribute to different activities. For example, one person may find volunteering at a local hospital very rewarding, whereas another person may find that same activity to be unpleasant. Two, activity theory assumes that psychological and social needs are stable over the adult years. However, it may be that a change in life circumstances (e.g., widowhood) can alter significantly the psychological and social needs of an individual. Three, activity theory presumes that individuals have a high degree of control over their social situation. But, do all older people have the means to reconstruct their lives, replacing old activities with new ones? Probably not—it is more likely that middle and upper class people have the economic resources to facilitate such changes. Old people with very little money may find it very difficult, even if they want to, to replace old friends or find activities that can compensate for lost ones. Four, activity theory has not been able to generate a generally agreed-upon conceptualization and measurement of activity (Achenbaum & Bengtson, 1994). With different researchers conceiving of, and measuring, activity in many different ways, it is difficult to gain a sense of an accumulated body of research that addresses if and how activity is related to adjustment in old age.

Disengagement Theory.

Cumming and Henry's (1961) disengagement theory is, on one level, the direct opposite to activity theory. In contrast to activity theory, **disengagement theory** holds that individual adjustment in old age is accomplished through withdrawing (disengaging) from social life, letting go of social roles and activities. On the other hand, disengagement theory represented a new approach to theorizing on aging in that it shifted focus away from the individual and to the wider social structure. The fundamental proposition of disengagement theory is that aging is accompanied by a *mutual withdrawal* of individuals and society. That is, the society withdraws from the individual, which is viewed as functional for society; at the same time, the individual wishes to be less involved in social interaction. Thus, the process is normative and agreed on by all concerned (Cumming, 1963). Further, the disengagement process is inevitable and universal because it makes for social equilibrium—there are minimal disruptions to society when an old and socially withdrawn person dies.

Cumming (1963) elaborated on the original formulation of disengagement theory by adding a relationship between personality and style of disengagement. She argued that there are two main personality types. One is the *impinger*, who is active and exhibits flexibility. The other is the *selector*, who is more cautious and subdued by nature. These two types react differently to disengagement. The impinger, who is generally considered "young" for his or her age for a long time, faces the physical losses of old age with anxiety and eventually withdraws in order to reduce confusion in his or her life. On the other hand, the selector, who has always been more withdrawn throughout life, reacts to old age with increased apathy for his or her social environment (Kart & Kinney, 2001). In general, this theory holds that impingers are more able to disengage in a nontraumatic way.

Disengagement theory created quite a reaction within gerontology, with gerontologists either "for" or "against" it, often quite vehemently. For the most part, however, subsequent research failed to find empirical support for disengagement. Also, some research suggests a social class dimension to disengagement; for example, Atchley (1971) found that retired university professors tended to be very much psychologically engaged in their profession, even if not socially engaged. Other occupations do not offer the same opportunity for involvement. Also, it is interesting that the research testing disengagement theory has tended to focus only on one side of the disengagement equation—individuals withdrawing from society. Very little research has taken disengagement theory to task on its proposition that society benefits from the withdrawal of its senior members.

The controversy around disengagement theory has continued, although not as vigorously as in the 1960s and 1970s. Hochschild (1975) argues that the theory contains three problems that have contributed to its continued controversy. One, the theory is hard to actually disconfirm (which is not a desirable quality for a theory). This is because Cumming and Henry (1961) created a number of categories for people who did not engage (for example, they could be unsuccessful disengagers, exceptional people who re-engage, or disengagers who were "off-schedule" and would presumably eventually disengage). Two, the concept of disengagement is so broad that there may be many different types of disengagement, both psychological and social. For example, there can be disengagement from friends, disengagement from social activities, disengagement from material possessions, and so on. As a result, theoretical propositions can multiply, and researchers can spend a lot of years testing them empirically. Three, disengagement theory does not pay attention to what the older individual is thinking or feeling. Behaviour that looks like disengagement to the researcher may not be viewed that way by the individuals involved. For example, retirement—to the outside observer—exemplifies disengagement. But, Crawford (1971), on the basis of a study of English men, found that different men give different meanings to it: retiring *back to* something, retiring *from* something, and retiring *for* something. This disjuncture between objective reality (retirement, in this case) and subjective meanings kept the door open for further research on disengagement (Kart & Kinney, 2001).

Newer Theories

Until the early 1980s, disengagement theory and activity theory were the dominant theories within social gerontology. Individual adjustment in later life was the focus of gerontological study. Even though disengagement theory introduced social structure to aging theory, research within both theoretical perspectives focused on aging individuals and satisfaction. Since then, a substantial number of new theories have been proposed and some more general social theories have been applied to the study of age and aging. We will now look at five of them—continuity theory, social exchange theory, age stratification theory, aging and modernization theory, and political economy of aging theory—going in general from the more micro to the more macro in focus. We will then give special attention to the life course perspective, given its recent popularity.

Continuity Theory.

Like the activity and disengagement theories, continuity theory is a uniquely gerontological theory that focuses upon individual adjustment in later life. **Continuity theory** holds that as people age, they make choices in an effort to preserve ties with the past. Continuity can be both internal and external. Internal continuity refers to the coherence of a personal structure of ideas (based on memory). External continuity refers to the constancy of familiar environments and people. However, it is not the case that successful adjustment to old age means that people should remain in the past or should behave exactly as they did in midlife (Kart & Kinney, 2001). Atchley (1989) reports that older people classify the degree of continuity in their lives as: too little, optimum, and too much. Too little continuity occurs when people perceive that their lives are unpredictable or discontinuous. This is associated with low levels of satisfaction, since individuals are not able to use their prior coping skills and strategies successfully. Too much continuity occurs when people feel that their lives are too predictable. New and/or enriching experiences do not occur. Optimum continuity exists when the pace of change in people's lives is in line with their personal preferences, personality, and societal expectations. Thus, continuity does not imply no change; rather, it means that new experiences occur against a backdrop of familiarity. Also, continuity is not necessarily the same thing for all individuals. Some individuals, throughout their entire lives, particularly in later life, prefer quiet activities and a lot of "me" time; others want activity and a high level of social involvement. Therefore, a degree of correspondence between midlife and later life is important for adjustment to old age, according to continuity theory.

While continuity theory is considered one of the main social gerontological theories, it has not been tested very much. And it has limitations. Perhaps the most obvious criticism is its lack of consideration of structural factors—if life is unpredictable because of a severe shortage of money (the result, for example, of low wages and seasonal work in the fishing industry, no private pension, and a work-related injury that led to "early retirement"), how is one to cope "successfully" in old age? Another query is: Is it agist to assume, as continuity theory seems to, that midlife is the standard for old age? Also, continuity theory does not take into account maladaptive behaviours in midlife; presumably, they would not become adaptive if continued into old age (Kart & Kinney, 2001).

Social Exchange Theory.

A variant of social exchange theory, originally set forth by George Homans (1961), has been applied to the subject of gerontology, especially by Dowd (1975; 1980). **Social exchange theory** is concerned with person-to-person interaction, focusing upon the calculations and negotiations that transpire between individuals as they seek to maximize rewards and minimize costs in their interactions. Rewards can be either material (e.g., money, property) or nonmaterial (e.g., affection, approval). Costs refer to the loss of rewards. Social exchange theory rests on the propositions that people want to profit (i.e., receive more than they give) in their social interactions and that profit consists of a perception that rewards outweigh costs. The ability to profit from a social interaction depends upon the resources that persons bring to their exchange relationships. Exchanges work best and are most satisfying when the resources that individuals have are approximately equal—this makes for interdependency and not dependency. When one of the persons in a social relationship has substantially fewer resources, his or her ability to profit from the exchange is reduced.

Dowd (1975; 1980) argues that older persons find themselves with fewer resources in exchange relationships. Since they cannot reciprocate, they are often forced to offer their compliance to others. And, having to do what other people want you to do is not an envious position to be in. Rather than be compliant, older people can choose to withdraw from relationships. For example, Sarah Matthews (1979), in a study of a centre for older women, observed a high rate of dropout, which, through interviews, she determined to be a calculated decision made by the older women to avoid the costs of interacting with the middle-aged staff at the centre who viewed them as old and, therefore, dependent. In other words, persons with perceived disadvantages (few exchange resources) can protect themselves and their identity by avoiding people who define them in negative terms.

It is important to note that the resources that a person has may not be as important as the resources that he or she is *assumed* to have. In our society, it is assumed that older people lack resources—for example, that they have out-of-date skills and knowledge and that they have inadequate physical strength. These assumptions underestimate the resources of older people, creating situations in which the seniors become powerless. For example, an older man is assumed by a prospective employer to be unable to work at a job requiring the use of a computer; an older woman is assumed by the police to have misplaced an item that she says has been stolen. The fact that the man is a computer wizard and that the woman has a wonderful memory may not figure into these social interactions. Thus, social exchange theory is a "bridging" theory (see Table 2.1) because it incorporates the agism of the wider society into the person-to-person social interactions in which older people are engaged.

In an important empirical test of social exchange theory, Kart and Longino (1987) found only moderate support for the theory. In a study of 1,346 retirement community residents in the United States, they report low inverse relationships between support (emotional, social, and instrumental) given, emotional and social support received, and life satisfaction. In other words, both seniors who gave more and those who received more had lower levels of life satisfaction. According to social exchange theory, we would expect only those who received more to be unhappy (due to lack of reciprocity). The finding that those who gave more were less satisfied is unexpected and is not consistent with social exchange theory's postulate that persons with more exchange resources will have more satisfying social relationships. A more recent study, however, finds higher levels of psychological well being among elders with more exchange resources but also reports that social exchanges are not a very important determinant of well being (Liang, Krause, & Bennett, 2001). Nevertheless, this theory, especially given its "bridging" of individuals and society, has potential; reformulations based on empirical findings are needed.

Age Stratification Theory.

Age stratification theory was initially developed by Matilda White Riley and her colleagues (1972). Unlike the other theories considered so far, age stratification theory is concerned with all age groups and not just the aged. It is more macro in focus, and views age not only as a characteristic of individuals but also as an important and dynamic element of the wider society.

The elements and processes involved in age stratification theory are presented in Figure 2.1. The age structure of a society consists of four primary elements (these are the boxes in Figure 2.1). The first element is *age strata*, which refers to groups that are based on age (e.g., youth, adults, the aged) and that have unequal status and opportunities in society; Riley (1971) argues that age strata share many commonalities with social classes, especially their hierarchical nature. As individuals age, they move from one stratum to another. The second element is *age-related capacities*. Each stratum differs from the others in the contributions that it makes to the wider society; that is, each stratum is characterized by age-related capabilities. These capacities depend on both biology and social/cultural definitions. The third element is the *social roles* based on age that are available to people. Some roles are directly linked to age (e.g., one must be 16 years old to drive; 65 years is considered the entry point for old age); other roles are only indirectly related to age. Regarding the latter, a society's normative system specifies the appropriate ages for persons to take on (or give up) given roles. We expect, for example, that undergraduate students will be approximately 18 to 23 years old; we expect that people will not be married at age 17 years. As this role linkage with age becomes looser, we can observe people in "off-time" roles (a 40-year-old first-year university student, a 16-year-old husband). However, the very fact that we notice they are "off-time" shows the workings of the age normative system. Fourth is *age-related expectations,* which refer to our expectations of how roles are performed by people of varying ages. For example, we do not expect a 20-year-old bride and a 40-year-old bride to act in the same way.

Figure 2.1 ELEMENTS AND PROCESSES IN AGE STRATIFICATION THEORY

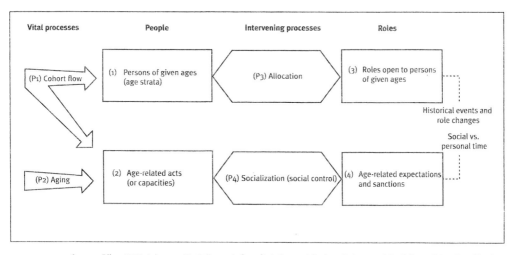

Source: Riley, M.W., Johnson, M., & Foner, A. (1972). *Aging and Society, Volume 3: A Sociology of Age Stratification.*
© Russell Sage Foundation, 112 East 64th Street, New York, NY, 10021. Reprinted with permission.

In addition, age stratification theory posits a set of processes that affects the degree of articulation between the above four structural elements and the patterning of individual lives. There are two basic processes and two intervening processes. The first basic process is *cohort flow* (the term *cohort* refers to a group of people who experience a given event at the same time; for example, everyone born in 1980 is part of the same birth cohort). Cohort flow refers to all the factors that contribute to the shaping of the age strata—fertility, in particular, mortality, and migration (as we saw in Chapter 1). Age stratification theory views cohort flow as a process, since a cohort is continuously undergoing change—it loses members (due to death, emigration), it can gain members (through immigration). Also, any given cohort is mobile, as it moves from one age stratum to another. The second basic process is *individual aging*, referring to the physiological and maturational changes that occur over time. However, the differences between age strata cannot be accounted for by age alone; therefore, age stratification theory proposes two intervening processes.

One intervening process is *allocation*, referring to the process of assigning and reassigning people of various ages to "suitable" roles. (Of course, role assignment is based on more than age, but age is one important criterion that we use.) Role allocation by age, which is also known as age grading, is based on a number of factors, such as cultural values, economic conditions (e.g., when the economy is healthy, people tend to marry at younger ages), and the general shape of the age structure, or population pyramids, as discussed in Chapter 1 (e.g., the large cohort of the "baby boom" may have delayed job opportunities for persons younger than the baby boomers). When any of these factors change, the system of role allocation by age occurs. The other intervening process is *socialization*—the learning and internalization of the age stratification system that is necessary to ensure the smooth transition of people from one age stratum to the next. We are socialized about the age stratification system through direct observation and participation in small groups, such as the family, through books and other forms of media, and by formal organizations.

Age stratification theory has been influential in social gerontology; however, its importance has waned with the general decline of structural functionalist-based theories and their status quo orientation. In dealing with criticisms—such as the static nature of the concept of age strata and its focus on social equilibrium—its proponents are "re-inventing" this theoretical perspective under a new name—the aging and society paradigm (Riley, Foner, & Riley, 1999). This theoretical perspective has introduced the notion of structural lag, referring to the disjuncture between the (limited) opportunities that our society affords older people and the growing numbers of competent elders. This represents a significant moving away from the concepts of age-related capacities and age-related expectations, so central to age stratification theory. Another new element is the idea of the emergence of an age-integrated society (Riley, 1997), in which age barriers are removed, and people of all age ages interact together—which turns the concept of age stratification upside down. Riley and her colleagues (1999) feel that age integration should demand the attention of the next generation of theory builders in social gerontology.

Aging and Modernization Theory.

Aging and modernization theory is most closely associated with Donald Cowgill (Cowgill & Holmes, 1972). It is a grand theory of the macro variety, attempting to establish universal principles regarding the status of the aged. Its most general and important proposition is that the status of the aged declines with increasing modernization. This idea was not new to Cowgill; early sociologists, such as Emile Durkheim and Max Weber in Europe and Ernest Burgess in the United States, expressed the same contention. However, Cowgill was the first to systemize this idea into a theory and generate testable hypotheses.

According to aging and modernization theory, four interrelated aspects of modernization are particularly salient in relation to aging. One aspect is the development of *health technology*, which includes improvements in sanitation and nutrition as well as curative and surgical medicine. Progress in health technology eventually operates to increase life expectancy, facilitating the aging of the population. With population aging, there is intergenerational conflict for jobs, which eventually results in the establishment of retirement. With retirement comes reduced prestige and reduced income for the aged. A second aspect is *economic modernization*, bringing with it many new specialized jobs, particularly in cities. The young will fill these jobs because they are more likely to have the training for them and they are more geographically mobile, that is, more likely to move to the urban centres where the jobs are. As a result, there is an inversion of status, with young people getting the better jobs and older people left in jobs that tend to become obsolete. The latter also creates a pressure toward retirement. Third, *urbanization* itself operates to lower the status of the aged. As young people migrate to urban areas, the role of the aged in the family changes. As elderly persons become geographically separated from their children and grandchildren, they become peripheral to the nuclear families of their children. Also, the upward social mobility of the children creates a social distance between the generations. Fourth, increases in *education* lower the status of the aged. In premodern societies, elders are the repositories of knowledge, an important role that reinforces their status. With increases in education, older people lose this role as their children gain more knowledge and have more skills than the parents have.

While Cowgill wants his theory to apply to all societies, he does recognize that societies will have unique characteristics (termed extraneous factors) that affect the way that modernization relates to aging. For the Western case, he identifies two unique factors. One is the work ethic, with its high value placed on industriousness, savings, time consciousness, efficiency, and individual achievement. These values serve to reinforce the decline in the status of the aged—people who no longer work. Second is the cult of youth, which is related to the work ethic and its emphasis on efficiency and so on. In a cult of youth, youth becomes a symbol of, and a means to, progress. By definition, then, older people are devalued—they are no longer young.

What about the future? With continued economic modernization, should we expect the status of seniors to decline further? In a revision to the initial theory, partly based on the research of Palmore and Manton (1974), Cowgill (1974) argues that the relationship between age status and modernization is likely curvilinear. In other words, the status of old people is relatively high in premodern and late modern societies and is low in the middle stages of development. What might account for rising status in late modernity? Possible factors include: a decline in the work ethic, which means that retirement is less harmful to status; increased affluence, so that societies can afford to provide adequate incomes to seniors; the differences across generations in education level narrow; increasing numbers of well-educated seniors become a political force (Cowgill, 1974).

While offering important insights, aging and modernization theory also has its limitations, and no longer enjoys the popularity it did in the 1970s. First, the concept of modernization in the theory is not well explicated and is used synonymously with a host of other terms, such as development, change, westernization, and progress. Indeed, it is often difficult to pinpoint when modernization actually begins, making tests of the theory very difficult. David Hackett Fischer (1977) argues that the decline of the status of the aged in the United States preceded any of the modernization changes that Cowgill's theory postulates as critical. Second, the theory, while aiming for universal applicability, appears to be ethnocentric, taking the West as the "standard." Third, researchers have challenged the linear conception of modernization that is implicit in aging and modernization theory. Modernization tends not to be linear and is a much more dynamic process than the way it is viewed in this theory. Fourth, aging and modernization theory homogenizes elders of the past; they were not all affluent, powerful property owners.

Political Economy of Aging Theory.

While political economy theory has a long history in the social sciences, it has been applied to the subject of the aged and aging societies only fairly recently. In Canada, the leading gerontologist using this perspective is John Myles (1984; Myles & Quadagno, 1991); Carroll Estes and Meredith Minkler are the gerontologists in the United States most closely associated with this perspective (e.g., Estes, 1979, Minkler & Estes, 1984); in the United Kingdom, relevant gerontologists include Alan Walker (1981, 1996) and Chris Phillipson (1982).

Canadian social gerontologists have tended to be more macro-focused than their American counterparts, and the political economy of aging has been a more important and more used perspective in Canada than in the United States. The basic premise of **political economy of aging theory** is that the experience of old age and the treatment of seniors can only be understood within the context of the economy (both national and international), the state, the labour market, and the intersecting class, gender, age and racial/ethnic divisions in society (Estes, Gerard, Zones, & Swan, 1984). Inequality by age is an important element of the political economy of aging perspective; it seeks to uncover the structural conditions that create age inequality and the way that older people are defined and treated (Quadagno & Reid, 1999).

The political economy of aging perspective originated from Marxist and neo-Marxist critiques of age stratification theory (Quadagno & Reid, 1999). Specific criticisms include that age stratification theory uses a static conceptualization of social structure; neglects political processes that create inequalities; ignores power relationships that play an important role in how roles and statuses are allocated; and does not consider the wide variation and diversity within age cohorts. The time had come for a social gerontological theory that focused on the dynamics of inequality and power relations, and the political economy of aging emerged to fill the bill.

According to Estes (1991: 31), the political economy of aging perspective is based on the following premises.

- The social structure shapes how older people are perceived and how they perceive themselves.
- Both labels applied to the elderly and social policy shape the experience of old age.
- Social policy and the politics of aging mirror wider social inequalities and the power struggles around them.
- Social policy reflects the dominant belief system that is crucial in enforcing, bolstering, and extending structured inequalities in the wider economic, political, and social order.

We can see that social policy—and the state that is responsible for it—are crucial elements of this perspective. The state is especially important in the lives of older persons, since they are more dependent on state policies than are younger adults. However, the state's primary purpose is to assure the well being of the economy. This means that older people, who are largely outside productive labour, are in a precarious and tension-filled relationship with the state. Yet, state policy is also responsible for meeting social needs. Thus, a central concern of the political economy of aging perspective is the dynamic between the organization of work (capitalism) and social needs and how the contradiction between the two affects the aging process and the experience of aging (Estes, 1991).

According to this perspective, the problems faced by older people are socially constructed, not biologically determined. The political economy of aging perspective is critical of the "structured dependency" (Townsend, 1981) of the aged, viewing age-related dependency as a construction of economic, political, and social factors in the 20th century West. The state, through the institutionalization of retirement, for example, has played a key role in the dependency of the aged. This perspective is also highly critical of institutionalized medicine—by applying a medical model to aging, it has created an equivalency between aging and illness, has helped create the idea that aging is a problem, and has individualized aging, making it appear to be the private problem of individuals. At the same time, medicine and many "helping professions" have become an "enterprise" with a vested interest in the view that old people are dependent and in need of their help (Estes, 1971).

The political economy of aging perspective is sympathetic to the critique of apocalyptic demography, discussed in Chapter 1. This perspective takes note of the state's creation of crisis as a way to promote its own agenda. As Estes, Linkins, and Binney (1996: 350) state, "(u)nderstanding the contemporary welfare state and its treatment of the aged requires... attention to *crisis construction and crisis management* by the state and its political leaders." [italics added] The socially constructed "crisis" of population aging has much to do with the distribution and control of capital and much less to do with the demographics of the changing age structure. As noted by Myles (1991: 304–305), the fact that a greater proportion of people (i.e., the aged) exist on public pensions means that "an ever-growing and increasingly important portion of the national wage bill [is]... removed from the market... [and] workers, in their capacity as citizens are able to claim a share of the social product independent of their capacity as wage earners." Such a shift is detrimental to the interests of capital; the state (aligned with capital) responds by constructing a "crisis" that allows it to "reform" pensions and health care, for example.

The Life Course Perspective.

The life course theoretical perspective, with Glen Elder (e.g., 1985; 1994; 2000) as its major developer, is generally considered the dominant perspective within social gerontology at the present time. It has roots in age stratification theory and also draws heavily on prominent American sociologist C. Wright Mills' (1959) call for a theoretical orientation that encompasses individual biography and history and the intersections of biography and history within the social structure. This call is for a theory that links macro (history, social structure) elements and the micro (or individual) level, and life course theory is considered the best attempt within social gerontology, to date, to make that linkage.

Before we look at the life course perspective, it is useful to distinguish among a number of concepts—life course, life span, life cycle, and life history. These terms are often used interchangeably; however, they do not refer to the same thing (Elder, 2000). *Life cycle* most precisely refers to the stages of parenthood, from the birth of the first child to the departure of all children (to set up homes of their own and, presumably, begin childbearing). Normatively, this cycle is repeated from one generation to the next, although, in actuality, some people will not have children and will not be part of an intergenerational life cycle. The life cycle comprises a set of ordered stages, with the important transition points being marriage, the births of the first and the last children, and the departure of the last child (resulting in the "empty nest" stage). In other words, the life cycle concept focuses upon the sequence of events and tells us little about age (e.g., marriage may be at 18 or at 30 years). A bigger limitation of the concept is its focus on "ideal" sequencing, which is increasingly being disrupted by common-law marriage preceding legal marriage and by divorce and remarriage. In other words, the concept has become less and less applicable to more and more people. *Life history* refers to a number of methods for collecting information about human lives over time. Information may be gained from either archival/administrative records or by interviews. Quite often, the former data source involves quantitative data, and statistical methods, such as life history event analysis, are employed. In contrast, interviews are more likely to yield qualitative data. Life history also refers to a self-reported narration of life; a narrative account by individuals in which the researcher takes a nondirective role, documenting the history only and not asking specific questions. *Life span*[3] refers to age-related biological and behaviourial changes from birth to death (Elder, 2000). This concept is most close to that of the life course. However, there is a difference between the span of a life time and the course of a life (Hagestad, 1990). The concept of life course is more macro; the life course reflects how society gives both personal and social meanings to the passage of time in a life. *Life course* can be defined as "trajectories that extend across the life span, such as family or work; and by short-term changes or transitions, such as entering or leaving school, acquiring a full-time job, and the first marriage. Each life course transition is embedded in a trajectory that gives it specific form and meaning." (Elder, 2000:1615) Thus, the focus of life course theory is on the transitions and trajectories that constitute an individual's life or the lives of similarly situated people.

The **life course theoretical perspective** is concerned with individuals as social personae, "tracing their pathways along an age-differentiated, socially marked sequence of transitions." (Hagestad, 151) These pathways occur over time. Time is an important concept within this theoretical perspective. There are three types of time: life time—or age; historical time—the historical era in which a life is embedded and the historical events that may affect it (e.g., Depression, war[s]); and social time—the ordering of life events/social roles by age-linked expectations and options (Elder, 1975; 1978). Research based on the life course perspective attempts to untangle the effects of age, history, and social structure on the pathways that make up the life course of individuals. The linking of age and historical time has benefited from the concept of cohort (persons born at the same time). If a historical event differentially affects people of different cohorts (or ages), then a **cohort effect** has occurred (Uhlenberg & Miner, 1996). For example, the Vietnam war era (and the protests that accompanied it and helped form a counterculture in the 1960s) had a different effect on the youth of the time than on middle-aged persons. On the other hand, if a historical event has the same effect on persons for all cohorts (ages), a **period effect** has occurred. The events of

September 11, 2001 may be of this variety. Both period and cohort effects show the impact of historical influences on individual lives (Elder, 2000).

Age and social time are linked by the notion of normative timing. That is, societies have expectations about the "appropriate" age for persons to take on (or exit from) social roles—these are sometimes called *social clocks*. Some of these expectations are formal (e.g., retirement at age 65 years); many more are informal, embedded in wider social and cultural norms. Settersten and Hagestad (1996) argue that age norms have three characteristics: (1) they are prescriptions for behaviour; (2) they are supported by widespread consensus in society; and (3) they are enforced through mechanisms of social control. Research indicates that individuals in Canada and the United States perceive age guidelines and express age preferences for role transitions (Gee, 1990; Settersten & Hagestad, 1996; Veevers, Gee & Wister, 1996); however, there is debate about whether these guidelines and preferences constitute age norms or not.

According to life course theory's main architect, Glen Elder (2000), it is organized around four major principles.

1. *The life course of individuals is embedded and shaped by their historical and geographical placement.* This principle is in reference to the cohort effect discussed earlier. That is, when societies are undergoing rapid social change, different cohorts are exposed to different structures of opportunities and constraints and to different cultural values. For example, persons born in the earlier years of the baby boom (in Canada, those born between 1946 and 1952) faced much competition for jobs (due to the size of the cohort), but in a generally expanding economy in which jobs were quite plentiful, and were exposed to a culture of youth resistance. In contrast, their children (who are of a relatively small cohort, due to the low fertility of the boomers) faced less competition for jobs, but due to economic recession, there were very few jobs around when they reached young adulthood, and they were exposed to a culture of youth consumption (designer labels and so on). Thus, the life courses of baby boomers and their children will vary due to economic and cultural differences. Also, within each cohort, variations will occur in terms of geography. For example, the "hippie" movement was more pronounced in large cities; the economic recession of the early 1980s hit certain parts of Canada harder than others.

2. *The impact of a transition or event depends on when it occurs in a person's life.* Social change or major events affect individuals differentially according to their age at the time of the change/event; this is sometimes called the "life stage principle." For example, if a country has compulsory military service, usually young people are conscripted and the military service tends not to have far-reaching consequences for the rest of their lives. However,

during war time, older people are engaged in military service. Late entry into the military in World War II had life-long consequences, such as increased risk of divorce, increased risk of work–life instability, and negative physical health effects in later life (Elder, 1987; Povalko & Elder, 1990). Similarly, giving birth at age 15 years will likely negatively affect the educational attainment of the mother and consequently her work opportunities and earnings; we would not expect this if a mother has her first child at the age of 30 years.

3. *Lives are lived interdependently.* This principle is sometimes called "linked lives." Given that we all live in networks of shared relationships, the actions of one person can affect the lives of other persons. This is most easily seen in the family context. For example, if a young woman has a child at a very young age, she also makes her mother a grandmother at a young age. Research on African American women in Los Angeles shows that young motherhood can be associated with a rejection of responsibilities by grandmothers, with care being shifted up a generation to great-grandmothers (Burton & Bengston, 1985). In contrast, women who become grandmothers at an "expected age" (i.e., their late 40s) are happy to take on the grandmother role. Canadian research (Mitchell & Gee, 1995) on the homeleaving phenomenon also shows the effects of linked lives. Children who leave and return home (boomerangers) several times are viewed by parents as having a disruptive effect on their lives and their marriages; children who leave home and do not return, or return only once or twice, do not negatively influence the marital satisfaction of their parents.

4. *Individuals construct their own life course through their choices and actions, contingent upon the constraints and opportunities provided by history and social circumstance.* This principle gives centrality to the concept of human agency within life course theory. Individuals are not just passive recipients of whatever history and social structure present them with; they have agency, and can make good or bad choices or act wisely or unwisely. Life course theory does not reduce individual behaviour to a stimulus–response model, in which all individuals respond in a given way to a set of social factors. Thus, two people in the same historical and social situation may act differently; for instance, one may choose to drop out of school at age 16 years, while the other goes to university; one may choose to remain in a bad marriage, and the other may leave it. The concept of planful competence has emerged to explain the different choices/actions of individuals; that is, persons who in their youth are future oriented and efficient are more likely to make "good" life-course decisions (Clausen, 1993). However, it seems that planful competence only holds when there are real opportunities open to individuals (Shanahan, Elder & Miech, 1997); when

the economy is very bad, for example, no amount of planful competence helps individuals construct their life course in a favourable way. This suggests that different historical and social circumstances will affect the likelihood of certain choices/actions being taken. For example, obtaining a divorce before 1969 in Canada was very difficult; the chances of going to university are better now than they were 50 years ago.

The life course perspective is a dynamic one; it focuses upon the complex interrelationships among biographical time, social time, and historical time. As such, it has much to deal with and much left to do. To "do," longitudinal data over several years are needed; something that is severely limited in the Canadian case. Hagestad and Dannefer (2001) identify a number of critical issues for this theoretical perspective and the research emanating from it. They suggest that the theory has yet to articulate a clear conception of social structure, with the effect that—despite the basic tenets of the theory—research has tended to be micro-oriented. Thus, we know more about lives at the micro-level than we do about lives at the macro-level. The failure of life course theory to conceptualize social structure adequately may account for some of the difficulties in research on social time. Social time may involve more than individually internalized social clocks, which have been a significant research focus. How much of social time involves normative expectations, and how much involves the structural needs of economic organization? A more macro-oriented conceptualization of social time may be needed.

Similarly, the concept of "linked lives" has been studied as to individual relationships (e.g., mothers and daughters) but the role of macro-factors, such as social policy, in the linking of lives has not been considered. Also, some researchers have registered skepticism about the life-stage principle—that the effects of social change depend on the age of individuals. For example, Elder (1974) found that young people were more negatively affected by the Depression than were the older people. However, it may not necessarily be the case that the young are the hardest hit. If people have invested many years in something that becomes useless/redundant/not socially valued, because of major social upheaval, they may be more negatively affected than young persons who have invested little.

The concept of agency—which does explicitly focus on the individual—contains some problems as well. Settersten (1999) argues that life course theory to date has not paid attention to *how* individuals shape or change structures, and the reverse; he calls for an "agency within structure view." Also, life course theory may establish individual agency and social structure as an artificial dichotomy. In addition, agency is implicitly assumed to be a "good thing" in itself; life course theory neglects the "dark side" of agency, for example, risk, stress, and uncertainty (Settersten & Hagestad, 2001). Relatedly, we cannot necessarily assume that individual agency is effective in producing or shaping social structural change; we need to know the conditions conducive to efficacy of individual agency—conditions that are likely social in origin.

Emergent Theories

In recent years, some new theoretical perspectives have been applied to social gerontology. Here we consider two of them—the feminist perspective and critical gerontology. While neither are "neat" theoretical packages, both, in varying ways and in varying degrees (depending upon what is being focused upon), share tenets with the political economy of aging perspective.

Feminist Theory.

There is no "one" feminist approach, either overall or with respect to aging. **Feminist theory** ranges from liberal feminism (which holds that men and women are equal and should have equal rights) to radical feminism (which focuses on women's subjugation due to patriarchal arrangements and argues that society must be fundamentally reorganized to address this problem). Within gerontology, a wide range of feminist approaches exists as well (Lopata, 1995). Given this diversity, providing the full scope of feminist gerontological theory is not possible here. Rather, our discussion is limited to general principles with which most feminist gerontologists would agree.

Feminist gerontology theory is based on the premise that gender is a fundamental organizing principle of society, operating over the life course of individuals. This does not mean that women and men are somehow "different"; rather, it implies something much more important—that gender is a structured aspect of our society. In other words, gender is socially constructed (not biologically determined) and the social construction of gender permeates all aspects of our society. With regard to biological determinism, leading feminist scholar Michele Fine (1992) states that feminist work must be intolerant of what is considered inevitable and natural. Since gender is an organizing principle of social organization, it is implicated in social stratification and inequality. Indeed, gender stratification—which occurs in work, family, leisure, and so on—is one of the ways in which patterns of (male) advantage and (female) disadvantage operate.

Gender and age operate together to lower the status of women as they age. As Garner (1999: 4) writes: "Much of western society's view of women's worth is associated with a socially defined social attractiveness that clearly equates youth with beauty and the ability to attract men. Therefore, women lose their social value simply by growing old." However, while women lack social, economic, and political power, this does not mean that they must accept this. Resources permitting, women have individual agency to resist social definitions of powerlessness. Indeed, one of the goals of feminist gerontology is to empower women to resist societal definitions and rules. Gee and Kimball (1987), in one of the earliest feminist gerontological works in Canada, argue that older women do, in fact, resist their social and political marginality through the development of rich interpersonal ties.

Feminist theory has implications for the practice of research, that is, methods. Feminist methods call for a dismantling of the power hierarchy between the researcher and the researched. Thus, older persons are transformed from "subjects" of research to real people engaged in a mutually beneficial (research) relationship. Relatedly, feminist research and theory begin with the premise that the knowledge brought to the research venue by older persons is just as valid as the knowledge of the professional researcher; this is the concept of *multiple knowledges*. One task of the feminist researcher, then, is to give "voice" to the marginalized, often silenced members of our society, such as older women, validating their experiences and their worth as individuals. However, feminist theory goes beyond this—seeking to empower older women and to play an advocacy role for them. Thus, feminist scholars do not feel satisfied with pointing out, for example, the severe financial situation of many older Canadian women; they seek to alter pension policies and so on to change this situation. Ideally, this is done collaboratively with older women and not just on their behalf, as participatory research is a hallmark of much feminist work. However, if some older women are physically or mentally limited in advocating for themselves, feminist scholars will operate alone.

The empowerment of older women is best seen in feminist practice, that is, for example, working with older women who require some type of social service. Feminist practitioners seek to empower older women through helping them establish new roles, identify their strengths, and use their knowledge (Garner, 1999). This is often done in small groups, in which older women share their experiences (and come to understand the social structural roots of problems shared), validate each other's sense of self-worth, and sustain each other through the development of meaningful relationships. While feminist practice aims to promote the independence and self-sufficiency of clients, it, of course, also supports the client's rights to services and resources and serves an educative function regarding older women's rights.

Critical Theory.

Critical gerontology is similarly not a neat theoretical "package." It could be viewed as a paradigm, rather than a theory. Here, we examine it as a theory. In Chapter 3, we discuss it as a paradigm. It has roots in the Frankfurt School (neo-Marxism), postmodernism, the humanities, and feminism (Achenbaum, 1997). Also, it has sometimes been integrated with the political economy of aging approach (Estes, 1999). In this case, the concept of moral economy is added to that of political economy, with *moral economy* referring to the shared moral assumptions that underlie norms of reciprocity in a society. The moral economy approach makes explicit the cultural beliefs and values that underlie social policies and practices that affect seniors. For example, the Canadian moral economy has valued equity and access to health care for all, including older people, far more than that of the United States (Clark, 1999). It remains to be seen if the Canadian collectivist orientation will survive the ongoing onslaught to health care; if it does not, we will know that our moral economy of what is "right" has changed in a fundamental way.

The essence of critical gerontology is reflexivity. That is, **critical theory** seeks a self-awareness and a deconstruction of the assumptions underlying "mainstream" social gerontological theories and research. At the same time, it focuses upon a critique of the existing social order and its treatment of the aged, especially by exposing assumptions and myths that maintain the status quo. Relatedly, and in keeping with the centrality of reflexivity, critical gerontology seeks to provide us with an understanding of the meaning of aging and old age.

In its extreme forms, critical gerontology represents a significant attack on mainstream gerontology because it questions the importance of causation—a central component of explanation, itself the defining characteristic of theories. In this way, critical gerontology can be viewed as part of the postmodern turn in social theory, discussed earlier. Some forms of critical gerontology reject causation in the call for a rich understanding of life that is intrinsically situational—affected by history, culture, geography; it is believed that the search for causes can only hinder our understanding of aging and old age. Critical gerontology assumes that the nature of aging is fluid (i.e., ever-changing), context based, and subject to individual agency. This nonstatic assumption about what aging is represents a fresh approach to social gerontology related to the humanities as much as to the social sciences. Thus, the scientific search for generalizable knowledge is underemphasized, in favour of a more humanities-oriented understanding of fluidity and context in aging. However, critical gerontology retains some links to the social sciences. For example, like feminist gerontology, critical gerontology rejects hierarchical power relationships between the researcher and the researched—and, thus, is still wedded to the idea of doing social research. And, critical gerontology has made an important contribution by increasing the reflexivity and awareness of other gerontologists about their (untested) assumptions about aging and old age.

CHAPTER SUMMARY

This chapter has introduced you to a wide variety of theories within social gerontology and to some broad theoretical concerns of the discipline. It has been shown that social gerontology is not devoid of theories, despite the criticisms of a vocal minority about the state of theory. The issue seems to be less that there are no theories and more that a considerable amount of research in social gerontology does not make its theoretical underpinnings explicit.

Key ideas to remember from this chapter include:

- Theory and research are intimately related; one is useless without the other.
- The defining feature of theory is its provision of explanations. Theories can be distinguished from facts (the building blocks of theories), empirical generalizations (findings that are found repeatedly), models (descriptive linkages of empirical generalizations), and paradigms (world views that underlie theories).
- The barriers to theoretical development in gerontology include: research driven by the need to solve immediate problems; the general difficultly with "grand theories;" and the postmodern turn.
- Theories are important because they: integrate knowledge; offer explanations; provide predictions; and can offer ways to solve problems.
- The three major foci in social gerontology are the aged, the aging process, and age as a dimension of social structure.
- Micro-level theories deal with the aged and the aging process; macro-level theories deal with age as a dimension of social structure. Another distinction among social gerontological theories is between interpretative and normative approaches. These two axes—level of analysis and assumptions about the individual–society relationship—form the basis for a way to classify theories in social gerontology, as seen in Figure 2-1.
- The early theories—role theory, activity theory, and disengagement theory—all focus on the adjustment of individuals to aging. In addition, disengagement theory is concerned with the wider society; its chief tenet is that aging is accompanied by a mutual withdrawal of individuals and society. Disengagement theory, and critiques of it, along with activity theory dominated social gerontology in the 1960s and 1970s.
- The newer theories, ranked from more micro-focused to more macro-focused, include continuity theory, social exchange theory, age stratification theory, aging and modernization theory, and political economy of aging theory. Life course theory—which links micro- and macro-levels—is the dominant theory currently.
- The life course perspective conceptualizes time in three ways: life time, social time, and historical time. Its four central principles are: the life course of individuals is embedded in and shaped by their historical and geographical position; the impact of a transition or event depends on when it occurs in a person's life (the "life stage" principle); lives are lived interdependently ("linked lives"); and individual agency is an important factor in the construction of a life course, contingent upon macro-level constraints and opportunities.
- Emergent theories include feminist gerontology and critical gerontology. Neither is a unified perspective, but both share tenets with the political economy of aging theory. Feminist gerontology is based on the premise that the social construction of gender permeates all aspects of society and aging. Critical theory's main contribution is its focus on reflexivity—of both researchers and the researched.

KEY TERMS

Theory, **(p. 34)**

Theoretical perspectives, **(p. 34)**

Facts, **(p. 34)**

Empirical generalizations, **(p. 35)**

Models, **(p. 35)**

Paradigms, **(p. 35)**

Grand theories, **(p. 37)**

Micro-level of analysis, **(p. 39)**

Macro-level of analysis, **(p. 39)**

Role theory, **(p. 41)**

Activity theory, **(p. 42)**

Disengagement theory, **(p. 42)**

Continuity theory, **(p. 44)**

Social exchange theory, **(p. 45)**

Age stratification theory, **(p. 46)**

Aging and modernization theory, **(p. 49)**

Political economy of aging theory, **(p. 50)**

Life course theoretical perspective, **(p. 53)**

Cohort effect, **(p. 53)**

Period effect, **(p. 53)**

Feminist theory, **(p. 57)**

Critical theory, **(p. 59)**

STUDY QUESTIONS

1. This chapter has argued that theory *is* important. Why is theory important? What do you think is its most important function? What would happen if there were no theory?

2. Identify the barriers to theory development in social gerontology. Do you think that one may be more important than the others? Why?

3. Why is the distinction between micro- and macro-levels important in social gerontology? Do you think this distinction has caused any problems in our understanding of aging?

4. Choose a topic of interest to you. How would this topic be approached by political economy of aging theory? by life course theory? by feminist gerontology? Create two or three research questions that each theory might ask regarding your topic.

SUGGESTED READINGS

Aquino, J.A., Russell, D.W., Cutrona, C.E., & Altmaier, E.M. (1996). Employment status, social support, and life satisfaction among the elderly. *Journal of Counseling Psychology, 43* (4), 480-489.

Bengtson, V.L., Burgess, E.O., & Parrott, T.M. (1997). Theory, explanation, and a third generation of theoretical development in social gerontology. *The Journal of Gerontology: Social Sciences, 52,* S72-S88.

Bengtson, V.L. & Shaie, K.W. (Eds.). (1999). *Handbook of theories of aging*. New York, NY: Springer.

Birren, J.E. & Bengtson, V.L. (Eds.). (1988). *Emergent theories of aging*. New York, NY: Springer.

Caro, F.G., & Bass, S.A. (1997). Receptivity to volunteering in the immediate postretirement period. *Journal of Applied Geronotology, 16* (4), 427–441.

Marshall, V.W. (1996). The state of theory in aging and the social sciences. In R.H. Binstock & L.K. George (Eds.), *Handbook of aging and the social sciences* (4th ed) (pp. 12–30). San Diego, CA: Academic Press.

Settersten, R.A. Jr. (1999). *Lives in time and place: The problems and promises of developmental science*. Amityville, NY: Baywood.

ENDNOTES

1. The correct answer is "Honey, I'm home."

2. Marshall's (1996) original classification scheme contains more than 11 theories. However, only the theories discussed in this chapter are placed in the scheme.

3. Within demography, the term *life span* refers to the maximum number of years that members of species can live, for example, approximately 120 years for human beings at the current time. The definition of life span in this chapter corresponds with its meaning in psychology and sociology.

Knowledge Building and Older People

Learning Objectives

In this chapter, you will learn about:

- Research in social gerontology.
- The focus of gerontological research on the explanation, description, and exploration of aging as a social process for both applied and policy purposes.
- How to avoid human errors in studying older people, by adhering to three main principles central to scientific inquiry: empiricism, objectivity, and control.
- Perspectives that challenge these principles and contrasting beliefs about the nature of reality, the relationship

between the researcher and older person, and how to build knowledge.
- Three overarching worldviews— postpositivism, interpretative/constructivist theory, and critical theory—that all employ different research methodologies.
- The postpositivist tendency to use cross-sectional and longitudinal surveys, secondary data analysis, experimental and quasi-experimental designs; constructivists' usage of biographies, phenomenology, grounded theory, and

ethnography; and critical theorists' use of the best methods suited to their research questions that help them challenge unjust social structures.

- The entanglement of age, period, and cohort effects unique to the study of aging and how their effects can best be separated.

- The flaws within all designs, including longitudinal designs.
- The critical importance of participation of the older person.
- The importance of ethical research in social gerontology.

Introduction

Are you aware that older people who surf the net report a decrease in loneliness and an increased sense of mastery (White and McConnell, et al. 1999), or that two-thirds of middle-aged and older people report an active sex life (Wiley and Bortz, 1996)? Did you know that 20 percent of grandparent caregivers in skipped generation families (no parents, aunts, or uncles) are from First Nations in Canada (Fuller-Thomson, 2002), or that the physical abusers of older people are not always caregivers (McDonald, 1995)? Contrary to what many people think, widows who live below the low-income measures for Canada express satisfaction with their incomes (McDonald, Donahue, & Moore, 2000). Much to everyone's surprise, during one of the worst floods in Canadian history, the cognitive functioning and self-assessed health for older flood victims with the greatest exposure to the crisis actually improved a year after the event (Havens, 2001).

All of the above knowledge about older people comes from research by social scientists who study aging. Many of the results are not obvious or challenge common stereotypes of older people and their social conditions. Social gerontologists are able to go beyond the obvious or commonly held beliefs by the use of the scientific method in their study of older persons. Two major features of the scientific method attempt to safeguard against human errors commonly made by researchers. The ideas that all knowledge is provisional and that all knowledge is subject to refutation are at the heart of the scientific method, no matter what cherished beliefs we might hold about older people. In this chapter, we review what social researchers study and why research in social gerontology is crucial. We describe the "many ways of knowing" about older people, the goals and methods of scientific inquiry, and the unique issues faced by social gerontologists.

What Is the Nature of Research in Social Gerontology?

The study of aging in a social context is different from the study of physical aging. While a researcher in geriatric medicine might be interested in the physical effects of the frailty of older people on the risk of death, a social geron-tologist might focus more on the relationship between frailty and "aging in place" in the person's own home. The social study of aging is strongly rooted in the disciplinary research traditions of sociology, psychology, economics, anthropol-ogy, and the humanities. The central interest of the gerontologist is age—how it affects and is affected by such factors as the influence of ethnicity on aging, or vice versa, and the consequences of aging, including hospital utilization, widow-hood, rural/urban mobility, and grandparenting. The first research on aging tended to focus on the aged as a special group in the Canadian population. These early researchers were inclined to see most of older persons' social circumstances as social problems and explored ways to solve these problems by intervening with individual older people and their families, or at the societal level by advo-cating for and altering social policies. The research methods social gerontolo-gists employed tended to treat older people like a static group (all those Canadians over age 65 years) who were seen to be mostly the same with little appreciation of their heterogeneity.

More recently, aging is viewed as a dynamic process seen through the lens of a life course perspective (see Chapter 2) where researchers pay attention to, "...the location and measurement of events and the processes of aging *in time* (Alwin & Campbell, 2001). Social gerontologists attempt to study individuals as they move through both normative (retirement) and non-normative (a war) events across the life course on their way to later life, all within the context of an ever-changing society. For example, the horror of "9/11," when the World Trade Center was struck by terrorists piloting commercial passenger planes, will follow many New Yorkers into old age. The life experiences of children who are destined to grow up without their natural fathers or mothers, or men and women instantly thrust into widowhood will be undeniably different. Recent studies of Holocaust survivors show that some of the survivors are particularly vulnerable to the changes asso-ciated with the normal aging process (Conn, Clarke, & van Reekum, 2000). Elder's study (1974) of the Great Depression found that children who suffered economic deprivation and family disruption were more affected by these experiences than were teenagers. Thus, the focus of gerontological research has shifted to include the study of aging as a social process in addition to "the aged" as a static population category, taking what we call a "long view" of aging over the life course (Hagesstad, 1990). Today, social researchers in gerontology are continually search-ing for more suitable ways to capture the flow of aging in a dynamic society that does not stand still.

Generally, researchers in social gerontology are interested in how aging processes affect people, how aging affects society in general and how society affects the aging processes of individuals. Social gerontologists are also interested in the best ways to intervene to help older people improve their lives. For exam-ple, one researcher might want to know how leaving a job to care for an ill parent affects a woman's income in later life, while another researcher might want to know whether the Canadian pension system protects women against such contingencies. Another researcher with more applied interests might want to know what we could do to effectively help an individual woman faced with these circumstances. Every one of these researchers may be from a different discipline that leads them to examine different aspects of the same issue and to study different relationships between the many factors involved. In the above example, the sociologist would be more concerned about the relationship between caregiving and income in later life, while the economist is more likely to focus on the capacity of the pension system. Furthermore, the two researchers might work together in partnerships or in multidisciplinary teams, in an attempt to capture the multidimensional nature of aging processes.

The *Canadian Association on Gerontology* (CAG), founded in the 1970s, which publishes the *Canadian Journal on Aging*, represents the wide diversity of research activities across the country. The Association has six active divisions: the biological sciences, health sciences, educational gerontology, psychology, the social sciences, and social policy and practice, all of which represent the full research spectrum (Martin-Matthews & Béland, 2001). Canadian research in gerontology ordinarily runs the gamut from curiosity-driven research about why things are the way they are to more applied research for policy and program development and for interventions, such as counselling for older persons (Chappell, 1995; Gee, 1997).

Why Do We Conduct Research?

To Err Is Human

When we observe older people on our own, we often make errors that scientific enquiry can help us overcome. Often, our observations are inaccurate and selective; we sometimes overgeneralize; we might engage in "ex post facto hypothesizing"; we can be illogical, and sometimes, we prematurely stop the inquiry before we have all the information. Sometimes, we let our ego get in the way of our observations (Rubin & Babbie, 2001). As a visitor to a nursing home, you may conclude that the staff are rude to the residents, when, in reality, the offenders were the visitors to another resident. On the basis of a few cases, namely, your retired aunt and her two friends who complain about their new seniors' housing, you may wrongly conclude that seniors housing is a poor living arrangement for all older persons. **Ex post facto hypothesizing** means that you deduce something after the fact. For example, you were kind enough to take your older uncle and three of his friends to the hockey game, thinking that this would be a treat because they love hockey. When you arrive at the arena, they seem somewhat uncomfortable and a little agitated and want to go home before the end of the second period—something you never would have expected. Your new hypothesis is that the noise and the crowds were overpowering for them, a sensible line of reasoning, but one that may not be correct. You would not know if you were correct until you tested your hypothesis by collecting factual information from your uncle and his friends. Being illogical can also be problematic. Inferring that the neighbour next door neglects her old mother because she works all day is illogical because the link between the evidence and conclusion is weak.

The familiar saying, "Don't bother me with the facts," is a good example of premature closure. The problem of **premature closure** can be seen in earlier research claims that retirement was a chronological guillotine, where people were believed to die shortly following retirement. (McDonald & Wanner, 1990). If social gerontologists had stopped studying retirement, the finding that certain people self-select themselves for retirement due to illness prior to retirement would not have been discovered. Ego involvement is another way of saying that sometimes we have a vested interest in our views, a serious problem that can cloud our vision. An excellent example is how some social gerontologists continue to claim that most elder abuse is the result of the unreasonable demands of caregiving. It is somewhat awkward for a social gerontologist to have to report that a family member purposely caused physical harm to an older relative, especially in light of the burgeoning research report that families are supportive of their older members. It is also easier to blame the abuse on the demands of caregiving than to face the fact that the family member perpetrated a crime and could be reported to the police (McDonald & Wanner, 1990).

The Purpose of Social Science Research.

Scientific enquiry helps prevent gerontologists from going astray in their attempts to understand the social processes of aging. Social scientists, like all scientists, are committed to explaining observed relationships or patterns of behaviour in the social world of older people. They want to reliably answer questions such as: Why do some older people and not others become depressed? Why do some people go back to work when they retire? Why does the erroneous belief persist that the aging of the Canadian population will bankrupt the health care system? Why are some older people abused by their families?

Explanatory research helps to answer these "why" questions and leads to the development and testing of theories that help us understand social behaviour (see Chapter 2). In addition, by identifying and understanding patterns of behaviour like elder abuse, sometimes we can predict who will be abused and design preventive programs accordingly (Singleton & Straits, 1999). The ultimate aim of social gerontologists, then, is to produce valid and reliable knowledge that explains the social processes of aging, knowledge that is less subject to the errors of judgment noted above.

Although explanation is the ultimate goal of the social scientist, exploration and description are considered to be two additional **goals of science**. Social gerontologists may pursue the simple goal of exploration when they know very little about a topic, such as the aging of gay couples. There is very little knowledge available about how gay couples grow old together and whether they face the same issues as everyone else (Whitford, 1997). In this instance, the researcher would have to first explore if there were any differences between homosexuals and heterosexuals before testing any theories about the differences. If the researcher wanted to describe gay couples in Canada, the goal would be different again. The social gerontologist would want to provide a description of gay couples as to how many there are, where they live, how long they have been together and so on, with the aim of obtaining facts, rather than opinions about this type of relationship in old age.

The goals of the social gerontologist, then, are to explore, describe, and ultimately explain the processes of aging. To achieve these aims, social gerontologists follow a number of standardized methods and procedures.

Scientific Guidelines.

Social gerontologists adhere to the guidelines for the scientific method and follow a common process of justification (Singleton & Straits, 1999). These guidelines also provide assistance in evaluating the quality of the existing research as reported in the ensuing chapters. While these scientific rules or guidelines are often subject to dispute, they provide a blueprint for collecting data, which minimizes the chances of committing the errors examined above. The three key principles are empiricism, objectivity, and control (Singleton & Straits, 1999).

Empiricism relies on evidence gathered systematically through observation or experiment and means that research results can be reproduced and verified by other social scientists following the same rules. Empiricism is distinct from explanations involving the supernatural or the doctrine that all values are baseless and that nothing can be known. In short, the type of information based on intuition, unsupported opinions, or "New Age" psychics is not part of science because social scientists limit their questioning to those phenomena for which empirical data can be collected.

Reliability and validity relate to the adequacy of measurement. Reliability refers to our confidence in the scores that we obtain from a measure; validity refers to how well the measure represents the concept assessed. The technical meaning of **reliability** is the extent to which the scores reflect true scores, rather than error in measurement. Different types of reliability include:

- Test–retest reliability—similar results with repeated use of a measure.
- Alternate-form reliability—similar results with the use of different forms of a measure.
- Internal consistency—high correlations among the different items of a measure.
- Inter-rater reliability—similar results using different raters.

A **reliability coefficient** estimates the level of reliability. These coefficients range from 0 to 1, with an estimate of 0.7 considered close to adequate reliability, and an estimate of 0.8 considered adequate. Classical measurement theory provides meaning to most forms of the reliability coefficient. The value of the coefficient (∞)

represents true differences between people, whereas $1 - \propto$ estimates the amount of error. Therefore, for a coefficient of $\propto = 0.8$, the meaning is that 80 percent of the variability in responses reflects true differences between people and 20 percent reflects error in measurement.

Reliability is affected by: situational effects at the time of measurement; the complexity of the items; the presentation of items; and the length of the measure. Situational factors include fatigue and stress. A test battery that is too long may weary older people or become boring and tiresome. Researchers try to minimize such effects. Many older people react adversely to the stress of the research setting. Stress can distract respondents, with adverse effects on the accuracy of responses. Harkins, Chapman, and Eisdorfer (1979) provide an example in which older women adopted a lax strategy toward the naming of correct responses in a recognition memory task. The use of this strategy masked lower capabilities to acquire and store information, compared with younger women.

The use of complex items can reduce reliability and it is always safe to assume that older people respond more accurately to simple items. In part, this is related to educational attainment. Statistics Canada (1999) reported that 62 percent of seniors have not completed high school. Literacy is an issue, with about three-quarters of seniors falling within the lower literacy grades (Government of Ontario, 1998). Such findings make it imperative that the items have simple wording and sentence structure. If the items are poorly understood, people respond in ways that sacrifice accuracy. Presentation of items is also important. Response set refers to a mode of responding in which the respondents show a bias toward one or the other response alternative (e.g., "yes" or "no"), rather than responding to the item content (Stones, 1976a; b). Findings with older people show evidence of response set (e.g., a string of "yes" responses), which is associated with lower education, low status of former occupation, and low fluency with words (Kozma, Stones, & McNeil, 1991). Thus, items must be presented in ways that minimize response set. Also, sensory deficiencies are present in many older people. Such deficiencies make it difficult for them to read small print or hear spoken presentations. Many self-report measures used with older people use large print to ensure readability.

Finally, reliability is related to the number of items in a measure. Classical measurement theory explains why. This theory assumes that a single measure taken from a person contains two components: a *true score* (t) representing the true position of that person on that measure; and an *error* component (e) that is random in that it has no correlation with the true score. Let us assume that a test contains one or many items and that the score on the test is the average score per item ($\bar{u}$). For a single item, the expression $\bar{u} = t + e$ defines the score. On the other hand, for a multi-item test, (1) the average true score is t because the true score is the same for all items, (2) the average error score tends toward zero because the random errors tend to cancel each other out (i.e., $\{\Sigma e / n\}$ _ 0), and the average score approaches the true score ($\bar{u} = t$). Consequently, we can deduce from classical measurement theory that reliability increases with the length of a measure.

As noted above, **validity** refers to how well our measure represents what we want it to. Effects on validity include no only random error, which sets an upper limit to validity, but also systematic error. These types of errors differ in that the former (i.e., random error), but not the latter, shows no correlation with true scores.

There are two main reasons for systematic errors: (1) the scale may not measure the concept its developer meant it to measure; and (2) the responses may show bias. The most complete way to avoid the former is through construct validation (Anastasi & Urbina, 1996). Although there is no fixed path to ensure construct validity, the methods include:

- Defining the construct precisely. (A **construct** refers to a higher level of abstraction that cannot be easily measured. Sometimes concepts such as "role" or "political attitude" will be referred to as a construct, rather than a concept, because of the level of abstraction involved.)
- Making sure the items fully represent the concept (content validity).
- Correlating the measure with other measures of the concept (criterion validity).
- Assessing differences on the measure between groups known to differ on the concept (e.g., a depression measure with patients diagnosed or not diagnosed with depression).
- Predicting future outcomes (predictive validity).
- Ensuring that the measure shows no confounding with other concepts (discriminant validity).

A biased measure shows the influence of something more than its substantive concept. Examples include responding in ways that are socially desirable or extreme. Kozma and Stones (1987; 1988) studied whether measures related to mental health are affected by social desirability. The findings indicated minimal bias at any age. Extremity bias refers to a tendency to choose extreme response alternatives. The Elder Abuse Attitude Test (EAAT), discussed in Chapter 6, shows evidence of extremity bias despite evidence of content and discriminant validity (Lithwick, Reis, Stones, MacNaughton-Osler, Gendron, Groves, & Canderan, 1997; Stones & Pittman, 1995). Consequently, it has been concluded that the test scores reflect two effects: (1) valid attitudes toward elder abuse; and (2) a tendency by some respondents to choose extreme responses, regardless of the item content.

Objectivity means that gerontological researchers strive to remove bias from their studies that are rooted in emotion, conjecture or intellectual partiality—a goal rarely, if ever, achieved. At best, social scientists take objectivity to mean that a group of scientists can agree on the results of a given observation, until new observations appear to refute the earlier ones. Because of the requirement for objectivity, the logic, method, and analyses of research studies should be reported step by step so that they can be accurately reviewed by peers in gerontology. In essence, "...objectivity is the product of a community of thinkers, each offering unsparing criticism of ...claims that the others make." (Nagel, 1967, as reported in Singleton & Straits, 1999: 31).

The need for **control**, the third guideline followed by social scientists, assumes that procedures have been used in the research study to eliminate, as much as possible, sources of bias and error that would discredit their results. While a researcher may have a "pet" explanation about why so many older people watch television (Lindsey, 1999), the same researcher must also consider alternative explanations of the television-viewing patterns of older adults and use proce-dures to rule out these alternatives. The researcher's "cherished" hypothesis may be that older people watch more television because they have nothing else to do, but the researcher must first rule out competing reasons, such as the possibility that older people have less income so they avoid expensive entertainment, such as going to the movies. Almost all procedures and techniques used by social geron-tologists are designed to achieve control of alternative factors, which is not an easy task, since people cannot live out their lives in a controlled environment, such as in a laboratory.

The three principles informing scientific activity are generally utilized in the scientific process that is represented in Figure 3.1. Social scientists follow one of two systems of logic depending on how theory is employed in the process. As depicted in Figure 3.1, there is a chain of events that social scientists can enter into at any point, depending upon their interest. Arbitrarily, starting at the top of the dia-gram, theories generate hypotheses or predictions; hypotheses are checked against observations in the world; the observations give rise to generalizations about the data collected; and the generalizations either support, contradict, or indicate the need to modify the theory. In this case, starting with theory, that is, going from the general to the particular, is an example of a **deductive approach** to research.

For example, if a social gerontologist employs a political economy perspective to examine the effect of ethnicity on income in old age, he or she might hypothesize that membership in a visible minority group is associated with lower income in old age, where ethnicity is treated as a structural variable that affects people's life chances and resources. The researcher would then interview visible minorities about their income in old age and determine if the observations reflected his or her hypothe-sis. The researcher might find out that only visible minority women have lower incomes in old age and would then adjust the theory to reflect gender differences.

If the researcher starts with observations, an **inductive approach** is utilized, which goes from the particular to the general. In the inductive approach to research, the gerontologist would first collect data from visible minorities about their aging experiences and, from the data, discover a number of patterns, one being that women from visible minorities have problems with their incomes in old age. This information, which is grounded in the data, could then be used to formulate a theory about aging within a visible minority group. At the outset, the researcher had no firm views on what would be found—the theory emerged from an examination of the data.

Figure 3.1 THE SCIENTIFIC PROCESS

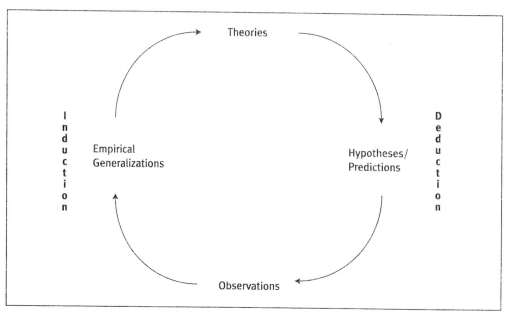

Source: Adapted from Walter Wallace, *The Logic of Science in Sociology* (Chicago, IL: Aldine-Atherton, 1971). Used by permission.

Systems of Knowledge

Some of the scientific rules or guidelines we presented above are currently contested in the social sciences and the debate has spilled over into gerontology (Haldemann & Lévy, 1995). Two aspects of the scientific method that attract considerable debate are ideas about the nature of reality and the quest for objectivity—issues at the heart of the study of knowledge or what philosophers call *epistemology*. Some scholars argue that there is no reality, and all we can do is examine each individual's subjective reality, while others counter that there is a "real" reality we can know, although not perfectly. Not surprisingly, those who favour a subjective reality usually believe that it is impossible to be objective, while those who believe there is an imperfect (but knowable) reality emphasize the pursuit of objectivity. Rather than enter into the debate, we present the different ways of "knowing" that are open to social gerontologists in their study of aging. While the epistemological differences might be insurmountable (Lincoln & Guba, 2000), gerontologists do not hesitate to take advantage of the complementary nature of the many methods available to them. Today, there are studies in gerontology that use several methods together, which results in a richer understanding of aging processes (McDonald, Donahue, & Moore, 1997; Laub & Sampsom, 1998).

The various philosophical views that researchers hold about the nature of reality, objectivity, and how to collect information about social behaviour are sometimes called **paradigms** (Kuhn, 1970) or systems of knowledge. A paradigm (as noted in Chapter 2) or system of knowledge is an organizing tool that helps us understand the world view of a researcher and, thus, has important consequences for the practical conduct of research and our understanding of the research. Systems of knowledge are, of course, not mutually exclusive and frequently overlap with each other. A system of knowledge usually has at least three components: (1) a view of reality (ontology); (2) an epistemology that is about the nature of the relationship between the researcher and the subject; and (3) a methodology that specifies a way to gain knowledge about the world and how we know what we know is true (Lincoln & Guba, 2000). Research in gerontology commonly falls within three major paradigms: (1) positivism/postpositivism, (2) interpretive approaches, and (3) critical gerontology (Lincoln & Guba, 2000).

This is not to suggest that these are the only knowledge systems available to social gerontologists. Knowledge production is continually evolving, to the extent that there are almost always newer systems of thought hovering on the horizon. Arguments have been mounted for an ethnic or race paradigm that would look to a different epistemological framework to describe the experiences and knowledge systems of people outside the dominant paradigms mentioned in this chapter. Beginning work draws on oral history and critical race theory to unmask racism (Stanfield, 1994; Ladson-Billings, 2000). A feminist paradigm that starts with the standpoint of women's experiences and knowledge has also been examined by a number of scholars (Harding, 1987; Code, 1991; Olesen, 2000) and has been used in gerontology by a number of researchers (Browne, 1998; Neysmith, 1999; Ginn, Street, & Arber, 2001). Postmodernism (see Katz, 1996) as Pauline Rosenau (1992) declares, "haunts" all systems of knowledge, calling into question the very foundation and core of the social sciences and poses challenges to every paradigm.

Postpositivism.

Positivism in the social sciences represents an attempt to transfer the principles of the physical sciences directly to human behaviour, but over time and use, the principles became more accommodating of human behaviour. Today, a number of social scientists practise a more flexible form of positivism called **postpositivism**. This group of scientists tends to subscribe to the scientific principles noted above, although in a more flexible manner. They subscribe to the views that reality can be known, although not completely, that the aim of observation is to be objective but is never perfectly achieved, and that the methods used to study aging are mainly quantitative in nature as seen in Figure 3.2. Quantitative methods rely more on the production of numerical data, which is presented in the form of generalizable statistical findings to represent aging processes. A simple measure of the health of older people-a rating—scale ranging from excellent, very good, good, fair, to poor—has been found to be remarkably accurate (Menec & Chipperfield, 2001). When we state that 27.9 percent of Canadians 65 years of age and over rate their health as very good (Statistics Canada, 1999), we are providing a reliable statistical snapshot of the health of Canadians over age 65 years.

While postpositivist gerontologists strive to be objective, they recognize that their studies are value laden. Their approach to theory is usually on the deductive side of the scientific coin (testing theory), although their research can also be inductive, especially if their goal is to explore a new topic. The studies within the postpositivist tradition favour three main types of research designs: (1) the social survey, (2) secondary data analysis, and (3) experimental and quasi-experimental designs. Postpositivists also have a way of deciding if their research findings can be classified as knowledge. Social gerontologists working within this system of knowledge judge their information to be knowledge if the research results are valid and reliable, that is, the measurements are not open to error.

The Social Survey.

Surveys are probably the most widely used method within the postpositivist paradigm. A survey is best used when social gerontologists want to study a population that is too large to examine directly (Fowler, 2001). This method basically uses a set of standardized questions contained in a questionnaire that can be administered by face-to-face conversations, telephone, mail, e-mail, or fax to older

Figure 3.2 COMPONENTS OF A PARADIGM

Components of a paradigm

Ontology
→ Postpositivism
→ Interpretive/constructivist
→ Critical theory

→ **Nature and form of reality**
→ Real reality imperfectly known
→ Reality socially constructed
→ Historical reality

Epistemology
→ Postpositivism
→ Interpretive/constructivist
→ Critical theory

→ **Relationship between the knower and known**
→ Reality is independent of the knower
→ Reality is dependent on the knower
→ Reality is transactional between knower and known

Methodology
→ Postpositivism

→ Interpretive/constructivist
→ Critical theory

→ **How do we gain knowledge?**
→ Cross-sectional and longitudinal surveys, secondary analysis, experimental, quasi-experimental designs
→ Biographies, phenomenology, grounded theory, ethnography
→ Social action research

persons, agency personnel, policy makers, and so on. Surveys can be used for explanatory, descriptive, and exploratory purposes, they can provide a "freeze-frame" of a population at one point in time (cross-sectional survey), or they can be a longitudinal study that interviews older people at several points in time. Surveys can be used in applied ways, such as determining if older persons' needs are being met in a specific community, or if a meals-on-wheels program successfully provides meals for house-bound rural seniors. While surveys can be small and local as in the cross-sectional survey of 1,406 community dwelling seniors in Manitoba (Chipperfield & Segall, 1996), they can also be large national surveys, such as the cross-sectional *Survey on Ageing and Independence* (1991), which used face-to-face and telephone interviews of over 20,000 Canadians 45 years of age and older. The data from surveys can also be used over and over again for different research purposes by other gerontologists who did not participate in the original design of the study or the collection of data (secondary data analysis).

Most researchers who work within the postpositivist framework would agree that random samples are more useful than nonrandom samples. A random sample ensures that each older person has an equal chance of being chosen for a study. As a procedure, random sampling is more likely to represent the heterogeneity of older people in the Canadian population, an important issue because research has shown repeatedly that there is increasing variability with advancing age (Dannefer, 1988).

Early research studies in Canada were sometimes not randomly selected and were, therefore, unrepresentative of the older people in the larger population. For example, the pioneer longitudinal study, the *Ontario Longitudinal Study of Aging* carried out between 1959 and 1978, was not a random sample and dealt only with the work and retirement of men. Although a very important study in the history of Canadian research because it was the first major longitudinal study, it completely overlooked the circumstances of women, as well as those of people from diverse ethnic groups. The social gerontologists using this study can only draw conclusions about the men in the sample because the sample was not randomly drawn, so there is no certainty that the findings apply to the Ontarian or Canadian population as a whole.

A related issue facing gerontological researchers has to do with statistically rare populations, which means certain subgroups in the population that are small (Kalton & Anderson, 1989). When social gerontologists attempt to locate people from "rare" groups, such as the oldest old (85+), physically abused seniors, or Chinese immigrant caregivers, these hard-to-reach populations require the use of special sampling techniques. Sometimes, researchers will oversample a certain group, such as First Nations older people, in order to have enough respondents to do a suitable statistical analysis.

While surveys are usually done relatively quickly and can be cost-effective, there are a few issues that have to be considered. When conducting surveys with older persons, compared with younger persons, research has found that older people have a tendency to have a higher nonresponse rate, especially in telephone interviews; the interviewer appears to have an influence on the older respondents' answers to questions; and older people seem to give more "don't know responses" (Herzog & Kulka, 1989). Specific effort must be made to try to counter each of these tendencies (through the training of interviewers, call backs, and so on).

Secondary Data Analysis.

Secondary data analysis, or secondary analysis, refers to the study of existing data initially collected for another purpose (Liang & Lawrence, 1989; Black, 1995). A researcher interested in the relationship between the average number of hours women spend in caregiving and the women's physical health might use a national data file, such as the *General Social Survey*, to analyze this relationship. The *General Social Survey* developed as a yearly survey was to track social trends and provide immediate information on policy issues in Canada. Most university libraries in Canada house the public-use version of this data file, which means all identifying information has been removed from the file. That is, no individual who participated in the survey can be identified; everyone is anonymous.

Secondary data analysis uses data from many sources besides surveys, such as archival data (Vital Statistics), administrative files based on data from the records of organizations, such as social agencies or hospitals, and the census data sets (Black, 1995). Secondary analysis can be used for any of the three purposes of research and is attractive because the analysis is inexpensive, requires few people, and takes less time. Secondary analysis is particularly useful for comparative studies that examine differences in aging processes across cultures or societies.

There is little doubt that secondary analysis has made an enormous contribution to gerontology in Canada. The *Aging in Manitoba Study* (AIM) is an excellent example. In a 30-year period of analyses of the AIM data by at least 60 researchers, the contributions include more than 20 student theses and dissertations, 300 journal articles, book chapters, and conference presentations; and the study has been cited more than 2,000 times in mainstream journal articles (Havens, 2001). The value of secondary analysis has been further emphasized by the recent move of the Canadian government in its *Data Liberation Initiative*, which, in partnership with Canadian universities, has made large national survey sample data files more easily accessible to Canadian researchers and their students. Most recently, Research Data Centres (RDCs) devoted to secondary analysis are scheduled to be established at nine Canadian universities across Canada. The goal of the RDCs, managed by a partnership between Canadian universities and Statistics Canada, is to help strengthen the country's research capacity in social research and to support the policy research community using existing data files.

Secondary data analysis, like all research methods, presents challenges to researchers. Although this methodology provides an opportunity for researchers to have access to large national, random samples that are often longitudinal, these surveys frequently leave out variables that the researcher might be interested in studying (Kasl, 1995). For example, a survey of interest may not measure mental health or stress levels, or it may not measure the concepts in a way that is consistent with the researcher's own theoretical perspective. If a social gerontologist is interested in a subjective measure of caregiver burden and the data file of interest only offers number of hours of caregiving per week, the researcher will have to abandon that particular data file or work around this shortcoming. In brief, the challenge to the researcher using secondary data files is to be able to work with the information that is available in the data file (Black, 1995).

Experimental and Quasi-Experimental Designs.

The classic experimental design is undoubtedly the gold standard for the post-positivist paradigm, mainly because it comes closest to meeting the three criteria required for causation: temporal ordering, where the intervention clearly comes before the outcome, covariation, where the intervention and outcome change together, and, lastly, the control of extraneous factors. In the classical experimental design, the aim is usually to find out the effect of aging on such factors as memory and cognition or if an intervention, such as attendance at a senior centre, is effective in combating loneliness. Experiments essentially require random assignment to the group that will receive the intervention, called the experimental group, and to the group that receives nothing, referred to as the control group. Random assignment means that each group is comparable to the extent that the control group should represent what the experimental group would have been like if it had not received the intervention. An intervention is introduced to the experimental group but not the control group, and if there is a difference between the experimental group and the control group after the intervention, then the intervention is deemed to have had an effect (Singleton & Straits, 1999; Rubin & Babbie, 2001).

For example, a study of a family intervention program comprising caregiver education, stress management, and the development of coping skills was hypothesized to reduce the burden of care in caregivers of Alzheimer's disease patients. The effectiveness of the family intervention was assessed by measures of psychological distress and depression of the caregivers before and after the family intervention (Marriott, Donaldson, Tarrier, & Burns, 2000). Caregivers were randomly assigned to one of three groups: the family intervention or experimental group or to one of two control groups—a group that was given no treatment but was simply interviewed and a control group that received no interview and no family intervention. At the end of the experiment, there were significant reductions in stress and depression in the family intervention group, compared with the two control groups.

Experimental designs with random assignment are, more often than not, difficult to achieve. Sometimes, these designs are not feasible from an ethical standpoint because it might mean delaying or denying a service to an older person. Withholding help from a physically abused and confused older person is out of the question. There is also the problem of intervention fidelity, where the researcher is not sure that the intervention (e.g., counselling) was delivered to the experimental group as exactly intended. For example, if three therapists provide therapy to subjects in the experimental group, some therapists may have better skills than others, or they may have better judgment, which will make the services delivered somewhat different. When this occurs, each older person in the experimental group might receive a slightly different version of the counselling, and one would not be measuring the same intervention. Client recruitment and retention is also a serious problem, since the researcher often has to wait for referrals to a program and people sometimes drop out of a study if they find out they are in the control group. In addition, it is unlikely that we could ever control all the factors in the environment that would influence the aging process.

Given some of these problems, researchers often turn to quasi-experimental designs, which are distinct from classical experiments because they do not use random assignment and sometimes they may not even have a control group. They do, however, have some of the characteristics of classical designs. An example would be a study that has an experimental group that receives an intervention but, instead of a control group, it has a comparison group that is not randomly assigned and, therefore, probably is not equivalent to the experimental group. In a study of the effect of training professionals to train their colleagues to detect substance abuse by older clients, an experimental group was given a training program, and a comparison group of professionals who were matched with the experimental group on several factors (years of experience and level of education) was not trained (Peressini & McDonald, 1998). Although the program apparently improved the knowledge of the experimental group, the researchers could not rule out alternative explanations because the professionals were not randomly assigned to the experimental and comparison groups, even though there was an attempt to match them on important factors, such as level of education.

As can be seen, postpositivists tend to use highly structured research methods that are informed by gerontological theories. Their goals are to understand social reality that they believe can be known to some degree. Postpositivists usually treat their results as tentative and expect them to be tested in the future according to set procedures. For these gerontologists, research is an unending and self-correcting process that strives to be as free as possible from political, ideological, and personal influences, against which the scientific method is a safeguard.

Interpretive Approaches.

A research paradigm that contrasts with postpositivism is called the **interpretative/constructivism** approach to knowledge generation (Lincoln & Guba, 2000). Social gerontologists who work within this paradigm or system of knowledge hold the view that you cannot adequately understand people by depending on objective measurements. They do not encourage research participants to be separate and apart from the researcher in an attempt to be objective. The researcher hopes to establish meaningful relationships with participants because the researcher wants to investigate the deeper meanings of the person's experiences. While a postpositivist is interested in how, on average, older people rate their health on a standardized scale, interpretive researchers would like to explore the meaning of health to older people and the place of health within the context of their whole life.

Interpretive/constructivist researchers do not believe that objective reality can be known even if there is one. (see Figure 3.2). Generally, they are interested in how people interpret and construct their social world and as a result, believe that there are multiple realities that are equally viable. The relationship between the researcher and the older person as the subject would be subjective and transactional, not objective in nature. The older person would be seen as an active participant in the research process, and an attempt would be made to capture the person's life in a holistic manner (Matsuoka, 1991). While theory is definitely important to interpretive researchers, they are more inclined to generate theory from their data (the inductive approach, see Figure 3.1) than to test theory. The methodologies employed by interpretive researchers fall within the broader category of qualitative research that explores the meanings of specific human experiences and generates "thick" descriptions of these experiences. Rather than statistics, the words, meanings, and conceptualizations of people are at the foundation of this approach.

Scholars within this research tradition have an embarrassment of riches when it comes to selecting a specific methodology—biographies, phenomenological approaches, grounded theory, case studies, and ethnographies, to name but a few (Creswell, 1998). In addition, each of these broad traditions contains a multitude of data collection practices. In-depth interviews with subjects and/or with key informants (people in the "know") and participant observation are the mainstays of the qualitative approach. In-depth interviews with older persons may be spread over a number of interviews, depending on the purpose of the study and the amount of information to be collected. Participant observation requires the researcher to engage in prolonged participation as a member in a group, a community, an agency, and so on. The degree of membership varies from being a declared member of the group in the role of researcher to participating as a complete member of the group where the identity of the researcher is not known. Content analysis is another technique sometimes used that covers a variety of ways to analyze text: any documents, formal records like medical files or agency files, newspaper editorials, advertisements, television shows, movies, and videotapes.

While qualitative methods vary somewhat, the underlying assumption is that a researcher can obtain a more complex understanding of older persons and their worlds from ordinary observations and conversations (Sankar & Gubrium, 1994). Their standards for warranting knowledge are shifting in the direction of ethical considerations but were originally anchored in credibility (equivalent to validity) and dependability (equivalent to reliability) of the data. These procedures for "checking " the data for authenticity often include review by those being studied. Here, we look at the four most common qualitative methods to study older people.

Biographies.

Biography covers a broad genre of approaches that provide methodological tools for studying the "lived experience of aging" (Wallace, 1994). Biographies include biographical studies, wherein the life story of a person is written by someone else; autobiographies where the life story is written by people about themselves; the life history, which reports on an individual's life and how it reflects the cultural themes of society, and oral histories, which are used to collect people's experiences of significant historical events.

While generally portraying the meaning of being and growing old, scholars do not agree on the epistemological stance to be adopted by the biographer (Tierney, 2000). Some researchers use biographies to reveal the objective facts in a person's life, others seek subjective interpretations of a life narrative, and still others emphasize that the life course is a social construction made up in the interaction between the researcher and the subject. A life history study by Wallace (1994) asked families to tell their life stories about how a family member came to be institutionalized in a nursing home. The goal of the study was to understand how families make the experience meaningful. The stories were analyzed as to where they began and ended, and what they included as relevant. It was discovered that the stories were very long and encompassed a multitude of family changes (Wallace, 1994). The task of the biographer, then, is three-fold: (1) to have the time to collect information over a lifetime; (2) to learn about history; and (3) to focus on the ordinary, instead of the extraordinary, the marginal, or the deviant (Denzin, 1984).

Phenomenology.

As with everything else in the interpretive paradigm, there are a number of different schools of **phenomenology** to choose from: the descriptive school, which attempts to describe the essence of an experience; the interpretive school, which looks for the systematic interpretation of meanings of experiences, and the "Dutch" school, which combines the two preceding approaches (Moustakas, 1994; Creswell, 1998). Central to this approach, however, is the attempt to capture the fundamental, lived experience of an individual in reference to a specific concept or phenomenon.

An excellent example of a phenomenological study is one done by Berman (1994), who asks, "What is it like to be old?" To answer the question, he studied the published personal journals written by people in later life and found a marked disjunction between chronological age and felt age. In a study of widows, researchers explored how women interpreted their financial situation in widowhood and how they constructed their poverty to be normative (McDonald, Donahue, & Moore, 2000). Phenomenological studies are sometimes difficult to implement because the method requires the researcher to hold their own personal experiences in abeyance and "bracket" their own preconceptions of the phenomena under study. It is often difficult for us to set aside our own views and approach a study with a completely open mind (Moustakes, 1994).

Grounded Theory.

While phenomenology emphasizes the meaning of experience, the intent of **grounded theory** is to discover theory or add to theory already developed. This methodology was first developed by sociologists Glaser and Stauss (1967) who argued that theories should be "grounded" in the data. Today, there are several strands of grounded theory, but overall, it is a very specific, highly developed set of procedures for generating a middle-range social theory. As the researcher collects data, insights and questions are generated and are pursued through further data collection. As concepts emerge from the data, the researcher engages in theoretical sampling of related events and activities, until no new information about the concepts emerges (Schwandt, 1997). In a study by Price (1998), a grounded-theory approach was used to generate a four-stage theory about the retirement transition of professionals. Her data indicated that women progress through the decision to retire, to relinquishing professional identity, to re-establishing order, and, finally, to developing a retirement life. In a study of caregiving sons, a typology of the son caregivers was developed—the dutiful son, the strategic planner, and the son who shares the care—information that has implications for service and program intervention for caregivers (Harris, 1998).

Even though grounded theory served at the front of the "qualitative revolution," which helped make qualitative methods acceptable to gerontologists and other social scientists, it has been critiqued as having an underlying positivist theme, mainly by postmodernists (Charmaz, 2000). Glaser's approach comes closest to traditional postpositivism with its assumptions of an objective external reality, a neutral observer who discovers data, and an unbiased reading of the data. Like other qualitative methods, though, it has made an important contribution to understanding the empirical worlds of aging persons by giving them voice and representing their reality as accurately as possible.

Ethnography.

Ethnography usually involves the description and interpretation of a social group or a culture and is both a process and an outcome. Ethnographers are "...outsiders wearing insider's clothes, while gradually acquiring the language and behaviours that go along with them" (Tedlock, 2000). The product of their efforts is usually an understanding of the intermingling perceptions of people and their patterns of behaviour, customs, and way of life. Ethnography, with its roots in anthropology, has been extended beyond sociology and is now used as a methodology in cultural studies, in women's studies, folklore, literary theory, and performance art. At the heart of ethnography is the assumption that by entering into a close and prolonged relationship with people in their everyday lives, ethnographers can begin to understand better the behaviours of their subjects (Hammersley, 1992). Participant observation is one of the main ways that data are collected when using this method.

An eight-month study of the process of discharge decision making for older patients in a large acute care hospital in Toronto uncovered a number of interesting processes (Wells, 1997). Over the eight months, the study used participant observation, interviews, and content analysis of the hospital charts to collect data. Some of the more important results indicated that the process of discharge from hospital was not tied to clinical outcomes for the older patients, but that discharge was related to nonclinical factors, such as the patient's social situation and the requirements of the hospital to reduce prolonged hospital stays. Professionals in the hospital consistently held low expectations for the older patients, while the patients thought the opposite. By the end of the study, the patients' perceptions turned out to be more accurate (Wells, 1997)! The results of this study had serious ramifications for the care of older people in hospitals. As this study illustrates, the challenge to the ethnographer is to have the time for prolonged observation.

Critical Theory.

The last paradigm we consider is the **critical paradigm**, which builds on an array of intellectual traditions, including those of Karl Marx and Max Weber, the writings of scholars from Frankfurt, Germany, in the 1930s, and, most recently, Jurgen Habermas (Estes, Linkins, & Binney, 2001). In Chapter 2, it was noted that critical theory is not a "neat theoretical package." Here, it is viewed as an underlying paradigm. It will be recalled that critical gerontology provides an approach to social gerontology "...that provokes and challenges assumptions, and that is grounded in a commitment, not just to understand the social construction of aging, but to change it" (Minkler and Estes, 1999). The distinguishing features of this perspective are to unmask the oppression of vulnerable people and to effect change through a mutual process of research (Rubin & Babbie, 2001). Critical theory cuts a wide swath to cover feminism, empowerment practices, race and ethnic studies, and, at its outer boundaries, postmodernism (Katz, 1996; Kincheloe & McLaren, 2000). When critical theorists make claims to be scientific, they attempt to offer rigorous explanations for the causes of oppression, such as economic dependence or ideological beliefs. These beliefs, in turn, are verified by empirical evidence and are framed by available economic and social theories in the process. Their explanations are also normative and critical, since they imply negative evaluations of current social structures.

The overall aim of the research process is to foster people's awareness of their oppression and to encourage social–political action. This paradigm generally subscribes to the view that reality is shaped by social, political, cultural, class, and gender divisions. Researchers in this tradition are not disinterested social scientists but, rather, share a transformative relationship with the research subjects in the research process. The type of research associated with this system of knowledge has been variously labelled social action research, participatory action research, critical ethnography, and participatory ethnography. In essence, the researcher discovers the meanings of situations to the participants (what it is like to be financially abused) and helps link these experiences to oppressive social, political, and economic structures (carelessness of banks) so that action can be taken by the participants (e.g., meeting with bank representatives to establish a monitoring system to protect older persons' bank accounts). Although there are a number of different versions of the method used, the differences are mainly about the degree to which the subjects participate in and control the research process and the extent of the social action. Many types of data collection techniques are used, from focus groups to surveys, to in-depth interviews. The criteria for claiming knowledge is whether the research participants experience some form of emancipation.

Improving the Quality of Life of Canadian Seniors is a national example of action research (Raphael, 1999). The goal of the project was to collect information about the factors affecting the quality of life of seniors in eight cities across Canada (Halifax, Quebec City, Montreal, Ottawa, Toronto, Regina, Whitehorse, and Vancouver). Seniors in each of the cities directed the activities of the projects and were supported by a local coordinator and a university researcher. For example, in Toronto, the research was directed by a Seniors Coordinating Committee, which utilized the knowledge and skills of seniors to explore and act upon government policy decisions that influenced the quality of their lives. The seniors wanted to know what government policies were affecting seniors, how these policies influenced their quality of life, what factors led governments to make the decisions they made, and what action could be taken to improve the quality of seniors' lives. In Toronto, 16 focus groups with seniors explored nine key policy areas from housing to belonging to a different ethnic community. The conclusion was that all three levels of government do not listen well to seniors' voices. With their results in hand, the seniors are designing "action plans" to address the issues that were raised in the research (Raphael, Brown, & Wheeler, 2000; www.utoronto.ca/seniors/).

Although we have not provided a review of all the research methodologies open to social gerontologists, it should be fairly obvious that there is a profusion of methods from which to choose. How one picks a method and/or combination of methods is guided by the research process. Normally, researchers are guided by the research questions they wish to answer (Chappell, 1995) and by their theoretical interests. A researcher interested in how older people feel about widowhood is more likely to choose a qualitative approach to answer the question than another researcher who would use a quantitative approach to determine the average income of Canadian widows. A feminist researcher may prefer a type of standpoint that sees the world from the point of view of a woman, to inform her work, while a political economist would prefer critical theory. Another researcher wanting to know how older people feel about their incomes in old age might combine both approaches and use a theoretical framework that accommodates both methods, perhaps, the life-course perspective. We are certain, though, that we require as many methodological options as possible, to address questions about aging processes. The complexity of the flow of cohorts through the age structure of society and through time demands nothing less (Riley, 1998).

The Challenges in Studying Aging

Although there are many different ways to approach the study of aging and a multitude of opportunities for methodological pluralism, there are several issues unique to aging that challenge the social gerontologist. In this section, we consider the dilemma of age, period, and cohort effects, the main concerns in collecting data from older persons, and special ethical considerations.

The Quandary of Age, Period, and Cohort Effects

An awareness of old age as a life-long journey embedded in a changing social context poses fundamental methodological issues for social gerontologists (Riley, 1998). If a researcher finds in a cross-sectional survey conducted in the 1990s that the frequency of computer use is less in older age groups than in younger age groups, what would be the reason for the difference? Could the difference be a result of the aging process; being part of the "older generation" who did not have computers in "their day"; or due to the fact that older people tend to be retired and do not go to school, work, or university, where computers are easily accessed? The cross-sectional survey, a "freeze-frame" of behaviour at one point in time, tells us there are differences between age groups but cannot tell us why. In our example, there is the possibility that three factors have influenced the changes between the age groups over time: aging, period, and cohort effects.

That older people do not use computer technology as much as younger persons do may be a result of growing old—an **aging effect**. Perhaps, as people grow older, they find that they have less ability to maneuver a mouse and, therefore, do not use computers as much (Czaja & Sharit, 1998). There is also the possibility that the differences between the age groups might be a cohort difference. A **cohort** refers to a group of individuals born around the same time and who often share a common history, including the social, economic, and cultural influences during this time. Older people today did not grow up in the company of computers and do not feel as comfortable around them as do younger cohorts. For example, the baby-boom echo, born between 1980 and 1995, have grown up with computer technology, whereas those born between 1940 and 1946 grew up with television. Those born between 1915 and 1919 grew up with radio.

Another explanation for the differences among the age groups could be a result of the fact that the majority of older Canadians are not in the workforce and live on limited incomes. A major event that had a far-reaching effect on the Canadian economy during the study was the recession of the early 1990s. Older individuals with their restricted incomes saw the yields on their savings precipitously reduced (McDonald, Donahue, & Moore, 1997). They may have wanted a computer, but the recession created so much economic uncertainty that they did not spend their money on what they probably saw as a nonessential luxury. The recession in the early 1990s in Canada had a significant effect on all Canadians and is called a period effect. **Period effects** are any historical or major event that occurs at the same time the researcher is measuring some aspect of the aging process. Common examples of period effects offered by researchers are world wars and depressions because they have had such a profound influence on all age groups. It is worth remembering, however, that more ordinary events, such as a simple technological innovation, for example, e-mail, can also affect people in vital ways. Finally, there is the possibility that the differences in the use of computers may be a result of the combination of aging, period, and cohort effects.

The problem social gerontologists face is disentangling age, period, and cohort effects. In the early days of gerontological research, investigators made the mistake of interpreting cross-sectional age differences as if they referred to the process of aging. This type of mistake has been referred to as the "**life course fallacy**" (Riley, 1998). For example, in their examination of intelligence and aging, researchers found that younger age groups scored higher on intelligence tests then did older age groups. Many concluded that intelligence declined with age, but they were confusing age-related development and cohort effects (Schaie & Hofer, 2001). It was later found that older age groups have lower levels of education, compared with younger age groups, which account for the difference, rather than age-related changes in intelligence (Albert, et al., 1995). Fortunately, there are a number of designs researchers can use to circumvent this type of mistake.

Research Designs Specific to the Study of Aging

Longitudinal designs can help determine the "...impact of age versus cohort versus time or period..." in samples of aging people (Havens, 1995: 121). This type of design allows researchers to directly observe changes in individuals and groups as they age and the consequences of these changes. By interviewing older people every year prior to retirement and every year after retirement, the reasons for and the nature of the transition have been better understood. Data collected from a cross-sectional survey could never truly capture what factors lead to changes in the work status of older people (see Chapter 12). Although these designs are very expensive and time consuming, in the last decade, there has been increased recognition that longitudinal methods can be used over shorter time intervals and that existing data sets can be turned into longitudinal data by adding another round of data collection (Schaie & Hofer, 2001).

Panel Designs

The most often used type of longitudinal study is the panel study, in which the same individuals in a sample are repeatedly surveyed about various aspects of their lives. In the United States, some studies span decades (such as the *Baltimore Longitudinal Study of Aging*, which started in 1958 and is still in progress). Depending on the study, people might be surveyed every year or could be surveyed up to every 10 years. The very first longitudinal study of aging in Canada mentioned above, the *Ontario Longitudinal Study of Aging*, started in 1959 and had annual follow-up for 20 years (Black, 1995; Havens, 1995). The *National Population Health Survey*, which started in 1994, interviews the same panel of Canadians every two years about their physical, mental, and social health. One of the explicit aims of the study is to examine the "...changes that people experience as they grow older." The federal government has made a commitment to fund this study for 12 years. Another longitudinal panel study in Canada is the *Survey of Labour and Income Dynamics* (SLID), which is the first national data file to collect data on the fluctuations in income that a typical family or individual experiences through time. The SLID, started in 1993, follows the same respondents for six years, and uses a split-interview format (people are interviewed twice a year) so that each panel is interviewed 13 times over a spread of six years.

The *Canadian Study of Health and Aging*, started in 1991, followed up 10,263 elderly people using 18 study centres across Canada. The initial purpose of the study was to examine the prevalence of dementia and its subtypes by age and gender. This study was administered in two languages, and over 70 investigators were involved. Most recently, the Institute for Aging, one of the Canadian Institutes for Health Research, is deliberating on the establishment of the *Canadian Longitudinal Study on Aging*. The goal of this study will be to examine the molecular, genetic, and cellular aspects of aging, together with the psychological and social aspects of aging—certainly an innovation in the history of Canadian gerontology (Healthy Aging: From Cell to Society, 2001).

Simple longitudinal designs, although more powerful than cross-sectional surveys, have their limitations. Sometimes, the duration of the study is too short to capture period effects, and unless there is more than one birth cohort sampled, the study can suffer from "cohort-centrism." For example, the *Survey of Labour and Income Dynamics* is timely because it captures up-to-date changes made to the Canada/Quebec Pension Plan in the late 1990s and researchers can gauge the effects of this policy change (period effect) on retirement incomes. Riley (1987; 1998) warns against the "fallacy of **cohort-centrism**," which erroneously assumes that members of all cohorts will grow older in the same way as members of one's own cohort. We should expect that research findings will change quite substantially as cohorts with differing experiences move in and out of the older population (due to death). The early baby-boomers (born between 1947 and 1959) are probably less likely to listen to the "Spice Girls" in their old age than upcoming cohorts.

Cohort Designs

An exceptionally useful longitudinal design, cohort analysis, allows researchers to study cross-sectional age-related differences, to observe age-related changes in a cohort over time, and to compare cohorts of the same age at different historical periods. Moreover, cohort analysis allows the researcher to study change across the life course. These designs, usually referred to as cohort sequential designs, follow more than one cohort longitudinally. The *Aging in Manitoba Study* (AIM), started in 1971 (Havens 1997; Havens, 2001), conducted three independent cross-sectional studies of older Manitobans in 1971, 1976, and 1983. All three groups were then followed up over time. The 1971 and 1976 groups were re-interviewed in 1983 to 1984, 1990, 1996, and 2001, and the 1983 group was re-interviewed in 1990, 1996, and 2001. Currently, AIM is the largest continuous population-based longitudinal study of aging in Canada. Figure 3.3 (next page) illustrates the design of this study.

Researchers using the AIM study can examine different age groups in any given year—they can compare the health of those aged 60 to 65 years with those 66 to 70 years of age from the cross-sectional survey in 1983 to 1984. They can also examine the same individuals aged 65 to 70 years at a minimum of three different time points, from 1971 to 1983 to 1990, to examine age changes within their cohort. Period effects can also be discerned by making comparisons of those who are the same age (e.g., 70 years) in 1971, in 1983 to 1984, and in 1990. Finally, researchers can assess patterns across the life course from one cohort to the other. While health may have deteriorated rapidly across the life course (three time points) for the 1971 panel, the 1976 panel did not show as rapid a decline over three time points. Figure 3.4 (next page) illustrates how a cohort sequential design can function.

In Figure 3.4, using hypothetical data, the various possible comparisons can be seen more easily.

Event History Analysis

Another tool that is useful to social gerontologists is event history designs (Hirdes & Brown, 1994). In research on aging, gerontologists are often very interested in when a particular life event will happen. For example, the bulk of the research

Figure 3.3 DESIGN OF *AGING IN MANITOBA STUDY* (AIM)

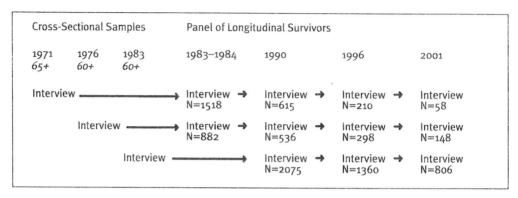

Source: Adapted from Chipperfield J.G., Havens, B., and Doig, W. Method and Description of the Aging in Manitoba Project: A 20-Year Longitudinal Study. *Canadian Journal on Aging*, 16(1): 612, 1997. Used with permission. Up-dated by B. Havens.

Figure 3.4 A HYPOTHETICAL COHORT SEQUENTIAL DESIGN

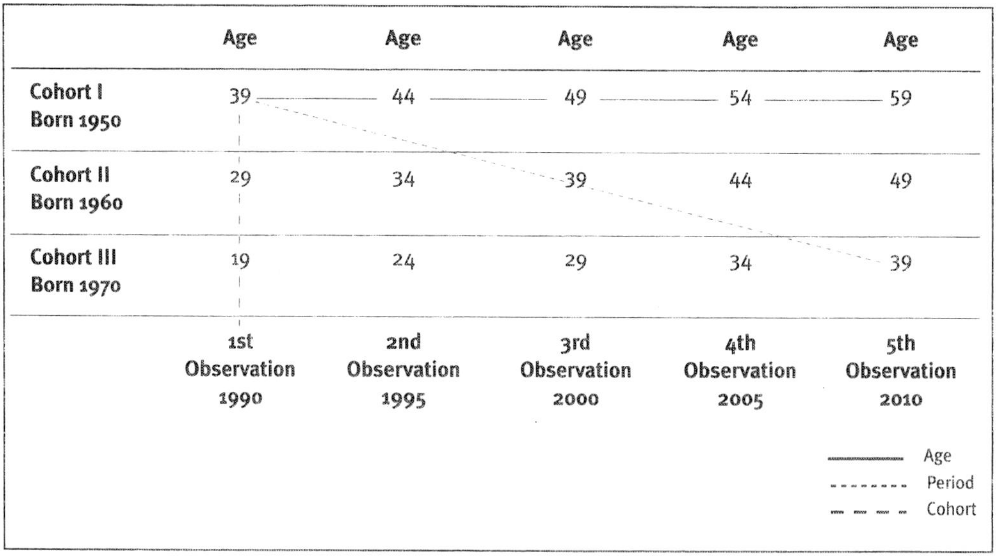

	Age	Age	Age	Age	Age
Cohort I **Born 1950**	39	44	49	54	59
Cohort II **Born 1960**	29	34	39	44	49
Cohort III **Born 1970**	19	24	29	34	39
	1st Observation 1990	2nd Observation 1995	3rd Observation 2000	4th Observation 2005	5th Observation 2010

—————— Age
- - - - - - Period
— —— — — Cohort

Source: Adapted from Morgan and Kunkel, *Aging: the Social Context*, p.18, copyright 2001 by Pine Forge Press. Reprinted by permission of Sage Publications.

on retirement has attempted to predict the age of retirement from paid employment, an issue that has serious ramifications for the costs of some government pensions. If people work longer they will spend less time in retirement, which can ultimately be cheaper for government. Event history analysis examines when and how particular events happen and their causes for individuals or groups (Alwin & Campbell, 2001). On the basis of the use of longitudinal data, the technique identifies how much time passes before an event occurs, the rates of occurrence of the event, and how the rates may change over time. In the last decade, in Canada, more and more workers who retire are actually returning to work. An event history analysis of a longitudinal data base, such as the SLID, would tell us how many years retirees spend in retirement before they go back to work, why they go back, what the national rates are for the reversal in any given year, and how the rates have increased or decreased over time.

Life Review

Other longitudinal designs already mentioned above are retrospective designs that include the use of diaries, letters, life stories, memoirs, biographies, and other kinds of data obtained by asking people to comment on the past (Alwin & Campbell, 2001). These retrospective studies compare events and periods within the life of a single individual, focusing on time-marked events, relationships in the family, work, and community in a historical, cultural context. The "life" in the life review is the observant person moving through the changes encountered across the life course (Clausen, 1998). These studies help provide "contextual realism," although they cannot be considered "statistical designs" (Alwin & Campbell, 2001). They are retrospective, since people are looking back over their lives, unlike panel studies that are inherently prospective because they measure attributes of individuals at regular intervals as they move forward in life. Sometimes these two features are combined when panel members are asked to fill in past history about jobs, family, and health, so there is often an interface between qualitative and quantitative approaches.

Related Methodological Issues

Although longitudinal designs are the strongest designs for studying age-related changes, they still have difficulties. Attrition from a longitudinal study can occur due to death, illness, and relocating, or because people no longer wish to participate in the study. For example, by the first follow-up in 1983 to 1984 of the AIM study, 58.6 percent of those respondents interviewed in 1971 or 1976 had died (Chipperfield, Havens, & Doig, 1997). For all designs, there are also measurement problems where a measure used at an earlier time is culturally unsuitable in later years or where it is difficult to determine the intervals between measurement. A related issue refers to constructing culturally sensitive instruments when some of the respondents do not speak either of the two official Canadian languages. **Back translating** of questionnaires (translating from English to the target language and back to English to see if they are similar) and using bilingual interviewers helps but is not foolproof. Some concepts simply are not the same across cultures (Biribili, 2000). As an illustration, the reluctance among Chinese respondents to acknowledge pride in a study of self-esteem carried out in Shanghai was not a translation problem but, rather, a matter of values. North Americans view pride in a positive light, but the Chinese in this study valued humility, so from their perspective, a negative answer to the question would have really been a positive answer (Yu & Zahang, 1987). The main problems with retrospective life reviews are fairly obvious because they are essentially cross-sectional. There is the problem of differential survival of the respondents. By definition, it is the life histories of survivors, who might have different histories than those who did not survive, that are studied. There is also the problem of the reliability of recall (Alwin & Campbell, 2001).

Data Collection

Besides design flaws, there are also issues related to collecting data from older people. Difficulties in obtaining data can be related to the diminishing capacity of the respondents over time. Some respondents may suffer "sensory decrements, language erosion, cognitive deficits, chronic illnesses," or any combination of these. There is also the problem with maintaining gender ratios representative of the population because of the difference in mortality rates between men and women in later life. In life review studies, the rather demanding claims placed on a respondent that go well beyond a single interview can be onerous in terms of time and the "work" required to remember and locate archival materials.

Ethics

A number of potential ethical hazards can be identified in the conduct of research with older individuals, especially the frail-old. The risks are somewhat similar to those for the general population, but the frail-old have the potential to be more vulnerable to unethical treatment. The three most common problem areas that have been identified regarding the ethical treatment of any human subject include potential harm, lack of informed consent, and privacy. In the case of older people, harm can range from the simple process of collecting data, which can seriously inflict fatigue or stress on the respondent, to the withholding of a potentially beneficial experimental treatment from subjects in the control group. Withholding a new or innovative treatment can be a dangerous practice because the older person might not live long enough to receive the treatment at a later date. A particularly poignant problem is the termination of a research project, especially a longitudinal project, where a meaningful social relationship has developed between the older person and the research team. The older person could be left feeling lonely and isolated, although the researcher did not intend to cause harm.

Particularly relevant to the study of older people are the many issues surrounding informed consent. Frequently, it is difficult to determine who may give consent when the person is cognitively impaired and, if he or she is not impaired, the unintentional threat of losing a service or a treatment may coerce an older person into participating. Even the promise of attention from the researcher may be enough to compel an older person to participate.

The right to privacy is the individual's right to decide when, where, to whom, and to what extent his or her behaviour will be revealed (Singleton & Straits, 1999). The right to privacy is a very easy right to violate, especially with a captive audience, such as elderly persons in hospitals and nursing homes, where there is little privacy to begin with and no family member may be present to advocate on behalf of the older person.

The vast majority of social researchers do not plan to harm their subjects in any way. Nevertheless, to help ensure that a researcher does not engage in a potential violation of ethics, the Research Ethics Boards at Canadian universities and ethics panels in most institutions and agencies approve the research before it can begin. All research conducted under the auspices of these organizations is subject to a thorough review by ethics committees, which ensure that researchers are ethically accountable. No research project can be implemented until the researcher is granted ethical approval.

CHAPTER SUMMARY

This chapter has reviewed the goals and methods of scientific enquiry in social gerontology. The focus of gerontological research has shifted from the study of the aged as a static category to the explanation, description and exploration of aging as a dynamic social process. Generally, researchers in social gerontology are interested in how aging processes affect the individual and society and how society affects aging processes. They like to take a "long view" of people as they move through transitions in their life span. To avoid human errors in studying older people, researchers adhere to three main principles central to scientific enquiry: empiricism, objectivity, and control. Researchers employ either deductive (theory testing) or inductive approaches (theory development) in the scientific process.

Although many gerontologists follow these principles, a number of new perspectives or paradigms have emerged over time that adopt contrasting beliefs about the nature of reality (ontology), the relationship between the researcher and the subject (epistemology) and how to gain knowledge about the world (methods). The various paradigms or systems of knowledge, therefore, employ a number of methodologies that match their worldview. Postpositivists who attempt to understand reality use methodologies such as cross-sectional and longitudinal surveys, secondary data analysis, and experimental and quasi-experimental designs. In contrast, interpretive researchers, who believe in a subjective reality, attempt to capture the meaning of the human experience as it is expressed in the aging process and rely on a distinct set of methodologies such as biographies, phenomenology, grounded theory, and ethnography. Critical theorists, on the other hand, expose the injustices sometimes suffered by vulnerable people and try to change the social and cultural structures and/or policies that are the culprits. All types of methodologies are put to use in this paradigm, so the feature that distinguishes it from the others is the involvement of older people in the control and direction of the research process and the commitment to social change.

It is extremely important to appreciate that paradigms overlap and that researchers who do not always agree on a specific worldview select among the many methodologies open to them. Indeed, many employ several methods at the same time in one study. An awareness of these overarching paradigms in social gerontology is not only helpful in situating research studies in the burgeoning body of gerontological literature but also provides a guide to understanding how research questions, theory, and methods are linked or should be linked in a study.

Notwithstanding the methodological pluralism found in social gerontology, there are a number of issues that are unique to the study of aging. The disentangling of age, period, and cohort effects—partially achieved by the use of longitudinal designs, such as panel and cohort designs, event history analysis, and life reviews—is a significant issue facing all gerontologists. If gerontological research does not unravel these effects, the conclusions drawn can have dire consequences for older people. Nothing is perfect in the world of research and longitudinal designs also have problems with follow-up, measurement, time intervals, and language, while all designs are subject to the capacity of the older person to participate in the study and their willingness to do so. It is up to the researcher to ensure that no harm befalls the older person, that he or she is fully informed about the study, and that privacy is protected at all costs.

Knowing the subject matter of gerontology, and with an understanding of theory and research, we now have a framework for reviewing research studies. The next section begins to put this knowledge to the test as we explore the commonalities and diversities of aging.

KEY TERMS

Ex post facto hypothesizing, **(p. 66)**

Premature closure, **(p. 67)**

Goals of science, **(p. 67)**

Empiricism, **(p. 68)**

Reliability, **(p. 68)**

Reliability coefficient, **(p. 68)**

Validity, **(p. 70)**

Construct, **(p. 70)**

Objectivity, **(p. 70)**

Control, **(p. 71)**

Deductive approach, **(p. 71)**

Inductive approach, **(p. 71)**

Paradigms, **(p. 73)**

Postpositivism, **(p. 73)**

Interpretive/constructivism, **(p. 78)**

Biography, **(p. 80)**

Phenomenology, **(p. 80)**

Grounded theory, **(p. 81)**

Ethnography, **(p. 81)**

Critical paradigm, **(p. 82)**

Aging effect, **(p. 84)**

Cohort, **(p. 84)**

Period effects, **(p. 85)**

Life course fallacy, **(p. 85)**

Cohort-centricism, **(p. 87)**

Back translating, **(p. 89)**

Study Questions

1. Choose a research topic of personal interest to you in gerontology. Do you think you could be objective about the topic? How would you go about avoiding human error in your study?

2. What are the differences between the three major world views used to study the aging process? Do you prefer one over the other, and if so, why? Do you think you could feel comfortable in the use of any of the three approaches?

3. If you consider your own life and that of your grandparents, what would be the some of the differences that might influence your own aging and that of your grandparents? What are the sources of these differences?

4. What ethical obligations do researchers in social gerontology have to older people?

Suggested Readings

Giele J.Z. and Elder Jr., G.H. (Eds.) (1998). *Methods of Life Course Research: Qualitative and Quantitative Approaches.* Thousand Oaks, CA: Sage Publications.

Gubrium, J.F. & Sankar, A. (Eds.) (1994). *Qualitative Methods in Research.* Thousand Oaks, CA: Sage Publications.

Martin-Matthews, A., and Béland, F. (2001). Northern Lights: Reflections on Canadian Gerontological Research. Special supplement on the occasion of the 17th World Congress of the International Association of Gerontology. *Canadian Journal of Aging,* Vol 20 suppl. 1. (all articles).

The Gendered Life Course

Learning Objectives

In this chapter, you will learn about:

- How men's and women's family life courses differ.
- How gender affects the life course of paid work and retirement.
- The interrelationships between gendered family and work life courses.
- How life courses have changed over the last 100 years, more so for women.

Introduction

Gender is an important characteristic of individuals. Males and females differ biologically and genetically (XX versus XY chromosome composition). As a determinant of behaviour, however, learning is more important than biology, and one important component of our learning occurs through gender role socialization. That is, girls learn to be girls (and, later, women), and boys learn to be boys (and, later, men). What they learn, however, is dependent upon what the wider society deems gender-appropriate behaviour. Gender-appropriate behaviour varies tremendously cross-culturally, and it can also vary over time in societies undergoing change. Thus, while gender is a characteristic of individuals, it is one that is socially determined and socially constructed. However, gender is more than a characteristic of individuals; it is also an important—even a defining—aspect of social organization. In other words, our society is structured to advantage and privilege males.

As noted in Chapter 3, age is both a characteristic of individuals and an aspect of social structure. Just as our society allocates roles and responsibilities to persons on the basis of their ages, it also differentially places people on the basis of their gender. However, age and gender are not just two social markers; rather, age and gender intersect or interrelate. This means that one cannot be understood apart from the other. To understand aging, one has also to consider gender. For example, the "difference" between a young man and an old woman is greater than that between a young man and an old man. This chapter examines how aging and gender intersect by focusing on the different life pathways of men and women in Canadian society. However, it is important to remember that there are variations among women and among men. While gender is a very important dimension of people's lives, it does not eliminate the effects of other factors, such as social class, race/ethnicity, region, and so on.

Our discussion of the gendered life course is couched in the context of two revolutions that are transforming societies, such as Canada. One revolution has already been discussed in Chapter 1—the longevity revolution, or increased life expectancy (and its effect on population aging). Second is a gender revolution, in which women's roles have substantially changed with a majority of women now engaged in the paid labour force. As Moen (1996:172) writes: "Both [revolutions] are challenging old norms and ideologies about age and gender, as well as producing a **structural lag** in the roles and resources available to men and women." [bold added] Also, it can be added that these revolutions are themselves interrelated; as we saw in Chapter 1, women have benefited more from the increase in longevity.

Before we look at the substantive issues involved in the gendered life course, a methodological caveat is needed. By its very nature, the life course is a temporal phenomenon. This means that the best data to assess it are longitudinal, ideally panel data on the same individuals as they go through life. However, such longitudinal data are in short supply in Canada, and we almost always have to rely on cross-sectional data. By looking at cross-sectional data at different points in time, we can draw a general picture of life course progression. However, as discussed in Chapter 3, we run the risk of confounding age, period, and cohort effects. Another difficulty in assessing the life course is that "it isn't over 'til it's over." So, for example, if we are looking at today's 20-year-olds, we do not know what their life course will be like in 50 years from now, when they are 70 years old. If we have the data, we can compare today's 20-year-olds with people who are now, say, aged 60 years when they were 20 years old (i.e., 40 years ago). While such a comparison can tell us some things, it is not useful in assessing the life course of today's 20-year-olds-much of their lives has not happened yet. No data, not even the best panel data available, can help with this problem.

Overview of the Changing Life Course

Two general dimensions of life course change can first be highlighted—related to the longevity and gender revolutions identified by Moen (1996). One dimension deals with the mortality reductions that were discussed in Chapter 1. The life course today is more predictable in that most deaths occur in later life. The unpredictabilities associated with loss of children, siblings, and spouses at a young age have lessened considerably. People can expect to enjoy many years in which parents and adult children jointly survive (Gee, 1990). While other unpredictabilities in life (e.g., divorce) have increased, they do not take away from the great strides made in reducing deaths at young ages. The other dimension relates to gender change. In the past, the life courses of people were highly gendered (although early deaths led to deviations, such as young widows working for pay to support their children). Men began working after their schooling was completed and continued working full time until retirement or until they could no longer; women's life courses were dominated by domestic tasks, and any work outside the home was secondary to that domestic work (although in farm settings, women did much work that directly contributed to the family income). Men's life courses were played out in the public sphere and women's in the private sphere, increasingly so as urbanization replaced farm life. As we progressed through the 20th century, this gendered public/private sphere distinction broke down. Women came to play a much bigger role in paid labour; however, norms continued to stipulate that work in the home remain the purview of women. Women's lives became more fluid; they entered and re-entered the paid labour force over their life course. However, the workplace remained dominated by a male model of early and continued full-time employment (until retirement), and thus, women's involvement in the public sphere of paid work has been treated as marginal. At the same time, their unpaid work in the home has been taken for granted and undervalued.

The male life course was affected first by the institutionalization of retirement (and then mandatory retirement—which continues to exist in most Canadian provinces—and then by an increasing trend of leaving and re-entering the paid labour force in later life, as discussed in Chapter 12. Retirement has less meaning in the female life course. When does a woman retire if she is a full-time home-maker? Even if a full-time worker, a woman's domestic work continues after departure from the paid labour force. If her husband is ill, that domestic labour can increase to become a "full-time job" but without pay. Thus, the life courses of men and women continue to be gendered, but in different and more nuanced ways than in the past.

The Gendered Family Life Course

Women and men experience their families' lives in different ways. In this section, we examine some aspects of the difference between the genders in the taking on of family roles and the timing of family role transitions.

Marriage and Cohabitation

The vast majority of Canadian women and men marry at least once. Today's family life course varies from that of the past, however, with regard to common-law marriage/cohabitation. Cohabitation was virtually unheard of before the 1970s (although it may have been practised—invisibly—more than was thought); it was derogatorily referred to as "living in sin" and "shacking up." Now, it forms a part of the family life course for many Canadians, particularly in the province of Quebec (where it is called *union libre*). Data from the 1996 Census reveal that approximately 8 percent of Canadians (or 1.84 million persons) over the age of 15 years live in common-law unions, a 108 percent increase since 1981 (when the Canadian Census first began collecting data on cohabitation) (Wu, 2000). Put in different terms, about 14 percent of all unions in Canada are common-law unions. However, there are strong provincial/regional variations. In Quebec, about one-quarter of all unions are cohabiting unions; in the Yukon and the Northwest Territories, the figures are even higher, approximating 30 percent. In contrast, in Prince Edward Island and Ontario, less than 10 percent of unions are common-law unions.

Cohabitation varies by age and gender as well. In terms of age, as one might expect, younger persons are more likely to be cohabiting. For example, nearly 17 percent of Canadians aged 25 to 29 years are currently cohabiting—more than double the percentage (7 percent) among those aged 45 to 49 years. Regarding gender, men have higher rates of cohabition than do women. However, these figures are about current cohabitation only; from a life-course perspective, we want to know the numbers/proportions who have *ever* cohabitated and about the transition to cohabitation. In Quebec, 36 percent of women and 41 percent of men have ever lived in a common-law union; for the rest of Canada, the figures are 25 percent and 26 percent, respectively (Wu, 2000). In other words, the gender difference in the likelihood of cohabitation exists for the Quebec population only.

It is important to look at *premarital* and *postmarital* cohabitation separately. Looking first at premarital cohabitation (cohabitation that precedes a legal marriage), by age 35 years more than 70 percent of women and approximately 63 percent of men have ever lived in a common-law union. Therefore, women have higher rates of premarital cohabitation than do men, which is consistent with the fact that women marry (legally) at younger ages. A different picture emerges for postmarital cohabitation, however. Men are more likely to make the transition to postmarital cohabitation. For example, among divorced or separated persons aged 45 to 54 years, 10.8 percent of women and 15.1 percent of men are currently cohabitating, and 30.9 percent of women and 42.8 percent of men have ever cohabited (since their marital breakup) (Wu, 2000). Overall, women are more likely to live in premarital common-law unions and men are more likely to live in postmarital common-law unions.

Whether it is a cohabiting relationship or a legal marriage, the ages of the men and women at the beginning of the union are different. Women tend to marry (or cohabitate with) men who are older than they are. For example, the median age at first marriage for men is about 29 years and for women 26 years (Beaujot & Bélanger, 2001). While this age discrepancy was larger in the past (Veevers, 1984), it is still an important phenomenon. The fact that women marry (or cohabitate) at younger ages than men do establishes what is called a **mating gradient**. The younger spouse (the wife in most cases) will have fewer resources, for example, less schooling, less job experience, less income. These small differences cumulate over time; the husband's job will be given priority, since it is more important to the economic well being of the family. So, for example, the couple may move because of the husband's job; the wife will quit her job and have to start over again. Over time, then, the initially small economic difference between the husband and wife becomes a substantial gap—this process is termed the mating gradient. While other factors are also implicated in women's lower economic status, it is important to know that a relatively small age difference between a wife and her husband is involved as well. Gee (1995a) argues that women face greater social pressures to marry and to marry early, helping establish a subtle process that increases women's economic dependency.

Fertility

The birth of children is an important transition in the life course of both men and women. However, we primarily have data only for women.[1] In part, this represents administrative convenience for the government (which is responsible for most data collection on fertility in industrialized countries, such as Canada), but it also reflects a sexist bias in which women are assumed to be the primary parent due to biology alone.

A dramatic change in the life course of Canadian women is a reduction in the number of children they bear. As we saw in Chapter 1, this decline in fertility is the primary cause of population aging. Table 4.1 shows the average number of children ever born to women at the end of their reproductive lives (generally taken to be ages 45 to 49 years) from 1941 to 1991.[2] In 1941, these women (birth cohort of 1986 to 1991) bore 4.2 children on average; in 1991 (birth cohort of 1946 to 1951), the comparable number was 2.2—a decline of approximately 50 percent. The women who produced the Canadian baby boom are represented in the data for 1971 and 1981 in Table 4.1; they bore on average 3.3 children. The baby boom, then, really did not encompass a large increase in children ever born to mothers, media coverage to the contrary. It is more accurate to say that the baby boom represented a stall in the overall trend of declining fertility in Canada in the 20th century. The baby boom was the result of a change in the timing of women's life course events, rather than a substantial increase in fertility. In the years of the baby boom, women married at younger ages and had their children at younger ages than did women both before and after them (Gee, 1980). Because of the pyramidal shape of the Canadian age structure in the mid-20th century, the proportionately large numbers of younger women led to greater numbers of babies being born (even though completed family size was only slightly elevated).

Table 4.1 also shows a convergence in the fertility behaviour of Canadian women. Not only are women having fewer children, they are also much more likely to have two children. Indeed, it is sometimes claimed that the two-child family has become the norm. At the same time, the percent of women having large families (six or more children) has plummeted. One reason for this convergence is a rapid fertility decline starting in the mid-20th century in Quebec, well known for its traditional pattern of very large family size—although First Nations fertility levels remain high (Suwal & Trovato, 1998).

Table 4.1 AVERAGE NUMBER OF CHILDREN EVER BORN TO EVER-MARRIED WOMEN AGED 45 TO 49 YEARS, AND PERCENT OF EVER-MARRIED WOMEN AGED 45-49 YEARS WITH TWO CHILDREN EVER BORN AND WITH 6+ CHILDREN EVER BORN, CANADA, 1941–1991

YEAR	CHILDREN EVER BORN	2 CHILDREN	6+ CHILDREN
1941	4.2	15.5%	27.9%
1961	3.1	22.5%	14.9%
1971	3.3	22.0%	15.1%
1981	3.3	22.9%	12.2%
1991	2.2	38.1%	2.6%

Source: Adapted from Statistics Canada, "Family over the life course," Catalogue No. 91-543, 1995.

However, these data—by their very nature—speak to the past. We have to wait until today's young women are in their late 40s to know how many children they will have. Will more of them end up with no children, that is, never make the transition to parenthood? It is difficult to say, but it is important to keep in mind that levels of childlessness in the past were not particularly low. For example, among ever-married women born around the turn of the 20th century, approximately 13 percent never bore any children (Beaujot, 1995). Among ever-married women born in the middle of the 20th century, the comparable figure was approximately 10 percent. Whatever percent of today's young people may remain childless, the reasons may be somewhat different from those in the past. Childlessness may be either voluntary or involuntary. In the past, it is probably true that a higher proportion of women were childless for involuntary reasons, including infertility/sterility (of either the man or the woman) and the early death of husbands. However, it is possible that involuntary childlessness may increase, especially if women wait until late ages to try to become pregnant. We can already see evidence of this in the growth of fertility clinics and the use of reproductive technology to assist in impregnation (and the associated risks of multiple births and the psychological trauma of a high rate of failure). We do know, though, that young Canadian adults have not embraced the idea of childlessness. Data from the 1995 *General Social Survey* reveal that only 6.6 percent of men in their 20s and 4.6 percent of similarly aged women intend to have no children (Beaujot & Bélanger, 2001).

While fertility has converged to a two-child average, some women go on to have a third child. What are their characteristics? Women who have a third child are more likely to have had their first child under the age of 25 years; have had a short interval between their first and second children; not be engaged in the paid labour force; not have a high school diploma; be born in a country other than Canada, the United States, and Europe; attend religious services frequently; and have two children of the same sex (Beaujot & Bélanger, 2001). Among Canadians with two children, the 15 percent who intend to have a third child are more likely to be regular attenders at religious services, Catholic, and in a remarriage (Wu & Wang, 1998). These sets of findings suggest that gender role orientations may lie at the heart of differences in fertility. Indeed, two Canadian studies find that gender role systems are an important determinant of family size, although in somewhat different ways. Jayachandran (2000) reports that couples who have an egalitarian gender role structure have fewer children; Matthews (1999) shows that women have fewer children than they desire because they have not been able to establish a satisfactory gendered division of labour in everyday life.

One of the recent changes in fertility behaviour in Canada is a postponement in the age at which couples have children. This is in sharp contrast to the baby boom mothers/parents, who married and bore children at the youngest ages in our history. The median age at first birth is now approximately 26 years for women and 29 years for men (Beaujot & Bélanger, 2001). However, compared with other family life course events, the spread around the average age at first childbirth is large

(Rajulton & Ravanera, 1995). In other words, while the overall trend in age at first childbirth is getting older, there is considerable variation around the average, and some people continue to have children at young ages. So, while there is convergence in the number of children born, the age at which the first child is born varies quite substantially. It is important to keep this variation in mind; the media have tended to focus on late-age first-time mothers only, and it is easy to forget that young mothers exist as well. Early age at childbirth (and to a lesser degree, early age at marriage) is associated with becoming a lone parent in both Canada and the United States (Smith, 1998), which, in turn, is a major predictor of economic hardship. However, late age at childbirth does not guarantee economic advantage. As shown by Grindstaff (1996), even late age at the commencement of childbearing does not protect Canadian women from economic disadvantage in terms of labour force participation, the securement of full-time work, and income.

The life course of Canadians has changed, as noted above, by the emergence of cohabitation as a common and accepted form of family living. When common-law marriages first gained popularity, children tended not to be born into them. However, in more recent years, children are increasingly being born into common-law marriage situations. For example, of all children born in Canada in 1983 and 1984, 9.8 percent were born into a common-law union; just 10 years later, 20.4 percent of children were born (in 1993 and 1994) into one (Marcil-Gratton, 1998). (In Quebec, the figure for children born in 1993 and 1994 is 43.1 percent.). If one adds the figure of 20.4 percent to the percentage of children born to single mothers (about 9 percent), we can see that around 30 percent of children are now born outside (legal) marriage (Marcil-Gratton, 1998). Of course, these children can later live in a family with legally married parents, but the emerging trend is for parents in common-law unions not to marry eventually even when they have children. Thus, the link between (legal) marriage and childbearing (and child rearing) appears to be weakening. In keeping with the life course principle of "linked lives," the changing behaviour of parents has implications for their children. As we will see, common-law unions tend to be more temporary than legal marriages; therefore, the children of such unions are more likely to live in lone-parent families headed by their mother. For example, children born into a common-law union in which the parents do not subsequently marry are three times more likely to experience family breakdown than children born into a legal marriage not preceded by a common-law union (Marcil-Gratton, 1998). Also, they are more likely to experience family breakdown at a younger age. And, as we will see later, families headed by mothers tend to be poor.

Divorce and Remarriage

Canada has seen a "revolution" in divorce in the last 35 years, in large part due to changes in divorce law. In 1969, there was a major liberalization in divorce; until then, adultery was the only legal grounds for divorce. A further liberalization in divorce law occurred in 1986, again making it easier for unhappy marriages to end by reducing the period of separation needed to be eligible for divorce. Consequently, divorce is now a relatively common event in the life course of men and women, although it is difficult to know how many of recent marriages will dissolve (as with fertility, we have to wait and see). However, among people born in the middle of the 20th century, 39 percent of men and 34 percent of women were no longer living with their (first) spouse after 25 years (Beaujot & Bélanger, 2001). With the recent increases in common-law unions, however, data on divorce prevalence become less meaningful. As argued by LeBourdais and Marcil-Gratton (1996), we need to have much better data on common-law marriages and their dissolutions in order to get a true picture of marital breakdown. This is especially true for Canada, compared with the United States, given much higher rates of common-law union formation in Canada.

However, there is a relationship between divorce and cohabitation. Numerous studies have shown that persons who cohabitate and then legally marry are more likely to divorce (e.g., Hall & Zhao, 1995). Estimates by Beaujot (2000) suggest that the risk of divorce is double for marriages preceded by common-law unions. Therefore, despite the everyday belief that "trial marriage" operates as a testing ground to ensure marital success and longevity, empirical research reveals the opposite. It appears that persons who cohabit before marriage are a self-selected group who have more casual attitudes about relationships and are, thus, more prone to divorce if "the going gets rough." (Hall, 1996) Thus, the recent increase in cohabitation could lead to higher levels of marital breakdown—among both the common-law unions themselves and the marriages that may follow them. It will be recalled that women are more likely than men to engage in premarital cohabitation. Thus, women are more at risk of divorce after a premarital union that leads to marriage.

Rates of remarriage have declined, although about one-third of marriages involve at least one spouse who has been previously married. Recent data show that remarriage after divorce is more likely for men; 64 percent of divorced men but only 52 percent of divorced women remarry (Beaujot, 2000). Relatedly, we have seen that men are more likely than women to be in postmarital cohabiting unions. Therefore, women are more likely to be living alone (if there are no young children) or heading a lone-parent family (if children are present) than are men. At least in part because of these differential postdivorce outcomes, women are more negatively affected economically by divorce than are men. Galarneau and Sturrock (1997) studied the financial effects of separation for Canadians who separated between 1987 and 1993. For persons with children under the age of 18 years living in the home, women experienced a 23 percent reduction in income in the first year and a 5 percent reduction after five years. For men, after five years, income had increased by 15 percent. Those who went on to form another union made gains after five years—18 percent for men and 14 percent for women. However, women were much less likely to form a postdivorce union.

Some argue that lower remarriage rates among women are the result of women's greater financial independence (e.g., Beaujot, 2000); the same argument has been made about divorce—that is, that increased divorce rates reflect women's financial independence as a result of their labour force participation. It has been found that in Canada, in marriages since 1969, women's labour force participation has not played a causal role in increased divorce (Hou & Omwanda, 1997). It has not yet been established whether women's participation in the labour force is a factor in their decreased likelihood of remarrying after divorce. However, given the negative financial implications of divorce for women, it seems likely that other factors are involved.

Lone Parenting

Women are far more likely to be lone parents than are men (McQuillan & Belle, 2001). This has always been the case; however, in the past, the major reason was the (early) death of husbands. In contrast, the main reasons today are never-marriage and marital dissolution (of both legal and common-law marriages). Of families with at least one child under the age of 18 years, nearly 20 percent are headed by a lone parent, with 16.4 percent headed by a lone mother (McQuillan & Belle, 2001). Lone parent families differ not only in the likelihood that the mother will head them but also in their economic well being. Female-headed lone parent families face a high likelihood of poverty. As shown in Figure 4.1, nearly one-half of lone female-headed families (with at least one child aged under 18 years) have incomes below Statistics Canada's Low Income Cut Offs (LICOs). Part of the reason for the economic problems of female-headed lone parent families is the failure of fathers to provide (even court-ordered) child support (Richardson, 1992).

In the light of information showing paternal noninvolvement associated with divorce and nonmarriage, Dumas and Péron (1992: 107) refer to an emerging "matriarchy" in the Canadian family. Gee (2000) argues against this interpretation, suggesting that rather than an end to **patriarchy**, what we are now witnessing is a shift in power (over women) from individual men to the state. Examples of the state becoming more involved in family life include legislation related to the best interests of the child and to parental fitness. Patriarchal control over the family continues, but in a different guise.

Same-Sex Unions

We have virtually no data on the numbers of persons in same-sex unions or their characteristics. However, we would be remiss in failing to mention this increasingly acknowledged and probably growing phenomenon of family living. It is likely that more men than women are engaged in same-sex unions (if we accept that more men than women are homosexual), and it is also likely that at least some portion of the group of persons in same-sex unions has had previous heterosexual

Figure 4.1 PERCENTAGE OF FAMILIES BELOW LICO BY FAMILY STRUCTURE FOR FAMILIES WITH AT LEAST ONE CHILD UNDER 18, CANADA: 1996

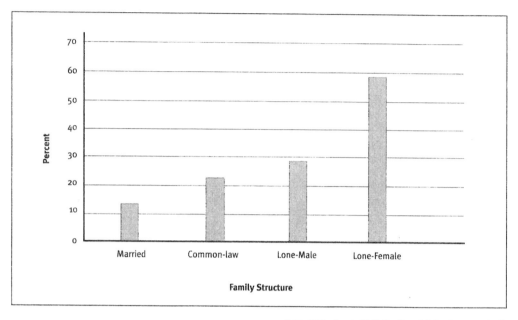

Note: LICO refers to Statistics Canada's low income cut-off.

Source: McQuillan, K., and Belle, M. "Lone-Father Families in Canada, 1971–1996."
Canadian Studies in Population, 28(1), 2001, pp. 67–88.

marriages and/or has children. Information about the family life course of homosexuals awaits the collection of data by federal bureaus, such as Statistics Canada. The collection of official data on common-law unions was the subject of much debate in the 1970s but came to pass in the 1981 census. Lobbying by gay groups for official recognition in the census took place prior to the 1996 and 2001 censuses; it appears to be just a matter of time before we have such data.

Widowhood

Women are much more likely to be widowed than are men. For example, among Canadians aged 75 to 79 years, more than one-half of women are widows, compared with less than 16 percent of men who are widowers (Martin-Matthews, 2000). Overall, among the population aged 65 years and over, widows outnumber widowers by a factor of five to one. This differential is due, in large part, to the facts that women live longer than men, as we saw in Chapter 1, and that women tend to marry men who are older than they are, as discussed earlier in this chapter. Also, women are much less likely to remarry after widowhood than are men after widowerhood (Martin Matthews, 1991; Wu, 1995). About 14 percent of widowers remarry, compared with only 5 percent of widows. And, widowed men remarry much sooner than widows. As a result of these combined trends, elderly women are much more likely to live alone. Among the Canadian population aged 75 years and over, 40.1 percent of women and 27.4 percent of men live alone (Gee, 1995b).

The Family Life Course of Older People: Present and Future

The family life course of the seniors of today is comparatively uncomplicated. They are the parents (for the most part) of the baby boomers, and were young at a time in Canadian history characterized by probably the highest degree of gendered behaviour. People tended to marry at relatively young ages, with husbands being older than their wives. They went on to have children, three on average. Divorce was not common, especially in the earlier part of their lives (although this does not mean that marriages were necessarily harmonious). Most marriages ended with the death of the husband. Women tended not to be major players in the labour force, certainly not when their children were young; when they were bringing up their children, a man's wage could support a family, and it was expected that men would "work" and women would look after the home and the people in it. This highly gendered division of labour was constraining, and it is no wonder that a women's movement developed in the 1960s. It also created economic vulnerability for women; they needed to stay married for financial reasons. When widowed (or abandoned in the pre-divorce liberalization days), women tended to fall into poverty (especially since husbands' benefits, if any, usually died with them).

In the 1970s—when today's seniors were middle aged—things started to change. Large scale increases in women's labour force participation began. On the family front, divorce became much easier, fertility started to decrease substantially, age at marriage began to increase, and cohabitation was beginning to become an acceptable living arrangement. All this *suggests* a decrease in the gendered division of labour and an increase in women's opportunities and life options. However, as noted by Moen (1996), structural lags still exist in the longevity and gender revolutions transforming our society. Women are still economically vulnerable, and often "one man away from poverty." The mating gradient still exists (for both marriages and common-law unions)—even if age at marriage is later for both men and women now—and continues to work to the financial advantage of men. Women, upon divorce or common-law union dissolution, are likely to head lone-parent families, which, as we have seen, are at high risk of poverty. To understand more about this structural lag, we turn our attention to the work life course.

Gender and the Work Life Course

We are all aware of the huge increases in women's labour force participation that have occurred in the last 30 years or so. This trend, along with that of men, is shown in Table 4.2. In 1976, 42 percent of women were in the paid labour force; in 1999, the comparable figure approaches 55 percent. At the same time, male labour force participation has declined—from 72.7 percent in 1976 to 66.8 percent in 1999. Differential age patterns by gender are involved in these opposing trends. Among women, an increase in the labour force participation of the young (particularly young mothers) is implicated. In contrast, among men, as discussed in Chapter 12, declines in the labour force involvement of older men (voluntary and involuntary retirement) drive down male labour force participation rates. The overall increase of women in the paid labour force—so that now approximately 46 percent of workers are women—would lead us to conclude that gender equality is being approached in the workplace. However, an examination of the characteristics of women's labour suggests that much change will be needed before that conclusion can be made.

The Gender Wage Gap

The wage difference between men and women in full-year, full-time employment is quite substantial—women earn approximately 72.5 percent of what men earn. The gender wage gap has reduced—it was 58.4 percent in 1967—but it is still appreciable (Shannon & Kidd, 2001). What causes it? Research in Canada has demonstrated that in any given year, *less than one-half* of the gap is due to differences between men and women in wage-determining characteristics, such as education, work experience, union status, and industry/occupation. The rest of the gender wage gap cannot be accounted for and is typically attributed to gender discrimination. This state of affairs exists despite the existence of "equal pay for equal work" and pay equity ("equal pay for work of equal value") legislation in most Canadian jurisdictions.

The gender wage gap is smaller for younger workers than for older workers (Gunderson, 1998; Statistics Canada, 1998). The gap is also smaller for persons with a university education but has actually fallen more since 1980 for those with less than a university education. Given women's increasing educational attainment, there would appear to be grounds for optimism about the future of the gender wage gap. However, Shannon and Kidd (2001) project that a substantial gap will still exist in 2031.

Part-Time Work

The above discussion of gendered wage differences relates to full-time workers only. However, men and women differ in their engagement in part-time

Table 4.2   MALE AND FEMALE LABOUR FORCE PARTICIPATION 1976–1999

	Women aged 15 Years and Over		Men aged 15 Years and Over		
	Total employed (000s)	% of all women employed	Total employed (000s)	% of all men employed	Women as a % of total employment
1976	3,630.7	42.0	6,145.5	72.7	37.1
1977	3,716.3	42.1	6,198.4	72.0	37.4
1978	3,891.7	43.2	6,320.5	72.0	38.1
1979	4,131.3	45.0	6,526.4	73.0	38.8
1980	4,339.3	46.3	6,630.9	72.8	39.6
1981	4,546.9	47.6	6,749.9	72.8	40.2
1982	4,510.9	46.5	6,436.2	68.4	41.2
1983	4,606.6	46.9	6,420.5	67.4	41.8
1984	4,746.7	47.7	6,553.4	68.0	42.0
1985	4,927.4	48.8	6,689.9	68.6	42.4
1986	5,118.9	50.1	6,860.1	69.5	42.7
1987	5,299.3	51.2	7,021.3	70.3	43.0
1988	5,532.1	52.7	7,178.2	70.9	43.5
1989	5,699.1	53.5	7,287.3	71.0	43.9
1990	5,806.2	53.7	7,277.8	69.9	44.4
1991	5,790.6	52.7	7,060.0	66.8	45.1
1992	5,789.6	52.0	6,970.4	65.0	45.4
1993	5,827.5	51.6	7,029.9	64.6	45.3
1994	5,934.0	51.9	7,177.0	65.2	45.3
1995	6,058.4	52.3	7,298.5	65.5	45.4
1996	6,116.6	52.1	7,346.0	65.0	45.4
1997	6,266.2	52.7	7,508.3	65.5	45.4
1998	6,479.0	53.8	7,661.4	65.9	45.8
1999	6,665.3	54.6	7,865.8	66.8	45.9

Source: Statistics Canada, "Women in Canada," Catalogue No. 89-503, 2000, p. 116.

work. Just under 30 percent of women work in part-time employment; this compares with approximately 10 percent of men (Statistics Canada, 2000b). This overall gender difference is matched by a difference in the age patterns of part-time labour by gender. Men are more likely to work at part-time jobs in their later working years, whereas women are more likely to work part-time when they are younger and have very young children in the home. This employment pattern of women has long-term consequences for their income, since part-time work tends not to have pension benefits. And it is a pattern that is not necessarily of their own choice. While some women choose to work part time, others can find only part-time work. Even the choice to work part time may not be an entirely free one, given the household workload that women continue to have (Baker & Lero, 1996).

Women's Wages in the Family

As a result of the gender wage gap and women's greater likelihood to work at part-time jobs (as well as the mating gradient), the contribution of women's income to total family income is quite small. As shown in Figure 4.2, women's share of the income in dual-income families (both married and common-law) is less than one-third. It is also notable that this share has not increased appreciably since the mid-1960s. It remains the case that women are "junior partners" in their

Figure 4.2 **EARNINGS OF WIVES AS A PERCENTAGE OF TOTAL INCOME IN DUAL-EARNER FAMILIES,* 1967–1997**

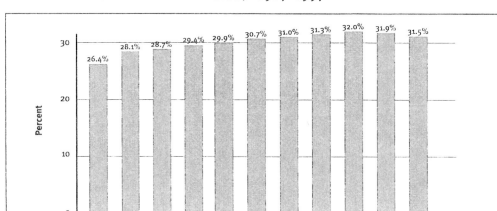

*Includes those in common-law unions.

Source: Statistics Canada, "Women in Canada," Catalogue No. 89-503, 2000, p. 145.

marriages and lack power as a result of their proportionately lower financial contribution (Grindstaff & Trovato, 1990). However, women's incomes are important to families; it has been estimated that approximately 40 percent of Canadian families would be poor if both parents did not work outside the home (Duxbury & Higgins, 1994).

Labour Force Segregation

Women and men tend to work in very different occupations, as shown in Box 4.1. Women are concentrated in a relatively few types of jobs—jobs in which other people are helped, for example, secretarial work, nursing, elementary school teaching, waitressing, and so on. Men are, on the other hand, concentrated in jobs in which people "do" things, rather than "help" people. This is not to suggest that all men have "good" jobs (for example, manual labour is one of the main male occupations), but there is a greater likelihood that men will have jobs in which they are owners and/or managers. The information in Box 4.1 also shows industrial segregation by gender. Men and women work in nonoverlapping industries. A good portion of the wage difference between men and women can be accounted for by their differential occupation and industry placement.

Why do men tend to concentrate in certain jobs and industries and women in others? Three different types of explanations have been put forth to explain labour force differentiation by gender (Armstrong & Armstrong, 1994). One type of explanation focuses on the biological differences (such as in physical strength) between men and women, suggesting that these differences channel men into certain types of jobs and women into others. However, in today's workplace, brute strength is needed in very few jobs, and there does not seem to be any biological reason why men can be owners and managers and women cannot. Another set of explanations focuses on the ideas constructed by societies about what is appropriate work for women and for men, ideas that are transmitted from generation to generation by socialization and internationalization (by both females and males). Armstrong and Armstrong (1994) favour a third set of explanations—called **materialist explanations** based on political economy theory—that focus on the interacting material conditions of life in both the home and the workplace. The material conditions of family life mean that most women have to work for pay. At the same time, there has been a growing need for cheap and flexible labour. Women have been forced to take on marginal jobs for this reason, and also because of their household duties. The gendered segregation of work, in turn, leads men and women to develop different kinds of consciousness, which are passed on to children. As Armstrong and Armstrong (1994: 222) state: "Thus, the division of labour between the household and the formal economy perpetuates the segregation in the labour force, and the division of labour within each unit encourages the development of sex-specific attitudes and behaviour patterns."

Box 4.1 The Gendered Nature of Occupational Segregation

Leading Women's Occupations*
Stenographers and typists
Nurses
Telephone operators
Elementary school teachers
Babysitters, maids, etc.
Nursing assistants and aides
Waitresses and hostesses
Sewers and tailors

Leading Men's Occupations*
Loggers
Operators, road transport
Carpenters
Farmers and stock-raisers
Labourers
Owners and managers—manufacturing
Owners and managers—trade
Owners and managers—community, business, and personal services

Industries in Which Women Predominate **
Community, business, and personal services
Finance, insurance, and real estate
Trade
Public administration

Industries in Which Men Predominate **
Construction
Resource extraction
Manufacturing
Transportation and communications

* Occupations in which one gender comprises more than 75 percent of job incumbents.
** industries in which more than 55 percent of workers are of one gender.
Source: Adapted from Armstrong & Armstrong, 1994, pages 32, 70, and 72.

The Intersection of the Family and Work Life Courses

The relationship between work and family over the life course differs dramatically for men and women. It is not an exaggeration to say that the family and work life courses for women *do not intersect very well*. Despite the fact that most Canadian women work outside the home for a considerable period of time, both family and work life are structured on a one-earner (male) model. Women are still the primary homemakers and carers of others. Yet, the workplace is based on the assumption that workers do not have significant family/domestic responsibilities. Since work and family do not mesh for women, they end up making personal (private) accommodations. These accommodations may be made on the home front (e.g., having fewer children, lowering housecleaning standards); Bittman (1999) shows that the reliance on market substitutes (e.g., housecleaning services, fast food) is key in women's adaptations to domestic work overload. Workplace accommodations are also common (e.g., refusing promotions, working part time). A vivid illustration of the conflict that women face in balancing work and family can be seen in Figure 4.3. As women have increased their labour force involvement, they have decreased the number of children they have. The direction of causation is not clear, however. Is it that women have fewer children because they work; or it is that women work outside the home because they have fewer children? It is likely that the direction of causation runs both ways. It is interesting to note, though, that Canadian mothers have lower incomes than Canadian women who have never had children (Phipps, Burton, & Lethbridge, 2001).

Figure 4.3 TOTAL FERTILITY RATE AND LABOUR FORCE PARTICIPATION RATE OF WOMEN AGED 25–44, CANADA, 1953–1998

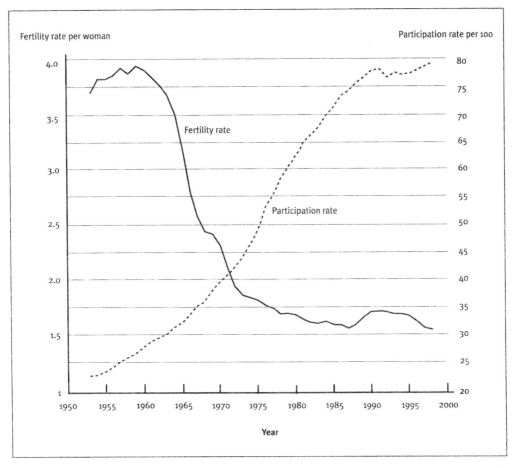

Note: LICO refers to Statistics Canada's low income cut-off.

Source: Beaujot, R., and Bélanger, A. *Perspectives on Below Replacement Fertility in Canada.* Discussion paper 01-6. London: UWO, Population Studies Centre.

The reason why women make accommodations is clear. Women continue to be the managers of the household, the cooks and the launderers, and the caregivers of others—husbands, children, parents. This unpaid work is not considered to be "real" work and is undervalued. At the same time, work is not "user -friendly" to women and families in many ways. (1) The care of children and elders cannot always be done around rigid workplace hours; hence women are absent from work for family reasons more than men—6.7 days per year for women versus 1.1 days per year for men (Statistics Canada, 2000b). These absences also annoy employers, who tend to make conclusions about women's lack of work commitment. (2) Most workplaces do not provide childcare facilities, and the workplace hours (9 a.m. to 6 p.m., Monday to Friday) of most daycare centres may not correspond with women's work hours. A national childcare policy has been promised several times by different federal governments, but nothing has come to pass. (3) Most professional, "career-type" occupations contain age-related expectations about career progress. That is, one is supposed to make "her" mark when young (in the 20s and 30s), when the demands of childbearing and child rearing are most onerous.

As noted by Gee (2000), some employers are beginning to recognize the family–work conflicts of their female employees and are offering flexible hours (flex time), family-related leave, childcare, and the like. However, only large employers can afford these supportive options, leaving out a majority of women workers. Public policy changes would be of more benefit to more women. However, in the current environment of government cutbacks, such policy changes seem highly unlikely. At the same time, the reduction of social services reinforces and heightens women's obligations for the care of others.

The overall situation of women's employment and work–family conflict does not bode well for the future of Canadian women as they age. On the one hand, due to low fertility, older women will have few children to assist them should they become frail in later life. And, given the instabilities in marriages and common-law unions—and lower rates of remarriage than in the case of men—it is possible that more women in old age will be partnerless. Martin-Matthews (2000) projects that as many as one-half of women entering old age in 2025 will not be in any marriage. Being "unattached" is a major predictor of women's poverty in later life. It is sometimes assumed that older women in the future will be in much better financial shape than their mothers and grandmothers because of their participation in the paid labour force. However, the characteristics of female employment, as outlined above, suggest caution in making that assumption.

CHAPTER SUMMARY

In this chapter, we have looked at a number of facets of change and continuity in the gendered life course, focusing on family and work. We have seen that the intersection of history and biography has operated in different ways for men and for women.

Key ideas to remember from this chapter include:

- The gendered aspect of the life course has changed over time. On the surface, gender differences are smaller; however, a more nuanced examination reveals that gender is a structured dimension of our society and that the life course continues to be gendered, although in more subtle and indirect ways than in the past.

- Men and women are both marrying at later ages. However, an age difference between husbands and wives continues, creating a mating gradient.

- Cohabitation is a new form/stage of the family life course for both men and women. Women are more likely to be premarital cohabitators and men are more likely to be postmarital cohabitators.

- One of the most dramatic changes in the family life course is declining fertility. Family size has converged around a two-child-family norm. The average age of (first) childbearing is older (especially compared with the baby boom period), but there is considerable variation in age at first motherhood. A recent fertility trend is that children are now much more likely to be born into common-law unions.

- Divorce is a more commonly experienced life course event, although divorce data are becoming increasingly less meaningful with the growing incidence of common-law marriages. Divorce has negative economic consequences for women but not for men. Despite commonsense thinking and media portrayals, marriages preceded by cohabitation are more likely to end in divorce than marriages in which couples do not live together beforehand.

- Remarriage after divorce is decreasing, partially due to increases in cohabitation. Men are more like to remarry after divorce than are women.

- Women are more likely to be heads of lone-parent families, due to their lower remarriage rates and an increased tendency for children to be born to unmarried women. Lone-parent families are at very high risk of poverty and experience a shift from patriarchal control from men to patriarchal control by the state.

- Women are much more likely to experience the life course event of widowhood. Among the population aged 65 years and over, widows outnumber widowers by a factor of five to one. Factors contributing to this gender differential include women's greater longevity, the fact that husbands are older than wives, and the higher rates of remarriage among widowers.

- The family life course of today's seniors is relatively uncomplicated, compared with that of younger Canadians. Today's seniors are less likely to have a history of cohabitation, divorce, and remarriage. The seniors of the future, on the other hand, will have had more complex family histories, and proportionately more of tomorrow's older women will have a life course involving paid labour.

- While family life course change has been substantial, there is a structural lag in the family–work interface for women. Women's labour force experience is marked by lower wages, part-time labour, and segregation by occupation and industry. Women's salaries make up only one-third of family income in dual-earner families.

- Both family and work life are based on a male, one-earner model. Accordingly, women make private accommodations to deal with work–family conflict.
- The characteristics of female paid labour, along with the accommodations women make, do not lead us to believe that the economic situation of younger women will be significantly better than that of today's elderly women. Their economic status may be further compromised by a greater likelihood of being "unattached" in later life—a major predictor of poverty in later life.

KEY TERMS

Structural lag, **(p. 95)**

Mating gradient, **(p. 98)**

Patriarchy, **(p. 103)**

Materialist explanations, **(p. 109)**

STUDY QUESTIONS

1. Interview some of your friends, and ask them how many children they expect to have. Consider what factors may lead to their having fewer children than they expect.

2. What are the advantages and disadvantages of cohabitation? Do they differ for men and women?

3. Identify the major life course changes that have occurred, and are occurring, for men and for women. What are the major points of difference?

4. What public policy measures would help alleviate the work–family conflicts experienced by women?

SUGGESTED READINGS

Armstrong, P. & Armstrong, H. (1994). *The double ghetto: Canadian women and their segregated work* (3rd ed.). Toronto, Ontario: McClelland & Stewart.

Beaujot, R. (2000). *Earning and caring in Canadian families.* Peterborough, Ontario: Broadview.

Beaujot, R., Gee, E.M., Rajulton, F., &. Ravanera, Z.R (1995). (Catalogue No. 91-643E). *Family over the life course.* Ottawa, Ontario: Statistics Canada.

Gunderson, M. (1998). *Women and the Canadian labour market.* Scarborough, Ontario: International Thompson Publishing for Statistics Canada.

Moen, P. (2000). The gendered life course. In R.H. Binstock & L.K. George (Eds.), *Handbook of Aging and the Social Sciences* (5th ed.) (pp. 179-196). San Diego, CA: Academic Press.

ENDNOTES

1. Exceptions are the Canadian General Social Surveys of 1990 and 1995, both dealing with Canadian families.

2. Data on children ever born are collected by the Canadian Census in years ending in "1" only. Data from the 2001 Census are not available at this time.

The Cultural Context of Aging

Learning Objectives

In this chapter, you will learn about:

- The importance of ethnicity and race in understanding aging.
- The ethnic origins of older Canadians.
- The immigration status of older Canadians.
- The visible minority status of older Canadians.
- Theorizing about ethnicity and aging.
- Health, wealth, and support of older ethnic minorities.
- Policy and practice with aging minorities.

Introduction

Virtually all countries in the world are ethnically diverse in that their populations are made up of groups of people with different ethnic ancestries. Canada is unique in this regard with complex patterns of ethnic and linguistic diversity represented in various regions of the country. Indeed, in Canada, the census lists 113 ethnicities in the population (Statistics Canada, 1993). Ranking next to the United Kingdom, Singapore, and the United States, Canada is one of the most ethnically and racially diverse countries in the world (Pendakur & Henneby, 1998). In a multicultural society like Canada, the aged population clearly is not a homogeneous group. In 1996, 27 percent of the population 65 years of age (Statistics Canada, 1999) were members of ethnic groups. To be an older member of an ethnic group, especially an older ethnic minority, is to experience environments substantially different from mainstream Canada.

Ethnogerontology is a new field in social gerontology that studies the influence of race, ethnicity, national origin, and culture on individual and population aging. Originally, ethnogerontology arose from a concern about the disadvantages experienced by ethnic minorities in the United States (Hooyman & Kiyak, 1999). The limited but growing research in ethnogerontology has shown that ethnicity and race have a profound influence on the aging experience, whether it be as a consequence of expectations for aging and preferred lifestyles, intergenerational differences, living arrangements, family supports, the use of ethnospecific health and social services, the problems of racism and discrimination, or any combination of these factors (Blakemore & Boneham, 1994; Hooyman & Kiyak, 1999). As an illustration, some Inuit do not subscribe to the view of healthy and active aging as the formula for successful aging that is promoted by Canadian culture. Rather, Inuit value the transmission of accumulated wisdom and knowledge to the young, an alternative view with implications for how Inuit will live their life and how they will relate to younger generations (Collings, 2001).

In this chapter, we review how ethnicity and race influence the aging process, the ethnic makeup of Canada past and present, we theorize about ethnicity, and we explore the current circumstances of older Canadians with diverse ethnic backgrounds.

Ethnic Membership and Aging

Defining Ethnicity and Race

Ethnicity.

As would be anticipated, there are many ways of conceptualizing **ethnicity** and **race**. Some of the more common themes that appear in definitions of ethnicity include: ancestral origin, a homeland or land of origin, a shared history of one's people and a shared identity, a language, sometimes a religion and, sometimes, a culture or subculture (Driedger & Chappell, 1987; Ujimoto, 1995; Vallee, 1998; Isajiw, 1999). An ethnic group may be said to exist if group membership is defined by means of a characteristic normally "inherited" from one's parents, if the group has a distinct social structure, and if the shared ethnicity is recognized by individuals (ethnic identity) and by others (De Vries, 1995). It is important to remember that culture is only part of ethnicity and that culture and ethnicity should not be used interchangeably (Li, 1990). People of the same ethnicity do not necessarily share a common culture, the English, the Irish, and the Scottish being an illustration.

Ethnicity is one of the main factors that stratifies or contributes to the ranking of the social structure in a multicultural society like Canada. Within the social hierarchy, ethnic groups are perceived to have relatively different statuses, depending upon whether they belong to a majority ethnic group, such as the British groups in Canada (e.g., English, Scottish, Irish, and Welsh), or a minority group that comprises all other ethnic groups (Isajiw, 1999). Majority ethnic groups, because of their advantage of size, usually determine the nature of the societal institutions, and their culture becomes the overarching culture of the society within which minority groups coexist. The dominance of the majority group over the minority groups contributes to inequalities in a number of areas, especially when the minority groups are perceived to be a threat to the majority group's higher ranking in the social structure and, hence, resources.

In the Canadian case, it is important to remember that Canada's French–English dualism has led to parallel institutions divided along linguistic lines so that Quebec is an exception to this observation. Although the French are a minority within the larger Canadian society, they are a charter group that has had a major impact in shaping the Canadian national character. In contrast, the position of the First Nations peoples of Canada is quite different. Canada is also a "new world country," where the First Nations peoples have become a minority in the face of successive waves of immigrants who have subsequently been incorporated into the larger society (Laczko, 1997:112).

Within this complex plural structure is a larger web of interlocking hierarchies that allocate the resources of society according to power–dominance criteria not only associated with ethnicity, but also with age, gender, and class (Calasanti, 1996). In essence, these statuses and their intersection influence a person's life chances, in terms of education, labour force participation, living arrangements, health status, and, ultimately, the quality of life in old age (McPherson, 1995). To illustrate the effect of the combined forces of being a woman, an immigrant, and belonging to a visible minority, visible minority immigrant women in Canada experience a 7 percent wage penalty, compared to their nonvisible-minority counterparts (Pendakur & Pendakur, 1996).

Although some scholars see ethnic membership in a group to be largely involuntary by virtue of recruitment at birth and socialization by parents and the community, others see ethnic identity to be partly a matter of subjective choice (Blakemore & Boneham, 1994; Anderson, 1991; Isajiw, 1999). Both conceptions have important implications for aged ethnic group members. In the former case, changing ethnic identity can be a demanding psychological and social experience, as when moving to a different country. In the latter case, the self-identification with a specific ethnic group may act as a resource, providing a behavioural script and material resources to deal with new experiences, such as aging (Berry & Kalin, 1990). It is likely that both processes coexist, although more empirical support for these observations is required.

What is relevant is the implication that ethnic identity can wax and wane over the life course. One of the more important gerontological questions is whether ethnic identity is lost, retained, or strengthened in old age. Ethnicity may or may not encompass minority status, since many Canadians (mainly ethnic groups of European origin) belong to Caucasian ethnic groups, who, although may preserve their ethnic way of life and at earlier times were considered to be minorities (e.g., Italians), are generally considered to be part of the dominant group.

A number of scholars have warned that definitions of ethnicity warrant some caution in their usage. As is the case with aging in general, the variations within ethnic groups are often overlooked to the detriment of the aging individual (Dietz, John, & Roy, 1998; Whitfield & Baker-Thomas, 1999). As an example, in Canada, there are 11 First Nations language groups made up of more than 65 distinct languages and dialects represented among First Nations seniors (Health Canada, 1998a). Analysis of the *First Nations Peoples Survey* (1991) indicates that 55 percent of First Nations peoples over 65 and 44 percent of those over 55 claim a First Nations language as their mother tongue—factors that have to be recognized in communicating with First Nations seniors (Health Canada, 1998:4).

While earlier studies often compared ethnic groups without paying heed to what generations were being compared (Burr & Mutchler, 1993; Kamo & Zhou, 1994), today, researchers are more careful (Kobayashi, 2000; Hsu, Lew-Ting, & Wu, 2001). A generational approach to studying older ethnic group members takes into account the importance of socioeconomic and political conditions encountered by each generation and, therefore, the different experiences of each generation and the nuances of the intergenerational relationships. The effect of the Holocaust, such as post-traumatic stress disorders suffered by many older Jewish Canadian survivors, has affected their relationships with the second generation. For instance, one study indicated that the role of a second-generation caregiver may be exaggerated by the transgenerational influence of the Holocaust (Safford, 1995).

Race.

Race and ethnicity are not synonymous. Race refers to physical appearance or, more specifically, the appearance of physical differences. Race is a category devised by others that places persons with similar biological traits into a group.

Essentially, race is a constructed social phenomenon (Isajiw, 1999). These traits, in themselves, are not necessarily an identity-generating force because people tend to identify with their racial characteristics only as a response to being categorized and excluded by others in dominant positions. As a case in point, a participant in a study of Japanese Canadian families stated, "I don't think of myself as Japanese. I'm a Canadian. The only reason I have to qualify my Canadian identity is because I look Japanese." (Kobayashi, 2000:193). What is more, race is a socially constructed category, whose label can have real consequences for any Canadian. Despite the fact that Black workers have education comparable with non-Blacks, they suffer higher levels of unemployment than the Canadian population as a whole (Torczyner, 1997). This socially constructed category has a consequence that undoubtedly will stretch over a lifetime and be felt in old age. The concept of race also overlooks the ethnic diversity found in racial groups, such as the differences between African Canadians and those from the Caribbean (Foster, 1996). Without dwelling on the finer distinctions, race and ethnicity are different concepts that are not interchangeable, but both are important to the study of the aging process.

The Influence of Race and Ethnicity.

The study of older persons within their own ethnic group and in relation to other ethnic groups is important for a variety of reasons. First, different societies respond to the challenges of aging in different ways, and by understanding these processes, we can better understand what is culturally determined and what is age determined, and ultimately, the effect of ethnicity on age changes. Today, researchers are no closer to answers as to whether or not aging "levels" ethnic or racial differences (Rosenthal, 1983, 1986). The age-as-leveller concept posits that ethnic minorities seem to do as well in the later years of their lives because aging challenges social, psychological, and physical abilities in unique ways that cut across ethnic boundaries (Williams & Wilson, 2001). One of the main research controversies in the United States centres on the "crossover effect" that African American mortality rates exceed those of Caucasian Americans until, at some age later in life, deaths among African Americans "cross over" and then decline relative to Caucasian Americans. The reasons behind this crossover effect are attributed to selective survival and adaptation factors that cause those who survive to be more "hardy" (Markides, et al., 1990). It is unclear, however, if the effect is a result of errors in collecting the date of birth of African Americans, or is a result of using cross-sectional surveys to study age effects (Williams & Wilson, 2001:168-169).

Second, by identifying culturally conditioned values in an older person's heritage, we can better understand their response to the aging process, since ethnicity can act as a filter, influencing beliefs, behaviours, and interactions with society. In a study of 362 younger and older Arab and Jewish people in Israel, ethnic background had a significant impact on the sources of the meaning of life, such as family, communal activity, and interpersonal relationships (Bar-Tur, Savaya,

& Prager, 2001). Aging in an unfamiliar ethnic environment can cause distress for older persons; ethnicity may act as an integrating force to buffer the stresses sometimes associated with aging (Strain & Chappell, 1984; Jacob, 1994). One study of elderly East Indian immigrants in Calgary found that when traditional living patterns were reversed within immigrant families from India, the reported quality of life of the parents was poor. In traditional India, the norm for adult children is to live with their older parents, an arrangement that confers respect on the older adults. When this position is reversed, which is often the case with immigration, the parents feel a loss of status (Murzello, 1991). In contrast, in a longitudinal study of Korean immigrants to Canada, increases in social support from Korean family members and friends lowered depression scores but support from the broader nonethnic community had no effect on psychological distress (Noh & Avison, 1996).

Finally, incorporating the study of ethnicity into gerontology at the theory, research, and practice levels is necessary for understanding the aging of all old people. As the American gerontologist Calasanti has argued, using the knowledge gained from the standpoint of racial/ethnic groups exposes the racial/ethnic dynamics that shape aging experiences, including previously invisible aspects of the privileged group's experiences. Oppression is relational, "Oppression only exists to the extent privilege does, and vice versa" (Calasanti, 1996: 149). Framing the aging process to include both sides of unequal power relationships provides a more inclusive and complete picture of the aging process. There has been, however, little research done on the discrimination of elderly minorities in Canada or any minorities in Canada and most of the research in the United States pertains to African Americans and Hispanic Americans.

We do know that there are approximately 60,000 hate crimes committed annually in nine major urban centres. It is calculated that 61 percent of hate crimes are directed against racial minorities, 23 percent against religious minorities, 11 percent for reasons of sexual orientation, and 5 percent against ethnic minorities (Heritage Canada, 1998). It is difficult to imagine how a satisfactory old age is possible in a society where all Canadians do not have a right to dignity and respectful treatment, regardless of ethnic, racial, sexual, and religious differences.

Canada's Diverse Older Population

Ethnic Origin

Settlement and immigration have been the main constitutive factors in the history of Canadian society. First Nations peoples were the original settlers in the North, followed by the English and the French, the two charter groups that formed the basis for all future interethnic relations in Canada (Laczko, 1997; Isawij, 1999). As Figure 5.1 shows, immigration over the century has fluctuated, with the largest waves of immigrants arriving in the 1910s, 1950s and 1990s (Boyd & Vickers, 2000). The composition of immigrant groups has been influenced by a host of shifting conditions: Canada's membership in the Commonwealth; alterations in immigration policies; the ups and downs of economic cycles in Canada and around the world; the displacement of peoples by wars and political strife; and economic globalization. For example, one of the largest waves of immigration was a result of labour market demands and immigration policy. From 1900 to 1915 Canada's economy grew so rapidly that the government instituted aggressive recruitment campaigns to boost immigration and attract more workers. Lured by the attraction of good jobs, the immigrant population grew from 13 percent to 22 percent between 1900 and 1911.

In the early 1800s, over 15,000 Chinese came from China as contract labourers to work on the Canadian Pacific Railway (CPR). Thousands of Jews fleeing Russia started to arrive at the same time, followed by Hungarians who settled in Saskatchewan and Ukrainians who went to Manitoba. In 1899, the Doukhobors began arriving from Russia and settled in Saskatchewan and later in British

Figure 5.1 IMMIGRATION TO CANADA, 1860–2000

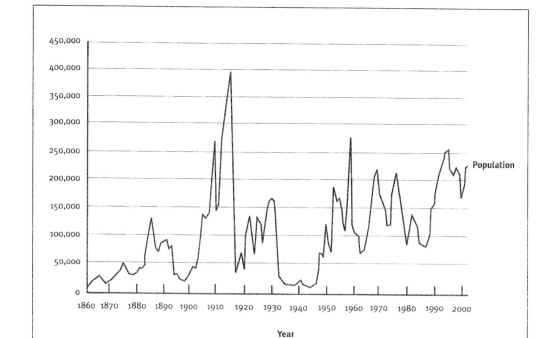

Source: Adapted from Citizenship and Immigration Canada, "*Facts and Figures, 2000: Immigration Overview.*" Reproduced with the permission of the Minister of Public Works and Government Services Canada, 2002.

Columbia. At the beginning of the 20th century, Indians, mostly Sikhs, came to British Columbia, as did over 8,000 Japanese and Italians who came to work on the CPR. As late as the 1950s, 80 to 90 percent of immigrants came from the United States and from European countries. This pattern began to change in the 1960s when immigrants from Asia and other regions outside Europe began to arrive in greater numbers. By 1994, Europe accounted for only 17 percent of immigrants, while immigrants from Asia rose to 57 percent (Pendakur & Henneby, 1998).

According to the Canadian Census, **ethnic origin** refers to the ethnic or cultural group(s) to which the respondent's ancestors belonged. About 56 percent of the total Canadian population reported ethnic origins of British, French, or Canadian (mainly English or French Canadians) in 1996 (Statistics Canada, 1998a). Of the total Canadian population who report an ethnic origin other than British, French, or Canadian, German is the most frequently reported ethnic origin, followed by Italian, First Nations peoples, Ukrainian, Chinese, and Dutch (see Table 5.1.)

First Nations peoples made up about 3 percent of the total Canadian population in 1996. The ethnic mix, however, varies by province because of the many different historical circumstances noted above. In Quebec, for example, Italian is the most frequently reported ethnic origin, followed by First Nations origin, once the British and French charter groups are taken into account. In the Territories, First Nations origin is the most frequently reported non-British or non-French ethnic origin.

When we turn to the older age groups in Table 5.1, in 1996, there were 3,265,632 Canadians who were aged 65 years and over who represented 11.45 percent of the total population of over 28 million. British, French, and Canadian origins still dominate the 65 years and over age category. Of the people 65 years or older, 41 percent identify British ancestry, 14.12 percent French, and 14 percent Canadian roots. Older Canadians of single or multiple German backgrounds constitute the largest reported ethnic identity group after the British, French, or Canadian groups. The next most frequently mentioned ethnic origins are Italian, other European (Scandinavian, Eastern European), Ukrainian, and Chinese. With few exceptions, the ethnic mix of Canada's older people reflects the aging of the longer established immigrant populations that arrived in Canada at earlier times.

It is, therefore, the case that some groups will have higher proportions of older persons within their ranks than the "young" ethnic groups. Comparing the two charter groups, it is evident that while 11.45 percent of the Canadian population are 65 years of age or over, the proportions of British (12.04 percent) and French (12 percent) are only slightly higher. Among the other 12 main ethnic origins reported, the European groups are the oldest groups: other Europeans (25.66 percent), Ukrainians (28.96 percent), Germans (21.04 percent), Hungarians (23.9 percent), and the Jewish (21.94 percent) have high proportions of elders that surpass the overall Canadian figure of 11.45 percent. In contrast, First Nations society is a young society, where First Nations seniors only account for 3.5 percent of the total First Nations population (Figure 5.2).

Table 5.1 ETHNIC ORIGINS BY AGE CATEGORY, CENSUS CANADA, 1996

Ethnic Origins*	PERCENT OF AGE GROUP		PERECNT OF TOTAL	
	0–64	65+	0–64	65+
	%	%	%	%
British	39.10	41.41	87.96	12.04
French	13.38	14.12	88.00	12.00
Canadian	19.24	14.60	91.07	8.93
German	2.26	4.66	78.96	21.04
Italian	2.43	3.33	84.92	15.08
Other European	1.16	3.10	74.34	25.66
Ukrainian	0.92	2.91	71.04	28.96
Chinese	2.89	2.24	90.89	9.11
Polish	0.84	1.51	81.10	18.90
Dutch	1.01	1.46	84.22	15.78
Jewish	0.60	1.31	78.06	21.94
South Asian	2.14	1.00	94.32	5.68
Hungarian	0.28	0.68	76.09	23.91
Other West European	0.25	0.63	75.08	24.92
Balkan	0.57	0.59	88.14	11.86
Portuguese	0.89	0.59	92.13	7.87
First Nations	1.84	0.57	96.14	3.86
Caribbean	1.16	0.49	94.82	5.18
Greek	0.51	0.42	90.50	9.50
Filipino	0.75	0.38	93.84	6.16
Other East/South-East Asian	0.58	0.38	92.17	7.83
West Asian	0.39	0.20	93.66	6.34
Vietnamese	0.41	0.17	95.05	4.95
Lebanese	0.31	0.16	93.75	6.25
Other Arab	0.35	0.15	94.71	5.29
Spanish	0.27	0.12	94.66	5.34
Latin/Central/South American	0.46	0.11	97.08	2.92
African	0.51	0.08	97.96	2.04
Asian	0.06	0.03	94.65	5.35
African/Caribbean	0.03	0.02	92.15	7.85
Other	0.34	0.26	91.03	8.97
Multiple Other	4.07	2.31	93.16	6.84
	100%	100%	88.55%	11.45%
TOTAL N	25,260,948	3,265,632	25,260,948	3,265,632

*Single ethnic origins based on selected single responses (those who provided one ethnic origin only) and multiple responses (those who reported more than one ethnic origin) created by Statistics Canada (1996). The top 14 ethnic groups are presented in order for the 65 years and over group.

Source: Adapted from Statistics Canada, "Individual File (public use microdata files): 1996 Census of Population," Catalogue no. 95M0013, April 1999.

Figure 5.2 IDENTITY OF FIRST NATIONS PEOPLES 65 YEARS AND OVER, 1996

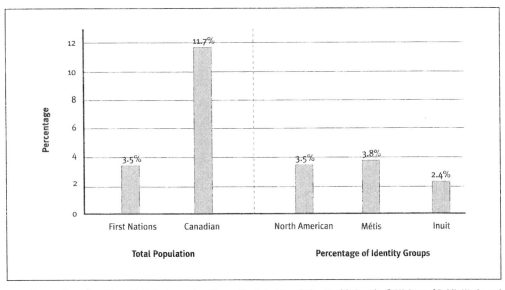

Source: Reproduced from *Statistical snapshop No. 15: Aboriginal Population*, Health Canada. © Minister of Public Works and Government Services Canada, 2002. http://hc-sc.gc.ca/seniors aines/pubs/factoids/en/no15.htm

Because Statistics Canada changed the format of the 1996 ethnic-origin question, it is almost impossible to compare the results from the 1981, 1991, and 1996 censuses. However, several significant shifts in the composition of the Canadian population can be noted at a broad level. While the French seem to maintain their ethnic identity, there has been a slow but gradual decline in the proportion of the British in the total population, currently down to about 28 percent from a high of 57 percent in 1901. As well, in the last 40 years, there has been a dramatic increase in the Asian category. The proportion of Asians, although small in comparison to other categories, more than doubled from 1951 to 1971 and increased seven-fold between 1971 and 1991, to 9.2 percent of the total population (Isawij, 1999:56). The Caribbean groups also increased substantially in 1968 through 1976. In sum, from the 1960s onward, there has been a reversal of the proportion of Caucasian to non-Caucasian immigrants, particularly Asians, who constituted the largest groups of immigrants arriving annually in Canada in the 1990s. Obviously, it will take some time for population shifts to wend their way through the system to change the composition of the older Canadian population. What is significant is that the shifts indicate an increasingly greater role of the non-British and Non-French ethnic groups among the elderly individuals of Canada.

Recognizing the changing ethnic landscape of Canada and the fact that Canada's older population is somewhat diverse at the moment, it is not as diverse as are the younger cohorts. While 36 percent of those 65 to 74 years of age report at least one ethnic origin other than British, French, Canadian, or First Nations, 44 percent of Canadians aged 19 to 24 years report different origins (Mata & Valentine, 1999). At the end of the 21st century the older population will look very different from the current population. We now turn to an examination of this diversity among older Canadians.

First Nations Peoples

Of the total First Nations population in Canada, 3.5 percent is 65 years of age or over, while 3.5 of the North American Indian population and 3.8 percent of the Métis population is 65 years of age or over, compared with 11.7 percent for the total Canadian population. Only 2.4 percent of the total Inuit population is age 65 years or older (see Figure 5.2). Even though the Royal Commission on First Nations Peoples estimates that the percentage of First Nations seniors is expected to grow between 1996 and 2016 to 7 percent of the First Nations population (74,000), it still is well below the 11.7 percent for all seniors (Health Canada, 1998a). The projected growth in the number of seniors varies by First Nations group and by place of residence. Future growth is projected to occur among registered Indians and Métis people living in urban areas. In 1995, the life expectancy of First Nations women was 76 years, compared with 80 for non-First Nations women and 68 years for men, compared with 75 for non-First Nations men (Health Canada, 1998a).

Older First Nations peoples are a significant link with First Nations culture. Seniors are the most likely First Nations people to know and use a First Nations language: almost twice as many senior First Nations people (54 percent) speak a First Nations language, compared with their younger counterparts (Statistics Canada, 1999). About 95 percent of Inuit between 55 and 64 years, and all Inuit over age 65 years, reported using a First Nations mother tongue at home. The highest concentration of First Nations people is in the North (where they originally settled) and in the prairies with approximately 67 percent of older Registered North American Indians living on a reserve (Statistics Canada, 1999).

An examination of Table 5.2 shows that First Nations people over age 65 are more likely to be widowed, two times as likely to reside with older children over 14 years of age and to live in larger households than are non-First Nations persons. Their education level is lower than non-First Nations seniors, they tend to be in managerial positions, but they also are more likely to be found in unskilled labour. They are less likely than the rest of Canadians to be employed.

Immigrants to Canada

Immigrants or foreign-born first-generation older people are usually persons who are, or have been, landed immigrants in Canada. A **landed immigrant** is a person

Table 5.2 SELF-REPORTED FIRST NATIONS STATUS BY SELECTED VARIABLES
FOR THOSE AGED 65+ YEARS, CENSUS CANADA, 1996

Characteristics	TOTAL		MEN		WOMEN	
	First Nations	Non-First Nations	First Nations	Non-First Nations	First Nations	Non-First Nations
	%	%	%	%	%	%
Current Marital Status						
Married	41.3	57.6	51.0	75.8	32.9	43.9
Separated or divorced	12.6	6.4	13.4	6.8	12.0	6.1
Widowed	36.7	29.9	21.7	11.6	49.5	43.8
Never married	9.5	6.1	14.0	5.8	5.6	6.3
Number of Children at Home						
None	53.3	82.2	56.1	84.1	50.2	79.8
<14 years old	4.3	0.3	5.6	0.5	3.0	0.1
>14 years old	42.4	17.5	38.3	15.4	46.8	20.1
Household Size						
Mean	2.71	2.07	2.76	2.22	2.67	1.95
Std. deviation	1.74	1.12	1.72	1.05	1.75	1.15
Educational Level						
High school or less	95.5	84.9	93.7	81.9	97.1	87.2
Postsecondary	4.5	15.1	6.3	18.1	2.9	12.8
Occupational Category						
Professional/managerial	35.7	29.0	31.4	32.7	42.4	21.9
Skilled worker	38.1	49.7	33.3	45.1	45.5	58.5
Unskilled worker	26.2	21.3	35.3	22.2	12.1	19.6
Below the line	31.4	19.2	28.2	13.2	34.2	23.9
Labour Force Activity						
Employed	7.4	7.7	10.0	12.1	5.1	4.3
Unemployed	0.7	0.4	0.9	0.5	0.5	0.3
Not in the labour force	92.0	91.9	89.1	87.3	94.4	95.4

Source: Adapted from Statistics Canada, "Individual File (public use microdata files): 1996 Census of Population," Catalogue No. 95M0013, April 1999.

born in another country granted the right to live in Canada permanently by immigration authorities. A relatively large proportion of older people in Canada are immigrants; 27 percent of the population aged 65 years and over in 1996 were immigrants, compared with only 17 percent of the total population in the same year. It is important to remember that the majority of older immigrants currently living in Canada have been here for a very long time. In fact, 61 percent arrived before 1961; 24 percent came in the 1960s and 1970s, while about 15 percent arrived between 1981 and 1996 (Health Canada, 1998). The current older population "aged in place" in Canada. Today, older people immigrate to Canada in smaller numbers. In 1997, about 3 percent of people (less than 6,000) who immigrated to Canada were 65 years of age or older.

Of the immigrants arriving in 1997, 90 percent were **family-class immigrants**, 6 percent were **refugees**, and four percent were **economic-class immigrants** (Health Canada, 1998a). The Family Class category in the *Immigration Act* stipulates that Canadian citizens and permanent residents have the right to sponsor the application of close relatives (spouses, dependent children, grandparents, brothers, and sisters). Family-class applicants are not assessed under the point system but are assessed for good health and character. Most importantly, the sponsor has to commit to support and house the applicant for up to 10 years, sometimes a problem for some families (McDonald, et al., 2001). Refugees are defined by the 1951 United Nations Convention on Refugees as people who may fear prosecution for reasons of race, religion, nationality, or political ideology and are outside the countries of their nationalities and who are unwilling to seek protection from those countries. Economic class immigrants come to Canada for the purposes of business.

It is not always clear why older people immigrate to Canada. In a nonrandom study of newcomer older immigrants (65+ years) who did not yet have landed immigrant status, the newcomers were asked why they came to Canada and if they had much choice in the matter. Those who answered that they had a choice (80 percent) indicated that they wanted to live with their children already settled here; they knew there were better health and social services for old people in Canada and they liked the democratic political environment. Those who did not want to come to Canada to settle came because their children wanted them to help family or they had no choice because they were married or lived alone in their home country (McDonald, et al., 2001). A refugee will have different care needs from those of an older person who comes into Canada as a family-class immigrant.

When we look at Table 5.3, we can see that Europeans represent almost half of all foreign-born seniors (49 percent of age group), with Eastern Europeans holding a large share. Immigrants from the United Kingdom are the next largest group. These settlers came to Canada in the wake of World War I and World War II but prior to the 1970s. The proportion of seniors among immigrant groups is fairly evenly distributed among the British and European seniors. A little less than one-third of foreign-born people from the United Kingdom are elderly, compared with about 31 percent of Eastern Europeans. On the other hand, of the people who came from central Asia, 6.03 percent are age 65 years or older. Today, Canada's newest residents tend to be Asian born. Almost 6 in 10 immigrants who arrived between 1991 and 1996 were from Asia (Chard & Renaud, 1999). Of the

Table 5.3 ELDERLY AND NONELDERLY IMMIGRANTS BY PLACE OF BIRTH

Place of Birth	PERCENT OF AGE GROUP		PERCENT OF TOTAL	
	0–64	65+	0–64	65+
	%	%	%	%
United Kingdom	11.07	22.41	69.88	30.12
Northern/Western Europe	5.35	9.46	72.63	27.37
Eastern Europe	6.92	14.93	68.52	31.48
Southern Europe	9.06	11.80	78.28	21.72
Other Europe	8.21	12.90	74.92	25.08
United States	4.90	6.18	78.84	21.16
Central/South America/Caribbean/Bermuda	12.91	4.22	93.49	6.51
Africa	5.30	1.89	92.95	7.05
West/Central Asia & Middle East	4.87	1.47	93.97	6.03
China/Hong Kong	10.10	7.06	87.03	12.97
East/Southeast Asia	12.48	3.88	93.79	6.21
Southern Asia	7.82	3.41	91.51	8.49
Other	1.01	0.39	92.39	7.61
Total	100.00	100.00	82.44	17.56
TotalN	4,184,676	891,252	4,184,676	891,252

Source: Adapted from Statistics Canada, "Individual File (public use microdata files): 1996 Census of Population," Catalogue No. 95M0013, April 1999.

6,000 older immigrants to Canada in 1998, close to 43 percent were from Asia (McDonald, et al., 2001).

When we consider the demographic characteristics of immigrants aged 65 years and over, compared with nonimmigrants of the same age, Table 5.4 indicates that both male and female immigrants immigrated when they were younger than age 45 years. Both men and women are more likely to be married, they are likely to have more children living at home, and they are likely to live in larger households. Their levels of education are slightly higher than the Canadian born, and they are more likely to be in professional/managerial professions than are Canadian-born seniors.

Table 5.4 IMMIGRATION STATUS BY SELECTED VARIABLES FOR THOSE AGED 65 YEARS, CENSUS CANADA, 1996

Characteristics	TOTAL		MEN		WOMEN	
	Immigrants	Non-Immigrants	Immigrants	Non-Immigrants	Immigrants	Non-Immigrants
	%	%	%	%	%	%
Current Marital Status						
Married	60.3	56.4	78.8	74.2	45.3	43.3
Separated or Divorced	6.2	6.5	6.1	7.2	6.2	6.1
Widowed	29.7	30.1	11.4	11.9	44.6	43.5
Never married	3.8	7.0	3.7	6.7	3.9	7.1
Number of Children at Home						
None	78.0	83.5	79.0	86.0	76.7	80.6
<14 years old	0.5	0.2	0.8	0.4	0.2	0.1
>14 years old	21.5	16.2	20.3	13.6	23.1	19.3
Household Size						
Mean	2.44	1.93	2.54	2.09	2.36	1.81
Std. deviation	1.48	0.91	1.40	0.85	1.54	0.94
Educational Level						
High school or less	80.9	86.6	74.8	84.9	85.8	87.8
Postsecondary	19.1	13.4	25.2	15.1	14.2	12.2
Occupational Category						
Professional/managerial	32.2	27.8	37.0	31.0	22.7	21.9
Skilled worker	45.5	51.2	39.8	47.1	56.9	59.0
Unskilled worker	22.2	21.0	23.1	21.9	20.4	19.2
Labour Force Activity						
Employed	7.9	7.6	12.0	12.2	4.5	4.2
Unemployed	0.4	0.4	0.5	0.5	0.3	0.3
Not in labour force	91.7	92.0	87.4	87.3	95.2	95.5

Source: Adapted from Statistics Canada, "Individual File (public use microdata files): 1996 Census of Population," Catalogue No. 95M0013, April 1999.

Visible Minorities.

Visible minority is defined by the *Employment Equity Act* as "persons, other than First Nations peoples, who are non-Caucasian in race or non-white in colour." (Boyd & Vickers, 2000:3). Only a relatively small portion of Canadians 65 years of age and over are members of a visible minority group. According to the 1996 Census, 6 percent of the total population 65 years of age and older (or 200,000 seniors) were part of a visible minority group. In comparison, 9 percent of those aged 45 to 64 years, 12 percent of those aged 25 to 44 years and 14 percent of those aged 15 to 24 years were members of a visible minority group in the same year (Health Canada, 1998b).

As seen in Table 5.5, of all the visible minorities over age 65 years, about 40 percent are Chinese, 19 percent are South Asian, and 18 percent are Black. In

Table 5.5 SENIORS AND NON-SENIORS BY VISIBLE MINORITY STATUS, CENSUS CANADA, 1996

Visible Minority Status	PERCENT OF AGE GROUP		PERCENT OF TOTAL POPULATION	
	0–64	65+	0–64	65+
	%	%	%	%
Black	18.27	12.86	95.72	4.28
South Asian	21.08	19.33	94.49	5.51
Chinese	26.09	39.60	91.20	8.80
Other	34.56	28.20	95.07	4.93
Filipino	7.33	7.19	94.13	5.87
Arab/West Asian	7.75	6.18	95.17	4.83
Latin American	5.71	2.71	97.08	2.92
Japanese	1.99	4.32	87.90	12.10
Southeast Asian	5.52	3.50	96.13	3.87
Korean	2.05	1.63	95.21	4.79
Other	2.22	1.61	95.59	4.41
Multiple	1.98	1.08	96.66	3.34
Total	100.00	100.00	94.02	5.98
Total N	3,006,405	191,070	3,006,405	191,070

Source: Adapted from Statistics Canada, "Individual File (public use microdata files): 1996 Census of Population," Catalogue No. 95M0013, April 1999.

the "Other" category, which accounts for 28 percent of visible minorities, 7 percent are Filipino, 6 percent are Arab or West Asian, and 4 percent are Japanese. Smaller still are Southeast Asian (3.5 percent), Latin American (2.71 percent), and Korean (1.63 percent). The visible minorities are mainly "young" groups, with smaller proportions of older people than in the case of the total Canadian population, with the exception of Japanese. In 1996, 12 percent of all those in the Japanese minority population were over the age of 65—the same figure for the Canadian population. As Table 5.5 indicates, only about 9 percent of the Chinese are age 65 years or more, a smaller share than that for the total population, although it has the second largest share for older visible minorities over age 65.

The visible minorities have a slightly different profile than non-visible minorities as indicated in Table 5.6. Overall, the women are more likely to be widowed; they are twice as likely as non-visible minorities to have young adults in the home; and their household size is almost twice the size of that of non-visible minorities. Although they have a small advantage educationally, they are less likely to hold professional or managerial jobs than the non-visible minorities, although there is no difference in employment levels.

The majority of visible minorities live in cities, which also applies to the aged members of visible minorities. Seven out of every 10 visible minority persons in Canada lived in just three major metropolitan areas: Toronto (42 percent), Vancouver (19 percent), and Montreal (13 percent) (Statistics Canada, 1998b).

To summarize this section, Canada's population over age 65 is diverse but not as diverse as the upcoming younger cohorts, who will eventually age and change the ethnic composition of Canada's older people. In light of current immigration patterns, we can expect to see further declines in the numbers of those of British ancestry, an increase in the number of First Nations seniors in urban areas, and an increase in the numbers of visible minority elderly in urban areas as well. According to Statistics Canada's projections, the number of Canadians in visible minority categories is expected to increase to 7.1 million by 2026 from 2.7 million in 1991 (Kelly, 1995). As a proportion of the overall population, visible minorities will constitute 20 percent of the population in 2016. The Chinese will continue to be the largest visible minority group and are projected to reach 2 million in 2016. The proportion of Canadians who are of Chinese ancestry is estimated to grow to 5 percent in 2016. Blacks are expected to become the second largest visible minority group (1.3 million), followed by South Asians as the third largest visible minority group (1.2 million), a switch from what we saw in Table 5.1. West Asians and Arabs will remain the fourth largest group (1 million) but are expected to increase at the fastest rate (Kelly, 1995). The vast majority of visible minority adults live in urban areas so that they will be aging in a city as opposed to a rural environment. Although the impact of the projected demographic changes

Table 5.6 VISIBLE MINORITY STATUS BY SELECTED VARIABLES FOR THOSE AGED 65+ YEARS, CENSUS CANADA, 1996

Characteristics	TOTAL		MEN		WOMEN	
	Visible Minority	Non-Visible Minority	Visible Minority	Non-Visible Minority	Visible Minority	Non-Visible Minority
	%	%	%	%	%	%
Current Marital Status						
Married	56.4	57.7	80.0	75.5	38.4	44.2
Separated or divorced	5.8	6.4	5.7	6.9	5.8	6.1
Widowed	33.0	29.7	11.2	11.7	49.5	43.4
Never married	4.9	6.1	3.1	6.0	6.3	6.3
Number of Children at Home						
None	59.4	83.6	61.7	85.6	56.5	81.2
<14 years old	1.3	0.2	1.8	0.4	0.8	0.1
>14 years old	39.2	16.2	36.5	14.1	42.7	18.7
Household Size						
Mean	3.74	1.96	3.76	2.12	3.72	1.84
Std. deviation	1.96	0.95	1.94	0.88	1.97	0.98
Educational Level						
High school or less	83.7	85.0	75.6	82.3	89.8	87.1
Postsecondary	16.3	15.0	24.4	17.7	10.2	12.9
Occupational Category						
Professional/managerial	25.7	29.2	31.0	32.8	16.7	22.3
Skilled worker	41.6	50.3	33.3	45.9	55.7	58.7
Unskilled worker	32.7	20.5	35.7	21.3	27.6	19.0
Labour Force Activity						
Employed	7.7	7.7	11.5	12.2	4.8	4.3
Unemployed	1.0	0.3	1.6	0.5	0.5	0.2
Not in the labour force	91.3	92.0	86.8	87.4	94.7	95.5

Source: Adapted from Statistics Canada, "Individual File (public use microdata files): 1996 Census of Population," Catalogue No. 95M0013, April 1999.

is uncertain, they do foretell a slightly different older, urban population that may have different needs. Whether we are prepared for these changes in Canada is highly questionable. We have little research on aging and ethnicity or, for that matter, on any minority groups and even less about new arrivals in Canada.

Theorizing about Ethnicity

Canadian gerontologists have not only conducted relatively limited research on ethnicity and aging, they have also engaged in minimal theory development. It has been suggested that elderly members of ethnic groups have been too small to warrant much attention until recently, at least in the United States (Hooyman & Kiyak, 1999). This is not to say that there is a general lack of acceptance of the importance of incorporating the factor of diversity into research on aging but, rather, that it has not been fully realized by social gerontologists (Hendricks, 1996).

In multicultural countries, such as the United Kingdom, the United States, and Australia, the focus of most of the research has been almost entirely on inequality, usually on the additive disadvantage of being old and belonging to a visible minority group (Dowd & Bengston, 1978). In Canada, the limited research activity has been directed more at ethnic groups generally (French and English) and not specifically at minority groups and the inequalities they face. One Canadian researcher has argued that research on diversity has been given short shrift because the sociological aging theories of inequality (e.g., age stratification, political economy) are not well suited to research on diversity and need to be rethought (McMullin, 2000). Whatever the cause, most theorizing has not overtaken the multiple jeopardy hypothesis, its competitor, the age levelling hypothesis, or the buffer hypothesis, which we will consider in this section.

Shared Perspectives
Assimilation and Modernization Theories.

Conventional sociological theories have been the foundation of both gerontological theory and general theories of ethnicity (see Chapter 2). One broad perspective that has been applied to the study of ethnicity and aging is modernization theory (see Chapter 2). Modernization theory links the lower status of older people to the increasing industrialization of a society as when simple societies are transformed into complex urban societies (Driedger & Chappell, 1987; Kim, et al., 2000). The theory has been used in a variety of ways, but mainly to explain differences among societies at different stages of industrialization as in the case of developing countries (Olson, 1990). It can be used to study ethnic groups on a continuum of modernization and their attendant status. Modernization theory has been critiqued as being inconsistent with reality. Less modernized families do not necessarily support their ethnic elders any more than do modern families (Rosenthal, 1983).

Cut from the same structural functionalist cloth is the **essentialist approach** to understanding ethnicity, one of the oldest in sociology and anthropology. The argument is that "ethnicity is something given, ascribed at birth, deriving from the kin-and-clan structure of human society and something more or less fixed and permanent" (Isajiw, 1999: 30). It involves a set of "ready-made" attributes and an identity that an individual shares with others from birth. Offshoots of this approach treat ethnicity as a matter of identity, including what forces help maintain it or impel it to change. When scholars investigate **assimilation** and **pluralism** of ethnic groups, the core issue is about ethnic identity (Li, 1990:5).

Assimilation theories go back to the Chicago School of sociology (e.g., Robert Park, W.I. Thomas, & F. Znaniecki) and suggest that minority groups will assimilate and lose their separate ethnic identities to a melting pot or through conformity or amalgamation with the dominant group (Driedger & Halli, 2000). Over time, the theories have been modified substantially to capture the many possible levels of assimilation or acculturation (Glazer & Moynihan, 1963; Driedger & Halli, 2000). Early studies of ethnic identity addressed how older persons managed their ethnic identity in the face of aging and how identity changed from first generation to second and third generations, particularly among Japanese Canadians (Sugiman & Nishio, 1983; Ujimoto, 1987; 1995). The data in a recent study of foreign-born Chinese who had immigrated to Vancouver and Victoria when older (average age 55 years) showed that 49.3 percent stated they felt more Canadian than Chinese; 36.9 percent felt more Chinese, and 14.1 percent felt equally Canadian and Chinese (Gee, 1999.)

Assimilation theories lost some of their lustre over the years in the face of wide variations between and within ethnic groups and in response to multiculturalism policies in Canada that promoted pluralism (Fleras & Elliot, 1992). Spurred on by the complexity of ethnicity and its many levels and manifestations, researchers developed a multitude of continuums that ran between assimilation and pluralism on a variety of levels, to include external and internal processes (Li, 1990; Driedger & Halli, 2000). Pluralism suggested that ethnic groups retain a separate identity and do not always assimilate but still manage to live amicably in the Canadian community. Pluralism today usually refers to the Canadian multicultural mosaic that, at least in theory, values diversity (Fleras & Elliot, 1992).

Although assimilation may not be the norm, it is still studied in great detail in Canada. One of the main markers of ethnic assimilation is language and the degree to which people use their language at home (De Vries, 1995). The assimilation of older ethnic Canadians was studied using 1981 census data, and it was concluded at that time that there was enormous variation among ethnic groups in the use of mother tongue and home language (Driedger & Chappell, 1987). Today, the majority of older Canadians speak at least one official language, but still, they are less likely than younger people to speak either English or French. In fact, in 1996, 4.4 percent of Canadians over age 65, did not speak either official language, compared with about 1 percent for younger age groups. In 1996, 11 percent of people 65 years and over, compared with 9 percent of younger people aged 15 to 64 years, spoke only a language other than English or French in their home (Health Canada, 1998b). The 11 percent of older Canadians speaking a nonofficial language in their home increased from the 7 percent in 1981, and is likely a reflection of changes in immigration patterns and the fact that older people maintain some aspects of their ethnic identity.

Age Stratification and Ethnic Stratification.

Other approaches that cross-cut gerontology and ethnic studies are the structural frameworks used to explain aging and ethnicity. The theories in aging (age stratification and political economy, and **ethnic stratification** in ethnic studies) operate on the assumption of inequality in the social structure—because of age in the case of aging and because of ethnicity in the case of ethnic groups. In relation to ethnicity, various ethnic groups are differentially incorporated into the larger society (aided and abetted by prejudice and discrimination) and membership in different groups confers different levels of resources, prestige, and power. The indicators of education, occupation, and income typically have been used to measure these positions. The **multiple jeopardy hypothesis** in gerontology represents the union of these two approaches (Markides, 1983; Gelfand, 1994). A combination of old age and ethnic minority status was the focus of interest in the early years of the jeopardy hypothesis. If one was old and belonged to an ethnic group, especially a visible minority group, one was doubly disadvantaged. The jeopardy studies expanded to include multiple negative statuses, adding female gender and low social class to minority status and age. The alternative hypothesis, the **age levelling hypothesis**, noted earlier, was used to refute this hypothesis and proposed that age effects cut across all racial and ethnic lines (Cool, 1981), levelling out inequalities found earlier in life.

Support for this hypothesis has been lukewarm at best (Penning, 1983, Havens & Chappell, 1983; Wong & Reker, 1985), while a number of scholars have found little evidence to support the hypothesis (Chan, 1983; Havens & Chappell, 1983; Lubben & Becerra, 1987). The promulgators of the hypothesis found in their own cross-sectional study of African, Mexican, and Caucasian people some support with regard to income and self-rated health, but little support when it came to psychological well being (Markides, Liang, & Jackson, 1990). Specifically, there was evidence that many minority elders expressed high levels of psychological well being, a finding to be repeated in a number of studies (Miner & Montoro-Rodriguez, 1999; Koybayashi, 2000). In other words, the external indicators of income, education, and occupation missed the mark; the social psychological processes of group identification and interaction were equally important.

Some have called the influence of psychosocial factors the **buffer hypothesis** (Miner & Montoro-Rodriguez, 1999). A direct test of the role of family psychological factors, compared with structural factors (acculturation, socioeconomic status), in an American study of Hispanics, found that collectivistic family values held by older Hispanics were the most important factors correlated with high levels of well being (Miner & Montoro-Rodriguez, 1999:443). Conversely, a Canadian study of foreign-born Chinese elders found that ethnic identity was not a resource to compensate for low income. Gee (1999) found evidence that

Chinese immigrants with lower incomes were less likely to identify themselves as Chinese. The author hypothesized that a Canadian identity, instead of a Chinese identity, may be more helpful to the descendents of poor older Chinese. As is likely to become a repeated refrain, more theory development is required to understand aging and ethnicity.

Although some scholars (Markides, et al., 1990) suggest that the jeopardy hypotheses have come to the end of their run, much of the recent interest (McMullin, 2000) in diversity still addresses the same issues of multiple statuses, albeit from a broader base and within ethnic groups.

Constructing Ethnicity.

A recent trend in theorizing about ethnicity and aging is a constructivist perspective. Both age and ethnicity are negotiated and constructed in everyday life. As Nagel (1994: 162) observes "...culture is not a shopping cart that comes to us already loaded with a set of historical cultural goods. Rather, we construct culture by picking and choosing items from the shelves of the past and the present." At the outset, in social gerontology, political economists argued that age was a socially constructed category emanating from policies on aging, such as state pension plans. These gerontologists were joined later by feminists who added race and ethnicity to the mix, arguing that the experiences of ethnic minorities and older women were conditioned by the intersection of their social class, gender, and ethnic statuses, and conducted research showing how these factors affected experiences (Calasanti, 1996; Estes, et al., 2001). Exploration of the various ways in which ethnic minorities construct retirement or how older ethnic minority women in Canada foster and reshape their identities would be examples of this work. Dosa's study of aging Canadian Ismaili women who immigrated to Canada shows how life stories are an "...embodiment of a homeland that can be (re)imagined only in her new country"(Dosa, 1999: 268). In Kobayashi's (2000) study of third-generation children (sansei) and second-generation parents (nisei), she found that while the majority of Japanese children believed in the longstanding values of filial piety, fewer adult children reported feelings of identification with being Japanese Canadian.

The theories addressed above provide several different lenses through which we can examine ethnicity and its effects on the social and psychological aspects of aging. Unfortunately, the net result is often fragmentary. Most of the theories do not have the capacity to capture the effects of ethnicity at the structural level and its link to the psychological and family levels. The theories are especially weak in reflecting the effects of multigenerations within ethnic groups. To apply any of the aforementioned theoretical perspectives with confidence at this time would be a risky business. The life course perspective, with its emphasis on the complex interrelationships among biographical time, social time, and historical time and its potential to link the individual and the structural, has rarely been used in the study of ethnicity and aging. The perspective has been flagged as having promise

(Rosenthal, 1987; Ferraro, 1997) but there appears to be more discussion than application. In short, there is much theoretical work to be done.

The Wealth, Health, and Family Support of Ethnic Minorities

The Economic Resources of Older Minorities

In Table 5.7, Panels A, B, and C indicate that there is variation among minorities in terms of amount and sources of income, when compared with the population 65 years and over. All indicators show that visible minorities, followed by First Nations peoples and lastly, immigrants, are more likely to be below the Low Income Cut-Offs (LICOs) of Statistics Canada. A person falls below the LICO if he or she spends a higher proportion of income on necessities than does the average Canadian. Although there is overlap between immigrant groups and ethnic minorities, they are included to show how non-visible minorities fare. When compared with the 18.5 percent poverty rate for the majority population, the amount of poverty is extensive for all minority groups. All are economically worse off than the nonminorities: 33 percent of visible minorities, 23 percent of immigrants, and 31 percent of First Nations peoples 65 years of age and over are below the LICOs. The burden of the poverty is carried by women in all instances, with 10 percent more older First Nations and visible minority women below the income cut-offs than majority women.

It is important to note that, despite older immigrants' slight advantage in levels of education and occupation, a larger proportion of older immigrants are below Statistics Canada's 1995 LICOs, with more immigrant women below the cut-off than immigrant men (almost 27 percent). This finding is consistent with earlier research that found that elderly women immigrants were more likely to have lower incomes than Canadian-born men and women (Boyd, 1991). Income security is particularly important for women since they live longer than men and must stretch their retirement benefits further.

When sources of income are considered, the profile for immigrants to Canada looks very similar, although not identical, to that of nonimmigrant elders. As an overall indicator of difference, the total government transfer payments for both groups are less than $800 apart (Panel B). There is little doubt that this difference is a reflection of the time of their immigration to Canada. Most immigrants came to Canada prior to 1961, which would make many of them eligible for a full Old Age Pension by 1995.

On the other hand, visible minorities do not appear to benefit much from either the public or private pensions systems. They receive almost $3,000 less than non-visible minorities from government sources and even less from work-related pensions. These differences have to be interpreted with considerable caution, however. There is undoubtedly a difference between Canadian-born

Table 5.7A SELF-REPORTED MINORITY STATUS BY INCOME SOURCES FOR
THOSE AGED 65+ YEARS, CENSUS CANADA, 1996

PANEL A: IMMIGRANTS

	TOTAL		MEN		WOMEN	
	Immigrants	Non-Immigrants	Immigrants	Non-Immigrants	Immigrants	Non-Immigrants
Old Age Security Pension and Guaranteed Income ($)						
Mean	5,282.97	5,848.84	4,855.95	5,371.10	5,630.77	6,202.58
Std. deviation	3,020.17	2,485.60	2,815.59	2,405.98	3,134.38	2,484.44
Canada or Quebec Pension Plan ($)						
Mean	3,421.18	3,801.09	4,412.88	4,933.12	2,613.48	2,962.89
Std. deviation	3,088.09	2,908.88	3,125.57	2,735.86	2,809.50	2,744.69
Total Government Transfer Payments ($)						
Mean	10,010.55	10,766.20	10,801.62	11,748.20	9,366.25	10,039.09
Std. deviation	4,853.45	4,219.57	5,094.85	4,374.96	4,547.00	3,946.29
Retirement Pensions, RRSPs and RRIFs ($)						
Mean	3,714.05	4,774.92	5,747.30	7,520.04	2,058.06	2,742.32
Std. deviation	8,964.35	9,887.08	11,359.29	12,542.33	5,882.82	6,629.18
Income Status Low Income Cut-Offs, 1995						
Percent above the line	77.4	81.9	82.4	88.5	73.4	77.0
Percent below the line	22.6	18.1	17.6	11.5	26.6	23.0

Source: Adapted from Statistics Canada, "Individual File (public use microdata files): 1996 Census of Population," Catalogue No. 95M0013, April 1999.

visible minorities and immigrant visible minorities, at least in terms of their facility with the official languages, the quality of their educational credentials, and the barriers they may have faced in the labour market, which could affect the size of their pensions (Human Resources Canada, 1996). There is also the possibility of the timing of their immigration. Visible minorities made up the largest proportion of older recent immigrants to Canada and would not qualify for pensions and would be dependent on their families for economic support. In interviews with 142 newcomer seniors to Canada, next to language barriers, financial difficulties (35 percent of the sample) were reported to be a major problem.

Table 5.7B SELF-REPORTED MINORITY STATUS BY INCOME SOURCES FOR
         THOSE AGED 65+ YEARS, CENSUS CANADA, 1996

PANEL B: VISIBLE MINORITIES

	TOTAL		MEN		WOMEN	
	Visible Minority	Non-Visible Minority	Visible Minority	Non-Visible Minority	Visible Minority	Non-Visible Minority
Old Age Security Pension and Guaranteed Income ($)						
Mean	4,191.87	5,771.19	3,699.18	5,301.72	4,566.10	6,127.68
Std. deviation	4,079.72	2,502.11	3,761.17	2,399.83	4,268.13	2,519.29
Canada or Quebec Pension ($)						
Mean	1,818.95	3,828.02	2,272.03	4,962.59	1,474.81	2,966.47
Std. deviation	2,784.86	2,932.41	3,065.94	2,763.50	2,496.41	2,758.59
Total Government Transfer Payments ($)						
Mean	7,675.17	10,729.73	7,814.52	11,701.82	7,569.32	9,991.57
Std. deviation	5,578.70	4,270.06	5,806.15	4,428.92	5,397.16	3,990.18
Retirement Pensions, RRSPs and RRIFs ($)						
Mean	1,493.89	4,698.63	2,314.23	7,355.52	870.79	2,681.10
Std. deviation	5,755.01	9,839.87	7,555.12	12,443.86	3,744.64	6,582.51
Income Status Low Income Cut-Offs, 1995						
Above the line	67.4	81.6	68.3	88.0	66.8	76.7
Below the line	32.6	18.4	31.7	12.0	33.2	23.3

Source: Adapted from Statistics Canada, "Individual File (public use microdata files): 1996 Census of Population," Catalogue No. 95M0013, April 1999.

    While many new senior immigrants are pleased to be in Canada, the problems
of financial dependence surface repeatedly (McDonald, et al., 2001; Leung &
McDonald, 2002). Without their own economic resources, the fact that they are
often retired with little opportunity for employment, and the fact that they are not
eligible for full Canadian pensions or reciprocal pensions from their country of origin, visible and immigrant minorities have nowhere to turn, except to family.
Many are forced to live in multigenerational households, and although they often
participate in household chores and childcare to help out, they are still totally
dependent on family for most of their needs. That only 11 percent of newcomer seniors were able to make a financial contribution to their own families is most telling

Table 5.7C SELF-REPORTED MINORITY STATUS BY INCOME SOURCES FOR
THOSE AGED 65+ CENSUS CANADA, 1996

PANEL C: FIRST NATIONS PEOPLES

	TOTAL		MEN		WOMEN	
	First Nations	Non-First Nations	First Nations	Non-First Nations	First Nations	Non-First Nations
Old Age Security Pension and Guaranteed Income ($)						
Mean	7,413.90	5,679.02	6,993.77	5,208.18	7,773.58	6,036.56
Std. deviation	3,080.97	2,646.43	3,201.91	2,527.82	2,926.08	2,678.33
Canada or Quebec Pension Benefits ($)						
Mean	2,052.11	3,710.77	2,485.96	4,805.55	1,680.70	2,879.43
Std. deviation	2,768.63	2,961.69	2,968.29	2,852.67	2,527.09	2,766.17
Total Government Transfer Payments ($)						
Mean	11,432.40	10,551.47	11,845.05	11,474.93	11,079.13	9,850.22
Std. deviation	4,302.41	4,415.69	4,579.24	4,611.79	4,017.03	4,124.88
Retirement Pensions, RRSPs and RRIFs ($)						
Mean	1,203.31	4,511.60	1,841.04	7,061.28	657.35	2,575.46
Std. deviation	5,245.28	9,678.31	7,117.51	12,269.47	2,655.85	6,465.25
Income Status 1995 Low Income Cut-Offs						
Above the line	68.6	80.8	71.8	86.8	65.8	76.1
Below the line	31.4	19.2	28.2	13.2	34.2	23.9

Source: Adapted from Statistics Canada, "Individual File (public use microdata files): 1996 Census of Population," Catalogue No. 95M0013, April 1999.

(McDonald, et al., 2001). Their lack of independence in a reduced social world where everything is foreign, including the spoken language, becomes even more challenging if illness strikes or if their adult children have their own problems.

The economic circumstances of First Nations seniors is strikingly different and represents a legacy of poor education, high unemployment, residential segregation, inadequate housing, lack of social services, malnutrition, and poor health (Driedger & Chappell, 1987; Wister & Moore, 1998). Given a lifetime of racial discrimination and inequality, it is not surprising that the mainstay of First Nations peoples' income in old age is the public pension system (see Table 5.7C). Of all minority groups, they receive the largest total government transfer payments, making them the most dependent on government. As Panel C indicates, the proportion of older First Nations women living in poverty is untenable by any standard—34.2 percent of First Nations women compared with 23.9 percent for the rest of the older population. As Frideres observed in 1994, older First Nations people suffer from double alienation because they have remained outside the mainstream institutional structures of Canada as well as remaining outside changes in their own First Nations communities (Frideres, 1994:30).

The high poverty rates experienced by aging ethnic minorities and older ethnic women, in particular, is a serious problem in danger of being ignored. Most Canadians believe that the "poverty issue" associated with elderly persons has been solved, in light of the plummeting poverty rates for the older population as a whole (see Chapter 12). If there ever was a case for treating a private problem as a public issue, this would be an important example. As the dollars directed to health and social services for older people are shrinking, those with the fewest economic resources and with the weakest claim on the Canadian pension system are at risk of the greatest harm.

Health

Population-based information on immigrants' health status, disability, and life expectancy indicates that the **healthy immigrant thesis** applies to Canada (Chen, Ng, & Wilkins, 1996). Fundamentally, immigrants of all ages are healthy on arrival in Canada, but compared with native-born Canadians, they lose this advantage over time. Immigrants who come to Canada from Europe, the United States, or Australia and who have higher levels of education, occupational status, and higher incomes, report very good or excellent health, compared with those who come from Asia, Africa, and South America (Dunn & Dyck, 1998). This research would suggest that immigrant subpopulations require closer examination and that health varies by ethnic group membership. Several researchers have found that there are culturally specific belief patterns about illness and health that influence views on illness and health care utilization (Chung, 1994; Cook, 1994). In studies of different subpopulations of older persons, there is, however, a serious lack of information about health status and health utilization of aging ethnic groups that immigrated to Canada.

Data from the National Population Health Survey (NPHS 1996-1997) shows that ethnicity is related to health status. Less than 25 percent of seniors born in Canada, the United States, Europe, Australia, and Asia reported fair or poor health, while over 33 percent of seniors born in Central and South America and Africa reported fair or poor health. Those seniors who have lived in Canada for 10 years or more reported the same level of health as native-born older Canadians. Nonetheless, 40 percent of recent immigrants perceived their health to be fair to poor, compared with those who had lived in Canada for five years or longer

(Maurier & Northcott, 2000:48). The effect of race on the health of older Canadians suggests that there is a racial disadvantage, at least for seniors living in Ontario. Mauier and Northcott (2000), using the NPHS, found that approximately 40 percent of Caucasian seniors, compared with 33 percent of non-Caucasian seniors, in Ontario reported excellent to very good health. In light of the poor economic circumstances of First Nations peoples, it is not surprising the National Council on Aging asserts that the First Nations peoples are the most unhealthy Canadians.

Several investigations indicate that the prevalence of chronic diseases among the immigrant population converge with that of the Canadian population over time (Chen, Ng, & Wilkins, 1996). In a study of Chinese elders in British Columbia, it was found that they suffered from as many chronic conditions as the older Canadian population (Chappell, Lai, & Gee, 1997; Chappell & Lai, 1998). In contrast, older persons of First Nations descent have very high rates of disability, compared with the general older population. On the basis of the *First Nations Peoples Survey*, 1991, Wister and Moore (1998) reported that in the group of those 55 years of age and older, the rate of disability was 66.5 for all First Nations peoples, compared with 37.4 percent for non-First Nations persons of the same age (see Chapter 10).

In terms of information about mental health, there are few available studies in Canada although there is a growing body of knowledge in other countries (e.g., Pang, 1998; McCracken, et al., 1997; Black, et al., 1998). A representative study of elderly Chinese living in Calgary who were recent newcomers to Canada found that the overall prevalence rate for depression was twice that of the general elderly population in Canada and was more pronounced among female elders (Lai, 2000a; 2000b). As the author argues, this is a unique and serious health problem of Chinese elders that requires culturally sensitive health services. To underscore this observation, elderly Chinese women in the United States have a suicide rate that is 10 times that for older Caucasian women (Butler, Lewis, & Sutherland, 1998). A Canadian study of suicide showed that the only age group to have higher suicide mortality rates than those born in Canada are immigrants over the age of 65 (Strachen, Johansen, Nair, et al., 1990).

How ethnicity colours perceptions of health and health service utilization is not well understood in the Canadian context. In a study of Japanese, Korean, and Chinese Canadians 65 years of age and older, Uijimoto et al. (1995) found that elderly Koreans expressed the most dissatisfaction with their health, whereas in an earlier study of the mental health of Koreans, it was found that few had problems because they somatize mental health symptoms (Kim, 1987). Anthropologist Collings (2001), in his study of successful aging among Inuit, discovered that there was no such thing as good health in old age; what mattered was the ability to manage declining health successfully. Chinese elders in British Columbia did not perceive themselves to be as healthy as the general population of older Canadians, a finding similar to data reported for China (Chappell & Lai, 1998). Interestingly enough, they still reported the same number of chronic illnesses.

In this study, Chinese elders in British Columbia preferred Western medicine over traditional Chinese medicine. About half engaged in traditional Chinese care for minor and major illnesses, which the researchers found to be associated with religious beliefs and a preference for traditional Chinese medicine (Chappell & Lai, 1998:35). In contrast, an American study of the use of traditional Korean healers found chronic illness and high social cohesiveness predicted the use of alternative services (Pourat, Lubben, Wallace, & Moon, 1999). In the B.C. study of Chinese elders, a multivariate analysis indicated that the ability to speak English, immigration history, and the country of origin were *unrelated* to the use of health services (Chappell & Lai, 1998). What was noteworthy, however, was that 92.2 percent of the elders reported using physician services with some Chinese staff, probably because they had an opportunity to use their own language. Overall, service use of physicians and home care services were the same for Chinese elders as for the rest of the senior population.

The Ontario advisory Council on Senior Citizens (1993) claimed that two-thirds of First Nations seniors living in northern Ontario encountered language problems when using health care services. In the newcomer study, lack of information about services and language barriers were the two most important reasons why services were not used, even if they were needed (McDonald, et al., 2001). In the United States, an analysis of three national data files on service use found that living arrangements, health status, number of functional limitations, region, and health insurance affected utilization of service more than race or ethnicity (Markides & Black, 1996). At the same time, another study found that medical and psychosocial interventions that were ethnically sensitive increased ethnic minority utilization of services (Miller, et al., 1996). The need for research on ethnicity and health and service utilization is obvious. At this point, we cannot say what characteristics are shared across ethnic or minority groups or how each is unique. We do know that the health care system is not organized to take their needs into account.

Family Support

The relationship between ethnicity and the provision of support to older persons from family has always been a focus of Canadian gerontologists, although the research has been a trickle, rather than a stream. Support from family is important because it is known to enhance health, especially mental health (Health Canada, 1999; Falcón & Tucker, 2000), it is known to relieve stress (Noh & Avison, 1996), prevent loneliness (Williams & Wilson, 2001), and it is believed to contribute to a more culturally sensitive environment within the host society (Miner & Montoro-Rodriguez, 1999).

The underlying assumption driving the research is related to the earlier traditional–modern continuum for classifying ethnic groups. Presumably, more "traditional" ethnic groups have extended families available to them and, because of culturally conditioned norms of filial responsibility, are more supportive of older family members (Uijimoto, 1995; Keefe et al., 2000). For example, Strain and Chappell (1984) compared the social supports of older First Nations people with those of non-First Nations people and found that First Nations people had larger numbers of friends and relatives outside the home and had more contact with them than did non-First Nations people. Whether these patterns translated into more social support is unknown, but as a group, they had more people available to them for social support (Dreidger & Chappell, 1987).

The evidence for ethnic differences in support, both instrumental (e.g., transportation, financial) and affective (emotional) has been mixed. The earlier Canadian research found few differences among ethnic groups (Chappell & Penning 1984). Payne and Strain (1990) compared support patterns among the four ethnic groups that constitute the majority in Canada. They did not find any conspicuous differences among British, French, German, and Ukrainian ethnic groups, possibly because of the relative cultural similarity among the groups.

The research that examines more recent immigrants from a wider spectrum of ethnic and racial groups finds ethnic differences in support patterns. Using a nonrandom subsample from the CARNET Work and Family Survey, Keefe et al. (2000) discovered that twice as many respondents with ethnic origins of southern European, Asian, and East Indian, compared with those with British origins, provided three hours or more of help to senior members of their families. When they examined the norm of filial obligation and its relation to helping behaviour, they found that the relationship held for all ethnic groups. In other words, filial obligation was an important value to all groups. When they considered the effects of sociodemographic factors, they found that **co-residency** had the strongest influence on helping behaviour, followed by being female and older.

Other relevant Canadian studies have explored social support in single ethnic groups. Noh and Avison (1996) found that social support from Korean family members living in Toronto was more helpful than from the non-Korean community. Chappell and Lai (2001), who compared the level of life satisfaction of Chinese seniors living in Victoria (Canada) and Zuzhou (China), found that social support was more important to life satisfaction of the Chinese in Zuzhou. A closer look at social support indicated that living with others was important to the Zuzhou Chinese but nowhere as important as geographical location (i.e., living in Victoria versus living in Zuzhou). The authors concluded that the differences in contributions to life satisfaction between the Canadian and Chinese seniors represented cultural differences. Koybashi (2000), in her study of generational support between second-generation and third-generation Japanese Canadian families found that the value of filial obligation influenced the provision of emotional support and the quality of the support, but parents' health and socioeconomic status affected the provision of financial and service support.

Co-residency has typically been considered an indicator of a close-knit family with strong filial traditions that ensure support for elderly family members. The research is well established on co-residency of older persons with their adult children, but there is little data about the quality of support in these settings (see Chapter 11). The data clearly show that visible minorities, First Nations peoples, and, lastly, immigrants, live in larger-sized households than do their counterparts, a finding replicated in most North American research (Thomas & Wister, 1984; Boyd, 1991; Kamo & Zhou, 1994; Gee, 1999; Kritz, Gurak, & Chen, 2000). In Canada, Chinese are one of the minorities more likely to live in complex households (Government of Canada, 1996a: 5-6; 1996b: 5-6). Fewer Chinese senior immigrants aged 65 years and over (about 11 percent) live alone, compared with 25 percent for all immigrant seniors and 29 percent for Canadian-born seniors. Furthermore, a significantly higher percentage of Chinese seniors (65 percent) who do not live with their immediate family, live with other relatives, compared with 29 percent of all immigrant seniors and 18 percent of Canadian-born seniors. In other words, Chinese Canadian families tend to be larger because of these living patterns that can involve three generations (Li, 1998: 112). In Gee's study in Greater Vancouver and Victoria (1999), about half the Chinese elderly lived with at least one child in an intergenerational household setting.

Overall, most of the findings on co-residency suggest that later life living arrangements among immigrants are influenced by the timing of immigration and ethnic and racial characteristics, which researchers treat as indirect measures of ethnic preferences. For example, in an analysis of the living arrangements of older Canadian immigrant women, Boyd (1991) found that immigrant women were more likely than Canadian-born women to live in an extended family, especially if they were older at time of immigration, had a lower socioeconomic status, and had poor language skills in either of the official languages. That the women were less likely to be from Europe was suggestive of cultural preferences for co-residency. In a more recent study, Basavarajappa (1998) used the 1991 census data, and discovered that the propensity for immigrant groups to live in three or more generation households was influenced by lower incomes, the nonreceipt of pension benefits, a shorter time in Canada, and widowhood. He also noted that 28 percent of immigrants living in three-generational households lived in crowded conditions. Gee (1999) underscores one of the main problems in the co-residency literature—there is wide variation within ethnic groups when it comes to co-residency. In her study, Chinese widows who lived alone reported lower levels of well being, but they also indicated that they did not want to live with an adult child.

A number of researchers have attempted to untangle cultural preference from economic need as determinants of co-residency. Immigrants from poorer countries often cannot afford to support their parents in separate dwellings, nor can the senior immigrants support themselves because they are ineligible for government transfer payments, as noted earlier. Living together and pooling resources becomes a very helpful economic strategy for both generations. A number of studies, however, have controlled for economic need and still find that some ethnic minorities choose to live in multigenerational families (Speare & Avery, 1993; Tennstedt & Chang, 1998; Wilmoth, 2001).

As the discussion has shown, there is growing evidence that membership in an ethnic group is related to different patterns of family support, especially for more recent immigrants to Canada. Co-residency appears to be one of the more important determinants for receiving help from family although the reasons for co-residency are not entirely clear. As the ethnic composition of Canada continues to change, the research will have to explore these issues further.

Implications for Policy and Practice

It should be evident by now that policies and services need to be designed to take into account inter- and intra-ethnic differences among older people (Dreidger & Chappell, 1987; Keefe, et al., 2000; McDonald, et al., 2001). How these services should be designed is another question. Some scholars advocate that the needs of ethnic minority elders are best understood by members of their own groups and that these elders should be treated as distinct groups with their own sets of health and social services and polices. This view has lead to requests for research and training programs that give special attention to ethnic minorities, a call for ethnic minority practitioners to be employed as service providers and the recommendation that policies that influence the aged need to account for elderly ethnic minorities (Hooyman & Kiyak, 1999). Others have argued that social and economic inequalities across the life course should be alleviated and that services and policies should be culturally sensitive while being integrated into all services for the aged. Because we do not have enough research, the jury is still out on this matter, but in the meantime, the majority of social gerontologists recognize the many barriers ethnic elders might encounter when they require health and/or social services.

Language is a primary barrier to service, as is lack of knowledge of services, a reluctance to use formal Western health services stemming from different world views, the lack of transportation to services, the shortage of practitioners who are ethnically sensitive, and financial difficulties. In addition, given that most of the new senior immigrants to Canada have arrived through family reunification programs, there may be two generations of people who are new to Canada and who face the same issues (Keefe, et al., 2000). Some studies have, therefore, recommended that the services for ethnic seniors also take into account the situation of the elder's family—outreach to provide information about services, ethnically sensitive services for families, and services offered outside the working hours and close to ethnic neighbourhoods, when possible (McDonald, et al., 2001; Janevic & Connell, 2001).

A serious policy issue that requires immediate attention is the problem of poverty among First Nations peoples and visible minority seniors. Adjustments to pension policy and to immigration polices that do not penalize older ethnic citizens need to be examined.

Chapter Summary

In this chapter, we have explored the diversity of older Canadians. One of the most important observations of this chapter is the fact that there is little research or theory development on older ethnic groups in Canada. What is more, the changing composition of the older population makes clear the need for new data to respond to the changing policy and practice demands of an aging ethnic and more urban population.

Key ideas to remember from this chapter include:

- Ethnogerontology is a new field in social gerontology that studies the influence of race, ethnicity, national origin, and culture on individual and population aging.
- Definitions of ethnicity can include a number of dimensions that involve ancestral origin, a homeland or land of origin, a shared history of one's people, a shared identity, a language, sometimes a religion, and sometimes a culture or subculture.
- Race refers to physical appearance and is a category socially constructed by others that places persons with similar biological traits into a group.
- There have been shifts in the composition of the Canadian population. The French maintain their ethnic identity consistently; there has been a slow but gradual decline in the proportion of the British and in the last 40 years, there has been a dramatic increase in the Asian immigrants' category.
- Europeans represent almost half of all foreign-born elderly (49 percent), with Eastern Europeans holding a large share. Visible minorities make up 6 percent of the older population, and 4 percent of the First Nations population is 65 years of age or older.
- Most theorizing about aging and ethnicity has not developed past the multiple jeopardy hypothesis, its competitor, the age levelling hypothesis or the buffer hypothesis.
- Higher proportions of immigrant visible minority seniors live below the low income cut-offs of Statistics Canada, compared with the general population of seniors.
- Immigrants of all ages are healthy on arrival in Canada, but compared with native-born Canadians, they lose this advantage over time. There is limited research indicating that non-Caucasian seniors may have poorer health than the general population of seniors. The research is inconsistent on the influence of ethnicity on service utilization.
- There is growing evidence for ethnic differences in family support. Co-residency appears to be one of the more important determinants for receiving help from family, although the reasons for co-residency are not entirely clear.
- Whether ethnic seniors need ethnospecific services requires further research. Barriers to health and social services, especially language difficulties, strongly suggest that services, at minimum, be ethnically sensitive with relevant linguistic staff who understand ethnic differences.

KEY TERMS

Ethnogerontology, **(p. 117)**

Ethnicity, **(p. 117)**

Race, **(p. 117)**

Ethnic origin, **(p. 123)**

Landed immigrant, **(p. 126)**

Family-class immigrants, **(p. 128)**

Refugees, **(p. 128)**

Economic-class immigrants, **(p. 128)**

Visible minority, **(p. 131)**

Essentialist approach, **(p. 134)**

Assimilation, **(p. 135)**

Pluralism, **(p. 135)**

Ethnic stratification, **(p. 136)**

Multiple jeopardy hypothesis, **(p. 136)**

Age levelling hypothesis, **(p. 136)**

Buffer hypothesis, **(p. 136)**

Healthy immigrant thesis, **(p. 142)**

Co-residency, **(p. 145)**

STUDY QUESTIONS

1. Thinking about yourself and your family, do you think ethnicity has had any effect on how you live your life day to day? Do you think it will affect you when you are old?

2. What will the ethnic composition of the Canadian population be when you are old? Will it be different from today? What will be different?

3. Poverty appears to be a serious issue for older First Nations peoples and visible minorities in Canada. What are the possible solutions to this problem?

4. How would you settle the issue as to whether we should have an integrated or separate service system for senior ethnic minorities?

SUGGESTED READINGS

Blakemore, K., & Boneham, M. (1994). *Age, race and ethnicity: A comparative approach.* Buckingham, U.K.: Open University Press.

Chi, I., Chappell, N., & Lubben, J (Eds.). 2001. *Elderly Chinese in Pacific Rim countries.* Hong Kong: Hong Kong University Press.

Neugebauer-Visano, R. (Ed.). 1995. *Aging and inequality cultural constructions of differences.* Toronto, Ontario: Canadian Scholars' Press Inc. (pp. 31–67).

Ikels, C. (1990). The resolution of intergeneration conflict: Perspectives of elders and their family members. *Modern China, 16*(4), 349-406.

Attitudes and Aging

Learning Objectives

In this chapter, you will learn about:

- What attitudes are and how they are measured.
- How older people are treated and how this relates to agist attitudes.

- Older people's attitudes about abuse and violence.
- Older people's attitudes about their sexuality and health.

Introduction

This chapter examines attitudes in the context of aging. The chapter begins with a discussion of the concept of attitude, including definition, key assumptions, and measurement. The subsequent sections deal with attitudes toward older people and attitudes of older people. A key concept is agism, which refers to mainly negative, but sometimes positive, stereotypes about older people as a social category or social trends pertaining to that category (e.g, population aging). Some researchers consider agism to be so pervasive as to be almost invisible. Box 6.1 provides an example of agism in sexuality to illustrate this point. Other researchers are not so sure that agism has harmful effects. You be the judge after reading the chapter.

Box 6.1 Examples of Attitudes about Romance in Later Life

Marjorie Charles remembers a woman from St. John's telling 500 seniors in Cornerbrook that they were sexy. It was 13 years ago now—at the yearly convention of the Newfoundland Pensioners and Senior Citizens Federation. "And the funny thing was—she was right on the money," Marjorie recollects. "Even though she was young, from the university, and probably hadn't ever set foot inside a fish plant, which usually means she knew naught worth telling. But I was wrong about that, b'y, was I wrong! That woman knew people, really knew people. No matter the wrinkles on my face and fingers, a bit knurled with arthritis, that woman saw the person inside was the same as when I was 20."

Lee Stones has memories of that day, too. First terror, then amazement, finally joy mixed with humility. Strong emotions often accompany attitude change. The Federation's president wanted her to talk on *"Putting the Zing Back into Your Relationships."* He asked Lee to suggest ways to improve the romantic lives of older people. At first, Lee thought he was kidding. Did older people even have romantic lives? Sure, she sometimes saw some sweet old couple—probably married forever—holding hands in the park. But holding hands is far from passion, and is not passion the key to romance? Also, most of her grandmother's friends were widows. Surely, they were not lusting after romance, if only because of a shortage of men their age.

Just the thought of talking about romance to people like her grandmother gave Lee the shakes. The working families of her adolescent upbringing did not talk much about sexuality. The edict was "Don't you fool around and you won't get pregnant!" That was about all she remembered of her at-home sexual education. The idea of sex between her parents, even her grandparents (God forbid!) was not so much unspeakable as unthinkable. Such were the times a decade or more before the potency drug *Viagra* changed forever society's attitudes toward later-life sexuality.

But Mike Pickett, the Federation's president, was insistent. A few months later, after much reading, thought, and discussion about the topic, Lee arrived at the convention floor.

"That's she, that's the one." Marjorie Charles remembers pointing Lee out to a friend. "I even went up to her and said, 'We really, *really*, look forward to your talk,' thinking only of smut. Wasn't I the catty one?"

(continued)

Box 6.1 (continued)

Soon Lee found herself on stage before the microphone, hundreds of eager old faces looking up at her excitedly. "I controlled my nerves, but at a price," she recalls. "My heart thumped to the rhythm of a fast Newfoundland jig. I asked myself for the umpteenth time: What madness made me agree to this? Will they think me presumptuous, even a hussy?" And so, with much misgiving, she gulped in air and began.

"What was memorable," Marjorie recalls years later, "wasn't so much her advice but her assumption that we needed advice. She could have been talking to somebody of her own age. She didn't treat us like people sexually dead—and I must admit, I acted dead in that way—but just in need of awakening. I did wake up right there and then, and so did a lot of other people. We knew what we wanted, longed for even, widows like us. But we couldn't talk of it. Speak about sex and we'd face the youngsters' ridicule. Even our children—'specially our children. When she'd finished, we didn't just clap. Oh no! We cheered, drummed the floor with our feet, on and on, must've been for a good three minutes. What a racket, b'y! The reason was she saw us like we are and wasn't afraid to say so."

"I learned so much from those people," Lee says now. "I told them what I knew, as though to friends. Of course, I was unsure about whether I would shock them. But they shocked me. They shocked the sexual stereotyping right out of my head. I have no doubts now that people remain sexual to the end of their days. It was joyful to experience, but humbling because I'd been so wrong before. They changed my beliefs, my attitudes, and I think I changed theirs. What happened that day was that the formerly unthinkable (to me) or unspeakable (to them) became open to discussion."

Lee Stones continued to give talks on later-life sexuality to avid audiences across Canada. She co-authored a book on the topic (Stones & Stones, 1997) and often acts as consultant to long-term care facilities to help staff who are still reluctant to adjust for the sexual needs of residents. Two years after the Cornerbrook convention, Marjorie Charles had a romance with a tourist from Nova Scotia. They married and settled near Halifax.

A review of undergraduate textbooks on aging reveals that a full discussion of the attitudes of older people is largely absent—is this an example of agist neglect by textbook writers? The authors of these texts discuss the aging process and older people but fail to give the latter their voice. The section in this chapter on the attitudes of older people provides them a voice. Although the selection of issues was the responsibility of the present authors, the attitudes belong to older Canadians and Americans. The topics deal with violence, sexuality, health, life, and the self.

The Nature and Measurements of Attitudes

The Concept of Attitude

Social scientists have measured attitudes since the 1920s. The true home of the concept, however, is in social psychology, where attitude became and remains "distinctive and indispensable." (Allport, 1935: 198) Definitions of **attitude** refer to a *tendency* to *evaluate* an *object* with some degree of favour or disfavour (Eagly & Chaiken, 1993). The meanings of the italicized terms are as follows:

- A *tendency* is a mental state lasting at least a short time.
- An *evaluation* is a response that implies favour or disfavour. Responses can be positive or negative, and differ in their valence (i.e., extremity). Common forms of evaluative response include liking or disliking, approving or disapproving, and approaching or avoiding.
- The *object* of an attitude may be abstract (e.g., democracy), concrete (e.g., Lake Superior), collective (e.g., Canadians), or unique (e.g., your mother). The object can be a general or specific feature of the same entity (e.g., your mother, your mother when you were younger, your mother now). Common objects of interest to social scientists include policy issues (e.g., health, social, political), minority groups (e.g., stereotyping), behaviour (e.g., violence), other people (e.g., attraction), and the self (e.g., self-esteem). The object is not the same as the *target* of an attitude. A target is the person who experiences the attitude object (e.g., a senior as the victim of elder abuse). The object may be a person (or people) or behaviour, but the target is always a person (or a category of people).

Definitions denote the meaning of a concept but not its function. Psychologists consider attitude to intervene between an object and the evaluative responses to that object. They term such concepts a "latent variable," "hypothetical construct," or "cognitive schema." These terms signify that the concept is not directly observable but inferred from observation (MacCorquodale & Meehl, 1948). Concepts, such as learning, memory, and personality, are similar to attitudes in this respect. None is accessible to direct observation, but all intervene between a stimulus and response.

Assumptions about Attitudes

Theories about attitudes elaborate on their scope and structure. All theories make assumptions. The following assumptions were pivotal to the evolution of theories about attitude. Figure 6.1 provides a schematic that integrates the assumptions within a simplified framework.

First, psychologists distinguish between a **belief** and an attitude. A statement such as, "Older drivers are at high risk of dying in car accidents," expresses a belief, rather than an attitude. This belief may or may not be true, but does not by itself convey an evaluation. An attitude always conveys an evaluation. If somebody says, "Older drivers are a danger to themselves and others," "I feel anxious about all the older drivers on the road," and "I try to avoid being in a car with an older driver," it is reasonable to infer a negative evaluation. The truth of this attitude is not the issue because an attitude, like a belief, may have no basis in fact. The research on accidents does support a belief that seniors are at high

Figure 6.1 SCHEMATIC SHOWING INFLUENCES ON EVALUATIVE RESPONSE

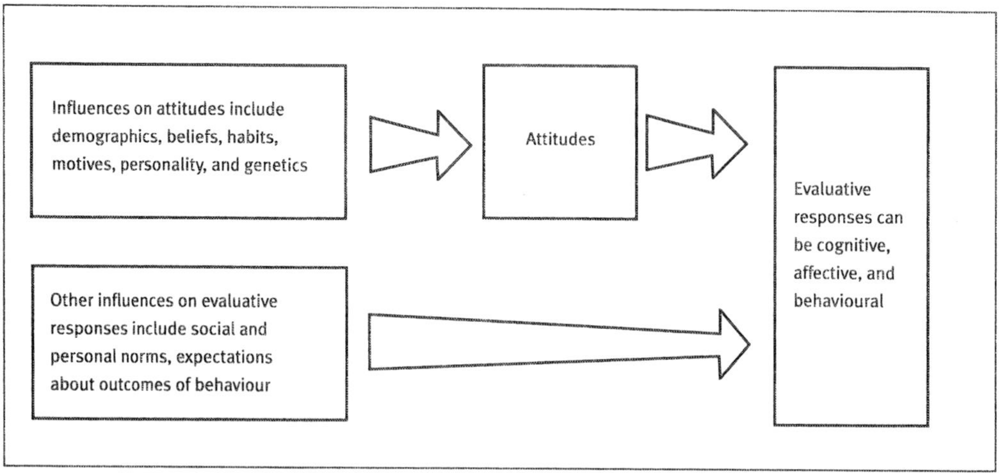

Source: Based on conceptualization by the author.

risk of fatality in automobile crashes. However, the findings on fatalities offer little credence to negative attitudes toward seniors who drive. The odds of dying in a car crash do increase with age, but the overall fatalities include more young people than old people (Bédard, Guyatt, Stones, & Hirdes, in press).

Second, psychologists use the concept of attitude to help to account for correlations between different kinds of responses. From the time of classical Greek philosophy, a useful tripartite model included cognitive, affective, and behavioural modes of response. Research showed the evaluative responses to correlate across these domains (Eagly & Chaiken, 1993). People with positive attitudes respond positively across the cognitive, affective, and behavioural domains, and vice versa for people with negative attitudes. Campbell and Fiske (1959) refer to such consistency as **convergent validity**. By this, they mean that the findings converge across categories of response. The complement to convergent validity is **discriminant validity**. This form of validity implies that responses should correlate more strongly within than across categories (e.g., cognitive responses should correlate more strongly with each other than with affective or behavioural responses). Without evidence for discriminant validity, there is no empirical reason to make distinctions among the response categories (i.e., the latter add nothing extra to our ability to predict responses). Because research findings provide good support for convergent validity but only weak support for discriminant validity (Breckler, 1984), current thinking considers the tripartite model as conceptually, rather than empirically, viable (Zanna & Rempel, 1988). It provides "convenient labels ...that would not necessarily sort out into three components on an empirical basis" (Eagly & Chaiken, 1993: 666).

Third, many social theorists incorrectly assumed that attitudes depend exclusively on learned experience. Campbell (1963) even defined attitude as an *acquired* condition. However, recent findings show a genetic influence on attitudes. An initial study compared the religious attitudes of identical and fraternal twins (Waller, Kojetin, Bouchard, Lykken, & Tellegen, 1990). Similarly, Eaves, Eysenck, and Martin (1989) showed a genetic influence on other attitudes.

Recent Canadian research on twins provides consistent evidence, with findings of a genetic contribution on 26 of 30 attitudes (Olsen, Vernon, Harris & Jang, 2001). Attitudes rooted in genetic or evolutionary disposition may be resistant to change because of life experience. Larose and Standing (1998) recently found that attitudes toward attractive and unattractive faces remain unchanged across the life span.

Finally, psychologists assume that attitudes have a predictive or even a causal relationship to behaviour. However, there was much debate about this issue during the 1970s. Wicker (1969) reviewed 42 mainly laboratory studies that included correlations between attitudes and behaviour. He found the correlations to be weak or nonsignificant in most of the studies. There were strong reactions to Wicker's paper. Hovland (1959), in an earlier account, had stated that attitude–behaviour correlations might be weaker in laboratory research than survey research because the attitudes studied tend to be less important to the respondents. Also, laboratory studies constrain the choice of actions to those chosen by the researcher, whereas people in natural settings express their attitudes by behaviours of their own choosing.

Probably the most compelling evidence was research showing a weak correlation of attitudes with discrete behaviours but stronger correlations with summed indexes of behaviour. Weigel and Newman (1976) provided an example in which they obtained correlations between attitudes toward environmental preservation with unobtrusive measures of behaviours taken six months later. The findings showed the correlations of attitude with discrete behaviours to average about $r = 0.32$, but the correlation with a summed index to be $r = 0.62$. The stronger correlation with the summed index was not a surprise. Somebody with a given attitude toward an object may express it unevenly for any number of reasons (e.g., fear of a social penalty if the attitude is unpopular), with attitude being only one among many influences on behaviour (Ajzen & Fishbein, 1975). Current theories tend to agree that generalized attitudes have implications for a range of behaviours, rather than strong effects on specific behaviours (Eagly & Chaiken, 1993).

Measurement of Attitudes

There are three main approaches to measuring attitude:

1. Thurstone's (1928) method of equal intervals proceeds in three stages. Judges rate statements for the degree of favour or disfavour toward an

attitude object. The items selected for inclusion are those that represent different levels on the evaluative dimension. Respondents rate their levels of agreement with each statement. This method fell into some disfavour because of its complexity.

2. Guttman's (1941) cumulative method uses statements ordinally graded for degree of favour or disfavour toward the attitude object. If the measure is truly cumulative, respondents should disagree with all items below a threshold level but agree with all those above that level. The threshold level reflects the attitude.

3. Likert's (1932) summative method uses statements rated by respondents for level of agreement. The scores are summed across items (i.e., with negative items reverse scored), and the attitude represented by the summed score. This method is currently the most popular.

Attitudes toward Older People

Dowd (1980) asserted that the status accorded to people in Western culture increases from youth to middle age but declines thereafter. This trajectory holds true regardless of the age, social class, or gender of respondents. The consequences include a stereotyping of older persons that is usually negative but sometimes positive in direction (Palmore, 1990). The name for such stereotyping is **agism**.

Is agism a social issue in Canada? Researchers disagree about this matter. Some consider agism not to characterize Canadian society. Schonfield found that approximately 20 percent to 80 percent of his respondents agreed with the stereotypes about (some or all) older people— "and that 20 percent could be convicted" of agist stereotyping, a proportion he considered "insufficient to justify the generalization that ours is an ageist society." (Schonfield, 1982: 269–270) Twenty percent is not a majority, but it is certainly a significant minority. Imagine the outcry if researchers were to find that 20 percent of our population "could be convicted" of racist stereotyping, homophobia, or religious stereotyping. Would not the reaction toward such (hypothetical) findings include, at the very least, a ferment against such bigotry? It probably would. Stones and Stones (1998) refer to agism as a "quiet epidemic" that contributes to benign neglect or indifference toward older people as a social category, rather than active antagonism. It is important to stress that agism refers to stereotyping of older people as a social unit, rather than behaviour toward specific older persons. A person with agist attitudes may have excellent relationships with older acquaintances, but hold stereotypical attitudes toward the category to which those acquaintances belong. Agism becomes a social problem only if it impacts on older people.

Research findings on agism derive from many sources, including undergraduate attitudes (Knox & Gekoski, 1989), literary and dramatic productions (Berman & Sobkowska-Ashcroft, 1986, 1987), humour (Palmore, 1971), health care (Butler, 1975), and legislative processes (Stones & Stones, 1998). The number of studies showing predominantly negative attitudes is legion. A recent compilation of research on the attitudes of college students toward seniors, accessible at one university library, includes nearly 40 references (Montgomery, 2000). Knox, Gekoski, and Kelly (1995) provide a useful tool to assess stereotypes and attitudes toward age groups. The Age Group Evaluation and Description (AGED) Inventory contains evaluative factors of *Goodness* and *Positiveness*, and descriptive factors of *Vitality* and *Maturity*. Assumptions about low vitality among the aged probably contributed to the opinions expressed by Lee Stones about sexuality in later life prior to her interaction with the targets of those attitudes (see Box 6.1).

Students' knowledge and attitudes about aging benefit from exposure to positive information. Couper (1994) indicated that the prevailing educational philosophy in North America ignores aging as a topic during the high school years, thereby providing the students with little information to counter agist attitudes. Several studies show that college students' knowledge and attitudes about older people show improvement with positive information. Palmore (1988) found that knowledge about aging increased with education and that courses on gerontology were beneficial. Matthews, Tindale, and Norris (1985) found education in gerontology to result in increased knowledge about aging in a Canadian context. Canadian studies by Knox, Gekoski, and Johnson (1984) and Gfellner (1982) found more positive attitudes among students having positive interactions with older people. A review of studies about medical students' knowledge and attitudes about aging surprisingly concluded that instructional modules in geriatrics have little impact (Beullens, Marcoen, Jaspaert, & Pelemans, 1997). The probable reason is that such modules deal only with sickness. The authors cite courses on gerontology and interaction with healthy seniors as ways to promote positive attitudes and recommend their inclusion in the medical curriculum.

There is also evidence that negative information contributes to negative attitudes toward an aging population. Kojima (1996) examined population opinion surveys in Japan conducted in 1990 and 1995. The proportions of respondents having positive attitudes toward an aging population fell from 5 percent to 3.5 percent between 1990 and 1995, the proportions having neutral attitudes fell from 43 percent to 38.5 percent, whereas the proportion having negative attitudes increased from 52 percent to 58 percent. The low proportions with positive attitudes reflect concerns about population aging. Kojima attributed the changes from 1990 to 1995 to extensive media coverage of record-low fertility rates during the intervening period and attendant policies to slow the rate of population aging.

Agist attitudes may do tangible disservice to older people. Nowhere is this more apparent than in health care. Pulitzer Prize-winning author Robert Butler (1974) addressed a Symposium on Geriatric Medicine as follows: "Medicine and the behavioural sciences have mirrored social attitudes by presenting old age as a grim litany of physical and emotional ills." In nursing homes, he spoke of a policy of **pacification**—the overuse of medication as a substitute for humane attention through diagnosis and careful treatment (Butler, 1975). This was but one example of poor health care conditional upon the old age of the patient. More than a decade later, van Maanen (1991) and Honeyman (1991) echoed Butler's sentiments to the Canadian Medical Association. Evidence from Canadian nursing homes also supports Butler's comments about pacification. Although Canadian homes use psychotropic medication no more than those in other countries, the physical restraint of residents is more frequent in this country (Canadian Institute of Health Information, 1998).

Agist attitudes also support the assumptions of "apocalyptic demography" (see Chapter 1) that influences health care policy (Gee & Gutman, 2000). The assumptions that age brings about illness, the treatment of illness incurs fiscal costs, and an expectation of escalating cost with population aging seem to provide compelling reasons to reconsider health care policies. However, the evidence suggests otherwise—it is minimally demography but mainly other factors that contribute to projections about health care expenditure (Evans, McGrail, Morgan, Barer, & Hertzman, 2001; Reinhardt, 2001). Evans and colleagues liken the apocalyptic demography hypothesis to a "zombie" that keeps walking despite its evident death. The zombie keeps on walking, Evans and colleagues argue, because it supports increased income to health care providers, distracts attention from poor practices within the health care system, and provides a rationale for greater corporate involvement in health care (i.e., privatization). It is an example of the use of agism (i.e., the assumption that age inevitably brings sickness and a high cost of care) to serve the economic interests of others. Evans and colleagues conclude that "we have nothing to fear from the aging of the population, only from those who continue to promulgate the fiction." (Evans, McGrail, Morgan, Barer, & Hertzman, 2001: 188).

Finally, agist attitudes in the legislature may also do disservice to older people. Lubomudrov (1987) examined congressional misrepresentations in the United States used to influence the legislative process. He identified negative (e.g., older people as poor, frail, ill-housed, and so on) and positive stereotypes (e.g., older people as well off, politically potent, and so on), both of which treat older people as a homogenous entity, despite abundant evidence that they are not. Stones and Stones (1998) refer to the Newfoundland and Labrador Human Rights Code as one example of legislation that discriminates against older people. Under the terms of this Code, a senior may be denied access to public places or private dwellings, denied service, harassed, and even become the object of hate literature. Why is this? Because age is a prohibited ground for discrimination under the Code only between age 18 and 65 years. It is not because the legislators were overtly agist that seniors were omitted from the Code, but simply because agism was unrecognized and, therefore, rendered invisible.

Attitudes of Older People

Violence and Abuse

Attitudes toward Violence.

Seniors are less likely than younger people to be victims of **violence**. Statistics Canada reports that in 1997, the homicide rates were approximately 2.5 victims per

100,000 for people aged 15 to 44 years, compared with 1.5 victims aged 65 years and older. Despite this lower risk, more older Canadians, like those in the United States (Dowd, Sisson, & Kern, 1981), express fear of violent crime. Figure 6.2 shows the percentages of respondents in 1993 who felt unsafe when walking alone in their neighbourhood after dark (Statistics Canada, 2000). Fear increased with age, with women expressing greater fear than men.

Attitudes toward Abuse.

In contrast to fear of violence, attitudes about elder **abuse** are less negative in seniors than in younger people (Stones & Pittman, 1995). An awareness of elder abuse as a social issue in Canada emerged in the 1970s. The legal, helping, and educational professions became involved in the following decade, when Health and Welfare Canada (1990) provided funds to tackle the problem at a national level by its sponsorship of research and educational projects. Box 6.2 provides a definition of elder abuse and a brief discussion of current knowledge and its limitations.

Researchers began to study elder abuse by asking questions mainly of relevance to those professions interested in detection, treatment, and prevention. A major issue concerned the "under reporting" of abuse, which refers to a failure to report suspected abuse to the relevant authorities. Subsequent studies explored the

Figure 6.2 PERCENTAGE OF CANADIANS FEELING SOMEWHAT OR VERY UNSAFE WALKING ALONE IN THEIR NEIGHBOURHOOD AFTER DARK

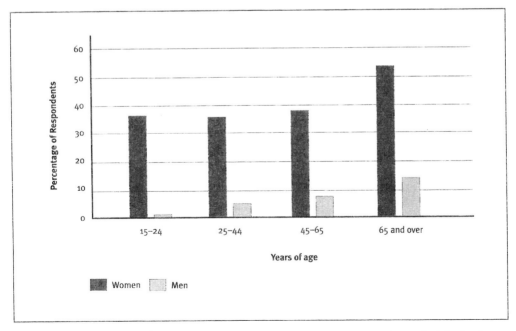

Source: Statistics Canada, 1999

Box 6.2 The Meaning and Scope of Elder Abuse and Neglect

Hudson (1991) added to our understanding of elder abuse and neglect by providing a standard definition agreed upon by a panel of experts. This definition refers to abuse as a special case of harmful behaviour that occurs in the context of a trust relationship. Abuse refers to destructive behaviour, while neglect refers to a failure to provide required help. The people that seniors should be able to trust include unpaid caregivers (e.g., a relative, a friend) and professional helpers (e.g., a doctor, a lawyer). Behaviours not considered examples of abuse include those by confidence tricksters who prey on older people. Such crimes are not examples of abuse because the criminal is a stranger, rather than somebody in a position of trust.

Definitions similar to that by Hudson (1991) are in use throughout Canada (e.g., British Columbia Inter-Ministry Committee on Elder Abuse, 1992). Although such definitions capture the global meaning, they do not distinguish between types of abuse. One way to classify cases pertains to the kind of harm done (e.g., damage to the physical, mental, or financial well being of seniors). Another way pertains to the type of social expectation the behaviour violates (e.g., legal, ethical, professional, or social standards of acceptability) (Stones, 1995). Although the latter accords more closely with legal logic, the former provides categories that are more concrete.

A political, rather than scientific, agenda prompted a dawning awareness of elder abuse and neglect as social problems in Canada. Although elder abuse emerged as a social issue in the United States in the 1970s, involvement at a federal level began in Canada a decade later (Health and Welfare Canada, 1987). At that time there was no real knowledge about the extent of the problem in this country (i.e., its *prevalence*), the number of new cases (i.e., its *incidence*), or its nature or etiology (Kozak, Elmslie, & Verdun, 1995). Subsequent research by Podnieks, Pillemer, Nicholson, Shillington, and Frizzel (1990) provided an estimate of the extent of the problem. These researchers used a random sample telephone survey to estimate the prevalence of elder abuse and neglect among seniors living in the community (Podnieks, 1992). They concluded that 4 percent of elderly Canadian community residents are victims of abuse or neglect each year. The most frequent forms relate to the loss of material possessions, followed by chronic verbal aggression, physical violence, and neglect.

Kozak, Elmslie, and Verdun (1995) point out some enduring limitations to our understanding of elder abuse and neglect.

1.   The measures used in elder abuse surveys have limited evidence of validity.

2.   Other Canadian prevalence estimates are much lower than 4 percent. Examples include a mean prevalence of 1 percent among clients of four community care agencies (Chesworth, Curtin-Telegdi, Dalby, Hallman, Hirdes, Kirchhner, Poss, & Tjam, 2000). This study used a measure designed for use in community care settings.

3.   No Canadian study provides a meaningful estimate of the extent of elder abuse and neglect in institutions.

4.   Prevalence studies provide a poor means to predict ongoing trends. Prevalence estimates include both old and new cases. There is no way to know whether the rate reflects an increase or a decrease in new cases, or a steady state.

5.   Incidence studies estimate only the frequency of new cases. No Canadian study provides an estimate of incidence rate.

(continued)

Box 6.2 (continued)

6. The most comprehensive incidence study to date is the *National Incidence Study* in the United States (Administration on Aging, 1998). This study used a complex system of *sentinels* to report on cases of elder abuse in community settings that otherwise escaped detection. The findings indicate an incidence rate of 1 percent nationwide, with only one case in five reported to the Adult Protective Services.

7. Many social theorists liken elder abuse to an *iceberg*, with only a small proportion of cases coming to the attention of the legal and helping professions (Administration on Aging, 1998). The reasons usually given for under-reporting include the shame felt by seniors reluctant to disclose their experiences of abuse or their fear of the family disruption that might result from such disclosure.

Books that provide in-depth discussion on elder abuse and neglect from a Canadian perspective include McDonald, Hornick, Robertson, and Wallace (1991) and MacLean (1995).

meaning of elder abuse in the wider community (Moon & Williams, 1993). The comparisons included professionals and the public, younger and middle-aged people, different occupations, and ethic minorities. A Canadian study by Stones (1994) compared the attitudes of seniors and professionals. These studies found overall similarity between the attitudes of professionals and the public but also some differences (Hudson & Carlson, 1998). Payne and Berg (1999) found the attitudes of nursing home professionals to differ from those of the police and college students. Older Korean American women were less likely to perceive abuse than African Americans or Caucasian Americans (Moon & Williams, 1993). Childs, Hayslip, Radika, and Reinbert (2000) found that middle-aged respondents rated examples of psychological abuse more severely than did younger people, an age trend consistent with that of the Canadian research discussed next.

The Canadian research proceeded in four stages. The first step was to compile a comprehensive inventory of elder abuse and neglect items from the literature. The examples included physical abuse (e.g., hitting), psychological abuse (e.g., berating), financial abuse (e.g., stealing), and neglect (e.g., inadequate provision of care). The second stage involved the addition of items obtained from focus groups with seniors and professionals. Third, pilot testing of an early version of the tool resulted in a 112-item final measure called the *Elder Abuse Survey Tool* (*EAST*; Stones, 1995). Fourth, over 550 seniors and professionals provided responses to this tool. Subsequent research resulted in two derivative measures. The *Elder Abuse Attitude Test* (*EAAT*; Stones & Pittman, 1995) was a short form with high reliability and validity. The *Senior Behaviour Inventory* (*SBI*) included items on beneficence, which a panel of 25 judges rated as *not* examples of "poor treatment" of seniors (Lithwick, Reis, Stones, Macnaughton-Osler, Gendron, Groves, & Canderan, 1997). Box 6.3 shows the full set of EAAT items and an abbreviated set of beneficence items.

Box 6.3 Abbreviated Senior Behaviour Inventory (SBI)

The following items refer to how people sometimes behave toward seniors. They only refer to behaviour by someone a senior has reason to trust. That person could be a relative or someone who takes care of the senior. That person could also be someone paid to help or look after the senior's affairs (e.g., doctor, nurse, homemaker, lawyer.) The questions do *not* refer to how strangers treat seniors. Do you understand the kinds of people the questions refer to? Please indicate whether the behaviours below are (1) not abusive, (2) possibly abusive, (3) abusive, (4) severely abusive, or (5) very severely abusive toward a senior if done by someone a senior has reason to trust. Remember that the questions do not apply to acts by a stranger.

Item	Not Abusive	Possibly Abusive	Abusive	Severely Abusive	Very Severely Abusive
EAAT items					
Steals something a senior values					
Pushes or shoves a senior					
Lies to a senior in a harmful way					
Opens a senior's mail without permission					
Withholds information that may be important to a senior					
Unreasonably orders a senior around					
Tells a senior that person is "too much trouble"					
Fails to provide proper nutrition					
Disbelieves a senior claiming to be abused, without checking					
Nonabusive (beneficence) items					
Asking a senior to contribute toward his/her own expenses					
Asking a senior to help with household chores					
Not buying an expensive watch a senior asked for as a birthday gift					

Findings showed the strength of negative attitudes toward elder abuse and neglect to decrease with age (Stones & Bédard, in press). Figure 6.3 shows this trend in both genders. Stones and Pittman (1995) explored possible reasons for the effect. They found that attitudes toward elder abuse correlated with those toward

Figure 6.3 NEGATIVE ATTITUDES TOWARDS ELDER ABUSE BY MEN AND
WOMEN OF DIFFERENT AGES

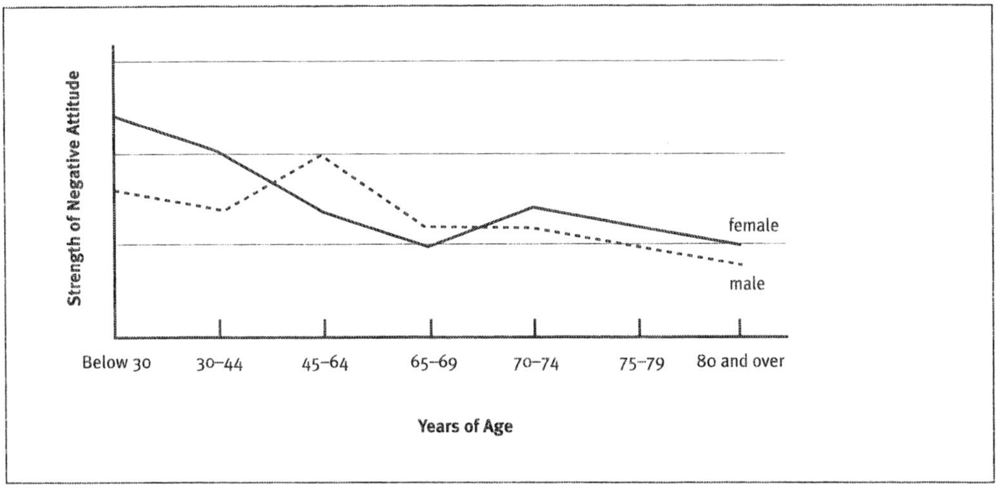

Source: Adapted from Stones & Bédard (in press).

child and spouse abuse, but not with attitudes towards other issues in social
morality (i.e., acceptable limits to physical and verbal behaviour, the responsibilities of the victim and family in abusive situations, abortion, capital punishment, illegal drug use, organ donation, and euthanasia). Consequently, attitudes
toward elder abuse appear to belong with a set of attitudes toward domestic
violence issues.

Earlier research in social psychology provides another way to interpret these
findings. Lindville (1982) distinguished between "in groups," to which the respondent belongs, and "out groups," to which the respondent does not belong. When
young people rate items about elder abuse, they express attitudes toward an "out
group," but when seniors rate the same items, their attitudes are toward an "in
group." Lindville (1982) found that attitudes toward "out groups" tend to be
more extreme than toward "in groups." In one study, she found the attitudes of college students toward (positive or negative) vignettes of an older person to be
extreme, relative to comparable vignettes of someone their own age. By extrapo-
lating this reasoning to attitudes about elder abuse, Stones and Pittman (1995)
suggested that young people have more extreme attitudes than older people
because their ratings are from an "out group" perspective, whereas seniors rate
elder abuse items from an "in group" perspective.

Stones (2000) reported other evidence consistent with this interpretation.
Older respondents living in either the community or institutions rated two sets of
elder abuse items. The first set consisted of *generic* items that were examples of

abuse that could happen to any senior, regardless of residence. The second set of *institutional* abuse items referred only to abuse in an **institutional residence**. Both groups of seniors belong to an "in group" with respect to generic abuse, but only the institutional residents belong to an "in group" with respect to institutional abuse. Consequently, Stones (2000) predicted no differences between the residential groups on the generic items but more moderate ratings by the institutional group on the institutional abuse items. The findings confirmed these predictions, with a minimal difference between groups on the generic items but more extreme attitudes toward institutional abuse by the community residents. Attitudes toward elder abuse, therefore, appear to differ by whether or not the respondent belongs to the target population.

Changing Attitudes toward Abuse.

Education is a key concept in the prevention of abuse and neglect. Podnieks and Baille suggest that attitude change is among the aims of elder abuse education: "Education is not only about acquiring information, it is also about changing attitudes, behaviours, and values." (Podnieks and Baille, 1995: 81). The targets of elder abuse education they identify include not only professionals but also caregivers, the public, children, and seniors themselves. The attitudes of seniors may influence their help seeking in situations of abuse.

Little evidence is available that attests to the outcomes of elder abuse education. Although one study found the reporting of elder abuse to be higher in communities with higher levels of training, this training was of professionals, rather than the public (Wolf, 1999). Podnieks and Baille's (1995) review of elder abuse education cites no research on outcome evaluation for any age group. A recent exception was a study in Quebec that aimed to change beliefs and attitudes in ethnic communities (Lithwick, Stones, & Reis, 1998). The intervention in this study included two phases. The first phase included four sessions on elder abuse with members of Community Senior Mistreatment Committees. The second phase involved a community awareness initiative organized and discharged by each committee. The committees had an average of 16 members drawn from the same ethnic community. The members included men and women with a mean age of 58 years. Committee members completed a battery of measures, including the Senior Behaviour Inventory (SBI), before and after the intervention.

The results showed differences in knowledge and attitudes before and after the intervention. Although the largest gains in knowledge concerned resources to help mistreated seniors, findings with the Senior Behaviour Inventory showed that attitudes toward elder abuse and neglect were harsher after the intervention. Because the beneficence items on the SBI showed no such change, these findings suggest that education about elder abuse and neglect has effects that are specific to elder abuse and neglect, rather than an effect on overall beneficence.

Sexuality

Like Lee Stones in Box 6.1, the pioneering investigators of human sexuality largely neglected later life issues. Less than 1 percent of the data collected by Kinsey and his colleagues (1948, 1953) were from people aged over 60 years, and they devoted only seven pages out of 1,646 to later-life sexuality. Similarly, Masters and Johnson (1966) studied only 31 people aged over 60 years for their seminal publication. Sexual agism seems to influence science as well as inform popular opinion.

Sexuality in later life became a frequent focus of research only during the 1980s. Surveys by Brecher (1985) and Starr and Weiner (1988) and findings from the Duke Longitudinal Study of Aging (Palmore, 1981) refuted earlier beliefs that sexual dysfunctions and a loss of sexual interest inevitably accompany aging. Although changes with age in physiological functions have effects on sexual expression, sexual performance is neither impossible nor even difficult for the majority of older people. Table 6.1 shows some frequent physiological changes, together with advice on dealing with such changes. Although Meston (1997) cautioned older people not to expect the sexual vigour of young adulthood, he joined others (Stones & Stones, 1996) in warning against a self-fulfilling prophecy in which sexuality dissipates in later life. Such stereotyping of the self or others has roots in prejudice and ignorance, rather than in knowledge.

Studies during the 1990s added to knowledge about the sexual attitudes and behaviour of older people. The designs used in this research—in contrast to some surveys from the previous decade—satisfied exacting scientific standards. Examples include an extensive survey by the American Association of Retired Persons (AARP, 1999). This survey included 639 male and 745 females, with a mean age of 60 years, randomly sampled from a panel of people aged 45 years and older. The response rate exceeded the 60 percent stipulation adopted by many prestigious medical publications (e.g., the *Canadian Medical Association Journal*).

The past decade also witnessed the introduction of the drug sildenafil (*Viagra*) in 1998. This drug was the first effective oral medication to assist men with erectile dysfunction. An explosion of interest in later-life sexuality greeted its appearance. The drug quickly gained acceptance, with over 7,000,000 consumers in the United States alone. An Internet page by Pfizer, *Viagra's* manufacturer, claims that physicians across the world now dispense four tablets every second (www.viagra.com).

Measures of Sexual Attitudes and Behaviour.

Measures of **sexuality** include cognitions (e.g., sexual thoughts, fantasies, erotic dreams), affect (e.g., sexual desires), and behaviour (e.g., frequency and type of sexual behaviour). Composite measures used in many studies include ratings of sexual satisfaction. The following discussion examines the trends on these indexes in later life, factors that modify the trends, and other issues relevant to sexual attitudes in later life.

Table 6.1 PHYSIOLOGICAL AGE CHANGES IN MEN AND WOMEN

CHANGES IN MEN	CHANGES IN WOMEN
Erection takes longer.	Vaginal lubrication is both slower and diminished.
The erection may not be as hard.	The vaginal walls thin and become irritated more easily.
The ejaculation takes longer, may feel less intense.	The vagina may change shape to become shorter and narrower.
It takes longer after ejaculation before the penis can become erect again (maybe leading to a decreased frequency of intercourse).	The clitoris becomes more exposed to irritation, and may decrease in size very late in life.
The man is aroused less easily.	The bladder and urethra (through which urine passes) become more susceptible to irritation and bacterial infection.

Effects of Physiological Changes and Consequent Advice to Older People

The positive effect of these changes is that the older man is more in control of his sexuality than the younger man, less a slave to it. Much better for him to take sex slowly, to have the time to enjoy its full sensuality. It is much better for her, too.	The older woman should take extra care to maintain cleanliness, use lubricants, and keep sexually active. Even a short abstinence may cause older women to experience temporary discomfort when resuming sex.

Source: Based on conceptualization by the author.

Sexual Cognition and Desire.

See Table 6.1 for a list of physiological changes in both men and women as they age. In addition, the AARP (1999) study reports on sexual thoughts and desires. More men than women thought about, fantasized, or desired sex on a weekly basis, with the percentages decreasing with age for both genders. In the 45 to 59-year cohort, more than 80 percent of men and 50 percent of women reported weekly thoughts and desire. Although the rates were lower in the oldest cohort, this was not because of a cessation in sexual interest. The percentages of people aged 75 years and older who thought about or desired sex at any time were more than 80 percent for men and more than 40 percent for women. Age, therefore, affected the rates of sexual thoughts and desires, rather than bringing about a termination. Wiley and Bortz (1996) found compatible trends among men and women enrolled in a program on sexuality for older adults. Three-quarters of the men and half of the women desired to increase their level of sexual activity.

Sexual Behaviour.

The sexual behaviours surveyed by AARP (1999) included intercourse, oral sex, masturbation, kissing and hugging, sexual touching, and caressing. The proportions engaging in these activities decreased with age, with two exceptions. Males showed no significant decrease in kissing and hugging; and the frequency of masturbation was low in females at all ages. The steepness of the decline with age was greater for females than for males on all the behaviours, except for masturbation. Figure 6.4 illustrates some of the trends.

Findings that sexual intercourse becomes less frequent with age are supported by Skoog (1996), Matthias, Lubben, Atchison, and Schweitzer (1997), and Bortz, Wallace, and Wiley (1999). By the age of the oldest cohort in the AARP (1999) survey, the most frequent forms of sexual expression were physical contact without penetration (e.g., kissing, touching, hugging, caressing). The findings affirm that earlier research which simply counted the frequency of intercourse provided an incomplete understanding of later-life sexuality.

Sexual Satisfaction.

Sexual expression takes many forms, and sexual satisfaction relates more to quality than quantity.

Figure 6.4 PERCENTAGE OF MEN AND WOMEN OF DIFFERENT AGES HAVING SEXUAL COGNITIONS, DESIRES, CONTACT, OR INTERCOURSE AT LEAST WEEKLY

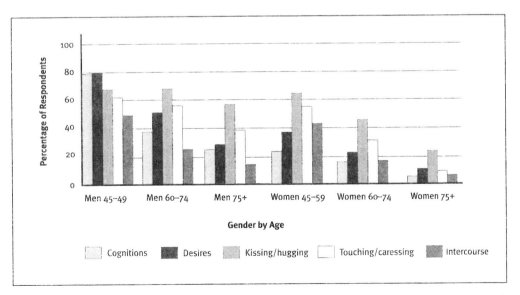

Source: Based on AARP (1999).

Females had higher ratings of sexual satisfaction than males in the AARP (1999) survey. This finding was consistent with other research (Matthias, Lubben, Atchison, & Schweitzer, 1997). The ratings in the AARP survey also showed limited evidence of decline with age. More people in the 45 to 59-year cohort chose response alternatives of "very satisfied" or "somewhat satisfied," compared with the older cohorts. The most frequent response in the oldest cohort was "neither satisfied nor dissatisfied." The proportions expressing dissatisfaction were relatively low for any age or gender group.

Modifiers of Sexual Expression: Absence of a Partner.

A main barrier to sexual expression is the absence of a primary sexual partner. The AARP survey found that men without partners were younger than women without partners, men were more likely to be married or never married (52 percent versus 19 percent) and were less likely to be widowed (21 percent versus 49 percent). More than 85 percent of men and women with partners were married.

The most frequent descriptors of a sexual partner in the AARP (1999) survey included "my best friend" who "loves me deeply." Respondents endorsed both descriptors with a frequency of about 75 percent. Sexual proficiency descriptors ranked much lower. People with partners were more likely to engage in most forms of sexual behaviour on a weekly basis. An exception was masturbation, which was frequent in men, with or without partners, but infrequent in women. People with partners also gave higher ratings of sexual satisfaction than those without partners.

Men without partners were more likely to engage in all forms of sexual behaviour than women without partners. The contributing factors probably include attitudes toward sexuality. Men were more likely than women to report that sexual activity was important to their quality of life, less likely *not* to enjoy sex, and less disapproving of sex outside marriage. Men without partners expressed the most dissatisfaction on sexual satisfaction ratings.

Modifiers of Sexual Expression: Health.

The AARP (1999) survey showed that people who were disease free and taking no medications had the highest frequencies for sexual cognitions, desires, and behaviours. Surprisingly, there were no effects of disease or medications on ratings of sexual satisfaction. Other research showing that **health** promotes sexual behaviours include Bortz, Wallace, and Wiley (1999) and Dunn, Croft, and Hackett (1999). Of particular concern are depression and psychological reactions to physical illness. Araujo, Durante, Feldman, Goldstein, and McKinlay (1998) report adverse effects of depression on sexuality. Buzzelli, di Francesco, Giaquinto, and Nolfe (1997) found that sexual problems following a stroke related more to psychological factors than to the physical condition. This finding echoes previous clinical observations that adverse psychological reactions to physical illness contribute to lowered sexuality, particularly among males (Stones & Stones, 1996).

More males than females sought treatment for sexual problems in the AARP (1999) study. Half the males with such problems took *Viagra*. Although patient satisfaction with this drug exceeded 85 percent to 90 percent in some trials, Steers (1999) cautioned that expectations are often unrealistic. He considered the drug to be an effective treatment for erectile dysfunction, not a miracle-cure for all sexual problems, many of which reside in the relationship with the partner.

Attitudes toward Sex in Institutions.

As indicated in Box 6.1, Lee Stones became an advocate for the rights of nursing home residents to sexual expression. The issues are complex because they involve not only the residents and their families but also the staff of the institutions. There is also the issue of ethics.

Long-term care brings special challenges because a significant proportion of residents have some form of dementia. Lichtenberg (1997) believes that sexual expression in older adults, with or without dementia, brings different ethical challenges. For the cognitively intact, the issue of privacy is primary to their ability to enjoy sexual relations. For people with dementia, the question of their competency may be paramount. Although there is no good reason to exclude people with dementia from enjoying a sexual relationship, it is important to respect their desires and ensure an absence of coercion or unwanted persuasion.

A study by Walker, Osgood, Richardson, and Ephross (1998) compared the attitudes of the staff of long-term care facilities with those of older people, including residents of nursing homes. More of the staff than older people considered sexuality to be an important concern. However, the older people were more tolerant about homosexuals residing in nursing homes, and more older people thought the staff should facilitate access to erotica. On the other hand, more older people than the staff thought family members should be informed if residents formed a romantic attachment.

Although many long-term care institutions now provide privacy rooms to facilitate the sexual enjoyment of cognitively intact residents, there is little evidence on the outcome of such initiatives. The barriers to overcome include not only the attitudes of the staff but also those of the residents, whose attitudes may reflect feelings of benevolence, envy, or concern toward those having romantic liaisons.

Health, Life, and the Self

A premise of **psychoimmunology** is that attitudes affect disease processes. Herbert and Cohen (1996) summarized the current state of knowledge with a model in which:

1. Psychological states affect central nervous system activity, hormonal responses, and behaviour.
2. These have effects on the immune system.
3. The immune system affects disease susceptibility.

An implication of the model is that positive attitudes may promote health and hasten recovery from disease. Positive attitudes are important to seniors' descriptions of successful aging. Christine Knight (1999) asked seniors from the same communal complex to nominate their peers who exemplified successful aging. When subsequently asked to describe the seniors with most nominations, the overarching theme was positive attitude. Although some frequently nominated seniors had poor health or physical disability, their peers considered these conditions not to impede successful aging. These findings affirm the importance older people attach to positive attitudes.

Attitudes toward Health.

Manulife Financial (1999) recently sponsored a Canadian study of health attitudes and behaviour. This telephone survey included a representative sample of 1,000 Canadians 18 years and older living in households, with a response rate weighted for regional demography exceeding 60 percent (Stones, 2001). Findings from the survey add to knowledge about the attitudes of Canadians toward their health.

When asked about diseases considered the biggest health threat in the new millennium, people of all ages ranked cancer, stress-related illness, and cardiovascular disease (i.e., heart disease and stroke) as the most threatening (Figure 6.5). Figure 6.5 also shows differences across cohorts. Compared with younger people, the oldest cohort (65 years and older) considered cardiovascular disease a higher threat and acquired immune deficiency syndrome (AIDS) a lower threat. These findings are consistent with age differences in disease susceptibility. Within the oldest cohort, men thought cardiovascular disease to be the biggest threat, but women thought cancer more threatening. This gender difference is opposite in direction from disease-specific mortality rates for older men and women living in developed countries—Murray and Lopez (1996) report that more men than women over 60 years die of cancer, and more women than men die of cardiovascular diseases.

The Manulife study measured subjective ratings of health relative to age peers. The findings showed that older people rated their subjective health as highly as those younger, with no differences between men and women. The absence of cohort differences is consistent with other findings. Health Canada (2000) reported that 78 percent of seniors described their health as good, very good, or excellent. The AARP (1999) survey similarly showed that just over 80 percent of people aged 45+ years evaluated their health as good, very good, or excellent, without major differences because of cohort or gender. Kozma, Stones, and McNeil (1991) noted that ratings of perceived health were high among older Canadians. These findings confirm that most older people evaluate their health positively. In addition, other research suggests that subjective health relates to objective health outcomes. Seniors with negative attitudes toward their health made more visits to physicians and used prescribed medications more frequently than

Figure 6.5 ILLNESS CONSIDERED THE BIGGEST HEALTH THREAT OF THIS MILLENNIUM BY AGE AND GENDER

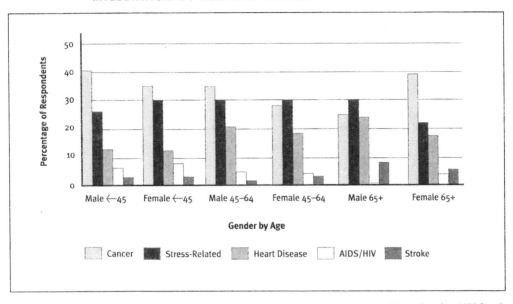

Source: Based on AARP (1999).

did seniors with positive attitudes (Sita, Stones, Csank, Knight, & Gauron, in press).

Another index relevant to health attitudes measured in the Manulife survey concerns the frequency of worrying about health. The findings showed no differences across cohorts, although women worried more than men at all ages. The gender difference may result from such conditions as anxiety (McDougall, 1998) or depression (Weissman et al., 1996) that tend to affect women more frequently than men. Analysis of the Manulife data supports this interpretation, with more women than men who endorsed a depression item that correlated with worrying about health.

Attitudes towards Life.

Older people generally have positive attitudes toward their life as a whole. The most frequent responses to global measures of happiness and **life satisfaction** are "happy" or "very happy." These global measures also show the following:

1. Moderate stability across the adult life span (Mussen, Honzik, & Eichorn, 1982; Stones et al, 1995);
2. Limited influence because of demographics, such as gender and socioeconomic status (Kozma, Stones, & McNeil, 1990);

3. Substantial influence on measures of happiness because of genetic variation—Lykken & Tellegen (1996) estimated that nearly 80 percent of the variation in stable evaluations of well being is because of genetics.

The AARP (1999) survey of people aged 45 years and older provides further information about attitudes toward quality of life. The survey included a 10-step ladder, on which respondents indicated their standings in the past (five years ago), present, and future (five years hence). This measure is similar to the one developed in Canada by Schonfield (1973). The findings indicate that all cohorts and both genders gave higher ratings for the past compared with the present and the present compared with the future. The respondents also indicated that health, vigour, physical activity, and good spirits were necessary to retain quality of life. Another recent study examined factors that impede quality of life (Cutler & Whitelaw, 2001)—concerns about finances, chronic pain, memory loss, health support, and being useless.

An issue studied extensively in Canada concerns the causal direction of the relationship between global attitudes (e.g., happiness, life satisfaction) and specific life evaluations (e.g., satisfactions with respect to health, housing, finances, and the self). The global and specific measures generally show a moderate correlation, that is, they are somewhat related to one another, but the direction of causality continues to provoke debate (Stones, Hadjistravopoulos, Tuuko, & Kozma, 1995). Two opposing models are the bottom-up and top-down. The **bottom-up model** assumes causation to proceed from the specific to the global, whereas the **top-down model** assumes global attitudes to influence specific life evaluations. Although the bottom-up model continues to influence Canadian research (i.e., we think this way) (Michalos, Hubley, Zumbo, & Hemmingway, 2001), directional comparison with empirical data generally finds the top-down version receives more support (Stones & Kozma, 1986; Kozma, Stone, & Stones, 1997, 2000). The top-down model is also more consistent with findings on the enduring stability and heritability of attitudes.

Attitudes toward the Self.

It is probably true that most people of any age like themselves most of the time and have a good sense of **self**. Findings of positive relationships between self-esteem and global life attitudes support this proposition (Kozma, Stones, & McNeil, 1991). Most people also like how they look (AARP, 2001). However, when asked to rate looks and feelings, compared with age peers, interesting cohort differences emerge (Montepare & Lachman, 1989).

With respect to physical attractiveness, a national telephone survey of over 2,000 Americans found mean rating by men and women to be 6.4 on a 10-point scale (AARP, 2001). These findings suggest that most people think themselves attractive but not too attractive, with no differences between the genders. When asked to give the age of peak attractiveness, the mean lay within the middle-age span but was somewhat older in older respondents. This finding suggests that as people age, their attitudes towards physical beauty shift in a chronologically upward direction.

Subjective age refers to ratings of looks and feelings relative to age peers. Findings by Montepare and Lachman (1989) showed a trend for subjective age to become younger as chronological age advanced. Teenagers had a subjective age older than their years, whereas middle-aged and older respondents evaluated themselves as subjectively younger than their age. This trend was stronger in women than men. Although subsequent research invariably replicated Montepare and Lachman's (1989) cohort effect, not all studies found a gender difference. Sata, Shimonka, Nakazato, and Kawaai (1997) recently replicated both effects in Japanese over 1,800 respondents aged 8 to 92 years. This finding shows that subjective age transcends the North American culture. The change from an older to a younger subjective age occurred for males in their early 20s and for females in their teens. Findings from Manulife's survey in Canada showed differences with age but not gender (Stones, 2000). Compared with the youngest cohort, more men and women in the older cohorts rated themselves subjectively younger than their age. Other findings from these studies indicate that subjectively older respondents reported greater distress (e.g., depression, low self-esteem, low life satisfaction, poor health, or fear of aging) than those subjectively younger.

An interesting insight from the findings on subjective age concerns an implicit agist bias among respondents beyond young adulthood. The majority of middle-aged and older people rated themselves as younger than their peers. Is this a favourable evaluation? Heady and Wearing (1998) refer to a **sense of relative superiority** to explain why most people evaluate themselves more favourably than others their age. If rating yourself as younger than your age implies a favourable self-evaluation, then, by default, a self-perception of yourself as older than your age is unfavourable. If Heady and Wearing (1988) are correct in assuming that unfavourable evaluations connote a sense of relative inferiority, then middle-aged and older people evaluate older age with a negative bias.

CHAPTER SUMMARY

The definition of attitude is a tendency to evaluate an object with favour or disfavour. Although attitudes have implications for behaviour, the relationship is stronger with respect to behaviour across a range of situations, than with behaviour in any specific situation subject to other influences.

Researchers have studied attitudes toward older people more frequently than the attitudes of older people. The term used to describe stereotyped attitudes toward older people is *agism*.

Key ideas to remember from this chapter include:

- Although some researchers argue that agism is not a pervasive phenomenon, the evidence suggests otherwise. There is evidence for agist attitudes in such diverse fields as literature and the arts, health care, legislature, and humour. These attitudes are mostly negative. Although negative agist attitudes may have limited consequences for specific behaviour toward an older person in a specific situation, attitudes do contribute toward policies toward older people as a collective entity. An example was the poor treatment of seniors in health care, where until recent times they were a neglected minority. Gee and Gutman (2000) conclude that although the health care system is now more sympathetic to older patients, agism still contributes to health policy by blaming population aging for the present and future ills of the health care system itself.
- Studies of the attitudes of elderly persons include those toward elder abuse, sexuality, health, life and the self. Elder abuse and neglect refer to behaviour toward older people by those in positions of trust. Attitudes toward elder abuse show reasonable consistency throughout society but differ somewhat among different professions, with differences also noted with respect to minority group membership and age. Compared with younger people, older people generally rate examples of elder abuse as lower in severity. This finding is consistent with other research showing attitudes lower in extremity when rating an "in group" rather than an "out group" with seniors belonging to the former and young people to the latter when rating examples of elder abuse for severity.
- Because older people evaluate elder abuse in a less harsh manner, compared with young people employed in helping professions, they may be less inclined to report instances to the relevant authorities. Research in Montreal suggested that education about elder abuse contributes to changing such attitudes to a level more typical of that of professionals (Lithwick, Stones, & Reis, 1998).
- Until recently, sexuality in later life was a taboo topic. It was not a suitable topic for discussion in polite company and was ignored by the research community. The past decade witnessed an explosion of interest, with the potency-enhancing drug *Viagra* becoming one of the most prescribed medications. Although sexual behaviours, thoughts, and desires decline with age, particularly among women, the research indicates that interest remains intact for most people to a very advanced age. The ratings of sexual satisfaction also remain high.
- Attitudes regarding health, life satisfaction, and oneself show minimal change with age. These findings suggest that contrary to agist myths, the majority of older people retain positive attitudes about themselves and their life situation, despite decrements in their health and functional capabilities.

KEY TERMS

Attitude, **(p. 153)**

Belief, **(p. 153)**

Convergent validity, **(p. 154)**

Discriminant validity, **(p. 154)**

Agism, **(p. 156)**

Pacification, **(p. 157)**

Violence, **(p. 158)**

Abuse, **(p. 159)**

Institutional residence, **(p. 164)**

Sexuality, **(p. 165)**

Health, **(p. 168)**

Psychoimmunology, **(p. 169)**

Life satisfaction, **(p. 171)**

Bottom-up model, **(p. 172)**

Top-down model, **(p. 172)**

Self, **(p. 172)**

Subjective age, **(p. 173)**

Sense of relative superiority, **(p. 173)**

STUDY QUESTIONS

1. Define the term *attitude*. Discuss the nature of relationships between attitudes and behaviour.

2. Is agism a pervasive problem in Canada?

3. What are the best ways to reduce agism?

4. Do older people have similar attitudes toward elder abuse as younger people? Critically evaluate the evidence.

5. Discuss the common belief that older people have little interest in sexuality.

6. Do older people have negative attitudes toward their health and their lives?

SUGGESTED READINGS

Hudson, M.F. & Carlson, J.R. (1999). Elder abuse: Expert and public perspectives on its meaning. *Journal of Elder Abuse and Neglect, 9*, 77-97.

Kozma, A., Stones, M.J., & McNeil, J.K. (1991). *Subjective Well-Being in Later Life*. Toronto, Ontario: Butterworths.

Matthias, R. E., Lubben, J. E., Atchison, K. A., & Schweitzer, S. O. (1997). Sexual activity and satisfaction among very old adults: Results from a community-dwelling Medicare population survey. *Gerontologist, 37*, 6-14.

Olson, J.M., Vernon, P.E., Aitken Harris, J, & Jang, K.L. (2001). The heritability of attitudes. *Journal of Personality and Social Psychology, 80*, 845-860.

Physical Competence and Aging

Learning Objectives

In this chapter, you will learn about:

- Ways to distinguish levels of physical competence.
- Ways to measure physical competence at the respective levels.

- How age and historical changes affect physical competence.
- Age differences in different sports and the implications for understanding age effects on elite physical performance.

Introduction

This chapter examines physical competence and aging. Physical changes with age occur at levels ranging from the cellular to whole body functions. Not all such changes occur because of the simple passage of time. Age changes may also reflect the effects of disease, disability, lifestyle, and the environment. Rowe and Kahn (1987) were among many who emphasize the significance of these distinctions, which are evident not just from comparison of individuals with different life histories and lifestyles but also from differences between successive cohorts. The effects of age and cohort relate not only to physical functioning but also to physical structure, with height providing an instructive example.

Shephard acknowledged that people lose height with age mainly because of compression of the intervertebral disks and increasing kyphosis (i.e., curvature) of the spine (Shephard, 1978: 20-22). However, the reasons you are probably taller than your grandparents of the same gender include not only your youth. Any tall person will tell you that people in medieval times were shorter than people today; how else could they fit into those suits of armour in European museums, which look made for children, not fighting men! Because of improved living conditions and diet, Shephard (1978) commented that height increased by one centimetre per decade in Britain during the 20th century, which, in terms of absolute magnitude, approximates the loss of height per decade after 40 years of age.

Sport provides numerous examples of age and cohort effects on physical performance. In 1954, Roger Bannister became the first athlete to run a mile in less than four minutes. He was 25 years old. Although Bannister stopped running after an accident in the 1970s, an algorithm provided by the World Association of Veteran Athletes (WAVA, 1994) suggests his time today (i.e., at age 73 years) would be around 5 minutes and 45 seconds had he continued to train and compete. In other words, the estimated loss in performance by an elite miler over the past half-century is approximately 20 seconds per decade. Contrast this estimate with the changes in the world mile record over the same period, which now stands at 3 minutes 43 seconds. The change over 50 years is less than the estimated intra-individual change per decade.

The reasons why athletes today perform at higher levels than their predecessors include advances in training and technique and participation by athletes from countries previously not much involved in international sports. Bannister's training for his world record attempt was minimal, compared with that of modern milers, with an emphasis on speed rather than endurance. Endurance training conditions a runner to run longer distances at a fast pace. Consequently, it was not surprising when Daniel Komen broke the eight-minute barrier for running two miles in 1997—a pace equal to Bannister's but over twice the distance. Like most of the current male world record holders in longer-distance running, Komen hailed from Africa. On a much lesser level, an author of this book (Michael Stones) broke a personal record by completing just over eight miles to win the United

States one-hour race-walk in 1979. Twenty-two years later, the top three finishers in the United States two-hour race-walk completed over 16 miles at the same pace as Stones but maintained twice as long. The reason once again was probably a greater commitment to endurance training. These examples give credence to the premise that the importance of the subject matter of gerontology includes age change within the context of cohort and historical trends.

Gerontologists study physical competence to answer questions about what people of different ages usually do or are capable of doing. The term for what people usually do is **usual competence**. Developmental research on usual competence attempts to elucidate influences on time-dependent abilities during specified periods in history. The term for what humans are capable of doing is **elite competence**. Research on this topic tries to provide an understanding of the limiting factors on performance as people age. Typical questions posed by researchers within these two paradigms include the following:

1. What are the usual levels of competence for people of different ages?
    *   What kinds of measurement tools are useful?
    *   What influences usual competence at different ages?
    *   What types of intervention are of benefit?
2. What are the maximal levels of competence shown by people of different ages?
    *   What are the appropriate paradigms for research?
    *   What are the barriers to maximal competence at different ages?

This chapter examines both usual and elite competences in physical performance. Although all human performance involves some kind of movement—blinking an eye, pressing a key, lifting an object, running a marathon—the performances described in this chapter are those that involve the larger muscle groups and require energy expenditure beyond the resting level.

Usual Competence

The study of usual competence proceeds from either of two conceptual perspectives. The first involves a *typological* grouping of people according to level of competence. This approach is useful in the applied field because people of different abilities

*   face different kinds of challenges;
*   require different tools to provide sensitive measurement; and
*   need different kinds of intervention.

The second perspective proceeds from a classification of process, rather than of people. A popular *type of aging* model tries to differentiate change because of the passage of time from other influences on competence.

The Typological Perspective

Spirduso (1995: 338-355) described a hierarchical approach to understanding and measuring physical competence in old and very old people. She identified five groups on the basis of differences in competence.

Physically dependent people are unable to perform some or all of the basic activities of daily living, such as walking, bathing, dressing, and eating. People in this category need assistance with the basic tasks of life, regardless of whether they live independently or in an institution. The reasons for physical dependency include debilitating physical illness and progressive neurological disorders, such as Alzheimer's disease and related dementias.

Several Canadian provinces routinely use versions of the Resident Assessment Instrument (RAI) to measure relevant functions (Hirdes, et al., 2000). The RAI tools for long-term care and home care provide sensitive measurement at this level of competence when completed by qualified and trained assessors. These tools have an advantage over alternative tools for assessment because their design incorporated guidelines for care planning. Consequently, intervention can follow directly from measurement. The development of the RAI tools is under the auspices of an international body called *InterRAI*, in which John Hirdes, of the University of Waterloo, and Catherine Berg, of McGill University, act as Canadian representatives.

Physically frail people are able to perform the basic activities of daily living but lack the competence to undertake a full range of instrumental activities, such as housekeeping, cooking, and shopping. They are frequently homebound and require help from relatives or professional caregivers to remain independent. Their **frailty** may result from chronic or acute diseases, accidents, and lifestyle. Spirduso (1995) reported that the predictors of physical disability most frequently reported in research include hypertension and arthritis, with cardiac disorders, cancer, bone injury, diabetes, obesity, smoking, and a high alcohol intake sometimes reported. Assessment at this level includes the RAI for home care, other measures of activities of daily living, and measures of adaptive mobility (e.g., Kemen & Suurmeijer, 1990; Tinetti, 1986). The main purpose of intervention is to postpone further deterioration.

Balance provides a useful example of the difficulties encountered when trying to measure specific competences in physically frail people. Balance is an important skill because poor balance contributes to falls that may result in premature morbidity and mortality in older people. Although the time a person can stand on one foot provides a common measure of static balance in healthy adults (Stones & Kozma, 1987), it is beyond the capabilities of most frail people. Although an "easier" task involves the measurement of sway in bipedal balance (i.e., standing on two feet), Lord, Clark, and Webster (1991) found 3 percent of residents in a hostel for the aged to be unable to balance unaided on a hard floor and a further 20 percent to show such incapacity on a compliant (i.e., soft) floor. Tinetti (1986) described an index more sensitive to the range of competences of the physically frail by measuring balance while sitting in or rising from a chair.

People classified as **physically independent** have competence in the basic and instrumental activities of daily living and are able to undertake light physical work and recreation (e.g., walking, gardening, golf). The majority of older people belong to this category. They do not suffer from debilitating disease of sufficient severity to threaten independence, but most of them neither participate in fitness activities nor concern themselves unduly with good health habits. Because such people are able to function independently, such measures as the RAI tools and activities of daily living tests fail to provide sensitive discrimination. A Canadian tool appropriate for assessment at this level is the *Standardized Test of Fitness* (1981), which is similar to the AAHPERD (American Association for Health, Physical Education, Recreation, and Dance) field test developed in the United States (Osness, 1987). Such tests measure competences related to balance, endurance, flexibility, and strength. Intervention based on findings from such tests aims to improve physical fitness.

Another perspective on measurement at this level (and beyond) takes account of a broader range of functions than measured by tests of fitness. The concept of biological or functional age originated in Canada with the work of Murray (1951) at Dalhousie University. Researchers in other countries soon incorporated this concept into their own research (Heron & Chown, 1967; Borkan & Norris, 1980). The aim was to "find out how old a person *really* is" through assessment of physical and cognitive functions while statistically controlling for chronological age. Applications envisaged for the concept included medical decisions (e.g., adjustment of the dosage of anesthetics administered to elderly people during surgery based on biological age) and the provision of an alternative to chronological age for decisions about mandatory retirement.

Although Costa and McCrae (1980) offered a scathing criticism of the early functional age research (e.g., because the model implies that aging is a unitary process, the statistical methods were controversial, and the anticipated rates of aging unconfirmed), other researchers refined the concept and its measurement. Borkan and Norris (1980) developed functional age profiles that discriminated between survivors and those deceased in longitudinal research. Botwinick, West, and Storandt (1978) were similarly able to predict survivorship, with a composite functional age index providing higher prediction than any component measure. Webster and Logie (1976) used a functional age battery to discriminate between women with exceptional health versus those with average health. Stones and Kozma (1988) found a simple four-function index (i.e., flexibility, vital capacity or lung volume, balance, and coding) to have high reliability and to show greater sensitivity to the effects of physical fitness training than any component measure. They also reported on a re-analysis of earlier data on six measures of psychological and physical fitness (Heron & Chown, 1967) that provided a reliable index.

So, how useful are functional age batteries? Spirduso (1995) concluded that such batteries have neither improved much on chronological age as a descriptor of the aging process nor proved capable of predicting rates of aging. On the positive side, she also concluded that such batteries were successful in discriminating groups differing in health and survival status, being sensitive to improved health behaviours. Although it is unlikely that functional age will replace chronological age in societal decision making (e.g., about retirement) in the near future, the batteries' use in research and for medical prognosis is likely to continue.

Physically fit individuals exercise two or more times weekly for reasons of enjoyment, health, and well being. They generally have good health habits, do not smoke, and refrain from excessive alcohol intake (Spirduso, 1995).

Measures of physical **fitness** for people within this category include field tests, such as the *Standardized Test of Fitness* and AAHPERD tests. Although these tests are relatively inexpensive to administer, there are limitations to the accuracy of the information they provide. The measurement of endurance fitness provides an example. Chodzko-Zajko (1994) noted that laboratory-based exercise stress tests provide the *gold standard* measure of endurance (i.e., cardio-respiratory) fitness in people who are physically fit. Such tests require a person to exercise to or at near maximal capacity, with endurance fitness indexed by maximal oxygen uptake. The field tests measure endurance fitness based on submaximal exercising while (for example) stepping up and down or walking a half-mile. Although such estimates are reasonably accurate at younger ages, there are indications that the algorithms underestimate the levels from laboratory measures in older people (O'Hanley, Ward, Zwirren, McCarron, Ross, & Rippe, 1987).

The main purpose of intervention for people within this category is to encourage them to continue to **exercise**. Larkin and Kipness were among the first in Canada to develop an exercise program for older people. This program, *Fitness with Fun and Fellowship* (3F), started in St. John's, Newfoundland, in 1977 and continues to this day with an enrollment of several hundred participants. As the name indicates, the aims of the program include making exercise an enjoyable experience within a socially supportive context. The participants exercise in groups graded according to fitness, with the context enriched by background music chosen to be lively and uplifting. The fitness instructors offer encouragement and support to all participants, with social support enhanced by many social events throughout the year.

The reasons why people terminate participation in exercise programs include illness, life changes, and personal factors. Stacey, Kozma, and Stones (1985) found participants who dropped out of the 3F program to be relatively unhappy and with high-trait anxiety. This finding is not altogether surprising, but unfortunate in light of evidence that regular physical exercise can contribute to improvement in feelings of well being (King, Taylor, & Haskwell, 1993).

Physically elite people are those who score at the highest fitness levels for their age (Spirduso, 1995). They *exercise* most days and many compete in age-class or open-class athletic competitions. These older athletes enjoy sport, believe it to be beneficial, and relish the challenges of competition. For many of them, later life athleticism is a continuation of life-long habits of competitive physical activity.

The Type of Aging Perspective

This perspective classifies processes rather than people. The **type of aging model** tries to differentiate change because of the passage of time from other influences on competence and habitual performance. The term used to denote change attributable only to age is an **age intrinsic effect**, with other normative effects often associated with age termed *age extrinsic*.

The type of **aging** model described by Stones, Kozma, and Hannah (1990) includes the four levels shown in Table 7.1. Primary aging includes two levels, termed by Rowe and Kahn as *successful* and *usual* aging. Successful aging refers to changes owing only to the passage of time (i.e., age intrinsic change). Usual aging refers to nonpathological changes commonly observed within a population but brought about by lifestyle or life situation. Examples include the loss in endurance fitness with age, which Smith and Gilligan (1983) estimated to be 50 percent because of age and 50 percent because of disuse of endurance capabilities. Similarly, Spirduso (1980) found old racquet sport players to retain faster reaction times than nonathletes, which Stones and Kozma (1988) interpreted as showing the effects of practice on speed of reactions. The third level of secondary aging refers to changes because of chronic disease, and the fourth level of tertiary aging has relevance to impending mortality.

Although this model is conceptually simple, the respective contributions of age-intrinsic and age-extrinsic effects are subject to continued revision. An example is skin wrinkling, formerly considered a largely age-intrinsic effect but now known to show strong effects because of exposure to the sun and other factors (Warren, et al., 1991). Another concern is that age-intrinsic and age-extrinsic effects may be interactive, rather than additive. Osteoporosis provides an example of pathological bone loss, probably brought about by a combination of age-intrinsic loss of bone mass exacerbated by factors related to inadequate nutrition and low

Table 7.1 TYPES OF AGING

CLASSIFICATION	SUBCLASSIFICATION	ALSO KNOWN AS	INFLUENCES
Primary	Successful	Healthy	Age
	Usual		Lifestyle
Secondary			Disease/disability
Tertiary		Terminal drop	Impending mortality

Source: Based on conceptualization by the author.

physical activity. A further limitation is that some chronic illnesses are either underdiagnosed (e.g., hypertension) or not diagnosed until the symptoms are relatively advanced (e.g., Alzheimer's disease), both of which may confound practical applications of the model. However, none of these concerns discredits the model's intent to provide clarity to distinctions among the processes contributing to change in time-dependent abilities, the understanding of which continues to evolve as new evidence accumulates.

Usual Competence and Performance at Different Age Levels

The most extensive studies of age, gender, and physical activity effects on physical competence in this country used data from the *Canada Fitness Survey* (Kozma & Stones, 1990; Kozma, Stones, & Hannah, 1991). The tests in this survey measured the number of pushups and situps within one minute, endurance fitness by a stepping test, handgrip **strength**, and trunk forward flexion. The ages of the more than 6,000 participants ranged from the 20s to the 60s. The findings indicated most loss of competence with age for the pushup and situp tests, followed by the step test, followed by handgrip strength and flexibility, with generally greater losses by males than females.

These findings accord with a model proposed by Stones and Kozma (1986) to account for age trends in athletic performance. This model suggests that the extent of age loss in physical competence is greater for activities with higher rates of expenditure of the available **energy**. The available energy derives from different sources depending on the duration of activity, with the energy available for a one-minute task estimated to be 35 percent of that available for 10 seconds of maximal effort (Astrand & Rodahl, 1977: Table 9.1). The pushup and situp tests expend energy at a high rate because they engage a large muscle mass in near-maximal effort for a full minute. The stepping test also involves a large muscle mass but the effort is submaximal. Handgrip strength involves contraction of a small muscle mass for a very brief interval, and flexibility taxes energy only minimally. Consequently, the findings support the Stones and Kozma (1986) model. However, a caution about the scope of the model—that it emphasizes power to the exclusion of other facets of activity (e.g., degree of neuromuscular coordination)—is worth bearing in mind.

A large study in the United States also provides support for Stones and Kozma's (1986) model. Kovar and LaCroix (1987) measured five work-related physical activities in a sample of nearly 10,000 participants aged 55 to 74 years:

- Mobility—walking a quarter-mile and walking up 10 stairs without resting.
- Endurance—standing and sitting for two hours.
- Freedom of movement—reaching up overhead and reaching out to shake hands.

- Fine motor movement—grasping with fingers.
- Strength—stooping, crouching, or kneeling, and lifting or carrying 10 or 25 pounds.

Fifty-eight percent of the sample group completed all the tasks successfully. Of the remainder, the proportion that had trouble or was unable to complete the tasks increased with age and was higher for women than for men. The tasks associated with the steepest loss of competence with age were lifting a 25-pound. weight and standing on two feet for two hours. Of all the tasks, these two require the highest rates of energy expenditure over the short term and long term, respectively. Compared with tests associated with lesser energy expenditure or that tax neuromuscular coordination, older people show the greatest loss of competence in activities requiring the highest expenditure of available power.

Competence refers to what people can do; **performance** to what they actually do. A number of methods are available to measure habitual levels of physical performance in people of different ages. These measures include standardized retrospective interviews (van der Suiijs, 1972), retrospective activity questionnaires (Morris, Chave, Adam, Sirey, & Epstein, 1956), and current time budget diaries (Durin & Passmore, 1967). Indexes of habitual performance derived from such measures usually consist of the sum of the products of the time expended in different activities and their corresponding energy costs. Expressions of the latter include rates of energy expenditure (i.e., kilocalories, kilojoules), oxygen consumption, relative load (i.e., oxygen consumption compared with the maximal oxygen intake), multiples of basal metabolic rate (METs), and changes in heart rate. A Canadian measure of physical performance indexed the frequency of exercising enough to "get sweaty," with findings of moderate reliability and correlations with fitness indexes (Godin, Jobin, & Bouillon, 1986).

Levels of habitual physical performance by people of different ages differ depending on the period of history when the researchers collected the data. Andersen Masironi, Rutenfranz, and Seliger (1978) reported that before 1970, the time spent in demanding physical activity and the total energy cost of that activity declined with age in each gender. This trend was evident in several countries (e.g., Czechoslovakia, Norway, Sweden, United States), and associated with a substitution of less strenuous pursuits (e.g., walking, gardening) with more strenuous pursuits (e.g., sport) after young adulthood. Such declines in habitual performance with age have implications for physical competence. Shephard (1969) compared the then-current findings on endurance fitness in the United States with the 1938 findings by Robinson. The comparison showed lower levels of fitness in the more recent data, which Shephard (1969) attributed to lower levels of strenuous physical activity in the decades immediately following World War II.

Findings after 1980 show higher levels of physical activity among older people, compared with earlier surveys. Stephens, Craig, and Ferris (1986) reported on the frequencies of the participants in the *Canada Fitness Survey* classified as "adequately active" (i.e., people whose activity is sufficiently frequent and strenuous to promote endurance fitness). Using data from the same survey, Kozma, Stones, and Hannah (1991) reported on the frequencies of people classified as "active" (i.e., people who regularly engage in physical exercise for at least three hours per week). The findings indicate that although few older people fell within the "adequately active" category, more people aged over 60 years were "active" than people aged 40 to 59 years. Although a probable contributing factor was the *ParticipAction* campaign sponsored by the federal government to promote increased physical activity in Canada during the 1970s and 1980s, findings from other countries likewise show relatively high levels of exercising by older people. The examples include findings from Japan, where Harada (1994) reported higher rates of at least weekly participation in exercise or sport by people aged over 60 years, compared with middle-aged people. A prolongation of such trends bodes well for the retention of physical competence as 60-year-olds continue to age.

Elite Competence

The only people to possess elite competence fall within Spirduso's (1995) *physically elite* category, which she estimates to include 5 percent of the population at each age level. So, why study elite competence if it is so rare? There are several reasons:

1. We study many conditions that pertain to small segments of the population with the hope of deriving benefit from the knowledge gained. Such conditions in later life include Alzheimer's disease and related dementia, which affects an estimated 8 percent of the Canadian population aged above 64 years, and elder abuse, with an estimated Canadian prevalence of 4 percent.
2. The study of elite competence can clarify the processes of usual competence, including factors that promote and hinder competence as people age.
3. Because elite physical performers are active, fit, and healthy, comparisons of their physical performances at different ages are more likely to reflect age intrinsic trends—uncontaminated by disuse and secondary aging effects—than comparisons of the same activities by non-elite persons.
4. The study of past and present trends in peak performance may facilitate prediction of the absolute limits of physical performance as people age.

Research on elite competence gained impetus from studies of games, such as chess. Chase and Simon's (1973) research with chess players of different proficiencies elucidated cognitive processes contributing to superior performance. The same dominant paradigm of comparing people at different levels of proficiency found application in studies of occupation, recreation, and sports. A predominant paradigm for the study of age trends in elite physical competence is the analysis of performance in sports.

The study of age trends in sports is a recent phenomenon made possible by increasing numbers of older participants during the past three decades and by the emergence of national and international governing bodies in sports, such as track and field events and swimming. These governing bodies compile records for various age-classes of athletes with the same rigour as the Olympic body and the associations responsible for screening national and world records in open-class competition. Spirduso (1995) states that most people within her *physically elite* category are active competitors in sports; moreover, it is because of their training and competition that they are physically elite. Consequently, the study of sports performance enables an analysis of what they do best.

Distinctions within Sports Performance

Skilled performance in sports involves at least five dimensions, two of which relate to structural parameters made explicit by the rules of that sport. The other components have relevance to level of performance within those rules.

Individual versus Team Sports.

Sports always pit one **athlete** against others or one team against others. Such activities as boxing, squash, and snooker are individual sports that pair two athletes in direct competition. Although some such athletes may represent a larger team (e.g., Lennox Lewis won the Olympic heavyweight boxing championship as a member of the Canadian Olympic team), the defining feature of an individual sport is that the winner is always the best performing athlete, regardless of any team affiliation. Individual sports with more than two athletes per event include track and field competitions, swimming, and motor racing. Although such events theoretically pit each athlete against all the others, this provision is not always true in practice. The exceptions include events within such sports as cycling and motor racing. Competitors in the Tour de France cycle race belong to teams with a designated star. The team expects its supporting members to assist the star, not to cycle for personal glory.

The defining feature of team sports is that the winner is a team of two or more people, rather than a single competitor. The active members may be fixed (e.g., doubles tennis) or variable (e.g., ice hockey) throughout an event and may serve different functions on the team (e.g., attacker, defender, goalkeeper). The winning performance may be an aggregate of individual performances (e.g., relay races) or the outcome of coordinated team effort (e.g., scoring more goals than the opposition).

Closed-Skill versus Open-Skill Sports.

This distinction relates to the quality versus the outcomes of physical activity. Judges evaluate the quality of movement in closed-skill sports against consensual criteria usually based on esthetics and difficulty. The aim of the athletes is to produce in competition a pattern of motion that excels against these criteria. Examples of individual closed-skill sports include figure skating, diving, and gymnastics. Synchronized swimming provides an example of a closed-skill team sport.

The measures of performance in open-skill individual sports include such dimensions as time (e.g., racing), distance (e.g., jumping, throwing), and weight (e.g., weight lifting). Other outcomes in individual and team sports include the number of points attained or goals scored according to the rules governing that sport.

In addition to differences in evaluation, closed- and open-skill sports differ in the relevance of the environment to performance. The organizers of closed-skill sports make every effort to ensure a uniform environment, regardless of the venue of the competition. Athletes in open-skill sports adapt their performance to accommodate variation in context. Such variation includes physical parameters, such as topography (e.g., golf) and climate (e.g., outdoor sports). Activity by the opponent usually provides the major source of contextual variation in open-skill events, with the competitors trying to introduce unexpected variation to outwit opponents.

Physical Effort.

Physical **effort** includes duration and intensity components, which involve different sources of energy. The energy provision for **endurance** activity—prolonged effort over an extended time—is *aerobic* in origin, with increased respiration supplying the oxygen necessary to sustain a higher rate of metabolism. The energy provision for brief strenuous effort is of *anaerobic* origin, meaning that it derives from within the muscle tissue without increased oxygenation.

Sports differ in their demands on energy. Long distance racing (e.g., cycling, running, skiing, swimming) emphasizes duration of effort, rather than intensity. Jumping, lifting, and throwing place the highest demands on intensity, with sprinting a little less. Boxing requires both endurance and strength, with the distribution of effort varying with time and position in team sports, such as basketball, soccer, and rugby. Some sports involve little physical effort. Frayne wrote about baseball that "except for the pitcher and catcher, nobody does much of anything for long periods but stand around and wait." (Frayne, 1990: 307). Cricket is similar. The lowest end of the physical effort continuum subsumes darts and table sports (e.g., billiards, snooker, pool) that require no strenuous physical effort at all.

Coordination.

All sports require a coordinated pattern of movements at the intrapersonal level, but only team sports involve interpersonal **coordination** among the members of a team. Intrapersonal coordination increases mainly through practice (e.g., golfers endlessly practise their swing), but every so often, an athlete introduces an improved pattern, which is subsequently copied by peers. Examples include Dick Fosbury, who introduced the famous "Fosbury flop" to high jumping in the 1968 Mexico City Olympics, and Mexican Daniel Bautista Rocha, who succeeded with a new style of race-walking at the 1976 Montreal Olympics.

Although intrapersonal coordination in closed-skill sports results in a fixed movement pattern, such coordination in open-skill sports contributes to adaptive motion. Archers adjust the angle of the arrow and pull on the bowstring, depending on the velocity and direction of the prevailing wind. Racing drivers vary their movements (e.g., steering, gear shifting) to maximize speed depending on immediate conditions, and jockeys ride different horses on different courses in different ways. Consequently, intrapersonal coordination in open-skill competitions serves to ensure a flexible range of responses to varying environments. All team sports require interpersonal coordination. The outcome of many a game depends on having a player in the right position at the right time. Coaches and managers assist the process of coordinating players, with their jobs at stake if the team's cohesion fails.

Strategy.

Closed-skill sports generally require minimal use of **strategy** in actual competition. The planning and practice for a simple or complex sequence of movements occur well before the event, in which the athlete tries to execute a display as nearly perfect as possible. Strategy in open-skill sports aims to maximize the athlete's options in the changing contexts of competitions. Some open-skill competitions, such as archery, darts, jumping, lifting, sprinting, throwing, and swimming, require low use of strategy. Actions by the opponents in such sports make little difference to the strategy deployed by any particular competitor, and many such events are of brief duration. Sports requiring a higher use of strategy are usually of prolonged duration, in which the opponent contributes to contextual change, and include most team sports.

Abernethy, Thomas, and Thomas (1993) hypothesized differences between high- and low-strategy tasks in the relative importance of knowledge, experience, and skill as performers advance from earlier adulthood to older age. In high-strategy sports, they hypothesized knowledge and experience to gain importance at the expense of skill. In low-strategy sports, they hypothesized experience to be most important and knowledge the least important, with skill occupying an intermediate position but declining in importance with age.

Age Differences in Different Sports

The preceding distinctions provide two ways to classify sports: (1) classification based on structure, and (2) classification based on the skills required. Classification based on skill is the more useful for inferences about age effects on sport performance. The four categories of skill are as follows:

1. Closed-skill individual and team sports for which the performance comprises a fixed form and sequence of movements.
2. Open-skill individual and team sports that require high effort but low strategy.
3. Open-skill individual and team sports requiring high strategy but low effort.
4. Open-skill individual and team sports involving both high effort and high strategy.

There are several ways to obtain inferences about age effects on sports performance based on comparison within or across categories:

1. Comparison of the ages of the youngest and oldest elite competitors.
2. The mean age at peak performance.
3. Statistical modelling of age-class records within categories.
4. Analysis of the career statistics of elite competitors.

None of these methods is definitive, and not all are applicable to all categories of sports (e.g., statistical modelling is appropriate only to sports that maintain age-class records). Consequently, the following discussion includes all the methods. It is also important to remember that records continue to be broken. The age trends reported in the following pages are current for today but may undergo modification (to a lesser or greater extent) in future decades.

Closed-Skill Sports.

Athletes in closed-skill sports attain peak performances when very young. Fu Mingxia of China never practised a full set of dives before becoming a member of the national junior team when aged 11 years. Less than three years later, she won the world championship and became the youngest Olympic champion in history. At the same 1992 Barcelona Olympics, a male Chinese diver won a gold medal at the age of 13 years. Elite gymnasts also peak when very young, with 14-year-olds regularly appearing in elite competitions. So do figure skaters. Tara Lipinski of the United States became the Olympic champion in 1998 at age 15 years. Her age was younger than that of another figure skater, Sonja Henie, who previously was the youngest Olympic champion in an individual event.

Elite athletes within this category often retain peak performance levels for a decade or more. Approximately 15 percent of Olympic triple gold medal winners (i.e., winners of the same event in three successive games) competed in closed-skill sports. However, few such athletes participate in elite competitions beyond the age of 30 years. Many elite skaters become professional entertainers during retirement. Gymnasts, such as former Olympic champion Olga Korbut, who enchanted the world during her competitive era, coach upcoming gymnasts when they retire. These examples illustrate compensation, wherein athletes teach others the skills they formerly practised.

Open-Skill Sports Requiring Effort Rather Than Strategy.

These sports include lifting (i.e., weight lifting and power lifting), rowing, swimming, and track and field events. Although cycling might also be included, cycle races involve more strategy than the other events within this category, with the winner rarely racing flat-out throughout the race. It is probably for this reason that age-class differences in cycling records tend to be lower than in the other sports (Spirduso, 1995).

The youngest world record holders and Olympic champions for sports in this category are swimmers, with ages in their teens or early 20s. Stones and Kozma (1995) noted the ages of world record holders in freestyle swimming were younger for longer distance (1,500 metres) than short distance (50 metres) events. They suggested that swimmers lose more competitiveness with age as the demands on endurance increase. Stones, Farrell, and Taylor (2001) noted a similar trend in runners. With the exception of the young race-walker Wan Yan, none of the youngest or oldest world record holders and Olympic champions competed in endurance events.

Comparison of age-class differences in national and world records provides a means to evaluate effects on performance associated with the duration and intensity of effort. Despite the methodological limitations associated with such comparisons (e.g., changes in training and motivation with age, variation in the number of competitors at different ages and over time, extrapolation mainly from cross-sectional trends), the trends show strong consistency over 20 years of study. These trends suggest that performance decreases with age depending on the duration and intensity of effort. Findings from swimming and track and field provide illustrations (Hartley & Hartley, 1984; Stones & Kozma, 1996).

More than 37,000 swimmers compete in events sanctioned by United States Masters Swimming. This organization ratifies and compiles age-class records at 50-metre, 100-metre, and 200-metre distances for each of freestyle, backstroke, breaststroke, and butterfly (with records also documented for longer freestyle events). Figures 7.1 and 7.2 express the 1999 age-class records for events no longer than 200 metres as multiples of the 1999 world open-class records. Because a multiple is a ratio of the age-class record to the world record, a multiple of 2 means that the record time by an older swimmer is twice the duration of the world record for that event. Figure 7.1 relates performance to age and race distance, with gender and stroke averaged out. Figure 7.2 relates performance to age and stroke, with gender and race distance averaged out. The figures do not provide separate plots for gender because the trends against distance and stroke are comparable, even though females have higher performance losses with age than males.

The figures show age differences in performance to vary with distance and stroke. Figure 7.1 shows the age differences to increase with race distance. The age-class records were higher multiples of the world record with each increase

Figure 7.1 USA AGE-CLASS SWIMMING RECORDS AS MULTIPLES OF WORLD OPEN-CLASS WORLD RECORDS (AVERAGED OVER GENDER AND STROKE)

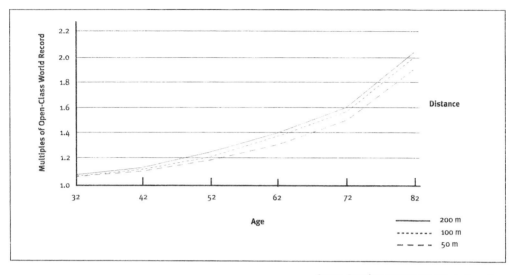

Source: Based on conceptualization by the author.

Figure 7.2 USA AGE-CLASS SWIMMING RECORDS AS MULTIPLES OF WORLD OPEN-CLASS WORLD RECORDS (AVERAGED OVER GENDER AND DISTANCE TO 200 METRES)

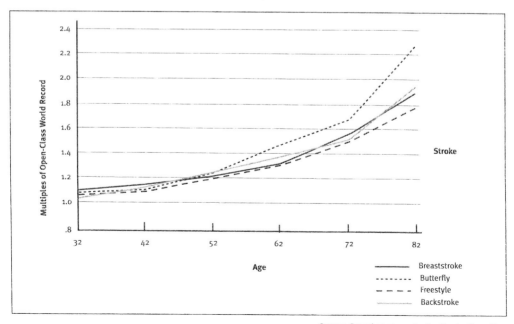

Source: Based on conceptualization by the author.

in race distance, with the size of the difference increasing with age. Because the longer events require more endurance than shorter events, these trends indicate a higher performance loss with age with increasing endurance demand. Figure 7.2 shows the age differences to relate to stroke, with the performance loss after middle age being highest in the butterfly and the lowest in freestyle swimming. Because the intensity of effort is highest in butterfly and lowest in the freestyle—as measured by oxygen uptake and the force exerted in tethered motion (Astrand & Rodahl, 1977, pp. 586–589)—these trends indicate that age differences increase with intensity of effort.

The preceding analyses of 1999 swimming records replicate those with records set 20 years earlier if analyzed in similar ways (cf. Hartley & Hartley, 1984; Stones & Kozma, 1984). Those findings also showed age differences to vary with distance and stroke. Findings with track and field records show similar consistency (Stones & Kozma, 1996), despite an ongoing improvement in performance over the decades. Although cross-sectional trends indicate a steeper age decrement than longitudinal trend, comparisons across events provide inferences that are similar despite this distinction (Stones & Kozma, 1982).

The First World Masters Track and Field Championship took place in Toronto in 1975, giving rise to the biennial World Veteran Games. These competitions regularly attract over 5,000 athletes from across the globe. The governing body is World Masters Athletics (formerly known as World Association of Veteran Athletes, or WAVA), which ratifies and compiles world and regional age-class records for men and women aged 35 years and older. Stones and Kozma (1981) provided the earliest comprehensive analysis of age differences in the WAVA records.

The following trends for age differences in track and field performance were noted:

1. Age decrement was lower in the sprints than in other short duration events, such as hurdle races of similar distance and the jumps and throws.
2. Age decrement was lower in the sprints than in longer running races.
3. Age decrement was lower in the race-walks than in running races of long duration.

These findings led them to hypothesize that performance decreases with age depending on the intensity and duration of the effort required. Their reasoning was as follows:

- The steps in sprinting require a low intensity of effort, compared with the leaps in hurdling, the take-off step in jumping, or the whole body thrust in throwing.
- The demands on endurance are lower in sprinting than in longer distance running.
- The steps in race-walking require a low intensity of effort, compared with those of running (i.e., race-walking steps are shorter and do not propel the body upward).

Stones and Kozma (1996) were able to replicate the age trends across events with subsequent age-class records. The same trends also persist in WAVA world age-class records for 2001. Figure 7.3 provides an illustration by showing the percentage loss in performance from age category 40 to 44 years to 60 to 64 years for representative events from the sprinting, jumping, long distance running, and race-walking categories. The 100 metres and long jump are short duration events that differ in the required intensity of effort, and the 10,000 metre walk and run are long duration events that differ in the required intensity of effort. Figure 7.3 indicates that performance loss, averaged over gender, is lower in the 100 metre sprint than in the long jump and 10,000 metre run, and lower in the 10,000 metre race-walk than the 10,000 metre run. These findings replicate those reported 20 years previously, providing impressive consistency that age decrement relates to the intensity and duration of effort.

The findings on running and race-walking are also important because they dispel two persistent myths about age effects on athletic performance. Conventional thinking suggests that endurance lasts better than speed as people age. Undergraduate gerontology texts continued to perpetuate this myth until very recently (Rybash, Roodin, & Santrock, 1991, pp. 92–95). Why else would so many middle-aged and older people compete in marathon and half-marathon races and so few in the sprints? The answer is that although older athletes compete in longer races, most are relative novices, few are elite, and fewer still break open-class records or place well in a field of elite but younger peers. These runners participate for joy, fitness, and health, not because age takes little toll on endurance.

Figure 7.3 PERCENTAGE PERFORMANCE LOSS FROM AGES 40 TO 60 YEARS OF AGE IN AGE-CLASS WORLD RECORDS FOR THE 100 METRES, LONG JUMP, AND 10,000 METRES

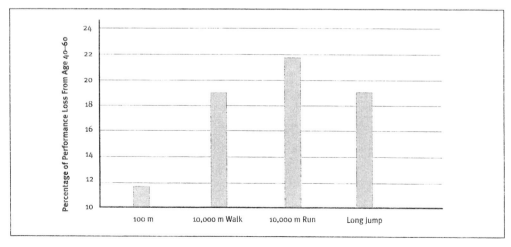

Source: Based on conceptualization by the author.

The second myth is that performance in long duration events declines with age because of declining endurance capability, lower training, and decreased motivation. The lower age decrements in race-walking than running are intriguing because both events tax endurance capabilities comparably (i.e., based on the percentage of maximal oxygen uptake while racing), and no evidence suggests that race-walkers differ from runners in training or motivation. Although rarely cited as a contributing factor to age decline, race-walking and running differ in the intensity of effort by the supporting leg as it kicks from the ground to propel the body forward. This intensity is lower in race-walking than in running because of the rule in walking that one foot must always maintain contact with the ground. A consequence is that race-walkers take shorter steps than do runners, with no upward propulsion of the body. Does the intensity of effort at the initiation of each new step have relevance to the size of age decrements? The following analysis suggests that it does.

WAVA (1994) published tables of times expressed as proportions of world age-class records for various race-walking and running events. These tables are widely used in track and field because they enable comparisons of performance across age, gender, and event groupings. The tables also include mathematical projections to ages beyond those for which ratified world records existed at compilation. Figure 7.4 provides estimates of the speed of running or race-walking 5,000 metres based on the WAVA tables. The lines in Figure 7.4 represent estimates for athletes performing at 90 percent of the age-class world record for that age, with the estimates at the older ages being projections, rather than based on actual

Figure 7.4 HYPOTHESIZED SPEED FOR THE 5,000-METRE RUN AND RACE-WALK BY MALE ELITE ATHLETES OF DIFFERENT AGES, AND ACTUAL SPEEDS BY WORLD RECORD HOLDERS AGED 90 TO 94 YEARS

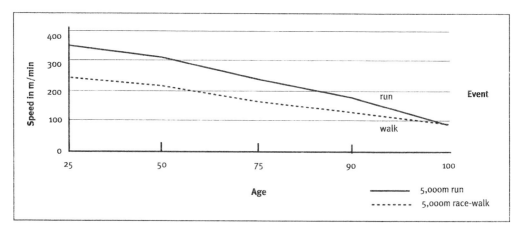

Source: Based on conceptualization by the author.

times. Although the hypothesized speeds not surprisingly get closer with age, given the lower age decrement in race-walking than running, what is surprising is that the estimates actually converge at age 100 years. However, is this projection realistic? The annotations to Figure 7.4 show that the hypothesized convergence underestimates the age at which it occurs. WAVA records for 2001 show the world record at age 90 to 94 years to be actually faster for the race-walk than the run at the 5,000 metre distance, and the speeds at the 10,000 metre distance to differ by only 10 metres per minute. In other words, very old elite athletes race-walk about as quickly as they run. The probable reason is that the steps of very old runners involve no greater thrust against the ground than those of race-walkers of comparable years.

Open-Skill Sports Requiring Strategy Rather Than Effort.

This category includes such sports as archery, baseball, bowling, cricket, equestrianism, fencing, golf, motor racing, and yachting. Although competitors in such sports may become elite performers in their teens, their careers often extend beyond those in any other category of sport. Galen Spencer won an Olympic gold medal in archery when aged 64 years. Spirduso (1995) noted that more than half the bowlers in the American Congress Hall of Fame who lived to be at least 60 years of age maintained high average scores over careers spanning 25 to 57 years. Stones, Farrell, and Taylor (2001) report that the youngest and oldest major league baseball players this century were respectively aged 15 and 59 years, with the peak ages for home runs and batting averages to be 27 years. Career spans in cricket are comparable with baseball. Seven Pakistanis played for their national team in their mid-teens, and four cricketers from different countries were members of their respective national teams when aged over 50 years. In equestrian sport, the youngest and oldest qualifiers for the National Finals Rodeo in the United States were 15 and 59 years, respectively. England's most famous jockey, Lester Piggot, won his first race at the age of 12 years and announced his retirement when aged 59 years, to end a career spanning 47 years. The career of Ivan Osiier in fencing lasted nearly as long; he competed in Olympic fencing competitions over a 40-year span. The same span applies to Magnus Konow in yachting, who competed in the Olympic Games for over 40 years. The youngest and oldest golfers to win a national championship (i.e., in Sri Lanka) were aged 12 and 54 years, respectively. Racing drivers attain prominence at a later age than in other sports within this category, but the oldest competitors and winners of Grand Prix motor racing events were aged in their 50s.

Spirduso (1995) reports findings on differences in golf performance between Professional Golf Association (PGA) tour players' records and those of players in the PGA Senior tour. The older golfers were comparable with the younger players in their putting ability and percent sand saves, but their driving distance averaged 10 yards less than that of the younger golfers. Consequently, the only deficiency because of age was that associated with a high intensity of effort.

Open-Skill Sports Requiring Strategy and Effort.

Individual sports ranging from boxing to tennis, and most of the popular team sports, require both high physical effort and a high use of strategy. Figure 7.5 illustrates the age extremes of elite participants in individual and team competitions, with the ages ranging from the mid-teens to the mid-40s. Stones, Farrell, and Taylor (2001) provide examples of the youngest and oldest elite competitors in different sports, including basketball players (youngest, 18 years; oldest, 43 years), Wimbledon tennis champions (youngest, 15 years; oldest, 43 years), and international soccer players (youngest, 17 years; oldest, 42 years).

Athletes with the longest careers at the top levels of team sport tend to play in positions that require the least physical effort. Stones and Kozma (1995) provide an example from soccer, in which more than half the oldest professional players in the top European leagues were goalkeepers. Goalkeepers, such as Alan Shilton (England) and Dino Zoff (Italy), even represented their countries in World Cup competitions when aged in their 40s. However, very few athletes in this category compete at elite levels in their 50s. Notable exceptions include Sir Stanley Matthews (soccer) and Gordie Howe (ice hockey).

Figure 7.5 **AGE RANGE OF YOUNGEST AND OLDEST ELITE COMPETITORS IN DIFFERENT CATEGORIES OF SPORT**

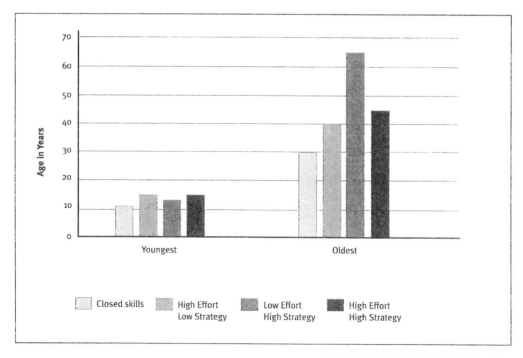

Source: Based on conceptualization by the author.

Statistical analysis of performance indexes can illustrate changes within athletic careers. Ice hockey provides a good example because the players contribute to their team's performance in different ways. Three useful indexes are games played, points scored (i.e., points = goals + assists), and penalty minutes. Games played and points scored reflect positive contributions to a team. Although the number of penalty minutes is supposedly a negative index (i.e., because the team plays short handed), the contribution is positive if earned for effective enforcement. Figure 7.6 illustrates changes on these indexes for the 50 players (excluding goalkeepers) who played in the National Hockey League (NHL) for at least 12 consecutive seasons within the epoch from 1973 to 1993. These players averaged over 70 games per season during their first 12 seasons.

The findings show increases in the number of games, points, and penalties from the first to the second season. Points scoring continued to increase beyond the mean of the preceding seasons for each of the third, fourth, and fifth seasons, whereas games played and penalty minutes showed no such changes. It was not

Figure 7.6 CAREERS IN NATIONAL HOCKEY LEAGUE BY SEASON: PENALTY MINUTES, GAMES PLAYED, AND TOTAL POINTS

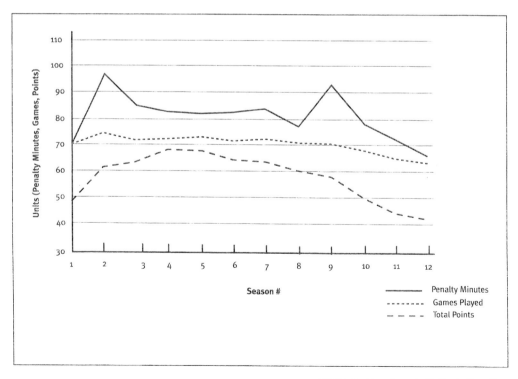

Source: Based on conceptualization by the author.

until the ninth season that the next significant change appeared: penalty minutes increased beyond the mean of the preceding seasons. This change may indicate compensation for an impending decrement in points scoring skill. Consistent with this hypothesis, each subsequent season saw significant decreases in the points scored and games played, with decreases in penalty points during each of the last two seasons.

These findings suggest that players with long careers in the NHL show no decrement in averaged performance for nine seasons, after which their contributions decline steadily. Stones and Kozma (1995) provide examples from different sports of the ways in which athletes compensate for changes in skill toward the end of their careers (e.g., a striker in soccer may fall back to become a schemer). The ice hockey players reacted to impending changes in points scoring with an increase in penalty minutes. Because penalty minutes usually result from aggressive play, this form of compensation is consistent with the classic scenario linking frustration (i.e., with declining skill) to aggression.

CHAPTER SUMMARY

The discussion on usual physical competence in this chapter distinguished among five categories of people—physically dependent, frail, independent, fit, and elite—and four types of aging processes—successful, usual, secondary, and tertiary. These two organizational schemes, not surprisingly, overlap.

Key ideas to remember from this chapter include:
- Physically dependent and frail people suffer from chronic disease and disability, which are manifestations of secondary aging. Approximately 25 percent of the population aged 65 years and older are deficient in at least one instrumental activity of daily living and fall within these categories.
- Independent and (to a lesser extent) fit people exhibit usual aging effects because of disuse of physical capabilities and other aspects of lifestyle. These categories subsume about 70 percent of the older population.
- Physically elite people comprise the top 5 percent of the population, with their levels of physical decline providing the best-known data for the estimation of age intrinsic effects.
- Encouraging historical trends over the past two decades indicate an increase in the frequency of exercising by older people. Because exercise promotes fitness, the anticipated consequences include the prolonged retention of physical competence.
- The findings on usual competence complement those on elite competence for activities requiring high effort but low strategy. There is more loss of competence with age for tasks more taxing of the available energy. In both short-duration and long-duration events, performance

decreases more with age for activities having a higher rate of energy expenditure. Similarly, performance decreases more with age with longer performances of a given activity.

- The model of Stones and Kozma (1986) postulates age loss to vary with the rate of expenditure of available energy. However, this model applies only to competences involving low use of strategy. Figure 7.5 shows elite competence to endure longer for activities involving high strategy.

- The youngest elite performers are aged in their teens for all categories of sport; the oldest performers participate in high strategy sports. The reasons include the facility among elite athletes to compensate for loss of strength, endurance, or speed.

- There is a lesson here for all of us: if a 64-year-old archer can win an Olympic gold medal by the effective use of experience and strategy, we too can use strategy to retain competence in most of the physical challenges that confront us.

KEY TERMS

Usual competence, **(p. 178)**

Elite competence, **(p. 178)**

Physically dependent, **(p. 179)**

Physically frail, **(p. 179)**

Frailty, **(p. 179)**

Physically independent, **(p. 180)**

Physically fit, **(p. 181)**

Fitness, **(p. 181)**

Exercise, **(p. 181)**

Physically elite, **(p. 181)**

Type of aging model, **(p. 182)**

Age intrinsic effect, **(p. 182)**

Aging, **(p. 182)**

Strength, **(p. 183)**

Energy, **(p. 183)**

Competence, **(p. 184)**

Performance, **(p. 184)**

Sports, **(p. 186)**

Athlete, **(p. 186)**

Effort, **(p. 187)**

Endurance, **(p. 187)**

Coordination, **(p. 187)**

Strategy, **(p. 188)**

STUDY QUESTIONS

1. Explain why no single set of measures can provide for sensitive and useful evaluation at all levels of physical competence.

2. Approaches to understanding usual physical competence include the typological and types of aging models. Compare and contrast these models.

3. What are the strengths and weaknesses of the types of aging model?

4. What is "elite physical competence"? Why do researchers study elite competence? How does an understanding of elite competence enhance our understanding of age effects on usual competence?

5. Describe age changes in swimming and track and field records. What are the implications for understanding age effects?

6. Compare age effects between sports involving a high or low use of strategy. What are the implications for understanding age effects?

SUGGESTED READINGS

Kaprio, J. & Sarna, S. (1994). Decreased risk of occupational disability among former elite male athletes. *Journal of Aging and Physical Activity, 2*, 115-126.

Shephard, R.J. (1987). *Physical Activity and Aging* (2nd edition). Rockville, MD: Aspen Publishers.

Spirduso, W.W. (1995). *Physical Dimensions of Aging.* Champaign, IL: Human Kinetics.

Stones, M.J. & Kozma, A. (1996). Activity, exercise and behavior, in J. Birren & K.W. Schaie (Eds.). *Handbook of the psychology of aging* (5th edition). Orlando, FL: Academic Press.

Mental Well Being and Mental Disorder

In this chapter, you will learn about:

- Is it a fact that most people are happy? Does the shape of the happiness distribution reflect reality or some artefact in measurement?
- Are happy people born happy or are people made happy?
- From what soil sprang our institutions to care for the mentally ill and frail senior—benevolence or expedience?
- Do older people experience unhappiness in different ways from younger people?

Introduction

If we think of mental health as a continuum ranging from bliss to extreme misery, mental well being refers to the upper half-range of this continuum and mental disorder to the lower half-range. We all wish mental well being for ourselves and those we cherish. Since the time of the classical Greek philosophers, there is documentation that mental well being is what most of us want the most in life. Evidence reviewed in this chapter suggests that over 80 percent of people in our part of the world succeed in this aim. Consequently, a stranger visiting our shores would surely express surprise at how little effort we make to understand mental well being, compared with mental disorder. Even the language used to describe the two poles of mental health reflects this difference in emphasis. There is really only one word in our culture to describe the positive extreme: bliss and its synonyms (e.g., ecstasy, delight). Whereas at the negative pole such terms as depression, anxiety, psychosis, and psychosomatic disorder express very different kinds of mental distress. The reason is, of course, that ours is a problem-oriented culture. The presence of mental well being is not a problem requiring a solution; mental disorder is a problem for the afflicted person and society.

The chapter begins by examining some background issues. Because mental well being and mental disorder are attributes of individuals, the initial subsection refers to the measurement of individual differences, with an illustrated example in Box 8.1. As noted in the introductory chapters, especially Chapter 3, accurate measurement is the underpinning of any good research. It is impossible to overstate the significance of reliable and valid measurement of individual differences.

Measures of individual differences include single and multi-item scales, physiological measures, and observations of behaviour. The scaling on these measures has implications for the meaning of the scores and the kind of statistics used to analyze them (see Appendix 8.A). The terms for summary statistics used to evaluate measures of individual differences are **reliability** and **validity** (as discussed in more detail in Chapter 3). The former refers to the confidence we can have in the scores provided by a measure and the latter to the confidence we invest in the measure itself. The research described in this chapter all derives from measures with adequate reliability and validity. Chapter 3 describes the means of their appraisal.

Another issue concerns the contributions of personality. Two main paradigms of personality theory with implications for mental health include trait models and stage models. **Trait models** assume that the structural foundations of personality retain stability throughout most of adult life, whereas **stage models** assume changes across the life span. The final sections review the state of current knowledge on mental well being and mental disorder as they relate to aging. The section on mental disorder focuses on depression, which is the most frequent emotional disorder in later life.

Box 8.1 Stability and Change in Character

Mary McKeown is nothing if not a shrewd judge of character. In her 80s now, she recently participated in a research project on mental well being in later life. Once the data collection was over, Mary insisted that the young researcher stay for a cup of tea before returning to the university. Then, she proceeded to tell him her opinions about life development, which was what she wanted to do the minute he told her the purpose of his research.

An immigrant to Canada, Mary brought with her, from Scotland, a toy mailbox designed to stimulate perceptual problem solving in infancy. The "letters" were plastic geometric shapes—like a star or a square—that the child "mailed" by pushing them through corresponding shapes cut in the lid of the box. When the infant succeeded in mailing all the letters, well, the idea was to pull off the lid, take out the shapes, and do it all over again! All Mary's three children loved that toy.

The pieces of wisdom Mary imparted to the young researcher came from her observations that each child used a different strategy to solve the mailbox problem and continued to deploy that basic strategy throughout life. She thought it showed that the basics of character were present in infancy and changed little—all her children now being in their 60s.

The oldest child, Rachel, would persist doggedly at the game—using whatever combination of insight and trial-and-error worked—never giving up until she mailed the last letter. Rachel's life course exemplified the potency of dogged determination. Intelligent and intuitive, though without the natural brilliance that made academic work easy, she consistently made the honour roll at school and university, usually while working at more than one job to help pay her way. She applied to the graduate program of a well-known business school, which offered her a place even without her finishing an undergraduate degree. It took her a year to complete a two-year MBA program and she never looked back. The rest is history—a job as troubleshooter in the automotive industry, sent to Europe to sort out problems in their Paris plant, back home with a promotion, marriage, off to the main plant in the United States, two children, promoted to the very top of her company in Canada, her children now at university, and Rachel soon to retire. Mary is very proud of her.

Matthew could never stick at anything for long. A brilliant, inquisitive, but impatient infant, he would play the mailbox game only until he made a mistake. Then he would stop playing, do something else, and come back to finish mailing only on some later whim. Matthew made the honour roll at school because of cleverness alone, certainly not because of the effort he made. A dropout from university, he became a hippie, travelling around Europe, Asia, and Australia, working at menial jobs in each country he visited just long enough to earn enough to finance a journey to some other exotic place. He returned to Canada in his late 20s for a journalism degree. Subsequently employed by a national newspaper in England, he became a foreign correspondent for most of his career. Only in his 50s did he return to Canada once more, this time as editor of a newspaper. Two years later, he took early retirement. He spends his retirement, not surprisingly, travelling abroad.

Sarah had a different way of playing the mailbox game. The first time she failed to mail a letter, she would lift up the lid, put all the shapes in the box, and with a radiant smile proclaim, "That was easy!" Mary remembers that Sarah never had much respect for conventions or rules. Often in trouble at school, but invariably able to overcome any difficulties by charm, she left without a high school

(continued)

Box 8.1 (continued)

diploma. A period of delinquency was followed by a spell in the armed forces, then she began to settle down. Sarah's attractiveness and charm earned her work in sales. She left sales to become a dancer, returned to sales, married, separated, worked again for a while, married for a second time, and became a mother. Always happy and charming, she continues to live life according to her own conventions.

The point made by Mary is that each of her children used strategies to overcome problems that changed very little from infancy on. The way her children played the mailbox game provided Mary with insight into their characters. Rachel was persistent, Matthew impatient and easily bored, and Sarah intuitive, charming, and unconventional. Mary believes that each person is born with a unique character and that upbringing and later experiences allow that character to develop but never change its basic form. Do you think she is right?

Personality as a Mental Health Resource

Trait models and stage models differ in presumptions about stability and change in personality. Costa and McCrae (1980; 1990) proposed that the most important features of **personality** reduce to just five traits, known as the "big five." These five traits are as follows:

1. Neuroticism—anxiety, depression, emotional distress
2. Extraversion—sociability, assertiveness, warmth
3. Openness to experience—willingness to take risks, seek out new experiences
4. Conscientiousness—organization, efficiency, dependability
5. Agreeableness—empathy, sensitivity, cooperativeness

Their research design included the administration of paper-and-pencil tests to huge numbers of people of different ages, with the traits identified by the use of a statistical procedure known as factor analysis. The findings provided evidence of stability of the mean levels across age groups, and some evidence of stability over time, suggesting that the **big five traits** retain stability over time. At least two of these traits—neuroticism and extraversion—correlate with mental well being such that people lower on neuroticism and higher on extraversion tend to be happier (Kozma, Stones, & McNeil, 1991). These two traits also show substantial contributions of **heritability** (Bouchard & McGue, 1990), meaning that **genetics** contributes substantially to their development.

There is persuasive evidence that personality traits provide a stable resource (or impediment) for **mental health**, which contrasts with the beliefs people have about personality changes. Krueger and Heckhausen (1997) asked young, middle-aged, and older people to describe how their own personality would change during subsequent decades of life. The respondents believed that age brought about more undesirable than desirable changes on four of the big five traits (i.e., neuroticism, extraversion, conscientiousness, and agreeableness). Theorists, such as Cumming and Henri (1961), and McAdams and de St. Aubin (1992), considered middle-aged people to emphasize generative concerns in their lives (e.g., contributing to their family and society), whereas the concerns of older people emphasize a review of the accomplishments and failures of their past life. Although much of such research is open to criticism because the measures lack the reliability and validity of those used by Costa and colleagues, age was associated with differences in aspirations and concerns. Consequently, it appears that although the foundations of personality remain stable with age and contribute to mental health (i.e., the big five traits), the peripheral aspects of personality may undergo transformation as people age.

Mental Well Being

Mental well being refers to a subjective evaluation of the overall quality of life. The various terms used to describe the concept include happiness, life satisfaction, morale, and trait affect. Although these terms convey different nuances of meaning, measures of mental well being correlate highly, regardless of the label used to identify the index—a person scoring highly on a measure of morale is likely to score similarly on any other measure of mental well being, and vice versa. These high correlations led Stones and Kozma (1980) to conclude that all the indexes measure essentially the same construct, known throughout most of Western history simply as **happiness**, which is the most desired of human conditions (Box 8.2). Measures of mental well being show a strong negative correlation with measures of depression, suggesting the latter to lie at the opposite end of the continuum (Kozma, Stones, & Kazarian, 1985).

Concepts related to mental well being but with more restricted meanings include (1) **life domain satisfactions**, which refer to satisfactions with specific aspects of life (e.g., finances, health), (2) temporally specific mood states, and (3) affective style—also termed affectivity. Measures of these concepts correlate highly with measures of mental well being.

Age and Gender Trends

Mental well being generally shows minimal differences with age and gender (Kozma, Stones, & McNeil, 1991). However, gender differences may appear in self-reports of depression. Figure 8.1 (page 207) shows responses from a representative Canadian sample to the *Manulife Health Styles Survey* (Stones, 2001). Agreement with a life satisfaction item was high at all ages and for both genders. Although few respondents agreed that they were "frequently depressed, down-hearted, or blue," more females than males agreed with this item. Findings reviewed later in this chapter show a similar gender difference in the prevalence of clinical depression.

Box 8.2 Mental Well Being as the Most Desirable Human Condition

Mental well being occupies a unique place in Western value systems. A thought game played since the time of the classical Greek philosophers involves a question-and-answer sequence. The questioner asks a respondent what that person desires most in life. Upon receiving an answer, the questioner asks a new question: "Why do you want that?" and repeats this same question until the respondent can provide no further reason for the last answer given. Typical question-and-answer sequences are as follows:

Questioner	Respondent 1	Respondent 2	Respondent 3
"What do you want most in life?"	"Right now? Money!"	"A responsible job after graduating."	"To meet someone and fall in love."
"Why do you want that?"	"So I can pay my tuition and buy a car."	"Because I think I have the ability to build a solid career."	"I'm a romantic. Eventually raising my own family is important to me."
"Why do you want that?"	"It'll make my life so much easier."	"Mainly because I want to make a *real* contribution to society."	"To feel excited about life, and fulfilled—doing the things I think are most important."
"Why do you want that?"	"I'll be happy, man!"	"So I can feel satisfied that I've done some good, made a difference to how things are."	"It'll make me content. If I never fall in love, I'd miss out on something very special."
"Why do you want that?"	"Just wanna be happy, man."	"That's it, really. I just want to be satisfied with my life."	"Being content. That is as good as it gets."

For thousands of years, the last answer has always been the same. People want to be happy. The classical Greek philosophers considered happiness to be the most valued of any human condition. Because of their thought games, they considered happiness to be:

- Valued for its own sake
- Not valued for the sake of anything else
- The most prized of any human condition because only happiness is valued for itself and no other reason.

The concept known throughout most of history as "happiness" now falls under a rubric of mental well being. This latter subsumes subtle differences in meaning associated with such terms as happiness, contentment, and satisfaction. Stones and Kozma (1980, 1989) wrote about historical changes in theorizing about happiness. In thousands of years, there were only three basic models.

1. Throughout most of history philosophers considered mental well being to be a consequence of virtuous activity—only the "good" could be happy.

2. During much of the past two centuries, thinkers represented happiness as the balance between pleasurable and unpleasant experiences. This affect balance model presumes that happiness is contingent on external influences that occasion pleasure or displeasure. An environmentalist perspective on happiness influenced political thought (e.g., the right to pursue happiness is part of the United States' Constitution) and helped justify the introduction of welfare systems in the 19th century.

3. During the past two decades, it became apparent that mental well being included a stable component. Researchers associated this stable component with personality traits and genetic dispositions. A debate about the respective contributions of internal and external influences on mental well being continues.

Figure 8.1   CANADIAN AGE AND GENDER TRENDS FOR SELF-REPORTED LIFE
SATISFACTION (LS) AND DEPRESSION

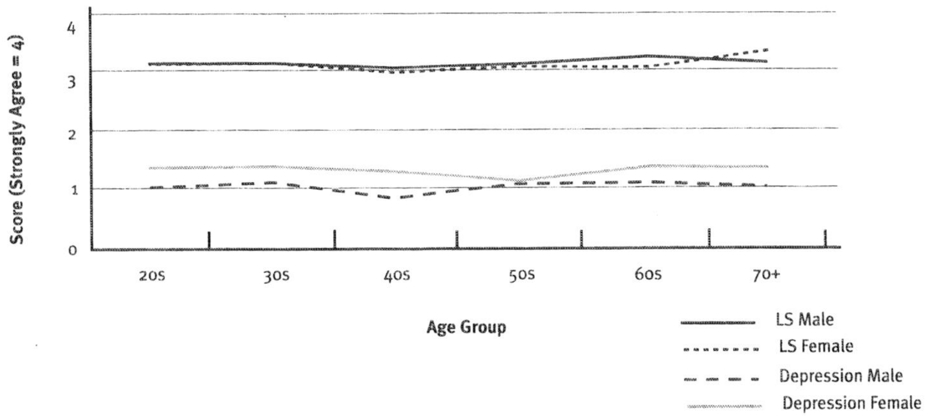

Source: Based on conceptualization by the author.

Longitudinal findings also suggest that mental well being remains stable with age. Atkinson (1982) was probably the first to show minimal effects on stability because of major life changes. Studies by Kozma and Stones (1983) and Costa, McCrae, and Zonderman (1987) confirmed this impression. Mussen, Honzig, and Eichorn (1982) examined measures taken twice over 40 years, finding stability to account for 15 to 30 percent of the total variability within measures. Stones, Hadjistravopoulos, Tuuko, and Kozma (1995) examined studies previously reviewed by Veenhoven (1994), concluding that the stable component of well being averages 40 percent or more over 10 years. Lykken and Tellegen (1996) reported comparable findings with a 10-year stability estimate of 50 percent. Consequently, the evidence is abundant from both cross-sectional and longitudinal research that mental well being measures retain considerable stability as people age.

Despite evidence to the contrary, a myth that mental well being decreases with age continues to persist in our culture. Earlier textbooks on gerontology make frequent reference to losses associated with aging (e.g., in health, income, intimacy) as contributing to an expectation of declining mental well being. Shmotkin found evidence that older people also believe this myth. Most devalued their present and future expectations of life satisfaction in relation to the past: "respondents of age 51 years and over evaluated the past increasingly higher than the present, and respondents of age 66 years and over evaluated the past even higher than the future." (Shmotkin, 1991: 264). However, the actual distributions of well being scores fail to support these expectations, with no loss found within the age range cited by Shmotkin (1991). It is time to put this myth to rest. (See Figure 8.1.)

Distributions of Mental Well Being

Although measures related to mental well being are not strongly associated with demographic indexes (e.g., poverty) within and across countries (Diener, Sandvik, Seidlitz, & Diener, 1993; Myers & Diener, 1995), one of the most frequently replicated findings to emerge during the past half-century is that most people score within the positive half-range on these indexes. If the index is on a 10-point scale (i.e., such that 10 is the most positive and 1 the most negative), the average score within the general population approximates 7 to 8 (Heady & Wearing, 1988). Figure 8.2 includes a recent distribution of mental well being scores among Canadians. More than two-thirds of respondents rated themselves above the scale midpoint. Statisticians refer to such distributions as **negatively skewed**, meaning that most scores cluster near the positive pole with a tail at the negative end. Findings of negative skew on mental well being measures transcend countries and demographic strata within countries (e.g., age, gender, social class) (Michalos, 1991; Near & Rechner, 1993). In other words, the findings from different coun-

Figure 8.2   DISTRIBUTION OF MENTAL WELL BEING SCORES FOR
CANADIANS: NORMAL DISTRIBUTION AND THEORETICAL
DISTRIBUTION

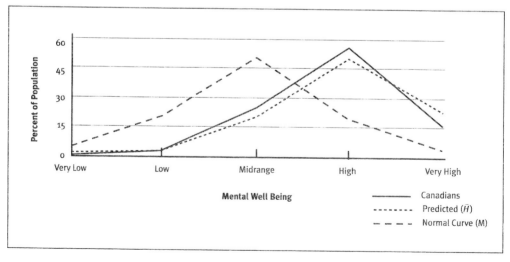

Source: Based on the difference between scores on life satisfaction and depression items in the *Manulife Health Styles Survey* (Stones, 2001).

tries, people of different ages, men and women, the rich and the poor are consistent. Such findings are obtained from a range of measures that include:

- Mental well being, life domain satisfaction, and affect indexes (Andrews, 1991; McNeil, Stones, Kozma & Andres, 1994).
- Absolute and comparative estimates of well being (e.g., personal well being compared with age peers) (Heady & Wearing, 1998).
- Self-ratings, multi-item scales, and ratings by other people (Kozma & Stones, 1988).
- Unipolar measures and indexes of the balance between positive and negative affect (Kozma & Stones, 1980).

The few exceptions to the rule that population distributions have negative skew include near-midrange levels of mental well being for black South African youth during the Apartheid era (Moller, 1992), residents of North American nursing homes (Stones & Kozma, 1989), and residents of psychiatric institutions (Kozma & Stones, 1987). The lowest mental well being scores on record include findings from South Africa, where older Zulu returning migrants in the 1980s provided scores below the midpoint on the scales. However, apart from the South African studies and studies of institution residents, the majority of findings indicate that community residents show mainly positive scores on mental well being measures.

Heady and Wearing (1988) wrote that some researchers appear defensive about findings that most people score highly on mental well being measures. The reasons are that traditional models in the social sciences convey an impression that unhappiness, rather than happiness, should be the prevailing condition (e.g., the "social pathology" and "relative deprivation" models in sociology; the "medical/clinical" model in psychology; the "rational actor" model in economics). Such theorizing evoked scepticism about mental well being measures, despite considerable evidence for their content and concurrent validity. Several theorists offered reasons for the negative skew in the distributions.

Some of these interpretations cite measurement error as the reason why most people obtain high scores on measures of mental well being, whereas others offer a substantive rationale. Because the error interpretations—if they are correct—cast doubt on the validity not only of research on mental well being but also of all research with self-report measures, it is important to discuss these interpretations as well as those of a substantive nature.

Error Interpretations.

The error interpretations include **response set**, **extremity set**, and **impression management**. Response set signifies a bias toward a particular response category (e.g., "yes" or "no"), extremity set a tendency to endorse extreme responses, and impression management a bias toward responses that are socially desirable.

Response set has relevance only to scales with categorical responses (e.g., the *Short Happiness and Affect Research Protocol*, or *SHARP*, of Stones, Kozma, Hirdes,

Gold, Arbuckle, & Kolopack, 1995, contains only "yes" and "no" response alternatives). Studies of response set found no evidence for response set on mental well being measures in the majority of older people, but some evidence in those of very advanced age, low education, low socioeconomic status, and impaired cognition (Kozma, Stones, & McNeil, 1991, pp. 40–43). On a balanced scale, such as the SHARP (i.e., a scale with equal numbers of items for which a "yes" or "no" response indicates higher well being), response set should result in a total score near the midpoint of the possible range. Consequently, response set cannot explain findings that most people score highly on such scales.

Extremity set refers to a tendency to choose extreme responses (e.g., the highest alternative on a five-point scale). However, the distributions had similar meaning, regardless of whether the extreme responses indicted high (Michalos, 1985) or low (Mann, 1991) mental well being or affect (Larsen & Diener, 1987, pp. 9–11).

Impression management includes biased responding because of concerns about **social desirability** or fear of consequences. Hirdes, Zimmerman, Hallman, and Soucie (1998), for example, suggest that patients in institutions may fear repercussion if they express concerns about their care. Studies of impression management typically include two main features in the research design. First, participants complete self-report measures of mental well being and impression management (e.g., social desirability), and the two are correlated to see if those high on social desirability have high well being scores. Second, "experts" estimate the level of mental well being of each individual who provided self-report data. An expert is someone with good knowledge of a person providing self-report data (e.g., a close family member, a primary care provider). The reasoning is that even if respondents bias their self-ratings to create a good impression, the experts should provide an unbiased estimate of mental well being.

The findings with this type of design provide no good evidence for impression management, regardless of age or residence (i.e., community versus institution). The mental well being estimates showed a high correlation between self-report and expert report, with no comparable correlation between self-reported mental health and social desirability (Diener et al., 1991; McCrae, 1986). The same studies showed comparable distributions of scores with self-ratings and expert ratings, with means of 7 to 7.5 on a 10-point scale, and comparable variability around the mean. Consequently, the findings provide no support for a measurement error interpretation.

Substantive Interpretations.

Substantive interpretations acknowledge that skewed mental well being distributions reflect reality, rather than measurement error, but attempt to explain the absence of a normal curve shown in many other individual difference traits. Although there is no consensus among theorists, the following ideas hold some promise.

Findings that intrigued Heady and Wearing (1988) were that most people consider their own happiness to exceed that of their age peers. Because, by definition, half the population falls below the average, there is an obvious incongruity. Consequently, they hypothesized a *sense of relative superiority* that is "a prop which most human beings have in place to support a high absolute level" of mental well being (p. 501). This hypothesis—one of the first attempts to explain skew as other than error—assumes that perceived superiority to others is a cognitive trait possessed by most people.

Although this hypothesis has some intuitive appeal, it fails to explain some of the findings described in the preceding section. Those findings showed that self-reported mental well being was no higher than estimates of that person's well being by an expert judge. If you rate yourself happier than your peer because you feel superior to that peer, does it not follow that the peer's rating of you should be the lower? A finding that the two ratings are likely to be comparable does not fully discredit Heady and Wearing's (1988) hypothesis, but does cast some doubt on its range of application.

A mathematical model of happiness by Stones and Kozma (1991) assumes mental well being to vary around a steady state. The mathematics derive from an adaptation of the well-known logistic difference equation with terms that include:

1. Happiness at time t (H_t)
2. Personality (P)
3. Outside influences on happiness (I)
4. Stable happiness ($\bar{H}$), which is affected by P and I

The model predicts happiness to show stability over time, with individual differences determined by personality. Although transient outside influences may raise or lower levels of happiness, the model predicts such effects to dissipate over time. The following expresses the form of the relationship of stable happiness to personality:

Equation 8.1 $$\bar{H} = \frac{P-1}{P}$$

Other sections of this chapter discuss the contributions of personality to mental well being. It is sufficient, for present purposes, to acknowledge that they are present and are strong. Because there is good evidence that many such traits have bell-shaped distributions, it is also reasonable to suppose that the distribution of P in Equation 8.1 is bell-shaped. What happens if we generate a distribution of $\bar{H}$ from a normal distribution of P and compare that theoretical distribution with one derived empirically?

Figure 8.2 provides a comparison of theoretical and empirical distributions of mental well being. The theoretical distribution is of stable happiness ($\bar{H}$) computed from a normally distributed person parameter (P) using Equation 8.1. The empirical distribution shows mental well being scores from a survey of Canadian households. The index was the difference between scores on life satisfaction and depression items (Stones, 2001). The finding that the theoretical and empirical distributions are similar is in accordance with Stones and Kozma's (1991) model. Of course, this support does not prove that the model is correct, but it does suggest that skewed distributions in mental well being scores can be reconciled with interpretations based on a normal curve.

Models of Mental Well Being

Stones, Hadjistravopoulos, Tuokko, and Kozma (1995) described three basic **models of mental well being** termed *bottom-up, top-down,* and *up-down.* Figure 8.3 illustrates these models.

Bottom-Up Models.

Bottom-up models assume mental well being to be a reactive state, with outside influences mediated though situational appraisal (e.g., life domain satisfaction, perceived burden, hassle). Clyburn, Stones, Hadjistravopoulos, and Tuokko (2000) examined several models of the impact of caring for Alzheimer's disease patients on the mental well being of family caregivers. A bottom-up model received the most support in a Canada-wide study. This model assumes that objective features of caregiving (e.g., disturbing symptoms, institutional support) affect the

Figure 8.3 THREE MODELS OF MENTAL WELL BEING

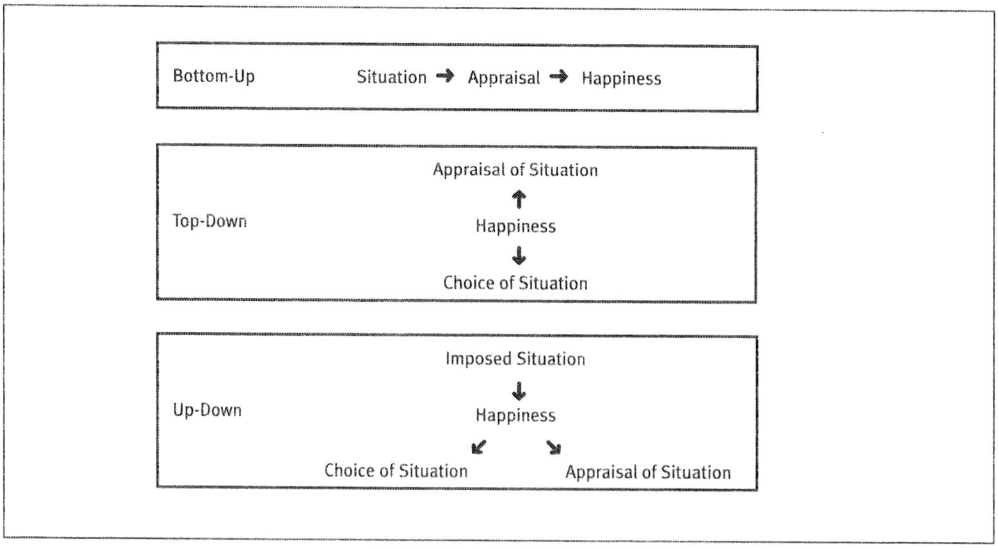

Source: Based on conceptualization by the author.

appraisal of caring (i.e., perceived burden), which, in turn, affects mental well being (i.e., a depression scale). However, the support received by bottom-up models varies with the type of research design.

1. *Cross-Sectional Research:* A considerable amount of other research used cross-sectional data to test support for bottom-up models. However, the support received is fairly limited. Michalos (1991) studied students from across the world, hypothesizing that demographic factors (e.g., income) correlate with situational appraisal (e.g., financial satisfaction), which correlate with mental well being. Numerous studies of elderly populations similarly examined the relationships of mental well being with demographic and situational appraisal indicators (Kozma, Stones, & McNeil, 1991). The findings show that although situational appraisals have moderate correlations with mental well being at any age, knowledge about demographics or life situation has almost no predictive value. Myers and Diener wrote about the prediction of mental well being as follows: "Knowing a person's age, sex, race, and income (assuming the person has enough to afford life's necessities) hardly gives a clue." (Myers & Diener, 1995: 17). In other words, mental well being has almost no relationship with any demographic index or life situation measure.

2. *Experimental Studies:* Bottom-up models also fare badly in experimental research. Kozma, Stone, Stones, Hannah, and McNeil (1990) used positive and negative mood inductions to determine the effects on mood and mental well being. These inductions required the participants to imagine or recollect experiences in their own lives that made them either happy (i.e., positive mood induction) or sad (i.e., negative mood induction). The induction brought about substantial change in mood but with no effect on mental well being. These findings provide no evidence that mental well being increases or decreases in response to experimental manipulations shown to change mood.

3. *Therapeutic Interventions with Institution Residents:* Therapeutic interventions for older people include psychosocial programs intended to promote mental well being. A well-known intervention is **reminiscence** therapy in which participants reminisce about experiences and feelings in their past. Butler (1963) suggested this kind of intervention provides an opportunity to review past life and thereby provide a continuity of meaning with present experiences. He reasoned that for the majority of older people, participation in the intervention should promote mental well being because it facilitates adaptation to the present situation. Other forms of psychosocial intervention aim to increase the personal control and daily responsibilities of institution residents. The rationale is that the loss of personal control associated with institutional life causes a loss of mental well being.

Interventions that increase such control might bring the levels back to approach the pre-institutional level.

Findings from such studies provide some of the strongest support for bottom-up models. A factor contributing to this success is undoubtedly the low levels of mental well being that are prevalent in institution residents. That is, they have lots of room to improve. Because the reason for these levels probably has more to do with the institutional environment than personality, it is conceivable that manipulation of that environment might contribute to a reversal of such effects.

Rattenbury and Stones (1989) studied the effects of reminiscence intervention on the mental well being of senior institution residents. Although previous studies on the effects of similar intervention in community settings provided little evidence of effectiveness, the institution residents had low levels of mental well being prior to the intervention. Their research design had different groups of participants reminisce about their past life, discuss current issues, or receive no treatment. The findings showed major improvement in mental well being by both treatment groups but no change in the control group. The authors concluded that participation in the group discussion, regardless of content, contributed to a gain in mental well being.

A subsequent study examined the effects of reminiscence over 18 months in five institutions (Rattenbury, Kozma, & Stones, 1995). Compared with a control condition that received no treatment, the participants in therapeutic reminiscence showed higher mental well being over the period, with dramatically reduced rates of morbidity and mortality. These effects, associated with the intervention, were independent of pre-existing levels of illness and disability.

Langer and Rodin (1977) studied the effects of increasing choice and responsibility in senior institution residents. One group of participants received information about choices in the institution and encouragement to take on extra responsibilities. Many of them did. Another group received positive messages about life in the home but no encouragement to assume additional responsibilities. Compared with the control group, the group that took on extra responsibilities showed improved mental well being and lower subsequent morbidity.

We conclude from these studies that if the reasons for low mental well being include the environmental context, changes to that context can produce beneficial change. Outside the institutions, most people are able to fashion a context more or less to their liking. The three things that people want from that environment are those that therapeutic intervention in institutions tries to provide. People want:

1. Someone to love
2. Something to do
3. Something to look forward to.

Institutions ignore the importance of these basic requirements for mental well being at the peril of their residents.

Top-Down Models.

Top-down models assume that mental well being is more unchanging than change-able (Lykken & Tellegen, 1996). Mental well being in this model is a trait-like, rather than state-like, entity that affects the choice and appraisal of situations. The model envisions that happy people do things that make them happy, elicit pleasing behaviour from others, and get over troubles quickly. Unhappy people tend to avoid intimacy or new encounters, elicit unfavourable reactions from others, and brood over troubles. A happy person exposed to adversity tempers that appraisal with an optimistic outlook. An unhappy person exposed to a fortunate occurrence still considers the "cup to be half empty." The model proposes that because people appraise situations from positive or pessimistic perspectives, life domain satisfactions generally correlate with mental well being, even though demographic indicators do not. An extreme example of the model is bipolar dis-order, with afflicted individuals behaving at different times like very unhappy or very happy people. Lykken and Tellegen (1996) cite this disorder as evidence that mood precedes behaviour in causal sequence, rather than vice versa.

Support for top-down models includes evidence not found and evidence found. The former includes a failure to obtain convincing evidence that unfavourable or favourable life experiences affect the long-term stability of men-tal well being (Atkinson, 1982; Costa, McCrae, & Zonderman, 1987). People adapt even to the gravest misfortune, such as acquired paraplegia, and winning a lottery does not ensure happiness. Chamberlain and Zika (1992) hypothesized that recent hassles might contribute more to an explanation of mental well being than major life events. However, their findings showed prior level to be a stronger predic-tor of present happiness than recent hassles. Similarly, Kozma, Stone, Stones, Hannah, and McNeil (1990) found minimal changes in mental well being to emotion evoking situations that do affect mood.

Research on personality provides a considerable body of evidence in sup-port of the top-down model. Personality traits and other stable resources that correlate with mental well being include extraversion, neuroticism, meaning in life, perceived **control**, and optimism (Kozma, Stones, & McNeil, 1991; Deiner, Suh, Lucas, & Smith, 1999). Because these dispositions, like mental well being, retain stability over time, the findings suggest that mental well being belongs with a constellation of other stable traits. However, the strongest evidence to support the top-down model derives from research on heritability.

A well-established research paradigm to estimate heritability compares monozygotic and dizygotic twins. Monozygotic twins have exactly the same genetic inheritance, whereas dizygotic twins are genetically as similar as any sib-lings with the same two parents. Refinements to the design include comparisons of each type of twin reared together or apart (e.g., because of adoption). Findings provide evidence for a considerable contribution by heredity to the mental well being of younger and older adults. Lykken and Tellegen (1996) estimate that approximately half the total variability between individuals at any given time—and 80 percent of the variability between individuals that is stable over time—is because of heredity. These findings indicate that after accounting for temporary fluctuations (i.e., possibly because of measurement error), only 20 percent of the differences between people in mental well being arise because of environmental differences, with 80 percent attributable to genetic differences.

Consequently, they suggest trying to be happier may be as futile as trying to be taller. They might also have said that trying to remain unhappy is as futile as trying to be shorter. However, other evidence provides indications to the contrary. Previously cited findings of low mental well being in elderly institution residents are unlikely to be because unhappy older people choose to live in institutions. There is ample evidence that disability and illness, rather than mood, precipitate entry into institutions and that the latter negates options taken for granted by community residents. Findings of the benefits to mental well being from reminiscence and other therapeutic interventions are also difficult to comprehend from a top-down perspective. But surprisingly these apparent inconsistencies are capable of reconciliation.

Stones, Hadjistravopoulos, Tuuko, and Kozma (1995) produced estimates of change after therapeutic intervention within the 20 percent range suggested by Lykken and Tellegen (1996). They computed the magnitude of change to stability of mental well being in reminiscence studies. Change in mental well being because of the intervention accounted for 10 percent and 20 percent of the stable variability between people over the time of the intervention. Does this mean that 90 percent and 80 percent of the variability remained stable? Most certainly. Does it mean that the change because of the intervention was insignificant or even futile? Most certainly not. The intervention made participants happier and reduced the likelihood of illness and death—by no means a futile accomplishment. The difference in interpretation is one between size and significance: sometimes changes of small statistical size have immense clinical significance.

Up-Down Models.

Up-down models include all features of top-down versions but also incorporate bottom-up assumptions that external influences affect mental well being. Bottom-up influences are more likely to be negative than positive because of high means in the general population that leave little room for upward movement. Gains in mental well being with therapeutic intervention represent a normalizing trend, in which treatment serves to alleviate a deleterious environment. It is for this reason that Figure 8.3 refers to situational effects on mental well being as "imposed," meaning that such situations are unwelcome and chosen (if at all) for reasons of necessity, rather than desire.

Up-down models are consistent with previously cited findings that mental well being shows:

- Stability over time
- The influence of personality and heredity
- Correlations with life domain indicators, burden, hassles, and mood
- Low levels in an imposed environment
- Gains with therapeutic intervention in the context of an imposed environment.

A further prediction is that top-down effects outweigh bottom-up effects within the general population because community residents choose their situations freely. Several studies used research designs that evaluated the stability versus change in mental well being while taking account of environmental contributions. Findings across a range of ages provide support for an up-down model in which top-down effects provide the stronger contribution (Kozma, Stone, & Stones, 2000; Mallard, Lance, & Michalos, 1997; Stones & Kozma, 1986).

Although the preceding findings support Lykken and Tellegen's (1996) contention that mental well being is more unchanging than changeable, few studies have addressed the reasons for low mental well being among people living in imposed situations. One such study examined spare time use and mental well being in 1200 black South Africans aged 16 to 25 years during the time of Apartheid. It is perhaps because of the youth of the sample that this research failed to elicit much excitement within gerontology, although the findings could allude to any imposed context (e.g., nursing homes). Moller's (1992) findings significantly challenge bottom-up lore that happiness reflects the balance between the number of happy and unhappy moments (Diener, Sandvic, & Parvot, 1991).

Moller (1992) found only 50 percent of the sample reported satisfaction with life, with the remainder either ambivalent or dissatisfied. Similar proportions considered life to be rewarding, frustrating, exciting, or boring, with another 50:50 split between those positive or negative in future outlook. These distributions contrast dramatically with those of Canadians the same age, whose ratings showed 90 percent endorsement of life satisfaction. The South Africans' life satisfaction is also at odds with findings from their time-use diaries. More than 90 percent of the sample pursued at least one "best liked" activity per day, with only 35 percent engaging in a disliked activity. Of the total activity units, 94 percent were liked activities and 89 percent undertaken of free choice. The author writes that: "Superficially seen, black youth in South Africa lead very normal lives: they spend approximately one-third of their time sleeping, working in jobs, or learning at school, and on leisure activities, including obligatory domestic duties." (Moller, 1992: 339). What they do, the diaries show, they mostly enjoy. The balance of happy and unhappy moments was highly positive. How can these findings be reconciled with their low life satisfaction? Spontaneous additions to the dairies gave clues about the respondents' discontentment with life. Crime, delinquency, riots, low opportunity for advancement, school boycotts, and pressures toward involvement in political conflict considerably limited their options and freedom of choice.

Although these young people created for themselves micro-situations that provided a preponderance of happy moments, it was the macro-situation that negated wider options and made them dissatisfied. Moller's (1992) finding made proponents of both bottom-up and top-down theories very uneasy. Perhaps that is why they left it to languish. Evidence for low mental well being despite a preponderance of happy moments and the presence of powerful macro-situational effects are difficult to explain other than with an up-down model.

Do Moller's findings have relevance to gerontology? There is no comparable study in nursing homes, in which residents live in an imposed macro-situation. However, there is evidence that the micro-situations preferred by residents are mainly passive. Findings from one Canadian city with the Minimum Data Set 2.0 (Morris, Murphy, & Nonemaker, 1995) showed that the most preferred activities of nursing home residents were listening to music, talking to people, and watching television. These were the only activities interesting to a majority of residents who were not bedfast. However, fully two-thirds of residents were inactive for the greater part of the day, participating in no activities. Are the residents inactive because of limited options—resulting in unhappiness and early death? Langer and Rodin's (1977) research suggests an affirmative answer, with the means of intervention not only possible but shown to be effective over the past quarter-century.

Mental Disorder

At the opposite end of the mental heath continuum to mental well being is mental distress. Mental distress encompasses many types of **mental disorders**. **Psychiatry** is the medical speciality concerned with the diagnosis and treatment of such disorders. **Geriatrics** is the medical speciality dealing with illness in older people. Their intersection is the subspeciality of **psychogeriatrics**, which focuses on the mental health problems of older people. Both psychiatry and geriatrics occupied lowly positions on the medical hierarchy for most of the past two centuries. A reason is that our society stigmatized both the mentally ill and the financially impoverished elderly for much of this period. Nova Scotia geriatrician Roy Fox (1991) proffered this mocking depiction of geriatrics as viewed by colleagues in other branches of medicine: "A second-rate speciality looking after third-rate patients in fourth-rate facilities." Psychiatry's reputation fared no better in medical circles and public awareness.

For reasons that were more political (regarding the mentally ill) or economic (for the impoverished elderly) than anything else, institutional care became the accepted form of treatment for both populations. Depictions in Europe (Townsend, 1962) and North America (Butler, 1974) during the past half-century raised concerns about the quality of life in institutions for the aged. Psychiatric institutions elicited even harsher criticism. Researchers, such as Laing (1960), Goffman (1961), and Szasz (1961), provided powerful critiques, and movies, such as *One Flew Over the*

Cuckoo's Nest, made the failings of psychiatry conspicuous to wide audiences. Such practices as frontal lobotomy and the overuse of electroconvulsive shock earned psychiatry much notoriety. Some former psychiatric patients formed support networks, called *psychiatric survivors*, which continue to provide support and advocacy at local and provincial levels (e.g., the Psychiatric Survivor Action Association of Ontario, with an Internet site at www.icom.ca/psaao). This section of the chapter traces the history of institutional care in North America, before discussing common forms and treatment of mental disorders in later life.

Institutional Care for the Mentally Ill and Impoverished Elderly

Early Models

North America imported models of institutional care based on experiences in Europe at the beginning of the 19th century. Large metropolitan mental asylums created during that century still exist in Canada, although with substantial reductions to the inmate populations since the 1980s, when advances in pharmacology made community care viable for many residents.

European psychiatric **institutions** before the 19th century were terrible places. The behaviour of mentally ill people scared the public and baffled physicians. The theology of a preceding era perceived many forms of social deviance as examples of *sin*. Although we now consider crime an act of volition and mental illness a loss of volition, the medieval theologian Thomas Aquinas interpreted mental illness as possession by the devil. Residues of this thinking remained as the 18th century drew to a close. Consequently, custodial institutions felt able to justify cruel treatment of the incarcerated mentally ill as purging them of sin.

Such treatment horrified Philippe Pinel, who became the administrator of a mental asylum in Paris. Incarcerated patients lived in gloom and squalor, tormented by brutal custodians, subjected to pitiless intervention (e.g., bleeding, blistering, emetics, purging), and some kept in shackles for decades. Pinel's observations led him to introduce a more humane model of institutional care (e.g., hiring more humane attendants, providing adequate nutrition, making the environment more pleasing). Evidence of therapeutic success resulted in the wider adoption of this model. Comparable innovations at the York Retreat in England (established in 1796 by Quaker William Tuke) resulted in calmer patients, despite the use of few restraints or medicaments. Another notable event of that era was clergyman Francis Willis's cure of the mental illness of King George III, after his physicians failed miserably and noticeably. These successes heralded a change in institutional culture from punishment to the provision of care. The new world imported this model from Europe.

By the middle of the 19th century, a purely religious interpretation of insanity was on the wane in North America, with a rational (or medical) outlook gaining credence (Jiminez, 1987). This changing outlook raised questions about how to care for the mentally ill in rural areas, who, looked after by their families, wandered freely about their communities. Such a familial model of care was less viable in the industrialized cities, which became the home to increasing numbers of American families after the first half of the 19th century.

Rothman (1971) described the introduction of institutional care to the United States as coinciding with governmental anxieties about a disintegrating social structure. During the first half of the 19th century, with high rates of immigration and a large exodus from rural areas to the cities, the government of President Jackson faced a period of unprecedented social upheaval. Its response to the perceived crisis included the creation of mental asylums, poor houses, and prisons as ways to prop the crumbling social structure. Consequently, the early evolution of North American psychiatry accorded with a political agenda to restore social order. Although such analysis applies to change at a macro-level of societal intervention, other researchers used similar concepts of social control to describe the micro-level treatment of patients within institutions. Goffman (1961) referred to "total institutions," in which the freedom of residents to act independently is made subservient to the smooth running of the organization.

Although institutional care for elderly persons also began for political reasons, these were due more to economics than social control. Forbes, Jackson, and Kraus (1987) describe the evolution of institutional care from its beginnings in Europe. After King Henry VIII dissolved the monasteries of England and Wales, the task of sheltering the old, poor, and vulnerable fell to the parishes. The parishes built poor houses, also known as work houses, in which residents did work in exchange for food and shelter. Poor houses were unhappy places, without heart or dignity. The little care provided to the sick was by other inmates, known as pauper nurses, who were usually untrained older women. Discipline was strict, and living conditions were deliberately made harsh to discourage all but the most destitute from seeking poor relief. The parish wanted no parasites to feed. Nevertheless, the old and infirm had no choice, as the alternative to the poor house was death.

This was the culture transported across the North Atlantic. It had little tolerance of the old. If aboard ships arriving in New England or Nova Scotia, elderly persons, those maimed, mentally ill, and vagrant were unwelcome. They were sent back home so as not to increase pauperism in the "Brave New World." However, the need for institutional care was pressing. Before long, poor houses opened throughout Canada patterned after those in Europe. These institutions mixed elderly persons with the poor, sick, disabled, widowed, vagrant, and drunk, unless they were demented and sent to mental asylums. Seventy-six such institutions still existed in Ontario and 24 in Nova Scotia by the 1920s. Across Canada, more than 250 institutions for dependent and disabled people existed by the early 1940s, with two-thirds of the residents aged over 60 years.

Current Models.

Psychiatric hospitals remained the main places of residence for severely ill patients throughout most of the 20th century. The treatments received by patients included physical intervention, such as prefrontal lobotomy, electro-convulsive shock therapy, and pharmacological therapy—but with psychoso-cial interventions, such as occupational therapy, group therapy, behaviour therapy, and therapeutic communities—becoming part of standard practice. The effectiveness of psychiatric intervention came under increasing scientific scrutiny with standards and procedures for evaluation similar to those used in physical medicine.

Major changes in psychiatry occurred during the past quarter-century for two reasons. First, a consensus on diagnostic criteria and the publication by the American Psychiatric Association of successive editions of its *Diagnostic and Statistical Manual* facilitated the reliable diagnosis of mental disorders, which, in turn, contributed to the more accurate evaluation of treatment modal-ities. Second, the success of long-acting tranquilizers in patients with psychosis, mood stabilizers in bipolar affective disorder, selective serotonin reuptake inhibitors in depression, and cognitive–behavioural intervention in neurosis meant that many patients were now treatable with short-stay institutional care, or as outpatients, who would formerly have required prolonged institutional care. These developments contributed to the evolution of a community psy-chiatry model and the demise of the older psychiatric institutions in the 1990s, with short-stay inpatient care mainly provided in the psychiatric wards of acute care hospitals.

Poor houses failed to survive as a model of institutional care in Canada much beyond World War II. At this time, the introduction of new provincial and federal health funding plans changed the treatment of the old and infirm from a culture of despair to one of health care, with an emphasis on services to meet needs. An outcome was a more than 10-fold increase in the elderly population under institutional care from World War II to the early 1990s. However, the new nursing homes proved expensive, with the lack of acknowledged criteria for admission and good assessment tools, resulting in inequitable admission practices. Many people in nursing homes had no real need for that level of care, and oth-ers in pressing need of such care remained without a bed for long periods. Two developments occurred during the 1990s to redress such anomalies as these. First, the provinces normalized their criteria for admission to nursing homes, with standardized assessment tools introduced to measure need. Second, a home care model evolved that provided assistance to residents in their homes, thereby enabling them to retain independence for longer. Such functions are now the responsibility of multi-purpose agencies that function as gatekeepers with respect to the allocation of home care services and decisions about admission to nursing homes (e.g., the Community Care Access Centres in Ontario).

Advances in Evaluation.

Although the quality of care in institutions for both psychiatric patients and elderly individuals continues to improve, complacency remains the enemy of progress. An influential school of thought suggests that comprehensive and regular assessment provides the key to enhancing quality of care. One such family of tools includes Resident Assessment Instruments (RAIs) used in Canada and many other countries throughout the world (Hirdes, et al., 2000).

The RAI family includes Minimum Data Sets for use in long-term care (MDS 2.0), home care (MDS-HC), and psychiatric institutions (RAI-MH). The version for long-term care became a mandated tool for all licensed nursing facilities in the United States early in the 1990s, and mandated for use in Ontario chronic care hospitals in the mid-1990s. The development of the mental health tool (MDS-MH) took place in Canada under the direction of John Hirdes of the University of Waterloo, who was the leader of an international development team. This tool is now in regular use in psychiatric institutions throughout Ontario.

The primary aim of the RAI tools is to provide basic information for care planning purposes. However, the tools have other uses that include comparison of quality of care across facilities and estimation of funding needs based on the distribution of problems within the resident population (i.e., known as *case mix* funding). The available evidence suggests that the RAI tools fare fairly well for all three purposes, not least because international usage tools makes possible comparison not just within provinces or countries, but across countries.

Examples of the use of the MDS 2.0 include reports by the Canadian Institute on Health Information on the quality of care in Ontario chronic hospitals (CIHI, 1998). The findings include higher rates for physical restraint in Ontario facilities than reported for nursing homes in the United States and Europe (Ljunggren, Phillips, & Sgadari, 1997). Although institutions justify the use of physical restraint for reasons of safety—to prevent residents falling—the high Canadian rate suggests that other countries succeed in preventing falls with less use of restraint. In contrast, the Ontario institutions have a lower prevalence of untreated cases of depression than most other countries. These comparisons provide guidance with respect to changes needed to improve care. Because the Canadian facilities appear to provide lower (i.e., more frequent restraint use) and higher (i.e., depression treated more frequently) standards of care than other countries, we now have indications about those aspects of care that need improvement.

Diagnosis and Epidemiology of Mental Illness

Since the time of Hippocrates, physicians included conditions now considered mental illnesses in their classifications of disease (Kendall, 2001). They treated these conditions in much the same way as physical disorders, using potions, medicaments (i.e., types of medicine), and other forms of physical intervention.

Challenges to this belief that mental illness is like other diseases occurred at two periods in history. The first followed Thomas Aquinas's attribution of mental illness to supernatural possession. The second occurred late in the 18th century, when physicians influenced by Cartesian mind–body dualism considered mental illness a disease of the mind, rather the body. The psychoanalytic schools emerging of the end of the 19th century exemplify this philosophy, treating mental illnesses as psychogenic disorders amenable to psychotherapy. Medical opinion continues to show unease about this issue. Although modern physicians continue to treat mental illness with physical methods, the very title of the American Psychiatric Associations *Diagnostic and Statistical Manual of Mental Disorders* (DSM-IV, 1994; underline added) perpetuates a dualistic philosophy, albeit with some reluctance (i.e., as indicated in the introduction to the manual). However, the DSM-IV continues to be the "Bible" for psychiatric diagnosis in North America.

Epidemiology is the study of the frequency of diseases. In the early 1980s, the National Institute of Mental Health in the United States sponsored the *Epidemiological Catchment Area Survey (ECA)* to provide the first comprehensive survey of mental disorders (Myers, et al., 1984). This survey continues to influence thinking about the frequencies of different mental disorders at different ages (U.S. Department of Health and Social Services, 1999). The findings in Table 8.1 suggest that with the exception of severe cognitive disorder (i.e., see Chapter 9 for a discussion of dementia), the prevalence rates are lower among people aged 55 years and older, than in younger adults.

Table 8.1   BEST ESTIMATE OF ONE-YEAR PREVALENCE RATES FOR ADULTS AGED 18 TO 54 AND 55+ YEARS, ON THE BASIS OF EPIDEMIOLOGIC CATCHMENT AREAS, U.S.A. DEPARTMENT OF HEALTH AND SOCIAL SERVICES (1999)

DIAGNOSIS	PREVALENCE 18–54 YEARS	PREVALENCE 55+ YEARS
Any anxiety disorder	13.1%	11.4%
Any mood disorder (major depression)	7.1%	4.4%
Schizophrenia	1.3%	0.6%
Somatization	0.2%	0.3%
Antisocial personality disorder	2.1%	0%
Anorexia nervosa	0.1%	0%
Severe cognitive disorder	1.2%	6.6%
Any disorder	19.5%	19.8%

Source: U.S. Department of Health and Social Services (1999).

Other than severe cognitive impairment, the most frequent disorders in later life concern anxiety and mood. Phobias are the most frequent disorders at any age. Agoraphobia is probably the most devastating phobia because a person fearful of public places (elevators, planes, open spaces) suffers a restricted life, frequently becoming housebound. Agoraphobia is also distinctive because of *panic attacks* that occur for no apparent reason. Although major depression in later life (i.e., as diagnosed by DSM-IV criteria) is no more frequent than at younger ages, the following section shows that susceptibility to minor depression may be high in later life.

Depression in Later Life

Depression stands opposite to mental well being on a mental health continuum. The symptoms of depression cited in DSM-IV (1994) include:

- Depressed mood (dysphoria)
- Loss of pleasure (anhedonia)
- Sleep disturbance
- Appetite disturbance
- Loss of energy
- Difficulty in concentration
- Low self-esteem
- Psychomotor retardation or agitation
- Suicidal thoughts.

For a diagnosis of **major depression**, at least five symptoms, including dysphoria or anhedonia, must be present for most of nearly every day during a two-week period. The worldwide prevalence of depression indicates higher rates among women than men and among unmarried (e.g., divorced, separated) than married people (Weissman, et al., 1996). Depression in older people increases the risk of mortality from physical illness (Schultz, Beach, Ives, Martire, Ariyo, & Kop, 2000) and suicide (U.S. Department of Health and Social Services, 1999), contributes to cognitive decline in the nondemented elderly (Yaffe, Blackwell, Gore, Sands, Reus, & Browner, 1999), and is an early manifestation (rather than a predictor) of dementia (Chen, Ganguli, Mulsant, & DeKosky, 1999).

Although the prevalence of major depression declines with age (i.e., a one-year prevalence of 5 percent or lower in older people), an inference that older people have a lower susceptibility to depression is contentious. There is evidence that older people may present symptoms of depression differently from younger people. Such presentation includes a more frequent appearance of anhedonia than dysphoria ("depression without sadness") and unexplained somatic complaints (Gallo & Rabins, 1999). Consequently, it is possible that depression is an underdiagnosed condition in later life and that patients without a dysphoria are at risk of undertreatment. The 1999 Surgeon General's report on mental health agrees. This report includes discussion of a proposal for a new diagnostic entity of "minor" depression to encompass individuals with an otherwise atypical presentation of depression (U.S. Department of Health and Social Services, 1999).

A psychological model of depression—the **tripartite model**—also distinguishes between anhedonia and dysphoria, albeit with different terminology. This model includes as components low positive affect (anhedonia), negative affect (dysphoria), and somatic arousal (i.e., symptoms associated with bodily excitation) (Joiner, 1996; Watson et al., 1995). Anhedonia in this model is specific to depression, somatic arousal to anxiety disorders, with negative affect present in both conditions. Epidemiological research suggests dysphoria to be a more frequent condition than anhedonia. A study of lifetime histories of depression in people aged over 65 years revealed that 15 percent of men and 33 percent of women reported dysphoria of at least two weeks' duration, whereas 8 percent of men and 16 percent of women experienced anhedonia for a similar duration (Steffens, et al., 2000). In elderly institutionalized populations, anhedonia, rather than dysphoria, may be the more frequent condition. Using a six-point scale of positive and negative affectivity, Figure 8.4 shows community residents to have higher positive affect than negative affect, whereas institution residents had dramatically lower scores for positive affect (Stones, 2000). These findings suggest that depression in institutions mainly involves a loss of pleasurable experiences.

Reports on the treatment of depression claim success in 60 to 80 percent of cases (U.S. Department of Health and Social Services, 1999), with the main forms of treatment including pharmacological intervention, electroconvulsive shock therapy, and psychosocial intervention. A Canadian innovation in the treatment for depression in older people was physical exercise (McNeil, LeBlanc, & Joyner, 1991). Subsequent research confirmed that its effectiveness was comparable with

Figure 8.4 POSITIVE AND NEGATIVE AFFECTIVITY IN OLDER COMMUNITY AND INSTITUTION RESIDENTS

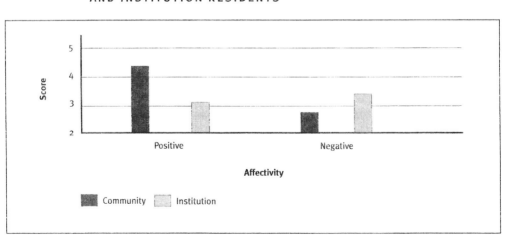

Source: Based on conceptualization by the author.

anti-depressive medication (Blumenthal et al., 1999). Because such findings show treatments for diagnosed depression to be successful in most cases, the resolution of issues about the accuracy of diagnosis in older people is of pressing concern.

CHAPTER SUMMARY

Key ideas to remember from this chapter include:

- Mental health is a continuum ranging from well being to distress.
- The distribution of mental well being shows negative skew, with the bulk of people located at the high end and a tail at the low end.
- Approximately 80 percent of people at any age report that they are happy, and about 20 percent have a medical diagnosis indicating some form of mental distress. Although some theorists suggest that error in measurement contributes to the shape of negative skew, the evidence suggests otherwise. In fact, Stones and Kozma (1991) showed how a skewed distribution could result from normally distributed precursors.
- Mental well being does not vary much with age in survey research, with no difference between gender groups in life satisfaction but more frequent reports of depressed mood in women than men. A diagnosis of clinical depression is also more frequent in women.
- Although mental well being has low correlations with demographic indicators, remains stable despite changes in life conditions, and shows resistance to transient life changes that affect mood, the levels are low for residents of restrictive environments, such as long-term care institutions. The probable reasons include a lack of choice, compared with life outside.
- Psychosocial intervention in an institutional setting is able to reverse such decrement to some degree, with attendant benefit to morbidity and mortality. However, mental well being outside the institutions relates more to personality and genetic dispositions than to life conditions. The relationship is so strong that some researchers conclude that trying to be happier is likely to be no more successful than trying to be taller.
- The treatment of mental disorder evolved from an institutional model to one emphasizing community care. Similarly, care of older people evolved from the poor house to a combination of nursing home and home care. Although the current models continue to receive their share of criticism, it is important to acknowledge the immense progress in humanitarian care that has occurred during the past few decades. Ongoing advances include the development of comprehensive and regularized assessment protocols for purposes of detecting problems, monitoring change and developing care plans.
- Although older people have rates lower than young people for most diagnosed mental disorders except cognitive impairment, the findings on depression may be misleading. The ways in which old people express depression—depression without sadness—shows a profile of low positive affect (or anhedonia), rather than depressed mood (or dysphoria). The Surgeon

General's 1999 report on mental health acknowledged this problem, which may result in the underdiagnosis of a disorder that responds well to treatment in an elderly population.

KEY TERMS

Reliability, **(p. 202)**

Validity, **(p. 202)**

Trait models, **(p. 202)**

Stage models, **(p. 202)**

Personality, **(p. 204)**

Big five traits, **(p. 204)**

Heritability, **(p. 204)**

Genetics, **(p. 204)**

Mental health, **(p. 204)**

Mental well being, **(p. 205)**

Happiness, **(p. 205)**

Life domain satisfactions, **(p. 205)**

Negatively skewed, **(p. 208)**

Response set, **(p. 209)**

Extremity set, **(p. 209)**

Impression management, **(p. 209)**

Social desirability, **(p. 210)**

Models of mental well being, **(p. 212)**

Reminiscence, **(p. 213)**

Control, **(p. 215)**

Mental disorders, **(p. 218)**

Psychiatry, **(p. 218)**

Geriatrics, **(p. 218)**

Psychogeriatrics, **(p. 218)**

Institutions, **(p. 219)**

Epidemiology, **(p. 223)**

Depression, **(p. 224)**

Major depression, **(p. 224)**

Tripartite model, **(p. 225)**

STUDY QUESTIONS

1. Older people tend to rate their present level of life satisfaction as lower than the level in earlier life. Does such a trend imply that mental well being decreases with age? Discuss the evidence.

2. We assume that life conditions affect our mental well being more than personality and genetics. Evaluate whether or not the evidence supports this assumption.

3. Most people in our society are happy. Is this statement borne out by the facts?

4. Evaluate levels of support for bottom-up, top-down, and up-down models of happiness.

5. Do older people differ from younger people in the frequency of psychiatric disorders?

6. Do the experience and expression of depression differ between old and young people?

SUGGESTED READINGS

Diener, E., Suh, E., Lucas, R.E., & Smith, H.L. (1999). Subjective well being: Three decades of progress. *Psychological Bulletin, 125,* 276–302.

Gallo, J.J. & Rabins, P.V. (1999). Sadness without depression: Alternative presentations of depression in later life. *American Family Physician, 60,* 820–826.

Myers, D.G. & Diener, E. (1995). Who is happy? *Psychological Science, 6,* 10–19.

Stones, M.J., Rattenbury, C., & Kozma, A. (1995). Empirical findings on reminiscence. In B.K. Haight & J. Webster (Eds.), *The art and science of reminiscing: Theory, research, methods, and applications.* Washington, D.C.: Taylor & Francis.

Appendix 8.A MEASUREMENT THEORY: SCALING

Scores fall into four kinds of scales:

1. *Nominal* scales include responses that differ in kind but not level (e.g., male or female).

2. *Ordinal* scales order responses according to size (e.g., Grade 10 implies more education than Grade 5).

3. *Interval* scales have equal intervals between adjacent scores (e.g., the difference between 5 and 10 degrees Celsius is the same as between 10 and 15 degrees Celsius).

4. *Ratio* scales are interval scales with an origin of zero. This enables comparison of the ratios of scores (e.g., a person aged 80 years is twice as old as somebody aged 40 years, who is twice as old as somebody aged 20 years).

   The logic of scaling implies that scores are additive for interval and ratio scales but not for nominal or ordinal scales (e.g., two children in Grade 5 do not have the same combined education as one child in Grade 10). Because most statistics assume the scores to be additive, nominal and ordinal data require different methods of analysis (Siegel, 1956). Although these challenges continue to occupy statisticians, modern statistical packages include procedures to analyze complex data below the interval level (SPSS, 1999).

Cognitive Competence and Aging

In this chapter, you will learn about:

- The barriers with age to the processing of sensory information.
- Whether and how age impairs different aspects of intelligence.

- How people continue to retain cognitive expertise and creativity with age.
- The effects of lifestyle and disease on cognitive expertise.

Introduction

Cognition refers to thoughts and perceptions as distinct from feelings and volitions. The work performed by cognition is on information, which at the earliest stage of reception is nothing more than the activation of some cells, rather than others, in a sensory receptor. In a seemingly miraculous way, the cognitive system:

*   Detects patterns in this activation
*   Decides whether the pattern is important
*   Holds it in memory long enough for integration with subsequent patterns
*   Maybe changes the total integrated pattern to accord with information processed in similar ways seconds, minutes, hours, weeks, years, and even decades before—the residues of which still endure within the brain—and retains that changed pattern, perhaps forever.

The term for the residues of previous information processing that reside within the brain is **memory**. Memories fall into two main categories: memories of information processed at a particular time, known as memories for episodes; and memories integrated into composite structures not specifically related to particular episodes, which fall under the rubric of *knowledge*.

An amazing feature of the human brain is that it is able to manipulate information stored in memory in similar ways to information received through the senses. The brain is able to detect differences, similarities, and incongruities between different bits of knowledge and create new knowledge or hypotheses about information not yet received. This kind of processing is analogous to intelligence and creativity, and its application to resolving important but uncertain issues in life goes by the term **wisdom**.

All the processes described thus far are susceptible to influences associated with age. Knowledge accumulates with experience and experience accumulates with age. On the other hand, old age may bring an increase in impediments that hinder the processing of information, whether from sensory sources or residing in memory. Such impediments include those associated with lifestyle and disease.

Sensory Sources and Information

Information acquisition begins at the sensory system. This section reviews changes with age in the important sensory systems that underlie the acquisition of visual and auditory information, as well as **senses** relevant to taste, smell, touch, temperature, pain, and the position of the body in space.

Vision

Recent reviews of vision suggest that two kinds of change occur at different ages (Fozard & Gordon-Salant, 2001; Kline & Scialfa, 1996). Changes in the outer parts

---

Box 9.1 On Not Growing Old

Consider the following people. What do they have in common?

Winston Churchill of Great Britain

Mao Tse-tung of China

Benjamin Franklin, the inventor

Michelangelo, the painter

Asa Gray, the botanist

Wilhelm Wundt, the father of modern psychology

Goethe, the author of *Faust* and other literary masterpieces

Cervantes, who wrote *Don Quixote*

Maggie Kuhn, founder of the *Gray Panthers* group of social activists

George Burns, the entertainer

None of them let age stand in their way of doing what they wanted. The world we know is like it is today because of the likes of Churchill, Mao Tse-tung, and Charles de Gaulle of France, all of whom led the governments of their countries when in their 70s. Asa Gray and Wilhelm Wundt both contributed seminal works to their respective sciences at ages beyond 75 years, and Franklin invented the bifocal lens when nearly 80 years old. Goethe, Cervantes, and Michelangelo all produced their most famous literary or artistic creations at an age now termed the golden years. Maggie Kuhn pioneered a revolution for seniors when herself a senior. George Burns, who died when 100 years old, was performing and acting well into his 90s. In the last interview we saw him give, he was still talking about how much he loved his late wife Gracie, and he was still cracking jokes with sexual innuendo.

None of these famous people ever grew old.

Source: Lee and Michael Stones (1996), *Sex May Be Wasted on the Young.*

---

of the eye, such as the cornea and lens, begin to occur in many people between 35 and 45 years of age. These changes include a loss of flexibility in the lens resulting in a decrease in the eye's ability to change shape to view objects at different distances— termed a difficulty in *accommodation*. This problem particularly affects vision for objects close to the eye, a condition termed *presbyopia*, which is why the first glasses usually acquired by people with previously normal vision are reading glasses.

Another change is a yellowing of the lens with age. This change results in a reduction in the amount and quality of light passing through the lens to reach the retina. Because yellow absorbs the shorter wavelengths, the light at the retina of older people is deficient particularly at the blue-green end of the spectrum. However, the main problem caused by yellowing is that compared with younger people, older people need more illumination to view objects, with colour constancy maintained by compensatory mechanisms.

Other changes to the eye include the development of cataracts and a decrease in pupil size with age. Both these conditions make more illumination a necessity for older people. Cataracts mainly affect people in their 70s and older. The condition results in opacity of the lens, which blocks light from reaching the retina. Another consequence of opacity is glare, which results from scattering of the light as it passes through the lens. Susceptibility to glare presents particular problems for driving at night because the headlights of oncoming cars result in glare even in people with unimpaired vision. Although cataracts afflict up to 25 percent of people aged over 75 years, the condition is now amenable to simple surgical correction.

Because additional consequences of the preceding changes extend to deficiencies with age in depth perception and field of vision, it is not surprising that the number of people requiring visual correction increases with age. The U.S. National Center for Health Statistics (1994) estimates that less that 50 percent of people in any cohort up to 44 years of age require corrective devices but that the proportion increases to 80 percent or more in older cohorts.

The second category of change includes effects on the receptor cells in the retina. Two such effects are *senile macular degeneration* and *glaucoma*. The former affects the macula, which is a part of the retina particularly relevant for acute vision. A consequence of this condition is a loss in visual acuity, which, if severe, may necessitate the use of a strong magnifying glass for pursuits such as reading. Glaucoma involves high intraocular pressure that damages the optic nerve and affects the visual field. Although both senile macular degeneration and glaucoma are diseases mainly affecting people over 55 years of age, the majority of older people show evidence of retinal damage (Fozard & Gordon-Salant, 2001), suggesting effects associated with normal living, regardless of diagnosed disease.

Hearing

Losses in hearing, like vision, begin to be noticeable by midlife. Fozard (1990) noted that one person in five had hearing difficulties between the ages of 45 and 54 years, compared with three-quarters of the population aged over 75 years, with the rates higher for males than females. Although external factors, such as wax accumulation, contribute to impaired hearing, the main cause is damage to the cochlea, which is the main neural receptor. This damage includes a loss of hair cells, which are the ear's equivalent to retinal cells in the eye, and problems of metabolism within the inner ear.

Two of the more prominent forms of hearing loss are *presbycusis* (a loss of reception of high frequency sounds) and *tinnitus* (the presence of high-pitched background noise). The former means that older people generally have more difficulty than those younger in hearing notes higher than bass notes in music, with the problem greater in men than in women. Tinnitus distracts and annoys those afflicted.

From a functional perspective, the main problem associated with hearing loss is the reduced ability to understand speech, which often leads to feelings of social isolation with its concomitant dilemmas. Bergman et al. (1976) found that various difficulties increased with age in the following order (i.e., from least to most):

- Normal speech
- Rapid speech
- Listening to one speaker among many
- Listening to speech in the presence of reverberation or echo
- Listening to interrupted speech.

These findings suggest that rapidity and distraction augment hearing difficulties in older people. They also point to ways to make speech more intelligible (e.g., slow paced speech without interruption or external distraction). The conventional hearing aid provides only a partial solution because it amplifies the background noise as well as foreground speech. Advances in hearing aid technology and the acoustic ecology hold the promise to rectify some of these problems (Fozard & Gordon-Salant, 2001).

Taste and Smell

Sensitivity to taste and smell show slight decline in late life, with some suggestion that sensitivity to sweet and salty tastes shows greater loss than sensitivity to bitter and sour tastes (Stevens, Cruz, Marks, & Lakatos, 1998). The implications are that older people may enjoy their food less than at a younger age and be less aware of smells indicating the putrefaction of food and the presence of other toxins that cause unpleasant odour, posing a danger to themselves and others.

Touch, Temperature, and Pain

Gescheider (1997) reported that vibrotactile sensitivity declined substantially with age, especially with high frequency stimulation. Losses in temperature sensitivity also occur with age (Stevens, Cruz, Marks, & Lakatos, 1998), which may put older people at risk of hypothermia during the cold Canadian winters.

The research on pain is inconsistent about whether pain sensitivity decreases with age, although there is some evidence that older people under-report low-intensity pain but not high-intensity pain (Harkins, Price, & Martinelli, 1986). Confounds in the naturalistic study of pain include the involvement of personality and emotion—not just the painful stimulus—and the greater susceptibility of older people to disease and disability associated with pain. Hadjistavropoulos (2001) indicates that pain is a significant problem for many older people, with a seven-day prevalence of pain in 50 percent of Canadian nursing home residents and 24 percent experiencing daily pain (Proctor & Hirdes, 2001).

Kinesthesis

Kinesthesis refers to awareness of the body's positioning as it moves through space. Simoneau and Liebowitz (1996) reviewed evidence indicating a loss of kinesthesis with age (e.g., reduced ability to touch one's nose with eyes closed). Low kinesthesis has implications for poor gait and balance and a higher susceptibility to falls.

Acquisition and Retrieval

Memory refers to the acquisition and retrieval of information. A model derived from James (1890) and elaborated by Atkinson and Shiffrin (1968) continues to provide a framework for structuring discussions about memory and aging. This model includes three stages of sensory, short-term, and long-term memory, as illustrated in Figure 9.1. The position of the circles in Figure 9.1 represents the temporal sequence of information acquisition (i.e., the inner circles represent earlier stages). The area of the circles represents both the duration of storage and the amount of information retrievable from the respective stores.

Figure 9.1 THE THREE STAGES OF MEMORY

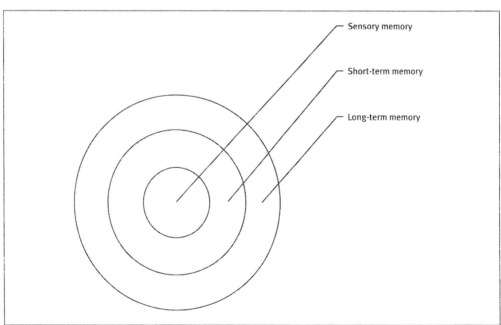

Source: Based on conceptualization by the author.

Sensory Memory

This store holds information received from the environment for a very brief interval. The terms for memory traces associated with different sensory systems include *icons* if the information is visual and *echoes* if auditory. The information persists in these stores only long enough for processing and subsequent transfer to a store of longer duration (e.g., the sound of a word before comprehension of its meaning). Although studies on the masking of previous by subsequent visual information suggest a limited age effect on iconic memory, the minor age differences in sensory storage are unlikely to contribute greatly to any deficiencies in short-term memory (Craik & Jennings, 1992).

Short-Term Memory

Short-term memory is an intermediate stage between sensory memory and long-term storage. It corresponds to the time information resides in consciousness while being processed for transfer to long-term memory. A distinction made between types of short-term memory includes *primary memory* and *working memory*, such that the former refers to passive storage and the latter to active manipulation of information.

Primary Memory.

Tests of primary memory include the *Digits Forward* subtest of the Wechsler Adult Intelligence Scale (WAIS; Wechsler, 1958), in which performance is the longest sequence of digits a respondent is able to recall after a single auditory presentation. Other tests of memory span use a nonmeaningful sequence of words, rather than digits. Most people are able to recall a string of six to eight digits, with no appreciable decline until very late in life, except in cases of pathology affecting cognition (e.g., dementia) (Craik & Jennings, 1992).

Working Memory.

Working memory involves mental manipulation of the information in consciousness into a form appropriate for long-term storage (Baddeley, 1986). An example is the *Digits Backward* subtest on the WAIS, in which the respondent recalls the presented sequence in reverse order. Recall on this test is typically lower than on the *Digits Forward* test by one to two digits and, unlike the latter, declines with age.

Hultsch and colleagues (1992) report further evidence that working memory declines with age in both cross-sectional and longitudinal research paradigms. However, the reasons for this deterioration remain unclear. Salthouse and Babcock (1991) suggest that the deficiency may reside in processing, rather than in capacity or storage.

Long-Term Memory

Long-term memory refers to a large capacity storage system in which memories reside over prolonged durations. There are four main categories of long-term memory:

1. Episodic memory refers to the remembering of discrete events.
2. Semantic memory includes knowledge about concepts or events not necessarily associated with a single episode of acquisition (e.g., the provinces of Canada).
3. Procedural memory involves the retention of skill (e.g., driving).
4. Prospective memory is remembering to do something at a future time.

These four categories, although conceptually distinct, may show some correlation. There is ample evidence that people with higher general knowledge perform at higher levels on episodic memory tasks (Hultsch et al., 1993). Because general knowledge involves retrieval from semantic memory, a relationship is evident. Similarly, the effects of disease have implications for a range of cognitive performances, with the generalized memory loss in dementia being an extreme example. However, evidence also suggests that the memory systems operate independently. Tulving, Hayman, and MacDonald (1991) reported on the cases of a brain-injured person with amnesia for past episodes in his life but retention of semantic and procedural memories (e.g., he remembered that his father taught him to play chess and the skills involved in playing chess but failed to remember any game he ever played). In a recognition task, Parkin and Walter (1992) provided evidence that while younger people report that they *remember* items previously presented, older people more often report *knowing* that the items were present. This distinction between remembering and knowing appears to relate to retrieval from episodic and semantic memory, respectively.

Acquisition of Information into Long-Term Memory.

The process of acquisition relates to the kinds of activity performed in working memory. Older people can organize material for later retrieval as effectively as young people can (Bäckman, 2001). Older people are particularly disadvantaged with unfamiliar information, material presented at a fast rate, and tasks that require effortful, rather than automatic, processing (Hasher & Zacks, 1979). These deficits may indicate diminished resource capacity, low motivation, or the persistence of less effective processing strategies dating from their school years. However, when taught mnemonic techniques to aid retrieval, the recall of older people improves. These findings suggest that older people are, indeed, able to learn new ways of learning.

Retrieval from Long-Term Memory.

Shonfield and Robertson (1966) were the first to show that the loss with age in the recall of information is less than the age loss in recognition of that information.

One reason for this discrepancy may be that recall invokes only episodic memory, whereas recognition brings semantic memory into play (e.g., the respondent may "know" an item through familiarity but not "remember" it from the learning trials). Because older people rely more on semantic memory than episodic memory at retrieval (Parkin and Walter, 1992), their performance may benefit accordingly.

Another reason relates to organization. In order to recall information, a respondent has to retrieve not only the specific content but also the organization imposed on that content during acquisition. The necessity to retrieve organization is less pressing in recognition because the task itself provides cues to organization. An example is the recall of prose, which has a higher level of organization than the typical word list task used in studies of memory, and which shows less loss associated with age. Older respondents show less loss with age in the recall of well-organized prose, compared with poorly organized prose, and similarly benefit in word list learning after instruction on how to organize the material during acquisition (i.e., as compared with conditions without such instructions) (Hultsch, 1971). Craik and Jennings (1992) provide compatible evidence with findings that the presence of retrieval cues disproportionately benefits recall by older persons, compared with younger persons.

A stereotype about old people is that they live in the past, remembering more about events decades past than current events. If this stereotype has any validity, issues remain about whether reminiscing about the past occurs because of a failure to acquire or retrieve recent memories or because earlier life events were more significant (e.g., the lyrics of Bruce Springsteen's song, *Glory Days*, suggest the latter). Our earliest memories usually date from about 4 1/2 years of age and coincide with the development of the self-concept. Rubin (1999) reported that older adults have a higher frequency of autobiographical memories for the period from 10 to 30 years of age than for any other period. His interpretation is consistent with a *Glory Days* hypothesis that these memories were for events significant in the lives of the respondents. Similarly, Fitzgerald (1988) found that especially vivid memories by older people dated from a period of late adolescence to early adulthood.

Evidence on the retrieval of very old memories indicates considerable retention. Bahrick and Wittlinger (1975) studied memory for high school classmates, the accuracy of which they checked against corresponding high school yearbooks. Their findings indicated that recall fell sharply during the three years since leaving school but remained consistently above 60 percent until 25 years after graduation, after which time it continued to decline. Name and picture recognition showed minimal decline for 34 years after graduation, consistently remaining at about 90 percent, after which it declined steeply. These findings suggest that although distortion and inaccuracies may be present in long-term memory, memories from late adolescence persist with considerable accuracy for decades after the event.

Metamemory

Metamemory refers to people's knowledge and beliefs about memory, including their own memory. Hess and Pullen (1996) pointed out that older people more frequently have negative evaluations of their memory, compared with young adults, report more memory failures, and expect to perform worse in memory testing. The main age difference in metamemory concerns *self-efficacy*, which refers to beliefs about one's own memory (Hertzog, Dixon, & Hultsch, 1990). However, Hess and Pullen's (1996) review shows the relationships between metamemory and actual memory performance to be minimal.

Intelligence

Ideas about **intelligence** and its measurement underwent successive revisions during the past century. Galton (1883) in England measured intelligence by the ability to process sensory information, with the more intelligent person presumed to make finer distinctions in modalities, such as hearing, taste, and weight discrimination. Binet in France attempted to differentiate between children failing at school because of low intelligence from those failing for other reasons (e.g., low motivation). The Binet and Simon (1905) test measured ability to solve cognitive problems, rather than make sensory discriminations, and its success was such that other countries adopted Binet's ideas about intelligence as well as his methods of measurement. Spearman (1927) in England supported Binet's assertion that intelligence includes a single ability to solve problems whatever the nature of the task presented. Wechsler (1958) in the United States developed the Wechsler Adult Intelligence Scale (WAIS) using different tasks to measure intelligence in different spheres of functioning. The WAIS also used a different procedure from Binet to compute the level of intelligence, or *intelligence quotient*, which involved comparison of performance with those by people of similar ages. However, others in the United States challenged the assumption of intelligence as a single ability, suggesting instead that intelligence comprises different and distinguishable mental abilities termed *primary mental abilities* (Thurstone, 1938). The multiple abilities model persists to the present day, although with variation in the ways of classifying these abilities.

Thurstone's (1938) model, and modified measure, endures in research on aging by Schaie and colleagues, with primary mental abilities that include:

- Verbal comprehension—evidenced by the ability to understand verbal information
- Word fluency—the ability to solve anagrams, to generate instances of a category
- Number—involved in arithmetic calculation
- Spatial orientation—concerned with spatial aspects of problem solving
- Associative memory—mainly relevant to rote learning

- Perceptual speed—speed of making distinctions in spatial problems
- Inductive reasoning—which involves the extraction of rules linking the elements in a problem.

Other classifications include a distinction between *fluid* and *crystallized* intelligence (Horn, 1982). **Fluid intelligence** refers to mental abilities not acquired by learning from one's culture but which may reflect individual differences in the integrity of the central nervous system. Horn (1982) assumed fluid intelligence to increase with the maturation of the central nervous system to the end of adolescence but to decline thereafter because of age changes and other deleterious effects on the brain. **Crystallized intelligence** refers to problem solving skills acquired from the culture. Such skills include the verbal abilities learned during school and from life experiences thereafter (e.g., vocabulary, practical reasoning, concept formation). Although Horn (1982) supposed crystallized intelligence to continue to increase with new learning throughout the life span, there is evidence for deterioration in advanced old age (Schaie, 1996).

Sternberg (1984) distinguished between applications of intelligence to the inner world and the external environment and their juxtaposition. Baltes (1993) differentiated the mechanical processes of intelligence from their pragmatic application, which can continue to increase to advanced ages.

Age Trends in Intelligence

Cross-sectional findings on adult intelligence suggest overall declines with age that affect some tasks and abilities more than other skills. Wechsler (1972) noted steeper declines on spatial tasks, rather than verbal tasks, which were due only partially to declining speed of performance. Schaie and Willis (1993) found verbal ability and numeric ability to show no substantial loss until age 60 to 70 years, compared with the other primary mental abilities that begin to deteriorate about three decades earlier. Horn (1982) reported that fluid intelligence begins to decline steadily after young adulthood, whereas crystallized intelligence continues to increase until advanced age.

Problems in the interpretation of cross-sectional data include a confounding of the effects of cohort and age in the research design. Schaie (1996) showed that successive cohorts born during the earliest two-thirds of the 20th century had progressively higher scores on such tests as inductive reasoning, verbal meaning, and spatial orientation. These increases across successive cohorts probably relate to higher levels of education and better nutrition and medical services. A consequence is that cross-sectional comparison between different cohorts usually provides an overestimation of the effects of aging.

Longitudinal research negates any confounding with cohort differences because the same cohort contributes data at two or more intervals of time. Canadian longitudinal studies (Arbuckle, Maag, Pushkar, & Chaikelson, 1998;

Schwartzman, Gold, Andres, Arbuckle, & Chaikelson, 1987) found low losses over 40 years or more (i.e., to age 65+ years)—but a slight gain if given extra time to solve the problems)—with gains more likely on verbal tasks and losses more likely on spatial tasks. Those individuals with more years of education and who were more active were also the more likely to show higher intelligence at all ages.

Other researchers studied different cohorts over intervals of three decades or more. Schaie (1996) reported little or no decline until age 60 years, slight decline until the mid-70s, followed by more pronounced deterioration. Although confounds in longitudinal studies include higher rates of dropout and death among those scoring lower on tests of intelligence, these trends persist even after correcting for such error. Consequently, it is fair to conclude that intelligence remains close to the levels in earlier life until long after the retirement age of 65 years.

Cognitive Expertise

Who is an expert? An expert is not just someone with an acknowledged skill; the term implies more than just competence. Although most people are competent at skills practised routinely in everyday life (e.g., driving), expertise connotes a higher degree of exclusivity. **Experts** are people who are not only competent, but who consistently show exclusive competence relative to their reference group (Salthouse, 1991).

These people fall within either of two categories: (1) Those who are *normatively exclusive* perform at the upper extreme of the normal distribution for an everyday skill (e.g., reading, typing, doing arithmetic). This form of expertise is always relative to the population of a culture at a specific point in history. Findings in the previous section on intelligence showed that successive cohorts in the United States during the 20th century increased in verbal comprehension skills. Although all people possess some degree of verbal comprehension skills, expert status implies (at the very least) an exceptional vocabulary. (2) Other experts have *exclusive skills* not possessed by the majority of the population. An undergraduate in Canada able to surf the Internet for hard-to-find information hardly has exclusive skills in computer expertise. The skill is less common among Canadian seniors (although getting more so) but qualifies as an exclusive skill in the developing countries with a scarcity of computers for everyday use. Good equestrian skills border on exclusivity in the modern era but were common a hundred years ago. Again, the evaluation of exclusive skills is relative to culture and history.

Studies with relevance to expertise fall within three main paradigms:

1. Comparisons between experts and others regarding the attributes of expert performance
2. Research on creativity
3. Studies that attempt to elucidate the properties of wisdom.

Expert Performance.

Typing is a skill possessed to some level of competence by many people in modern Canadian society. Expert typists are those able to type accurately at high speed. Salthouse (1984) examined the skills of younger and older typists differing in their level of typing proficiency. Using laboratory tests of reaction time, tapping speed, and coding skill, he found deficiencies of a direction and magnitude expected with age. If these attributes relate to typing expertise, the expectation should be of declining typing proficiency with age. Surprisingly, this was not the case, with typing speed being uncorrelated with age but predicted instead by the expert or novice status of the typists. The older expert typists showed the expected loss in reaction time and tapping speed, but compensated by scanning the printed text less frequently, thereby providing more time to plan successive keystrokes. By using this form of compensation, they were able to retain proficiency despite deterioration in the component skills.

Charness (1981; 1985) studied chess experts. He found that among players matched in skill, the older players were less able to recall positions accurately. However, they compensated for this deficiency by their ability to choose the best possible next move from among alternatives. In other words, they used the knowledge acquired from years of experience to compensate for deficiencies in memory and processing. He reached similar conclusions from studies of bridge players.

These findings suggest that experts use the knowledge acquired through extended practice to compensate for losses in basic mental abilities. Charness pointed out that laboratory tasks make it less possible to compensate with knowledge for declining mental abilities. The same is also true of real life performances that require speed, endurance, or strength but little knowledge or strategy. Findings from Chapter 7 on physical competence are consistent in showing that superior performance in later life is less frequent in high effort but low strategy pursuits.

Creativity.

Creativity is a poorly understood concept, although one that differs from intelligence in the opinion of most theorists. A frequent distinction made by researchers is that intelligence implies *convergent thinking*, in which the respondent selects one correct response from several alternatives (e.g., the meaning of the word *antiquary*; the next number in a sequence beginning 1, 1, 2, 3, 5, 8...). A precursor of **creativity**, on the other hand, is *divergent thinking*, in which the respondent generates multiple instances of a concept (e.g., possible uses of a sock). Convergent thinking may or may not require an extensive knowledge base to solve the problem, but creativity in the real world usually requires an extensive knowledge base from which the creative act can emerge.

McCrae, Arenberg, and Costa (1987) conducted a comprehensive study of intelligence and creativity across the adult age span. They measured intelligence by a vocabulary test and creativity by four divergent thinking tests. The design included both cross-sectional and longitudinal methods of data collection. The findings indicated no relationship between vocabulary and divergent thinking, with the latter showing modest declines with age. These findings complement those by Ruth and Birren (1985), who found creativity to decline with age in cross-sectional research.

Findings on creativity outside the constraints of academic research vary according to the criteria used to define a creative act or production. Early research suggested that the frequency of products judged as exceptionally creative peaked when the originators were aged in their 30s, thereafter showing gradual decline (Lehman, 1953). Dennis (1966) examined the total productivity, rather than single masterpieces, of long-lived scholars in various disciplines, finding that their 60s was the most productive decade. Simonton (1990) concluded that the periods of high productivity coincided with the highest rate of producing masterpieces, with the ratio of the two unrelated to stage of career. What are we to make of these apparently discrepant findings?

Part of the answer is that creativity in the real world may take second place to other concerns as people age. Simonton (1990) suggested that for many creative people the need to be creative becomes secondary to a need to be wise. Successful people in our society often find themselves taking on positions with administrative responsibility in their later careers, which limits the time available for creative output. It is also true that the desire to foster creativity in others supplants for many people the desire to be creative oneself. Another reason is that once an innovator achieves success with a creative piece of work, social and commercial pressures may encourage that person to produce more of the same, rather than chance something different. It is for reasons like this that some successful novelists and painters subsequently opt to reproduce variants on the pattern that brought them their first success. Such considerations suggest that declines with age in the output of truly creative productions may have less to do with waning creative prowess with age than with social influence that reward other than creative pursuits.

Wisdom.

Baltes and Staudinger (1993) suggested that *wisdom* implies good judgment in important but uncertain matters of life. The basic dimensions of wisdom include the *mechanics of mind* and the *pragmatics of mind*. The former refers to the basic information processing system, and the latter to factual and strategic knowledge and their relationship to problem solving in real life situations. Consequently, wisdom implies the application of expert knowledge that includes knowledge:

- About the basic pragmatics of life (both factual and strategic)
- About the uncertainties in life
- About context
- That is appreciative of the relativism of values and goals in life.

Baltes and Staudinger (1993) suggest that three factors affect wisdom. First, wisdom is likely to increase with the knowledge gained through life experience. However, not everyone has the requisite life experiences and aging brings about some decrement in the mechanics of mind. Second, personality traits, such as openness to experience, may foster one's knowledge about uncertainties and relativism. Third, specific experiences relevant to decision making may promote wisdom about those life domains. Consequently, the hypothesized relationship of wisdom with age may be secondary to its relationship with favourable life experiences.

Influences on Cognitive Expertise

Health and lifestyle, not surprisingly, have effects on cognition. Several cross-sectional and longitudinal studies show that hypertension contributes to less favourable outcomes with age on a range of cognitive measures in middle-aged and older people (Schaie, 1990; Schultz, Elias, Robbins, Streeter, & Blakeman, 1986). Hultsch, Hammer, and Small (1993) reported that self-reported health, level of alcohol intake, smoking, and physical activity all predicted mental competences in older people. A term used to describe the effects of habitually low levels of physical activity is **hypokinetic disease**, the effects of which on cognition became the focus of considerable research. These studies are important because hypokinesis is a preventable condition in most middle-aged and older people.

Hypokinetic Disease.

Studies of hypokinetic disease fall into three categories: (1) studies of old people exposed to a single dose of **exercise**; (2) cross-sectional comparisons of physically active and inactive people of different ages; and (3) studies of activity intervention.

Single Doses of Exercise.

Three such studies found temporary gains in cognition from a single dose of very low-intensity exercise among very sedentary older people. All three studies used a controlled design with random assignment of participants to conditions. Diesfeldt and Diesfeldt-Groenendijk (1977) and Stones and Dawe (1993) found gains in verbal memory with nursing home residents aged in the 80s. Stones and Dawe (1993) reported that the exercise raised the heart rate of residents by only two beats per minute to produce a gain in semantic memory of more than 20 percent. Diesfeldt and Diesfeldt-Groenendijk (1977) reported a gain in verbal memory of 35 percent. Molloy, Beerschoten, Borrie, Crilly, and Cape (1988) studied hospital outpatients mainly in their 60s. They also found improvement on some cognitive tasks after a bout of acute exercise. Although these studies did not examine the duration of the beneficial effects, we presume them to be temporary because the exercise was too brief to produce any increase in long-term physical fitness.

Cross-Sectional Studies of Exercise and Cognition.

The cross-sectional studies typically compare younger and older participants classified as regularly active or inactive. The activity classification in different studies includes participation in sport, scores on activity indexes, and appraised fitness. The cognitive measures used as the dependent variable include those considered likely to show effects because of activity or fitness (e.g., reaction time, tapping, neuropsychological tests), with the activity groups usually equated on aspects of cognition thought not to be sensitive to activity effects (e.g., verbal intelligence). A problem with this kind of design is that the selection of participants is not random. The participants in the physically active conditions self-select themselves according to lifestyle and may differ from inactive participants on dimensions other than activity and fitness (e.g., nutrition, smoking, alcohol intake).

Findings with cross-sectional studies consistently show favourable levels of proficiency associated with a younger age and higher activity, sometimes with an age by activity interaction (Stones & Kozma, 1988; Dustman et al., 1984). Such interactions have interpretative significance because a greater discrepancy between active and inactive participants at older ages may suggest that activity postpones decline on activity-sensitive aspects of cognition. An early study by Spirduso (1975) found age by activity interactions using reaction time, with no age difference in the active participants but a performance loss with age in the inactive. Spirduso and Clifford (1978) found somewhat similar trends, as did Stones and Kozma (1989) with one of two coding tasks. Others such as Dustman et al. (1990) and Spirduso, MacCrae, MacCrae, Prewitt, and Osborne (1988) found no interactions using a range of cognitive and motor tasks.

Kozma and Stones (1990) offered a reinterpretation of Spirduso's early findings, which involved comparisons between racquet sport players of various ages and nonathletic control groups. Although Spirduso hypothesized that fitness was responsible for the absence of age effects in the reaction times of racquet sport players (e.g., the retention of cardio-respiratory fitness might postpone the onset of age-related hypoxia), Stones and Kozma (1990) argued that practice, rather than fitness, was the causal agent. Playing a racquet sport involves the frequent practice of quick reactions, which are less practised in everyday life, and the *use it or lose it* principle might account for the findings. They provided evidence that specific practice and habitual activity both contribute to tapping performance. They measured tapping speed using up and down and back and forth movement patterns. With the up and down task, the older participants were slower in hand tapping, but there were no age differences in foot tapping. The researchers attributed the latter to the habitual practice of a closely related form of movement in everyday walking. With the back and forth task, tapping speed was higher at younger ages and among the more active participants, with no interaction. This task involves a form of movement not practised in everyday contexts and feels quite unfamiliar. Consequently, their findings support a *use it or lose it* interpretation of age effects for familiar movements but suggest that habitual activity (e.g., fitness) predicts proficiency with unfamiliar movements.

The *use it or lose it* principle also shows applicability in early work on age loss in writing speed (La Riviere & Simonson, 1965), and subsequently in a variety of expert–novice paradigms (Allard, 1993). Spirduso articulated this principle at the cellular level with her assertion that "cell aging is influenced to a large degree by the amount of activity in which the cell is involved." (Spirduso, 1980: 860).

Exercise Intervention.

Models of aerobic exercise intervention suggest that gains in cardio-respiratory fitness benefit the central nervous system (e.g. decreased hypoxia, improved neurotransmitter functioning), resulting in improved neuropsychological performance. Animal studies consistently support this model with findings of improved performance after exercise intervention (Dustman et al., 1994). The findings from comparable studies with humans proved disappointing by comparison. The review of 12 controlled studies of aerobic training effects on human neuropsychological performance by Dustman et al. (1994) showed only one study with gains substantial enough to make a difference to everyday functioning.

The reasons for the discrepancy between the animal and human studies may include:

- A longer duration of exercising, relative to life span, in the animal studies (e.g., interventions with rodents typically lasted three to 12 months compared with three to four months in humans).
- Older sedentary humans may have other diseases that limit the potential for cognitive gain.
- It is possible that the prior fitness level of human participants limits the potential for therapeutic gain.

Stones and Kozma (1996) noted some evidence for the latter. They estimated the baseline cardio-respiratory function in the Dustman et al. (1984) study to be 20 percent below the normative age mean but to have risen to the level of the normative mean at the end of the intervention. The only other studies in which the participants were comparably unfit at baseline were much less successful in their attempts to promote fitness (Blumenthal et al., 1989; Madden, Blumenthal, Allen, & Emery, 1989). Because Dustman et al. (1984) was the only study to report substantial gains in neuropsychological performance, it is conceivable that the latter depends on both low baseline fitness and a substantial gain in fitness through exercise intervention.

Diseases That Impair Cognition

The two main conditions associated with impaired cognitive competence in later life are dementia and delirium. **Dementia** at this age most frequently takes the form of Alzheimer's disease or vascular dementia. Both involve a progressive deterioration in cognitive competence because of changes within the brain, but vascular dementia has a different etiology and includes signs of focal neurological damage. **Delirium** is a disturbance of consciousness and cognition associated with a medical condition, the use or withdrawal of drugs, or other conditions. Table 9.1 shows the basic diagnostic criteria for the three conditions in the fourth edition of the Diagnostic and Statistical Manual of the American Psychiatric Association (DSM-IV).

A large study that estimated the prevalence of dementia in Canada was the Canadian Study of Health and Aging (Canadian Study of Health and Aging Working Group, 1994a). The study divided the country into five regions and sampled representatively from community and institutional settings but excluded the territories, First Nations reservations, and military units. The total sample included 9,000 persons aged 65 years or older. All participants received initial screening using a standard measure to identify cognitive impairment. All institution residents and those living in the community with impaired scores on the screening tool received a clinical examination to diagnose

Table 9.1 DSM-IV DIAGNOSTIC CRITERIA FOR DEMENTIA AND DELIRIUM

Dementia includes disorders with multiple cognitive deficits. The most common type in later life is Alzheimer's disease, with vascular dementia of lower prevalence.

Alzheimer's disease can be of early or late onset (65 years), and occur with delirium, delusions, or depressed mood. Diagnostic criteria include the following:

A. Both (1) memory impairment, and (2) at least one of language impairment, motor impairment, impaired recognition of objects, impaired executive functioning

B. The preceding result in impaired social or occupational functioning, and represent a decline from previous levels

C. Gradual onset and continuation of symptoms

D. The symptoms are not because of other forms of illness.

Vascular dementia includes criteria A and B (above), and also:

C. Focal neurological signs or symptoms

D. The deficits do not occur exclusively during a delirium.

Delirium includes a disturbance of consciousness and cognition, associated with a medical condition, substance use or withdrawal, or multiple or unspecified etiology. The criteria include:

A. Disturbance of consciousness

B. Disturbance of cognition

C. Development over a short period

D. Evidence of a contributing condition.

Source: Adapted from "Delirium, Dementia, and Amnestic and Other Cognitive Disorders," APA.

dementia. The definitions of dementia and Alzheimer's disease were those conventionally used.

The findings indicated that 252,600 (8 percent) of all Canadians aged 65 years or over met the criteria for dementia. Half of these people resided in institutions, and two-thirds were female, with the prevalence rate increasing with age. The specific rates for Alzheimer's disease and vascular dementia were 5.1 percent and 1.5 percent, respectively. The authors estimated that if the prevalence rate remains constant the number of Canadians with dementia would double during 1994 to 2021 because of demographic changes in the population.

Risk factors for dementia found in the Canadian Study of Health and Aging included family history, low education, and head injury, with low risk associated with arthritis and the use of nonsteroidal anti-inflammatory drugs. These risks are similar to those previously reported (Canadian Study of Health and Aging Working Group, 1994b).

There is a predictable stage-by-stage progression of cognitive decline in Alzheimer's disease (Reisberg, Ferris, de Leon, & Crook, 1982). The symptoms in sequence include forgetfulness, then confusion, failure to recognize familiar people, loss of memory for recent events, disorientation, and finally the loss of all verbal ability. Other dysfunctions that accompany cognitive decline include those listed in Box 9.2 as well as loss of control over bodily functions and personality change.

Delirium differs from dementia because its (1) onset is abrupt, (2) duration is usually brief, and (3) appearance coincides with that of another disorder. Martin, Stones, Young, and Bédard (2000) found that nearly 20 percent of consecutive admissions to an acute hospital experienced an episode of delirium, usually beginning within three days from admission. Precipitating factors included illness, medication, and the loss of control brought about by relocation to an unfamiliar (i.e., hospital) setting and associated medical procedures.

Box 9.2 Correlates of Dementia in Nursing Homes

Findings from approximately 400 cases in the Resident Assessment Instrument Health Infomatics Project (2000) show 43 percent with a diagnosis of dementia.

Significant correlates of dementia include:

* Cognitive impairment
* Lack of social involvement
* Behavioural disturbance
* Limitations in everyday activity.

Source: Stones, 2000

....

Figure 9.2 SCORES ON COGNITIVE IMPAIRMENT AND SYMPTOMS OF
DEMENTIA SCALES BY NURSING HOME RESIDENTS WITH OR
WITHOUT DIAGNOSED DEMENTIA

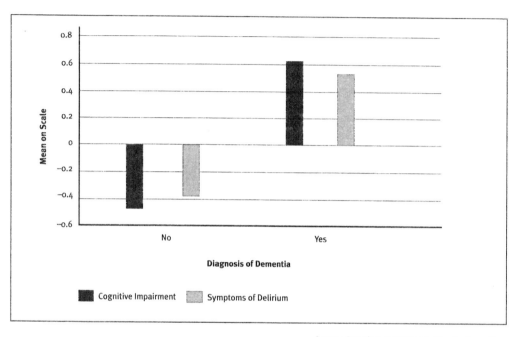

Source: Based on conceptualization by the author.

Delirium has adverse implications for early discharge and subsequent placement, especially if physicians in acute hospitals mistake the symptoms of delirium for dementia. Although such misdiagnosis tends to be less frequent now
than a few years ago, patients with dementia do exhibit some of the symptoms
associated with delirium. Figure 9.2 shows standardized scores on indexes of
cognitive impairment and symptoms of delirium. Seventy-seven percent of the
residents with dementia and 33 percent without dementia had more than one
symptom indicating disturbed consciousness and cognition associated with delirium, but in only 5 percent of total cases were the symptoms of recent origin.
These findings highlight the importance of abrupt onset of symptoms for the
diagnoses of dementia and delirium.

CHAPTER SUMMARY

Cognition refers to a set of processes that enable us to monitor information from the environment,
filter that information, store some components in memory, integrate them with previous and sub-

sequent information, make decisions, and behave in ways anticipated to change the environment. The processes of cognition include the sensory system, memory, intelligence, creativity, and wisdom.

Key ideas to remember from this chapter include:

- The sensory system shows some deterioration with age in most modalities. However, many such changes are correctable to some degree (e.g., the use of glasses or hearing aids), and do not impair a person's capability to function effectively.
- Memory consists of several systems that appear to have some degree of independence. Sensory and primary memory show minimal effects of aging throughout most of the life span. Working memory, which involves a higher level of processing, does decline with age. Acquisition of information into long-term memory is less effective in older people, and particularly if the information is presented rapidly or with few cues to organization. The provision of retrieval cues facilitates retrieval from long-term memory, with particular benefit to older people. Beliefs about memory include lower perceptions of efficacy in older people.
- Despite deficiencies, longitudinal studies show intelligence to remain intact until very late in life, the output of creative productions not to decline in frequency, and wisdom to increase with accumulated favourable life experiences. With respect to specific competences, most people retain cognitive expertise until very late in life in the competences important to them.

Baltes and Baltes (1990) relate the retention of specific expertise to a strategy of *selective optimization with compensation*, meaning that older people:

- Select those activities important to them
- Continue to practise those activities
- Compensate for deficiencies in basic processing abilities by the use of knowledge or other means to retain competence

It is for such reasons that the famous people named in Box 9.1 were able to function at exceedingly high levels during old age

Deficits of relevance to cognitive performance in older cohorts include:

- Decreased sensitivity in processing sensory information
- A slower speed of information processing and working memory deficiencies
- The use of less effective memory acquisition strategies
- Poor recall
- Belief about memory that is unfavourable

Impediments to the retention of cognitive expertise in later life include disengagement from those activities, disease, and an unfavourable lifestyle. The latter includes physical inactivity, associated with a range of adverse consequences termed features of *hypokinetic* disease. Although physically active people perform at higher levels on tasks related to cognition, the available evidence on aerobic exercise intervention suggests that the benefit on neuropsychological performance is highest in those with very low aerobic fitness before the intervention.

Diseases with direct effects on cognition include delirium and dementia. Delirium has an abrupt onset that coincides with illness or trauma, and is a reversible condition. Dementia has an insidious onset, is progressive, and at the present time is irreversible. Dementia affects one person in 12 aged 65+ years, with a prevalence that increases with age.

KEY TERMS

Cognition, **(p. 230)**

Memory, **(p. 230)**

Wisdom, **(p. 230)**

Senses, **(p. 230)**

Metamemory, **(p. 238)**

Intelligence, **(p. 238)**

Fluid intelligence, **(p. 239)**

Crystallized intelligence, **(p. 239)**

Experts, **(p. 240)**

Creativity, **(p. 241)**

Health, **(p. 243)**

Hypokinetic disease, **(p. 243)**

Exercise, **(p. 243)**

Dementia, **(p. 245)**

Delirium, **(p. 246)**

STUDY QUESTIONS

1. Some sensory processes show deterioration with age. Which of these processes are the more likely to affect an older person's functioning and well being? Give reasons.

2. Describe the various types of memory. Which types show the greatest changes with age?

3. Does intelligence deteriorate with age?

4. How strong is the evidence that people retain creativity in very advanced age?

5. Is *use it or lose it* a good prescription for retaining cognitive competence in later life?

6. Describe the main conditions associated with impaired cognition in later life. What are the main risk factors?

SUGGESTED READINGS

Baltes, P.B. & Baltes, M.M. (Eds.). (1990) *Successful Aging: Perspectives from the Behavioural Sciences*, Cambridge, U.K.: Cambridge University Press.

Hultsch, D.F., Hertzog, C., Dixon, R., & Small, B.J. (1998) *Memory Changes in the Aged*, New York, NY: Cambridge University Press.

Kaszniak, A.W. (1996) The role of clinical neuropsychology in the assessment and care of persons with Alzheimer's disease, in R.J. Resnick and R.H. Rozensky (Eds.), *Health Psychology through the Life Span*, (pp. 239–264). Washington DC: American Psychological Association.

Schaie, K.W. (1996) *Intellectual Development in Adulthood: The Seattle Longitudinal Study* New York, NY: Cambridge University Press.

Health, Health Beliefs, and Personal Health Practices

Learning Objectives

In this chapter, you will learn about:

- Which aspects of health decline as we age and which aspects improve.
- The lay explanations seniors use for their symptomatology and how, as we age, we begin to interpret some symptoms and bodily changes as a normal part of aging (although many are not).

- Whether or not discrete personal health behaviours, such as nutritional intake, exercise, sleep, and so on, cluster with one another in order to constitute identifiable lifestyles.
- The effect that social structure, our socioeconomic status, gender, and age, have on our health.

Introduction

Thus far, we have been reading about the physical aspects of aging, cognition and aging, personality and aging. In this chapter, we turn to an examination of health and illness. The chapter begins with some statistics that provide us with a picture of the health and illness of Canada's seniors. We then discuss the distinction between being sick (which includes both disease and illness) and health, and the more general concept of well being. The chapter then turns to a discussion of the determinants of health, with a major focus on health beliefs, personal health practices, and social structure.

Health During Old Age

As we have seen in Chapter 1 on demographics, life expectancy is increasing and life expectancy of women continues to surpass that of men. When looking specifically at seniors, the remaining life expectancy after one reaches age 65 years is also increasing. In 1996, a 65-year-old person could expect to live another 18.4 years, approximately half a year more than in 1991, three years more than in 1971, and five years more than in 1921. Senior women have more years remaining than senior men (20.2 years after age 65 for women, almost four years more than for a 65-year-old man).

Unfortunately, the common image that our health declines as we age is, indeed, true of our physical health. And it is chronic conditions that particularly afflict us in old age. Indeed, 82 percent of all seniors living at home within the community (not in long-term care institutions) suffered from at least one chronic health condition in 1996. Senior women suffer more from chronic health conditions than do senior men (85 percent versus 78 percent). As shown in Table 10.1, the most common chronic health problem is arthritis and rheumatism, followed by high blood pressure, food and other allergies, back problems, chronic heart problems, and cataracts. Fewer but still a substantial proportion of seniors also experience restriction in their daily activities due to health problems. Overall, the figure is 28 percent, rising among the old-old to 50 percent of those age 85 years and over. Although we are used to diagnosing diseases and chronic conditions, pain is a problem for a substantial number of seniors; 25 percent suffer chronic pain or discomfort, increasing to 37 percent among those age 85 years and over. Most are taking some form of medication, either prescription or over-the-counter (84 percent), and the majority are taking two or more (56 percent). This figure increases to 65 percent among those age 85 years and over. Pain relievers are taken most often; 62 percent had used them in the previous month (Statistics Canada, 1999).

As noted in Chapter 8, Mental Well Being and Mental Disorder, illnesses of the mind are viewed as diseases by the medical profession and are typically believed to have physical causes (e.g., serotonin levels that are too low). Dementia is considered to be a disease, even though the physical cause remains undetected.

Table 10.1 MOST PREVALENT CHRONIC CONDITIONS* AMONG CANADIAN
SENIORS LIVING AT HOME

Arthritis and rheumatism	42%
High blood pressure	33%
Food or other allergies	22%
Back problems	17%
Chronic heart problems	16%
Cataracts	15%
Diabetes	10%
Chronic bronchitis or emphysema	6%
Asthma	6%
Urinary incontinence	6%
Sinusitis	5%
Ulcers	5%
Glaucoma	5%
Migraine headaches	4%
Effects of stroke	4%

*As diagnosed by a health professional.
Source: Statistics Canada, "A Portrait of Seniors in Canada," Catalogue No. 89-519, October 1999, p. 62.

As noted previously, seniors are more likely than younger persons to suffer from dementia, the most prevalent form of which is Alzheimer's disease. However, the vast majority of seniors are not likely to suffer from dementia. *The Canadian Study on Health and Aging* (1994), Canada's first and only national study to establish the prevalence of dementia, has revealed that between 6 and 8 percent of seniors suffer from this disease. Three-quarters of those who are elderly and suffer from dementia reside in a long-term care facility. More seniors—28 percent—suffer from memory problems.

Despite their health problems, seniors perceive their general health to be good, very good, or excellent (78 percent). This decreases to 71 percent among those age 85 years and over. Among those in this older age range, women are more likely to rate their health as only fair or poor (Statistics Canada, 1999). This is consistent with measures of psychological well being. Data from the 1994 and 1995 *National Population Health Survey* (NPHS) reveal that while 28 percent of

Canadians have a high sense of coherence (a view of the world that life is meaningful, events are comprehensible, and challenges are manageable), those over age 75 years are three times more likely than 18- to 19-year-olds to score high on a sense of coherence. Similarly, self-esteem and mastery improve with age, peaking in middle adulthood, followed by only modest declines in the later years. In other words, while Canadian seniors are far more likely than younger Canadians to suffer from physical illnesses and conditions, they exhibit favourable and often better psychological well being than do younger adults (Federal, Provincial, and Territorial Advisory Committee on Population Health, 1999).

Causes of death record only our physical bodily malfunctions. Heart disease and cancer are the leading causes of death among both older men and older women (30 percent and 26 percent, respectively, of all deaths, although the rates are higher for senior men than for senior women in both instances). Deaths from respiratory diseases rank third and strokes fourth. Seniors are somewhat less likely to commit suicide than are younger adults. Among seniors, there were 14 suicides for every 100,000 in 1996, a rate that is higher for men than for women (26 versus 5 per 100,000) (Statistics Canada, 1999).

In summary, while women live longer than men, they are more likely to suffer from both chronic conditions and limitations in their activities of daily living. And while older Canadians are more likely to suffer from physical health declines than are younger adults, they appear in many ways to be psychologically more resilient than is true of younger Canadians. Furthermore, while they suffer many physical declines, the majority of elderly Canadians do not suffer from mental decline to the point of dementia. Although chronic conditions, by definition, are not fatal, they can, nevertheless, seriously affect the quality of our lives. Because of the prevalence of chronic conditions in old age, there is a major concern in social gerontology with quality of life rather than only quantity of life.

Wellness

We know much more about illness and disease than we do about wellness and quality of life. This is because **health** has typically been defined in terms of absence of disease. However, we want to distinguish not only between health and **sickness**, but between **disease** and **illness**. The term *sickness* includes both disease and the experience of illness (Segall & Chappell, 2000). People experience illness; physicians diagnose and treat disease. Disease is a modern biomedical concept related to changes in specific organs of the body caused by pathogenic agents, such as germs. Modern medicine believes that each disease has a particular cause or specific etiology; it attempts to control the causes, for example, through drug therapy, surgery, or both. This has often been described as a **mechanistic model** because disease is viewed as objective, as an altered functioning of the biological organism, that is, the human body. Disease constitutes deviation from normal biological functioning.

Box 10.1 Mrs. G.

Mrs. G. is 84 years old. She has been widowed for five years, an experience for which she was totally unprepared—she expected her husband to outlive her. Since they had lived in different countries of the world, and away from their Canadian-born children, widowhood meant a return to Canada and settling in a new city without friends nearby. One son lived nearby. She was determined to live on her own near a senior centre, to become active and involved, and to make new friends. She did all this. Now at 84 years, she is taking medication for high blood pressure, has persistent skin cancer on her cheek, which keeps recurring even after the physician removes it, and has recently experienced a fall that has left her wrist painful and swollen. Probably most disturbing is her very noticeable short-term memory loss—she cannot remember where she put the groceries she just bought, she cannot find her purse, she cannot remember whom she had lunch with earlier in the day, and so on. However, she is still managing on her own, with family and friends close by, although there is now discussion that she should enter assisted living.

If you ask her how her health is, she will respond immediately and enthusiastically about how good it is. She will comment on the fact that she is still very mobile and living on her own and able to do most things that she wants to do. Medication will not be mentioned unless you specifically ask her if she is taking any, and then she will note that she is taking just a little for blood pressure. And if you explicitly ask her about her memory, she will tell you how well she is doing. If you further ask if she forgets the odd thing every once in a while and perhaps give her some examples, she will tell you that yes, it is frustrating that some nights she spends hours looking for her wallet or a letter or some other object. She will go on to tell you how, compared with others her age, she is doing much, much better. They are all taking many more medications and many of them can hardly walk at all. She will tell you how lucky she is to have her children who call or drop in and attend to her needs. She will add that she does not know what she would do without them.

While there is no dispute that the biomedical model of disease has seen some important success against acute infectious diseases, its appropriateness becomes questioned with an older population, where chronic degenerative diseases are most prevalent. These diseases result from multiple etiological factors and have no known cure. Partly because of the growing elderly population and, therefore, the increase in the incidence of chronic conditions for which medical treatment has been inadequate, medicine has increasingly come under attack. In addition to its inability to deal with chronic conditions, medicine also does not give credence to the individual's experience of the disease. Illness is the subjective psychosocial phenomenon that individuals experience when they are not feeling well. Illness, as opposed to disease, is based on personal perception, evaluation, and response to symptomatic conditions.

Part of the difficulty when talking about the concept of health arises because we tend to take health for granted unless we experience illness. We tend not to notice our health when we are feeling fine. It is typically when we feel ill that the lack of good health becomes apparent. However, as stated half a century ago by the World Health Organization (1948), good health is more than the absence of illness and disease. Within a positive definition, it is a state of complete physical, mental, and social well being. This includes subjective feelings as well as the adequate performance at the physical, psychological, and social levels of functioning.

More recently, the concept of **wellness** has become popular, referring to a broader concept that usually includes, but extends beyond, good health. Litva and Eyles (1994) describe feelings of healthiness as a sense of psychosocial well being. Emotional well being is related to such factors as a sense of control and coherence and feelings of purpose, belonging, and satisfaction with one's life. Wellness is often spoken of as including a level of fitness, which may refer to physical and mental fitness, as well as social fitness (being able to perform one's social roles and the demands of everyday living adequately).

Health, it might be noted, does not mean the same thing to all people and furthermore, people who are living with chronic illness may, nevertheless, define themselves as being in good health. For example, arthritis is becoming a normal part of later life. Seniors suffering from arthritis may consider themselves healthy. Indeed, as we saw in the preceding section, when seniors are asked about their perceptions of their health, the majority say that their health is good to excellent. Health and illness, therefore, are relative terms, and they are constantly evolving. They are not static. For example, it was not long ago that stress was not considered an illness or a predictor of disease. It is common now for workplaces to allow stress leave when it is certified by a physician that the individual is suffering from that condition. Interestingly, Litva and Eyles (1994) report that when they asked individuals to define health, they did so in general and abstract terms, focusing on physical aspects, often in terms of the absence of disease and illness. However, when asked to talk about the personal meaning of being healthy, they spoke about quality of life issues and psychological well being, such as feeling happy, enjoying life, and feeling good about oneself.

Another important distinction is that between personal or individual health and population health. **Population health** involves a multidimensional approach to health but encompasses a societal, rather than an individual, focus. It refers to all members of a group or a society, including those who are healthy and those who are ill, those who are at risk and those who are not. Often, we measure population health by examining individual health in the aggregate (such as men versus women, young versus old). In addition, though, population health also includes societal measures, such as the proportion of gross national product spent on health and the numbers of physicians available per 100,000 of the population.

Because of the traditional emphasis on biomedical disease, we are much better at measuring sickness than at measuring wellness, and we have more information about diseases than about health in old age. Nevertheless, increasingly, attention is focusing on wellness. It is important to examine all aspects of health, especially given that physical health declines but psychological health increases in old age. As we learned in Chapter 4, many aspects of aging are gendered. Whenever examining health among seniors, it is important to recognize gender differences, an area to which we now give specific attention.

Gender Differences in Health

There are numerous differences between women and men in both the diagnosis and experience of health and illness, differences that extend into old age. This was evident in the figures provided at the beginning of this chapter on life expectancy, chronic conditions, and psychological well being, as well as causes of death. While the gap between men and women has narrowed slightly in recent years, women still outlive men. Relatedly, the major causes of death differ by gender. While the top two causes of death are the same for women and men, a slightly higher number of males die of cancer than of heart disease. The reverse is true of women. Men are more likely to die from motor vehicle accidents and suicide (especially younger men). Part of women's higher life expectancy today is due to a reduction in the deaths that used to be associated with pregnancy and childbirth.

The extent to which these differences will dissipate as women take on lifestyles more similar to those of men is unknown. However, female lung cancer rates are increasing as smoking rates increase among young women, whereas male lung cancer rates are remaining stable or decreasing. Breast cancer rates among women are increasing at a faster rate than is true for prostate cancer among men. Data from the *National Population Health Survey of Canadians* in 1994 reveals that women are more likely than men to report multiple health problems associated with chronic conditions, such as arthritis and rheumatism, high blood pressure, back problems, and allergies. Furthermore, women are more likely to have taken medications for their problems than are men, even when birth control and menopause-related drugs are excluded. Women are also more likely to have consulted a physician about their health problems (although there was no gender difference in contacts with other health professionals, such as dentists and physiotherapists) (Millar & Beaudet, 1996).

Contrary to the argument that as women and men adopt more similar lifestyles, they will experience similar health problems, is the argument that the factors influencing each are different. Denton and Walters (1999), for example, find that social structural factors such as being in a high income category, working full time, caring for a family, and social support are stronger determinants of health for women, whereas for men, it is personal health practices, such as smoking and alcohol consumption. In addition, the multiple roles of women, such as parenting and being employed, can result in role overload and role conflict and, therefore, strain in their experience of health. Increased stress and excessive demands in time and energy (the double day for women) are major factors in psychological distress and poorer health.

Social acceptability due to socialization and to traditional roles may mean it is more acceptable for women than for men to adopt the sick role. They may be more willing to admit to being sick and to accept help in dealing with their health problems. Women discuss their health more freely than do men, they discuss it with many more individuals, they are more accepting of a wider variety of health actions, and they are more likely to seek the help of a professional (Kandrack, Grant, & Segall, 1991). Men, on the other hand, have been traditionally socialized to deny experiencing symptoms of illness and disease, are reluctant to adopt the sick role, and discuss their health concerns with far fewer people (Cameron & Bernardes, 1998). The extent to which women's and men's socialization and life experiences differ will influence how these differences extend into later life. For current cohorts, old age will be a gendered experience.

While feminism as an ideological perspective developed only recently, the perspective, nevertheless, has much relevance to those who are seniors today and has much to offer in our understanding of health and illness. Irrespective of the variety of feminism, the perspective is critical of the biomedical model of disease, which does not take the whole person into account, excluding social, psychological, and spiritual factors. Furthermore, the biomedical model privileges the expertise of physicians while discounting the feelings and experiential knowledge of women, both as those who experience health and illness and as informal caregivers (see Chapter 13). As noted by Hooyman (1990), women have a major role in the health of families and yet have been largely uncompensated and unrecognized for their contributions. Because so much of women's caring work is invisible and unpaid, that is, it takes place in the private sphere, and because the labour of nurturance and health maintenance have been devalued, they have received relatively little attention until very recently.

This perspective is important for those who are seniors today, irrespective of whether they are aware of it or accept it. Those who are seniors today lived most of their lives within a greater traditional and paternalistic division of labour than will be true of the baby boom generation as it becomes seniors. Women's role as nurturers and as caregivers, if anything, is more characteristic of those who are elderly today than may be the case in future cohorts.

Determinants of Health

As our conceptualization of health is multifaceted, it should not be surprising that the determinants of health are also multiple. Canada has been a world leader in recognizing this fact. In 1974, the then-federal minister of health Lalonde published a new perspective on the health of Canadians, acknowledging that not only formal health care services but also human biology, lifestyles, and environment are major determinants of health. A decade later, then-federal minister of health Epp (1986) extended this perspective with a framework for health promotion characterizing health as an essential part of everyday living. Health was portrayed as a resource for living, influenced by our circumstances, beliefs, culture, and socioeconomic and physical environments.

Box 10.2 Cross-Cultural Comparisons

Historic cultural differences between Asia and North America would suggest a very different aging experience in these two different parts of the world. Much is heard of the respect and care provided for seniors in China in contrast to the neglect and alienation of seniors in North America. In Canada, most seniors are not employed and when their spouses die, they tend to live alone. The focus within the capitalist society is on autonomy and independence, together with a youth orientation. Historically, the Chinese have valued and practised filial piety (*xiao*) and a reciprocity known as *ci*, referring to kindness in rearing children and Chinese familism (*Tianlun zhi le*) and to harmonious family relations and happy family life. Indeed, in 1979, it became a legal obligation of children to care for their elders.

Recent comparative data from seniors living in Shanghai and those living in Victoria, British Columbia, suggest that there are similarities as well as differences. Up to three-quarters of those living in Shanghai have no more than Junior High formal education and two-thirds rent, rather than own, their dwellings. Indeed, fully 42 percent have no independent room of their own within their living accommodations. Fully two-thirds live in what are known as old-style lodges, which typically have shared washrooms, often at the end of the hall. There is no universal old-age security payment, and a substantial proportion (fully a quarter) receive financial help from their children and grandchildren, which is their major source of income. In all these ways, they are distinctive from seniors in Canada. Furthermore, they perceive their health to be worse, and the objective data would suggest that their perceptions are correct. That is, they seem to suffer from more chronic conditions and from more symptoms (such as chills and flu, being sad or depressed, agitated itchy skin, indigestion). We have already learned that poverty is related to ill health, so this is not surprising. The Shanghaians are less likely to be receiving services, either of a physician or other health care workers.

However, like seniors in Victoria, and in Canada generally, Shanghaian seniors have others whom they can turn to. In an emergency, or in terms of who their confidants and companions are, the historical value of males emerges. They are much more likely to turn to their sons than is true of Canadian seniors. And most have family and friends nearby.

Another similarity emerges when examining happiness among Shanghaian seniors. The major predictors of happiness or life satisfaction are their social support and their health. Furthermore, these are the same factors that emerge consistently in research on happiness among seniors in Canada, and in North America generally and, indeed, in Western countries. The form that the social support takes varies (sons are more valued and more popular in Chinese society), but the importance of social support is clearly similar. That is, what brings us happiness in old age seems to span cultural boundaries.

Source: Chappell, N.L. (2001). *Family Care of Seniors in Shanghai; Similarities and Differences with the West.* Paper presented at the International Symposium on Chinese Elderly, Shanghai, October.

There is no disputing the biological determinants of health (Figure 10.1), including individual genetic endowment and the functioning of various body systems, such as our immune and hormonal systems. Hereditary factors may well make us susceptible to a variety of diseases, but this does not exclude other environmental factors as being influential in the onset and development of diseases. The environment includes both the physical environment and the social environment. The importance of the physical environment is recognized in legislation to ensure clean drinking water, increasing concerns about clean air to breathe, and exposure to hazardous waste. This is the traditional area of public health. New dangers are becoming recognized in today's post-industrial society, such as industrial air pollution, second-hand smoke, and acid rain.

The physical environment also includes the built environment, such as the workplace and housing. Housing is especially important as we age because the physical environment can mean the difference between independence or dependence. For example, if a senior has difficulty going up and down stairs but lives in a place where there are no steps, this lack of mobility does not make him or her dependent. Most people, including seniors, express a preference for staying in their own home, a concept referred to as **aging in place**. This does not mean that they necessarily wish to live in a particular house for their entire lives, but rather that as they settle into a place in their later middle years and early old age, they

Figure 10.1 **DETERMINANTS OF HEALTH**

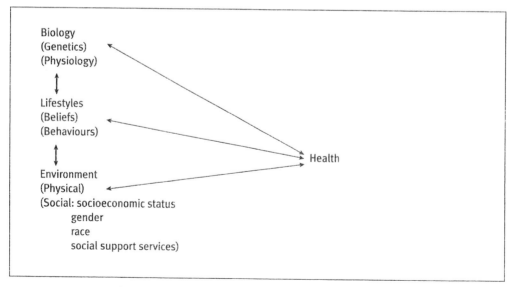

Double-pointed arrows indicate reciprocal effects.

do not wish to be uprooted to a place where they cannot take their personal belongings that have history and meaning attached to them, from a space that has become familiar and easy to maneuver, from a location that they know well and from which they can meet their needs, and be put in an environment that is unfamiliar, distant from family and friends, and/or institutional-like.

A type of housing receiving much attention in Canada and elsewhere at the present time is known as **assisted living** (also known as supportive housing), where individuals live usually in apartments that provide, at minimum, a general on-site manager who checks on them and is available for more than physical maintenance of the building, a personal alarm system in case an emergency arises, and congregate meals for those who wish to partake in such. Assisted living is for those whose health has begun to deteriorate and is a built environment that allows them to age in place. Health care services, including services that are provided in assisted living environments, are a determinant of health, particularly for those who have fallen ill. However, they do little to promote health and wellness. More is said about health care services in Chapter 15. They do have a role in risk

---

Box 10.3   Abbeyfield Houses

Abbeyfield housing was founded in 1956 in London, England, by Richard Carr-Gomm. Abbeyfield was the name of the street where the founders met. The name commemorated a charitable medieval abbey. Initially, Carr-Gomm began Abbeyfield as a charity caring for lonely people in the East end of London.

Today, Abbeyfield houses involve volunteers who set up and manage each house, where residents pay their share of the costs. Each house has a housekeeper, who looks after the house, provides meals, and cares generally for the residents. All residents have their own rooms, furnished as they wish, where they are assured privacy and the right to invite visitors. The three principles of Abbeyfield are:

1. Many elderly people everywhere suffer from loneliness and insecurity and so need care, companionship, and practical support in their daily lives.

2. The elderly still have an important role to play in the lives of their families, friends, and communities.

3. Within each community, individuals can actively help the elderly to have a secure and happy life by offering them a home of their own within the companionship of a small household.

Abbeyfield offers a home within a home for seniors who are relatively fit but no longer willing or able to live alone or are at risk if living alone. It offers a family-style home, balancing privacy, companionship, security, and independence. The primary criteria for eligibility are age and loneliness, together with health and compatibility with the other residents. As of Spring 2001, there were 1,100 Abbeyfield houses world-wide, with 25 in Canada and another 10 houses planned or under construction.

Source: *Abbeyfield Newsletters*. Vol 9 No. 1, Spring 2001, & Vol 9 No 2, 2001 & *Abbeyfield Newsletters*. Vol 9 No. 2, 2001.

reduction (for example, providing immunization) but do little to provide people with knowledge and skills to adopt healthy living practices. The focus in this chapter is on the social and social-psychological determinants of health: health beliefs, health behaviours, and social structure.

Two types of determinants of health are examined in greater detail here. One refers to **personal health determinants**, which take place at the individual level and include beliefs and personal health behaviours. The other refers to **structural determinants**, which occur at the societal level and include, for example, the social and economic environment, gender, race, and social support. In examining these determinants, we are interested in the determinants of health and wellness, not simply the determinants of disease or disease avoidance.

Health Beliefs

Health beliefs, also referred to as lay conceptions of good health, are personal determinants of individual and population health. We all have our beliefs about what makes us healthy and what makes us ill. These beliefs give meaning to our experiences when we are healthy and help us interpret the meaning of and determine the actions we will take when we fall ill. Interpretive frameworks for explaining health and illness have been classified as professional (scientific, modern, and expert) and popular (nonscientific, traditional, and lay), each offering a set of ideas of shared meaning. The lay public often draws on both belief systems. In our discussion of seniors and aging, we have particular interest in commonsense models of chronic illness. In a study of older adults' meaning and management of chronic illness, Segall and Chappell (1991), report that most believe that medical care is necessary for such conditions as high blood pressure; 38 percent also believe that some home remedies are better than prescribed drugs for treating illnesses. That is, consulting a health professional does not preclude self-treatment with, for example, home remedies.

Stoller (1993) reports that among her sample of seniors, the most common symptoms included joint and muscle pain, fatigue, and a runny or stuffy nose. These seniors offered both medical and nonmedical interpretations of these symptoms. Medical interpretations included a flare-up of a chronic disease or condition, other medical conditions, or something they caught from someone else. Nonmedical (popular) interpretations included normal aging, lifestyle, stress, weather, or season of the year. The most common medical explanation for a symptom was flare-up of a chronic condition, and the most common nonmedical explanation was weather or season of the year. Often, seniors cite multiple causes.

Among Chinese seniors in Canada, Chappell and Lai (1998) report that beliefs in traditional Chinese medicine, which offers a holistic view of the person and their surroundings, coexists with their strong beliefs in Western medicine and the utilization of Western health care services to the same extent as the host society. It should also be pointed out that while we often think of subcultures, such as the Chinese seniors or the aboriginal seniors, as having traditional lay beliefs, mainstream Caucasian Canadians also have their beliefs in home remedies. Chicken soup, not sleeping with the window left open, or not getting wet to avoid catching a cold, and so on would be examples.

In contrast to the expert belief system of medicine, which is relatively closed, the lay health belief system is more open and flexible. The two are sometimes related to one another and sometimes reinforce one another. Child birthing rooms are now a regular part of hospitals, through the influence of the wishes of women; similarly the treatment of breast cancer among women has been heavily influenced by the desire of women to have their own experiences heard and to be part of therapy. In some jurisdictions, aboriginal healers are brought into the process as cultural brokers within hospitals (Kaufert & O'Neill, 1990). There is now scientific evidence that one of the substances in licorice root protects the lining of the stomach against erosion by stomach acid, supporting the longstanding use of the licorice plant in folk medicine as a laxative and a digestive aid (Segall & Chappell, 2000).

Importantly, many older adults normalize their symptoms by referring to them as simply part of the normal aging process. In Stoller's (1993) study, over half attributed at least one of their symptoms to normal aging, and even more did so for such symptoms as vision problems, constipation, indigestion, and sleep difficulties. Kart (1981) also documented seniors' tendency to attribute many of their symptoms to "normal aging," even symptoms that were not inevitable consequences of the aging process. And Leventhal and Prohaska (1986) found that common everyday health concerns (general symptomatology) are more likely to be attributed simply to "aging" as one grows older. Older adults are more likely to interpret such symptoms as weakness and aching as simply part of aging, rather than as warning signs of specific illnesses.

Chronic illness, as opposed to general symptomatology, however, is not usually attributed to the aging process among older adults. Segall and Chappell (1991) found that half the older adults (age 50 years and over) did not know what caused their chronic illness and could not offer a specific cause. Those who could tended to name heredity, biophysical factors, or lifestyle factors. Only 2 percent attributed chronic illness to old age or the aging process. Recall from above that Blaxter (1983) found that her middle-aged respondents similarly did not attribute chronic illness to the aging process.

Other Beliefs.

Besides cause, another important belief that we hold about our illnesses is that of controllability, that is, whether or not the disease can be managed by the individuals themselves, other persons in the informal network, or the formal health care system. Within this area, there has been interest in researchers in the concept of the general locus of control and, more specifically, health locus of control; it has been studied in relation to self-rated health, self-initiated preventive care, and behaviour during illness episodes, including use of physician services and compliance with medical regimens (Lau & Hartman, 1983; Sieman & Sieman, 1983). Typically, distinctions are made between **internal locus of control** and **external locus of control**, with the former referring to personal or self-control beliefs that emphasize personal mastery of health and illness and the latter emphasizing provider or powerful other control that focuses on faith in health care professionals and also chance health outcomes where health is beyond all control. And there is research suggesting that there is a relationship between having a strong internal locus of control and favourable health outcomes. It is believed that this operates through the adoption of healthy lifestyle behaviours. That is, those who believe they have some control over their health are more likely to adopt healthy lifestyles (Peterson & Stunkard, 1989).

There is inconsistency in the findings of research focusing on age-related differences in locus of control beliefs. Lachman (1986) reviewed the literature in this area. Equal numbers of studies find that the strength of internal locus of control beliefs increase as we age, as find that such beliefs decrease as we age. Still other studies report that such beliefs remain stable throughout adulthood and old age. Lachman (1986) believes the inconsistency is due to methodological problems, including study design, sampling, and measurement, and that both multidimensional and domain-specific beliefs must be studied. Lachman's own research found significant differences by age only for external locus of control (both control of powerful others and belief in chance outcomes) but not in the internal dimension. That is, older adults come to believe more in the salience of external factors while maintaining their belief in their own control over their health. The findings support this researcher's contention that control beliefs may change with age or remain stable, depending on the domain being examined.

Furthermore, Shewchuk, Foelker, and Niederehe (1990) adapted measures of locus of control that had been developed for younger adults (for example, not using employment items) and revised the scales so that they were more applicable to older adults. They could not confirm the three-factor structure that has become so accepted as locus of control (internal–personal; external–provider; and external–chance). In addition, it may well be that one's sense of control over the cause or onset of an illness is different from the sense of personal control over the course of the condition and its management. This distinction has not been studied in relation to the locus of control concept (Chappell & Segall, 2000).

There are, of course, many other beliefs surrounding health and illness. Generally, they have received less attention in the research literature. One such belief is that of susceptibility. Interestingly, Najman (1980) argued for a concept of general illness susceptibility. This is contrary to the biomedical model in which each illness is believed to have a specific cause. As noted above, however, the general lay public appears to accept a notion of general susceptibility in that they believe in family susceptibility. Some health economists, such as Evans and Stoddart (1990), have argued that the biomedical model errs in its focus on specific causes for particular diseases and that researchers should be examining a host response of the individual. This is especially important for research on diseases because at the present time, the vast majority of research dollars is targeted to finding a cure for specific illnesses, such as cancer. If the **host response** or **general susceptibility hypothesis** is valid, then as one discovers a cure for cancer, another illness will simply emerge as important, for example, HIV/AIDS. In other words, those individuals who are susceptible will simply develop another illness. This is a contentious issue that has not been resolved through research to this point. Leventhal and Prohaska (1986) have reported that older adults have an increased sense of susceptibility to chronic conditions, such as heart disease and high blood pressure. The extent to which these chronic illnesses are an expected part of later life and, therefore, become normalized as simply part of old age is not yet known.

Another health belief that has received even less attention in the literature is belief about seriousness, that is, how serious the disease or condition is. We also know little about beliefs related to stability versus changeability of conditions, their temporary or permanent nature, and the predictability of the symptoms of the illness. Yet, all of these beliefs go together to help the individual make sense of the illness experience.

As is obvious from the foregoing, research on health beliefs has focused primarily on beliefs about the nature of illness. It is about making sense of illness, rather than making sense of either good health or preventing disease. An exception is research conducted by Prohaska, Lenenthal, Lenenthal, and Keller (1985) who examined age differences (20 to 39 years, 40 to 59 years, 60 to 89 years) in lay beliefs about the preventability of illness. They asked about a variety of health behaviours, such as eating a balanced diet, avoiding too much physical exertion, getting enough sleep, and having regular medical checkups. They report that while the frequency of health maintenance activities increases with age, there is no

Box 10.4 Health Beliefs

CAUSE OF THE ILLNESS

Susceptibility

Controllability

Seriousness

Changeability

Permanency

age group difference in beliefs about the effectiveness of these health actions. In other words, belief in the efficacy of these health practices in preventing specific illnesses (such as colorectal cancer) is similar across all three age groups. An exception is that older adults believe they are more vulnerable to these types of illnesses, that they are more serious for them, and they are less likely to consider mild symptoms, such as tiredness, as an indicator of illness.

In an analysis of the 1990 *Health Promotion Survey*, Penning and Chappell (1993), report that while the vast majority of Canadian adults believe that a change in their personal lifestyles would improve their health and well being, the proportion decreases as one ages. Older adults are less likely than younger adults to expect positive changes from increased exercise, stopping smoking, better dental care, or increased relaxation. Similarly, in regards to the benefits of reducing environmental pollution, fewer older adults believe in the benefits than do younger adults, and fewer men than women believe in this effect. Similar results are evident when examining social environmental changes, such as improving income or moving to a new neighbourhood. Older adults are less likely to perceive a benefit and in this instance, women are less likely to perceive a benefit than are men.

Lay conceptions of health are multidimensional and complex. Several studies suggest that for the lay public, an absence of disease is important in their view of health but that it also includes a sense of wholeness as in healthiness. As noted earlier, individuals can perceive themselves as healthy while living with disease; here, a sick individual nevertheless considers himself/herself healthy or in good health (Blaxter, 1990). In fact, older adults living with multiple chronic conditions typically report good health. Segall and Chappell (1991) found that fully 74 percent of their respondents described their health as being good or fair for their age, even though, on average, they were living with four different chronic conditions. As noted earlier, most older adults perceive their health as being good to excellent when compared with others their own age. In other words, individuals can view themselves as healthy while living with disease and chronic conditions. It relates to a sense of overall well being and refers primarily to a psychological, rather than physiological, state.

Our interest in beliefs evolves not only around understanding the experiential nature of health and illness but also because they are related to health behaviours. We turn next to a discussion of the health behaviours. This discussion draws the same distinction between health and illness, those behaviours oriented toward maintaining health and those oriented toward our behaviour when we become sick. It will not be surprising that there is more research on illness behaviour than on health maintenance behaviour.

Personal Health Behaviours

Illness behaviour refers to activities surrounding the interpretation of symptoms being experienced and action taken in response to the condition. **Health behaviour,**

in contrast, is activity undertaken in order to prevent disease or detect it at a symptomatic stage as well as activities with the intention of promoting one's health, that is, positive health behaviour. This includes risk-avoiding behaviour, such as wearing seatbelts and not smoking, and preventive medical care, such as having dental checkups and regular physical exams. However, positive health behaviour also includes such activities as regular exercise, rest, and nutritional intake. That is, many daily routine activities, such as eating nutritious meals and getting enough sleep, are part of health maintenance and health improvement (Mechanic, 1999).

Over two decades ago, Harris and Guten (1979) referred to **health protective behaviours** to describe activities we routinely engage in to protect our health, as any behaviour that is intended to protect, promote, or maintain one's health, irrespective of whether it has been demonstrated to, in fact, be related to health and irrespective of the individual's perceived or actual heath status. In their research, they identified three dominant positive health actions: nutrition, relaxation (sleep, rest), and exercise (recreation) activities. In 1985, Green used the term **self-health management** to refer to what we generally do or routinely engage in, in terms of personal health practices, including both health-protective behaviours and illness-treatment activities. This includes our own monitoring of our health status by evaluating the meaning of symptoms and bodily conditions and deciding on a course of action. This may include doing nothing, getting more rest, speaking to others about the condition, self-medicating, and so on.

Green argues that self-health management encompasses, but is broader than, self-care behaviour, including self-care practices plus mutual aid, plus membership in self-help groups. **Self-care** refers to any behaviours that are lay-initiated through a process of self-determination. Self-care necessarily includes lay control over the decision-making process and the management of health care resources. Segall and Goldstein (1989) argue that the "essence of self-care is self-control," since it necessarily incorporates notions of autonomy and responsibility.

Self-Care.

Self-care, with the recognition of the role that self-care plays, is especially important because it changes the nature of the relationships between participants in the health care system by recognizing the valuable knowledge that individuals/patients bring to that system. It also acknowledges lay persons as primary providers of health care and that they are actively involved in managing their own health. Self-care, in fact, is the central and fundamental component of health care; health professionals are just one of many informal and formal resources available to individuals for managing their own health. Some researchers include the utilization of health care services as part of self-care, others do not. There is consensus that self-care includes health protective behaviours, symptom evaluation, and various self-treatment practices. Often, the use of preventive medical services is included. It also includes self-referral and use of informal social networks as a health resource. The concept of self-care points out that we are all health care providers and health producers, as well as health care consumers. Self-care is the basic, primary, and dominant form of health care practised by individuals (Dean, 1981; Levin & Idler, 1983). Dean (1986) has estimated the predominance of self-care at 75 percent of the management of everyday illness episodes.

Self-care takes on particular significance in later life because of the chronic conditions experienced in that period; because of a pattern of co-morbidity, where typically several chronic health problems coexist at one time; and because traditional acute-care treatment provided by the health care system is less likely to be effective. Self-care at this time of life also becomes more complicated. Self-care of chronic illness includes self-monitoring, managing drug therapy at home, deciding whether to take prescribed and nonprescribed medications, and treatment to manage symptoms, especially pain and discomfort. There are, in addition, any number of emotions that accompany chronic illness, including, frustration, anger, and depression, that must be managed when they arise. Often, one's daily life must be adjusted in order to maintain one's activities.

Personal Health Practices.

Individuals engage in any number of **personal health practices**, some of which are believed to be positively related to health and others negatively so. Exercise, rest, and good nutrition are all potentially beneficial. However, smoking and alcohol consumption are potentially harmful. Similarly, environmental protection and home safety practices can have health consequences (such as having smoke detectors in the home). The *Health Promotion Survey* of 1990 asked Canadians about a number of personal health practices. On some traditional health behaviours, seniors do better than younger adults. Whereas 30 percent of adults report either missing breakfast or having only coffee or tea for breakfast at least once in the past week, this proportion decreases from about 40 percent between the ages of 15 and 29 years to 9 percent at age 70 years and over. This is true for both men and women. When it comes to exercise (vigorous activities, such as aerobics, jogging, sports, or brisk walking), half the adults report exercising at least three times a week, with the frequency increasing with age (20 percent of those aged 15 to 49 years, 28 percent of those aged 50 to 59 years, and 35 percent of those aged 60 years and over). This is true of both men and women.

In the case of smoking, 29 percent of Canadian adults report being current smokers, with relative stability for individuals less than 60 years (30 to 36 percent) and declining to 22 percent among those aged 60 to 69 years, and down to 14 percent among those 70 years and over. While 81 percent of Canadian adults have at least one alcoholic drink a month, older adults are less likely to do so than younger adults, and women are less likely to do so than men. However, the use of medications (including tranquilizers, diet pills or stimulants, antidepressants, codeine, Demerol or morphine, sleeping pills, and aspirin or other pain relievers) increases as we age. For example, older adults, especially older women, are much more likely to use sleeping pills (the figure overall is 7 percent within the last year, but 20 percent among those 70 years and over—18 percent of men and 21 percent of women report using sleeping pills). Similarly, only 2 percent of those aged 15 to 29 years report using tranquilizers, but 11 percent of those aged 70 years and over (in this case, there is no significant difference between men and women). These findings are relatively stable between 1990 and 1996 to 1997 (Statistics Canada, 1999).

In terms of environmental protection and home safety practices, however, older adults are least likely to engage in such activities as recycling paper, bottles, or cans, or purchasing recycled goods. They are, however, just as likely to undertake composting. When asked whether they had done anything with the intent of improving their health during the last year, half the adults say that they did so. Regardless of age, women are more likely to do so than men. However, the proportion decreases with age for both men and women. Older adults are the least likely to report increasing their exercise, changing their eating habits, or undertaking other types of change for the purpose of improving their health. Similarly, when asked if there is anything they intend to do in the following year in order to improve their health, older adults are less likely to have such intentions. In other words, older adults tend to engage in the long-held traditional beliefs about what one does in order to have good health (exercising, eating a good breakfast, and so on) but they are less likely to engage in activities that reflect new thinking about how to improve health, such as environmental practices (e.g., recycling).

When talking about personal health behaviours, often, we are referring to aspects of people's lifestyles, taken to mean a general orientation toward life. Interestingly, existing research suggests that individual behaviours are not highly related to one another. That is, because one exercises does not mean that one eats particularly nutritious meals or that one does not smoke or drink. The one exception seems to be smoking and drinking, which are moderately correlated with one another (Kronenfeld, et al., 1988; Krick & Sobal, 1990). Stephens (1986) reports similar findings when analyzing national data from the *Canada Health Survey*. Because of this lack of correlation between the various behaviours, some authors have examined whether or not certain behaviours cluster with one another, depicting a lifestyle, rather than individual behaviour. Contrary to much other research, Harris and Guten (1979) found that some behaviours appear together empirically and, on this basis, postulated five clusters of health protective behaviours:

1. Personal health practices—routine daily positive health actions, such as getting enough sleep, relaxation, eating sensibly, watching one's weight, doing things in moderation, and avoiding overwork.
2. Safety practices—other daily living activities in the home, such as checking the condition of electrical appliances or the car, fixing broken things

right away, keeping emergency phone numbers near the phone, having a first aid kit.

3. Preventive health care practices—the usual preventive medical behaviours, such as seeing a doctor or a dentist for regular checkups.
4. Environmental hazard avoidance—these behaviours include avoiding parts of the city with a lot of crime or pollution.
5. Harmful substance avoidance—not smoking or drinking.

They report that preventive health care practices are unrelated to any of the others; visiting a health care professional is unrelated to positive health actions.

Importantly, measurement difficulties may be the reason why these behaviours do not cluster with one another in most research. For example, it might be important to distinguish between routine exercise and exercise that is unplanned, and to document actual nutritional intake of a variety of foods; greater detail on activity patterns informs us whether some individuals, for example, eat well and exercise during the week, but then eat less healthily and do not exercise on the weekend. Part of the problem is that there is no consensus in theory or practice as to what constitutes "lifestyle." It is a way of life that involves individuals' beliefs, attitudes, values, and behaviours, but beyond that, we do not have a good understanding of this area.

Conceptually, Dean (1989) argues that discrete practices should be defined as self-care behaviours, whereas behaviours that cluster together and interact with the cultural, social, and psychosocial factors could be referred to as lifestyles. Researchers, to date, have been unsuccessful in identifying clusters that constitute lifestyles, perhaps because they are looking for logically consistent behaviours, whereas it could be that many individuals behave in complex and not always logical ways (such as bingeing or drinking a fair amount of alcohol at a party but many times eating well and not drinking alcoholic beverages). Backett, Davison, and Mullen (1994) argue that we seem to trade off positive and negative aspects of health-related behaviour constantly to balance out our overall health, rather than choosing certain types to the exclusion of others.

Despite this lack of clarity, the concept of lifestyle appears to be here to stay, for some time at least. Evans and Stoddart (1990) suggest one of the reasons for this popularity is because lifestyle is within the control of the individual and because of the belief that if we could figure this out, it has the potential to have the largest effect on health about which we are able to do something. This gains in importance with aging of the population and, therefore, the increase in chronic degenerative diseases for which medicine has no cure. Lifestyle behaviour becomes emphasized in terms of regulatory and preventive self-care practices to delay the onset of such conditions but also for restorative self-care for managing daily living with chronic conditions.

While personal health practices are largely within the control of the individual, many of the determinants of our beliefs and actions are much broader and outside this realm. We turn now to a discussion of some of those factors, notably of social structure as a determinant of health.

Social Structure as a Determinant of Health

Simply put, **social structure** is the pattern of interrelated statuses and roles within society and within subgroups of society that constitute a relatively stable set of social relations. This entails an interrelated set of rights and obligations within a system of interaction. George (1990) describes social structure as the relatively stable pattern of social organization based on a system of social roles, norms, and shared meanings that provide regularity and predictability to social interaction. Examples of social structural variables include age, socioeconomic position, and formal roles, such as positions or memberships in an organization or group. Age, for example, defines our occupancy and performance in roles (legal eligibility to attend school, drive a car, drink alcohol, vote, receive a pension).

Social class refers to one's structural position in society and is also referred to as socioeconomic status (SES). It is most often measured in terms of one's income but also often in terms of education and/or occupation and, irrespective of the measure used, it is related to our health. There is no disputing that poverty is related to poor health. Basic necessities are required for life: food, clothing, and shelter. Absolute material deprivation is unhealthy. This is why most countries, including Canada, have basic welfare measures to ensure a minimum level for people to live. Beyond this, however, there is now much research documenting the fact that SES is related to one's health. Those of higher social class have better health than those of lower social class; this has been demonstrated for numerous indicators of health, including mortality, morbidity, functional ability, and perceptions of health. This relationship has persisted over time despite the fact that the causes of mortality have changed away from primarily infectious disease. This relationship, furthermore, is strongest in the middle years. Mustard, Derksen, Berthelot, Wolfson, and Roos (1997) identify those aged 30 to 64 years; Torrance, Zhang, Feeny, and Boyle (1992) identify those aged 45 to 64 years; and Wilkins, Adams, and Brancker (1991) identify those aged 25 to 64 years as the age groups with the strongest correlations between SES and health. This is not surprising, given that older individuals are no longer part of the workforce. The relationship between SES and health holds even when controlling for other factors, such as nutritional intake, exercise, and social support. Although the relationship is not as strong during old age, nevertheless, it is still evident (Hay, 1994).

As Williamson (1996) describes it, the relationship between social structure and health is the power of social structure over life and death. Furthermore, since social structures can be modified, illness is potentially preventable. Indeed, Wilkins et al. (1991) have examined how regional disparities in death rates in Canada have changed, showing a decrease from five years in 1941 to 1.5 years in 1986, during a period that saw both major economic growth and national investment in equalizing educational opportunities despite continuing regional differences. That is, social structural change was evident in this time period.

In addition to the importance of poverty for ill health, recently this work has been extended to include the concept of the **social gradient**. The social gradient refers to the fact that those with fewer socioeconomic resources have more ill health; inequality per se is bad for health. We now know that it is not only the poorest of society who experience more health problems and die sooner, but that those with fewer socioeconomic resources than others, irrespective of how high up they are in the societal hierarchy, experience more ill health. Those on the second-highest rung of society are in better health than those on the third-highest rung but in worse health than those on the highest rung. This refers to the distribution of inequality in society. Inequality per se is bad for health, irrespective of the absolute levels or material standards of living (beyond basic necessities). This gradient is continuous; there is no threshold before or after which it does not apply. Furthermore, it is the distribution of inequality *within* a country that matters, presumably reflecting standards of living within that country. So, for example, diseases with the steepest gradients vary from country to country (Wilkinson, 1996). In Canada, men with the lowest 5 percent of earnings before retirement are twice as likely to die between the ages of 65 and 70 years when compared with men in the highest 5 percent of earnings; furthermore, those in the top earning category, on average, enjoy 12 more years of good health than do low-income earners (CIAR, 1991).

This means that the ways in which a society structures opportunities for its citizens and the ultimate availability of a variety of positions become relevant for our health. It is important, at the same time, to recognize that all individuals have a variety of reference groups in their lives. One can hold a position of value and importance within the local community, within the family, or within a sports club and, provided that the group is salient in one's life, it could have a positive health influence. In other words, we all do not have to be prime minister in order to have good health. The social gradient has been interpreted in Canada, by such economists as Evans and Stoddart (1990), to mean that it is income and wealth that are related to health and that we should, therefore, turn our efforts to producing wealth. However, as Wilkinson (1994) asks, is the individual's desire for more income a desire to improve his or her relative standing in society, or is it a request for more wealth rather than wealth per se? That is, is the equation of social position with material standards in Canada due to the fact that Canada is a capitalist country in which income is a major determinant of social status?

Poland, Coburn, Robertson, and Eakin (1998) argue that it is equity and **redistributive justice** (ensuring that a country's wealth is shared by those less fortunate) that is the key to improving a society's health; it is not wealth and prosperity per se. Research on unemployment (another structural factor) and health supports this argument. Although unemployment is generally related to ill health, in parts of the country with high overall unemployment rates, this relationship is weaker (D'Arcy, 1988). In areas where unemployment is the norm, it is not as strongly related to health differentials. This is a complex area of study and as Judge et al. (1998) note, factors potentially affecting the relationship between equity distribution and health must also be taken into account. Such measures would include, for example, measures of prosperity (perhaps average national income) and characteristics of the welfare system. Measures of equity presumably need to take into account taxes, cash benefits, and household composition.

Understanding Why.

And, knowing that social structure affects health does not tell us why or how this relationship works. Some authors, such as Syme (1994), argue that it is one's control or influence over one's own actions and perhaps feeling that one is contributing to the larger society that is critical; the Determinants of Health Working Group of the National Forum on Health suggests it is through self-esteem, sense of control over one's life, and resiliency that this relationship may work (Renaud, et al., 1996). While it is not well understood, the clear suggestion is that social–psychological factors, such as coping, self-mastery, and a sense of control are all relevant here. How precisely these connections take place is not known, but it is believed that the social environment affects us psychologically, which, in turn, affects us physiologically. For example, the immune system is the body's primary defence against bacteria, viruses, and cancer. Stress alters the immune system. The nervous and immune systems talk to one another so that the social environment can influence biological responses through the nervous system. Hormonal systems also respond to stress (Evans & Stoddart, 1990).

Increasingly, research is investigating the biological pathways through which social factors are related to health. For example, Cohen, Tyrell, and Smith (1991) inoculated volunteers with one of five viruses or a **placebo** (a substance that, unknown to the individual, has no effect), for all participants who had completed a variety of psychological stress measures. They were quarantined and monitored. Respiratory infections and clinical colds increased in relation to the dose injected, as the psychological stress of the individual increased, for all five viruses in the study. Despite the now-acknowledged connections between health and SES, our understanding of how this relationship operates is just starting to be investigated. It is, however, worth noting that non-Western cultures do not embrace the mind–body dichotomy as does Western medicine. The Ayurvedic tradition of south Asian medicine or traditional Chinese medicine see the mind and body as parts of the same whole.

Gender.

It is also important to note that women and men experience social class positions differently. Not only are opportunities for women structured in ways that are different from those for men (Canadian women were worse off in 1992 than they had been five years earlier; women working full time in 1990 earned only 67.6 percent [now 73 percent] of the amount that men earned; National Action Committee on the Status of Women, 1992), but similar positions may have differential meanings. For example, unemployment might be important for men for different reasons from those for women because until recently, men were expected to be employed whereas women not necessarily so. Women have been more the nurturers and more likely to have close friends, to be the kin keepers and network builders within the family, and to reach out to others. This is as true in old age as when we are younger (Chappell, 1992; Moore & Rosenberg, 1995). Because of these differences, women have also been excluded from many labour force opportunities, and women who are elderly today lived in a time when these gender divisions of labour were more typical than today.

In addition, as noted earlier, women suffer from more symptomatology than do men, although they have a longer life expectancy. The extent to which these gender differences reflect the set of indicators that have dominated health research (such as mortality, morbidity, and functional ability) is not known. If other indicators are studied more extensively, such as happiness and stress, differential results may be forthcoming.

Cultural Minority Status.

Race also shows differential health experiences. Typically, being a member of an ethnic minority is highly correlated with poor health, with the First Nations peoples a dramatic example in Canada. Canada's Royal Commission on Aboriginal Peoples (1996) documents the interrelationship between health and race:

- The life expectancy of registered Indians is 7 to 8 years shorter than that of non-First Nations Indians (statistics were not available for other groups of First Nations peoples).
- Unemployment rates, incidence of low educational attainment and welfare dependency are higher in First Nations communities.
- The incidences of violence, physical and sexual abuse, and suicide are higher in First Nations communities.
- First Nations peoples are increasingly affected by such conditions as cancer and heart disease.
- Children in First Nations communities have higher rates of accidental death and injury than other Canadian children. Many First Nations communities have higher rates of infectious diseases, such as tuberculosis and AIDS, than non-First Nations Canadians.

Importantly, the leading causes of death among First Nations infants (respiratory ailments, infectious and parasitic diseases, accidents) are all indicators of inadequate housing, unsanitary conditions, and poor access to medical facilities. Similarly, rates of death among adults due to infectious and parasitic diseases are consistently above national levels and they reflect differences in lifestyles and living conditions. First Nations reserves often lack central heating, proper ventilation systems, adequate water sources, and sanitation facilities and have fire hazards from wood stoves, improper air circulation, and overcrowding (Young, 1991; Wotherspoon 1994).

In Canada, as is true in the United States, members of cultural minorities also tend to be economically disadvantaged so that differentiating the effects of socio-economic status from competing explanations, such as cultural minority status, is difficult. Nevertheless, the National Forum on Health concluded that the consequences of hardships among First Nations peoples are similar to those experienced by others in similar economically disadvantaged circumstances. First Nations peoples, however, are more likely to be living in circumstances that are bad for their health. Zong and Li (1994) concluded from a study of 118 countries that economic conditions and nutritional levels, not cultural influence implied in race, were responsible for differences between countries in life expectancy and infant mortality rates.

Economic advantage is related to health in more indirect ways as well, to the extent that it also means affordability of good nutrition, living in healthy environments, and so on. Poor people have few choices in where they live and the food they eat. Fast foods, cigarettes, and alcohol are all relatively accessible in our affluent society, and the poor choose what is accessible, but that means that they must forgo other choices. That is, with money in our capitalist society come the conditions, opportunities, and amenities that allow for a healthy life. Whether or not our children will attend university is influenced by where we live, parental expectations, and peer pressure (Marmot, Kogevinas, & Elston 1987).

CHAPTER SUMMARY

This chapter has examined health and illness in old age, emphasizing the importance of incorporating a sense of healthiness as well as a sense of sickness. The domination of medicine within our society together with people's focus on health, primarily when they become ill, has meant that research has concentrated much more on disease and illness than on health and well being—a distinction that is very important.

Key ideas to remember from this chapter include:

- While women live longer than men, they are more likely to suffer from both chronic conditions and limitations in activities of daily living than are men.
- Despite physical health declines as we age, our psychological well being seems to improve.
- Gender differences in health are important; women experience more symptomatology in old age than do men; men, however, die younger; that is, the conditions that they experience are more likely to be fatal.
- A major focus in gerontology is an understanding of how we can maintain and enhance quality of life in old age, not simply extend the quantity of life.

- The determinants of health, including health beliefs, health behaviours, and the social structure, influence our health and are all relatively new areas of study in which we have much to learn. However, they are also all factors that we can change in order to improve our health. Although we often think of social structure as being less influenceable than individual factors, governments and community groups can, in fact, effect change.

- Some health beliefs change as we age (such as the tendency to normalize some symptoms as simply part of aging), others remain stable (such as the actions we should take to help promote and maintain our health). Health beliefs tend to include scientific/expert as well as lay/popular explanations about why we become ill, the course of the illness, and its controllability.

- The general susceptibility hypothesis argues for a host response of the individual to illness. If this is true, those who become ill with one illness would simply contract another if that illness were conquered.

- Despite the attention paid to sickness and treatment, self-care is the most predominant form of care.

- Personal health behaviours can be positive, neutral, or negative. Positive health behaviours and negative health behaviours may represent two dimensions, rather than opposite ends of one dimension. To date, researchers have largely failed to demonstrate a clustering of lifestyle behaviours that would represent a lifestyle.

- Socioeconomic status predicts health. Not only are those living in poverty in worse health, the social gradient suggests that those doing less well than others are in worse health than those others.

KEY TERMS

Health, **(p. 254)**

Sickness, **(p. 254)**

Disease, **(p. 254)**

Illness, **(p. 254)**

Mechanistic model, **(p. 254)**

Wellness, **(p. 256)**

Population health, **(p. 256)**

Aging in place, **(p. 260)**

Assisted living, **(p. 261)**

Personal health determinants, **(p. 262)**

Structural determinants, **(p. 262)**

Health beliefs, **(p. 262)**

Internal locus of control, **(p. 264)**

External locus of control, **(p. 264)**

Host response or general susceptibility hypothesis, **(p. 265)**

Illness behaviour, **(p. 266)**

Health behaviour, **(p. 266)**

Health protective behaviours, **(p. 267)**

Self-health management, **(p. 267)**

Self-care, **(p. 267)**

Personal health practices, **(p. 268)**

Social structure, **(p. 271)**

Social class, **(p. 271)**

Social gradient, **(p. 272)**

Redistributive justice, **(p. 272)**

Placebo, **(p. 273)**

STUDY QUESTIONS

1. In old age, women and men reveal many differences in their health. Discuss what those differences are and the possible reasons for them.

2. Health has different aspects and different meanings. Discuss what these are and their relevance in old age.

3. How do health beliefs differ in older age from when we are younger, and why is this important for our health?

4. The concept of the host response, if confirmed, will profoundly change how we think about research and treat illnesses. Explain.

5. Do personal health behaviours represent a "lifestyle"? Explain why or why not.

6. What is the social gradient, and what implications does it have for population health?

SUGGESTED READINGS

Dean, K. (1989). Self-care components of lifestyles: The importance of gender, attitudes and the social situation. *Social Science and Medicine, 29*(2), 137–152.

Evans, R.G., & Stoddart, G.L. (1990). Producing health, consuming health care. *Social Science & Medicine, 31*, 1347–1363.

Hay, D.I. (1994). Social status and health status: Does money buy health? In B.S. Bolaria & R. Bolaria. (Eds.), *Racial minorities, medicine, and health* (pp. 9–51). Nova Scotia & Saskatchewan: Fernwood Publishers and University of Saskatchewan.

Litva, A., & Eyles, J. (1994). Health or healthy: Why people are not sick in a Southern Ontario town. *Social Science and Medicine, 39*, 1083–1091.

Mustard, C.A., Derksen, S., Berthelot, J.M., Wolfson, M., & Roos, L.L. (1997). Age-specific education and income gradients in morbidity and mortality in a Canadian province. *Social Science and Medicine, 45*(3), 383–397.

Poland, B., Coburn, D., Robertson, A., & Eakin, J. (1998). Wealth, equity and health care: A critique of a "population health" perspective on the determinants of health, *Social Science and Medicine, 46*(7), 785–798.

Families and Aging

Learning Objectives

In this chapter, you will learn about:

- Difficulties in defining families.
- Common myths about the family lives of elder Canadians, past and present.
- How the longevity revolution has affected Canadian families.
- The structure of aging Canadian families, especially regarding marital status and living arrangements.
- Issues concerning midlife families, including "sandwiching," the departure of grown children from the family residence, and the intergenerational stake.

- The exchange relationships between elderly parents and their children and the issue of private transfers across generations.
- Grandparents and characteristics of the grandparent–grandchild relationship.
- Aspects of the life course transition to widowhood, an especially common transition for older women.
- Characteristics of sibling relationships in later life.
- Conflict and abuse in aging families.

Introduction

The family is a key social institution in all societies, and Canada is no exception. Within gerontology, there has been a substantial amount of research done on families—proportionately more than in the "standard" social science disciplines—in part because of a focus on caregiving (dealt with in detail in Chapter 13), which tends to be done by family members. However, this chapter does not focus on caregiving (and its attendant challenges and positive features for both caregivers and care recipients). It has already been pointed out in this book that the majority of elders in Canada are quite healthy and do not require much, if any, care. In this chapter, the focus is on the overall characteristics of the family structure and family relationships of Canadian elders. The possibility and reality of age-related health decline and its effects on family members will not be ignored, but it not a major concern of this chapter.

In keeping with the life course perspective introduced in Chapter 2, a distinction is made between midlife families and "old" families, depending on the age of the family members. Of course, midlife families will eventually become "old" families as time goes by, and midlife families will often interact with the members of old families. Considerable attention will be placed on the life course perspective of linked lives, especially regarding intergenerational relationships.

What Does "Family" Mean?

Most of us are part of a "family," and the definition of what a family is seems self-evident. However, it is not easy to capture, for empirical purposes, what a family is or is not. On one level, the standard definition of family as a "group of people related together by blood, marriage, or adoption" seems straight-forward enough. *The difficulty lies in drawing the boundary between families.* If you are a 20-year-old woman living with your brother and your parents, is this four-person unit your family? What about your aunts, uncles, and cousins? What about your grandparents? Are you all one big family? What about the siblings of your biological aunt's husband—are they included in your family? Your cousin's common-law husband? Your recently divorced uncle's second wife and her grown-up children?

Statistics Canada has been engaged over many years in efforts to define the term *family*, and its definitions of family (and household) appear in Box 11.1. These definitions are important in that many researchers depend on them for their studies of families in Canada, and policy makers and politicians use them in formulating family and family-related policies. In making its definitions, Statistics Canada reflects normative understandings of family. In Canadian society, we tend to divide families into nuclear versus extended forms. The **nuclear family** is a co-residing unit of parent(s) and dependent children. We further distinguish nuclear families into two types: the family of orientation and the family of procreation. The **family of orientation** is the family into which a person is born (or adopted)—and typically consists of co-residing parents (or a lone parent) and dependent children. The **family of procreation** is the family formed when an individual marries (or lives common-law) and has children of his or her own (or adopts them); it typically consists of a co-residing couple (or lone parent) with dependent children.

In Canada, it is assumed that these two families live in different households—that is, when you marry and have children, you no longer live with your parents. This common understanding is reflected in the Statistics Canada definition of *census family*. So, as an individual grows up, he or she moves from one census family (in which he/she is a dependent child) to another census family (in which he/she is part of a couple and likely has dependent children). Since an individual can only be a member of one census family at a given point in time, this normative understanding of family life means that family membership changes over time—as a result of the requirement that nuclear family members must co-reside and must live in the same household.

The **extended family** consists of family members who do not co-reside. Thus, when you grow up and no longer live with your parents, they move from being members of your nuclear family to being members of your extended family. Other non-co-resident kin are also members of your extended family, for example, your

---

Box 11.1 Definitions of Family and Household

CATEGORY	DEFINITION
CENSUS FAMILY	A currently married (legal or common-law) couple with or without never-married children or a lone parent with at least one never-married child, living in the same household.
ECONOMIC FAMILY	Two or more persons who are related to each other by blood, marriage, common-law, or adoption, living in the same household.
PRIVATE HOUSEHOLD	A person or a group of persons (other than foreign residents) who occupy a private dwelling.
FAMILY HOUSEHOLD	A private household that contains at least one census family.
NON-FAMILY HOUSEHOLD	A private dwelling that consists of one person living alone or a group of persons who do not constitute a census family.

Source: Adapted from Statistics Canada Website, 1996 Census Dictionary-Final Edition,
http://www.statcan.ca/english/freepub/92-351UIE/free.htm.

married brother and his wife and children, and so on. Individuals and families differ in terms of where the line is drawn between kin and non-kin. For example, some will include third cousins as part of their extended family; others will adopt a narrower definition of the extended family.

One's family/household status can become very complicated. Let us follow a hypothetical case of a female, using the family and household definitions in Box 11.1:

1. She grows up with her parents and sister (census family).
2. At 20 years of age, she moves out to live with her girlfriend (non-family household).
3. At 22 years of age, she and her sister live together (economic family, non-family household).
4. At 23 years of age, she lives alone (non-family household).
5. At 24 years of age, she goes back to live with her parents (census family).
6. At 25 years of age, she marries and lives with her husband (census family).
7. At 28 years of age, she divorces and goes back to live with her parents (economic family, family household).
8. At 29 years of age, she lives with her grandmother after her grandfather dies (economic family, non-family household).

This is an extreme example, but it serves to highlight the complexities of categorizing people as members of families/households (or not). Part of the complication stems from our normative practice of making co-residency a defining characteristic of families, that is, of privileging the nuclear family form over the extended family form. This practice has implications for aging persons. As long as an older person is married, he or she is considered part of a (census) family—but *not* part of the family of his/her ever-married adult children *unless* they live together; in that case, we have a situation of a family household (but this is not common practice in Canada, as we will see). If a woman becomes widowed and she and her granddaughter then co-reside—as in the hypothetical case above—she becomes a family member again, but in a non-family household.

When we consider the family lives of older persons, we need to break down the assumed connection between families and households, between family membership and co-residency. Connidis (2001) emphasizes that nearly all older persons in Canada are family members, regardless of household living arrangements. As we will see, the majority of elderly Canadians do not live with their children or other family members. However, they are clearly enmeshed in the lives of their children, grandchildren, siblings, and other family members. Separate residence does not mean family estrangement. Rather, separate residence means we have to examine family ties among Canadian elders with a lens that does not focus only on nuclear families.

Myths about the Family Lives of Older Persons in the Past

It is commonly thought that the family life of older persons was "better" in the past than it is in contemporary times. We have images of a golden past in which "grandma and grandpa's" house was the hub of a large, happy, and harmonious family of children and grandchildren. The house, although not lavish by today's standards, was big—to accommodate the large and ever-growing family. This image also serves as a standard by which to gauge today's families—which do not measure up, purportedly abandoning their elderly family members in the embrace of materialist consumption.

There is something very wrong with our picture of the past, however. It does not take into account the cruel demographics of life in past generations. Infant and child mortality rates were high so that the loss of young children for parents and siblings was not uncommon. For example, although Canadian women among those born in 1860 bore, on average, 4.9 children, only 3.2 survived to the age of 20 years (Gee, 1990). Maternal mortality was also high so that some families would lose the mother/wife (Guyer, Freedman, Stobino, & Sondik, 2000). Life expectancy at birth in the 19th century was well below 60 years so that proportionately few people survived to old age. These mortality conditions meant that the odds of even three generations of a family being alive at the same time were quite low. The increasing likelihood of a child having at least one parent alive when that child is aged 40, 50 and 60 years is shown in Table 11.1, which provides a vivid portrayal of the longevity revolution. More than one-half of persons born in 1860 would be "orphans" by the time they were aged 40 years; for persons born in 1960, 82 percent would still have at least one parent alive when they were aged 40 years (in 2000). Among the birth cohort of 1960, nearly one-quarter can expect to have at least one parent alive when they are aged 60 years; among the cohort of persons born

Table 11.1 PERCENTAGE OF PERSONS WITH AT LEAST ONE PARENT ALIVE AT AGES 40, 50 AND 60 YEARS: CANADA, PERSONS BORN IN 1860 AND 1960

AGE	PERSONS BORN IN:	
	1860	1960
40	42%	82%
50	16%	60%
60	2%	23%

Source: Adapted from Gee, E.M. (1990). Demographic change and intergenerational relations in Canadian families. *Canadian Public Policy, XVI*, 192.

a hundred years earlier, only 2 percent would have had a parent alive when they were aged 60 years. In addition, women born in the middle of the 19th century would, on average, be widowed before their youngest child left home (Gee, 1986).

Our image of the past also contains the assumption that earlier Canadian families lived in extended (not nuclear) families. Apart from the demographic constraints on multigenerational family living, there is no evidence that earlier generations of Canadians lived in multigenerational families, even if they could. The Western European family ideal—which came to Canada with the first European settlers—was nuclear family living (Laslett, 1979). Anglophone Canada clearly endorsed this ideal. Even in pre-Confederation Newfoundland—long considered the most "traditional" society in English-speaking North America—research reveals that extended multigenerational households were few; when they did exist, it was due to dire economic need or situations in which elders assisted younger family members (McDaniel & Lewis, 1998). In Quebec, on the other hand, there is some evidence of the ideal and the existence of the **stem family**. In the stem family, one son (not necessarily the eldest) remains at the parental home, bringing in a wife (and later children). Even so, most traditional Quebec families lived as nuclear units. In traditional First Nations societies, diverse family patterns existed, in line with differing kinship systems—kinship systems that, for the most part, were considerably more complex than that of populations of Western European origin.

Overall, these more collectivist-oriented societies preferred multigenerational living arrangements (Dunning, 1959). However, high mortality (particularly in the postcontact period, when infectious diseases brought here by European groups killed many natives, who lacked immunity) meant that most people lived in nuclear or nuclear-type units. Among the traditional Inuit, the few individuals who did live to an older age would, when frail, be left outside to die. In such cases, cultural values emphasize the interests of the group/collectivity over the interests of individuals. In general, we can conclude that "(t)he great extended families that became part of the folklore of modern industrial society were rarely in existence" (Hareven, 1992:7) and that most of our ancestors "remained poor, died young, and lived out their lives in nuclear families." (McDaniel & Tepperman, 2000)

Another image of the past relates to the treatment and status of the aged in earlier times. The image is one of older persons of the past being venerated, honoured, and well cared for by their children. The historical evidence, however, suggests that was not the case in Western countries and that wealth played a large part in the status/treatment of the aged of the past. Hanawalt's (1986) research on peasants in medieval England reveals much about premodern Western families and intergenerational relations. She finds considerable evidence of tension between aged parents and their children—with adult children wanting to gain control of family resources and older parents desirous of retaining control while being assured of care if they needed it. Contracts and wills were established if parents were unsure of receiving care from their families, with the outcomes of such nego-tiations dependent upon the wealth of the aged. If they had land and goods, they could negotiate with kin (or non-kin) for their care. If they lacked economic resources, elderly persons would come to depend on private charity. In Canada, maintenance agreements were used in an attempt by older persons to ensure economic security in later life (Snell, 1992).

It must be remembered that most people in preindustrial and early industrial times lacked property and wealth; Victor states that "ageing was, for most people, a time of pauperism, degradation and dependency" (Victor, 1994: 73). If elders could work for pay, the work was low-waged, heavy, and irregular; if they could not work, most families lacked the economic ability to support them. In this real-ity, the response in England was to establish poor houses (the Elizabethan Poor Laws), the beginning of state-sponsored support for the old. There is no evidence that state financial assistance for elderly persons decreased family ties or weakened the family (Quadagno, 1982); indeed, it is more likely that state support for the aged eased intergenerational tensions and reduced feelings of guilt in many who simply could not financially assist their elderly parent(s).

All in all, we can conclude that myths of the past over-idealize earlier fami-lies. There is no evidence that the majority of Canadian families ever lived in large, multigenerational households, or wanted to. High mortality meant that families lost members at all ages and that few families had older people in them. Among families in which there were older members, few had the economic resources to care for them. However, a "common sense" belief in the happy and large multigenerational family of the past, in which elders were treasured and well cared for, persists. Bengston, Rosenthal, and Burton (1996) term this dis-juncture between everyday belief and scientific evidence as one of the paradoxes about families and aging. There are several reasons for this disjuncture, which parallels the more general "crisis in the family" view that has received consider-able media attention and been promulgated by writers, such as Gairdner (1992) in Canada and Popenoe (1988) in the United States.

One reason is the rise of the conservative "family values" movement, with its agenda of a return to a more rigidly gendered society, back to "when gals were gals, and men were men" and "we didn't need no welfare state" (lines taken from "Those Were the Days" sung by Archie and Edith Bunker at the beginning of each episode of the TV show "All in the Family"). A less political reason for over-idealizing past families lies in a confusion between the definitions of households and families. If we view family life as occurring only within the confines of the nuclear family residing in a single household, we miss much of what goes on across generations in families.

We now move away from myths of families past to examine contemporary family life for middle-aged and elderly persons. We begin with structural dimensions, such as marital status and living arrangements, and then move to family ties—that is, the relationships among members of aging families. However, the distinction between structure and ties is somewhat artificial; they are interrelated in the same way that form and content are intertwined. Thus, we will go back and forth between family structure and family interrelationships/ties in the following discussions.

The Structure of Aging Families

Marital Status

We first look at the marital status of the older Canadian population (Figure 11.1). Marital status is important; for example, research shows that married elders are healthier and live longer than their nonmarried age peers (Thorson, 2000); widows are poorer than elderly married women (Martin Matthews, 1991); separated and divorced elderly persons do not fare as well as the widowed in terms of quality of life, economic status, and social support (National Advisory Council on Aging, 1994); and unmarried seniors, especially women, are more likely to be institutionalized (Gee, 1995). While there is diversity within each marital status grouping (for example, some widows are rich), marital status remains an important determinant of quality of life in the later years.

As can be seen in Figure 11.1, it is not possible to talk about marital status without considering gender as well. Older men are most likely to be married; even at ages 75 years and over, approximately two-thirds of men are married (in a first marriage), and an additional 10 percent are remarried (either legally or in a common-law arrangement—although common-law unions are not popular among current elderly persons). For women, on the other hand, the likelihood of being married decreases quite dramatically with age. Unlike men, at ages 75 years and over, less than one-quarter of women are in a first marriage, and only about 3 percent are remarried. The difference in the marital status of men and women lies in the differential likelihood of becoming widowed. By ages 75 years and over, nearly 65 percent of women are widowed, making widowhood for women "an expectable life event" (Martin Matthews, 1987). This gender difference is the combined function of women's greater life expectancy and of the age difference between spouses (that is, husbands are older than their wives).

Another important gender difference in marital status relates to remarriage. Men are more likely than women to remarry after being either widowed or divorced. Among people in their 70s in 1990 who had been previously married, 38 percent of men and only 15 percent of women had remarried (Gee, 1995). This difference in remarriage probability results from a set of factors, chief among them is demographic reality—that is, there are not many unmarried older men for women to marry, whereas widowed men have a wide choice of unmarried women. Related to this are sexist social norms that allow older men

Figure 11.1 MARITAL STATUS OF POPULATION AGED 55 YEARS AND OVER, BY GENDER AND 10-YEAR AGE GROUP, CANADA 1990

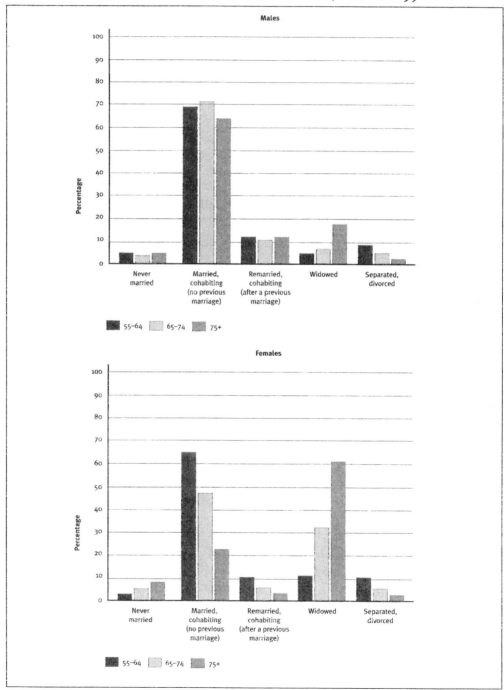

Source: Statistics Canada, "Family over the life course," Catalogue No. 91-543, 2000, p. 83.

to marry women who may be quite a bit younger than they are but do not see the converse as appropriate. There is also some evidence that older widows are less likely to desire to remarry than are widowers (Davidson, 2001); in one study, more than one-half of widows were strongly opposed to the idea of remarrying (Talbott, 1998). Relatedly, Canadian research shows that different factors predict remarriage for widows and widowers; for example, remarriage is positively associated with education among men but not among women, and the presence of children has a negative impact on widow remarriage but not on widower remarriage (Wu, 1995).

As shown in Figure 11.1, the marital status categories of never married, separated, and divorced are not common within the older Canadian population—and there is no strong gender difference, although women are somewhat more likely to be in these unmarried statuses. However, it is quite likely that a higher proportion of elderly individuals in the future will be divorced. This is not because a large increase in later-life divorce is expected; rather, more people are entering old age as divorced individuals. Martin-Matthews (2000) estimates—assuming no significant change in marriage, divorce, and remarriage rates—that as many as one-half of all women who turn 65 years in 2025 will not be in a marriage. If this is the case, widowhood will become a less common marital status for older women. The group of older women of the future to watch is the separated and divorced; they enter old age with even less income than widows (Gee, 1995). If there is a substantial increase in separated and divorced elderly women, the economic situation of older unattached women could worsen.

Living Arrangements

Who lives (or does not) with whom is an important dimension of family life—even though we must remember that families and households are not necessarily the same thing, as previously discussed. Nevertheless, living arrangements are an important issue for elderly persons, related to social support, family cohesion, economic independence, and age segregation.

Living arrangements are of course related to marital status—for example, it is rare for a married person to live alone, although this can happen in later life if one spouse is institutionalized. But there is no one-to-one correspondence between marital status and living arrangements; depending on a number of factors, for example, a widow may "choose" to live alone, with her daughter's family, with her sister, or in a nursing home. As we will see, there is considerable diversity in the living arrangements of elders, and gender, again, plays a determining role. It is important to remember that the living arrangements of elders are dynamic and subject to change. Change in marital status (usually widowhood) results in a change in living arrangements; similarly, declines (and improvements) in health can lead to change. Declines in health are associated with moves to institutions or to the households of relatives (Grundy, 1999; Pendry et al., 1999).

Living with Spouse (Only).

Approximately 60 percent of elderly men live with their wives only, in a couple household, and there is little difference between men aged 65 to 74 years and those aged 75 years and over (Figure 11.2). In contrast, only 44 percent of women

Figure 11.2 **LIVING ARRANGEMENTS OF POPULATION AGED 55 YEARS AND OVER, BY GENDER AND 10-YEAR AGE GROUP, CANADA 1991**

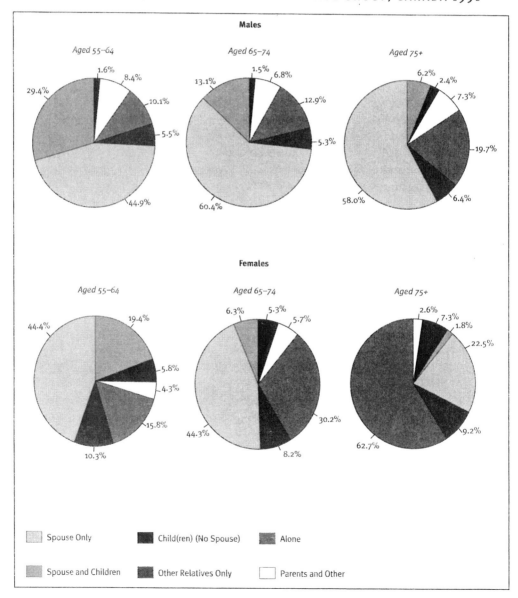

aged 65 to 74 years and fewer than one-quarter of women aged 75 years and over live with a husband. This gender difference is a direct function of differing rates of widowhood between men and women. It means that a majority of older men have a companion in the home, and someone who can assist with instrumental activities. While there is no guarantee that these older wives will be healthy and active, much research shows that older wives do a considerable amount of caring for their husbands (e.g., McDaniel & McKinnon, 1993) and that husbands tend to rely almost exclusively on their wives for social support (Antonucci & Akiyama, 1987). This gender difference also signifies that women are much more likely to experience changes in their living arrangements in later life, a fact that has implications for policy related to housing, health, and social support.

Living Alone.

Living alone is a common living arrangement for older women—30 percent of Canadian women aged 65 to 74 years in private households live alone, as do approximately one-half of women aged 75 years and over, as shown in Figure 11.2. For men, the comparable figures are about 13 and 20 percent, respectively. Living alone in later life is a growing phenomenon. In 1931, only 9.4 percent of the population aged 55 years and over lived alone; by 1991, the figure had increased to 20 percent (Gee, 1995).[1] While both men and women have experienced an increase in living alone, the trend is far more pronounced for women. This trend is not unique to Canada; all Western industrialized societies have witnessed a substantial increase in living alone, especially among older women, since the end of World War II (Wolf, 1990). What factors account for this large increase in living alone among older people, especially older women? Undoubtedly demographic factors (mortality and fertility) are important. As shown by Wolf (1995), using data from 21 industrialized countries from 1960 to 1992, three demographic variables are important in explaining the rise of living alone among older women. One is the higher increases in female life expectancy, as discussed in Chapter 1, which mean that there is a higher ratio of women to men at older ages now than in the past. Second is declining fertility so that elderly women have fewer children with whom to live. Relatedly, Canadian data reveal that nearly one-quarter of women aged 75 years and over have no surviving children (Gee, 1995). Third is the increased fertility of the second generation (i.e., the parents of the baby boom) so that grandparents have had to compete for space in the homes of the middle generation.

Other factors have been put forth to explain the increasing trend of living alone, but there is little consensus and much debate. One explanation centres on economic feasibility. That is, it is argued that the increase in living alone reflects the improved financial situation of elders that makes it possible for them to afford to live on their own (e.g., Holden, 1988). While this explanation has intuitive appeal, Wolf (1995), in an analysis of statistical data for 21 countries in North America and Europe over the period 1960 to 1992, finds no relationship between living alone and economic variables, such as Gross Domestic Product and expenditures on public pensions. In contrast, McGarry and Schoeni (2000), using U.S Census data from 1940 to 1990, find that improved pensions and a general increase in economic status are important factors leading to elderly widows' increased likelihood of living alone. Similarly, Costa (1999) reports that pension improvements account for a large part of the increase in unmarried elderly women living alone in the United States for the same period. In addition, McGarry and Schoeni (2000) report that economic improvements are much more important than sociodemographic factors, such as decline in number of children; in complete opposition to Wolf (1995).

Another explanation de-emphasizes economic and demographic factors, pointing instead to normative change regarding privacy, independence, and individualism leading to more elders wanting to live alone (e.g, Angel & Tienda, 1982). Mutchler, Burr, and Rogerson (1997) stress cultural factors as well, but also point out that cultural variables such as ethnicity are related to economic factors (e.g., affordable housing) in determining living arrangement patterns. Other researchers have emphasized other factors, such as health improvements that allow older persons to live independently (Grundy, 1999; Pendry et al., 1999).

Overall, we can conclude that economic, demographic, and cultural factors are all important in explaining the trend of increase in older women's propensity to live alone, but the jury is still out regarding the relative importance of these determinants.

Multigenerational Living.

National estimates of multigenerational living are hard to obtain for any of the Western industrialized societies, including Canada. This is because statistical agencies (such as Statistics Canada) define families and households in a way, as we have already seen, that focuses on nuclear living arrangements. However, some special tabulations performed by Statistics Canada on the 1991 Census data allow a clearer picture on the prevalence of multigenerational living than is typically available.[2] In 1991, 15 percent of men and 12 percent of women aged 65 to 74 years lived in a multigenerational context (defined as living with a child [with or without a spouse] or with a parent). Among persons aged 75 years and over, the figure is approximately 9 percent, with no marked gender difference. It should be noted that these data are conservative estimates of multigenerational living, since they exclude multigenerational living that "skips" a generation, such as grandchild(ren) and grandparent(s) living together, and they are limited to arrangements centred on the parent–child relationship (excluding, therefore, possible situations such as a elderly woman and her niece living together). These living arrangements would fall into the category "other relatives only." Approximately 7 percent of older Canadians live in "other relatives only" arrangements, but we cannot be sure if they are multigenerational (such as in the examples above) or single-generational (such as two elderly sisters living together). It is probably safe to assume that at least 13 percent of Canada's elderly population lives in some kind of multigenerational living arrangement. While this is not a large percentage, it is not inconsequential either.

Ethnicity and immigration status are associated with multigenerational living in Western countries, such as Canada. Families of Asian origins—and particularly immigrant families of Asian origins—appear to be the most likely to live in multigenerational arrangements in Canada (Gee, 1997), the United States (Phua, Kaufman, & Park, 2001; Wilmoth, 2001), and Australia (Neupert, 1997). For example, Gee (1997) finds, on the basis of a random sample of 830 Chinese elders— mostly foreign-born—residing in Vancouver and Victoria in the mid-1990s, that approximately one-half are living in a multigenerational household. This includes both married couples and widows living with children (and often grandchildren). It is not clear whether ethnic minority families are more likely to live multigenerationally due to preference (cultural ideals) or economic necessity. Some empirical evidence suggests that minority ethnic group elders have more favourable attitudes towards co-residency and express a higher degree of filial responsibility (Burr & Mutchler, 1999). Neupert (1997) reports that age, gender, and marital status do not explain the higher likelihood of ethnic minority aged to live in extended households and that propensity to prefer joint living arrangements is the key factor. However, this propensity contains a mix of cultural, economic, and social factors—and it is not clear how economic and cultural factors may play independent (or intersecting) roles.

Attitudes about multigenerational living with aging parents are related to the past living arrangements of persons. Specifically, persons who, as children, lived in a multigenerational household and/or who lived with their parents as adults before they married have more positive attitudes to living with aging parents (Goldscheider & Lawton, 1998). Szinovacz (1997) finds that living in multigenerational households when young predisposes persons to view multigenerational living positively *and* to actually bring aging parents into their homes. This research highlights a significant issue in multigenerational living arrangements—that is, who is living in whose house? Rosenthal (1986) argues that it is important to distinguish between multigenerational households located in the parent's home and those located in the child's home, finding that they differ along a number of dimensions, including stage of the family life course. That is, multigenerational households in the parent's home are most likely a nuclear family household continuing into the later years, whereas multigenerational households located in the child's home are most often situations in which a daughter is providing a home for her mother. Despite this crucial distinction, gerontological research has tended to assume that multigenerational living is the result of an aging parent or parents moving to a child's home, especially in the face of health declines (Grundy, 1999; Wolf & Soldo, 1988). Research on

Asian Americans shows that they are more likely than other groups both to live in their children's homes and to have adult children living in their homes (Phua, et al., 2001). In the case of elderly Chinese Canadians, Gee (1997) reports that more elders in multigenerational family settings are living in their child's home than in their own home—a reversal of the traditional Chinese pattern in which family elders owned property and exercised economic control over their children. This is also a reversal of the pattern reported by Ikels (1990) in mainland China, where the majority were living in the parents' home. It seems likely that the increasing Asian-origin population in Canada will lead to research that studies more closely the differences between multigenerational households headed by parents and those headed by children.

Structure of Extended Families

The combination of increased longevity and decreased fertility has led to more families that have family members alive at one time (or **vertical extension**) but each generation has fewer members (**horizontal extension**). This is sometimes referred to as the growth of **beanpole families** (Qualls, 1993), that is, situations in which four and even five generations are all alive. While there certainly has been an increase in shared life among family members, as Table 11.1 indicates, the occurrence of beanpole families is not as common as we sometimes think. Research by Uhlenberg (1993) and Winsbororough, Bumpass, and Aquilino (1991) shows that about one-third of Americans aged 45 to 64 years are members of four-generation families; the research also suggests that four-generational families will never be dominant and that five-generational families will be rare. As Rosenthal (2000: 52) states: "While the beanpole family, in the sense of generational depth, is probably more common than in the past, we need to be careful about making sweeping statements about its prevalence." One of the factors that needs to be considered in our thinking about beanpole families is the timing of childbearing. If the trend toward older age at childbearing continues, or even remains constant, it will be difficult to actualize beanpole families. If women have their first child at, say, age 35 years and several generations of women follow this pattern, how many generations could be alive at the same time—unless there is a huge increase in the human life span?

With the increase in divorce has come the formation of what is called **reconstituted families**—that is, families formed by remarriage and involving children from a previous marriage. It is sometimes thought that family reconstitution is having and will have an important effect on aging families. There is some evidence that the adult children of divorce have significantly less contact with their older parents than do adult children raised in a two-parent family (Webster & Herzog, 1995). However, we must not forget that reconstituted families were not uncommon in the past, and may even have been as common as they are now—the difference being that the cause of remarriage was the death of a spouse, rather than divorce. And we do know how family relations played out in the past in situations of remarriage after widowhood.

Midlife Families

Midlife families are ones in which the household "head" is (approximately) aged 45 to 64 years. They can be of any number of structures—e.g., a married couple living alone, a married couple (or lone parent) living with children, a married couple (with or without children) living in their own home along with one of their parents. Research on midlife families is not extensive, but there are three issues that are important for us to consider.

The "Sandwich" Generation?

The **sandwich generation** refers to midlife families, especially women, who are caught in the middle between the care demands of children and the care demands of aging parents. This concept has garnered considerable media attention of late, viewed as one of the negative implications of population aging. At least two books are devoted to the subject: *The Sandwich Generation: Caught between Growing Children and Aging Parents* (Zal, 1992), and *The Sandwich Generation: Adult Children Caring for Aging Parents* (Roots, 1998). In Canada, the hugely popular book *Boom, Bust, and Echo* by economist/demographer David Foot (1996) promulgated the notion of the sandwich generation.

An important Canadian study addresses the issue of the prevalence of such "sandwiching" (Rosenthal, Martin-Matthews, & Matthews, 1996), using data from over 5,000 persons aged 35 to 64 years in 1990. The researchers distinguish between those who have the structural *potential* to be "sandwiched" (i.e., have a living parent, a dependent child, and a paid job) and those who *actually* have an aging parent who needs their assistance and have competing intergenerational responsibilities. They find that 35 percent of women in their late 40s and much smaller proportions of women over the age of 50 years have the structural potential for "sandwiching." Among these women, the highest percentage in any group who provide assistance to a parent at least once a month is only 7 percent. Thus, actual "sandwiching" is not a common phenomenon. Caregiving to elderly parents tends to occur after dependent children have left the home. Penning (1995) reports similar findings. It is important to remember that the family members who are "caught in the middle" —although there are not huge numbers of them—face a very difficult situation and require a range of choices and supports that currently are often nonexistent. In a related study, Rosenthal, Matthews, and Marshall (1989) report that women under the age of 55 years are more likely to face competing demands, but their parents are typically not old and frail. In Chapter 13 on social support and caregiving, the more accurate term "serial caregiving" is discussed.

Empty Nests, Cluttered Nests, and "Boomerang Kids"

Midlife families have experienced considerable change with regard to the presence of adult children in the home. With the increased life expectancy of the 20th century, we came to expect that a married couple would have a period of time "on their own," after all the children had left home and established independent lives, and before the death of one of the spouses ended the marriage. Before the 20th century, however, this **empty nest** phase of life was not a reality for many couples. As noted by Gee (1986), it was not uncommon in 18th century Canada for a marriage to end through death before the last child had left home or shortly thereafter. However, by the middle of the 20th century, the empty nest had become an institutionalized life stage for most midlife couples. Early research on the empty nest was predicated on the assumption that it represented a difficult life transition, especially for mothers (e.g., Myers, 1984). However, subsequent research established that for the majority of women, the departure of children from the home was met with feelings of relief. Guttman (1994) and Helson and Wink (1992) report that empty nest women feel freer and more independent and confident.

In recent years, the empty nest has become increasingly "cluttered." Adult children are remaining home until later ages, and some adult children are returning (sometimes several times) to the parental home. As a result, rates of adult child–midlife parent(s) co-residency have increased in the last few decades. For example, in the Canadian case, in 1981 about one-quarter of unmarried adult children residing with their parents were aged 25 years and over; by 1996, the figures had increased to 33 percent for unmarried women and 40 percent for unmarried men (Boyd & Norris, 1999). Mitchell, Wister, and Gee (2002), using national data from the 1995 *General Social Survey*, find that the strongest predictor of young Canadian adults aged 25 to 34 years living at home is emotional closeness (when growing up) to the mother. Gee, Mitchell, and Wister (2001), using a Vancouver-based sample of 1,800 adult children aged 19 to 35 years, report strong ethnocultural differences in adult child–parent co-residence; Indo-Canadians display a high propensity for co-residency, followed, in order, by Chinese Canadians, Canadians of southern European origins, and then Canadians of British origins.

As noted above, one of the factors responsible for the cluttered nest phenomenon is young adult children returning (at least once) to the parental home, these adult children are sometimes referred to as **boomerang kids**. What are the characteristics of boomerang kids? Canadian research reveals that boomerang kids are not "failures" who have been unable to attain "full" adult status (Mitchell, 2000). A Vancouver-based study of 420 randomly selected families (both child and parent interviewed) reveals that boomerangers are more likely to be never married; be unemployed; and to have a step-parent in the parental home at the time of the survey (1993-1994) (Gee, Mitchell, & Wister, 1995). Approximately one-quarter returned home for reasons of financial difficulty, but another 19 percent returned home to save money (and many of these young adults indicated that they could afford to live on their own). Economic factors, then, play an important role in returning home. Mitchell (2000) notes that economic conditions and diminished opportunity structures are important factors in the return home of adult children. The availability of a welcoming family may be a source of inequality among today's young adults; those who are able to return home have social and economic advantages that others lack (Mitchell & Gee, 1996b).

As with the emergence of the empty nest phenomenon, initial "common sense" speculations are that boomerang kids create stress for parents and cause family disharmony. Media images of boomerangers as selfish and/or lazy and/or immature abound. However, research by Mitchell and Gee (1996a) finds that the presence of boomerang kids does not negatively affect the marriages of midlife parents. Mothers, in particular, are quite pleased to have their children back at home. Boomerang kids can have a disruptive family effect, however, if they "bounce" back and forth several times. This pattern, though, is not common.

Intergenerational Stake

It is commonly found that middle-aged parents feel closer to their children than their children feel toward them; the **integenerational stake hypothesis** has been put forth to explain this differential closeness (Bengtson & Kuypers, 1971). This hypothesis postulates that the younger generation and the middle generation have different developmental "stakes" in their relationship. The younger generation has a stake in developing its own autonomous ways of living and values. In contrast, the older generation has a stake in preserving what it has built. As a result of their differing stakes, the younger generation will tend to maximize differences between it and the next generation, whereas the older generation will tend to minimize differences. Overall, studies have found support for the intergenerational support hypothesis. Lynott and Roberts (1997) find that parents (and grandparents) perceive less of a generation gap than do children, although it is smaller for women. Also, over time, the perceived gap narrows. Giarrusso, Stallings, Bengtson, Rossi, and Marshall (1995) similarly find support for the existence of a generational difference in perceived consensus and closeness as a result of different stakes. These researchers also highlight the methodological point that perceptions of family relationships must be examined for *both* generations, in order to avoid bias in results.

Family Relationships in Later-Life Families

Intergenerational Relations and Transfers

Several misconceptions exist with regard to the relationships between elderly persons and their families, particularly their children. One misconception is that children abandon their elderly parents, and "dump" them in nursing homes as soon as they can. Important research by Shanas (1979) over two decades ago put that myth among social gerontologists to rest. She found that children provide substantial support to their aging parents and that the decision to institutionalize a parent, if it has to be made, is done with reluctance and only after all other avenues have been exhausted. Unfortunately, this is not always recognized by the general public and the media so that stereotypes of abandoned elderly people continue to surface. Shanas' research may have had another consequence, however. Once gerontologists became attuned to the care and assistance that children, especially daughters, were providing to their parents, research on caregiving became very popular. With that research has come the concept of caregiver burden—and images of (mostly) daughters overwhelmed by caregiving duties to their frail parent(s). Inadvertently, we may now have the impression that elders are terrible encumbrances to their families—reinforcing stereotypes of the aged as frail, dependent, and useless. However, most elders are in fairly good health, and most of the joint years lived by adult children and their parents are ones in which little, if any, caregiving is needed. These comments are not meant to dismiss the fact that some families face very heavy caregiving responsibilities that can extend for several years. (See Chapter 13 for a discussion of satisfactions of caregiving.)

It is important to realize that help and assistance *go both ways* between parents and children. The data in Table 11.2—from both Canadian and American sources—show that parents tend to give more help to children than they receive from them, until very advanced ages. We can also see that relatively low percentages of children are involved in giving help to parents and that daughters are more likely to help than sons. These data are quite rough in that they do not tell us what kinds of, and how much, help is being provided or received. The assistance being given/received falls into five categories of instrumental help—home maintenance, transportation, household help, personal care, and financial support. This represents a wide range of activities—it is one thing to drive a family member to a doctor's appointment (help with transportation) and quite another to give him or her a bath (help with personal care). Also, giving financial help does not involve much time, whereas cleaning a house can take up a whole day. Nevertheless, these data are sufficient to show that aging parents and their children are involved in relations of reciprocity and that help does not flow only from children to parents.

The provision of help among parents and children is related to age and life course stage (Stone, Rosenthal, & Connidis, 1998). Parents receive the most help when they are at advanced ages; children receive the most help from parents when they are bringing up their own children. This pattern reflects the changing needs of each generation over time. The help that children receive is instrumental assistance, largely in the form of childcare and financial assistance. Kobayashi (1999), in a study of Japanese Canadian families in British Columbia, reports high levels of financial assistance from parents to children. Less assistance with childcare is observed, in part because of the geographic distance between parents and

Table 11.2 HELP GIVEN TO CHILDREN BY PARENTS AND TO PARENTS BY CHILDREN

PERCENTAGE OF CHILDREN GIVING HELP TO PARENTS

Age of Parent:*		
65–69	14%	
70–74	16%	
75+	38%	
Age of Child:**	Daughters	Sons
45–49	15%	8%
50–54	22%	7%
55–59	18%	11%

PERCENTAGE OF PARENTS GIVING HELP TO CHILDREN

Age of Parent:*	
65–69	40%
70–74	48%
75+	16%

* Data taken from Spitze & Logan, (1992).
** Data taken from Rosenthal, Martin-Matthews, & Matthews, (1996).

children, a legacy of the internment of Japanese Canadians in several parts of the province during World War II. Soldo and Hill (1995) also report substantial amounts of money transfers from older parents to children (a median value of $1,650 in the preceding year). Limited research on aging gays and lesbians suggests they have less intergenerational supports, largely due to intrafamilial discrimination (Blando, 2001; Cahill, South, & Spade, 2000).

Up until now, we have focused on the *amount* of assistance flowing between the generations, as has most of the research. The amount of assistance is important and speaks directly to the issue of intergenerational equity. The intergenerational equity debate, introduced in Chapter 1, focuses on the fairness of transfers across generations. However, the debate has been framed in terms of public transfers, which appear to favour older people. The data here show us that private transfers are very important and appear to favour the younger generation (and its children). However, as McDaniel (1997) argues, we need to overcome the great divide between public and private intergenerational transfers, both theoretically and in terms of data collection. While the amount of intergenerational transfers is important to know about, other aspects of intergenerational exchange are similarly critical and not yet known. As Stone and Rosenthal (1998) point out, we need to know whether enough help is available when it is needed. Also, we need to know more about the meaning of help, the context in which it is given and received in everyday family life. Bengtson (2001) goes even further, arguing for the criticality of intergenerational emotional ties in our lives, and the need to know more about the strength and resiliency of intergenerational solidarity over time. Also, he suggests that with increases in divorce and step-families, multigenerational bonds may be becoming more important than nuclear family ties. In stark contrast, Eggebeen (1992) suggests that today's elders lack a tradition of family support, and that remarriages (step-families) inhibit intergenerational exchanges. The latter finding has been replicated by Pezzin and Schone (1999).

Grandparents

More and more people are becoming grandparents, and for longer periods. This is the combined result of increased longevity and a mid-20th century drop in the age at which women bore children. However, recent trends in increased childlessness, lower fertility, and later age at motherhood suggest that older persons in the future may be less likely to be grandparents and for shorter periods. At the current time, three-quarters of Canadians aged 65 years and over have at least one grandchild, and most have more than one (McDaniel, 1994). And it is believed that most future elders will be grandparents, although they likely will have fewer grandchildren due to reduced fertility levels. Until now, becoming a (first time) grandparent is an event that happens in midlife—not later life, as is sometimes assumed. Canadian research shows that Canadians become grandparents for the first time when they are in their late 40s or early 50s (Gee, 1991). Grandmothers tend to feel that this is the "ideal" age to take on this role, whereas non-grandmothers are less likely to think there is an "ideal age" to become a grandmother and, if they do, it is at an older age. Since grandparenthood status tends to commence in midlife, there can be competing demands on grandparents' time. Most will still be employed, and some may be dealing with the "cluttered nest" of late-leaving or returning children. However, with the birth of each successive grandchild, competing demands are likely to lessen.

Grandparents provide a considerable amount of assistance—both in kind and financial—to the families of their grandchildren (and great-grandchildren). Bass and Caro (1996) estimate that older Americans who provide help to grandchildren and great-grandchildren account for $17 to $29 billion per year in economic contribution. The vast majority of grandparents providing such help report that it is a source of pleasure and satisfaction for them. This, then, is another example of private transfers—this time to grandchildren and great-grandchildren—that directly challenges the idea of intergenerational inequity favouring the old. This example is an especially good one, since—in the imagery of intergenerational inequity—the elderly are pitted against children and viewed as "stealing" from them.

Grandparenting differs by gender. On the demographic level, because women live longer than men and have children at younger ages, they will be grandparents for a longer duration of time than grandfathers. Thus, grandmothers are more likely to have relationships with their grandchildren when they are both children and adults. In addition, men are more likely to be married grandparents, whereas women will be both married and then widowed grandparents.

Grandchildren, in general, feel emotionally closer to their grandmothers; among both male and female grandchildren (Roberto & Stroes, 1992). This may be related to findings (e.g., Hagestad, 1985) that grandfathers tend to give advice to their grandchildren, whereas grandmothers are engaged in a wider variety of conversation topics as well as activities. However, Hagestad suggests that this gender difference in grandparenting behaviour may be cohort specific. If that is the case, future grandmothers and grandfathers may be more alike in their interactions with grandchildren.

Grandparent–grandchild relations are also affected by lineage, or line of descent. Given the importance of the mother–daughter relationship in North American families, we would expect that maternal grandparents play a more influential role in grandchildren's lives than paternal grandparents (Rosenthal & Gladstone, 2000). This issue has not been studied very much, but there is some evidence that adolescent grandchildren feel closer to their maternal grandparents than their paternal grandparents (Van Ranst, Verschueren, & Marcoen, 1995) and that the maternal grandmother is the key grandparent in terms of feelings of closeness (Matthews, 1983, cited in Rosenthal & Gladstone, 2000).

The grandparent–grandchild relationship is affected by geographical proximity. The closer that grandparents and grandchildren live to one another, the more opportunities there are for contact and interaction. We know that grandparents tend to live close to at least some of their grandchildren. However, as noted by Rosenthal and Gladstone (2000), in Canada, we do not have exact data on the proximity of grandchildren and grandparents. Estimates, then, are inferred from data on geographical distances between older parents and their children. While this gives us a general idea, it does not capture geographical distance between grown-up children and their grandparents (likely to be mostly grandmothers).

The relationship between grandparents and grandchildren is mediated by the person (i.e., the children's parent and the grandparent's child) who connects them. This makes the grandparent–grandchild tie vulnerable, especially in the event of marital breakdown in the middle generation. If a marriage breaks up, the custodial parent may deny grandparents access to the grandchildren; this is more likely to happen, of course, to the grandparents who are the parents-in-law of the custodial parent (Gladstone, 1989). With increasing divorce rates, this is an issue of growing importance to grandparents. In Canada, a number of advocacy and "grandparents' rights" groups have emerged, working on behalf of grandparents who have lost contact with their grandchildren due to marital breakups (Kruk, 1995).

In a totally different vein, grandparents may end up parenting their grandchildren if their own child is unable or unwilling to do so. In Canada, we have no information on this phenomenon. However, researchers in the United States have been turning their attention to the issue of grandparent-headed households, which appears to be an especially fast-growing circumstance among African Americans. Overall, in the United.States, in 1997, 6.7 percent of families with children under 18 years were maintained by grandparents, although in some of these families, at least one parent was present as well—this represents a 19 percent increase since 1990 (Casper & Bryson, 1998). In the United States, the increase in grandparent-headed households reflects a whole range of social problems—drug and alcohol addiction, teen pregnancy, incarceration, AIDS, and so on—that are themselves related to poverty (Roe & Minkler, 1998-1999). Grandparents—and often at personal sacrifice regarding free time, working, and financial stress—are coming to the rescue of a growing minority of grandchildren whose parents are not able to raise them.

Widows

Most of the research on widowhood focuses on widows; as we have seen, women are much more likely than men to experience the death of their spouse. One of the most striking characteristics of elderly widows is their straitened economic circumstances; approximately one-half of Canadian elderly widows live in poverty (McDonald, 1997). This is so despite the fact that research evidence shows that older widows are more likely than other marital status categories to receive assistance from children (Eggebeen, 1992; Pezzin & Schone, 1999). The poor financial situation of widows highlights the penalties that women face due to their child rearing and domestic responsibilities that result in less paid employment over their life course, as discussed in Chapter 3. It also is a function of employer-sponsored pension plans that lack survivor benefits (Schellenberg, 1994). And, overall, it is testimony to the economic dependence of women on men. (Also see the discussion on pensions in Chapter 14).

One important research finding about widowhood is that it is not a cut-and-dried phenomenon that necessarily begins at the death of the husband. Neither is it the case that the way women experience widowhood is simply contingent on what happens after the husband dies (van den Hoonaard, 2001). The distinction between widowhood and nonwidowhood may itself be blurry for women. As Martin-Matthews (2000) emphasizes, widowhood is not only an event, it is a process of transition over time. Widowhood is one of the most difficult life transitions to make, and the bereavement process is usually long and painful. It is characterized by intense grief, depression, feelings of meaninglessness, and loss of identity. With regard to the latter, van den Hoonaard (2001) describes a number of cases in which the widow must deal with "who she is" now, given that "who she was" in the past was so closely connected to her husband and her role as wife. This (usually temporary) loss of identity was recognized in the first study of widows in North America (Lopata, 1973) and continues to emerge as an important theme in research on widows.

While most widows feel the loss of their husband and their role as wife very intensely, for some, the experience of widowhood is one that Martin-Matthews (2000: 331) terms an "ambiguous loss." This happens when the marriage was not successful and the husband was cruel or nasty. Given that today's elderly women were less likely to leave a bad marriage, some widows are relieved to be no longer married. Presumably, future cohorts of widows will be less likely to face the challenge of having to appear bereaved when they are actually glad, or at least relieved, their husband is dead.

Whether widowhood is an intensely painful process (which is the case for the majority of women) or a "blessing in disguise" (for the minority of women in very bad marriages), widows must renegotiate their relations with others. The mother–child(ren) relationship is one that changes with widowhood—in which a new balance must be achieved between them (Matthews, 1979; van den Hoonaard, 2001). The balance hinges on privacy and support. Widows want and need the support of their children, but they also want to maintain their own privacy—at least in mainstream North American society. Children may become overly protective of their mother and even treat her like a child. The postwidowhood negotiation with children involves reaching a "place" in which both the widow and the child feel they are contributing equally to the (changed) relationship—that is, the achievement of reciprocity (van den Hoonaard, 2001). Also, relations with friends change after a woman is widowed. Maintaining friendships with couples is particularly difficult, given the couple orientation of modern society. An "unattached" woman may be perceived as a threat by married women friends. Relatedly, relations with men must be renegotiated. As van den Hoonaard (2001) points out, most widows do not want to remarry. Nevertheless, they still want to have contacts and friendships with men. The challenge, then, is to work out new ways to relate with men that do not create the "wrong impression."

Another category of the widowed that is just beginning to receive research attention is gay widowers. To date, we do not even know how many gay widowers there are. Small sample research reveals that gay widowers' bereavement process may be made more difficult by an enforced privacy (if others do not know of their homosexuality) but that, overall, gay widowers are able, with time, to transform their lives in positive ways, much like widows (Shernoff, 1997).

Widowhood research has shifted its focus in recent years. In the past, the focus was on the difficulties that widows face. While these are real, widowhood— like any other change in status—creates opportunities for growth and development.

Thus, there has been a shift from a "doom and gloom" portrayal of widowhood to one that emphasizes creativity, strength, and positive development. At the same time, this new emphasis moves us away from the (often hidden) agist assumption that old age is a period of life in which positive developmental change cannot occur. Examples of this new trend in understandings of widowhood are van den Hoonaard's (2001) book on the "journey" through widowhood and an anthology of Canadian widows' stories entitled *Beyond Coping: Widows Reinventing Their Lives* (Hurd & Macdonald, 2001).

Sibling Relationships in Later Life

Until recently, most of the research on siblings was conducted in the context of childhood. However, with population aging and the growth of social gerontology, there has been some refocusing to adult sibling relationships. Norris and Tindale (1994:81) characterize this as a shift in viewpoint "from rivals to allies." Sibling relationships in childhood—which are not voluntary—can be very intense, filled with positive affect and assistance as well as with frictions and rivalries. In young adulthood and early midlife, sibling relations tend to attenuate somewhat, taking on the characteristics of (voluntary) friendship, as a result of competing demands, especially when children are born. There is more closeness between sisters than between brothers and between brothers and sisters. However, in late midlife, sibling ties tend to be reactivated by the declining health of the parents. The stresses of elder care may strain sibling relations, especially if siblings perceive an unfair division of labour. This is less likely to happen in families with only two sisters; they tend to share duties most equitably (Matthews & Rosner, 1988). In families with both brothers and sisters, the sisters are more likely to be engaged in parental caregiving. Sons in brothers-only families do not neglect their parents, but they tend to be reactive, rather than proactive—leaving it to parents to tell them what they need, rather than seeking ways to assist them (Connidis, 2001).

Approximately 80 percent of today's older persons have at least one sibling (Connidis, 2001). The next generation of elders (the baby boomers) are also likely to have at least one surviving sibling—due to the relatively high fertility of their mothers and increased longevity. The following generation (that is, the children of the baby boom) will be somewhat less likely to have a sibling in old age, although the one-child family has never yet enjoyed much popularity in Canadian society. Future generations of older persons will probably have more step-siblings and half-siblings, as a result of increased divorce and remarriage, although it is hard to be sure about this. Half-siblings and step-siblings are hardly a new thing; what is different is that now they are more likely the result of divorce, whereas in the past, they were the result of early widowhood. This raises the interesting (and yet unanswered question) as to how step-siblings and half-siblings define themselves in adulthood, in the past and in the present. Do they come to view each other as "real" siblings, or does the "kin tie" disappear with the years? Or does some combination of these two things occur? If so, what accounts for the difference? It is very possible that some of the siblings reported by today's elderly persons are half-siblings or step-siblings.

Many of the currently elderly people have a sibling who lives nearby (Connidis, 2001). Close geographical proximity is important to the maintenance of the sibling tie; in fact, Canadian research shows that geographical closeness is more important for sibling interactions than for older parent–adult child relations (Connidis & Campbell, 1995). Other factors that influence sibling contact in later life include gender, marital status, and parental status. With regard to gender, sisters are far more likely to see each other than are brothers and brother–sister combinations (Connidis, 1989a). Also, sisters are more likely to talk about issues of personal importance to them. Persons who are married are in less frequent contact with their siblings than are the unmarried. However the key factor is being never married (single); they are most likely to keep sibling ties activated. However, it is not the case that single seniors feel closer to their siblings (Connidis & Campbell, 1995). Connidis (2001) suggests that reciprocal feelings of obligation may be stronger in the case of the never-married. Persons who are childless are more frequently involved with their siblings than persons with children (Connidis & Campbell, 1995). The single and childless are more likely to live near a sibling, and Connidis (2001:211) suggests that the "salience of siblings to single, childless persons shapes decisions about where to live." In addition, the existence of a family "kin-keeper" (Rosenthal, 1985) is important; families that have an individual who takes on this role are more likely to keep in contact, and this role is particularly important to the maintenance of sibling relationships.

Sibling relationships are about more than frequency of contact, of course-they are also about emotionality and loyalty. Connidis (1994) reports that among Canadian adults aged 55 years and over, 70 percent say they are somewhat, very, or extremely close to at least one sibling. This sense of closeness comes from a history of shared life (siblings are the longest lasting kin tie); as Connidis (2001) notes, siblings rarely become close in old age if they have not been close in earlier life. Siblings are often confidants in later life; this is especially true for women and single and childless persons. Siblings are more likely to be confidants than companions in later life. Connidis (2001) attributes this to geographical proximity, a characteristic more common among friends than siblings. However, 77 percent of older Canadians consider at least one sibling to be a close friend (Connidis, 1989b).

Sibling relationships are of diverse types. On the basis of research on older siblings, Gold (1989) identifies a five-fold typology of sibling relationships. In order of their frequency, the five types are: intimate, congenial, loyal, apathetic, and hostile. Intimate relationships are very emotionally intense, with frequent contact between siblings. Congenial relations are quite similar, but less intense. Loyal relationships do not necessarily involve a great deal of contact but are characterized by a strong sense of family obligation. The majority of sibling relationships are one of these three types, but the existence of both apathetic and hostile sibling relationships reminds us that family relationships are not necessarily harmonious and close. In another study, it is reported that as many as 35 percent of pairs of brothers are disaffiliated, describing their relationship as not at all close, as characterized by disagreement on important issues, and/or as one in which their brother does not understand them (Matthews, Delaney, & Adamek, 1989). This leads directly to the next section, dealing with family conflict.

Family Conflict

Given the emotionality of family relationships, conflict is to be expected. That families are always, or are supposed to be always, harmonious units is a naive expectation grounded in the myths we hold about families (of the past and present). While disagreements and anger are unavoidable in families—at any stage of the life course—and are probably necessary for problem resolution, there are limits on the acceptable expression of conflict. In the last 20 years or so, there has been a growing realization that—in some later-life families—elder mistreatment occurs. This mistreatment can take several forms: neglect, physical abuse, psychological abuse, and financial abuse. Maltreatment of elders is not reserved to the family arena; indeed, it is possible that more maltreatment occurs outside the family than within it. For example, elders can be victimized along all four dimensions mentioned above: in institutional care facilities; "scam artists" often target the elderly; and neighbours can take advantage of elders in any number of ways.

We lack research on the topic of conflict in aging families. Bengtson, Rosenthal, and Burton (1996) suggest four reasons for this. (1) Respondents may not mention family conflict due to social desirability and/or reluctance, thus—through omission—portraying family life as more harmonious than it really is. (2) Researchers have not developed a clear concept of conflict. (3) Researchers who have studied family conflict have tended to use quantitative measurement scales, which is probably not the best approach to a subject that is inherently subjective and interpretative. (4) A clear classification scheme of issues of family conflict, which is needed for systematic investigation, has yet to be developed.

What, then, is known (or believed) about elder maltreatment? While the overall extent of elder maltreatment is not known, a national Canadian survey reports that approximately 4 percent of elders have been abused (at least once) since turning 65 years of age (Podnieks, 1992b). An American-based study estimates that about 3 percent of elders are victims of physical violence, verbal aggression, and/or neglect (Pillemer & Finkelhor, 1988). It also finds that spouses are much more likely to be perpetrators of maltreatment than are children. It should be noted that this study omits financial abuse, which is believed to be a common, and perhaps the most common, type of elder mistreatment (Bengtson, Rosenthal, & Burton, 1996), perpetrated either by family members or by unscrupulous businesses. However, we have the most "hard data" on physical abuse. A combination of media images of "granny bashing" and an understandable clinical focus on the most extreme cases of elder abuse have led to an overemphasis on violence and a lack of knowledge about other forms of elder maltreatment. Also, the estimates of elder abuse by both Podnieks (1992b) and Pillemer and Finkelhor (1988) are for community-dwelling elders. However, Spencer (1994), in a report for Health Canada, points to high levels of abuse amongst older persons who are institutionalized. Overall, it is likely that approximately 4–8 percent of Canadian elders have been abused.

Violence against aged family members has been related to four factors: (1) problems of the abuser, such as mental illness and drug addiction; (2) dependency of the abuser on the victim, particularly financial dependency; (3) social isolation; and (4) external stresses on family members (Pillemer & Suitor, 1990). Penhale (1999) also finds that the causes of domestic violence against older women are multifactorial, including dependency, social isolation, relationship difficulties, caregiver stress, and psychopathology. Men are more likely to be perpetrators of violence, whereas women are more likely to be implicated in neglect (Dunlop, Rothman, Condon, Hebert, & Martinez, 2000). Violence against dementia sufferers has received a considerable amount of research attention, in part because it appears that persons with dementia—especially if their disease leads them to act in aggressive and violent ways—are at increased risk of abuse (e.g., Buttell, 1999; Penhale & Kingston, 1997).

Part of domestic violence in old age is "merely" the perpetuation of wife abuse into later life (Phillips, 2000). Relatedly, Pillemer (1986) finds that adult child perpetrators of violence toward elderly parents are likely to have been physically punished as children or to have been victims of child abuse. At least to some degree, family violence against elders represents a continuation of behavioural patterns beginning much earlier in the family life course. The stresses of caregiving, in conjunction with mental health problems and dependency in later life are added causal factors.

Domestic violence in aging families is a hard issue to deal with. First, many cases of it are hidden; Wiehe (1998) estimates that approximately only one in 14 cases of elder abuse is ever reported.

Second, as Hill and Amuwo (1998) point out, elder maltreatment is more a social than a legal issue. A host of problems, some directly related to aging and health declines, contributes to elder abuse. In most cases, legal notions of guilt and punishment have little relevance. Also, if elders choose not to come forward to the courts, are "we" to take away their right of choice? Would that not be paternalism, reinforcing agist stereotypes of elderly individuals as incompetent and childlike? The direction to take, rather than a legal one, is to facilitate prevention. In some cases, that means prevention of violence much earlier in the family life course. Prevention can also be fostered by providing the right kinds of supports and services to deal with mental illness, caregiving stress, and social isolation.

CHAPTER SUMMARY

As we have seen, family membership and family ties are an important aspect of the lives of elderly Canadians. While most Canadian elders do not live with anyone other than their spouse, other family members play an important role in their lives. One of the most critical ways in which lives are linked is through families. Nevertheless, there is considerable diversity in older Canadians' family lives—related to age, gender, and ethnicity, for example.

Key ideas to remember from this chapter include:

- There are many definitions of family and household, as observed in Box 11.1. The most difficult issue in defining families is drawing a line around where one family ends and another starts. Another important issue is the distinction between families and households and our tendency to equate the two. When considering older families, it is important not to equate families and households, nor to privilege the nuclear family over the extended family.
- We need to free ourselves of myths about families and family life in the past; if we compare today's families against an idealized version of the past, contemporary families are guaranteed not to measure up.
- One of these myths is that families in the past were extended, consisting of multigenerational households. The demographic realities of the past, particularly mortality, did not allow many families to have three generations alive at the same time. Further, at least among Anglo-Canadians, extended families were not preferred.
- Another myth of the past is that elders were honoured and well cared for by their children. Most people were poor and could not afford to help their parents.
- Gender and marital status are closely related. In later life, women are likely to be widows, whereas men are likely to be married. This gender difference is the combined function of women's greater life expectancy and of the age difference between spouses (that is, husbands are older than their wives). Also, men are more likely to remarry if they are widowed or divorced.
- Gender is also related to living arrangements. Men are much more likely to live with a spouse than are women. There has been a substantial increase in living alone among older women in all industrialized countries. Reasons for this trend include demographic, economic, and cultural factors, but there is much debate about the relative importance of these factors.
- It is probably the case that approximately 13 percent of Canada's elders live in multigenerational households. Ethnic origin is related to the propensity to live multigenerationally; Asian-origin Canadians—and particularly those who are foreign-born—are more likely to live in three-generational households. An important distinction in multigenerational households relates to home ownership—is the multigenerational household located in the child's home or the elder's home?
- Beanpole families—consisting of four or five generations, but with few members per generation—are not as common as sometimes thought. Age at childbearing is an important consideration here; if women have their children at relatively late ages, the age gap between generations is lengthened, making it difficult to achieve beanpole families.
- Research findings are clear in showing that the image of midlife families "sandwiched" between the needs of dependent children and elderly parents is an exaggeration.

- Midlife families are experiencing a "cluttered nest," with children leaving home at older ages and adult children more likely to "boomerang" back.

- Research supports the intergenerational stake hypothesis, which holds that midlife parents feel closer to their children than their children feel toward them as a result of different developmental stakes. This generation gap, however, decreases over time.

- Private transfers between older parents and their children go both ways. Indeed, research indicates that elder parents give more to their children than they receive. This finding has implications for the intergenerational equity debate.

- Most Canadian elders are grandparents, and most experience the transition to grandparenthood in midlife. Grandparents contribute much to their grandchildren (and great-grandchildren), which is another important finding regarding intergenerational equity. Grandparenting differs by gender: women are more likely to be grandparents for a longer time, and the grandparent–grandchild tie is more emotionally close among grandmothers. This tie is mediated by the middle generation, and can have two opposite effects. In the event of a divorce in the middle generation, grandparents and grandchildren may be denied contact. In contrast, grandparents can become "parents" if persons in the middle generation are unable or unwilling to care for their children.

- Widowhood is an "expectable" life event for Canadian women and is associated with financial difficulty. Widowhood is both an event and a process over time; the process is emotionally painful (for most) and one necessitating a change in identity. Widows must negotiate new relationships with children and other family members, with friends, and with men.

- The importance of siblings varies over the life course. In later life, sibling ties are important to many people. The importance of sibling ties is influenced by geographical proximity, gender (sisters are closer than other siblings), marital status (siblings are more important to the never-married), and parental status (siblings are more important to the childless).

- Family conflict has not been studied extensively by social gerontologists. We know most about elder abuse—the most extreme form of family conflict/elder maltreatment but probably not the most common. It is estimated that approximately 4–8 percent of elders are victims of abuse and/or neglect in both home and institutional settings. Within the family setting, spouses are much more likely to be perpetrators of elder maltreatment than are children. Men are more likely to be physically abusive; women are more likely to be abusive through neglect.

- Violence against aged family members is related to four factors: problems of the abuser, such as mental illness and drug addiction; dependency of the abuser on the victim, particularly financial dependency; social isolation; and external stresses on family members. Part of domestic violence in old age is the perpetuation of wife abuse into later life. Elder abuse is more a social problem than a legal one, and social solutions are needed.

KEY TERMS

Nuclear family, **(p. 279)**

Family of orientation, **(p. 280)**

Family of procreation, **(p. 280)**

Extended family, **(p. 280)**

Stem family, **(p. 283)**

Vertical extension, **(p. 292)**

Horizontal extension, **(p. 292)**

Beanpole families, **(p. 292)**

Reconstituted families, **(p. 292)**

Sandwich generation, **(p. 293)**

Empty nest, **(p. 294)**

Boomerang kids, **(p. 294)**

Intergenerational stake hypothesis, **(p. 295)**

STUDY QUESTIONS

1. In what ways have declines in mortality affected families?

2. Identify at least four myths about aging families and family relationships. Why do you think they exist?

3. List ways that the families of ethnic minority elders differ from those of the "mainstream." What are the difficulties in trying to ascertain why these differences exist?

4. Discuss ways in which men's and women's family life courses differ.

5. Discuss how increasing divorce (and remarriage) is affecting older persons in their family lives.

SUGGESTED READINGS

Bengtson, V.L., Rosenthal, C.J., & Burton, L.M. (1996). Paradoxes of family and aging. In R.B. Binstock & L.K. George (Eds.), *Handbook of aging and the social sciences* (4th ed.) (pp. 253–282). New York, NY: Academic Press.

Blieszner, R. & Bedford, V.H. (1995). *Handbook of aging and the family.* Westport, CT: Greenwood Press.

Connidis, I. A. (2001). *Family ties and aging.* Thousand Oaks, CA: Sage.

Finch, J. & Mason, J. (1993). *Negotiating family relationships.* New York, NY: Tavistock/Routledge.

Hareven, T.K. (Ed.). (1996). *Aging and generational relations across the life course.* New York, NY:Walter de Gruyter.

ENDNOTES

1. The trend data on percentages of persons living alone are calculated on a base that includes persons in all types of households—private and collective.

2. Part of these data are shown in Figure 11.2.

Work and Retirement

In this chapter, you will learn about:

- The history of the institutionalization of retirement.
- A description of the "new" retirement as we know it today.
- The various definitions of retirement and their links to gerontological theories.
- The linkages between work and retirement—the different work experiences of men and women and

how they influence the transition into retirement and postretirement social and economic status.
- Why and when people retire, how they retire, and the consequences of retirement.

Introduction

Most scholars would agree that retirement is a social invention that emerged in modern industrialized societies at the start of the 20th century. As labour force participation rates of older workers began to plummet in most industrialized economies, retirement became a deeply rooted social institution by the end of the 1980s. As a social institution, retirement was designed to move the older worker out of the labour force in a systematic manner without causing unwarranted economic hardship, while solving the societal problem of what to do with an aging labour force. As a consequence, retirement emerged as the last segment of the life course and helped define old age as a distinct life phase, a phase chronologically set apart from the first phase, typically dedicated to education, and the middle phase, devoted to work. Understanding the emergence and development of retirement is, therefore, crucial to an understanding of the last phase of life, since retirement is not only the principal gateway to later life but is the conduit that links the institutional structures of work and nonwork to prepare the foundation for well being in old age.

The History of Retirement in Canada

The Pre-Industrial Agrarian Era

Retirement did not exist prior to the industrialization of Canada. People appeared to adjust their work with their diminishing physical capacities as they aged. As historian Andrejs Pakans has aptly observed, people "**stepped down**" from their work, but these actions referred to an informal process of withdrawal, which could be long and drawn out (Pakans, 1989: 176) or, sometimes, sudden and unexpected as a result of illness or accident (McDonald & Wanner, 1990). In agrarian Canada in the latter half of the 19th century, ownership of the family farm lent itself to stepping down because the farmer had the power to control the process. The farmer could continue to work but could also gradually reduce his more demanding tasks by delegating them to his sons and sons-in-law without losing control of the land. At a time determined by the older farmer, he would pass the farm on to his children, mainly his sons, with provisions made for the care and maintenance of himself and his wife in their old age. The promise of inheriting the farm served to maintain the interest of adult children in the farm and provided the mechanism for maintaining older people in their old age. Maintenance agreements were used to document the nature of the inheritance and the care to be provided to the older couple to make sure that the terms were implemented (Snell, 1992; 1996). Since the ownership of property was legally in the hands of the male, it is likely that women stepped down in tandem with their husbands, perhaps passing some of their more onerous tasks on to daughters or daughters-in-law, although this is not known. If a woman's husband died, her care in old age was passed on to her male relatives, such as sons. Often, the husband left explicit instructions as to how she was to be cared for, including which rooms in the house she could use (Cohen, 1988). If she remarried, the will usually stipulated that she lost her inheritance so that husbands often exerted control over their wives even from their graves.

Not all workers owned farms, although farming was the mainstay of the economy. Men tended to work in such industries as the fur trade, iron-making industries, timber firms, and water transportation (McDonald & Wanner, 1990), while the majority of women were employed as domestic servants (Cohen, 1971). Most people worked until they could no longer fulfill the responsibilities attached to their jobs, at which time they were moved to less onerous jobs that matched their capacities. The paternalistic nature of labour relations in the 1850s, driven by serious labour shortages, led to a personal concern for workers because employers were anxious to retain them in their firms (Pentland, 1981). There is some evidence that the Hudson's Bay Company offered a type of annuity plan that paid four percent on any of a worker's wages left in the care of the company, only if the worker was considered deserving. Katz (1975), in a study of citizens of Hamilton, found that businessmen, if they fared well financially, would retire and pass their business on to their sons. What became of the women who were domestics, took in boarders, or ran small businesses (such as taverns) is not clear. It is likely that they simply worked until they could cope no more. If they were destitute and bereft of family, they likely ended up in a poor house.

The evidence about retirement in pre-industrial Canada suggests that it was an ad hoc event and that it was a gradual withdrawal process taking the form of stepping down, both on the farm and in the workplace. For the farmer and entrepreneur, stepping down was rooted in the Canadian system of inheritance, while the paid worker was at the mercy of his or her employer as to whether or not he or she could step down to lesser tasks. Women, it would seem, were dependent on the family economy and were to be cared for by their male relatives in old age.

The Industrial Era

The industrial revolution in Canada, which spanned the period between the 1840s and the 1930s, caused a momentous transformation of Canada from a rural, agrarian society to an urban, industrialized society. This era is usually considered by historians to be a crucial time in the development of retirement because it was during this period that retirement began to take shape as an institutionalized phase of the life course. The development of retirement is consistent with the **life course institutionalization hypothesis** (O'Rand & Henretta, 1999: 181). This hypothesis suggests that over the long term, individual lives have become increasingly organized by institutions of the state and of the workplace. In this process, individuals have been freed from the bonds of family and the earlier paternalistic relationships of the workforce, as noted above. The bureaucratic structures of firms tend to be age based; so, for example, permission from an employer to continue to work is replaced by age as the criterion for retirement (Graebner, 1980). In the same vein, the availability of public or private pensions at a specific age encourages exit from the labour force at that age and tends to reduce individual discretion in the decision.

Snell (1996) addresses retirement in his history of aging in Canada. He argues that the effects of industrialization were gradual in Canada and that a minority of older workers were pushed out of the labour force into poverty. It was this minority who compelled the social activists in Canada to fight for pensions, which led to the establishment of the *Old Age Pensions Act* of 1927, a type of social assistance, subject to a means test. He goes on to show that the ungenerous administration of the Act led to activism on the part of elderly persons, which ultimately helped establish the *Old Age Security Act* of 1951, the first universal pension plan in Canada. With the universal pension came a steady income for older workers that made retirement a distinct reality for many Canadian older workers.

In this process, advanced industrialization significantly contributed to the trend that institutionalized retirement in several ways. Most importantly for older workers, firms became bigger and more bureaucratic, with specialized divisions of labour, hierarchical chains of command and centralized authority—all of which depersonalized the firm, making it almost impossible to meet the individual needs of older workers. At the same time, "scientific management" (Taylor, 1947) was introduced into organizations, which divided the production process into small, repetitive operations that emphasized physical efficiency and speed—a case of deskilling older workers. In the faster paced industries where technological change speeded up production levels even further, older workers had trouble keeping up, making them more vulnerable to unemployment (Haber & Gratton, 1994).

After having deskilled older workers, a problem developed, which was later solved by the Ford Motor Company. The traditional discipline attached to the crafts disappeared, and turnover rates of workers were high. To combat this problem, Ford created a set of graduations among identical jobs within the factory, establishing a false hierarchy based on seniority rather than skill. Because of seniority, older workers moved to the top of the hierarchy and ended up being paid more than younger workers for the same work. To avoid high costs and to be more efficient, management required a cutoff point. The cutoff was **mandatory retirement**, which usually was set at age 65. At about the same time, the "wear-and-tear" theory of aging was popular, which suggested that old workers were worn out and should retire. As Dr. William Osler, the great Canadian suggested, "...men above 60 years of age were useless..." (*The Globe*, 1905: 7). In short, a number of factors converged during industrialization that set the stage for the institutionalization of retirement. Some workers were forced out of the labour force, expedited by growing agism, and fixed time schedules for when to leave the labour force and under what circumstances, as in the case of mandatory retirement.

Pensions and the Institutionalization of Retirement

In 1908, the *Government Annuities Act* was passed as a delayed response to the majority report of *The Royal Commission on the Relations of Labour and Capital* in 1889, which detailed the more appalling labour force conditions of early industrialism. The Annuities Act was not particularly successful in reaching the people who needed it the most, namely, working class labourers who made up only 4 percent of the population (Bryden, 1974), nor did it treat women (who received lower returns for the same investment as men) fairly (Strong-Boag, 1993). Retirement, at this time, continued to be an ad hoc affair available to the wealthiest and those few privileged workers with a pension. The seeds had been sown, however, for the idea of retirement in both government and business.

As a result of the negative aspects of industrialization, some older workers were forced out of the labour force. Their poverty caused great concern on the part of social reformers and, after much debate in the House of Commons, the *Old Age Pensions Act* of 1927 was passed. There were three serious problems with this Act that made retirement difficult to achieve. First, the state could recover the cost of the pension from the pensioner's estate when he or she died, which violated the spirit of the Canadian system of inheritances. Second, the miserly amounts of pensions paid on the basis of a means test were too small to make retirement possible. Although considered the first "gender-inclusive" Act (Struthers, 1992), in the administration of the Act, officials maintained the gendered nature of marriage, making sure that women received lesser pensions than their husbands because women were still viewed as dependent on male relatives for their retirement income. What other family members, such as sons, *could* contribute to their mothers was more stringently considered in calculating women's pensions than in the calculation of men's pensions. This problem with the administration of the pension deterred parents interested in retiring because they did not wish to burden their children.

On the heels of the Great Depression and World War II, there was a demand for better pensions because Canadians desperately wanted to avoid the devastation wrecked by the Great Depression in the 1930s. The problems with the Act of 1927 also strengthened the resolve of Canadians to agitate for change. The *Old Age Security Act* of 1951, a universal, flat-rate pension plan, financed and administered by the federal government, operated on the principle of social insurance for older workers, as opposed to social assistance. At this time, the *Old Age Assistance Act*, a form of social assistance, was also passed for those aged 65 to 69 years and was based on a means test. Private pension schemes also grew during World War II in response to labour force shortages. Taken together, both public and private developments facilitated the spread of retirement, linking it to a specific age and normalizing the retirement experience for most Canadians. As can be seen in Figure 12.1, the labour force participation rates of men aged 65 years and over dropped substantially from 37.9 percent in 1951 to 26.2 percent in 1966 when

Figure 12.1 PARTICIPATION RATES FOR AGE GROUPS 55 TO 64 YEARS AND 65+ BY GENDER, 1946–2000

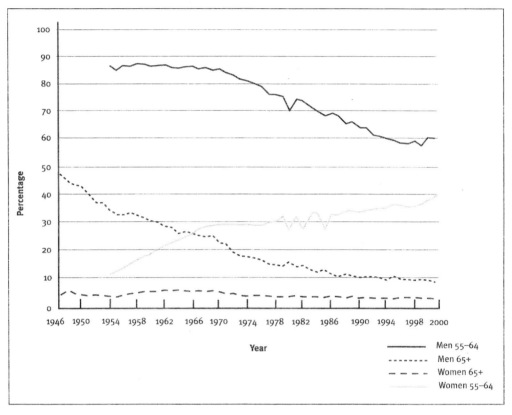

Source: Based on data from the Statistics Canada "Labour Force Historical Review" microdata file, Catalogue No. 71F0004, February 2002.

the next round of pension changes occurred. Women's rates remained stable during this time, because most women were not in the labour force in 1951. The labour force participation rates of women in 1966 was about 24 percent because the belief at the time was that a woman's place was in the home.

Through the 1960s, the *Old Age Security Act* was restructured to increase pension benefits and the qualifying age of 70 years was reduced by one year every year until it became age 65 in 1970. The Canada/Quebec Pension Plan (C/QPP) was added as a second tier to the pension system in 1965, as a compulsory, contributory plan with benefits linked to contributions based on waged labour. Because Canadians who were already retired would not benefit from the C/QPP, the Guaranteed Income Supplement was introduced in 1966, as an income-tested interim measure to be phased out when the C/QPP fully matured in 1976.

The third tier of the pension system included personal savings and assets, private pensions, and the Registered Retirement Savings Plan of 1957, to secure the idea of retirement. With the three tiers of the pension system firmly in place, retirement became economically attractive, was financially guaranteed by the state, and was felt to be a desired event by most Canadians.

The first national retirement study in Canada was conducted in 1975. It found that 75 percent of women were retired at age 63 years, while 60 percent of men were retired at age 65 years (Ciffin & Martin, 1977). By the 1980s, retirement was a widespread institution, which moved Canadians from the labour force into the last segment of the life course in an ordered and systematic manner—a shift that was age based and defined by the state through public pensions and by private pensions in the workplace (McDonald & Wanner, 1990; Myles, 1984). As seen in Figure 12.1, in 1989, only 11.1 percent of men 65 years and over were in the labour force, compared with 3.5 percent of women at the same age.

It is important to note that the labour force experiences of women were quite limited in the formative years of retirement, because most women did not work outside the home and, if they did, their work was considered secondary to the work of their husbands, who were the chief breadwinners. Also, if women worked, their unpaid work at home occurred simultaneously with their paid work in the labour force at a time when housework was hard physical labour. These two major differences indicate that women faced unique circumstances that made their link to the labour force more tenuous than men's—differences that ultimately call into question the accepted view of the history of retirement and its application to women (McDonald, 2002).

Retirement in the 21st Century

The Extent of Retirement

Today, in Canada, retirement is the norm for older workers. Canadians want to retire and preferably early. The *General Social Survey* of 1994 indicates that 8 percent of men intended to retire before age 55 years, 23 percent between the ages of 55 and 59 years, 14 percent at age 65 years, and 2 percent after age 65 years. Ten percent of men reported that they did not intend to retire, and 25 percent did not know when they would retire. In the case of women, 8 percent intended to retire before age 55 years, 20 percent between the ages of 55 and 59 years, 13 percent between 60 and 64 years, and 1 percent after age 65 years. Seven percent of the women did not intend to retire, and 36 percent did not know when they would retire (Monette, 1996). Women's more complicated work experiences due to the overlap of paid and unpaid work and the problem of negotiating family retirement makes their retirement more uncertain.

The desires of Canadians are reflected by their retirement behaviour when the precipitous decline in labour force participation rates are reviewed. As indicated in Figure 12.1, in 2000, 61 percent of men aged 55 to 64 years remained in the labour force, compared with 86.5 percent in 1953. For men aged 65 years and over, the labour force participation rate was 9.5 percent in 2000, compared with 47.5 percent in 1947, an amazing drop by any measure. Three observations can be made based on the data for men in Figure 12.1. Declines for men have been greater over age 65 years, although there has been a decline for all ages; the decline over age 65 years appears to have stabilized and, during the 1990s, labour force participation seems to have fluctuated somewhat. The fluctuations may represent such factors as government cutbacks that occurred during this time and corporate downsizing (Gower, 1997). Looked at another way, the median age of retirement for men in 1998 was age 61.8 years, down from the median age of 65.1 years in 1976, as shown in Figure 12.2.

The pattern for women's labour force participation, as seen in Figure 12.1, appears different from men's because the rates represent two trends: the dramatic

Figure 12.2 RETIREMENT AGE BY SEX

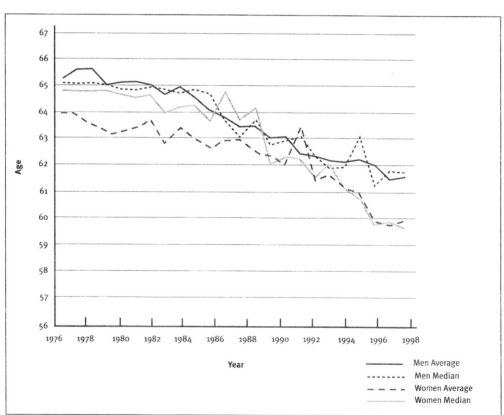

Source: Based on data from the Statistics Canada "Labour Force Historical Review" microdata file, Catalogue No. 71F0004, February 2002.

increase in women's labour force participation starting in the 1960s and the trend toward early retirement. The increasing midlife participation of women aged 55 to 64 years is evident in the figure. In 1954, only 12.9 percent of women aged 55 to 64 years were in the labour force, compared with 41.6 percent in 1999. In contrast, the labour force participation rates for women aged 65 years and over have never exceeded the rate of 6.3 percent in 1964 and have remained fairly stable since 1946, suggesting that the two trends offset each other for older women. An examination of women's median age of retirement is more telling. As shown in Figure 12.2, the median age of retirement for women dropped from 64.8 in 1976 to 59.8 in 1999.

Figure 12.3 clearly indicates women's labour force patterns in relation to those of men. Beginning in the 1970s, each successive cohort of women was in the labour force longer. In light of the larger baby boom cohorts, the participation rates rose dramatically, as seen in the cross-sectional rates in Figure 12.3. The decline in the participation rates of men, noted above, served to narrow the gap between the rates of men and women, and the participation profile of women has begun to resemble the same high and flat shape of men's rates (Sunter, 2001). The flat participation rates of women during the 1990s have been attributed to the full integration of women into the labour force (Beaudry & Lemieux, 1999) and/or that the participation rates of successive generations have become more similar leading to slower growth, although both observations are speculative (Sunter, 2001).

Figure 12.3 **PARTICIPATION RATES BY AGE AND SEX, CANADA 2000**

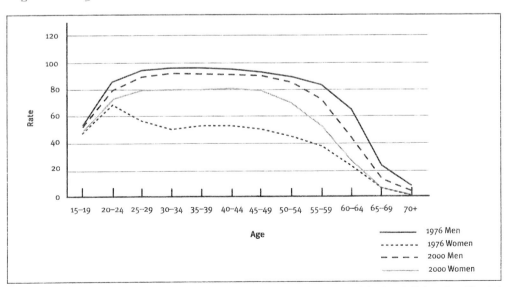

Source: Based on data from the Statistics Canada "Labour Force Historical Review" microdata file, Catalogue No. 71F0004, February 2002.

The data presented in all three figures indicate the pervasiveness of the age-based structure of the life course in Canadian society (as in most industrialized societies). The decline in men's participation has, over time, become more and more closely associated with age 62 for retirement. For women, waged labour has become more of a central element in their lives, thereby tightening the previous weak link between work and retirement. Most importantly, the patterns indicate that women's retirement will be different from men's retirement. Women's late entry into the labour force means, at a minimum, they will be playing pension "catch-up" to men.

The New Retirement

Having argued for the institutionalization of the life course, some researchers now debate whether or not the life course is "coming undone" (Guillemard & Rein, 1993), is simply becoming longer and fuzzier (Kohli & Rein, 1991), is more asynchronous (O'Rand & Henretta, 1999; Han & Moen, 1999), or, more vividly argued, represents a "...veritable revolution in the age structure of society" (Riley & Riley, 1994). In short, retirement does not always represent an abrupt transition from work to nonwork: it can be gradual, it can involve multiple exits, and it may never happen. Han and Moen (1999) capture the essence of the new arguments, when they conceptualize retirement as **clocking out**. Retirement is a multiplex process, governed by multiple institutional schedules and by the diverse pacing of individual biographies that intersect with institutional timetables, all of which lead to variability in the age of retirement. Guillemard (2000) specifically argues that the retirement pension system no longer regulates early retirement in Europe; rather, disability insurance creates the bridge between work and retirement. Henretta (1992) argues that the life course is still uniform but becoming more variable in timing. Gardyn (2000) argues that retirement is being reinvented to include not only second careers but also continuing education and volunteerism. Whatever the precise nature of the changes, most scholars agree that there have been some adjustments in the temporal order of the stages of the life course and changes in the time spent in the various stages.

Some of these changes have spilled over to the debates about retirement to the extent that there is some discussion of a "new" retirement, although what is "new" about the "new retirement" is not agreed upon by gerontologists. What is different about retirement today is that it is evolving into a process without a clear beginning or end; it is much less likely to be chronologically determined, it is not as tightly regulated by the state through public pensions or by one's relationship to the labour force, and there are a multitude of pathways leading to retirement. The evidence for these changes is growing.

While the continuing lowering of the age of retirement could still be argued to be tied to public and private pensions, a full 31 percent of Canadians reported, in 1994, that they did not know at what age they would retire. The group most uncertain, as noted above, was women: 36 percent of women did not know when they would retire, compared with 25 percent of men. The average planned retirement age of employed persons in this survey was 58.5 years for both sexes, well below 60 years, the age at which pensions first become available in the Canada/Quebec Pension Plan. Although the evidence is tenuous because of the lack of available data over time, there does seem to be a larger number of routes into retirement than was available in previous times. Two "new" routes that have come to the forefront in recent years would be retirement via early retirement packages and the need to provide care for a family member. In the *Survey of Persons Not in the Labour Force*, 26 percent of men and 12 percent of women indicated that they had retired unexpectedly because they were offered an early retirement package (McDonald, Donahue, & Marshall, 2000). In the *Survey of Aging and Independence*, only 5 percent of the women who were still employed identified caregiving as a possible reason for their retirement. However, in the *General Social Survey* five years later, at least twice that many women (13 percent) reported retiring to provide care (Monette, 1996). Another example is the use of disability benefits as a route into retirement. Disability benefits were originally intended to provide income for those who could not earn a living because they had a severe disability. However, in a number of countries, they were used as a vehicle to remove older workers from the labour force in response to high levels of unemployment. The uptake was so sharp that in 1990, recipients of disability benefits outnumbered those in receipt of unemployment benefits in 12 of 23 OECD countries (McDonald & Donahue, 2000).

Some Canadians have also reversed their retirement decision. Depending on the data file used, between 13 (*General Social Survey*, 1994) and 17 (*Survey of Aging and Independence*, 1991) percent of Canadians reversed their retirement decision and returned to the labour force, mainly to what have been called "bridge jobs" to retirement (Doerringer, 1990). In a small, nonrandom study of a telecommunications company in Canada, almost 47 percent of male and 25 percent of female early retirees went back to work (Marshall, Clarke, & Ballantyne, 2001). Most persons in Canada who went back to work took up part-time work, and they tended to be persons who had been forced to retire because of mandatory retirement provisions or because of early retirement packages (McDonald, 1997). In the United States, it is now estimated that between 30 and 50 percent of people move into their "final" retirement via partial retirement or use "bridge jobs" from their career jobs into retirement (Mutchler, et al., 1997; Quinn, 1999).

Perhaps even more revealing is the number of Canadians who have no intention of ever retiring. Eight percent of Canadians stated they had no intention of retiring—10 percent of men and 7 percent of women (Monette, 1996). Using the longitudinal *Health and Retirement Survey* in the United States, Ekerdt, Hackney, Kosloski, and DeViney (2001) showed that the uncertainty about the form and timing of retirement is substantial. In their analyses, 40 percent of workers aged 51 to 61 could not state how they would exit their job, and about 12 percent did not know the date or age of their retirement. They provide some evidence that the uncertainty was less likely among those who led a more "socially attended life," meaning a more public life influenced by people on the job, at home, and by friends.

To capture the new retirement dynamic, a host of terms have been proposed in the retirement literature. At the theoretical level, Atchley (1993) describes the **deconceptualization of retirement**, referring to the blurring of boundaries between work and retirement; Honig and Hanoch (1985) refer to **partial retirement**, meaning less than full-time work after retiring; Hardy, Hayward, and Lui (1994) identify **reverse retirement** or **spells of retirement** as pauses in ongoing careers; Quinn, Burhauser, & Myers (1990) describe **unretirement** as returning to work after being retired for a long period of time, and Rhum (1990, 1994) has tagged full-time or part-time jobs taken up after a career job is ended as **bridge jobs** to retirement, a designation that has become very popular in the retirement literature.

Although there is preliminary evidence that the very nature of retirement is changing, only time will define the magnitude and the permanence of these changes. More than 80 percent of Canadians currently remain retired, so change is slow. Recent evidence supports the idea that the institutionalization of retirement is still strong, at least in the United States. One study found that retirement anticipation was normative among older workers (Ekerdt, Kosloski, & Deviney, 2000), and another found that institutionalized retirement criteria have been strongly internalized to anchor people's self-definition as a retiree (Szinovacz & DeViney, 1999).

Explaining Retirement

Definitions

As would be anticipated, contemporary retirement research does not share a common definition of **retirement**. Even though retirement generally refers to late-life separation from waged labour, there are still many variations in definitions. Conceptually, retirement has been defined as an institution, an event, a process, a social role, and a phase (O'Rand & Henretta, 1999; Kohli & Rein, 1991; McDonald & Wanner, 1990). Usually, the conceptual definition chosen by a researcher depends upon what aspects of retirement the researcher wishes to explore.

As described above in the discussion of the history of retirement, retirement is usually seen as a social institution by those interested in broader societal issues, rather than an individual's retirement. As an institution, retirement functions to remove older workers from the labour force in a timely and orderly fashion, which is beneficial for the individual and society. Kohli and Rein (1991), for example, focus on institutionally based pathways, such as state policies and work regulations, that define retirement. In Canada, provincial policies supporting mandatory retirement may force people to retire against their will and would be an example of a state policy that defines retirement.

Retirement, as an event, usually refers to the formal end of employment, which, most of the time, is accompanied by some rite of passage, such as a party or special luncheon and the giving of a commemorative gift. Retirement as a one-time occasion has not been studied extensively by gerontologists, so we know little about the ceremonial aspects of the occasion. Retirement as a social role and the related concepts of retirement as a social process and phase have received far more attention from researchers. Those who study retirement as a social role are interested in knowing the rights and obligations of the retiree in the retirement role and, as a process, how the role is approached, assumed, and relinquished.

How researchers measure retirement also varies. The simplest and most commonly available measure is the one used above—labour force participation rate—a static measure that ignores how people may move in and out of the labour force. In addition, being out of the labour force does not necessarily mean that an older person is retired. Other measures that are often used are number of hours worked in the past year, nonparticipation in the labour force, a reduction in work responsibilities, age at which the person left his or her career job, receipt of social security benefits, receipt of a private pension, a self-definition of retirement, and any combination of the preceding indicators.

Recent analyses of the many measures of retirement concluded that there was no optimal measure of the term, all definitions have flaws (O'Rand & Henretta, 1999; McDonald, 1996). The standard definitions of retirement are somewhat inadequate in light of the "new retirement" noted above or in the case of women's retirement, since almost all definitions of retirement imply a relationship to the labour force and not all women have had such a relationship. How retirement is measured is important, however, for three reasons: (1) the measure determines who will or will not be included in the study; (2) whose perception of retirement matters; and (3) why research findings on the same issue may be contradictory.

Theories

Theories explicitly designed to explain retirement are few and far between and generally reflect the theories found in mainstream gerontology that have emerged over the last 50 years (see Chapter 2). Retirement, however, has usually played only a minor role in the classical social theories developed to explain the broader issue of social aging. Moreover, there has been an apparent reluctance by retirement scholars to undertake theory building, leaving little in the way of new theories. Most theories either focus on the micro-level of individual actors or the macro-level of social structure in explaining retirement (Estes, et al., 2001). Very few theories attempt to link both micro-perspectives and macro-perspectives.

Micro-Theories.

At the micro-level of theory development, many of the leading theories of social aging have been influenced by the functional paradigm, which explains social phenomena in terms of how they are functional to society. The early theories of disengagement, activity, and continuity shared the underlying assumptions of this approach and, as a result, emphasized the inevitability of physical, social and psychological aspects of the aging process, the importance of scripted roles, and how people adjusted to these roles. Thus, disengagement theory viewed retirement as part of a normal, mutual, and beneficial withdrawal of the individual and society from each other (Cumming & Henry, 1961). Activity theory, developed in opposition to the assumptions of disengagement theory, considered retirement a break in healthy activity, which had to be replaced following the withdrawal from work. Continuity theory (Costa & McRae, 1980) treated retirement as a discontinuity to be replaced with other forms of social activity. All three approaches assumed retirement to be natural, that the individual was responsible for the quality and quantity of his or her own level of social activity. Retirement could be potentially traumatic, since prescriptions were offered for how to accomplish retirement—no activity or plenty of activity. The difficulties with these theories were that retirement seemed to occur in a vacuum, unaffected by social, political, or economic factors (McDonald & Wanner, 1990).

Modern-day versions of these theories, the successful aging framework (Rowe & Krahn, 1997) and the productive aging framework (Estes, Mahakian, & Weitz, 2001; Holstein, 1992) are based on similar principles. Successful aging identifies the risk factors for unsuccessful aging along with the personal choices to be successful, while productive aging seeks to reverse the "decline and deficit" view of aging and replace it with the view that older people produce goods and services for society that are valuable. Both frameworks focus on activities and individual responsibility, and pay no heed to structural factors, such as race or social class. The end result is that these perspectives are in danger of "blaming the victim" if retirement does not proceed in a healthy and productive fashion.

Macro-Theories.

The macro-theories that touch on retirement—modernization theory and age stratification theory—are cut from the same structural–functional cloth. Life course theory currently exhibits fewer characteristics of functionalism but, in earlier times, was thought to belong to this paradigm. Modernization theory, developed by Cowgill and Holmes (1972), is a theory about how the status of the aged has declined over time with the modernization of society and how retirement facilitated this process. With the growth of an aging population, the intergenerational competition for jobs increased. The accompanying modern technological innovations, which were more suited to the young, meant that there were fewer suitable jobs available for older workers, and as a result of these two developments, retirement was created. Retirement, in turn, inevitably led to lower incomes, and lower incomes produced lower social status for the aged. Retirement in this theory is simply an inevitable outcome of the unidirectional evolution of society toward modernization.

According to age stratification theory, life is conceived of as a series of roles linked together on the basis of age. Behaviour is explained according to the role occupancy of a group of people who were born at about the same time and who share the same experiences as they move through the linked roles (Riley, Johnson, & Foner, 1972). Retirement is a role with the age criterion for entrance and exit as it applies to a cohort of people. Indeed, at the time of the development of the theory, if the retirement role was not carried out according to appropriate age norms (e.g., people retiring *precisely* at age 65 years), they were labelled "age deviants" (Nelson & Nelson, 1972). This theory has been criticized as relying on a static concept of social structure (Quadagno & Reid, 1999), which overlooks inequality based on race, gender, and social class. A newer version, the aging and society paradigm, introduces the idea of an age-integrated society, where age stratification disappears (Riley, Foner, & Riley, 1999; Riley & Riley, 1994). In this model, retirement would no longer be explained on the basis of the age criterion but no other criteria are offered to replace age.

Theories of the life course attempt to bridge micro- and macro-levels of analysis by simultaneously considering the individual and society as the unit of analysis. A four-faceted and recursive model, proposed by Giele and Elder (1998), considers the interrelationships between four key elements of the life course: (1) history and culture (which locate people in time and place); (2) the linked lives of social relations; (3) human agency; and (4) the timing of lives, funnelled through the intersection of age, period, and cohort effects. Essentially, the age structures developed by a given society (as borrowed from age stratification theory) provide road maps for moving through life within a context of historical and cultural change. Retirement would be one of life's age-graded transitions on the road map and is the last stage of the life course as noted above. Kohli (1988) and Moen (1996) are rare researchers who have taken account of the life course in explaining retirement. In different ways, both argue that there are significant links between the past and the present in the lives of individuals and that these links create a unique retirement for each individual, even though everyone is influenced by the same institutional characteristics of retirement. For example, two women with the same job, but with different records of work interruptions over their working lives, will have different incomes in retirement.

A broad critique of the life course as a theory is that it is more of a perspective or framework than a theory (Marshall, 1995a). More specifically, the life course perspective has been criticized on three counts on the basis of the nature of the research spawned by this approach. The identified problems include the minimization of the central position of social structure and social interactional processes as they affect the life course; a neglect of intracohort variability; and a neglect of the problem of individual choice—all factors very relevant to retirement (Dannefer & Uhlenberg, 1999: 309).

Alternative Theories.

To offset the one common flaw of inattention to structural issues in both the micro- and macro-theories, the political economy perspective emerged in the late 1970s and early 1980s with the work of Estes (1979), Guillemard (1980), Walker (1981), and Phillipson (1982). Although more a perspective than a theory, the political economy approach argues that aging is a socially constructed process that is conditioned by one's location in the social structure and the economic, political, and social factors that affect it (Estes, Swan, & Gerard, 1984). When retirement is explained within this perspective, it is seen as a marginal and dependent status occupied by the aged, which is the culmination of the effects of social, economic,and political processes prior to retirement. For example, Myles concludes, "Both the right to retire—and hence to become old—and the rights of retirement today, are the products of national legislation" (Myles, 1984: 175).

The political economy approach has recently undergone a metamorphosis and is considered to be part of critical theory by some theorists. Atchley (1993) was the first to propose a "critical gerontology of retirement," which would expose the hidden power struggles and patterns of domination influencing retirement. As an example, he reinterprets his own institutional view of retirement to show how removing workers from the labour force serves the interests of capitalists and is of questionable value to society. He argues that retirement, as an institution, ensures that society has no obligation to provide a job for an older worker who may wish to be gainfully employed. In addition, the institution reinforces the erroneous view that older workers are less productive. Phillipson (1999), using a critical approach to the study of retirement, argues that the changes we see today in work and retirement reflect the trends associated with the emergence of postmodern societies. The replacement of mass production with flexible forms of work, the globalization of social life, and the weakening of social security policies that govern the retirement transition generated the "new" retirement mentioned above. As an illustration, he invokes Beck (1992, 1994) and Giddens (1991, 1994) and their views on reflexive modernity to suggest that the self, as reflexive, can influence the retirement transition, thereby inventing more social constructions of retirement in the process.

The major criticisms of the political economy approach are diametrically opposed depending on which version is used to explain retirement. The versions emanating from the "Estes school" have been criticized for their over-reliance on structural explanations at the expense of neglecting human agency in the aging process and, by association, the retirement transition. The use of critical theory by Phillipson (1999) can be criticized on the same grounds as the reflexive modernity theory of Giddens and Beck, namely, that the role of structural factors are in danger of receiving short shrift.

The Link between Work and Retirement

The bridge between the work and retirement phases of the life course has been conceptualized in three ways, all of which have to do with inequality in old age. The first hypothesis, related to the life course perspective, emphasizes economic continuity over time and is called the **status maintenance hypothesis**. The competing hypothesis, the **status levelling** or **redistribution hypothesis**, posits that the links among occupation, income, and retirement are tenuous because social security "levels" income differences or redistributes income when the retiree receives public pensions. A newer hypothesis, also reflective of a life course perspective, is the **cumulative advantage/disadvantage hypothesis**, which postulates that a shift from work to retirement means an increase in the relative importance of differences in income—workers with more resources, such as education, will have "accumulated" more pension benefits by the time they retire than workers with fewer resources. Retirement is a critical threshold that can increase inequality. There is mixed support for the three hypotheses due mainly to methodological problems, including the measure of inequality and the use of cross-sectional versus longitudinal data. Frequently, distinctions are not made between men and women who, in practice, have different trajectories of inequality into retirement.

The Status Maintenance Hypothesis

According to this hypothesis, the effects of various statuses are maintained across the life course. In the case of retirement, a person's educational attainment influences the nature of his or her occupation and industrial placement to produce a certain level of income-related pension benefits and other types of economic resources. The pension benefits and the assets serve as the connection between work and retirement and operate to maintain the individual's relative status in later life (O'Rand & Henretta, 1999). The status maintenance hypothesis implies that postretirement inequality represents a continued effect of inequalities prior to retirement (Crystal & Shea, 1990).

A good example of this process would be the situation of female retirees in Canada. The well-documented inferior work conditions of women—their over-representation in the low-paying services industries, their high representation in contingent and part-time work, their work interruptions related to family responsibilities, and their overall lower incomes—are carried over into retirement. Examples of these postretirement outcomes are many: 39.9 percent of women have an employer-sponsored pension plan, compared with 42.3 percent of men; the income of women over age 65 years remains at about 62 percent of men's; and among women aged 65 years and over, some are twice as likely as men to have low incomes (Statistics Canada, 1999; 2000).

The Status Levelling or Redistribution Hypothesis

The status levelling hypothesis posits that old age and the increased dependence on public transfers that accompanies it, level status differences that developed in the workplace. The underlying rationale is that public transfers are distributed more equally than are wages and salaries and investment income. Workers at the lower echelons of the income ladder receive a greater rate of return to contributions to social security programs than wealthier workers because it is assumed that political institutions can mould the processes that determine income. In a cross-sectional study of Canadian men in the 1976 *Survey of Consumer Finances*, Myles (1981) found that government transfers substantially altered the relationship between education and income to reduce relative, as opposed to absolute, inequality. Prus (1999), using the same survey, provided support for the redistributive hypothesis, and more recently, Myles (2000), using the longitudinal aspects of the same data file, showed that small proportional increases from all public government sources, including the earnings-related Canada/Quebec Pension Plan, tended to reduce inequality in old age.

The Cumulative Advantage/Disadvantage Hypothesis

The cumulative disadvantage/advantage perspective proposed by Crystal and Shea (1990) incorporates the status maintenance conceptualization, but goes further. The inequalities created by work histories prior to retirement are perpetuated after retirement, in keeping with the status maintenance hypothesis, however, in a number of instances these inequalities become amplified by cumulative effects over time. Having the resources to purchase a house when young allows this asset to grow in value over time, whereas renting over the same time drains resources. In their study using American panel data, they found that income inequality within a cohort increased with age and that income inequality was the highest after age 64 in their sample. Pampel and Hardy (1994), using the *National Longitudinal Survey of Older Men in the United States*, found support for both hypotheses. They found that the effects of race, educational attainment, occupational status, and residence on family income changed only slightly after retirement, but private pension income differences within occupational groups increased inequality. Whatever hypotheses gain ascendancy as the research accumulates, the transition from work to retirement is crucial for most Canadians, since it helps set the parameters for well being in the later phases of life.

Issues in the Retirement Research: Who Retires, When, and Why

Undoubtedly, the most enduring theme in the retirement literature has been about the timing of retirement, which began with the spread of early retirement. Early retirement was considered to occur any time prior to the "normal age" of retirement at age 65 years, while late retirement was thought to be any time after age 65 years. Since the end of the 1980s, there has been a growing diversity in the age of retirement, with an increase in retirement for those between the ages of 60 and 64 years, a decline in those retiring right at age 65 years and an increase in people retiring after age 65 years. Knowing who retires when is a critical question, since the answer has significant consequences for individual Canadians and for Canadian society as a whole. As we have already seen, the timing of retirement helps define when a person is considered to be old, it lays the foundation for the economic well being of individuals and has implications for the economic stability of society at large.

The most frequently studied factors believed to affect the timing of retirement are: sociodemographic characteristics, health, potential wealth in retirement, the work environment, unemployment, and family contingencies.

Characteristics of Retirees

There is continuing controversy about the function of sociodemographic characteristics in the timing of retirement. The newer life course models have begun to show that early life circumstances, such as family of orientation or number of children, have a direct impact on retirement behaviour and sometimes serve to modify the effects of factors found to be significant in earlier cross-sectional studies. Overall, the life course research tends to support the earlier research about men, but not women, mainly because women were seen only in the role of homemakers, limiting the attention paid to women's retirement. The recent research has shown that unmarried men and unmarried women have a greater probability of retiring before age 65 years. Men with higher personal incomes and previous jobs in the core industrial sector of the economy (where jobs are the most stable and high paying), also tend to retire earlier. The level of a woman's household income, as opposed to her personal income, decreases the age of her retirement, highlighting the important place of marriage in women's economic security in later life (McDonald, 1997,1996; Peracchi & Welch, 1994).

The findings on the presence of dependants in the family are somewhat mixed. The presence of children in the family significantly reduces the probability of early retirement for men (Toma, 1999; Hayward, Friedman, & Chen, 1998) but not always for women. For example, Pienta (1994, 1999) found that the more children a women had, the greater were her chances of working full time in later life and that the later she had the children, the later she would work before retiring.

While the research is thin on the influence of race and ethnicity on the timing of retirement, several differences have been found, but most of these apply to the differences between African and Caucasian Americans (Flippen & Tienda, 2000; Hayward, Friedman, & Chen,1998). One Canadian study found that the odds of being retired are uniformly lower for all foreign-born groups in Canada, compared with the Canadian-born, after age and gender have been taken into account. People from Asia, Africa, and Latin America have the least chance of retiring early and tend to retire later than the general Canadian population (Wanner & McDonald, 1989).

Workers who work past the age of 65 are a small group—3.3 percent of women and 9.5 percent of men. Canadians who retire after age 65, in contrast to those who retire and go back to work after age 65, are well educated, with higher occupational status, are self-employed, married men and single women, and people in good health (McDonald & Wanner, 1990). Statistics Canada (1999) found that men aged 65 years and older worked in the primary industries, such as farming, while older woman gravitated to female occupations in clerical, sales, and service occupations. There is also growing evidence that men aged 65 years and over are increasingly likely to be employed past age 65 years.

In a study of professors still working after age 70, Dorfman (2000) found that they worked, not for the money, but because they enjoyed the work and because they felt their work was important to society. Hayward et al., (1998) recently showed that older Americans holding jobs that required more challenging cognitive skills tended to delay retirement.

The Health versus Wealth Debate

Researchers have asked if it is the "push" of poor health or the "pull" of a pension that leads to early retirement. On the one hand, early retirement has been viewed as an involuntary response to poor health, and on the other, a voluntary response to unearned income from pensions and assets that draws workers into retirement. The answers offered by scholars have varied over time, depending on the historical context and the interests of the researchers. In the initial retirement research, ill health was found to be a very important predictor of early retirement (Reno, 1971) but was viewed with some suspicion. At the time, early retirement was not the norm, so researchers thought that retirees might have used poor health as a cover for supposedly less acceptable reasons for retirement, such as pursuing a hobby. Today, this view is referred to as the **health justification hypothesis** and has received little support in the literature (Dwyer & Mitchell,1998: 3).

With the introduction of early retirement incentive plans, in the 1980s, the focus swung to pension income (both public and private) as the more important predictor of early retirement. The lure of early retirement pensions was thought to be so powerful that, at this time, actual policy changes to social security were instituted in the United States and Europe, making it less attractive to draw on pensions at younger ages (Wise, 1993). Some critics, however, thought that the influence of public pensions was overestimated in explaining early retirement (Rein & Turner, 1999; Epsing-Anderson, 1994). For example, it is difficult to explain why the rate of early retirement is lowest in countries with the most generous early public pension plans, as in Norway and Sweden (Epsing-Anderson, 1994). In contrast, other researchers were more inclined to think that early retirement represented a response to high unemployment rates and early pension options for retirement (Peracchi & Welch,1994; Kolberg & Epsing-Anderson, 1991)

The early 1990s saw a renewed flurry of interest in health as a major factor in the early retirement decision (McDonald & Donahue, 2000). The thinking was that healthy workers could continue to work and would not need to use expensive early pension options. Current research about reduced mortality and morbidity and the "compressed morbidity" of older workers implied that health should no longer be a main reason for early retirement (Council of Economic Advisors, 1999; Woodbury, 1999). Research surfaced that supported this view. For example, in an analysis of 12 years of American data, researchers found that self-reported work ability had increased among persons 60 years of age and older, which logically would negate early retirement (Crimmins, Reynolds, & Saito 1999).

While the research documenting improvements in workers' health is encouraging, some older workers genuinely suffer ill health and are forced to retire early. The most recent literature confirms that poor health is an important consideration in the early retirement decision (Dwyer & Mitchell, 1998; Quinn, 1999; OECD, 1998).

In Canada, the research has shown that illness and disability are the most important single reasons for early retirement. In the *General Social Survey*, 1994, retirement because of poor health was the most important reason for retirement, followed by personal choice, mandatory retirement policies, and feeling old (Table 12.1). Health was reported as a reason by slightly more men than women: 25 percent of men versus 22 percent of women (McDonald & Donahue, 2000; Monette, 1996). In an analysis of unexpected early retirement, the health reason reduced retirement income by over $7,000 a year in 1992 (McDonald, Donahue, & Marshall, 2000).

The most recent research also offers support for the pension side of the debate, although most research does not assess the relative importance of health and pensions. When changes to the Quebec Pension Plan (QPP) in 1984 and the Canada Pension Plan (CPP) in 1987 made substantial benefits available at age 60, Frenken (1991) reported that Canadians did not hesitate to respond. In 1984, three out of

Table 12.1 REASONS FOR RETIREMENT BY GENDER, *GENERAL SOCIAL SURVEY* 1994*

REASONS FOR RETIREMENT	PERCENTAGES		
	Women	Men	Total
Wanted to retire	21	24	23
Caregiving	13	...	6
Unemployment	9	10	10
Health	22	25	24
Early retirement incentive offered	4	10	7
Mandatory retirement policy	11	16	14
Spouse retired	7	...	3
Respondent felt old enough	9	11	10
New technology	...	...	...
Other reasons	4	3	3
Total	100%	100%	100%

* Overlap between categories has been removed. Following Statistics Canada guidelines, estimate cannot be reported because of insufficient cases.
Source: Created from data from Statistics Canada, "The 1994 General Social Survey," (public-use data file) Cycle 9, Education, Work and Retirement.

every four persons receiving QPP pensions were, for the first time, between the ages of 60 and 64 years. Two-thirds of new CPP beneficiaries were aged 60 to 64 years. Using a longitudinal administrative data file covering 1982 to 1994, to examine the age at which individuals begin to draw benefits from the CPP, Tompa (1999) found that income amounts from various sources had a significant impact on the take-up of CPP benefits, as did family characteristics and health status. He noted a definite trend to early take-up of CPP benefits, providing further evidence for the effects of pensions on retirement.

When private pension plans and other employee benefits such as health coverage are considered, there is growing evidence that they affect the early retirement decisions of a substantial number of individuals. Generally, more men than women who have a private pension plan have been found to retire earlier (Fronstin, 1999; Tompa, 1999; Monette, 1996). McDonald, Donahue, and Marshall (2000) found that 26 percent of men and 12 percent of women retired early and unexpectedly because they were offered early retirement incentive packages. In a study of a public utility company in Ontario, it was found that planned voluntary retirement was influenced most strongly by incentive packages for early retirement (Luchak,1997).

It is important to note that the voluntary nature of early retirement incentive plans is not always voluntary. Not all workers willingly choose this route into retirement and are sometimes coerced into accepting a package by the threat of layoffs and downsizing. In an American study, 49 percent of workers who elected to take an early retirement package indicated that it was not a desirable choice, one reason being that they did not wish to retire early (Gowan, 1998). In a Canadian study of a major telecommunications company, some workers leaving the company with an early retirement incentive program (ERIP) had a sense of ambiguity as to the degree of choice they had about the time they retired (Roberston, 2000). Marshall (1995b) calls this the "retirement incentive game," where the company offers the lowest possible retirement incentives to the worker in the hope that the older worker will accept the package in order to help reduce staff levels in the company. The worker, usually within a short time frame, must decide to take the package, hold out for a better package, or risk being displaced.

Work and the Timing of Retirement

The type of employment at the time of retirement has an effect on the timing of retirement. Within the Canadian context, workers who held nonstandard jobs, such as part-time work, temporary jobs, or self-employment, retired at later ages, possibly out of economic need. Among men, part-time workers retired, on average, at age 64.2, compared with age 60.8 years for full-time workers. Self-employed women retired at an average age of 60, compared with age 59 for salaried workers (Monette, 1996).

The type of occupation a person had prior to retirement, in combination with the type of employment (full-time, part-time or self-employed,) also affects the retirement age. For example, men who retired at age 60 years from sales and services were full-time employees with a job-related pension, while their colleagues in the same occupations who were self-employed without a pension retired on average at age 64 years. Similarly, salaried professionals with a pension retired at age 61 years, while self-employed professionals without a pension retired at age 63 years. All the data point to the importance of a pension in the early retirement decision.

Interest in job characteristics and their effect on the transition into retirement has revolved around the centrality of work in people's lives. Some studies have demonstrated that workers who were highly committed to their work or liked their work delayed retirement, while those with opposite views retired earlier (Hansson, DeKoekkoek, Neece, & Patterson, 1997; Reitzes, Mutran, & Fernandez, 1996; Richardson & Kilty, 1992). The work environment in comparison to the nonwork domain has also been studied as to which domain is more important in the retirement decision. As would be anticipated, several studies have shown both domains to be important. (Beehr, Glazer, & Nielson, 2000; Stetz & Beehr, 2000).

One of the more serious issues in the workplace is the presence of age discrimination. Several studies have found that age discrimination directed at the older worker has led to early retirement (Johnson & Neumark, 1997; McDonald, Donahue, & Moore, 1997). Although McMullin and Marshall (2001) reported little age discrimination in their study of garment industry workers in Montreal, they did report that age-related declines in dexterity and physical ability were rationales used to force workers to leave employment.

One need not look further than the Supreme Court of Canada and its decision on mandatory retirement to find sanctioned discrimination against older workers, even though 65 percent of Canadians do not support it (Lowe, 1991). A landmark ruling by the Supreme Court on December 7, 1990, upheld the principle of mandatory retirement, a decision that was reaffirmed in later rulings in 1992 and 1995 (Klassen & Gillin, 1999). The majority position of the court was that age discrimination was definitely a violation of individual rights but condoned mandatory retirement under Section 1 of the Charter of Canadian Rights and Freedoms as a "minor infringement" of people's rights in favour of the greater benefits that would accrue to Canadian society. While there is no federal statute that forces a worker to retire at age 65, the Supreme Court decision supported the mandatory retirement provisions in provinces that did not have provincial human rights legislation prohibiting mandatory retirement (Alberta, Manitoba, Quebec, and New Brunswick are the only provinces with such legislation).

The envisioned benefits to society include the creation of opportunities for job openings for younger people, a short-sighted reason favoured by corporations at a time when Canada was in the throes of a recession. There was no evidence to suggest that mandatory retirement created openings for younger workers because employers tended not to fill vacant positions (McDonald, 2000). Perhaps more disturbing was the message sent to Canadians about older workers. According to Klassen and Gillin (1999), the decision of the Court was based on the stereotyping of older workers as being less competent than younger workers and failed to provide the older worker with any protection against discrimination based on age. In addition, the decision was detrimental to women, who frequently have to work longer to accumulate pensions benefits because of interrupted work periods and their shorter time in the labour force (McDonald, 2000). The decisions were also short-sighted when considered within a global context. Many countries are now implementing policies to slow early retirement because they are concerned about the escalating public costs of social security and the possibility of worker shortages (McDonald & Chen, 1993). One of the important adjustments some countries (such as the United States, Italy, and France) have made is raising the statutory age of retirement.

The Spectre of Unemployment

The unemployment rates were high in Canada during two recent recessions: one in the early 1980s and one at the beginning of the 1990s. The accumulated effects of these recessions had a long-term influence on older workers that affected their retirement behaviour. Many researchers have been quick to suggest that a large portion of early retirement was actually unemployment (Hutchens, 1999; Tompa, 1999; Gee & Gutman, 1995; McDaniel, 1992). While the unemployment rates for older workers are relatively low in Canada—about 7 percent for both men and women aged 55 to 64 years, compared with 15 percent for those 15 to 24 years of age (Statistics Canada, 1999)—the move into retirement probably masks the actual numbers of older unemployed workers. However, part of the problem for older Canadian workers is that, although they are less likely to lose long-term jobs than are younger workers, they face longer periods of unemployment and instability in the labour force after job loss (Lauzon, 1995).

Using the *Labour Market Activity Survey*, Osberg (1993) found that the lack of jobs accelerated retirement among Canadian men substantially, by about one-tenth of the men aged 55 to 64 years. Tompa (1999) showed that individuals receiving employment insurance or who were out of the labour force were more likely to exit to retirement. Another good example of unemployment comes from the *Survey of Persons Not in the Labour Force*. Of those persons who retired unexpectedly early, 8 percent of men and 10 percent of the women stated that they had left work for retirement because their company closed, because they were laid off, or because of downsizing (McDonald, Donahue, & Marshall, 2000). The same study found that for every month of joblessness, family income in retirement was decreased by approximately $100 per year. In studies predicting early retirement, local unemployment rates have been significant factors (Tompa, 1999; McDonald, 1996). Workers who do not find jobs tend to be "discouraged out" of the labour force, a finding confirmed in the garment study in Montreal, where older workers who could not find jobs that matched their skills gave up looking and retired (McMullin & Marshall, 2001).

Confusing retirement and unemployment camouflages the debilitating circumstances older workers suffer. Older workers forced to retire early for want of a job may be too young to qualify for pension benefits, yet they still must support themselves and their families (McDaniel, 1997; LeBlanc & McMullin, 1997). In fact, the sharp uptake in disability benefits in industrialized nations has been viewed as a makeshift measure many older workers and their employers use to tide the workers over until they qualify for retirement benefits (Guillemard, 2000; McDonald & Donahue, 2000). An American study found that even if displaced workers managed to find another job, which, on average, took up to a year, they faced large wage reductions and were less likely than nondisplaced workers to work longer after their spell of unemployment. The researchers suggested that the workers were attempting to make up lost time in building their pensions. In separate studies of older displaced workers in Toronto and Edmonton, the human suffering resulting from the severe financial distress, the humiliation, and discouragement of looking for a job and the lack of available assistance, underscored the human tragedy endured by older workers (McDonald, Donahue, & Moore, 2000a; McDaniel, 1995).

A Family Approach to Retirement

With the increased labour force participation of women, family contingencies have taken on a whole new meaning for both men and women. In the early retirement literature, researchers considered women to be homemakers and "retired" only if their spouse was retired. As we saw earlier, in the history of retirement, women were essentially invisible workers and hence invisible retirees because they did not work for long in the paid labour force; rather, they were mainly unpaid workers in the home. Today, women's paid and unpaid work is publicly acknowledged, with the resulting recognition of the interdependence of life domains and their influence on retirement status. Researchers now investigate joint decision making for married and dual-career couples and the various routes they pursue into retirement and the effects of family obligations on retirement.

Originally, researchers reported equality in retirement decision making in dual-career couples because characteristics of both spouses influenced the decision to retire (Henretta & O'Rand, 1983). More recently, researchers have found that marital and spousal characteristics affect retirement timing, but the processes differ by gender. Using the Survey of Labour and Income Dynamics (1998), it was found that wives appeared more likely than their husbands to take their spouse's career and retirement into account when making their own decisions to retire. In a study of Canadian married couples, McDonald (1996) found that if a husband was older than his wife, her age of retirement increased, a finding not always supported in the American data (Szinovacz & DeViney, 2000). As well, the husband's higher levels of education, occupational prestige, and income led to lower retirement ages for the wife, while the husband's age of retirement was increased if the wife was the same age or older and had high occupational prestige (McDonald, 1996). In contrast, Tompa (1999) found that both men and women tend to make joint retirement decisions with their spouses.

The marital history of the couple may also have some bearing on retirement, since remarried widowers are less likely to retire, and remarried widows are more likely to retire (Szinovacz & DeViney, 2000). In one study, it was found that married Canadian women retired, on average, at age 56 years, that their retirement was voluntary, and that they were more likely to retire because they wanted to stop working. In contrast, widowed women retired later (age 61 years), and their retirement was less likely to be voluntary (McDonald, Donahue, & Moore, 2000b).

Family care obligations may also impinge on retirement decisions, usually for women, who provide the bulk of family care. In Canada, preliminary estimates indicate that between 13 and 15 percent of women in Canada retire for caregiving (McDonald, 1996; *Canadian Study of Health and Aging*, 1994). Interestingly, most Canadian women do not envision caregiving as a reason for retirement (Zimmerman, Mitchell, Wister, & Gutman, 2000; McDonald, 1996) For example, a Vancouver study found that actual retirement timing was affected by health and stress, a preference for early retirement, caregiving, and spouse's retirement, while pre-retirement women did not anticipate that caregiving or health/stress would influence the timing of their retirement.

Although there is considerable research on the effects of caregiving on employment, it is difficult to ascertain if caregiving in the years close to retirement leads to early retirement or if a spell of caregiving makes it difficult to rejoin the labour force when the caregiving is over (Pavalko & Artis, 1997). A Canadian study found that the age of retirement for women was reduced by almost six years, compared with less than a year for men (McDonald, 1996) if they retired for caregiving reasons. The costs of the early retirement of women for caregiving may be very high: forgone wages, nonwage benefits, and pension accruals. The average age women retire for caregiving is quite low: 48 years in the *General Social Survey*, 1994 (Monette, 1996), which raises the question as to what happens to the women when the caregiving is over. Will their family savings see them through retirement, will they have to go back to work, and, if so, will they secure a job? If they remain in retirement, will they live in poverty? These questions are only beginning to be addressed within the Canadian context.

Living in Retirement

Making the Transition from Work to Retirement

Most research has found that the vast majority of men and women suffer few, if any, ill effects as a result of the transition from work to retirement. Gerontologists today no longer consider retirement to be a crisis as they once did and now focus on the issues of planning for retirement, partial retirement, involuntary retirement, and reverse retirement as part of the transitional process.

Retirement Preparations.

Approximately 41 percent of Canadians aged 45 to 64 made no preparations for retirement in 1990, and if they did, about 25 percent devoted only two years to planning (Statistics Canada, 1992). People already retired reported that they paid off or avoided debts (64 percent), contributed to an RSSP (63 percent), and built up savings (59 percent) in preparation for retirement. Ever-single women were more likely to prepare for retirement than married women (McDonald, Donahue, & Moore, 2000b), and in a study of preparation for later life, it was found that people in better health were more likely than those in poorer health to make plans for retirement (Denton, et al., 2000). In contrast, American research that deals specifically with retirement found that poor health was related to increased retirement planning (Ekerdt, et al., 1996; Taylor & Shore, 1995). In a study of the relationship between job-related awards and retirement planning, workers with jobs high in intrinsic enjoyment or positive social relations were less likely to plan for retirement (Kosloski, Ekerdt, & DeViney, 2001). These researchers also discovered that more highly educated workers, older workers, and men were more likely to report having plans for retirement and to discuss them with friends and co-workers. In contrast, women were less likely to have plans or to discuss them with friends and co-workers.

Moen, Sweet, and Swisher (2001) have developed a model predicting retirement planning that takes into account five factors: the nature of the labour force, **biographical pacing**, financial resources, spousal considerations, and organizational location. In their study of dual-income couples, they found some support for their model, especially biological pacing. There was some suggestion that biographical pacing influenced the timing of retirement planning. Belonging to a different cohort indicated different times for the onset of retirement planning. Younger workers in this study reportedly started planning earlier than the baby boom cohort. (Moen, et al., 2001).

Involuntary Retirement.

Even though most Canadians experience a positive transition into retirement, people who experience **involuntary retirement**—about 27 percent of men and 22 percent of women—do not always fare well in the transition (McDonald, Donahue, & Marshall, 2000). Of the one in four Canadians who retired involuntarily, the primary reasons were poor health, mandatory retirement, and unemployment. Many involuntary retirees experienced lower incomes in retirement, dissatisfaction in retirement, and a decrease in overall well being, and rated themselves as having poorer mental and physical health (Schultz, Morton, & Weckerle, 1998; Sharpley & Layton, 1998). In a related process, the emergence of the "new" retirement has also contributed to what some scholars have referred to as "instability in the retirement transition," unstable exits involving moving in and out of the labour force. These exits were associated with adverse health effects for both men and women in a study of a telecommunications company in Canada (Marshall, Clarke, & Ballantyne, 2001).

Partial Retirement.

Contributing to the blurring of the boundaries between work and retirement is partial retirement, which is the most common pattern of postretirement work for

Canadians. Of the 17 percent of Canadians who went back to work after retiring in 1990, 79.6 percent worked part time and 20.4 percent worked full time. Two types of retirees are most likely to go back to work part time: professionals, whose skills allow them to find work fairly easily, and those forced out of work because of loss of jobs but who can find lesser jobs at the margins of the economy in smaller, less bureaucratized firms (McDonald, 1997).

There are many barriers to partial retirement, including the public and private pension systems. As an illustration, there are rules prohibiting working while collecting a partial pension under the C/QPP. Another serious obstacle is the problem of losing current income and future pension income while in partial retirement. Only 1 percent of an elite group of British Columbia government managers took up a deferred salary leave program when offered on a trial basis, highlighting the difficulties related to protecting present and future incomes (Lussier & Wister, 1995). This pattern has been evident in most industrialized countries, especially where older workers have been assured large pensions at full retirement (Latulippe & Turner, 2000).

Stages.

One of the first conceptual frameworks gerontologists used to study postretirement life was the idea that retirees went though stages as they moved through retirement. The classic stage model of retirement is based on continuity theory and suggests that retirees transit through the honeymoon phase, where retirees are satisfied with their new roles, then move to the disenchantment phase, where retirement may not live up to expectations, on to a readjustment phase, called the reorientation phase, which settles into a stable phase, ultimately ending in death (Atchley, 1976). There has been some empirical support for this model (Gall, et al., 2000; Theriault, 1994) but the evidence is slim. More recent models have attended to the gender issue. Monk (1997) found three main adjustment patterns for men (withdrawal, compensation, and accommodation), while Price (1998) uncovered a developmental stage model in interviews with professional women who went through three successive stages (decision to retire; relinquishing professional identity; and re-establishing order). The likelihood is that the stage approach to retirement adjustment is extremely complicated and depends on a broad array of interrelated factors for both men and women.

Well Being in Retirement

There has been extensive study of the impact of retirement on individuals, how people adjust to retirement, and the resources required for an individual's satisfaction with retirement. Given differences in research designs, time of assessment at postretirement, and the measures that are used to study adjustment and satisfaction, the findings can be confusing and are frequently inconsistent.

For instance, longitudinal studies have reported a negative relationship between well being in retirement as the length of time spent in retirement increases (Bosse, Aldwin, Levenson, & Workman-Daniels,1991). As we have also seen, the issue of retirement is distinctly different for women, and so, by definition, their situation in retirement is different. For example, Quick and Moen (1997) found that later retirement was associated with lower retirement quality for women, whereas the pre-retirement job was more important to the quality of men's retirement. In addition, the use of different measures of satisfaction give mixed results. Retirees have reported greater depression and loneliness, lower life satisfaction and happiness, and negative attitudes to retirement, when compared with workers (Rosenkoetter & Garris, 1998; de Grace, Pelletier, & Beaupre, 1994). Other researchers have established that retirement has a positive effect on the life of retirees, in the sense that older workers look forward to retirement and are satisfied in retirement (Sharpley & Layton, 1998; Gall, Evans, & Howard, 2000; Maule, Cliff, & Taylor, 1996).

Satisfaction.

Longitudinal studies have shown that recent retirees report the highest levels of satisfaction, whereas long-term retirees express less satisfaction (Ekerdt, Bosse, & Levkoff, 1985). Other studies report the opposite (Richard & Kilty, 1991; Beck, 1982), while at least one study has shown that life satisfaction remains constant from pre- to postretirement (Gal, et al., 2000). What we know about Canadians and their satisfaction with life in retirement is minimal. We do know that in the *Survey of Aging and Independence*, 83 percent of retired men aged 55 to 64 were satisfied or very satisfied with retirement, while the figure was 85 percent of retired women the same age. Eighty-three percent of retired men and 88 percent of women 65 years and over reported that they were satisfied or very satisfied with life. Almost half the respondents in the *General Social Survey* (1994) reported that they enjoyed life more, one year after retirement. There was no difference between men and women (according to analysis by the authors of the *General Social Survey*), a finding that does not match American data (Quick & Moen, 1997).

Health and Wealth.

The two main resources of the retiree known to affect the quality of retirement include health and wealth. Physical health consistently predicts adjustment to retirement for both men and women (Dorfman, 1995; Hardy & Quadagno, 1995; Hibbard, 1995). A Canadian study of the impact of pre-retirement expectations for income and satisfaction on the quality of men's lives six to seven years after retirement is an exception to the rule (Gall, Evans, & Howard, 2000). These researchers found that changes in physical health and psychological distress did not change the long-term quality of life in later retirement. The differences in findings may be attributed to the fact that the Canadian study was longitudinal, unlike most of the earlier studies.

Although research on physical health is in abundance, there has been less research on the adjustment to retirement and mental health. Controlling for age, gender, and marital status, Midanik et al. (1995) found that retirees, compared with those planning to retire, had lower stress levels. No differences were found between the groups on self-rated mental health status or depression. Another study found that self-esteem did not decline in the transition to retirement (Reitzes, Mutran, & Fernandez, 1996), while in a longitudinal study, anxiety levels steadily decreased with time in retirement (Theriault, 1994).

Like health, wealth has been found to be a significant resource in contributing to well being or higher satisfaction in retirement. Using 25 years of data from a panel study in the United States, researchers found that work history was the most important predictor of transitions into poverty after retirement, a condition most likely to affect women (McLaughlin & Jensen, 2000). In Canada, 49.1 percent of unattached older women were below Canada's Low Income Cut-Offs, compared with 33 percent of men (Statistics Canada, 1999). In a study of retired widows, it was found that low incomes severely constrained older women's activities and made day-to-day living a challenge. As an illustration, one widow reported turning her hearing aid off while at home because she could not afford the batteries (McDonald, Donahue, & Moore, 1997).

In the case of marital status, marriage is a double-edged sword. On the one hand, marriage has been shown to be a major economic resource that buffers women against poverty in retirement and, on the other, prevents women from building their careers and pensions because of their family responsibilities (McDonald, et al., 1997). One national study in Canada found that 49 percent of retired widows, 53 percent of divorced or separated women, and 28 percent of ever-single women lived below the Low Income Cut-offs for Canada, compared with 15 percent of married women (McDonald, et al., 1997). When marital support disappears, however, women's secondary poverty becomes all too evident in retirement (Logue, 1991). The finding that married and single women are more likely to find their income in retirement satisfactory, compared with divorced and widowed women, comes as no surprise.

Monette (1996) found that people who had been retired since 1980 believed that their financial situation had deteriorated since they retired. He found that the proportion of retirees who had reported that their financial situation had improved or remained the same since retirement was 81 percent among those who had retired before 1980, compared with 57 percent of those who retired between 1990 and 1994—the time of a major recession in Canada. It would seem that wealth in retirement, like everything else in gerontology, is sensitive to historical times.

CHAPTER SUMMARY

This chapter has provided an overview of retirement from its inception until the present day. On the basis of the retirement research, at this moment in time, we can conclude the following:

- Retirement is a social construction that evolved from a process of stepping down within the confines of the family into an age-based, society-wide institution, supported by a national pension system.
- The mould for retirement, as we know it today, is based on a linear, male, 19th century life course model, where a woman's place was in the home, supported by the husband as sole breadwinner.
- Historically, women have been invisible in the labour force and invisible in retirement, so we know little about their retirement history.
- Most Canadians want to retire, and they want to retire early, compared with about 8 percent of Canadians who say they will never retire. The four main reasons for retirement, in order of importance are poor health, a desire to retire, mandatory retirement, and unemployment. For women, the third most important reason for retirement is caregiving, compared with mandatory retirement policies for men.
- The new retirement has been characterized as having no clear beginning or end. It is not necessarily dependent upon one's age. It is not as tightly regulated by public or private pensions, and there are many routes into retirement, if one chooses to retire at all.
- There is a wide variety of definitions, measures, and theories explaining retirement that spans structural and individual circumstances and a few that attempt to show the interplay between the two. The life course perspective shows considerable promise in representing the complexity of retirement.
- The link between work and retirement has been studied in three ways, all of which concern inequality in old age and all of which have some empirical support. The three approaches are: (1) the status maintenance hypothesis, where the older person's situation remains the same after retirement; (2) the status levelling or redistribution hypothesis, which postulates that state pensions redistribute income to make old people more equal in old age; and (3) the cumulative advantage/disadvantage hypothesis, which claims that disadvantages accumulate over time and become magnified in retirement.
- Canadians who retire early tend to be married men and women, men who had stable jobs in the core of the economy, and men with higher incomes. Women with large household incomes were more likely to retire early. Late retirees were married men, single women, and people with good health and with opportunities to keep working. Immigrants to Canada also tend to retire later. People who go back to work after retirement appear to have high levels of education that make them attractive to employers.
- Mandatory retirement is a sanctioned form of age discrimination in Canada.

- Less than half of Canadians plan for retirement, most prefer part-time work if they work postretirement, and overall, most Canadians adjust to and are satisfied with their retirement, which good health and a decent income make possible.

Key Terms

Stepped down, **(p. 310)**

Life course institutionalization hypothesis, **(p. 311)**

Mandatory retirement, **(p. 312)**

Clocking out, **(p. 318)**

Deconceptualization of retirement, **(p. 320)**

Partial retirement, **(p. 320)**

Reverse retirement, **(p. 320)**

Spells of retirement, **(p. 320)**

Unretirement, **(p. 320)**

Bridge jobs, **(p. 320)**

Retirement, **(p. 320)**

Status maintenance hypothesis, **(p. 325)**

Status levelling or redistribution hypothesis, **(p. 325)**

Cumulative advantage/disadvantage hypothesis, **(p. 325)**

Health justification hypothesis, **(p. 328)**

Biographical pacing, **(p. 336)**

Involuntary retirement, **(p. 336)**

Study Questions

1. Having reviewed the history of retirement, what do you think retirement will look like 50 years from now? Do you think you will retire, and what would be your reasons for this decision?

2. Compare and contrast the different ways retirement has been conceptualized and their links to different theories.

3. Inequalities related to gender and ethnicity in employment over the life course usually translate into inequalities in retirement. Do you think social policy could be used as a tool to change these outcomes? If your answer is yes, describe these policies. If your answer is no, why do you think social policies will not work? Are there other ways to offset life-long inequities?

4. Given the fact that most older Canadians experience good health in retirement and that a sizable proportion go back to work after retiring, do you think we should abolish mandatory retirement? Why, or why not?

Suggested Readings

McDonald, L. (1996). Transitions into retirement: A time for retirement. Toronto, Ontario: Centre for Applied Social Research, Faculty of Social Work, University of Toronto.

McDonald, 1997. The link between social research and social policy options: Reverse retirement as a case in point. *Canadian Journal on Aging /Public Policy. Supplement 1997,* 90-113.

McDonald, L., Donahue, P., & Moore, B. 2000. Widowhood in retirement. 329-345. In F. T. Denton, D. Fretz, & B. Spencer. (Eds.), *Independence and Economic Security in Old Age.* Vancouver, British Columbia: University of British Columbia Press.

Gee, E., & Gutman, G. (1995). (Eds). Rethinking retirement. Vancouver, British Columbia: Gerontology Research Centre, Simon Fraser University.

McDonald, P.L., & Wanner, R.A. (1990). *Retirement in Canada.* Toronto, Ontario: Butterworths.

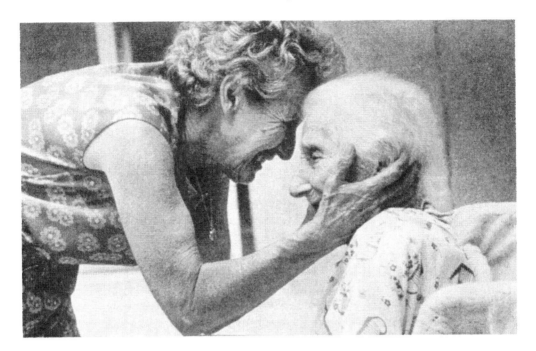

Social Support and Caregiving

In this chapter, you will learn about:

- What constitutes social support and why it is important.
- The relevance of social support for quality of life in old age.
- What are direct and indirect effects of social support.
- A number of role-specific interpersonal relations in old age, including spousal relationships, relationships with friends, children, and grandchildren, and other types of interactions.
- Caregiving, a specific type of social support that has critical importance as we age.
- The historical role of the informal network of family and friends in providing the vast majority of care to individuals when they become sick or disabled.
- The source of the overwhelming majority of care to seniors when their health declines and the predominant care system within society, although it is still largely an invisible care system.

Introduction

This chapter examines social support—what it is and why it is important in old age. As an area of research, social support has been popular for some time and researchers do not show any signs of lessening interest. Despite its clear importance, for both our well being and our health, as will be elaborated throughout this chapter, it still has not captured the attention of clinicians. Yet, social support has long been established as important for our health. Berkman and Syme (1979) demonstrated a negative relationship between social network and mortality over two decades ago, when a lack of involvement with others was associated with earlier death. Lubben and colleagues (1989) are among several researchers who have confirmed this relationship, in this instance between social networks and hospitalization. Less involvement with others is related to more hospitalization. Furthermore, the relationship is as strong as that between smoking and mortality, which led to the Surgeon General's warning on cigarette packages many years ago.

An argument can be made that interacting with others becomes even more important in old age than during the earlier years. In Canada's capitalist and individualist society, most older individuals do not work for pay and are, therefore, excluded from society's defining role. Their exclusion from the mainstream, furthermore, has not been replaced by socially sanctioned roles that provide meaningful places for them within society. However as we will learn in this chapter, this does not mean that seniors are all isolated and lonely, as portrayed in many stereotypes. Rather, the vast majority of Canadian seniors are embedded within social networks and lead active lives.

Social Support: What Is It, and Why Is It Important?

Other people are important throughout our lives; this is no different when we reach age 65 years than it is prior to that time. We do not live our lives in social isolation. Even those who do live in relative isolation and those who live alone are not necessarily those who feel lonely and isolated (Larson, et al., 1985). That is, one can be in a crowd and still feel lonely; conversely, one can be alone and not feel lonely. It is subjective measures of emotional connectedness with others (having confidantes and having companions) that are related to general well being (Chappell & Badger, 1989). Despite this fact, assessments by health care practitioners tend to measure social isolation in terms of such factors as living alone or having no children. It is assumed from these quantitative indicators that the individuals are at risk psychologically. Such assumptions are illustrative of the need for research on social support in old age. We know little about the circumstances when it is beneficial to have other individuals in our lives and when and for whom they are problematic. Nevertheless, the area is driven by a broad and common-sense understanding that **social interactions** are a necessary part of all our lives and can have critical implications for our happiness. Indeed, the fact that it is not well understood is part of the reason for interest in this area.

Social support is a broad term, used variously by researchers sometimes to refer only to positive interactions with others and at other times to encompass all interactions whether positive, negative, or neutral. The term "informal support" suffers from the same lack of consistency in its use by researchers. The confusion arises from the fact that the term "support" suggests positive interactions only and can, therefore, suggest that all interaction is necessarily positive, which, of course, is false. The terms "social network" and "informal network" do not have this value-laden implication. When reading the literature, though, one must look for the author's definition of the term because it cannot be assumed. Whichever term is used, it is multidimensional, unless a particular researcher specifies otherwise.

Early research in this area identified the affective and emotional aspects of social support. Lopata (1975) discusses the informal network as the primary support system involving the giving and receiving of objects, services, and social and emotional supports deemed by the receiver and giver as important. Cobb (1976) defines support as including one or more of: emotional support, that is, the person believes he or she is cared for or loved; information that leads the person to believe she or he is esteemed or valued; and the feeling that the person belongs to a network of communication and mutual obligation. Cohen and Syme's (1985) definition is slightly different, including the following three components: (1) the emotional function; (2) information that may or may not lead to confirmation or heightening of self-esteem; and (3) tangible support, such as assistance with activities of daily living.

Pearlin (1985) distinguishes among social network, group affiliation, and interpersonal interaction. The social network refers to the entire web of relationships with which the individual is involved either directly or indirectly; it includes all individuals with whom we have contact or exchange. Group affiliation is a narrower concept, including only those social relationships that involve active attachment to the group and, therefore, the social relations that we are likely to turn to for support. Interpersonal interaction is narrower still, including only active affiliations that involve relationships of trust and intimacy. For Pearlin, interpersonal interaction refers to individuals, rather than groups, and to qualitative, rather than quantitative, aspects of relationships. Similar to this schema, House and Kahn (1985) categorize social relationships as social networks, social support, and social integration. Social networks are a set of relationships that can be described in terms of their structure, using such terms as their density or homogeneity. Social support refers only to the functional content of social relationships, such as emotional concern, instrumentality, and information. Social integration and isolation refer to the existence or quantity of relationships.

The lack of consistency in the use of these terms is, to say the least, glaring! Refer to Table 13.1 to see the use of the various terms by these authors.

Notwithstanding the numerous terms, "social support" is often used generally to refer to any of these concepts.

The majority of research attention has focused on social networks (primarily their size but also, to a certain extent, their composition) and two of the functional aspects identified by House and Cohen (1985), namely, emotional support and instrumental or tangible support. The gerontological literature contains much less information on group affiliation, interpersonal interaction, social integration, feelings of belonging, or information.

There has been particular interest in the emotional aspects of social support including companionship and intimacy (having confidantes). The term **companionship** refers to having other individuals in your life with whom you can spend time and share activities. The term **confidantes** refers to having one or more individuals with whom we feel free to discuss personal matters and share emotional feelings and events. The same individual could be both confidante and companion, or the terms could refer to different individuals. Most Canadian older people report having both types of relationships. Chappell and Badger (1989) report that 96 percent of elderly persons have companions and 84 percent confidantes. Approximately half of all seniors living in the community name the same person as both.

There has also been tremendous interest in tangible or instrumental assistance during old age. This is referred to as assistance with **activities of daily living** (ADL) and can include basic activities (those considered necessary for survival, including both physical activities and personal care activities, such as the ability to walk or to be personally mobile, to eat on one's own, to wash and bathe, and to use the toilet).

Table 13.1 SOCIAL SUPPORT TERMS

	LOPATA	COBB	PEARLIN	COHEN & SYME	HOUSE & KAHN
Social network			X		X
Group affliation			X		
Interpersonal interaction			X		
Social integration					X
Social support					X
Emotional support	X	X		X	X*
Information		X		X	X*
Feeling of belonging		X			
Tangible support	X			X	X*

* All part of their term "social support."

Few seniors are impaired in all these areas. The loss of functioning in any one, though, can lead to long-term institutional care, especially if there is an absence of an informal network to provide assistance. **Instrumental activities of daily living** (IADL), refer to such activities as housework, preparing meals, household maintenance, transportation, shopping, and banking. These activities are important for independence but are not essential for survival. It is not uncommon for seniors to have family and friends who assist with these matters.

Different types of support may come from the same individual at the same time, and they may not be considered "support" by any of the parties involved. For example, a daughter may take her elderly mother shopping once a week and in doing so provide companionship, information, and tangible support, but neither may consciously consider any of these functions or even refer to this activity as "support." Furthermore, each may view the situation differently; the mother may consider the activity primarily companionship, and the daughter may consider it tangible support. Read the text in Box 13.1 and identify the different types of support and possible differing interpretations by those involved.

Box 13.1 Types of Support and Interpretations

It's 10 o'clock Saturday morning. Helen is 75 years old, widowed, and in relatively good health. She lives on her own, is independent, and is mobile. Her 40-year-old daughter lives in the city and every Saturday comes round to pick Helen up. They do grocery shopping together. Each does her own and pays for her own groceries. However, the daughter picks up a few special things that she knows her mother likes and slips them into her mother's bags while unloading the car back at her mother's home. Once the groceries are in the house, their routine is to have a cup of tea together and to chat.

The daughter is a single mom with two children aged eight and 10 years. Late afternoon, every Tuesday and Thursday, Helen takes the bus over to her daughter's home, prepares dinner for everyone and looks after the grandchildren, while the mother goes to her activities. The daughter comes home after work and eats with the family but then goes off immediately afterwards. They have been doing this for a number of years. Helen seems to get along well with her grandchildren, and the grandchildren look forward to her visits.

During the day, Helen takes the bus herself to go to her own activities, to see friends, see the doctor, go shopping, and so on. She has a couple of close friends with whom she shares many activities, and they have known each other for several decades. They do not like to be out after dark, so they typically see each other during the day. They talk on the telephone in the evenings and will call each other to discuss favourite television programs. However, when Helen is sick, it is her daughter who tends to her needs. Friends call and check on one another, but they themselves are elderly and find it difficult to look after each other if anyone becomes ill. Two years ago, though, when Helen was released from hospital and her daughter had to tend to her full-time job and her two children, her friends would come over for a few hours during the day to stay with her. Even then, with her fierce independence, she was determined not to have home-support workers or other service personnel within her home.

Debunking Myths

Available research, furthermore, reveals that many of society's stereotypes about old people are false. The vast majority of older Canadians are retired, not working in paid labour. In our modern capitalist society, those excluded from paid labour tend to be devalued. This is evidenced in agist attitudes, for example, in media portrayals of seniors, among school age children, among health care professionals (Achenbaum, 1995), and among employers faced with job applicants who are older (McDonald & Wanner, 1984). No socially sanctioned and valued role has developed for seniors in society. A common stereotype is that seniors are isolated and alone with their deteriorating health (see Chapters 7 and 10). Added to these longstanding issues are more current issues about working daughters, who may no longer have sufficient time to care for their parents and of low fertility rates that produce even fewer children to care for us in our old age. Mobility of children can mean that they live great distances from their elderly parents, and the technological age has evolved forms of knowledge that simply leave seniors behind.

No question that the majority of seniors are not in paid labour (as seen in Chapter 12); unfortunately, agist attitudes are evident within Canadian society, and seniors do not have socially sanctioned roles for a meaningful old age. This, however, does not translate into isolation and loneliness or a lack of connectedness with others. On the contrary, seniors confirm the notion of the **modified extended family**. As Litwak (1960) noted three decades ago, the extended family emphasizes mutual and close intergenerational ties among kin, the strength of intergenerational relations, continuity of responsible filial behaviour, and contact between the generations, all of which has been supported by gerontological research. Very few elderly individuals are socially isolated; the vast majority report having both companions and confidantes.

Research in the 1970s documented the variety and extent of social interaction during old age. This was particularly important in debunking common assumptions at the time that the nuclear family abandoned their seniors to long-term institutional care and that seniors were largely isolated from their families. Social gerontologists have demonstrated the falsity of these assumptions and debunked the myth of the abandoned elder (Chappell, 1992). This important phase of research on social support documented the type and extent of seniors' interaction. This research, though, assumed that the interaction was supportive, without measuring supportiveness directly (Sauer & Coward, 1985; Walker, et al., 1977). Indeed, sometimes social *networks* were defined in terms of emotional support, that is, beneficial interaction, although many benefits were assumed, not measured.

Researchers at this time documented the fact that the predominance of interaction in old age is with family and friends, that most elderly individuals have extensive social contacts, and that size of social networks does not vary significantly between those who are middle-aged and those who are older (Antonucci, 1985).

An average size of network for community living seniors in Canada is over 30 people (Chappell, 1992). There are elderly individuals who evidence decline in the amount and variety of social interaction, but this decrease tends to be characteristic of those who are old-old, in poor health, and have fewer economic resources. It does not characterize seniors as a group.

Much of the research has focused on marriage, which, during the later years, tends to characterize those who are young-old, rather than old-old. Older married couples tend to have higher incomes, better mental and physical health, assured companionship, and larger social networks (Verbrugge, 1979). For these reasons, it has been argued that marriage is good for people. Litwak (1985) characterizes the marital relationship as having face-to-face continual contact, long-term commitment, high affection, high duty to group survival, a common life style (age homogeneity), high number of peer ties, and meaningful everyday social interaction. Indeed, most seniors do have positive perceptions of their marriages and increased satisfaction over the younger married years (Lowenthal & Robinson, 1976), perhaps due to reduced competition from other roles and increased opportunity for companionship. There could also be a selectivity factor at work; those in worse marriages may not have stayed in them. Married men typically name their wives as their confidantes, whereas married women name their husbands plus children or friends; married men name their wives as their best friends, while women name their offspring or female age peers (Strain & Chappell, 1982; 1985). Married men's exclusive emotional reliance on their wives has led to much concern that older men are particularly at risk when they become widowed.

Given the differential life expectancy between men and women (as noted in Chapter 1) and the fact that women tend to marry men a few years older than themselves, widowhood is a normal life stage for most women. Men are less likely to become widowed, but those who are widowed are more likely to remarry then are women. The fact, though, that widowhood has become a normal life stage for women means they typically have many peers in the same situation with whom they can form friendships (Martin-Matthews, 1991). The proportion of seniors who have been divorced will increase as the baby boom generation ages, as will the proportion of the never-married. Single persons tend to nurture their relationships with their parents, siblings, and friends. When their parents pass away, their friends and siblings represent long-lasting ties. The little research in this area suggests that life-long singlehood promotes self-reliance (Johnson & Catalano, 1981). As more diverse forms of living together are evidenced in the baby boom generation than among those who are currently older (such as same-sex couples) and as these individuals age, we can expect to see more research appearing on such relationships.

The sibling relationship is also a special social tie; it lasts longer than any other family tie. Siblings share a common cultural background, common genetic pool, and earlier life experiences within the same family. Of those seniors today, approximately 80 to 85 percent have at least one living sibling, but less than half of those age 85 years and over do so. Seniors report feeling closer to siblings than any other relatives, except their own children and perhaps their spouses. They are especially important to the never-married, the childless, the divorced, and the widowed. Siblings tend to keep in contact throughout their lives and have been characterized as "standing ready" should help be needed (Connidis, 1989; Cicirelli, 1982; 1985).

Among intergenerational relations, the relationship with children has captured the interest of researchers to a much greater extent than that with grandchildren or other persons. Contrary to assumptions about the predominance of the isolated nuclear family, the majority of seniors have at least one living child and live with or near one child—no more than half an hour's drive away (Hanson & Sauer, 1985). Over 80 percent of seniors have at least weekly contact with their children (Rosenthal, 1987a; Chappell, 1989b); and more interaction takes place between older parents and their children than with any other kin. It is dominated by visiting, family get-togethers, and shared leisure activities. As early as 1963, Rosenmayr and Kockeis aptly coined the phrase **intimacy at a distance** to describe seniors' general preference not to live with their children but to maintain close ties.

These relationships are maintained even if there is geographic distance. Letter writing, phone calls, and today e-mail substitute for face-to-face contact. Those with less money tend to have larger kin networks and to live closer to one another. Women, furthermore, usually consider their relationships with their children as more important and more satisfying than do men, and there tends to be greater similarity of the views of children with those of their mothers than of their fathers (Connidis, 1989). Indeed, the mother–daughter tie is one of the closest.

We know much less about seniors' interactions with their grandchildren, although grandparenthood has many symbolic functions. Bengtson (1985) has written about four symbolic dimensions of this role: (1) someone who is simply there; (2) the national guard or family watchdog, who stands in readiness and provides necessary help; (3) arbitrator; and (4) active participant in the family's social construction of its history. "Being there" when needed provides stress buffers when there are family crises, such as illness, divorce, or unemployment (Hagestad, 1985). Grandparents provide a key function as symbols of connectedness, having the time to listen and being a link to the past. As noted in Chapter 1, more and more individuals are becoming grandparents and great-grandparents. Three-quarters of Canadians have at least one child, and over 90 percent of those with children are grandparents. Grandmothers tend to be involved in interpersonal dynamics, emphasizing the quality of the relationship, while grandfathers emphasize task-oriented involvements with grandchildren. Same-gender ties tend to be more prevalent among these generations, and the grandmother-granddaughter tie is reported to be the closest (Hagestad, 1985).

There is also a relative paucity of research on non-kin friendships in old age. Friendships are characterized by voluntary involvement, affective bonds, and consensus and less by obligation than our kin ties. One chooses one's friends and is also chosen by them. They can be long lasting. Friends tend to be age peers, to be similar to one another in such characteristics as gender and socioeconomic status, share common experiences, and similar world transitions. Chappell (1983) reveals friends are especially important for companionship, and Lee (1985) notes their importance for emotional support, friendship, affection, and quick integration. They are also more likely to fade away than to end on a bad note, allowing their reactivation, if circumstances permit. Seniors have accumulated a large number of social relationships simply by virtue of the amount of time spent meeting people throughout their lives. They, therefore, have a large number of relationships from which to draw and from which to form friendships (Matthews, 1986).

We know almost nothing about other relationships, such as cousins, aunts, uncles, and in-laws, and about instrumental relationships with shopkeepers, delivery persons, mail carriers, and so on. We do know that most persons do not belong to voluntary organizations, and most do not belong to seniors' organizations, even those who know about them (Stone & Huebert, 1988), the major exception being church membership.

In summary, early research in the area of social support focused on social interaction more than on social "support." It documented the extensiveness of social interaction in old age. The vast majority of seniors are immersed in social interaction and have many social ties. The stereotype of the isolated and alone senior applies to a minority of seniors, typically those who are old-old, frail, and poor. We know much more about seniors' interactions with their spouses and with their children than with other kin or non-kin relationships. This research, documenting the extent and type of social supports in the lives of seniors, continues today. In the 1980s, however, major attention turned to the extent to which this interaction was indeed "supportive" and to an examination of the relationship between social support and well being. We turn next to a discussion of this body of work.

Social Support and Well Being

Much of the research on the relationship between social support and well being in the later years assesses either a direct effect or indirect effect of social support on well being. Well being is measured either as the absence of physical or mental illness or more positively as happiness or health. The **direct effects view** argues that social support is important in meeting needs that require fulfillment on a more or less daily basis, regardless of whether the individual is experiencing stress or not. Simply being a member of a group or receiving support from others is beneficial, but it is mediated through one's perception, that is, through subjective support. While results of empirical research are not entirely consistent, in general, they support the direct effects view. Having social support is related to higher well being and a greater quality of life among seniors (Thomas, et al., 1985; Mancini, et al.,1980). Exceptions can be found in the literature; for example, Lin et al. (1979) report a very weak relationship between social support and well being. Because of the number of studies in this area, several reviews were conducted in the mid-1980s. They concluded that the direct effects view is valid, although the specific aspect of social interaction that is the most crucial is not always agreed upon. Cohen and Syme (1985) argue that it is the degree to which a person is integrated within the social network. House and Kahn (1985) argue that of all the measures of social support, network size is the most consistently related to health and well being.

The **indirect effects view** argues that social support is important for the quality of life during stressful events or crises. Social support mediates the effect of stressful experiences; it is protective against the harmful effects of stress. Many of the studies examining this view study individuals who have experienced stressful life events, such as widowhood, retirement, or illness. Kessler and McLeod (1985) conclude there is evidence for indirect effects in relation to particular stress episodes. They argue that emotional support has a pervasive indirect effect, while membership and affiliative networks do not. Generally, studies find that social support is related to quality of life and well being during times of stress with more support related to enhanced well being (House & Kahn, 1985). Antonucci (1990) argues that quality of social support shows a stronger relationship than quantity for both men and women but that the impact is greater for women. Furthermore, there is more evidence demonstrating a link between social support and mental health and between social support and mortality than there is for a link between social support and physical illness (Cohen & Syme, 1985).

An additional difficulty is that many of the life events used to measure stress also measure aspects of social networks. For example widowhood, retirement, and relocation all entail losses, discontinuation, or disruptions to social ties. And not surprisingly, there is research that does not support the indirect view. Andrews et al. (1978) do not find an indirect effect of the relationship between life events, stress, and physiological impairment when studying social support. There is little research, however, on the indirect effect of social support during ongoing chronic stresses and daily hassles, compared with major life events.

Part of the difficulty in this area, alluded to above, is the multidimensionality of social support. Researchers often measure different aspects of social support, making the drawing of general conclusions difficult. One can measure size of network, perception of emotional support, having confidantes, having companions, living arrangements, feeling of belongingness, group affiliation, and so on and then relate any one or more of these measures to any number of outcomes (life satisfaction, happiness, absence of depression, mental health, any number of psychological characteristics, any number of physical health systems). The multi-dimensionality of the concept of social support is difficult to capture empirically, and there are many aspects that have not been tackled to any extent by research to date. For example, in 1985, Pearlin hypothesized about the **specialization of support**, wherein different sources of support may be more effective for different problems or for different stages of a particular problem. Problems often have a natural history of their own and may call for different types of support at different times. Little is known about the specialization of support.

Part of the complexity of social support lies in the fact that social interaction can be negative as well as positive. Rook and Pietromonaco (1987) reveal at least four types of detrimental functions of close relationships: ineffective help, excessive help, unwarranted help, and unpleasant help. As Wortman and Conway (1985) poignantly reveal, healthy persons' efforts to cheer up individuals with cancer are unhelpful to the patients who find such unrelenting optimism disturbing and unauthentic. The study finds that minimizing problems is not helpful. For example, for those who have undergone a mastectomy, it is not helpful when others think that their major concern is the loss of their breasts. These individuals are more concerned about recurrence, death, and treatment side effects. This example is also a striking reminder that those who provide support and those who receive support may have divergent views of the interaction.

Added to the complexity is the fact that one requires longitudinal research designs to determine the causal relationship between social support and quality of life, but most research in this area is cross-sectional. Researchers, by and large, assume that social support, that is, beneficial social interaction, leads to enhanced quality of life, but we do not know if, for example, those with better well being or higher quality of life are more likely to engage in social interaction with others or to engage in supportive interactions with others. These options are not either/or, that is, the relationship could occur in both directions. In addition, we do not know if the relationship between social support and quality of life is spurious. The relationship may be due to some other factor, such as social competence, wherein the socially competent may have easier access to social support and may be more effective in negotiating the health care system, resulting in optimal care and treatment. Or the explanatory factor may be psychological coping, wherein those with appropriate coping skills are those who receive more social support and also have higher quality of life. Even if the relationship between social support and quality of life is not spurious, we do not know whether or not there is a threshold effect. Is there an optimal level of social support beyond which the benefits diminish and may even become negative? Is it the absence of social support or minimal social support that is more deleterious, under what circumstances, and for whom? Box 13.2 offers two scenarios with similar interactions, but the experience is negative for one person and positive for the other.

In summary, we have sufficient empirical evidence for both the direct and indirect views to conclude that there is a relationship between social support and quality of life. But we do not yet have a good understanding of whether or not it is due to another unrelated factor. If the relationship is not spurious, we do not

Box 13.2 Two Scenarios

Scenario 1. Mary is 78 years old, widowed, and with numerous health problems. She lives in an assisted living complex in a large city and is cognitively intact. She has full days booked in activities, Monday through Friday. These are organized through the complex administration. While she has her own full kitchen, where she makes her breakfast and snacks, she often eats in the main dining room of the building with others. Two of her children live in the same city and one elsewhere in the country. The two children who live in the city call her often and offer to have her come to their places for visits, either for a few hours or a few days, whatever she would like. Similarly, the child who lives at some distance calls often and invites Mary to come for short or extended stays. It is, however, difficult to get in touch with Mary because she refuses to have an answering machine or voice-mail, and her busy schedule means that she is often not at home. When asked, she will tell you proudly about her children and how wonderful they are to her. However, she seldom accepts the invitation to travel to a distance to see that child, and while she will visit her children in the city on special occasions, such as on their birthdays or at Christmas time, she finds that she is busy. She is not the grandmotherly type and does not know her grandchildren well but tries hard to remember when it is their birthdays and at least to send cards. She prefers the company of other seniors and has very close friends within the complex.

    Scenario 2. Heather, who also lives in the same complex, is 79 years old, widowed, and with deteriorating physical health. She, too, has children in the city and one who lives some distance away. Heather is also involved in many seniors' activities offered through the complex adminstration and busies herself seeing other people. Unlike Mary, Heather has given up just about all the activities that she would do in the evening. She no longer goes out at night, and she no longer bakes, sews, knits, and so on. She thoroughly enjoys and, indeed, longs for the company of others. She signs up for activities, seeking out social interaction. She is, therefore, usually home in the evenings when her children call, and when they do not call any particular evening, she would call them. She eagerly accepts invitations for visits and asks them to visit her more often. She finds the evenings sitting alone in her apartment to be long and wishes the time would pass more quickly.

know the processes through which the relationship occurs. Is it the provision of advice, information, and/or services that those with better social support receive, and is it that information and/or services that enhance their well being through better care? Is it the actual provision of services, tangible assistance from members of the social network, or is it through social control and peer pressure whereby we are pressured into healthy lifestyles? Is there a direct physiological link between our susceptibility to illness influenced through our neuroendocrinological and immune systems and our psychological and emotional well being that is affected by our social support? Any of these mechanisms may be operative singly or in combination with the others. We do not yet know.

Volunteering

Volunteering has changed throughout the century. At the beginning of the 20th century, there was a critical need for social welfare, a need that had been created by industrialization. Charity at this time was largely unorganized. That is, it involved individual, rather than organizational, efforts. By the 1940s, the state had become involved in social welfare with children's services and then transfer payments. The next two decades saw the growth of the welfare state in Canada, with societal institutions evolving in psychiatric care, criminal justice, services for the developmentally handicapped, and geriatric care. The 1960s and 1970s saw growth in the helping professions, including social work, physiotherapy, occupational therapy, speech pathology, psychology, psychometry, child development, and community development. By the latter part of the 20th century, professional human service workers had largely displaced lay persons, including volunteers, who, by implication, could not provide adequate service. The end of the century, though, marked a major shift, with government efforts to devolve responsibility back to the community and its not-for-profit sector (Graff, 1988; Gordon & Neal, 1997). A resurgence of interest in volunteering has been evident since that time.

Volunteering today, however, is different in substantial ways from 100 years ago. Societal developments over the last century have included the women's movement, which has impacted volunteerism, supporting the founding of new service-oriented organizations, such as rape crisis centres, shelters for battered women, and women's reproductive health services, which rely heavily on volunteers for direct service work. These organizations tend to be characterized by democratic decision making, involvement of service users, and relatively nonhierarchical structures. New ways of thinking emphasize the importance of understanding how social identities are influenced by social structural variables, such as class, gender, and race. There is increased awareness of the consequences of political and economic culture for lived lives. This has occurred within a climate of changing fiscal policies, in which there is less generous funding to voluntary organizations, when it is available at all. The devolution of service programs, previously provided by government to the voluntary sector, has enormously increased both the pressure and the opportunities for the voluntary sector. The partial withdrawal of government responsibility has meant that administrative and financial responsibilities for the social safety net for vulnerable persons and groups now fall to the community (Chappell, 1999).

The new environment for volunteerism has shifted the focus both for volunteers and for those who are served by them. The attraction for seniors to a workshop on "Designing meaningful new volunteer roles for retired persons," hosted at the University of Victoria in early 1997, is captured by Hadley:

> Themes of self-worth and the common good have emerged as central to today's discussion. Volunteerism, many have observed, has little to do with being a "do-gooder." It is about valuing the person and increasing the value

of social and human resources; it is about self-esteem, freely sharing one's talent and wisdom; it is about being valued, not paid; it is about empowerment, growth, and creativity; it is about enhancing the community's quality of life. It is also about having fun in the process...the third stage or "Troisième âge" of human development...is a time when we can give back to society the lessons, the wisdom and resources that we have derived throughout our long and productive lives...this "Troisième âge" is a special period when we can deepen our wisdom and personal sense of spiritual identity. Whatever emphasis each of us might place in this stage of life, our full engagement implies an enhancement of the common good. (Hadley, 1998: 42-43)

The 1987 *Canadian National Survey on Volunteer Activity* (NSVA) provides some of the most comprehensive data available anywhere in the world on volunteering activity. With the 1997 National Survey on Giving Volunteering and Participating (NSGVP), Canada has the richest national data on volunteering that exists. Two meanings of volunteering are captured within the 1997 NSGVP. Volunteering can be either formal or informal. **Formal volunteer work** is defined in terms of activity with an organization, frequently with paid staff. **Informal voluntary work** is not performed through an organization and includes, for example, helping a friend or a neighbourhood. The distinguishing characteristic of volunteering is that it is done without pay and of one's own free will. That survey also includes information on donations and civic participation in local associations and organizations, including attendance at meetings, voting in elections, and being informed about news and public affairs. That survey finds that individuals who participate in any one form of volunteering, for example, donating, formal volunteering, informal volunteering, and civic participation, are more likely to participate in other forms of volunteering as well. Our interest here is on formal volunteering through organizations. The area of informal volunteering receives much research attention, but it is not referred to as "volunteering" in the literature-rather, it is found within the research on social support, generally and, specifically, on caregiving (the topic of the following section in this chapter). Formal volunteering has not been a major area of interest among researchers. There is, though, some information on who volunteers, reasons for volunteering, and some of the perceived benefits of volunteering.

Formal Volunteering

Volunteering through an organization, then, is typically what is referred to as volunteering. In 1997, the NSGVP informs us that just under one-third of Canadians aged 15 years and over engaged in formal volunteering, constituting some 7.5 million Canadians. This was an increase over the one-quarter of Canadians who engaged in formal volunteering a decade earlier. One-third of volunteers accounted for fully 81 percent of all hours contributed, that is, a small proportion do most of the volunteering. Younger persons, those aged 15 to 24 years, as well as those aged 35 to 54 years, volunteer comparatively more than do other age groups. This has been stable from 1987 through to 1997. The one exception is younger individuals, those aged 15 to 24 years, who almost doubled their rate in the 10-year period, from 18 percent in 1987 to 33 percent in 1997. These younger individuals, though, contribute fewer hours than do their counterparts in other age groups. Furthermore, the number of hours they contribute has decreased over the decade (from 174 hours, on average, to 125 hours per year). Those with more income were more likely to volunteer than those with less income, and those with more education were more likely to volunteer than those with less education. In addition, those who volunteer when older were the same persons who tended to volunteer when they were younger (Statistics Canada, 1998; Hertzog, et al., 1989). Almost a quarter of seniors participated in formal volunteering (22 percent in 1987; 23 percent in 1997). Importantly, they contributed, on average, more hours per year than did any other age group (202 hours, compared with the next largest category of 160 hours for those aged 55 to 64 years, to a low of 125 among those aged 15 to 24 years).

The reasons those who volunteer do so are, according to Cohen, ideology and a need to fill leisure time with interesting activities. Hertzog and Morgan (1993) argue that formal volunteer activity serves three functions: social context, the exercise of competence, and feelings of usefulness. They go on to suggest that volunteer work can be viewed as an overall act of lifestyle focused around a formal arena of work and organizational activities. Drawing on the fact that most volunteers have been recruited through an organization to which they belong, these authors argue that individuals in specific roles and with certain types of personalities (such as extroversion), belong to certain types of organizations, such as religious organizations. They are recruited and, therefore, become engaged in volunteer work. Similarly, they hypothesize that professionals are more attracted to work and work-like activities as a result of positive work experiences and are, therefore, receptive when approached to participate in formal volunteer activities. Professionals are also probably offered more interesting and satisfying kinds of volunteer work.

Prince and Chappell (1994) reviewed the empirical research on reasons why seniors volunteer, and report that seniors, like others, have multiple reasons for volunteering. These reasons include the fulfillment of a personal need for affiliation, participation, social reform, sense of religious duty, or gaining social status. Okun's (1993) research finds that those motivated to volunteer in order to feel useful or productive and those who volunteer due to a feeling of moral obligation volunteer more often than do individuals volunteering for other reasons. Brennan's (1989a) analysis of the NSVA reveals that seniors and those who are younger report similar reasons for volunteering, except that fewer seniors volunteer in order to make useful contacts for employment purposes—not surprising. However, Zenchuk (1989) reports that senior volunteers are more motivated by a sense of obligation to the community and to religious obligations than are youth. Seniors do appear to be more motivated by altruism than self-interest (Stoller, et al., 1994; Midlarsky & Kahana, 1994).

In a multivariate analysis of the 1987 NSVA data, Prince and Chappell (1994) identified three independent and interpretable motivations for volunteering. Self-interest included the importance of meeting people, learning, accomplishment, pleasure, making employment contacts, using skills, using spare time, and self-benefit. Obligation included the importance of religious obligation, heritage obligation, community influence, community obligation, and obligation to an organization. Altruism included the importance of helping others and helping the cause. In this instance, both seniors and younger volunteers were just as likely to provide altruistic reasons or to say they volunteered out of self-interest. Senior volunteers, however, were more likely to list obligation, supporting Zenchuk's (1989) research around the same time, but contrary to Stoller et al.'s (1994) research just noted. In Prince and Chappell's Canadian analyses, the reason for volunteering was not related to frequency of volunteering, but this is contrary to research from the United States reported by Okun (1993).

The Benefits of Volunteering

A dominant theme within the literature on formal volunteering is that it is good for the volunteers themselves in addition to the recipients of the volunteering. In Canada, Graff (1991) has been a vocal and visible advocate within Canada of the benefits of volunteering, both for those who are served and those who do the serving. She argues that volunteering contributes to the health, vitality, self-esteem, and longevity of volunteers. The 1987 NSVA indicates that 93 percent of volunteers say that volunteering is very or quite important to themselves, while less than 1 percent say it is not important at all. Graff cites evidence, such as the 1985 Gallup survey in the United States, that reveals half the volunteers indicate they continue to do so because they like doing something useful and helping others and that a third say they enjoy doing the work and feel needed.

There is empirical research that supports these arguments. Aquino et al. (1996) find a relationship between volunteer work and life satisfaction, accounted for because of social support. Hunter and Linn (1980) report that volunteers have significantly higher life satisfaction, a stronger will to live, and fewer symptoms of depression, anxiety, and somatization. Caro and Bass (1997) also report a relationship between health and volunteering, as do Canadians Hirdes and Forbes (1993); membership in fraternal organizations is associated with less decline in health. However, Cohen (1989) does not find a relationship between volunteering and health.

These studies are primarily cross-sectional and, therefore, reflect the difficulty with cross-sectional data in terms of causality. We do not know whether or not the relationship between volunteering and quality of life is causal or reflects selectivity. That is, does volunteering maintain and enhance well being or do those who are in better health and are more satisfied with life volunteer? As noted in Wheeler and associates' (1998) review of 37 independent studies over 25 years (from 1968 to 1994), of which 34 were conducted in the United States and three in Canada, these studies typically use correlational designs. One therefore cannot infer causality. Nevertheless, these studies demonstrate that 70 percent of older volunteers enjoy greater quality of life than the average nonvolunteer; those involved in direct helping seem to derive greater rewards from volunteering than elders engaged in more indirect and less formal helping roles.

Furthermore, when looking at the benefits for those who are served, the clients, approximately 85 percent of the people with whom older volunteers work do better than people not receiving the services of volunteers. Greater help is received from volunteers engaged in enablement or counselling type roles than those engaged in other helping roles, such as advocacy, mediation, social brokering, or information referral. Even though many of these studies are not longitudinal, many control for the independent effects of health and socioeconomic status. In addition, the authors conclude that the effectiveness of counselling by older volunteers compares favourably with the effectiveness of paid professional social workers and that the most probable effective form is to have formal social workers in combination with older volunteers.

In other words, while we are in need of longitudinal studies in this area, the cross-sectional studies that are available do support the claims that volunteering is good for the health of volunteers. There is evidence to conclude that volunteering provides benefit for volunteers although it is not conclusive and it is likely that selectivity is operating. Selectivity does not mean that the results are false; it means that volunteering is beneficial for certain types of people, not necessarily for everyone.

Why Volunteering is Beneficial

Concluding that volunteering is good for the health and well being of volunteers does not tell us what it is about volunteering that leads to such benefits. Is it the social support received from the involvement? Is it the sense of feeling useful? Is it formal affiliation per se? Is it some combination of these? Many of the studies on participation and formal organizations will include data on social support and affiliation in a combined measure with several indicators of social support. It is, therefore, difficult to examine the effect of formal participation per se. The few studies that do allow examination of some of these different factors are inconclusive at this time. Moen et al.'s (1989) study of women's longevity finds an effect of formal social participation but none for informal relationships. However, Krause and colleagues (1992) report the opposite, with informal support having a positive effect on well being in later life while helping others within formal organizational contexts does not. They argue that informal support to others affects well being primarily by bolstering feelings of personal control. Ward (1979) similarly finds no significant independent correlation between amount of group activity and satisfaction. He does note that those whose participation has more of an active quality, such as planning or leadership, have higher life satisfaction than those whose involvement is less active, such as playing cards.

Young and Glasgow (1998) argue that formal voluntary participation is separate and distinct from the social ties that may be formed therein. Formal social participation was defined as voluntary activity in the context of a community organization with a name and an explicit purpose and excludes those that charge a fee for service. It is classified as either instrumental or expressive, and participation in religious organizations is kept separate. Instrumental participation includes, for example, membership in clubs, volunteer work, and local politics. Expressive social participation includes use of recreational services, cultural services, and educational services. A third category called compensatory adaptation includes using seniors' centres, the public, and public transportation and living within city limits where services are available.

They find, in a multivariate analysis controlling for sociodemographic characteristics and religious participation, that those who participate in instrumental community-oriented voluntary organizations have higher levels of self-reported health. This supports their argument that formal participation, irrespective of any informal ties that may be formed there, is a distinct phenomenon (their data are cross-sectional). Expressive social participation has a significant and strong effect on women's health but not on men's. Compensatory adaptation is negatively associated with men's health. There is, in other words, support for the claim that formal affiliation per se is related to good health. Many aspects remain unknown, though, such as: does participation per se in the external world act as an early warning system for volunteers, in which others notice when the volunteers themselves require assistance or are in need? (Chappell, 1999)

Young and Glasgow (1998) also examined seven studies demonstrating separate effects for formal participation (as distinct from an informal supportive component) on mortality. All seven studies were prospective, that is, longitudinal, and arranged from three to 30 years. All but one controlled for initial health status, and that one used a proxy. All report a positive relationship between formal voluntary participation and health.

A Special Type of Social Support—Caregiving

When the physical and/or mental health of the senior declines, social support typically turns to caregiving, sometimes called simply "caring." **Caregiving** refers to support provided to seniors because their health has deteriorated and they can no longer function independently as they once did. The defining characteristic is that this is social support that is required by the individual. This does not mean that the individuals involved necessarily define their interaction as caregiving or

Box 13.3 Canadian Caregiver Coalition

In November 2000, there was an inaugural meeting of the Canadian Caregiver Coalition, with a decision to incorporate it as a society in the province of Ontario in December 2001. The first annual general meeting will be held in 2003. The mission of the coalition is to come together with a unified voice to influence policy and to promote awareness and action to address the needs of caregivers of all ages across Canada.

Interestingly, a decision has been made not to refer to caregivers as "informal," on the argument that there is nothing informal about caregiving. Priority issues identified by the coalition, to date, include:

- National home and community care program
- Funding for support organizations
- Status of caregivers
- Compensation for caregivers
- Respite programs.

The coalition notes that family caregivers in Canada number 1.2 million and argue that they save the health care system approximately five billion dollars a year (equivalent to 276,000 full time employees).

as the provision of assistance. A daughter may take her mother grocery shopping as the mother may be unable to do this on her own, but the mother still may not define it as caregiving. Our needs for emotional support, intimacy, and companionship do not decrease because our health fails. These needs continue throughout our lives. Caregiving is a major area of interest in gerontology because, as noted in previous chapters, physical health declines in old age.

Despite media and governmental attention to the formal health care system, in fact, care and assistance from the informal network of family and friends has been the mainstay of care for seniors throughout history. Informal care refers to unpaid assistance from family and friends. There is some objection to the term "informal," on the grounds that there is nothing informal about caregiving. However, a distinction does need to be made between family and friends who provide care and are not paid and health care personnel who are paid and are typically referred to as formal caregivers.

Summarizing research on caregiving in industrialized countries, Kane et al. (1990) conclude that regardless of whether the country provides universal comprehensive health insurance or not, the informal network provides 75 to 85 percent of the total personal care received by seniors. Keating and colleagues (1999), drawing on the 1996 national *General Social Survey* (GSS) of Canada, distinguish among three groups of seniors receiving care assistance: (1) those with long-term health problems; (2) those experiencing a temporarily difficult time; and (3) those who receive assistance because of the way things are done within the family structure. They refer to those receiving care due to long-term health problems or disabilities as care recipients. Those with short-term illness problems and receiving assistance would also be considered care recipients.

Some of the confusion in this area is highlighted by looking at actual numbers of people receiving care. For example, almost 80 percent of nonseniors (those age 64 years or less) and 73 percent of seniors (age 65 years and over) living in the community (not in long-term institutional care) are receiving assistance. Of all the individuals receiving assistance, however, only 3 percent of those who are not seniors do so because of a long-term health problem or physical limitation. In other words, they are being helped often because of the way things are done (we help one another). The figure for seniors is 22 percent; 4 percent of seniors receive assistance because of a temporarily difficult time, such as a short-term illness or minor injury. According to this survey, just over one-quarter of Canadian seniors receive no assistance. This can include those who are independent and do not require assistance as well as seniors who require assistance but are not receiving any. Among those receiving assistance for long-term health problems, there are higher proportions of women than men, of the unmarried than the married, those older rather than younger seniors, and, not surprisingly, those in poor health. And overwhelmingly, they receive assistance with household tasks (fully 93 percent of them). That is, most seniors receiving care do so with instrumental activities of daily living and not with the basic activities of daily living that are required for survival.

Continuing to draw on data from the 1996 GSS (Keating, et al., 1999), caregivers (those providing assistance) are most likely to be female, rather than male (61 percent versus 39 percent). The mean age for caregivers is 44 for women and 42 for men, somewhat younger than is reported in some other studies. In the province-wide study of caregivers in British Columbia, Chappell and Litkenhaus (1995) find that 73 percent are female and that the mean age for caregivers in that province is 52 years. Of female caregivers, 54 percent in British Columbia are wives and daughters. Figures from the United States reveal that 72 percent of caregivers are women, and of these, 52 percent are wives and daughters (Stone, et al., 1987).

Furthermore, caregivers in the GSS are likely caring for two people, rather than just one individual. And 60 percent of caregivers have been doing so for two years or more. More women than men are primary caregivers and, therefore, shouldering the major responsibility for the organization and provision of care. Furthermore, women provide more total weekly hours of caregiving, and more women than men undertake tasks related to homemaking, personal care, and emotional support. Men are more likely to perform instrumental activities, such as home maintenance and repair. However, driving and finances are just as likely undertaken by men as by women.

The distinction between primary and secondary caregivers is an important one. The majority of research on caregiving focuses on the **primary caregiver** only.

In fact, little is known about others, and even less is known about the differential experiences of these two groups (Chappell, et al., 1996). Tennstedt and colleagues (1989) report that spouse caregivers are the least likely to receive assistance from others but that child caregivers and friends who are primary caregivers usually have secondary caregivers involved with them. When the primary caregiver is a child, she is usually a daughter or daughter-in-law, and the sons and sons-in-law as well as grandchildren living with her often act as secondary caregivers. Friends are more typically secondary than primary caregivers. Brody and associates (1989) report that among siblings who are caregivers, one tends to be the primary caregiver, with the others acting as secondary caregivers.

Another study (Amercian Association of Retired Persons and Travellers Company Foundation, 1989) reports that employed caregivers are more likely to have secondary caregivers helping them than primary caregivers who are not working for pay. We do not know whether employed caregivers are more likely to be secondary than primary caregivers themselves. Brody and Schoonover (1986) report that employed caregiving daughters give just as many hours to caregiving as their unemployed counterparts but that they are involved in different activities. It is not known whether employment adds stress to the life of the caregiver as an added demand or if it represents diversion and relief, reducing the stress of the caregiving experience. We also know little about whether the involvement of secondary caregivers is helpful or unhelpful to the primary caregiver. Not surprisingly, the little research available reveals contradictory findings with Jutras and Veilleux (1991) finding that secondary caregivers do help alleviate the burden for primary caregivers but Pruchno (1990) reporting that secondary caregivers do not reduce the burden experienced by primary caregivers. Chappell et al. (1996) report that 7 percent of caregivers self-identify as "sharing equally," rather than as a primary or a secondary caregiver. Caregivers sharing the task equally with others, though, are more similar to secondary than to primary caregivers. Other than labelling themselves as equal-sharing caregivers, they do not carry the task loads that primary caregivers do. Rather, in their study of Canadian caregivers throughout British Columbia, primary caregivers emerge as the distinctive group and are more likely to be female, not to be working in paid labour, and to be older (mid-50s, rather than mid-40s). They are also more likely to be spouses, to be caring for individuals who are more ill, and to report being closer to the care recipient than is true of secondary caregivers.

As noted above, the primacy of the marital relationship continues as we age and as health deteriorates. Because women tend to marry men a few years older than themselves and yet have longer life expectancy than their husbands, they tend to be there to provide assistance to their husbands as their health deteriorates in the few years before death. Older couples tend to cope by redistributing domestic chores, but there tends to be less relocation when the husband is the one who becomes disabled. This is because wives' traditional tasks include cooking, cleaning, and attending to their husbands' needs. Spouses, provided they are available, more than any other caregiver, are likely to provide care during periods of greater disability and illness and continue doing so even as their own health declines (Hess & Soldo, 1985; Chappell, 1992). The husband is likely not to be around when the wife's health deteriorates, so it is her child, daughter if there is one, who steps in to provide the care. Children are the next most frequent caregivers. Among the nonmarried (including the never-married, divorced, separated, and widowed) half name their children, 29 percent naming daughters and 20 percent naming sons (Chappell, 1990b). Caregiving roles of sons and daughters tend to be different and are often gender based, with daughters providing more hands-on and emotional care; sons providing more supervision and money, if and when needed. If, however, a daughter is unavailable either because there is not one or she is geographically distant, sons do provide the needed care (Horowitz, 1981).

Middle-aged children, primarily daughters, have been identified as the **sandwich generation**, **hidden victims**, and the **generation-in-the-middle** because they can have multiple demands, including having to care for aging parents, still raising their children, and working in paid labour. However, despite the popularity of this notion and the media attention given to it, it is not middle-aged adults with young children who are providing extensive help to their parents. It is, rather, children who no longer have their own children living at home who are doing this caregiving (Penning,1998; Rosenthal, et al., 1986). The terms sandwich generation, hidden victims, and generation-in-the-middle are misnomers. The term **serial caregiving** would be more appropriate because most women raise their children, then give care to their parents, then give care to their husbands, in succession, rather than simultaneously.

Caregivers to seniors can themselves be seniors, and in fact, among a sample of Canadian community living, Chappell (1989a) reports 22 percent of elders consider themselves primary caregivers to others. Of these, almost half provide care to a spouse, while 14 percent do so to an older parent. Among these elderly primary caregivers, 55 percent are female, and 45 percent are male, a much more equal gender split than is found among all caregivers. There are no gender differences in terms of whether it is a male or female who is providing care to a spouse or to a daughter. However, when looking at all caregivers, women are more likely to be providing assistance with both basic and instrumental activities of daily living than are men. For assistance with walking, dressing, bathing, and feeding, the caregiver is more likely to be female. The only exception is when going to the toilet—where the caregiver is overwhelming male, perhaps because of the physical strength required. In instrumental activities of daily living, women provide overwhelming help, such as with housekeeping, preparing meals, cutting toenails, and administering medications. Only with household maintenance do males predominate. Emotional support and informational needs are given by women in most instances. A traditional gendered division of labour is evident here.

Much less is known about caregivers other than spouses and children. This is partly due to a bias within the literature that tends to exclude other family members and non-kin from the study. An exception is a Canadian study by Penning (1990). She finds little assistance from relatives other than spouses and children, friends, and neighbours. There are conflicting reports about caregiving by siblings (Lopata, 1978; Martin-Matthews, 1987); and there is also little known about assistance provided by grandchildren. There is some suggestion that when grandchildren do help out, it is because their parents are primary caregivers (Tennstedt, et al., 1989; Chappell, 1990a). There is also little known about the role of friends in caregiving, although Chappell (1990b) finds that after spouses and children, friends are the next most frequent source of support cited. An American study (Barker & Mitteness, 1990) reports non-kin caregiving ranging from 5 to 24 percent. It is believed that friendship is particularly important for companionship (Lee, 1985), where similar interests and psychological dimensions may take precedence. Little is known about caregiving for those without family. Fischer et al. (1990) report that these individuals do have some support, but it is frequently characterized by a network of helpers, each of whom provides a few services. These authors characterize it as "care without commitment" because the caregivers have neither obligation nor authority. We do know that elderly persons without families are more likely to live in long-term care institutions.

Caregiver Burden

Without question, one of the major foci of research on caregivers for seniors has been stress and burden experienced by caregivers. Montgomery (1989) identified several terms commonly encountered in the literature, all capturing the essence of the meaning of burden (as a consequence of caregiving), including stress effects, caregiving consequences, and caregiving impact. George and Gwyther (1986) define **caregiver burden** as the physical, psychological or emotional, social, and financial problems that can be experienced by family members caring for impaired older adults. Tebb (1995) refers to it as the inability to be resilient. This can refer to any negative implications for mental health, for social recreational involvement, for financial difficulties, and/or for physical health problems that are a consequence of caregiving. It is commonly understood to have both objective and subjective components, with the subjective being particularly important because people's own definitions and assessments of the situation greatly affect their ability to meet their own needs. Objective burden often consists of such things as changes in daily routine, employment, and health, while subjective burden often includes emotional reactions, such as low morale, anxiety, and depression.

Much of the caregiving literature has focused on caregivers to sufferers of Alzheimer's disease and other dementias. The negative consequences of caring for those with dementia can include physical, physiological, and/or social repercussions. Those caring for dementia sufferers, compared with those caring for the physically frail, are more burdened (Zarit, 1983; George & Gwyther, 1986). It appears to be the behavioural manifestations of dementia that are most problematic for caregivers, rather than the condition per se (Chappell & Penning, 1996), and not all stages of the disease are as problematic as others. Among behavioural problems, certain ones are more problematic, such as agitation, violence, incontinence, wandering, the need to watch and control care receivers' behaviours, hallucinations, dangerous and embarrassing behaviours, and sleep disturbance. Among specific caregiving tasks, those that restrict or confine the caregiving time and space and those requiring personal bodily contact, such as bathing, dressing, and toileting, are more burdensome (Montgomery, et al., 1985). The relationship between the caregiver and the care receiver has been identified as important for the burden experienced by the caregiver. Close relationships between the two are associated with less burden (Morris, et al., 1988).

The psychological impact of caregiving has been well documented, whether looking at depression (Parks & Pilisuk, 1991), guilt, worry/anxiety, loneliness (Barusch, 1988), emotional stress and strain (Fast et al., 1999) lowered physical functioning, lower social functioning, or worse general health (Hughes, et al., 1999). Indeed, the negative psychological and emotional consequences of caregiving receive widespread acceptance. Burden is studied in its own right, as a predictor of other caregiving outcomes, such as well being or physical health, and the search for explanatory factors of burden receive much attention. There is inconsistency in the literature but predictors that do emerge include the care receiver's functional characteristics, gender, hours of caregiving, interruptions of paid employment, relationship between the caregiver and care receiver, health of the caregiver, and social support (Stull, et al., 1994; Chappell & Penning, 1996; Lawrence, et al., 1998).

The primary focus in the caregiving literature is on stress and burden during the caregiving experience. Fewer studies examine the bereavement of the caregiver, that is, adjustment of the caregiver to the death of the loved one. An implicit assumption, therefore, is that once the loved one dies, stress on the caregiver ceases (Montgomery, 1996). It also reflects an assumption that the importance of the role lies in the stresses and burdens, rather than in the satisfaction that is derived from caring for a loved one. However, the death of a loved one is dramatic, and the bereavement literature generally tells us that wives suffer greater depression than do bereaved husbands but that in time the depressive episodes for both tend to decline (Zisook & Shuchter, 1991). Among caregivers in particular, similar results are evident, revealing similar gender and relationship associations. That is, spouses tend to express more negative consequences, women more so than men, but over time they regain their equilibrium (Rudd, et al., 1999; Schulz, et al., 1997). The few studies examining the effect of nursing home placement report contradictory findings with some showing that the death of a loved one in a nursing home results in greater difficulty for the caregiver, with other research suggesting no differences between those with a loved one dying in a nursing home and those with a loved one who dies at home (Chappell & Behie, 2002).

This focus on the negative aspects of caregiving, specifically stress and burden, has been concomitant with a lack of attention to the positive or more satisfying aspects of the caregiving situation. But, when asked why they provide care, caregivers give a number of reasons, including love, affection, reciprocity, and commitment (Horowitz, 1985). Furthermore, one-quarter of family caregivers in one study claim that caregiving increases their satisfaction in life (Hooyman & Associates, 1985). Fitting and associates (1986) notice a similar figure of 25 percent of husbands claiming an improved relationship with their spouses after providing care. In the province-wide British Columbia study, Chappell and Litkenhaus (1995) report that the vast majority (93.4 percent) of caregivers can list rewards of caregiving. For example, over half name something that involves the personal relationship with the care receiver, such as seeing them happy and watching them improve, and the closeness of the relationship, and one-quarter cite being able to help as their reason. Fully one-third say that the caregiving relationship is the closest relationship they have ever had with anyone in their lives; over 40 percent say that it is as close as other relationships have been. Keating et al. (1999) report from the 1996 national GSS survey that the vast majority of caregivers state that they often feel that by helping they are giving back what they received from that other individual; over three-quarters say that they are giving back what life has given to them (87.7 percent) and it strengthens their relationship with their care receiver (88.7 percent).

Despite the evidence that caregiving is a burden, when one examines prevalence figures for the experience of burden and well being among caregivers, the majority of caregivers do not emerge as overburdened and unable to cope. In the British Columbia study, two-thirds say that they find caregiving stressful; two-thirds of those who find it stressful say that the burden is intermittent, and only 9.2 percent say it is extreme. When asked how well they think they are coping, over 90 percent say that they are coping well. In the national GSS survey, only 18.2 percent say that they felt burdened in helping others. Without denying that caregiving can be burdensome and that some might require assistance, nevertheless, it is time for gerontology to recognize that not all caregivers are burdened to the point of being at risk. Schulz and Williamson (1991) find depressive symptomatology stable among most caregivers and that most are able to meet their demands without becoming dysfunctional.

Yet, the focus on negative aspects on caregiving, such as burden, and the simultaneous lack of attention to the positive aspects of caregiving leave the impression that the vast majority of caregivers are on the brink of burnout and breakdown. Extensive research suggests that this is not the case. Rather, most caregivers are not at risk of burnout, at risk of giving up caregiving, or at risk of becoming a major user of the health care system. It is time to turn our attention to identifying the minority of caregivers who are at risk and need considerable help and to study the positive consequences of caregiving and the beneficial coping skills of caregivers. There is some research linking personality characteristics to better coping and less burden among caregivers. Individuals scoring higher on hardiness, sense of coherence, and personal resiliency are likely to report less burden and better overall well being, to use formal services less, and to be in better health (Mockler, et al., 1998; Braithwaite, 1998).

The fact that we know much less about the experience and lives of caregivers than the abundance of literature on burden would suggest is further evidenced in recent research on the meaning of caregivers having a break. Having a break, known as **respite**, refers conceptually to a pause in or temporary cessation of caregiving tasks and an interval of rest. However, in practice and in research, it is referred to primarily as a service or a group of services that provide periods of relief or rest to caregivers away from their caregiving tasks (Feinberg & Kelly, 1995). The services are considered respite care services when they explicitly target the caregiver, rather than the care recipient. In Canada, they typically refer to three types of services: (1) attendants who come to the house and look after the elder, while the caregiver leaves the home in order to do such tasks as shopping or stays in the home but tends to noncaregiver tasks, such as cooking or sewing; (2) adult daycare or day hospital programs, where the care recipient is taken for a few hours; and (3) respite beds in a facility, where the care receiver stays for days or weeks. Respite services aim to strengthen the efforts of informal caregivers to allow the loved one to remain within the community. Other aims include decreasing caregiver burden, providing caregiver education and training, avoiding or delaying institutional placement for the loved one, linking caregivers and care recipients to other community services, and preventing unnecessary hospital admissions (Kosloski & Montgomery, 1995).

However, use of respite services is low, with only a small proportion of those considered eligible using the service when it is offered. Among the many reasons offered for this include unfamiliarity with the service, cost, psychosocial conflict over the appropriateness of using respite care, philosophical values opposed to respite care, feeling a loss of independence, lack of understanding of bureaucratic structures, and negative attitudes toward the receipt of services (Rokowski & Clarke, 1985). Furthermore, research examining the effectiveness of respite services, when they are used, suggest they may have a moderate effect at best. Several studies report no effect, other studies report positive outcomes, such as lessened burden for caregivers, higher levels of self-efficacy related to caregiving, lower levels of depression, and improved physical health (Milne, et al., 1993; Nolan, et al., 1993; Gottlieb, 1995). Several reviews of the literature in this area arrive at inconsistent conclusions, arguing that it represents either a mild intervention or a moderate intervention (Kirwin, 1991; Lawton, et al., 1991; Knight, 1993).

One reason that can account for this lack of findings concerning respite services is methodological. Those not receiving respite services may be receiving respite (a break) through other means, such as a relative looking after the loved one for a period of time, the loved one being hospitalized for a period of time, and so on. Therefore, a typical methodological design that compares users of the services with those who are not using them is inappropriate, since they may actually be comparing respite services with other types of activities that provide respite to the caregiver. This is a major selectivity problem in the research on respite for caregivers, which requires a different research design in order to assess the adequacy of the services.

Chappell et al. (2001) argue that researchers and service providers alike have gone astray by conceptionalizing respite as a service, rather than as an outcome. Caregivers must be first asked to define for themselves what it means to have a break. Despite the emphasis on a task orientation (the provision of assistance with activities of daily living and instrumental activities of daily living) by both researchers and service providers, it is the emotional aspects of caregiving that appear to be the most important to both the caregiver and the loved one receiving care (Abel,1990; Hasselkus, 1988). Informal caregivers realize the importance of their invisible work, their decision making, and their protecting the elder's self-image, sense of identity, and autonomy. They see this as their most important task. Since caregivers view their role differently from researchers and service providers, it should be not be surprising that they view respite differently as well.

Using in-depth qualitative interviews and confirmation in a random sample of 250 caregivers in British Columbia, Chappell and colleagues (2001) derived a typology of what respite means to caregivers. It is very different from what researchers and service providers had assumed. Six meanings of respite were derived (Table 13.2). *Stolen moments* refers to brief periods away from the actual tasks of caregiving, involving activities or situations that temporarily take the caregiver away from caregiving tasks but maintaining the daily caregiver routine. It includes all manner of activities, such as taking the dog for a walk, taking a bath, cooking, having a haircut, grocery shopping, and so on—activities that are done in the time "stolen" from caregiving and generally refer to activities that have to be done anyway. They provide a break from actual caregiving tasks.

Connections refers to social involvement, that is, making connections with people in the world "out there," either in a social sense or as part of a support group. These caregivers perceive these contacts as providing a break in and of themselves. It is the interaction with others that was named as important.

Relief refers to separation from caregiving. It is distinct from *stolen moments* above in that caregivers specify that an activity is a complete physical and mental break away from caregiving tasks. It is an opportunity to distance both body and mind from the loved one. Such activities as going on a vacation or activities in closer proximity, such as elaborate bathing rituals, which serve the purpose of providing a complete break, would be examples.

Mental or physical stimulus includes challenges not associated with caregiving that engage the mind and/or the body in an all encompassing manner. Reading, intellectual pursuits, hobbies, involvement in work, and so on, as long as they are totally absorbing, would be examples.

Angst-free care receiver refers to caregivers who define a break as occasions when the care receiver is relatively happy, comfortable, angst free. It is not the person from whom they get the break but their condition.

Minimize the importance refers to those who claim they do not need the break, it is simply not an issue for them, they minimize the importance of having a break. Often, secondary caregivers and those with few caregiving responsibilities fall into this category.

These different meanings of respite, based on experiential evidence from caregivers themselves, reveal that fully half the caregivers define having a break differently from how the health care system and researchers have in the past, with the most prevalent category (*Stolen moments* at almost 50 percent) entirely new and unexpected.

Not one caregiver defined what a break is to them or spoke of the experience in relation to service provision. These meanings, nevertheless, have important implications for service delivery, pointing to the fact that policy makers and service providers must redefine respite as an outcome, rather than a service. Assessment protocols should ask caregivers what a break means to them and how they can best receive a break that is meaningful to them. New types of intervention based on the reconceptualization of respite as an outcome may see improved utilization rates of respite services. New interventions, such as instruction in self-care, may be appropriate. Another might be teaching strategies to reduce stress levels and to deal with anxiety and guilt. Interestingly, the meaning of respite for caregivers is unrelated to gender or to social class.

Table 13.2 **THE MEANINGS OF RESPITE ACCORDING TO CAREGIVERS: DOMINANT THEMES**

INTERNAL RESPITE	PERCENT OF CAREGIVERS INDICATING THEME	
Stolen moments	48.1%)	
Minimize importance	12.0%)	61.3%
Angst-free care receiver	1.2%)	
External respite relief	18.3%)	
Mental/physical boost	11.2%)	38.6%
Connections	99%*	9.1%)

N=241 caregivers to seniors in Victoria, British Columbia, Canada. *Figure does not total 100% due to rounding.
Source: Chappell, N.L.

CHAPTER SUMMARY

Interaction with others is a normal part of virtually everyone's lives. As human beings, we are social creatures. The concept of social support receives much recognition and research attention because of this. However, capturing the essence of social support in precise scientific terms and then being able to translate this into accurate measurement is another matter.

Key ideas to remember from this chapter include:

- Social support, particularly in gerontological research, has focused on emotional support, instrumental or task-oriented support and on social networks (their size and their composition).

- Early research in gerontology measured social interaction, assumed it was supportive, and debunked the notion that the vast majority of seniors were lonely and isolated. On the contrary, it documented the social imbeddedness and extensiveness of social ties in old age.

- Intimacy at a distance conveys the preference among seniors in relation to their children.

- Most research has focused on the marriage relationship and also the relationship of seniors with children. We know much less about other relationships, such as the sibling relationship, relationships with grandchildren, distant relatives, and so on.

- Research in the 1980s empirically examined the supportiveness of social interaction and confirmed a relationship between social support and well being. Social support is directly related to our well being; those with more social support have increased well being. Social support is also important for our well being during times of stress. Those with social support during times of stress have better well being than those without social support.

- Despite an abundance of evidence documenting the relationship between social support and well being, little is longitudinal; logically, one would expect the relationship could be reciprocal.

- Although there is relatively little attention focused upon organizational participation including volunteering, research suggests that volunteering is good for the volunteers' health. There may well be a selectivity factor operating, but among those who do volunteer, it appears to be beneficial.

- Caregiving is especially important as our health declines during old age. Informal caregiving from family and friends is the mainstay of care for seniors, not the formal health care system.

- Most of the research in this area focuses on the primary caregiver, that is, the individual providing most of the care to the loved one. Women predominate as caregivers, especially wives and daughters.

- Despite the popularity of the terms sandwich generation, hidden victims, and generation-in-the-middle to describe caregivers, research suggests a more appropriate term would be serial caregiving. In reality, women raise their children, then provide care to their parents, and then provide care to their husbands. This tends to happen in a serial fashion, rather than simultaneously.

- Typically, there is a gender division of labour when men and women are caregivers, with women providing more hands-on personal care and emotional support; men are more likely to provide advice and monetary assistance.
- There is a major emphasis in the caregiving literature on caregiver burden. This literature reveals the many stresses associated with caregiving, including psychological, physical, emotional, and economic.
- Despite the focus on caregiver burden, most caregivers can also name satisfactions they derive from this role, and most cope and are not at risk of having to forfeit this role or to receive health care services themselves.
- The fact that we have much to learn about the caregiving experience is vividly portrayed in the meanings of respite (having a break) for caregivers themselves. Fully half refer to stolen moments, a concept that is foreign to the thinking of researchers and service providers alike when they discuss respite for caregivers.

KEY TERMS

Social interactions, **(p. 344)**

Social support, **(p. 345)**

Companionship, **(p. 346)**

Confidantes, **(p. 346)**

Activities of daily living, **(p. 346)**

Instrumental activities of daily living, **(p. 347)**

Modified extended family, **(p. 348)**

Intimacy at a distance, **(p. 350)**

Direct effects view, **(p. 351)**

Indirect effects view, **(p. 352)**

Specialization of support, **(p. 353)**

Formal volunteer work, **(p. 356)**

Informal voluntary work, **(p. 358)**

Caregiving, **(p. 360)**

Primary caregiver, **(p. 362)**

Sandwich generation, **(p. 364)**

Hidden victims, **(p. 364)**

Generation-in-the-middle, **(p. 364)**

Serial caregiving, **(p. 364)**

Caregiver burden, **(p. 365)**

Respite, **(p. 368)**

STUDY QUESTIONS

1. What is social support, and why is it important as we age?

2. Why is Litwak's concept of the modified extended family appropriate for discussions of seniors in today's society?

3. Discuss the differential importance of various relationships, such as spouse, daughter, son, siblings, friends and so on, for seniors.

4. Discuss the relationship between social support and well being in old age.

5. Who are the caregivers to seniors, and what do they do?

6. How important is the notion of caregiver burden?

SUGGESTED READINGS

Abel, E.K. 1990. Daughters caring for elderly parents. In J.F. Gubrium, & A. Sankar (Eds.), *The home care experience: Ethnography and policy*, (pp.189–286). Newbury Park, CA: Sage Publications.

Braithwaite, V. (1998). Institutional respite care: breaking chores or breaking social bonds? *Gerontologist, 38(5),* 610–617.

Chappell, N.L., Reid, R.C. & Dow, E. (2001). Respite reconsidered: A typology of meanings based on the caregiver's point of view. *Journal of Aging Studies, 15*(2), 201–216.

House, J.S., & Kahn, R.L. (1985). In S. Cohen & S.L. Syme (Eds.), *Social support and health.* Orlando, FL: Academic Press.

Rosenthal, C.J., Martin-Matthews, A., & Matthews, S.H. (1996). Caught in the middle? Occupancy in multiple roles and help to parents in a national probability sample of Canadian adults. *Journals of Gerontology: Series B: Psychological Sciences and Social Sciences, 51B, (6),* S274–S283.

Yates, M.E., Tennstedt, S., & Chang, B.H. (1999). Contributors to and mediators of psychological well being for informal caregivers. *Journal of Gerontology: Psychological Sciences, 54B*(1), P12–P22.

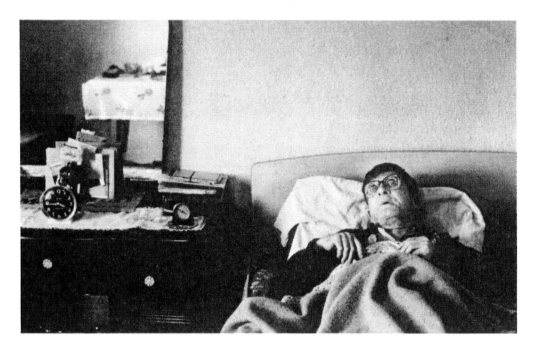

Pensions and Economic Security for Older Canadians

In this chapter, you will learn about:

- How Canada came to be awarded a B grade in "economics" by NACA, which, as we shall see, has a lot to do with the financial situation of Canadian women and with the situations of men and women who live alone.
- Changes in average income and total assets within the last decade.

- The development of the pension system and what the system looks like today.
- What the future might hold for the retirement income system and why it matters to all Canadians.

Introduction

The National Advisory Council on Aging (NACA) issued a *Report Card on Seniors in Canada*, which rated how well older Canadians were doing economically. They awarded a B grade, which meant good, but with improvements needed (NACA, 2001). See Table 14.1 for the indicators that were used to assign the grade. As we saw in Chapter 10, people's health and overall quality of life depend, to a great degree, on their economic status. At least one study discovered that the higher

Table 14.1 HOW WELL ARE SENIORS FARING ECONOMICALLY?

INDICATOR	DEFINITION	TREND DIRECTION INDICATES
Income	Mean income of seniors	Situation improving
	Mean income of households headed by seniors, compared with all households	Mixed situation
	Mean income of unattached seniors, compared with other unattached people	Mixed situation
Source of Income	Percentage of seniors' income derived from government pension programs, employer-sponsored pension plans and RRSPs	Situation improving
	Percentage of seniors receiving Canada and Quebec Pension Plan benefits	Situation improving
	Percentage of workers contributing to employer pension plans	Situation improving
	RRSP contributors and contributions	Situation improving
Income distribution	Percentage of Canadians in the lowest income group of Canadians	Situation improving
	Income level for one-fifth of seniors with the lowest incomes	Situation improving
	Low income within the seniors' population	Mixed situation
Assets and Debts	Number of $ in debts for every $100 in assets	Stable situation
	Total assets (both financial and nonfinancial)	
Economic Well Being	Self-assessment of economic well being by seniors	Trend unknown

Source: Reproduced from *Seniors in Canada: A Report Card* 2001, Health Canada. Copyright Minister of Public Works and Government Services Canada, 2002.

earnings of Canadian men prior to age 65 years were associated with low mortality during the ensuing nine years (Wolfson, et al., 1993). Furthermore, older persons who have wealth in the form of assets or income can either own, or afford to buy, goods and services that will allow them to exercise control over their own lives. In short, wealth at older ages contributes to an independent and healthy life for older persons. The pension system in Canada makes a significant contribution to the wealth of older people. As one recently retired woman stated about her old age pension, "I know some people groan about what they get, I say I'm thankful for what I'm getting because I never had anything before." (McDonald, et al., 1997:53). In contrast, a Canadian widow observed, "...there are women that aren't getting what I am because I get the Canada Pension, but I still think there are a lot that don't, and without that I don't know how they live..." (McDonald, et al., 1997: 56).

The Retirement Wage

As we outlined in Chapter 12, retirement is a modern social invention that marks the transition to old age. Some scholars further suggest that retirement would never have been possible on such a large scale unless there was a second invention, namely, the pension system, which has often been called the **citizen's wage** or the **retirement wage** (Snell, 1996; Myles, 1995). The public pension system is central to the development of the contemporary welfare state in Canada, as in most other capitalistic democracies, so much so that the welfare state has been hailed as a "welfare state for the elderly" (Myles & Street, 1995). Large government expenditures on elderly persons are responsible for this description. For example, in 1997, government transfers accounted for 54 percent of the income of people over age 65 years, compared with about 21 percent from private pensions (Lindsay, 1999).

Traditionally, welfare states have been portrayed as systems that curb the stratification created by market and social forces and, in the process, foster greater equality among citizens. The underlying theme is that workers are oppressed by capitalism, which buys and sells their labour and, in so doing, turns it into a commodity. However, with the advent of social rights based on citizenship, social protection for workers is institutionalized in modern social welfare policies in the form of social insurance and universal benefits, a critical transformation from social relief to social security. Although capitalists have greater resources in the market, workers, because of their numbers, have greater political resources. Workers will use their political resources to temper market processes and to extend their social rights. Theorists who use this approach tend to highlight the distinction between **social assistance**, with the aim to provide subsistence to those in need, and **social insurance**, which provides income security and continuity in living standards. It is this analytical framework, a power resources account, that most gerontologists use to explain the development of the retirement wage in capitalist societies, including Canada.

Social Assistance for the Older Worker

Until the introduction of the *Old Age Security Act* in 1951, destitute older workers relied on the good graces of their families, their employers, or social relief for help. At the time, there were isolated examples of private pension plans for older workers, such as at the Hudson Bay Company. The Company offered some protection for their fur traders who "...in case of sickness and old age" were allowed a pension in "any case that was deserving" (Simpson, 1975: 33–34). The Hudson Bay Company also offered a primitive annuity plan that paid 4 percent on any funds the fur trader left in the keeping of the company, but this was rare because workers were paid very little (McDonald & Wanner, 1990). *The Superannuation Act* of 1870 passed by the new Federal Government provided an early occupational pension plan for federal employees in order to "...get rid of persons who had arrived at a time of life when they could no longer perform their work efficiently" (Morton & McCallum, 1988: 6). The Act was as much a political strategy designed to rid the new government of officials inherited from an earlier government as it was a genuine retirement pension for civil servants.

It was the Grand Trunk Railway, later the Canadian National Railway, that established one of the first compulsory industrial pension plans in Canada in 1874. In order to impose discipline on a large body of employees spread across Canada, the company looked to the military for inspiration. Besides adopting uniforms, hierarchies, and strict regulations, the organization also introduced a contributory pension at age 65 years to shore up the worker's commitment to the company. Because the worker contributed part of his or her salary to the plan, they were less likely to leave the company, while the strongly held Canadian value of thrift was reinforced because pensions were a reward for saving. In the ensuing years, these types of benefits were offered by a growing number of businesses, such as banks, and became known as **corporate welfare**. An Imperial Oil employee observed that the private pension was "...a cold blooded business proposition" (quoted in Morton & McCallum, 1988: 11). Pensions at this time were a *gift*, designed to ensure that older workers did not antagonize their employers, such as by going on strike, in return for a secure old age income. Indeed, in 1910, in the course of an acrimonious strike, the Grand Trunk railway wiped out the pension rights of the workers who had struck the company.

Not wanting to take responsibility for the pensions of Canadians, the federal government emulated the railways and banks in their approach to pensions. In order to encourage individual responsibility for pension plans, the federal government took action on two fronts. It passed the *Pension Funds Societies Act* in 1887, which allowed workers in federally chartered organizations to set up pension plans to which their employer could contribute, and it introduced the

Government Annuities Act in 1908, a savings plan that offered reasonable interest rates to workers. These actions were followed by the *Income War Tax Act* in 1917, which allowed employer contributions to employee pension plans to be claimed as tax deductions. The problem, of course, was that few people were covered by such pensions or could set aside money from their paltry wages. Although the government of the day boasted that the *Annuities Act* would eliminate the need for a government program of old age pensions, in the last year of the existence of the Act in 1927, only 9,000 contracts were signed (Morton & McCallum, 1988).

In the 1880s, Bismarck instituted the first state pensions for working class men in a rapidly industrializing Germany:

> The State must take the matter into its own hands, not as alms giving but as the right that men have to be taken care of when, from no fault of their own, they have become unfit for work. Why should regular soldiers and officers have old age pensions, and not the soldier of labour? (quoted in Donahue, Orbach, & Pollack, 1960:351)

Canadian politicians were, however, indifferent to the plight of the "soldier of labour," although a number of organized groups, such as the Social Service Congress and the Trades and Labour Congress of Canada, demanded old age pensions for the poor. Witnesses to various parliamentary committees set up in 1911–1912, 1912–1913, and 1924 to investigate the viability of an old age pension system also provided evidence as to the devastation of industrialism and the inability of poor families to provide for their aged members (House of Commons Debates, 1921). Canada's first *Pension Act*, however, was enacted in 1919 for soldiers returning from World War I, a supposedly Draconian piece of legislation with stringent eligibility criteria (Finalyson, 1988: 9). Earlier in 1911, Newfoundland, still a British colony, introduced the first state-run old age pension program, which, true to the ethos of the day, did not include women because they were unpaid family labourers, even though about 13 percent of women worked in the paid labour force in 1911.

Canada's first national pension legislation promoted by the social crusaders J.S Woodsworth, and A.A. Heaps, both members of the Labour Party, was not enacted until 1927 and was nothing more than "...a classic piece of 'social assistance' legislation..." (Myles & Teichroew, 1991: 87). The *Old Age Pension Act (OAP)*, which established a cost-shared program between the provinces and the federal government, copied the Elizabethan poor laws, targeting benefits only to the poorest workers who were 70 years of age and over and indigent (making less than $350 per year). The pension, which was administered at the provincial level by Pension Boards, was worth $240 a year, or a maximum of $20 per month, and was subject to a means test. A worker could earn up to $350 a year including the pension amount—well below the average worker's wage of $2,460 per year. First Nations peoples, as defined under the *Indian Act*, were not eligible, nor were immigrants to Canada who were not British subjects. Women were eligible but were treated differently in the administration of the Act as we saw in Chapter 12. By the time the OAP was replaced by the *Old Age Security Act (OAS)* in 1951, less than half the population received benefits (Myles & Teichroew, 1991).

From Social Assistance to Social Security

Following World War II, a universal, flat-rate pension plan was instituted, on the advice of the *Joint Committee of the Senate and House of Commons on Old Age Security* in 1951, as a first step on the road to social security. The advice followed the recommendations of several strong lobby groups, such as the Canadian Congress of Labour and the Canadian Welfare Council, and was buttressed by the rise of Keynesian economics, which promoted government responsibility for economic growth and social security, an attractive policy following the Great Depression. The *Old Age Security Act* of 1951 was financed and administered by the federal government and operated on the principle of social insurance for all older Canadians. All Canadians aged 70 years and over were paid a flat rate of $40 per month and were not subjected to the unpopular means test of the 1927 Act. What is important about the *Old Age Security Act* is that eligibility was based only on age and on citizenship, so women were automatically included, independent of their marital status. At the same time, the *Old Age Assistance Act*, a form of social assistance equally shared with the provinces, was also passed for those aged 65 to 69 years, but was based on a means test. Through the 1960s, the *Old Age Security Act* was restructured to increase pension benefits and the qualifying age of 70 years was reduced by one year every year until it became age 65 years in 1970.

As Myles (1984) has shown, the problem with the flat-benefit structure was that retired workers were equally poor in an otherwise wealthy society (Myles, 1984). The benefit rates were not meant to replace market income, they were to provide a social safety net. The minister of national health and welfare (Paul Martin Sr.) was careful to make the point:

> I am sure that as this new program comes to be integrated into the existing pattern of retirement provisions provided by individuals, by employers, and in other ways, it will be recognized for what it is intended to be—not as a total retirement security scheme in itself, replacing and supplanting all others, but as the core, the keystone of a national savings and retirement plan, around which each individual in the country will be encouraged to build his own retirement security program in a manner and to an extent peculiarly suited to his own needs. (Paul Martin Sr. quoted in Clark, 1960: 239–240)

It was not long before Canada, along with a host of other countries with flat-benefit structures (e.g., the United Kingdom, Sweden), recognized that the benefits were not enough to allow workers to withdraw from the labour force without a drastic drop in their income, a problem that became glaring as inflation eroded the value of the benefits even further in the 1950s. Although the rate was raised in 1963, an automatic upward adjustment tied to the Consumer Price Index was instituted in 1972. Tinkering with the rates was not enough to achieve a sufficient level of income security to enable workers to retire, so a second tier of contributory pensions was added to the flat-benefit program.

The *Canada Pension Plan and the Quebec Pension Plan (C/QPP)* were introduced in 1965 as compulsory, contributory plans with benefits linked to contributions based on a person's earnings. The CPP was the result of considerable finagling between the federal government and the provinces, while Quebec opted to establish its own plan, the QPP. Equal contributions were required from the employee and the employer and were originally set at 3.6 percent of earnings in 1966, meaning the employee and employer each paid 1.8 percent of the contribution. The C/QPP, at the time, replaced approximately 25 percent of the average industrial wage.

The C/QPP is what Myles (1988) refers to as the citizen's wage because it is a hybrid combination of market-based and citizenship entitlements (it was open to all Canadian citizens). Even though market-based inequalities were part of the formula (contributions based on earnings), overall, the benefit formula was redistributive, with higher returns on past contributions to people in lower income groups.

In order to aid those already retired, the Guaranteed Income Supplement (GIS), an income-tested program and, thus, a form of social assistance, was introduced in conjunction with the C/QPP as an amendment to the *Old Age Security Act* in 1966. The GIS was originally an interim measure until the C/QPP matured in 1976, but is still with us today. For married couples, the GIS was calculated on their combined income and was less than double a single person's GIS because of the view that two could live more cheaply than one person. In 1975, an income-tested Spouse's Allowance (SPA), a controversial program that favoured heterosexual marriages, became payable to 60- to 64-year-old spouses of GIS recipients.

These initial pension programs were never meant to completely replace pre-retirement income, since the thinking at the time was that they were a platform upon which Canadians would build their own pension nest eggs. It was anticipated that the first two tiers of the pension system would eventually be complemented by a **third tier**—employer pensions (Registered Pension Plans or RPPs) and through individual savings in Registered Retirement Savings Plans (RRSPs), which were introduced in 1957 as an amendment to the *Income Tax Act*. Although RPPs and RRSPs were seen as part of the third tier of private income, they were actually publicly subsidized through tax concessions on contributions and monies that accumulated within the fund. Looked at another way, the pension system included government-administered pension programs, employer-sponsored pension plans, and pension plans purchased by individuals.

By the beginning of the 1970s, then, the Canadian Pension system was a complex package of public and private programs. The principal components of the three tiers were: (1) the Old Age Security system made up of the Old Age Security pension (OAS), (2) the Guaranteed Income Supplement (GIS), the Spousal Allowance (SPA), and the Canada and Quebec Pension Plans; and (3) private pensions comprising Registered Pension Plans and Registered Retirement Savings Plans.

At the outset, these three tiers of programs firmly established the structural design of the Canadian pension system that has endured over time. The prewar welfare state in Canada was a social assistance welfare state based on the poor law tradition and was designed to provide subsistence to the older worker and his or her family. In contrast, the postwar improvements introduced in the 1960s and 1970s aimed to provide a different welfare state built on social security that provided a modest but secure standard of living for older Canadians.

The culmination of these two major historical developments has resulted in a system that tends to have a dual nature in that it still has remnants of social assistance for the poor (GIS) alongside social insurance (OAS, C/QPP) usually taken advantage of by the more fortunate. Understanding this fault line helps explain some of the continuing debates about pensions that have occupied Canadians for the last 30 years. At some point in most pension debates, the issues ultimately revolve around the degree to which Canadians support social assistance or social insurance models or combinations of both, in their collective vision of the Canadian pension system. As a simple illustration, when *The Globe and Mail*, one of Canada's national newspapers, calls for the gutting of the OAS and C/QPP to be replaced by a universal super-RRSP for Canadians, the argument is for the further privatization of the pension system and the termination of the social insurance model for pensions (*The Globe and Mail*, 1995: D6).

The Great Pension Debate

The **great pension debate** (Townson, 2000; Myles & Street, 1995) during 1976 to 1984 erupted when it became obvious that the third tier of the pension system did not live up to expectations. Anticipated private pension coverage did not materialize, and RRSPs attracted few investors. Private pension plans covered about 39 percent of paid workers in 1965, reached 48 percent in 1980 and dropped back down to 45 percent in 1983 (Statistics Canada, 1996). As late as 1974, about one working woman in four had private coverage, mainly because so many women, then as now, worked in the services sector, where private pensions were the exception to the rule. Seldom was there coverage for self-employed or part-time male or female workers. As well, the C/QPP, which was originally designed to suit a linear, male economic life course of school, work, and retirement (see Chapter 12), did not match the more complicated lives of women. Even though women's participation in the labour force was escalating rapidly, only 53 percent of Canadian women were contributing to the C/QPP in 1976, compared with 94 percent of men (Dulude, 1981). More telling of the system's failure were the poverty rates. The most commonly used "poverty rate" in Canada—although there is no official poverty line in Canada—is the Low Income Cut-Offs (LICOs) developed by Statistics Canada, which essentially identify those who are worse off than the average individual or family. About 68.6 percent of Canadians aged 65 years and older had incomes below the LICOs of Statistics Canada—71.6 percent of unattached women and 68.6 percent of unattached men in 1980. Only 10 percent of female taxpayers were able to contribute to RRSPs in 1982 (Statistics Canada, 2000).

Both women's groups and the Canadian Labour Congress began to agitate for improvements in the system as the shortcomings quickly became obvious. More social insurance, like an expanded C/QPP and homemaker pensions, was the order of the day. However, the groups supporting these changes came up short in the face of a powerful lobby from businesses, which doggedly resisted any reform because they believed it was not good for business. A major review of the Canadian pension system was set into motion, accompanied by a national pension conference in 1981 and a blizzard of reports from numerous groups that swamped the public (e.g., reports from The Task Force on Retirement Income Policy, 1979; the Economic Council of Canada, 1983; Special Committee on Retirement Age Policies, 1979; the famous "green paper" by the federal government, 1982; the Royal Commission on the Status of Pensions in Ontario, 1980; and the Parliamentary Task Force, Canada, 1983). The end result of almost 10 years of debate was the *Pension Benefits Standards Act* in 1985 directed at setting minimum standards for private pension plans. With the arrival of the 1982–1983 recession, talk about pensions dwindled, only to be revived in the early 1990s on the heels of another recession.

In the 1990s, Canadians were subjected, once again, to a round of debates about their pension system that was driven by what Myles and Street (1995) labelled the **politics of the debt**. With a mounting national deficit, a high debt, and soaring rates of unemployment in the early 1990s, Canada concentrated on how to contain the costs of the public pension system, a rather dramatic turnaround from the 1980s debate. Seen in an international context, the "about face" was part of a larger attempt to contain the runaway costs of social insurance programs in many developed countries (OECD, 1998). The greying of Canadians and the anticipated costs of the pension system in the future were seen as the culprits responsible for many of Canada's economic woes, even though this was not borne out by the evidence (Gee, 2000). As a result, there were a number of changes proposed to ensure the viability of the pension system. Many changes were placed on the national agenda. There was fierce opposition from a number of quarters to changes that were made in how the OAS was administered and changes made to certain aspects of the C/QPP, which ultimately reduced the amounts of some benefits under the program. We now turn to a description of the pension system that is with us today.

The Current Canadian Pension System

Government-Administered Programs

The retirement income system is presented in Figure 14.1. Government administered programs include the Old Age Security Pension, the Guaranteed Income Supplement, and two programs that replaced the Spouse's Allowance and the Widowed Spouse's Allowance. Together, these programs constitute what is generally referred to as the **first tier of the pension system**. The Canada and Quebec Pension Plans are also administered by the federal government but are considered to be the **second tier of the pension system** because they are different in that they are based on labour force participation.

Figure 14.1   CANADA'S RETIREMENT INCOME PROGRAMS

Retirement Income Programs

Government | Employer | Individual

OAS/GIS[1] and the Allowance[1] | RPPs[3], Group RRSPs[4] | RRSPs[5]

C/QPP[2]

Provinvial Low Income Supplements

1. Old Age Security/Guaranteed Income Supplement; the Allowance and Allowance for the Survivor
2. Canada/Quebec Pension Plan
3. Registered pension plans
4. Group registered retirement savings plans
5. Registered retirement savings plans

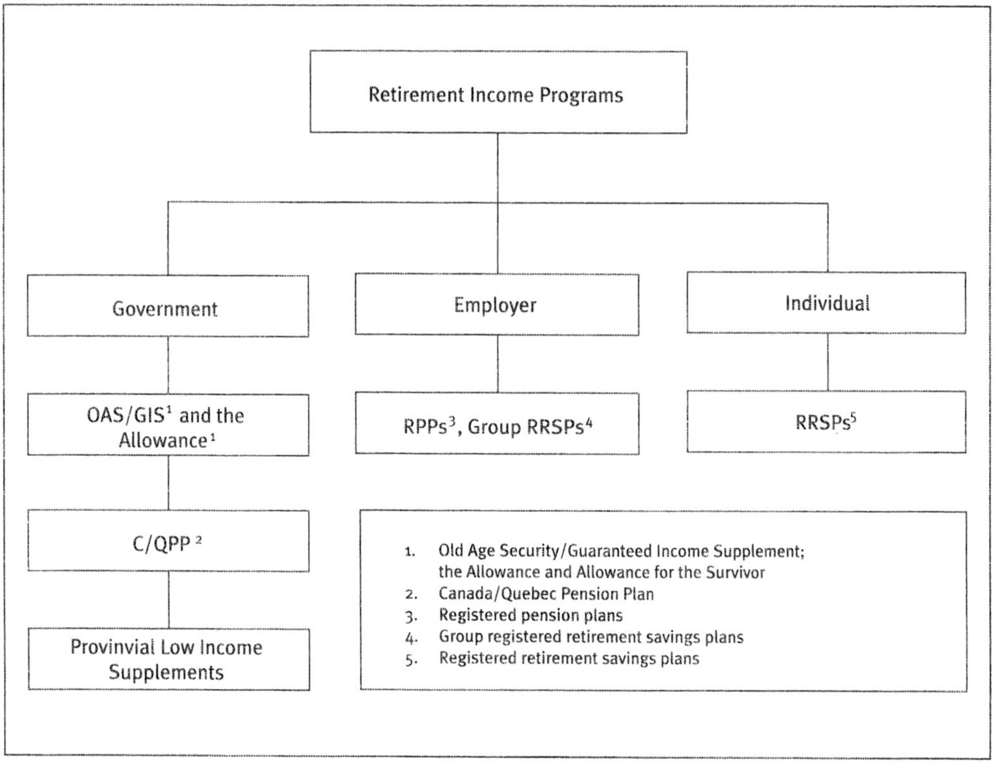

Source: Adapted from Statistics Canada, "Pension Plans in Canada: Statistical Highlights and Key Tables," Catalogue No. 74-401, January 1999, Figure 1.

Old Age Security (OAS)

The OAS is a flat-rate monthly benefit that is fully taxable. The program is financed from general revenues and is administered by Human Resources Development Canada. To be eligible for an OAS pension, a person must be 65 years or older and a Canadian citizen or legal resident of Canada and have resided in Canada for at least 40 years after reaching age 18 years. Partial pensions may be awarded, wherein a person can earn one-fortieth of their pension for each year spent in Canada after age 18 years. The OAS program also includes reciprocal agreements with other countries that allow time spent in another country to count toward the OAS and the Allowance.

The universal aspect of the OAS pension was terminated in 1989. It is currently means tested through a **clawback**. A person's pension is clawed back at a rate of 15 cents on every dollar of OAS benefits for every dollar of income over $55,309 (for 2001). Since July 1996, the government has imposed the clawback before paying the benefit, so the amount of OAS older people actually receive in any year depends upon the income they declared in their tax return the previous year. If a person has an income of $90,070 or above, he or she will not receive a pension.

The OAS rates are adjusted four times a year to reflect any increases in the Consumer Price Index. The average benefit paid in the second quarter in 2001 was $417.46, and the maximum benefit that could be paid was $436.55. At mid-year in 2000, 53 percent of OAS beneficiaries were women, compared with 47 percent of men (Human Resources Development Canada, 2000). In June 2001, 3.8 million OAS pensions were paid to Canadians and the cost to the national treasury for the month of April 2001 was over $2 billion.

The loss of the universal aspect of the OAS is a significant step in the development of Canada's welfare system for two reasons. First, the end of universalism heralds a renewed receptiveness to a social assistance model for the Canadian welfare state, one that targets dollars to those most in need and moves the federal government out of the pension arena. Second, the income level at which the clawback takes effect is not indexed to inflation below 3 percent, which means the cut-off level will decline each year so that, in the long run, most older Canadians will become subject to the clawback. In a "worst case scenario," it is predicted that by the year 2036, the pension legislation will generate a six-fold increase in the incidence of low income in Canada (Murphy & Wolfson, 1991). Whether this will unfold remains to be seen, but what is clear is that the OAS is fast becoming a social assistance program for the poor people and that there is a good chance that the trend will continue (Myles & Street, 1995). Most recently, the Association of Canadian Pension Management (2000) released a report calling for further restrictions on the eligibility for OAS and GIS. One recommendation was to consider assets as part of income when assessing eligibility for OAS. Effectively, this recommendation would mean that poor older persons would have to sell off their assets, like their homes, to qualify for a pension. Essentially, older people would have to spend their way into poverty to secure an OAS pension.

The Guaranteed Income Supplement (GIS)

The Guaranteed Income Supplement, a program that was intended to be phased out with the maturation of the C/QPP in 1976, is a vital component of the pension system. The GIS is a means-tested, nontaxable monthly benefit available to OAS recipients with low incomes. Generally, sponsored immigrants to Canada are not eligible for the GIS during their period of sponsorship, usually 10 years. Eligibility for and the amounts of benefits are determined by total family income in the previous year, which must be lower than a specific level. The rates for the third quarter of 2001 are presented in Table 14.2. A single person must have an income lower than $12,456, not including OAS, to qualify for the GIS, while a retired married/common-law couple would qualify if their income is under $16,244. The

Table 14.2 OLD AGE SECURITY BENEFIT RATES, 2001

Type of Benefit	Average Monthly Benefit April 2001	Maximum Monthly Benefit July–Sept.	Maximum Annual Income	Amount Paid April 2001
	$	$	$	$ M
Old Age Security	417.46	436.55	55,309	1,600.9
Guaranteed Income Supplement				430.9
Single Person	363.93	518.82	12,456	309.2
Spouse/Common-law partner of a nonpensioner	337.36	518.82	30,192	26.5
Spouse/Common-law partner of a pensioner	205.44	337.94	16,224	78.8
Spouse/Common-law partner of an Allowance recipient	258.86	337.94	30,192	16.4
The Allowance				33.3
Regular Allowance	278.77	774.49	23,232	17.6
Allowance for Survivor	484.57	855.05	17,064	15.7

Source: Adapted from Statistics Canada, "Pension Plans in Canada: Statistical Highlights and Key Tables," Catalogue No. 74-401, January 1999.

average monthly benefit is worth $363.93 for a single person, and the maximum benefit is worth $518.82 for a single person. Like the OAS, the GIS is indexed to the Consumer Price Index, which is adjusted four times a year. The GIS benefits are reduced by $1 for every $2 of income for single persons and by $1 for every $4 of combined income for married couples where both partners receive OAS.

Of the 1.32 million GIS beneficiaries in June 2000, 35.2 percent were men, and 64.8 percent were women. About 80 percent of all single recipients of GIS are women, an indication of who is most at risk for poverty in old age and who depends most on the social assistance or welfare component of the pension system.

The performance of the GIS in reducing poverty depends upon how poverty is defined and, as would be expected, there are many definitions, all of which are controversial. The LICOs, developed by Statistics Canada, although not considered an official measure of poverty, are the most widely used indicators in Canada. According to this measure, a single pensioner with the maximum OAS and GIS benefits would have an income in 2001 of $11,462.44, which is below the LICOs for rural areas at $12,142 and $17,571 for cities (1992 base for the year 1998). In June 2001, 13 percent of all single Canadians receiving the GIS received the maximum benefit (HRDC, 2001).

The Allowance and the Survivor's Allowance

The Spouse's Allowance (SPA) was available to Canadians aged 60 to 64 years who were married to a GIS recipient or to 60- to 64-year-old widows and widowers. The SPA program has been replaced with a new program called the Allowance, which took effect in July 2000 and extended the benefits to same-sex couples. The Allowance may be paid to the spouse, or common-law partner, of an old age pensioner or to a survivor. The same age regulations apply, that is, the person must be between the ages of 60 and 64 years and must have lived in Canada for at least 10 years after turning 18 years. To qualify, the combined yearly income of the couple, or the annual income of the survivor cannot exceed certain limits, which are established quarterly: $23,232 for couples and $17,064 for survivors in 2001. The Allowance is discontinued when the person becomes eligible for OAS. The maximum amount paid to a partner of a pensioner is the combined full OAS and the GIS at the married rate. Over the time that the SPA program was offered, Spouse's Allowance recipients were concentrated among women. Close to 90 percent of SPA recipients were women in 2000, a state of affairs that is likely to continue with the Allowance.

The former SPA discriminated on the grounds of marital status in so far as low-income individuals who had never married or who were divorced, separated, or married to a partner not yet 65 years were not entitled to benefits under the program. The SPA was unsuccessfully challenged in the Federal Court of Canada and was deemed a "reasonable limitation" under Section 1 of the Canadian Charter of Rights and Freedoms. The problem is likely to continue with the new

Allowance and may be challenged again in court. The Allowance, like the GIS, is too small to keep people above the LICOs.

The Canada/Quebec Pension Plans (C/QPP)

The Canada/Quebec Plans make up the smaller second tier of programs administered by government, but unlike the first level programs, the C/QPP is a compulsory plan financed by employees, employers, the self-employed and by CPP investments. The Canadian government does not fund the C/QPP. Contributions are paid on a portion of a worker's earnings that falls between specified minimum and maximum amounts of income. The maximum amount of income, equivalent to the average Canadian industrial wage ($38,300 in 2001) is adjusted annually, and the minimum has been frozen at the 1997 level of $3,500. A worker who makes $3,500 or less does not pay into the C/QPP, nor does his or her employer, and no contribution is required on earnings above the maximum amount. The contribution rate for 2001 was 8.6 percent—4.3 percent for the worker and 4.3 percent for the employer or 8.6 percent for the self-employed who pay both portions.

The CPP and QPP cover all workers between the ages of 18 and 70, whether they work full time or part time or are self-employed. The C/QPP allows for a flexible retirement age, since workers can retire and claim benefits at any time between the ages of 60 and 70 years. Those who claim retirement benefits prior to age 65 years receive an actuarially reduced benefit, and those who claim after age 65 years receive an actuarially improved benefit.

The C/QPP replaces approximately 25 percent of a worker's pre-retirement income, averaged over his or her annual lifetime earnings up to the maximum noted above. A worker's earnings and contributions over the years constitute a worker's **pension credits**. There are provisions in the Plan that allow a worker to drop or exclude periods of low or no income from the contributory period in the calculation of the average earnings on which the pension benefit will be based. Up to 15 percent of the months when the person's income was lowest in the contributory period can be excluded and is called the **general drop-out provision**. There is also a **child drop-out provision**, which accommodates child-rearing responsibilities, a feature very important to women. The period when a worker has a child under the age of seven years can be dropped from the calculation of pension benefits.

Besides retirement pensions, both plans also provide disability pensions, benefits to dependent children of deceased C/QPP contributors, children of disability recipients, surviving spouse/partner benefits, and lump-sum death benefits to help cover the costs of funerals. The rates for the main programs are presented in Table 14.3. The maximum rate for a new beneficiary is $775 per month and, as presented in Table 14.4, the C/QPP constitutes about the same proportion of income for men and women (21.1 percent for men, compared with 21.8 percent for women). The amounts, however, are quite dissimilar because the Plan, to a certain degree, reproduces the income differentials generated during the working years. Women received, on average, $307.12 for the month of June 2001 from the C/QPP, which is 57 percent of the $541.14 paid to men for the same month. Even though women's benefits are lower than men's, the proportion of women receiving CPP benefits is higher than in previous generations—about 60 percent of women aged 65 to 69, compared with 30 percent of women over the age of 85 years (Human Resources Development Canada, 2000).

It is important to note that pensions can be equally shared by partners so that each receives his or her own pension cheque, even though one partner may not have contributed. Where both partners have worked, the pension can be divided equally, even though one person may be eligible for a higher pension benefit. C/QPP pension credits can also be equally "split" on divorce or separa-

Table 14.3 THE CANADA PENSION PLAN AND THE QUEBEC PENSION PLAN

TYPE OF BENEFIT	NEW BENEFITS MAXIMUM RATE (2001)	
	$	$
	CPP	QPP
Retirement (age 65)	775.00	775.00
Disability	935.12	935.09
Survivors		
Under 65	428.70	—
Over 65	465.00	465.00
Death (lump sum)	2,500.00	2,500.00
Combined pensions		
Surv./Rtr.	775.00	775.00
Surv/Dis.	935.12	1,227,71

Calculation of CPP Maximum Monthly Rates for New Benefits

Retirement: 25% of 1/12 of the average Yearly Maximum Pension Earned for last five years

Disability: (retirement x 0.75) + flat rate ($353.87)

Survivors: 65 and over: (retirement x 0.60)

Source: Adapted from Statistics Canada, "Pension Plans in Canada: Statistical Highlights and Key Tables," Catalogue No. 74-401, January 1999.

Table 14.4 SOURCES OF INCOME BY GENDER AND FAMILY STATUS, 1997

| | | | | UNATTACHED PERSONS | | |
SOURCE	MEN	WOMEN	TOTAL	MEN	WOMEN	TOTAL
Employment	10.6	3.8	7.6	8.2	1.9	3.9
Investments	10.7	12.7	11.6	8.9	11.8	10.8
RRSPs	4.7	4.5	4.6	3.8	4.6	4.3
Income from Government Transfers						
OAS/GIS	21.2	38.1	28.7	25.2	37.2	33.4
C/QPP	21.1	21.8	21.4	21.3	23.4	22.7
Other	3.7	4.2	3.9	3.6	4.1	4.0
Transfers Total	46.0	64.2	54.1	51.1	65.8	61.2
Government Transfers Occupational	26.5	13.2	20.6	25.3	14.6	18.0
Pensions Other Money	1.5	1.7	1.6	2.7	1.3	1.7
Income Total	100%	100%	100%	100%	100%	100%

Source: Adapted from Statistics Canada, *"A Portrait of Seniors in Canada,"* Catalogue No. 89-519, Table 7.5, p.106 and Table 7.6, p. 107.

tion, even if one partner did not contribute. For these reasons, along with the child drop-out provision and the survivors benefit, the C/QPP has been described as woman "friendly" (Townson, 2000). In fact, the C/QPP has been credited with improving the financial situation of women in old age and has been shown to have reduced their poverty rates, at least through the 1980s (Myles, 2000).

The Canada and Quebec Pension Plans are very similar programs but not identical in that the federal and provincial governments administer the CPP and the Quebec government administers the QPP, which is also financed somewhat differently. The Canada Pension Plan can only be changed with the approval of two-thirds of the provinces, including Quebec. Both programs are coordinated so that credits accumulated are fully portable between the provinces, territories, and Quebec. The C/QPP program also includes reciprocal agreements with other countries that allow time spent in another country to count toward the benefit or permit the beneficiary to receive benefits from either Canada or the country in which the person previously worked. All C/QPP benefits are taxable and all benefits, except the death benefit, are adjusted at the beginning of each year according to the Consumer Price Index. During the fiscal year 1999–2000, more than 3.5 billion Canadians received approximately $18.8 billion in benefits (Human Resources Development Canada, 2001).

Originally, the CPP was a pay-as-you-go plan, which means that contributions made by employers and employees in the current workforce were used to finance the benefits of those who are retired. In a pure pay-as-you-go system, there is generally no fund from which benefits are paid.

In 1998, however, the financing of the CPP changed to become a partial pay-as-you-go system in response to concerns about the demands the future baby boom would place on the pension system. The federal government calls the new financing of the partially funded CPP **steady-state financing**. Under steady-state financing, the contribution rate increases sharply from 5.6 percent in 1996 to 9.9 percent in 2003 and is expected to remain at this steady rate thereafter. This approach will generate funds that exceed the amount that must be paid out to beneficiaries between 2001 and 2020 when the last of the baby boomers will retire. The excess funds will be transferred to a new CPP Investment Board created in 1998, which will invest the money and, over time, create a large enough reserve to ensure the viability of the Plan.

Other significant changes were also made to the CPP in 1998, which have resulted in slightly lower retirement pensions, the freezing of the death benefit at $2,500 down from $3,580 in 1997; the freezing of the $3,500 level at which contributions are exempt, and restricting who receives the combined survivor and disability/retirement benefits. Despite these changes, the C/QPP are sound programs that cover virtually all workers; they follow workers when they change jobs, and they are linked to inflation. Most importantly, they are accommodating to the needs of women.

Provincial and Territorial Supplements

Older persons living in Newfoundland, Ontario, Manitoba, Saskatchewan, Alberta, British Columbia, the Yukon, the Northwest Territories, and Nunavut receive income supplements on top of their federal income security benefits (National Council of Welfare, 1999). The amounts, based on need, vary from area to area and are administered on a variety of schedules. In 1998, a single older person living in the Northwest Territories would receive $1,620, compared with the $996 a person living in Ontario would receive. The benefits are not indexed to keep them current with the cost of living: benefits in the Yukon, British Columbia, and Ontario have not been raised since the 1980s. According to The National Council on Welfare (1999), there are more than 300,000 seniors receiving supplements that are valued at more than $250 million (National Council of Welfare, 1999). The problem with these benefits, according to the National Council of Welfare, is that they ignore the greater financial requirements of single older persons.

Looking at the overall picture for government administered programs, Table 14.4 displays the degree to which Canadians depend upon government transfers in their annual incomes. Government transfers account for 46 percent of older men's income, and 64 percent of women's income. In 1997, 38 percent of all income of women aged 65 years and over came from OAS/GIS, compared with 21 percent for their male counterparts (Lindsay, 1999).

In Table 14.4, unattached older persons, especially women, depend on government transfers even more—about 66 percent of women and 51 percent of men's incomes are from this source. Keeping in mind that no component of the program theoretically raises income over the LICOs, it begins to make sense why Canada was awarded a B grade by the NACA. At best, the system guarantees a very modest income to Canadians and is beginning to tilt toward more of a social welfare system than a social insurance system with the changes to the Old Age Security Pension.

Employer- and Individually Administered Programs

Almost all Canadians require other sources of income if they are to avoid a substantial drop in their income when they leave the labour force. As we indicated above, the employer pension plans and RRSPs are supposed to make up the rest of people's incomes in old age, usually up to approximately 70 percent of their pre-retirement earnings to maintain their standard of living prior to retirement (National Council of Welfare, 1999). This third tier of the pension system does not achieve this goal for most Canadians.

Employer-Sponsored Pension Plans

Employer-sponsored pension plans are also called registered retirement pension plans (RPPs), occupational pension plans, private pension plans, or company pension plans. At the bottom, the plans are a form of deferred wages, which postpone the receipt of some of a worker's current wages to provide income when the worker retires. These plans are provided by employers or by unions in both the public and private sectors of the economy, usually on a voluntary basis. The plans are called registered plans because they are registered with Canada Customs and Revenue Agency for tax purposes and, in many cases, with the federal or a provincial regulatory authority. By 1999, all provinces (except Prince Edward Island) plus the government of Canada had put into operation legislation to protect the rights of workers who belonged to pension plans.

At the beginning of 1998, 5.1 million workers were covered by occupational pension plans (Statistics Canada, 2000). More men than women were members of plans, although the number of female members did increase slightly in the last few years. The increase can be directly attributable to the growing number of women in the workforce and changes in legislation that allowed part-time employees, mainly women, to be covered. The gap between the number of men and women with membership has been closing because of women's increased labour force participation and the decline in men's participation. In 1993, men represented 57.7 percent of plan members, but in 1999, they represented only 55.4 percent of plan members.

Table 14.5 displays the extent of coverage of employer-sponsored pension plans in Canada. Experts use two ways of looking at private pension coverage, the percentage of *paid workers* who are covered by a plan and the percentage of the *labour force* who are covered by a plan. The labour force measure includes the self-employed, the unemployed, and unpaid family workers who do not have an employer–employee relationship. Including this group of people in the measure will reduce the percentage covered by an occupational pension so that knowing what indicator is used is important in appreciating the level of pension coverage.

According to Table 14.5, 40.6 percent of paid workers or 32.9 percent of the labour force enjoyed pension coverage. As Table 14.5 shows quite clearly, the coverage rate for paid workers has steadily declined, a drop from 45.1 percent in 1992 to 40.6 percent in 1998, and the decline has been more pronounced for men than for women.

An analysis of this drop found that a decline in union membership and a move to low coverage jobs adversely affected not all but most workers (Morissette & Drolet, 2000). Pension coverage dropped significantly for men, dropped slightly for young women, but increased for prime-aged women.

Table 14.5 COVERAGE OF EMPLOYER-SPONSORED PENSION PLANS: PERCENTAGE OF LABOUR FORCE AND PAID WORKERS

	1992	1994	1996	1998
Women				
Labour force	34.2	33.6	32.8	32.3
Paid worker	41.6	41.1	40.3	39.1
Men				
Labour force	37.5	35.6	34.3	33.4
Paid worker	48.1	45.3	43.4	41.9
Total				
Labour force	36.0	34.7	33.6	32.9
Paid worker	45.1	43.4	42.0	40.6

Source: Adapted from Statistics Canada, 1999, *"Pension Plans in Canada, Statistical Highlights and Key Tables,"* January 1, 1999, Catalogue No. 74-401-SIB, Table 3, p. 16.

Almost half the occupational pension members worked in the public sector in 1999 (46 percent of plan membership), and most plan members in Canada belonged to large plans with a thousand members or more, which represents only 4 percent of all plans in Canada (Statistics Canada, 2000). Generally, there are two types of plans: noncontributory plans, in which the employer makes all the contributions, and the contributory type, where both employer and employee pay a share. An employee might pay anywhere from 5 to 10 percent of earnings into a plan, which is tax deductible, and the employer's contributions, which are also tax deductible, will be calculated according to some contribution formula guaranteed to keep the plan actuarially sound. About 58 percent of plans were contributory in 1999 (Statistics Canada, 2000).

Within these two types of plans, various methods are used to calculate retirement benefits. The two most common methods are found in defined contribution plans and defined benefit plans. In defined contribution plans, pension benefits vary depending on the contributions accumulated for each individual and the return on the investment of these contributions. In this type of plan, both employers and employees contribute a fixed percentage of a worker's earnings into a fund for investment. In defined benefit plans, benefits are established by a formula specified in the contract with the employer. Defined benefit plans have the advantage of guaranteeing members a fixed percentage of their pre-retirement earnings and/or years of service, which does not occur in defined contribution plans. Even though membership in defined pension plans has dropped since 1993, these plans still covered 85 percent of total members in 1999 (Statistics Canada, 2000). Some observers have argued that there is a growing movement toward providing defined contribution plans that are cheaper to mount and make no guarantees about the amount of a pension (Townson, 2000).

Employer-sponsored pension plans and the C/QPP are now similar on a number of features. Ever since the federal and provincial governments agreed to tighten the standards governing private pensions and to make them consistent in each province in 1986, pension contributions are now locked-in and vested once a worker belongs to an employer's plan for two years. Locking in future benefits means that the benefits cannot be paid until a later date, usually at age 55 years and vesting means that workers have a right to future benefits from contributions that they and their employer have made, even though the worker may go to another job. If a worker goes to another job, his or her benefits are portable in that the worker is able to transfer vested pension benefits to the pension plan of the new employer, to an RRSP, or to an annuity. In addition, some part-time workers are now covered, survival benefits are available, and there is credit splitting upon divorce in some provinces, such as in Manitoba, where a 50–50 split is mandatory.

Employer-sponsored pension plans differ from the C/QPP on two counts—they do not cover everyone, and they are not indexed to inflation. Employees in the private sectors, in small firms and women employees are less likely to be covered by private pension plans. As is evident in Table 14.4, occupational pension plans make up only 13.2 percent of older women's income compared with 26.5 percent of older men's incomes—a dismal showing in both instances. Finally, inflation, which can make a pension worth less over time, is rarely covered by private pensions. For example, inflation protection is only provided in about half the defined benefit plans.

A very serious problem with private pension plans is that they are not a very useful source of retirement income for workers who make lower wages because they replicate the inequality found in the labour market. In 1996, only 10 percent of wage-earners making $20,000 or less belonged to plans. It is women who experience the brunt of this problem, since about 47 percent of women have incomes below $20,000. In addition, the average contribution to an employer-sponsored pension plan rises as income rises, so that persons with lower incomes (usually women) make lower contributions and, as a result, receive lower pensions. For example, a person making $10,000 would make an average contribution of $253, a small sum that will not add up to much in the long run. In contrast, a person making $50,000 would make a contribution of about $3,121 which could be substantial over time (National Council of Welfare, 1999:39).

To add to this disparity is the fact that workers with more income get a better tax break on their pension contributions than do poorer workers. Again, we can see why the National Advisory Council on Aging decided on a B grade for Canada. The occupational pension system does a poor job in covering most Canadians, is not inflation protected, and is not particularly useful to lower-income workers.

Registered Retirement Savings Plans (RRSPs)

While RPPs have been declining, Registered Retirement Savings Plans have been increasing, mainly because RRSPs are available to all workers, and RPPs depend upon whether a worker's employer offers a private plan. Canadians contributed $62 billion to C/QPP, RPPs, and RRSPs in 1998. Of this contribution, 43 percent went to RRSPs, compared with 27 percent for RPPs. Registered Retirement Savings Plans, first introduced in 1957, have become very popular in the last decade. In fact, the single most important financial asset for Canadian families in 1999 was the amounts held in RRSPs, accounting for 12 percent of their total assets, up from 4 percent in 1984 (Statistics Canada, 2001).

RRSPs allow taxpayers to save for their old age through tax breaks given by the government. A person is allowed to make an annual contribution of up to 18 percent of earned income to an RRSP to a maximum limit currently set at $13,500 if they do not have a private pension plan. Members of occupational pension plans have this limit reduced by an adjustment made by Canada Customs and Revenue Agency (CCRA). The worker can then deduct the full amount of the contribution from taxable income for that year. The money in RRSPs is usually invested, and the money made on investments is not taxed until the RRSP is terminated. People can cash in their RRSPs at any time, but at retirement, they usually buy an annuity that provides them with a regularly paid benefit. The annuities are taxable income, but after retirement, people are usually in a lower tax bracket and, as a result, pay lower taxes than they would have if they were still working. If a person does not use all their RRSP "room," that is, contribute their maximum allowable, they can carry over unused RRSP room to the following year, a rule that allows for flexibility for contributors. People may not contribute much in the lean years, but in more prosperous years, they can contribute more.

In 1997, 5.6 million individuals or 38 percent of all tax filers aged 25 to 64 made RRSP contributions, which totalled $22.8 billion. Men's contributions made up 64 percent of the total contributions, although they accounted for 56 percent of the contributors because men have higher incomes than women (Statistics Canada, 1999). There have been, however, greater proportions of women contributing to RRSPs in the last several decades. Twenty-six percent of all *female* taxpayers contributed in 1997, compared with only 10 percent in 1982. This figure, however, is still lower than the comparable figure of 33 percent of male tax-filers making a contribution in the same year. Women who purchased RRSPs in 1997 contributed, on average, about $3,400, about $1,300 less than men who contributed $4,700.

As seen in Table 14.6, the proportion of contributing tax-filers increases with level of income. In 1997, 4 percent of persons with incomes below $10,000 contributed to an RRSP, compared with 79 percent of tax-filers making over $80,000 per year. Contributions also increase with age (as does income), so that in 1999, 46.3 percent of people aged 45 to 54 years contributed to their RRSPs, compared with 37.6 percent of those aged 25 to 34 years (Palameta, 2001). In 1997, only 11 percent of tax-filers used almost all of their room, and as would be expected, the people who used their room had increased levels of income. Furthermore, most people do not regularly contribute every single year to their RRSPs. Only about 15 percent of RRSP contributors made a contribution each year between 1991 and 1997. Those persons who were not likely to contribute to an RRSP during the 1990s had incomes of less than $20,000 and tended to be women.

In 1997, about a quarter of the people who cashed in their RRSPs were 55 to 64 years of age, and the average amount they withdrew was $7,835, suggesting that these were, perhaps, early retirees who were using their RRSPs until their pensions kicked in at ages 60 and 65, or unemployed older workers (Statistics Canada, 1999). As seen in Table 14.4, RRSPs accounted for 4.7 percent of older men's income and 4.65 percent of older women's income in 1997 (Lindsay, 1999).

A rather large number of RRSPs were withdrawn by younger persons who clearly were not about to retire: over half the RRSPs withdrawn in 1997 were by persons under 45 years of age, and they withdrew, on average, $4,488. While the government allows Canadians to withdraw some funds from an RRSP to buy a home or for postsecondary education, provided the money is paid back within a specific period, these reasons covered less than 1 percent of contributors in 1995.

In a 1991 study, researchers found that one in five people who withdrew their RRSPs had no other source of income (Frenken & Standish, 1994). The implications are somewhat troubling, since a substantial number of people who have managed to set aside private savings for old age can use them for any life emergency and may deplete their resources long before retirement.

All things considered, RRSPs, like RPPS, are a strong savings vehicle for people in the higher income echelons, an average vehicle for those in the middle echelons, but not very helpful for Canadians at the bottom of the income ladder (see Table 14.6). Over half of the low-income earners have not contributed to an RRSP or to a registered pension plan. What is more, the people with higher incomes receive more tax assistance than do poorer people. In the progressive tax system of Canada, income taxes become higher as income increases, but the value of a deduction also increases with rising income. As an illustration, the tax deduction for a contribution of $1,000 is worth around $447 in tax savings to people in the highest tax bracket, while the same contribution affords only a $255 tax deduction for a person in the lowest tax bracket.

It is useful to remember that taxes not paid represent a reduction in government revenues. For example, the net loss of income to governments in 2003 as a result of RRSPs is projected to be over $9 billion. In the case of Registered Pension

Table 14.6 CONTRIBUTORS TO RRSPS BY LEVEL OF INCOME FOR ALL TAX-FILERS AGES 25–64 YEARS, 1997

Level of Income	All Tax-Filers	RRSP Contributors	Contributors as a Percentage of all Tax-Filers	Average Savings from RRSPs	No RRSP or PA*
$,000	Number ,000	Number ,000	%	$	%
< 10	3,495	146	4.2	828.37	45.7
10 < 20	2,766	590	21.3	1,410.87	27.6
20 < 30	2,440	986	40.4	1,699.03	14.4
30 < 40	2,092	1,153	55.1	2,288.24	6.8
40 < 60	2,394	1,576	65.8	3,185.00	4.0
60 < 70	893	677	75.9	4,796.45	.8
80+	628	499	79.4	8,188.92	.6
Total	14,709	5,628	38.3	—	100.0

* A PA, or pension adjustment, is an indirect indicator of who contributed to a Registered Pension Plan.
Source: Adapted from Statistics Canada, "Retirement Savings Through RPPs and RRSPs, 1991–1997," Catalogue No. 74F0002, Table 1, p. 23; Table S3, p. 42 and Table S7, p. 47.

Plans, the projected net loss is over $5 billion (Department of Finance, 2001). The cost of pensions, then, is not only limited to benefits paid but also to forgone taxes. When observers call for cutting the costs of the pension system, they often overlook this feature and choose to focus more on cutting the amounts of benefits, which, of course, hurts lower-income people more.

Why a B Grade for Canada?

Improvements in Income

With an overview of the retirement income system, it becomes easier to see how well the pension system protects older Canadians. In terms of income levels and measures of income distribution, the relative economic position of older persons in Canada, as in many industrialized nations, has noticeably improved over the last several decades. The improvement has been so dramatic that the National Council of Welfare has called it "...one of Canada's biggest success stories in social policy during the latter part of the 20th century" (National Council of Welfare, 2000: 79). As recently as 1980, close to 61 percent of unattached older men and 72 percent of older women lived below Canada's LICOs, as reported above. Comparative studies of low-income rates in the 1980s of older persons in six nations placed Canada near the bottom of the list as one of the underperforming countries. The gap between men's and women's incomes was considered to be particularly unacceptable.

Today, depending on the measure of poverty used, 20.8 percent of people 65 years of age and over live below the LICOs after taxes have been deducted. Close to 22.1 percent of unattached women, the lowest number ever, and 17.4 percent of unattached men, lived in poverty as of 1998 (Figure 14.2). Using a slightly different measure, which considers income before taxes have been removed, the equivalent poverty figures are 44.4 percent for all older unattached persons: 35.1 percent for unattached males and 47.9 percent for unattached females (Figure 14.3). These figures are more in line with how the poverty rates were originally used in the 1980s and are a better gauge of the gains in income.

The protection afforded by a family against poverty is extraordinary. As Figures 14.2 and 14.3 illustrate, the proportion of older persons in families below the LICOs is only 3 percent after taxes and 7.8 percent before taxes, and reflects the presence of a male income. Although we do not wish to enter into the debate about the choice of LICOs, the point remains that poverty has been reduced among the aged, but by any measure, too many older unattached persons are still poor. Moreover, Figure 14.4 shows that the incomes of older families have been declining while the incomes of the unattached have remained fairly constant since 1989.

Figure 14.2 PEOPLE AGED 65+ YEARS WITH LOW INCOME AFTER TAX

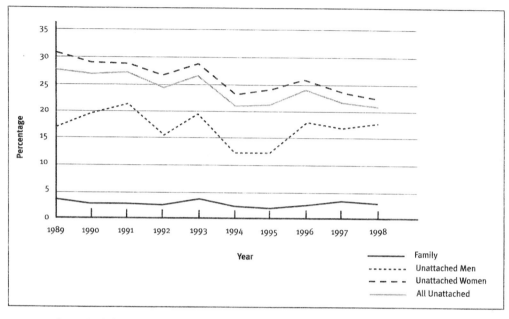

Source: Statistics Canada Website, www.statcan.ca/english/Pgdb/People/Families/famil19a.html (and famil19b.htm).

Figure 14.3 PEOPLE WITH LOW INCOME BEFORE TAX

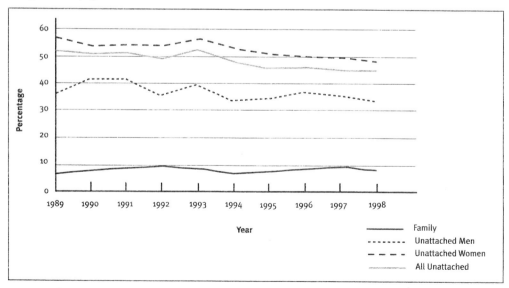

Source: Statistics Canada Website, www.statcan.ca/english/Pgdb/People/Families/famil41a.html (and famil41b.htm).

One of the major reasons for the turnaround in the circumstances of Canada's seniors is due to the maturation of the C/QPP, meaning that it has become fully operational as an increasing source of older people's incomes. The C/QPP was designed to come to maturity very quickly, so that full benefits were in place ten years after its introduction in 1966. As a result, recent cohorts who are more likely to be covered by the C/QPP have displaced older cohorts and, due to the increased labour force participation of women, more women are receiving their own C/QPP benefits. According to one study, the percent of unattached women receiving a C/QPP rose from 44 to 78 percent between 1980 and 1996, while married persons in families receiving one C/QPP benefit rose from 74 to 93 percent over the same period (Myles, 2000).

Unfortunately, the changes that have occurred are part of the planned maturation of the C/QPP and are not likely to continue in the foreseeable future. Changes that will occur are likely to be related to RRSPs and RPPs, which, as we have already seen, favour the wealthy over the poor, and men over women. So, while improvements have been made, the poverty of the seniors in Canada has not been eradicated, contrary to what many people believe. Changes still have to be made to accommodate the poor seniors, who are, mainly, women. The B grade assigned by NACA acknowledges this progress and the need for further improvement.

Figure 14.4 **AVERAGE TOTAL INCOME BY FAMILY TYPE FOR PERSONS AGED 65+ YEARS**

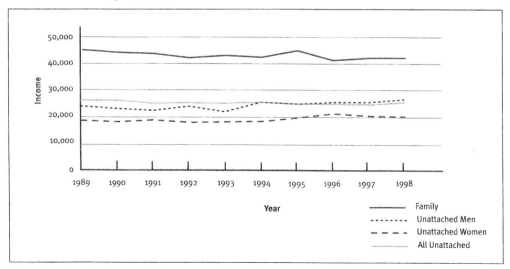

Source: Statistics Canada Website, www.statcan.ca/english/Pgdb/People/Families/familo5a.html (and familo5b.htm).

The Mismatch between the Lives of Canadians and the Pension System

Our review of the three tiers of the Canadian pension system shows where the flaws are and who is most vulnerable to their effects. Women, especially unattached older women, depend on the public pension system for most of their income and are unable to use the private pension system to their advantage. Unattached older men would be the next most vulnerable group at risk for poverty and their circumstances, especially for those in the secondary labour market, are similar to the situation of women. Men at both ends of the age spectrum have been affected by high levels of unemployment in the last decade, moving in and out of the labour force into a series of jobs that are frequently nonstandard in nature. Their wages have been stagnant, and as we saw earlier, they are now less likely to be covered by private pensions. In effect, one could argue that some men's career trajectories are beginning to look more like women's, rather than women's careers emulating those of men (McDonald, 1997). The fundamental problem with the pension system is that it was developed to meet the needs of the 19th century male worker who was a lone breadwinner supporting a family. The pension system today, with its emphasis on job tenure in a life-long career job, excludes many Canadians who do not match this profile. At issue, then, is the idea that pension policy does not match the life course of a substantial number of Canadians. Here, we make the argument as to why it does not match women's lives.

The financial situation of women in their later years is a function of their family and labour force histories. Many of today's older women are poor because they belonged to a cohort where the primary occupation of women was that of housewife and mother. As one widowed woman observed in a study of widows, "...I was born in the days when the men didn't want women to work...so women didn't work..., I mean there was no jobs for them anyway...." Another widow was told, "Mrs. X, I hope you realize that the policy is that when you are in the family way, you must give notice...." In the 1930s and 1940s, most women had to depend upon their spouses for support in old age, and if they worked, their job was "just a job" to bring home extra money (McDonald, et al, 1997: 38, 40). Most women did not have surviving spouse benefits if their husband died and had to rely on the public pension system, which, as we saw above, does not provide enough income to move a person over the LICOs. Indeed, in this particular study, 49 percent of the widows, who previously worked, lived below the LICOs in 1991.

Today, many economic analysts argue that the next generation of women, namely, the baby boomers, will have been in paid employment for most of their lives and will have their own private pensions and RRSPs, and most will receive C/QPP benefits. While all this may be true, there are at least two overriding factors that suggest that their pension incomes will still not be equal to men's pension incomes in old age. To the degree that the private and semiprivate (C/QPP) components of the pension system replicate the inequality in the labour market and as long as women have interrupted work histories due to family responsibilities, their ability to save and accumulate pension benefits will be affected.

Some of the more obvious patterns of women's labour force participation that will affect their pensions in the future are: women's concentration in non-standard and part-time work, their under-representation in unions, their over-representation in the services sector, and the continued distribution of their occupations in female employment. The number of women working in non-standard jobs, including temporary workers, part-time workers, self-employed workers, and multiple job holders, has increased from 35 percent in 1989 to 41 percent in 1999. Part-time employment continues to be the most common form of nonstandard work for women. Since the middle of the 1970s, 7 in 10 women have worked part time, even though a quarter of these women reported that they would prefer full-time work. In 1995, 43 percent of part-time workers earned less than $7.50 per hour, and less than 20 percent of part-time jobs were covered by an RPP. Close to 15 percent of part-time jobs fell below the basic exemption of $3,500 in the C/QPP.

Only 31 percent of women are covered by unions, a factor that has been directly linked to increased pension coverage, as reported above. In terms of the distribution of women's occupations, 70 percent of employed women in 1999 continued to work in teaching, nursing and related health occupations, clerical or other administrative jobs, and sales and services occupations, down from 78 percent in 1982. It is well known that female occupations traditionally attract lower wages. Women still earn 73 cents for every dollar earned by men. The female-to-male earnings ratio for full-time full-year workers was 72.5 in 1997 and shows signs of dropping, since the ratio was 73.4 in 1996 and 73.1 in 1995. When all is said and done, it comes as no surprise that the average income of women in 1997 was $19,874, compared with $30,169 for men (Statistics Canada, 2000).

Tomorrow's older women may have their own pensions, but their position will be only marginally improved because RPPs, the C/QPP, RRSPs, and savings all depend on earnings and length of time in the labour market. Unless these conditions are modified, a change in the size of women's benefits will be small. To add to women's problems, they outlive men, so their private pensions are more likely to be subject to inflation in the long run.

Family responsibilities are linked to women's work histories and have a significant impact in altering their work patterns and, therefore, their incomes in old age. Almost two-thirds of women who have ever worked, have had a work interruption in paid work of six months or more. Most women on maternity leave (86 percent) return to work within one year after giving birth, however, one study has shown that after a work interruption, women are not as likely to return to the same job or a full-time job if they had a full-time job prior to their interruption (Fast & Da Pont, 1997).

Another study found that if a labour force adjustment must be made to accommodate family responsibilities, it is usually women who make the adjustment (Townson, 2000). Of the men and women with family responsibilities who made adjustments in 1995, two-thirds of women adjusted their work schedules, compared with about one-third of men. The adjustments included part-time work, irregular schedules, voluntary job absences, and voluntary joblessness. In the face of a growing demand for the care of aging parents and relatives, women are also more likely to provide care: 15 percent of women, compared with 9 percent of men, cared for both children and an aging relative in 1996. The data from one study suggests that employed women provide elder care by carrying out some of their paid work at home and by working in their off hours (Marshall, 1998). While more research needs to be done to establish the exact effect of family responsibilities on women's work, and ultimately their financial security in old age, there is enough evidence now to suggest that their futures might not be as rosy as predicted.

The current pension system does not mirror the complexity of women's lives, or the lives of some men, lives that are characterized by multiple transitions in and out of the labour force with employment in more than one job, which is usually a contingent, nonstandard job. Pension policy barely recognizes the burden of institutionalized lower earnings for women or the costs of their unpaid work and ignores the multiple job changes that both men and women have experienced in the last 10 years. At its best, the pension system offers social welfare to the poor in the guise of OAS and GIS, which, in the final analysis, does little to relieve their poverty. While the C/QPP has great potential to accommodate people's lives, the size of benefits are small and have become even smaller with the adjustments made in 1998. Any improvements that are made to public or private pensions would have to start with a new vision of the life course in order to reflect the actual lives of Canadians, if it was to prevent poverty successfully.

Looking to the Future

Currently, most of the pension changes on the immediate horizon focus on tinkering with the pension system in order to save money by looking to the markets for solutions. The three main strategies that have been considered in Canada include: (1) raising the age of retirement as has been done in the United States, Germany, and Italy; (2) the introduction of partial retirement through the use of flex time, job-sharing, and part-time work as in Germany; and (3) the shift of pension costs from the government sector to the private sector, as in the United Kingdom. The last solution has been the solution of choice for Canada.

The pension debate in the 1990s, which resulted in cost-saving changes to the Canadian pension system—such as adjustments to increase contribution rates to the C/QPP, reductions in the size of C/QPP retirement and disability benefits, the move to a market solution to bolster the CPP, and the improvements to RRSP regulations—were, at the core, cost-cutting measures and nothing more. It is significant that nothing was done to curtail tax expenditures, the "silent" side of pension costs. Rather than expand benefits to the poor or find ways to improve private pension coverage, the system was more committed to contraction, a stand that does not bode well for Canada's poor seniors and that threatens any progress we have already made.

Today's pension policy does lean precariously closer to a social assistance model of income security, but has not gone all the way down the road to social welfare. The demise of the Seniors Benefit in 1998, intended to target only the poor and to save $8.2 billion in 2030, would support this view. Whether the emphasis is on reducing the role of the state in the provision of pensions and the downloading of costs to the private sector remains to be seen. Pension policy is a complicated matter influenced by changing economic conditions (such as a skittish stock market), the trends in people's behaviour (such as investing in RRSPs), lobbying by interest groups (such as corporations), and the political will of the Canadian people.

CHAPTER SUMMARY

This chapter has provided an overview of the history of the development of the pension system and how the system has changed and operates today. Some of the highlights of this chapter are:

- The prewar welfare state in Canada was a social assistance welfare state based on the poor law tradition and was designed to provide subsistence to the older worker and his or her family. In contrast, the postwar improvements introduced in the 1960s and 1970s aimed to provide a different welfare state built on social security that provided a modest but secure standard of living for older Canadians.

- The first private pension plans in Canada, which appeared before state pensions, were a result of a new set of management tools designed to encourage the loyalty of the workers to the company. When they were first offered they were considered a gift that could be revoked by the company at any time for any untoward behaviour on the part of the worker.

- Canada's first national pension legislation, the *Old Age Pension Act* (OAP), which established a cost-shared program between the provinces and the federal government, copied the Elizabethan poor laws, targeting benefits only to the poorest workers who were 70 years of age and over and indigent.

- The *Old Age Security Act* of 1951 operated on the principle of social insurance for all older Canadians and was financed and administered by the federal government. All Canadians aged 70 years and over were paid a flat rate of $40 per month.

- The Canada Pension Plan and the Quebec Pension Plan (C/QPP) were introduced in 1965 as compulsory contributory plans, with benefits linked to contributions based on a person's earnings. The pension has often been called the "citizens' wage" or "retirement wage" because it is a hybrid combination of market-based and citizenship entitlements.

- In order to aid those already retired, the Guaranteed Income Supplement (GIS), an income-tested program and, therefore, a form of social assistance, was introduced in conjunction with the C/QPP. The GIS was supposed to have been phased out but is still needed today.
- The principal tiers of the pension system today include: the first tier, comprising the Old Age Security pension (OAS), the Guaranteed Income Supplement (GIS), and the Allowance; the second tier, made up of the Canada and Quebec Pension Plans; and the third tier, comprising private pensions, including Registered Pension Plans and Registered Retirement Savings Plans.
- The universal aspect of the OAS pension was terminated in 1989 and is currently means tested through a "clawback." A person's pension is clawed back at a rate of 15 cents on every dollar of OAS benefits for every dollar of income over $55,309 (for 2001).
- The great pension debate of the early 1980s was about how the system could be expanded to provide a more adequate income for Canadians. The economic security of older women was one of the prime issues of concern. The "nondebate" about the pension system in the 1990s was about how to reduce the costs of the very same system in order to reduce the national debt and deficits.
- The Seniors Benefit, an income-tested plan, was proposed in 1995. The Benefit would have replaced the OAS and GIS and two tax credits directed to older people. The Benefit was dropped in 1998, given the strong opposition. Changes were made to the CPP instead, which essentially reduced benefits and increased contribution rates.
- The problems with private pension plans are that they are not indexed to inflation and they do not cover enough workers, while RRSPs are more useful for the wealthy than they are for the poor.
- Even though the economic security of older Canadians has improved since 1980 because of the maturation of the C/QPP, there still are too many Canadians who depend on the system for most of their income and who live in poverty.
- About 20.8 percent of people 65 years of age and over live below the low income cut-offs after taxes have been deducted. Older persons who do not live in a family are at the highest risk for poverty. About 22.1 percent of unattached women and 17.4 percent of unattached men have been living in poverty as of 1998.

KEY TERMS

Citizen's wage, **(p. 376)**

Retirement wage, **(p. 376)**

Social assistance, **(p. 376)**

Social insurance, **(p. 376)**

Corporate welfare, **(p. 377)**

Third tier, **(p. 380)**

Great pension debate, **(p. 381)**

Politics of the debt, **(p. 382)**

First tier of the pension system, **(p. 383)**

Second tier of the pension system, **(p. 383)**

Clawback, **(p. 384)**

Pension credits, **(p. 387)**

General drop-out provision, **(p. 387)**

Child drop-out provision, **(p. 387)**

Steady-state financing, **(p. 390)**

Study Questions

1. Do you agree with the National Advisory Council on Aging that the economic security of older Canadians is good but could use some improvement? If improvements are to be made to the public pension system, what changes would benefit you when you retire?

2. What are the differences between social insurance and social assistance, and how are they reflected in our national pension system? When you retire, do you think the system will lean more toward social insurance or social assistance?

3. What plans are you making now that will eventually influence your economic security in old age? Do you think the public pension system will be there to support you in your old age? Why, or why not? Will RRPs and RRSPs take on more importance in the future?

4. How do gender and marital status affect the size of private and public pensions? Do these factors have any influence on who lives above or below the Low Income Cut-Offs for Statistics Canada?

Suggested Readings

Denton, F.T., Fretz, D.,& Spencer, B. (2000). (Eds.) *Independence and economic security in old age.* Vancouver, British Columbia: University of British Columbia Press.

Ginn, J. Street, D., & Arber, S. (2001). (Eds.) *Women, work and pensions.: International issues and prospects.* Philadelphia, PA: Open University Press.

Myles, J. (2000). *The maturation of Canada's retirement income system: Income levels, income inequality and low-income among the elderly.* (Catalogue No. 11F0019MPE No. 147). Ottawa, Ontario: Statistics Canada and Florida State University.

O'Rand, A.M., & Henretta, J.C. (1999). *Age and inequality: Diverse pathways through life.* Boulder, CO: Westview Press, A member of the Perseus Books Group.

Health Care System and Policy

In this chapter, you will learn about:

- Jurisdictional issues, established with the formation of the country, that have impacted the evolution of the health care system, the historic development of Medicare, and the description of the health care system as it exists today.
- Health reform of the 1990s; what led to such questioning of the established health care system; the implications for Medicare of the challenges that have arisen; and the vision of a new health care system that promised to be more appropriate and more effective than the existing system.
- The actions of health reform, that is, what has been taking place since the mid-1990s to reform the health care system. This includes changes directed at medical schools, hospitals, physicians, and home care, as well as such concepts as regionalization and integration of services.

- An assessment of health reform as it exists at the beginning of the millennium, including a discussion of vested interests in the established system and of broader societal forces (such as

capitalism) and their effects on attempts at change.
- What the future holds if we continue with health reform as it appears at the present time.

Introduction

The health care system is of particular concern when studying an aging population because, as has become evident in earlier chapters, our physical health tends to decline as we age. To recap, these declines occur gradually over time, beginning long before official retirement. They tend to include chronic conditions, rather than acute conditions or infectious disease. Mental health, however, does not necessarily deteriorate as we age, although the prevalence of certain mental illnesses, such as dementia, does increase with aging. The health care services offered by society are important when we have difficulties with our health and are, therefore, important for an aging society. In examining the Canadian health care system, we are interested in knowing whether or not the services it provides are the most appropriate for the illnesses and disabilities suffered as we age and whether or not these services are effective in the treatment they provide. We can also ask: Is the major focus of the health care system on "health," that is, is there an emphasis on promoting the nation's health and preventing illness and disability? Is the system effective in these efforts?

In light of the health needs of an aging society that have emerged in the preceding chapters, this chapter examines the health care system that is in place to assist with promoting our health and coping with our illnesses and disabilities as we age. In order to do so, it examines the history of where we have come from and offers an assessment of where we are at this time. What the future holds cannot be fully known, given the constantly intersecting factors that continue to evolve. Nevertheless, some directions are clear; if Canada remains on the path of reform that it is currently on, some of the consequences are predictable.

Historical Roots of Canadian Health Care Policy

The health care system in Canada has been shaped beginning from Confederation in 1867. The *British North America (BNA) Act* made no mention of welfare measures. The government's contribution to this arena was restricted to poor relief administered at the local level. If an individual was needy, he or she relied primarily on religious organizations or private charities. Neither the federal government nor the provincial governments at that time were concerned with either income security or social service programs. The working assumption of the day was that persons were responsible for providing for the contingencies of life for themselves and their families; this included health care. Such **family-based welfare** is known as **residual welfare**.

The BNA assigned responsibility for quarantine centres and marine hospitals, together with special groups, such as the Armed Forces and Veterans, to the federal government. The provinces were responsible for other hospitals, asylums, charities, and charitable institutions. Importantly, any jurisdiction not specifically assigned to the federal government was necessarily to fall within the provincial domain, if it arose later. Because health and welfare were not specifically mentioned, they were provincial jurisdictions when they arose later (Bryden, 1974). This is why Canada, to this day, has a split federal–provincial responsibility for health care. Health care falls within the provincial jurisdiction, but the federal government, as will become clear below, plays a significant role through funding.

It is important to recognize that community care, that is, care in the community, was present within Canadian society long before the health care system was created. It existed largely on a volunteer basis. For example, the Grey Nuns, formed in 1838, visit the sick in their homes. The Victorian Order of Nurses was established in 1898 to provide nursing services in the home. Most provinces adopted workers' compensation laws between 1851 and 1928. Throughout this time, local government was involved in providing health care services, including, for example, medical services, hospital outpatient departments for the indigent (extremely poor) and near indigent, and public clinics for treating tuberculosis and sexually transmitted diseases. There were health insurance plans at this time, but there were not many, and they were operated by many industries. Public health was also being implemented: the collection of vital statistics; sanitary inspection; supervision of water, milk, and food; and the disposal of sewage and garbage (Government of Canada, 1970). What used to be referred to as **public health** is now often referred to as **preventive medicine**.

It was also during the latter part of the 1800s and the early 1900s that the public acceptance of medicine evolved. Louis Pasteur discovered that each disease has its origin in a particular microorganism, and Lister advanced techniques for sterilizing operating procedures in the late 1800s. The stethoscope, clinical thermometer, and hypodermic syringe were invented, as was the vaccine for smallpox. From 1900 to 1920, medical licensing laws were passed, medical schools were standardized, restrictions on entry into the medical field were enforced, and the income and status of the medical profession increased. It was a period, however, when private enterprise dominated the health care field, that is, doctors, dentists, and nurses sold their services privately. Similarly, drugs and medications were sold on the open market, and a physician prescription was not required in order to obtain them (Brown, 1979; Chappell, 1983).

The federal government entered the area of social welfare in a significant way well into the 1900s. The first old age pensions (started at age 70 years), for example, were instituted in 1927 (see Chapter 14). Later, after the Depression, which exposed the inadequacy of many private schemes for health care, the federal government entered into health care in a serious way. After a series of commissions, task forces, and reports, the Canadian government accepted the argument that the risks of illness were relatively easy to establish, relatively constant, and not subject to cyclical fluctuations or sudden emergencies and that the universal risks of sickness and invalidity in old age should be underwritten by the community as a whole. Thus, arguments for **equity in health care** for all Canadians were accepted, that is, the principle that no one should be disadvantaged in the receiving of health care because they could not afford it. Public insurance spreads the economic burden of care more equitably than does private insurance and lowers barriers to "needed" care. It provides a "just" system, to the extent that those who have more money are not more likely to receive better or more service and to the extent that most communities have services available and accessible to them (this has not always been the case in the remote rural areas of Canada).

Hospitals and Physicians

In the 1950s, during the economic upturn after the Depression, a research and training program and assistance for hospital construction were established. Hospitals throughout the country emerged as locations where complex medical procedures were performed. They quickly became a central focus of health care, which was a major departure from previous health care, which had been provided in the home. Hospitals were transformed and were no longer places where the poor went to die but now were the homes of skilled medical specialists, who utilized complex technologies in their trade (Coburn, et al., 1983). With the establishment of hospitals, the development of hospital insurance was inevitable, given the high costs of this care. In 1957, the *Hospital Insurance and Diagnostic Services Act* ensured hospital care, including outpatient clinics and medical and nursing schools, for the entire population. When this program was launched, the federal government agreed to share all costs of running acute care hospitals (excluding tuberculosis hospitals, sanitoria (institutions for the mentally ill), and care institutions (such as nursing homes and homes for the aged), which, to this day, are not included in Medicare). Only if the place of work was a hospital were nonmedical personnel covered, provided they were under the supervision of a physician. Hospitals, thereby, became the place for medical care.

At this time, medical care provided outside the hospitals was not covered. As the number of hospitals throughout the country grew and physicians became more hospital minded, accustomed to expensive therapies, and increasingly specialized, dollars flowed readily from the public purse. Physicians also became used to working with a cadre of paramedical workers to assist in their work, transforming them from independent entrepreneurs to participants in a major complex medical and industrial institution. In 1966, the *Medical Care Act* was passed, implemented in 1968, providing national insurance for physician services. Thus arose Canada's Medicare system of universal physician and acute hospital care. It ensured the growth of these fields because citizens paid for these services anyway and, on each visit, perceived them as "free." They had to pay for other health practitioners whose services they sought, either through additional insurance or out of their own pockets at the time of the visit.

All provinces and territories had become partners in the federal government's cost-shared medical insurance program by 1972. The federal government paid one-half of the funding, while the provinces paid the other half and delivered the programs. For their programs to be eligible, they had to meet certain criteria as set out by the federal government: universal coverage, reasonable access to services, portability of benefits, comprehensive services, and nonprofit administration by a public agency. These criteria are still in effect today. In 1977, the contractual agreements between the provincial and federal governments changed. The federal government felt it had no control over costs that were continually escalating, and the provincial governments were complaining of federal interference in an area of provincial jurisdiction. After much negotiation, new terms emerged in 1977. A system of cash grants was agreed upon, whereby the federal government would use a formula (spelled out in the *Established Programs Financing Act*) based on population size, gross national product, and the transfer of specific taxing powers to the provinces in order to contribute to the financing of Medicare. At the same time, through the Extended Health Care Services legislation, the federal government provided dollars for long-term care. This was the first time this had occurred and resulted in the development of provincial long-term care facilities (nursing homes) and home care/support programs.

By separating funds from specific health expenditures, the strategy limited the rate of growth of federal costs. It also gave greater control over health expenditures to the provinces, since the federal government removed the dictate that the money had to be used for physicians and acute care hospital services. Removing these strictures, however, did not assist the provinces because of the large medical hospital complex already in place. Rather, the result for the provinces was increased demand on provincial coffers. Some provinces implemented **extra billing** by physicians (additional charges to patients, over and above the payment schedule) and hospital user fees to raise more monies to cover costs. This resulted in concerns that reasonable access, as required under the terms of the agreement, was threatened. In 1984, the *Canada Health Act (CHA)* was passed by the federal government, allowing a reduction in the financial contributions from the federal to the provincial governments equal to the amount of extra billing and user charges implemented in the province. The CHA effectively ended these practices.

But the economic recession continued into the 1980s, and the federal government sought means to halt the continual rise in health expenditures. In 1986, the block funding legislation was amended to further reduce the rate of growth of federal contributions, with more reductions announced in subsequent years. The plan was to decrease steadily federal contributions to the provinces until they became nil—with timelines varying from province to province. In return, the provinces' taxing powers were to be increased. This action removed any power the federal government had for enforcing the five criteria of Medicare noted above; it no longer had any clout. If the provinces wanted to implement user fees, the federal government could no longer withhold any funds. Simultaneously, the federal government also lost its ability to ensure comparable services from province to province and left open a greater possibility for differing quality in health care in economically depressed areas, compared with other provinces (Segall & Chappell, 2000).

As the provinces struggled with their ever-increasing health care costs, media stories about declining quality in health care and private sector pressures arguing that public health care does not work were rampant. National polls demonstrated that Canadians overwhelmingly supported their universal Medicare and even saw it as a defining characteristic of the Canadian identity. In February 1999, the federal government re-entered funding with budget transfers to the provinces for health care once again. It came at a time of economic surplus when the federal debt had been paid off and has continued in subsequent budgets. In 2001, the federal government gave large transfers to the provinces, with few strings attached other than that the money had to be spent on health care (McDaniel & Chappell, 1999).

In summary, Canada's health care system evolved only in the mid-1900s after a severe economic depression and in times of economic prosperity. It was a reflection of societal beliefs in the credibility and hope represented by medicine for the health of the nation. The government embraced hospital care unquestion-ingly as the most appropriate care to ensure healthy individuals. Canada also embraced an equitable system, in which all citizens would receive health care on the basis of need, irrespective of ability to pay. While establishing a publicly funded and equitable insurance system, nevertheless, Canada did not choose to establish socialist medicine. Physicians are, by and large, paid on a fee-for-service basis for each service delivered. That is, physicians operate as private entrepreneurs with their incomes guaranteed. Citizens also have the right to choose the physician of their liking.

With no limits on the amount of money they could earn and no limits on the utilization of hospitals, in retrospect, the unprecedented growth of physician services and hospital treatment is not surprising. High-tech hospitals with expen-sive support staff became the place of physician care; there was no process put in place to assess whether or not this health care system was leading to appropriate and effective health care for the recipients of service, the patients. Health econo-mist Evans (1976) clearly demonstrated the dominance of physicians in this health care system a decade after universal physician insurance was implemented. He esti-mated physicians controlled approximately 80 percent of health care costs, even though only 19 percent of total health care expenditures were going directly to physicians. They largely controlled hospital utilization (accounting for about half of all health care costs, prescribing of drugs, ordering of laboratory tests, and, after the initial visit to the system, recommending return visits of patients). Physicians are the gatekeepers to the utilization of Medicare; they have expert knowledge not shared by patients and make decisions on the patients' behalf. The system is, to a large extent, **provider driven**, not user or patient driven.

The 1990s and Discontent

By the late 1980s, Canada's health care system had grown and matured. Canada, like virtually all other industrialized countries (the United States being the main exception), had universal Medicare for physician and hospital services. Each province had its own unique configuration of other services, including a variety of home care services (home nursing, home personal care, home physiotherapy, and so on) and other services (adult daycare, mental health teams, nursing homes, and so on), but there was no consistency in these programs, among provinces or jurisdictions, in terms of the services offered, referral mechanisms, or user fees charged.

Nevertheless, research demonstrated that in Canada, utilization of Medicare services was determined largely by the individual's need (ill health), rather than by nonmedical factors, such as financial status. Lower-income groups, seniors, and women receive more services because they have worse health than higher income groups, younger adults, or men. McDonald et al. (1973), Enterline et al. (1973), and Siemiatycki et al. (1980) for Montreal, Manga (1978) for Ontario, and Broyles et al. (1983) for Canada all demonstrated that the best predictors of the utilization of Medicare services are health needs and that economic factors do not adversely affect the use of these services. Furthermore, and importantly, this was different from the situation prior to the introduction of universal Medicare, when economic ability was related to whether or not one received these services. Similar findings had also been demonstrated in the United Kingdom (Rein, 1969a; b; Stewart & Enterline, 1961).

In addition, many studies applied the popular Andersen and Newman model (1973) for examining utilization of physician and hospital services. These authors argued that one could understand the utilization of health services in terms of social determinants, such as technology and social norms, the health services system, including resources and organizations, and individual determinants. Most research has focused on the individual determinants of the model, assessing the influence of three types of factors: (1) the predisposition of the individual to use the services, (2) the ability to secure services, and (3) the need for services. **Predisposing factors** exist prior to the onset of specific illness episodes such that individuals with these characteristics have a greater propensity to use services. They include demographic, social structural, and attitudinal–belief variables, such as age, gender, education, occupation, and a strong belief in the effectiveness of medical treatment. **Enabling conditions** allow the individual to use the service

Figure 15.1 DETERMINANTS OF SERVICE USE

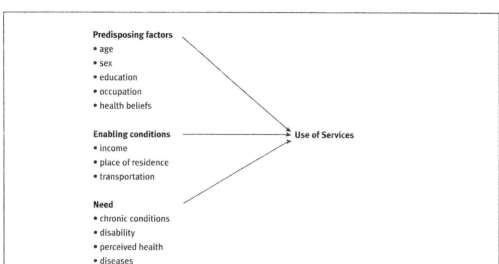

and include such factors as income or region of the country where one lives. **Need** refers to ill health, including chronic health conditions, physical disability, perceived ill health, and diseases (Figure 15.1). Need is the most frequent cause or predictor of service utilization.

Although the Andersen–Newman model has been criticized because it fails to tap the underlying decision-making processes that lead an individual to the doctor's office (finding and interpreting symptoms, seeking the advice of others, coming to a decision to use or not use services) and because it fails to take into account the broader structural context within which physician services operate, nevertheless, the extensive research using this model does support the notion that, where universal Medicare exists, need is the driving factor behind its use. Those in need are the ones who use the services.

The Discontent

However, Medicare was increasingly coming under attack. Both the provincial and federal governments were struggling with the constant spiraling costs of health care and were desperate to find ways, if not to prevent, at least to decrease the nonstop escalation. In addition, new research was questioning the long held belief that the decline in mortality since the turn of the century was due to medical treatment. Medical intervention is, even to this day, usually cited as the major reason for this decline. McKeown et al. (1975) show that the rise in medical care expenditures and, therefore, widespread medical intervention, began after almost all (92 percent) of the modern decline in mortality in this century had already occurred, except for the eradication of smallpox, which accounted for about 5 percent of the reduction. Rather, it would appear that public health measures, including rising standards of living (such as improved diet, improved hygiene, and increased natural immunity to some microorganisms), were the reason for the decline in mortality. McKeown and associates (1975) suggest nutrition was the major influence.

McKinlay (1977) identified medical interventions believed to account for the decline in 10 diseases (tuberculosis, scarlet fever, influenza, pneumonia, diphtheria, whooping cough, measles, smallpox, typhoid, and poliomyelitis) and the dates when the treatments for these diseases became available on a widespread basis and then related both these to mortality data, including cause of death. Only in the case of five of the 10 diseases was there a noticeable decline after the introduction of the medical intervention (influenza, pneumonia, diphtheria, whooping cough, and poliomyelitis); for the others, the medical intervention was introduced several decades after the major decline had already occurred. Furthermore, they noted that if all of the subsequent decline is attributed to medical treatment, at most, only 3.5 percent of the total decline could be contributed to medicine. In addition, Badgely (1991) reviewed Canadian research since the introduction of Medicare and concluded that there was little significant improvement, if any, in the disparities in longevity and the prevalence of illness between the rich and the poor.

Research was also revealing that medicine was not as scientific as the public often believes. From their research, Roos and Roos (1994) concluded that:

- Patterns of medical practice differ substantially from one physician to another.
- A significant amount of care is inappropriate, and the rate of inappropriate care is often as high in areas with low rates of the particular intervention as it is in areas with high rates.
- There is a lack of evidence of clear benefit from certain procedures (such as cesarean section), which suggests that some existing rates of intervention are too high.
- Clinical uncertainty explains some practice variation; that is, decisions or choices are not always grounded in evidence.
- Informed patients tend to prefer conservative treatment when there are risks involved.
- Both expert panels and cost effectiveness studies tend to overestimate the benefits of treatment.
- Applying practice guidelines does not guarantee low surgical rates.

Unexplained variation in surgical rates demonstrates the discretionary nature of medicine. Shapiro (1991) records variations in surgical rates among different areas of the province of Manitoba, citing differences of opinion among physicians in selecting patients for elective surgery, underestimation of risk, and possible overestimation of benefits associated with some procedures. Differences in hospital admission rates among geographical areas were due, in large measure, to the adoption of new procedures before the risks and benefits were fairly studied, physician practice style, and the way physicians deal with medical uncertainty. Lomas (1990) notes that international research demonstrates that between 15 percent and 30 percent of medical procedures are inappropriate.

Fee-for-service payment of physicians was exposed to be less than optimal. The evidence of inappropriate hospital utilization, especially under fee-for-service remuneration, are numerous. Controlled studies have found (Loyd, et al., 1991):

- Twenty-five percent to 45 percent lowering of hospital admissions and hospital days per 1,000 population achieved by health maintenance organizations (HMOs) relative to conventional fee-for-service.
- Twenty-five percent of hospital admissions to be inappropriate, on the basis of chart review.
- Large regional differences in controlled hospital admission rates, patient days per 1,000 and lengths of stay.
- Up to 33 percent disagreement from second opinion consultants regarding the necessity of elective surgical procedures.
- Large differences in surgery rates between HMOs and fee-for-service practice.
- Large geographical differences in surgery rates.
- Large vicissitudes in surgical rates through time unrelated to changing technology.
- Large changes in practice patterns affected by the Prospective Payment System in the United States.

(See Box 15.1 for findings about the use of medical technology).

Box 15.1 An Assessment of Medical Technology in Canada (Guyatt, et al., 1986)

- Technologies are too often accepted for use without evaluation.
- When evaluations are done, technologies are often put into use before they are complete.
- Technologies that have been evaluated and accepted for use are often used for conditions that were not covered by the evaluations.
- Technologies that have been evaluated, accepted, and used for their intended purposes are often utilized too much.
- Even for technologies that avoid all of these problems, value may be dubious, because there is an equally effective and less costly technology that is not being used.

At the same time, there was increasing recognition that the benefits derived from a medical approach may be reaching their limits. That is, spending more dollars on health care will not necessarily enhance the health of the population. The American government noted that only 10 percent of premature deaths are attributable to inadequate health services; 50 percent are attributed to unhealthy lifestyles; 20 percent to environmental factors; and 20 percent to human biological factors (General Accounting Office, 1991). Research was appearing throughout the industrialized world that national health insurance, while treating the ill, did nothing to prevent illness, disability, or disease and that poverty (as seen in Chapter 10) was a major correlate of ill health (Evans, 1994). The acute care focus of medicine became seriously questioned in terms of its appropriateness for an aging population in which chronic illness dominates, not acute conditions. A **medical paradigm** locates the disease process physiologically within the body, assuming that there are specific causes for diseases that can be discovered through biomedical research and that discovering them will lead to a cure. And, as noted some time ago by Estes (1979), old age itself has been defined as a problem that is considered resolvable through medical care. Yet, during old age, it is chronic conditions, such as cancer, heart disease, and frailty, that primarily afflict individuals. Medicine has no cures for chronic conditions. But the conditions of old age are frequently nonspecific and chronic, so there is always something more that the physician can try or check, raising the possibility of overservicing of seniors (Barer, et al., 1995).

Despite the concern of popular media that the aging of the population itself is a cause of the continually increasing costs of health care, the evidence suggests that this need not be. Rather, increased servicing of seniors is probably more related to physician beliefs and behaviours than to aging itself. That is, physicians are intervening but the evidence does not suggest that seniors are better off for it, and there are good reasons to believe that an acute care biomedical focus is not the most appropriate for an aging population. Roos et al. (1993) estimated a 29 percent increase in the numbers of seniors in Manitoba between 1971 and 1983, but a 73 percent increase in number of seniors in poor health. Similarly, Ford et al. (1992) report worse health and worse functional status for those aged 65 to 76 years in 1987, compared with the same group in 1975. That is, medicine may not be helping.

Even worse, there could be negative consequences from medicine itself. Illich (1976) introduced the concept of **iatrogenic illness**, or simply **iatrogenesis**, more than 20 years ago in order to convey this idea. Iatrogenic illness includes, in a narrow sense, those diseases that would have not occurred if sound and professionally recommended treatments had not been applied. However, in a broader sense, clinical iatrogenic illness refers to all clinical conditions for which remedies, physicians, and hospitals are the pathogens or the "sickening" agents. Such errors as when individuals are given the wrong drug, an old drug, or a contaminated drug, and harmful interactions of drugs would be included here, as would be cases where persons become addicted to prescription drugs or where antibiotics alter the normal bacterial flora of the body and induce a super-infection. Illich goes on to argue that depersonalization of diagnosis and therapy has turned malpractice from an ethical problem into a technical problem, where, within the complex technological medical environment of the hospital, negligence becomes "random human error" or "system breakdown"; callousness becomes "scientific detachment"; and incompetence becomes "a lack of specialized equipment."

Concomitant with the declining reverence for medicine is a growing acceptance, through research and at the grassroots level, of alternative approaches to health, including herbal medicines, non-Western approaches to holistic living, homeopathy, and so on. As Sinnott (2000) notes, where health is concerned, people choose whatever works. Interest in complementary systems of healing is booming and is now a multibillion dollar business in the United States. It is difficult to pick up a popular magazine or newspaper without reading about nutrition, exercise, home remedies, and other aspects of life that promise to maintain and/or improve our health (see Box 15.2 on p. 418). Health clubs, exercise groups, and "natural" and "health" food stores have all seen dramatic increases in their popularity throughout the 1990s.

In addition to medical intervention per se, the organization of the delivery of health care has also come under attack. Until recently, countries have been focusing their attention on equity, extending equal financial protection and access to health care services to most or all of the population and not on questioning the adequacy of the care being provided. No overall mechanism to evaluate interventions, to assess delivery efficiency or effectiveness, or to ensure cost accountability was established when the original programs were mounted. For the first time since medicine achieved prominence in health care in the industrialized world (about 100 years ago), the 1990s saw the buyers of care, both public and private, questioning the quality of that care. They started asking questions such as: How much of current medical intervention is warranted? Would some of the dollars currently spent on medical care have a greater effect on health and, therefore, be better spent on such things as home care, better housing, or air quality? How do we ensure that medical intervention is beneficial, rather than simply causing no harm? What is the effectiveness of many medical interventions? Are we organizing and delivering health care in the most appropriate and effective way?

A New Vision

By the late 1980s and early 1990s, the cumulative evidence concerning gaps and inefficiencies within Medicare and the widespread acceptance of a broader view of health and health care led to a major questioning of Medicare for the first time since it had been established. Of note, the criticisms of Medicare were not new, but the 1990s reflected an official acceptance of the criticisms and an apparent willingness to act on them—this was new. In addition, despite the criticisms of Medicare, there remained widespread acceptance of the principles of universal access and public funding, which that system is based upon.

With a political willingness to examine the health care system came a variety of commissions, task forces, and committees established at the provincial, territorial, and federal levels, all examining the health care system and possible reform. In the early part of the 1990s, Mhatre and Deber (1992) reviewed available reports from the various working groups and found remarkable consistency in the vision of a new health care system for Canada. These authors listed the characteristics that were shared among the various reports:

- Broadening the definition of health to include other aspects in addition to the biomedical aspects, such as the social and psychological aspects, with a collaboration of multiple sectors.

Box 15.2 Health in the Headlines

Woman's World, The Woman's Weekly, April 2, 2002

- Home remedies (for children's ear infections, diarrhea, hay fever, vomiting, itchy skin, and diaper rash)
- Pizza as protection against cancer
- New ways to beat stress
- Herbal supplement for premenstrual breast pain

Times Colonist, March 30, 2002

- Conditioning merits of golf
- Yoga at home
- Inner peace from gardening

Good Housekeeping, April 2002

- Exercise your brain, ways to fend off forgetfulness
- Green tea has a metabolic effect that leads to weight loss
- Importance of exercise for increasing metabolism

Allure, 2002

- Feeding your face with avocado, tomato, lettuce, strawberries, bananas
- Relaxation exercises can help physical symptoms
- Sunshine affects mood
- Stress and hair loss
- Oregano as a natural antidote to dangerous bacteria

- Shifting the emphasis from curing illnesses to promoting health and preventing disease.
- Switching the focus to community-based rather than institution-based care.
- Providing more opportunities for individuals to participate with service providers on making decisions on health choices and policies.
- Decentralization of the provincial systems to some form of regional authority.
- Improved human resources planning, with particular emphasis on alternative methods of remuneration for physicians other than fee-for-service.
- Enhanced efficiency in the management of services, through the establishment of councils, coordinating bodies, and secretariats.
- Increasing funds for health services research, especially in the areas of utilization, technology assessment, program or system evaluation, and information systems.

Subsequent committees, task forces, and work groups on health reform have reached virtually the same conclusions. There was widespread acceptance that a redistribution of both emphasis and dollars from medical and institutional care to a broader base of community health care services was required.

The new vision was embraced as promising a more appropriate system of care for less than, or at least no more than, the cost of the current Medicare system. The new vision reformulates the role of government from a provider to a partner in care and places greater emphasis on a reliance on family and community social care. The envisioned health care system embraces a broader paradigm of health, as noted in the report of the National Forum on Health (1997): being healthy requires a clean, safe environment, adequate income, meaningful roles in society, and good housing, nutrition, education, and social support. The National Forum concluded that Canadians strongly support the basic principles of Medicare and that they value equity, compassion, collective responsibility, individual responsibility, respect for others, efficiency, and effectiveness. That Forum also argued that the social and economic determinants of health merit particular attention, including the factors that lie outside the traditional health care system, such as unemployment, labour market conditions, and cultural status. The report of the National Forum on Health recommended that Canada's health care system must be expanded to publicly fund all medically necessary services, explicitly naming home care and drugs, and by reforming primary care funding, organization, and delivery.

Reforming Canada's Health Care System

By the mid-1990s, both levels of government were ready to take action. They wanted to reduce costs. Hospitals became the first target because they represented the largest single expense in the public health care system. In Canada, hospitals are private, nonprofit organizations provided with global budgets (excluding funds for medical technologies), which, until this time, had been provided few incentives for devising adequate information systems to allow them to assess cost per patient or per case. As Rachlis and Kushner (1989) had noted, hospitals are about the only business that has no idea what its product (healthy patients) costs to produce. Global budgeting makes it difficult for provincial ministries of health to influence actual hospital expenditures. Typically, this period saw closure of long-term or chronic care beds within hospitals (for example in Nova Scotia and Newfoundland), closure of entire hospitals (in Saskatchewan), and a moratorium on building long-term institutional beds (British Columbia). During this period, there were no increases or only minor increases to acute care hospital budgets, with small increases to community and home care budgets in many provinces (Chappell, 1993a; b).

Medical schools agreed to limit new admissions and postgraduate training by 10 percent, to implement tighter restrictions on foreign-trained physicians' practice, and to have differential fees to encourage physicians to settle in underserviced areas. Limiting the number of physicians is an important cost-cutting measure because their cost to the system is much greater than their own personal incomes. Because they largely have control over health care resources, including laboratory tests, hospital usage, and the ordering of prescription drugs, they cost the system far more than their own salaries. Some provinces also introduced aggregate caps on physician salaries through a negotiation with provincial medical associations. User fees are being charged in some areas where they did not exist before, such as for equipment in Manitoba; income testing is being imposed for higher room and board fees in long-term care facilities, such as in British Columbia; and private for-pay services are being established, such as for magnetic resonance imaging (MRI) in Alberta.

There are, as well, attempts to redistribute health care dollars from expensive acute care hospitals to less expensive home care. However, the increased dollars to home care (referred to as home support services in British Columbia) have resulted in a major shift of services away from chronic care for those in the community to more intensive short-term post-hospital acute care. Penning et al. (1998) reveal that in the Capital Health Region of British Columbia, there were fewer people receiving services; however, those who were receiving services were receiving more hours of service, as they were in greater need as measured by level of care. In other words, these data suggest there has been a reduction, not an expansion, of community home-based service. Home care is resulting in a redirection of services away from clients who are less needy and who, therefore, may have the greatest potential for prevention to more intensive medically focused post-acute care. Home care is providing more medical support and less social care. This is the experience with diagnostic-related groups in the United States when they became the funding formula for acute care hospitals. This resulted in earlier discharges from hospital and increased the demand for intensive post-acute home care with a restriction on social services available through home care (Estes & Wood, 1986). This interpretation is supported by evidence that surgeries are increasingly being performed on an outpatient basis to the point where some hospitals in Toronto are performing 80 percent of their surgeries on this basis (Deber, et al., 1998).

Recent research, also from British Columbia, demonstrates that these shifts are not cost effective. Hollander (2001) compared four health units in that province that differentially implemented cuts to home support services. Units that cut these homemaking-only services paid for more services for these individuals three years later through their greater use of hospital beds, increased use of home care services in the second and third years after the cuts, and increased rates of admission to nursing homes. The greater overall costs did not emerge immediately. In addition, a higher proportion of those who were cut from the service died. It is important to note that not all who were cut were worse off three years later. Approximately, one-third of the people who were cut were not worse off, and some had even improved. Some adapted by paying for services themselves or having family and friends provide more help. However, there was a group of people who deteriorated, and that deterioration brought them back into the system, raising overall costs for the entire group such that they cost significantly more to the health care system than was true of those who were not cut from these services. This suggests that such services as homemaking only are cost effective and that a preventive and maintenance function of home care should be taken seriously.

Other recent research, also from British Columbia, compared the costs of similar level of care clients remaining in their homes and receiving home care with those for clients in nursing homes. Hollander and Chappell (2001) analyzed data for the years 1987–1988, 1990–1991, 1993–1994, and 1996–1997. The results reveal that the costs for home care clients are 40 to 75 percent of the costs of facility care. The differential is greater for lower levels of care than for higher levels of care. Furthermore, the cost of home care is in the transitions, that is, those who change their type or level of care cost considerably more than clients who remain within their level of care, even though individuals in transition still cost less than facility care clients. The only home care clients who cost more than nursing home clients are those who die while on home care, and the increased costs are due to hospitalization of those individuals. That is, hospitalization and not home care is the cost driver. In a separate project, Hollander and Chappell (2001) examined the costs of nursing home care in Winnipeg and in Victoria, compared with those at the same level of care receiving home care in these communities, taking into account costs of informal care (that is, costs incurred by family and friends in caring for the senior). The conclusion was the same, even when informal care was costed at minimum wage—home care costs less for individuals at the same level of care than nursing homes.

By the end of the 1990s, most provinces (Ontario being the major exception) were implementing **regionalization** on the argument that it allows for integration and for decision making at the local level. However, in almost all instances, only hospital care and community care are integrated, excluding both physician payments and drug payments. It is, therefore, at best only partial integration, which excludes major decision makers (physicians) and cost escalators (drugs) from an integrated system. It has the disadvantage of marrying a well-established and powerful vested interest within the system (acute care hospitals) with a historically weak distant cousin (home care). There is the very real danger of the home care sector losing visibility and having even less influence than it had prior to regionalization.

Recent data from British Columbia. (Penning, et al., 2001) compared three regions. The data refer to regionalization of 1997 (re-regionalization has taken place in 2001, creating fewer regions by collapsing some of the earlier ones). These researchers demonstrate that there are few differences among the regions. All three had appointed rather than elected boards; provincially defined representation; responsibility for regional health planning, the distribution of regional health budgets, and the management of delivery of health services; global budgets provided on a needs-based funding formula, based on population size, demographic characteristics, and mortality statistics; and responsibility for acute hospital care, public health, adult mental health, home care, and home support and long-term residential care. None had responsibility for physician care, Pharmacare, alcohol and drug treatment, emergency services, or broad health-related areas, such as education and employment. They did differ in terms of the number of tiers within the organizational structure and related centralization of decision making, as well as the roles of stakeholder groups within the organizational structure. The socio-demographic makeup of the regions also varied. When examining the utilization of acute care hospital services, physician services, and community-based home support services prior to and for two years after regionalization, few regional differences were found.

Allan et al. (2001) examined all regions throughout the province from 1990–1991 to one year after regionalization. In terms of utilization by older adults, regional differences and visits to specialists, inpatient hospital separations, and home support clients remained constant. Differences in visits to general practitioners, outpatient hospital separations, and home nursing care clients all decreased. That is, there is some evidence that the regions are becoming more standardized in their health care, rather than more distinct, as one would expect as care moves "closer to home." Both studies report that the observed trends began long before regionalization and continued afterwards. A decrease in the supply of acute care and extended care beds began prior to 1997, with both admissions and lengths of stay decreasing. This decline continued after regionalization. However, extended care and day surgery rates increased prior to regionalization and decreased afterward. Utilization of physician services, especially specialist services, increased, an increase that was even greater after regionalization. Furthermore, outpatient hospital utilization rates increased prior to regionalization but declined recently.

In terms of community home care services, Penning et al. (2001) confirm their earlier findings, noted above, that community-based home support services declined prior to regionalization and continued afterward but that the intensity of servicing (hours of service received per client) increased. This increase in the intensity of servicing continued after regionalization (data up to and including 1999, that is, for two years after regionalization). There was also an increase in the numbers of massage therapists, dental hygienists, occupational therapists, naturopaths, and chiropractors prior to regionalization but a decline afterward. The recent decision by the provincial government to delist alternative practitioners from coverage in the provincial health care plan will no doubt lead to further decline in these utilization rates. There is also a decline in health record personnel, emergency response personnel, and nurses, particularly LPNs, prior to regionalization. This continued after regionalization. In addition, the settings (primarily hospitals) in which nurses are employed changed little after regionalization.

As Sullivan and Scattolon (1995) suggest, regional boards with no budget- or policy-setting authority will be unsuccessful in ensuring consumer participation. For public participation through consumer representation to work, administrative and budget authority over service provision must be provided. It is too early to tell whether regional populations in Canada contain too few people to affect economies of scale or the coordination of services. In British Columbia, the newly elected provincial government has just decreased the number of regions and some of the existing regions had already begun collaborating to order supplies and so on because their population base is too small.

More Reform Is Promised

At the time of writing, health reform is still very much in process and the outcome is not yet known. There is much discussion of embracing the primary care model, which holds the promise of integrated health care. Marriott and Mable (1998) note that primary care is defined in a variety of ways, one of which is as essential health care that is universally accessible to individuals and families by means acceptable to them and through their full participation. It is generally considered the first level of contact with the national health care system and delivered as close to home as possible. It includes health promotion, illness prevention, and curative, supportive, and rehabilitation services. It should lead to improved accessibility, quality, and coordination of services as well as responsiveness to individual needs. It is, in other words, more consistent in its image with the vision of health reform than many of the changes that have been taking place. Key elements include:

- The development of general practitioners working in a group environment that could also include a network of solo practices.
- The development of multidisciplinary teams, including general practitioners as well as others, such as nurse practitioners, counsellors, and nutritionists.
- Patient registration or rostering, whereby the organization is responsible for specific individuals, rather than a geographic area.
- Funding on a population or a capitation basis, that is, a set amount of dollars is provided per person.
- Core services, including health promotion, sickness prevention, diagnosis and treatment of illness, urgent care, 24-hour accessibility, and management of chronic illness.
- High quality, specific information or records that would allow for greater certainty for costing and better analysis of the benefits.

It is to be noted that while the vision includes health promotion and sickness prevention, there is still a primary emphasis on physician-dominated medical care. There is no necessary inclusion of home care, and they do not extend to the larger structural elements of the community, such as the workplace or educational institutions. Where health promotion and illness prevention are included, there is little evidence that it means more than providing information on healthy lifestyles, such as proper nutrition, or on the harmful effects of smoking.

It is clear that Canada's health care system is under reform. There are efforts to cut costs by decreasing or refusing increases to hospital budgets, putting caps on physician salaries, graduating fewer physicians, and encouraging care for individuals at home, rather than in hospital. There are attempts to deal with structural issues that have created a health care system that has operated in stove pipes or silos, in which funds are allocated to each sector with different rules. For example, physician services are paid through a fee-for-service mechanism, hospitals receive global budgets, and assistive devices receive a percentage subsidy. There has been no provision for the transfer of monies from one administrative unit to another, and historically, there is little interaction between them. This is a major reason for **integration**, noted above, in an attempt to merge the different sectors and levels of health care delivery. It does represent an attempt at structural change within the system.

Nevertheless, despite the change that is taking place, physicians as well as other fee-for-service providers, such as walk-in clinics and physiotherapists, are, by and large, based on a market allocation model, wherein practitioners are paid for their services to clients who choose to see them. Hospitals are still largely funded on a global budget basis. Reimbursement is a function of the volume and mix of services delivered. Even though caps have been imposed on physician salaries, they still operate within the fee-for-service system; caps just mean that there is ultimately a limit to the amount that they can make. There has, furthermore, been less visible action in terms of shifting the emphasis from curing illness to promoting health and preventing disease, providing more opportunities for individuals to participate with service providers in making decisions on health choices and policies, improving human resource planning and, in particular, alternative methods of remuneration of physicians, and enhancing efficiency in the management of services through councils, coordinating bodies, secretariats, and so on.

In addition, the saliency of women as recipients of care and as the majority of care providers—both as informal care providers, as noted in the earlier Chapter on Social Support and Caregiving, and as paid providers within the system—has received little attention. The top managerial positions (such as hospital CEOs) are typically filled by men. Despite the increased number of women entering this profession, there is now evidence from several countries that they, nevertheless, hit a glass ceiling, beyond which they tend not to be promoted. They are largely concentrated in traditional specialties, such as pediatrics, or as general practitioners (Lorber, 1993; Riska & Wegar, 1993). Other than physicians, the majority of health care workers are women. This is especially true among nurses and home care workers.

Women have little say in when and how health care reform happens. When they are consulted, they tend to be experts in medical or nursing practices (Armstrong & Armstrong, 1999). With the reforms taking place, it can be argued that there is medical retrenchment (see the following section on Vested Interests), leaving even less room for women's perspectives that have argued for the demedicalization of health, including diseases, such as breast cancer, and childbearing. With health care restructuring taking place, there is a clear shortage of nursing jobs, for example, in Ontario. In many instances where nurses are retained, they have little or no say in decision making; nurses are finding themselves in contracted-out positions, often with no career trajectory and little in the way of benefits. With home care being transformed into an intensive acute care support system and the dismantling of home care that offers long-term chronic support, the jobs that are being lost tend to be the housekeeping and homemaking positions that also belong to women.

A major issue for health reform is the fact that the health care system is not being created from scratch but must work with an existing system, affect change in that system, and create a new system. The existing structure of the system is, therefore, very relevant for any new system that evolves, as are vested interests within that system. Included within the area of vested interests is the private sector. We turn to that discussion now.

Vested Interests

Canada's health care system, Medicare, is universal and publicly financed but only includes a limited number of services, not all of health care. In addition,

Canadians have rejected a private health care system as is found in the United States. These basic facts are particularly important in health reform. Privatization has implications in terms of diminished control by citizens through government and increased control by business interests of multinationals over the health of Canadians. As health economist Evans (1984) noted decades ago, health care is not a market commodity like automobiles or appliances. Health is not something that applies only to the rich, nor is it a commodity about which the consumer can be expected to have perfect or even adequate knowledge to choose between alternatives. In supporting Medicare, Canadians have rejected the notion that health should only be for those who can afford it and that health care should be available as market forces dictate.

Profitization

Privatization has various meanings, including: anything that is not public and, thereby, referring to the size and scope of government involvement; to empower individuals and communities through increased reliance on families, churches, and other nonprofit institutions, rather than governments; laissez faire capitalism as free markets and the profit motive working to produce innovation, efficiency, good management, and responsiveness to individual choice. Relatedly, public and private arrangements are not dichotomies. Private includes for-profit as well as not-for-profit organizations. Charitable and non-profit sectors frequently work closely with government and may not charge for services. However, the discussion within health services generally refers to private as for-profit and has business and corporate connotations (Deber, et al., 1998). The concern as noted by Williams et al. (2001) has more to do with **profitization** of health care, that is, the provision of health services as a profit-making business than with privatization per se (doctors and hospitals have always been private providers under Medicare).

As a capitalist society, we can always expect there will be pressures toward privatization and profitization. And with health reform, we are headed in that direction. The proportion of private funding in health care increased from 23.6 percent in 1975 to 25.4 percent in 1990 (Armstrong, et al., 2001), and to 30.2 percent in 2000 (Mendelson & Divinsky, 2000). Compare this with the United States, where the private sector figure is 53.6 percent and with the United Kingdom, where it is 15.4 percent.

Increased profitization is consistent with the internationalization of capital so often referred to as "globalization" (Coburn, 2001). In the era of the free trade agreement, business influence within Canada increased greatly, to counter the perceived threat of capital mobility (the flight of capital from Canada). The Canadian government, threatened with reduced credit rating, higher interest rates, and/or withholding business investment in the 1980s, slashed government expenditure, reduced deficits, and paid down the debt. Canada became much more market oriented, and the power of the state was reduced. Trade levels with the United States have increased dramatically so that trade with the United States now far outstrips intra-Canada activity in virtually every region of Canada (Mendelson & Divinsky, 2000). The increased favour of a for-profit ideology brought with it a business-state coalition to rationalize health care. Part of the impetus came from American businesses, which, according to Armstrong (2001), had more or less saturated the American health care business market. By the mid-1990s, for-profit health maintenance organizations dominated the market in the United States and for-profit hospitals also became good business. Hospitals, for example, saw their aggregate profits rise by 25 percent in 1996. By the end of the 1990s, they were looking to Canada to expand their investment and demanded greater freedom to deliver health care business in Canada under the North American Free Trade Agreement (NAFTA).

Hospitals became central to the new business approach to health care. They were a focus not only because they represented the single largest expense within Canada's publicly funded system, but they were also most amenable to new strategies taken from the private sector, that is, business forms of management practices could be transferred to the running of hospitals. As hospitals became restructured, their appropriate business (acute care) became more narrowly defined, surgeries became shifted to outpatient status, and nursing positions were lost and downsized. Patient stays lessened, and services became contracted out. More and more of the care provided by hospitals became more narrowly defined, and day and outpatient services increased. More and more of the services that used to be provided within hospitals no longer fall under the umbrella of Medicare. For example, some rehabilitation services, provision of prescription drugs, nursing care, and custodial care became either not offered or offered under the rubric of home care. As such, it is outside of Medicare and, therefore, outside universally insured and publicly provided care.

Home care has been shifting more and more to a mixed mode of managed competition where the local health authority purchases services from a mix of not-for-profit and for-profit service providers on behalf of consumers (the Ontario Continuing Care Access Centres would be a major example). In Ontario now, as in British Columbia, citizens will be assessed for services but not necessarily provided with needed services, which are means tested. Such mixed mode of delivery is supposed to ensure competition and, thereby, keep the price down, despite the fact that there is evidence from other jurisdictions to suggest that for-profit firms are more likely to skimp on quality or select only consumers who are in the least need in order to keep profits up (Bendick, 1989; Williams, et al., 2001). In addition, managed care plans in the United States can drop coverage or reduce benefits if they are losing money. Furthermore, when for-profit multinationals buy home care agencies in Canada, profits, more often than not, leave this country. The problems unfortunately do not stop there. Under NAFTA, the Canadian government can allow for-profit entry into the health care field, but once it does, it cannot then return that area to public provision without providing compensation to those for-profit firms and must do so under the terms and conditions of an international, not a domestic, tribunal. Those for-profit firms have the right to compensation for the resulting expropriation of their future profits. It therefore becomes increasingly difficult and expensive, if it is possible at all, to reverse the for-profit trend.

It is well established that for-profit health care is more expensive than universal public schemes. For-profit health care is less expensive for governments, but consumers pay more. A large part of this increased expense comes not only through profits but also administrative overhead. Figures on percent of revenues spent on overhead in large American health maintenance organizations, in private plans in Canada not covered under Medicare, and for the costs of private prepayment in commercial health insurance carriers prior to Medicare in Canada, all range around the 26 percent mark. Cost of overhead within universal Medicare, however, is only 1 percent. In the United States, only 84 percent of the population is insured, while in Canada it is 100 percent, and Canada's system costs less: $2,250 per person in 1998, while the figure for the United States was $4,270 per person (Marmor & Sullivan, 2000).

While we have a vision of **health care reform** that argues for expanding the mandate under Canada's Medicare system, acknowledging the social determinants of health and arguing for a broader definition of health than simply medicine, we see a paradigm shift within society that has increased the dominance of capitalism and allowed it to become increasingly pervasive within health. Within this transformation, Medicare becomes more narrowly defined, and therefore, the territory for for-profit firms becomes expanded. With health reform has come an increased role for private clinics that used to be restricted mainly to specialized or elective services, with the public sector paying for the comprehensive mix of core services. We now see the purview of these private clinics extending beyond abortions, in vitro fertilization, and laser eye surgery and moving into the arena of private hospitals.

Importantly, for an aging population, the hollowing out of Medicare means that many of the home care and community support services required by seniors are the ones that are no longer available or are becoming privatized. Concerns that the aging of the baby boom generation will bankrupt the universal health care system are simply unfounded. It is the old-old, those aged 75 years and over, who use health care services disproportionately, and this population will grow from 5.8 percent of the population in 2001 to 6.7 percent in 2016. Even if it is assumed that this population currently accounts for fully 50 percent of health care expenditures, the growth in this segment of the population will add only about 1.1 percentage points to health care expenditures as a percentage of GDP. While this represents growth, it hardly warrants the alarmist writings one sees often in the media (Mendelson & Divinsky, 2000).

Pharmaceuticals

A powerful interest group that has particular relevance in any discussion of health care is the pharmaceutical manufacturing industry. The pharmaceutical industry is tied uniquely to physicians, since physicians are the only individuals who can prescribe drugs. (Prescription drugs are not part of Medicare, unless they are provided within an acute care hospital.) Payment schedules vary from province to province. Drugs, an essential element of our modern culture of health care, evidence a tremendous explosion of knowledge, whereby physicians and other health care workers, citizens, and governments are deluged with masses of often conflicting information (Segall & Chappell, 2000). In 1990, Lexchin estimated that there were 3,500 prescription products available to Canadian physicians. Known side effects and drug interactions continually emerge, as do computer programs to warn doctors and pharmacists. Most physicians stay current by relying on information from drug company representatives (detail men) who number about one for every 16 physicians (Rachlis & Kushner, 1989). This relationship, interestingly, is not viewed as one of a conflict of interest, but rather as experts (who are employed by the drug manufacturers) providing information to physicians.

Yet, as noted by the recent Saskatchewan Commission on Medicare, there is solid evidence from Ontario and Quebec that we often prescribe drugs poorly. To cite from that report, "Antibiotics are often prescribed for viruses where they are totally ineffective. An estimated 20 percent of elderly admissions to hospital are associated with an adverse drug reaction. Evidence from Ontario and British Columbia suggests that expensive drugs are routinely prescribed when cheaper drugs will do..." (Fyke, 2001: 72). In their review of evidence on prescription drug use among seniors, Tamblyn and Perreault (2000) conclude that the potential benefits of drug treatment are compromised by the underuse and overuse of prescribed medications for certain conditions, errors in the drug dose and duration of therapy prescribed, and suboptimal compliance. They note that drug-related illness is now cited as the sixth leading cause of mortality in the United States.

There has been an unprecedented increase in the cost of prescription drugs. In Ontario, from 1987 to 1993, the average price per prescription (excluding the dispensing fee) went from $12.48 to $24.09, a rise of 93 percent in comparison with an increase in the consumer price index during the same period of 23.1 percent. More than half the rise in these costs was due to the introduction of new patented medications. The year 1987 saw the introduction of Bill C-91, which extended the monopoly for new drugs coming on the market, abolished compulsory licensing, and gave the multinational manufacturing companies 20 years of patent protection for their products (Lexchin, 2001). Both NAFTA and the General Agreement on Tariffs and Trade (GATT) were used to eliminate compulsory licensing, which had allowed generic competitors to come on the market within five to seven years after the appearance of the original product, typically priced at 25 percent lower than the brand name product; and when there were three or four generics, the price differential would be 50 percent (Lexchin, 1993). In addition to these global agreements, however, the pharmaceutical industry invested heavily in Montreal; indeed a key feature of Quebec's industrial strategy has been the development of the pharmaceutical industry. The Quebec government is an affiliate member within the Pharmaceutical Manufacturers Association of Canada (PMAC). A perceived threat to the economic viability of the pharmaceutical industry, therefore, is also a perceived threat to the Quebec government, which could be used by separatists should the federal government take a position against PMAC (Lexchin, 2001).

In an effort to deal with increasing drug prices, provinces often increase the deductible for eligible Pharmacare programs or restrict the population groups (such as to seniors) who are eligible. Some provinces, specifically British Columbia, have introduced reference-based pricing (RBP) (whereby the cheapest of the most effective drugs with the least side effects is reimbursed through the provincial drug plan) in order to try to contain these escalating costs. Brunt et al. (1998) document the public relations campaign orchestrated by PMAC to convince the public that RBP was not acceptable on the argument that individuals under this scheme would receive the oldest and cheapest drugs only, that provincial economic needs were being placed before patient needs, that there would be multiple adverse effects on the quality of care and consequently on health, that bureaucrats and not physicians were making medical decisions, and that there was lack of consultation when developing the policy. The provincial government tried to counter this public media campaign with the messages that the profit motive of drug companies was driving the opposition to the policy, that the program means good stewardship of threatened resources, and that the policy offers flexibility and safety. The government had established an expert panel in order to decide which drugs were chosen to be reimbursable. Chappell et al. (1997) report a province-wide survey of seniors demonstrating their strong support for RBP and their view that the media campaign by the pharmaceutical manufacturers was driven by self-interest. PMAC sued the provincial government for lost revenues but lost in the courts. It is currently under appeal. The pharmaceutical manufacturers are now lobbying the federal government for permission to advertise directly to consumers.

Amid health care reforms, there seems to be no appetite among provincial or federal governments to add Pharmacare within the rubric of the *Canada Health Act* and, therefore, Medicare. In the early 1990s, Canada ranked at the bottom of a list of 24 OECD (Organization of Economic Cooperation and Development) countries on three measures of public drug spending:

1. The public expenditure on prescribed medicines as a percentage of total expenditure on medicines.
2. The percentage of the population eligible for pharmaceutical benefits under a public scheme.

3. The average percentage of a beneficiary's prescribed medicines paid by a
    public fund.

Since, in the meantime, provinces have been increasing deductibles and
patient co-payments in their public drug plans, this situation has not improved and
may well have deteriorated. At the time this study was reported, the United States
also ranked at the bottom of the list (Lexchin, 2001). In other words, the cost of prescription drugs is increasing, and there is no indication that this will be covered
through public plans or that costs will be maintained in the foreseeable future.

The Future?

Health care reforms of the 1990s opened the door for a greater role for private
interests within Canada's health care system. The entire discussion of the provision of health care has been reformulated. During the 1990s, the role of government
switched from being the provider of care, which it had been viewed as in the
past, to being the partner, one that enables and empowers individuals to exert
control over their lives (OECD, 1992). Partnerships have become a key concept and
are believed—at least so the rhetoric maintains—will improve the efficiency, effectiveness, and responsiveness of public organizations. This has represented a fundamental shift in the approach to health care in Canada and has facilitated a
greater role for private interests. This is within a climate in which the United
Nations Declaration of Human Rights (Article 25) recognizes the right to health care
as a human right, not a privilege. The need for health care for serious illnesses is
understood as a vital need, that is, a right to obtain fulfillment. This provides a
moral argument for legislation to establish equal access for all to basic health care,
and since it emanates from the United Nations, it is applicable to all countries
(Tranoy, 1996). Furthermore, Canadians strongly believe that their government's
role in social policy should not be minimized but, rather, that social policy is at the
forefront of defining Canadian identity (Peters, 1995). They consider health a
right for all; they do not want a two-tier system where those who cannot afford to
pay are disadvantaged.

Indeed, Canadians' strong support of the Medicare program is a reason
why we are witnessing the current strategy unfolding.The public's strong support of Medicare and outcries that it is being eroded mean that it is very difficult
for governments to dismantle this program explicitly. They must, therefore, be
seen to be maintaining Medicare. Current restructuring and redefinitions of
"acute care," which specify that only the most severely ill can receive immediate treatment, can be presented as improved efficiency in the delivery of
Medicare. The consequence, though, is to make Medicare even more medical
and narrow, contrary to the broadened vision for reform. It results in what
Williams et al. (2001) refer to as a "hollowing out" of Medicare. More and more
individuals, many of whom are women (since women experience more

symptomatology than men) and are elderly (the greatest users of health care services), are defined as being outside the protection of Medicare.

The recent Saskatchewan Commission on Medicare (Fyke, 2001) notes that the two biggest challenges of modern health care are accountability and sustainability. Unfortunately, many of the reforms being witnessed today will lead neither to public accountability nor to sustainability. Particularly for an aging population, public health, home care, chronic disease management, and mental health are of paramount importance and yet are receiving short shrift within the reform. While we agree that health care requires a cultural transformation, the major paradigm shift that appears to be taking place in Canada at this time is not the one that is going to lead to a more appropriate and more effective health care system for seniors. This is despite the fact that the vision of health care reform outlined a new health care system for Canadians that, indeed, would have provided more cost effective, more intervention effective, and more appropriate services for an aging society.

And at time of writing, we have another national commission examining the direction of health reform—the Romanow Commission. They are holding hearings across the country and examining available research to try to understand the best direction in which the health care system should evolve.They are well aware that research cannot answer all questions; values underlie decisions that are made. What is striking about Canada's National Forum on Health, the Saskatchewan Commission on Medicare, and other reports concerning reform of the Canadian health care system is that the vision seems to hold little resemblance to the actions that are actually taking place within the provinces. Whether or not this will continue to be the case with the Romanow Commission depends on its final report and recommendations.

However, the vision of health reform has allowed the opportunity to dismantle the health care system as we know it in this country. The call for a broader perspective on health, less medicalized health care, and less institutionalized health care have all allowed provincial governments to begin downsizing acute care hospitals, shortening lengths of stay, imposing caps on physicians' salaries, and so on, but governments have not, to date, demonstrated a willingness to expand community care outside the hospitals, to expand a definition of health beyond biomedicine, or to embrace other types of health care workers in addition to physicians. Current discussion surrounding assisted living for seniors (see Chapter 13 on Social Support and Caregiving) opens the door to allow further downsizing of long-term care institutions and offloading of costs onto seniors and their families. Expansion of assisted living (which has its place in the continuum of care for seniors) can allow for only those who are at higher levels of care to access long-term institutional care without governments subsidizing the cost of assisted living. This would ensure that families must bear that cost on their own.

The vision of health reform, in other words, has allowed for a shifting of the burden of care in old age from the public purse onto individuals and families even though this was not part of the rhetoric or the vision of health reform. The vision, in retrospect, has allowed the reforms to take place, but unfortunately, the reforms are primarily counter to that vision. While we do not know the health of seniors in the future and there are some studies that suggest reason for optimism (for example, Wilkins [1991] shows that some of the increased years of life are now disability free, and Fyke [2001] reports studies suggesting seniors are healthier now than decades ago), we do not know what the future will bring. We do know that with the aging of the baby boom generation, there are going to be significantly more seniors and they are going to expect a just and civil society to provide them with appropriate care.

CHAPTER SUMMARY

In this chapter, we have examined Canada's health care system, its historical roots, its evolution throughout the 20th century, and present day health reform.

Key ideas to remember from this chapter include:

- Canada's universal health care system, Medicare, emphasizes medical aspects of illness care covering only physician care and acute hospital care.
- Other aspects of care, particularly those that could be considered from a social perspective, are not covered in Medicare. These include, for example, home care, long-term institutional care, and care by alternative practitioners, such as chiropractors, massage therapists, naturopaths, and so on.
- Canada's health care system emphasizes the most expensive forms of care and revolves around illness treatment, rather than health promotion or disease prevention.
- Despite provincial jurisdiction to deliver health care, the federal government has, over the past century, played a critical role in health care through funding.
- Provincial discontent in what they perceived as federal interference within their jurisdiction, cumulative research suggesting there were more efficient and more effective forms of delivery, and widespread acceptance of alternative definitions of health, health promotion, and health care led to a new vision for health care for Canada in the early 1990s.
- The vision of health reform embraced a more appropriate health care system for seniors that included a broadened definition of health, a de-emphasis only on biomedicine, a de-emphasis on institutional care, a strengthening of community care, a recognition of the role of evidence-based decision making, a call for greater citizen participation in their own care, and for reorganization of the management of health care.
- The 1990s differed dramatically from the preceding decades in the political willingness to take action to change the health care system. By the mid-1990s, there was clear evidence of attempts at reform, including capping hospital budgets, closing hospital beds and, in some

cases, entire hospitals, limiting enrollment to graduate schools, and modest increases to home care budgets.

- By the late 1990s, there were major efforts at regionalization in most Canadian provinces and examination of primary health care models.

- Recent evidence suggests that regionalization and downsizing of acute care hospitals is not working to the extent that it is producing results that are inconsistent with the vision of health reform. Indeed, evidence suggests that the Canadian health care system is becoming more medicalized, rather than less medicalized, although there is some de-institutionalization taking place.

- The vision of health reform embraced in virtually all quarters of the country permitted a major change to our system. It has allowed some dismantling of some parts of the system without follow-through to build those aspects of the system that were deemed necessary within health reform.

- The voice of women and a women's perspective are difficult to find within health care reform.

- Health care reform has opened the door to privatization of the health care system.

- A powerful, established vested interest group within the health care system is the pharmaceutical industry.

- Despite the establishment of the federal Romanow Health Commission, the future for health reform is not optimistic when judged against the vision of health care reform.

KEY TERMS

Family-based welfare, **(p. 408)**

Residual welfare, **(p. 408)**

Public Health, **(p. 408)**

Preventative medicine, **(p. 408)**

Equity in healthcare, **(p. 409)**

Extra billing, **(p. 410)**

Provider driven, **(p. 412)**

Predisposing factors, **(p. 412)**

Enabling conditions, **(p. 412)**

Need, **(p. 413)**

Medical paradigm, **(p. 416)**

Iatrogenic illness, **(p. 416)**

Iatrogenesis, **(p. 416)**

Regionalization, **(p. 422)**

Integration, **(p. 424)**

Privatization, **(p. 426)**

Profitization, **(p. 426)**

Health care reform, **(p. 428)**

STUDY QUESTIONS

1. How did Canada end up with a primarily medical health care system?

2. What are the reasons for wanting to reform Medicare?

3. Why is the system within the vision of health reform a more appropriate system for seniors?

4. How are reforms "hollowing out" Medicare?

5. Why is health reform not optimal for seniors?

SUGGESTED READINGS

Armstrong, P., Armstrong, H., & Coburn, D. (2001). *Unhealthy times. Political economy perspectives on health and care in Canada.* Toronto, Ontario: Oxford University Press.

Badgely, R.F. (1991). Social and economic disparities under Canadian health-care. *International Journal of Health Services, 21*(4), 659-671.

Barer, M.L., Evans, R.G., & Hertzman, C. (1995). Avalanche or glacier? Health care and the demographic rhetoric. *Canadian Journal on Aging, 14*(3), 193-224.

Coburn D. (2001). Health, health care, and neo-liberalism. In P. Armstrong, H. Armstrong, & D. Coburn (Eds.), *Unhealthy times. Political economy perspectives on health and care in Canada.* (pp.45-65). Toronto, Ontario: Oxford University Press.

McDaniel, S.A., & Chappell, N.L. (1999). Health care regression: Contraindications, tensions and implications for Canadian seniors. *Canadian Public Policy, 15*(1), 123-132.

National Forum on Health. (1997). Canada Health Action: Building on the legacy. Volume I: The Final Report of the *National Forum on Health and Volume II: Synthesis Reports and Issue Papers.* Ottawa, Ontario.

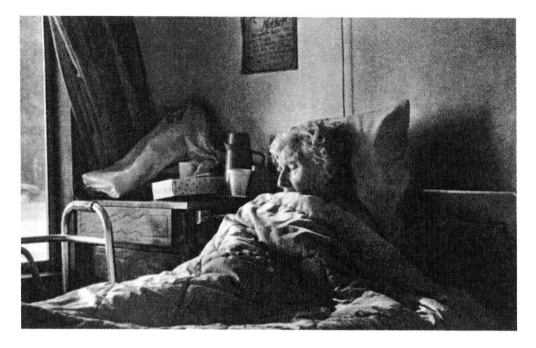

End-of-Life Issues

In this chapter, you will learn about:

- Place of death, that is, where do people die?
- Defining death, how do we know when people are dead?
- The process of dying, which is different from death. Various aspects of living with impending death are discussed.
- Understanding that those who are dying are still living and the important implications of this for care of the dying.
- Non-life-sustaining measures, euthanasia, and assisted suicide.

- Because some suffer from cognitive impairment, including dementia, during old age, the issue of making their wishes known for end-of-life decisions also arises. Competence and advanced directives are also discussed.
- Family and friends who must cope with the process of dying and ultimately with the death of a loved one.
- The funeral—rituals and business.
- Increased recognition of end-of-life issues.

Introduction

We all die; it is, as they say, a fact of life. However, death at the beginning of the 21st century differs from death occurring earlier in history. Now that most individuals can expect to live to old age, we know that most will die in old age. At the present time, this means that most will die after suffering from chronic illnesses and organ system failures. There is, in other words, a long trajectory of dying before one is dead. Furthermore, the juncture at which one is no longer simply living with chronic illness but is dying is not necessarily clear for either the individuals themselves, their family members, or the clinicians caring for them. As we shall learn in this chapter, death is not simply biological. There are social, psychological, and spiritual aspects to this process.

Death and Dying in the 21st Century

Death in modern society occurs overwhelmingly in hospitals. Heyland and associates (2000a; b) note that in Canada, 73 percent of deaths in 1997 occurred in hospitals. This is a significant rise from the 45 percent of deaths that occurred in hospitals in Canada in 1950. Approximately three-quarters of those deaths (i.e., those in hospitals) occurred among patients who were over 65 years of age. Only a third of institutionalized seniors, however, die in hospitals, compared with 72 percent of community-living seniors (Montgomery, et al, 1988). In other words, if you are in a long-term care facility when the end comes, you are likely to die there. If you are living in the community when the end comes, you are likely to be taken to a hospital and to die there. In part, this reflects the difficulty of knowing when "the end" is here, and therefore, the move to the hospital often represents an effort to cure or care for an ailment experienced by the living. In part, it also represents families', physicians', and the health care system's difficulty in accepting death. Indeed, hospitalization at the end of life can result in a prolongation of dying, rather than "a good death."

While suicide rates increase near the end of life, the reasons for this are not well understood and may not always simply reflect preemptive suicide, where death is chosen as a rational alternative to a demeaning and punishing decline (Prado, 1998). We understand little about the role of anxiety, fears, or threats of losing aspects of one's identity as reasons for suicide in late life. Suicide in old age, unlike suicide when younger, tends to happen among those who are married or single, have severe health problems, and have not attempted suicide before.

While death comes to all of us and is final, even its definition has become problematic in present-day society. Traditionally, when someone's heartbeat and breathing stopped permanently, they were considered dead. During the 20th century, the question arose as to whether or not an individual could be dead even though his or her heart was pumping blood and the lungs were working. The concept of whole-brain death, or just **brain death**, arose, allowing the declaration of death if an individual's entire brain ceases functioning.

Dying

While death is defined in biological terms, dying is also social, emotional, and spiritual. Over 30 years ago, Kubler-Ross (1969) developed her theory of five stages inherent within the process of dying. These stages were derived from her work counselling terminally ill patients. She argued that first there is denial, then anger, then bargaining, then depression, and, finally, acceptance. These stages are not necessarily linear or sequential and vary from person to person. It is important to recognize that there is the meaning of life in death and that dying involves more than biological changes.

As we saw in earlier chapters, most individuals today can expect to live to old age. During old age, we are likely to suffer from chronic conditions before we die. Older people, by virtue of their proximity to death, are assumed to accept death, that is, they do not find it frightening and need not even discuss death. Clarke and Hanson (2000), however, find that older individuals in the United Kingdom do want to talk about death, although they are not obsessed by or overly preoccupied with it. They appreciate the opportunity to discuss their impending death. It is a myth that just because one is aged, one is necessarily completely prepared for death. Some may be and others not.

Preparing for death can include a desire to bring meaning to one's life. Because of the prolongation of the dying process due to chronic illness in old age, there has been increased interest in spirituality and the meaning of life toward the end. As Bevans and Cole (2001) argue, as long as our focus is on technology, treatments, procedures, and documents, that is, on problems toward the end of life, the mystery of the end of life becomes ignored. When we talk about the meaning of life, we are talking about spirituality. Dying individuals can have **crises of meaning**, also referred to as **soul pain** (Kearney, 1966), where they experience a lack of meaning, coherence, or comfort with their life. Meaning refers to existential well being and is more than physical or psychological well being. Where an individual finds **spirituality** will vary from person to person because it refers to bringing integrity and coherence to one's life. For some, there may be a particular emphasis on religion; for others it may be on friendships.

Quality-adjusted life years (QALYs) refer to the duration of life in various compromised health conditions. The concept has been around for nearly 30 years. QALYs all score one full year of healthy life at 1.0. Less than optimal health receives a score of less than 1.0. There are different ways of computing QALYs. The standard "gamble technique" asks a respondent to make a hypothetical choice between continued life in their present state or a gamble that would result in either perfect health or death. A different method refers to time trade-off, in which individuals are asked how much time they would be willing to give up in order to be in a better state of health. Another approach uses a simple rating scale in which individuals rate health conditions on a scale ranging from 0 to 10 or 0 to 100.

Valuing Life

Lawton (Lawton, et al, 1999) prefers to approach the topic through death, anxiety, and the wish to live. While health-related quality of life considers the extent to which distress from illness or side effects associated with treatment reduce the person's wish to live, much less is known about the desire to live. Lawton argues that years of desired life is not determined entirely by quality of life but is mediated by an intervening cognitive affective schema referred to as **valuation of life (VOL)**. VOL is defined as the extent to which the person is attached to his or her present life due to enjoyment and the absence of distress, as well as hope, futurity, purpose, meaningfulness, persistence, and self-efficacy. VOL is considered an existential concept, capturing the concept of total reason for living. Lawton and his associates find that people do choose fewer years of life if life is marred by functional and cognitive impairment or pain. Cognitive loss is much less desirable than either functional impairment or pain. Pain is the least threatening of the three. They find that VOL predicts years desired to live independently of other measures of psychological well being and, therefore, contend that it is not simply another measure of positive mental health. They argue VOL is an attitude that motivates people for continuing to live longer and that its incorporation of purpose may be critical as a sustaining force in the desire to live.

In addition to valuation of life, one can have **fear of death**, refering to either fear of the unknown or fear of dying. Cicirelli (1999) has reported that fear of dying is associated with being younger, of lower socioeconomic status, female, white rather than black, and having a more external locus of control and less religiousness. Greater fear of the unknown is associated with having a more external locus of control, less perceived social support, less religiousness, and indirectly with being older, of lower socioeconomic status, male, and white rather than black (the research was conducted in the United States).

Individuals have been asked directly what the quality of the end of life means to them. Canadians sampled identified five domains of quality end-of-life care. They referred to: (1) receiving adequate pain and symptom management, (2) avoiding inappropriate prolongation of dying, (3) achieving a sense of control, (4) relieving burden, and (5) strengthening relationships with loved ones (Singer, et al, 1999). The role of religiousness seems to depend on the specific beliefs held by the individual. For example, beliefs that one's suffering is a reflection of punishment from God or that one has a forgiving God can affect one differently. And people can be afraid of dying without being afraid of death.

There could be a sense of no further time to make restitution or receive forgiveness from another individual, there may be guilt, and there may be despair. On the other hand, one could find great comfort in the belief that he or she will soon be with loved ones in an after-life. Some believe that religious coping is especially prevalent in old age because with impending death, there can be an existential or health crisis. Religious coping resources can allow the individual to integrate the self, to retain feelings of control over the environment, to continue with intimate relations with others, and to come to terms with mortality. Attendance at religious services declines somewhat among the near-deceased, probably due to physical decline. Feelings of religiousness and strength or comfort received from religion are either stable or increase slightly (Idler, et al, 2001). In other words, the general belief that our religious beliefs become much stronger near death does not receive empirical support.

Our discussion has emphasized life near death and concern beyond the physiological aspects of dying. This is in contrast to a medical focus on pain and suffering associated with death. Rather, quality of life at the end of life focuses on life, rather than death, even in terminally ill patients. Bradley and associates (2001) discuss the notion of quality of life trajectories because it suggests that dying is a social process that changes over time, rather than death as simply a biological event. Trajectory refers to a particular path and can include a change in the pattern of health status. In the matter of end-of-life trajectories, one could think of one trajectory as referring to sudden death from an unexpected cause, such as an accident or heart attack. A second trajectory could refer to a steady decline in health status from a progressive and fairly predictable disease, such as cancer. A third trajectory could refer to a long period of chronic illness with gradual decline and periodic crises, any of which may result in sudden death. Congestive heart failure would be an example. Note that all these trajectories define living near death in terms of health status. This is not surprising, given that death is defined in terms of physiological factors.

Quality-of-life trajectories, in contrast, would include all dimensions of living that characterize a **good death**. Reviewing the different domains, Bradley and associates (2001) report that between 20 and 70 percent of dying patients are inadequately treated for pain. Other common physical symptoms experienced by the dying include fatigue, drowsiness, nausea, dyspnea, and insomnia. A decrease in physical function and an increase in physical symptoms are related to nearness to death. Psychologically, it appears that depression increases with nearness to death and that suicide rates are higher among terminally ill adults than among healthy adults. Some individuals lack social supports to meet both instrumental and emotional needs at this time of their lives. And, as already noted, religious beliefs do not seem to change much with impending death. Those who are not religious are more likely to be depressed. Communication is also important at the end of life, both because the individual has sufficient information of the situation in order to maintain control and make decisions and because they can convey their wishes. When multiple dimensions of life are taken into account in examining quality of life near the end, it becomes clear that one may have poor physical health but the overall quality of life may still be high, even in the face of death. For some, social and spiritual health may have greater importance than physical health. Quality-of-life trajectories (rather than health-status trajectories) could include, for example, good psychological health, a strong sense of one's self and of control of one's dying process, loved ones close by, and good communication with health care professionals and with loved ones, whether in prolonged physical decline or in swift decline.

Discussions about dying, rather than death, about living during the end of life, and about quality of life near the end place the emphasis on continued life, even near death. This emphasis ensures the inclusion of psychological, social, and spiritual issues, in addition to physiological concerns. It leads to a particular type of care for those who are at the end of their lives. We turn now to a discussion of care at the end of life.

Care of the Dying

At the end of life, seniors want candid but sensitive communication; they also want respect and recognition and a multidisciplinary approach that focuses on medical needs as well as on psychosocial, spiritual, and emotional needs. High value is placed on **comfort**, a term that puts the focus on the person receiving the care, rather than on the provider. Comfort is subjective; only the individual knows whether or not she or he is comfortable. As noted by Hurley and associates (2001), physical comfort is part of overall comfort but it also includes a state of "contented well being," which includes both psychological and spiritual well being. The term comfort has been examined in terms of three different aspects. One includes a state of ease and contentment. Another is relief from discomfort. And another is transcendence or being strengthened and invigorated. Transcendence refers to being free to take control of one's own decisions and one's own destiny.

Comfort leads us to the broader issue of quality of care when we are dying, in a time in which chronic illness has extended the trajectory of dying and blurred the boundaries between when one is living with chronic illness and when one is dying. Advanced technologies need not be compatible with dying with dignity. Leading causes of death are now from chronic progressive organ system failure—heart disease, cancer, stroke. After interviewing persons with life-threatening illness, those caring for someone with a life-threatening illness, surviving family members or significant others, and professional caregivers, Teno and associates (2001) summarized the areas that they believe are relevant for quality of care:

- Spirituality and personal growth while dying
- A natural death in familiar surroundings with loved ones
- Symptom management
- Sensitive communication to allow decision making and planning
- Family and patient treated as a unit

- Absence of financial, emotional, and physical burden for family members
- Autonomy or right of self-determination for the patient.

Despite the fact that seniors themselves seem to know what they want for end-of-life care, research on health care providers, most notably physicians, suggests that seniors do not have a say in this decision and that health care professionals do not provide care that is consistent with the wishes of the seniors. Physicians often make their decisions about care to dying patients without much input from others (Baggs & Schmitt, 2000). In Israel, for example, physicians are more likely to use life-sustaining treatment than what the older adults actually want (Carmel 1999). Similarly, Schlegel and Shannon (2000) found in a study of nurse practitioners that a significant number were ill informed about legal guidelines and few actually incorporated advanced care planning into their clinical practice.

Now that death occurs primarily in old age from chronic illnesses, the dividing line between when one is ill and when one is dying is not clear cut. Chronic illnesses evolve in a gradual fashion. Determining when one is dying is, therefore, a clinical judgment. Relatedly, medical care tends to focus on survival, even survival at all costs. Interestingly, Kaplan and Schneider (2001) note that this tendency to prolong life at all costs is contrary to the Hippocratic corpus, wherein physicians are urged that when a disease is too strong for available remedies, the physician should *not* expect it to be overcome by medicine and urges the physician *not* to attempt what does not belong to nature.

The role of the physician at the end of life is important. Most adults want realistic estimates of how long they can expect to live. The issue, therefore, of physicians' communication with patients is one of particular importance near the end of life. Yet, more often than not, there has been a lack of communication, both because of the difficulty of definitive diagnoses and prognosis and because of a desire to maintain the hopes of the patient. In addition, there is often professional discomfort in discussing death. This is not an easy area; the physician must maintain a balance between honesty and compassion (Bradley, et al, 2001). Yet accurate communication can be especially important so that individuals have an opportunity to prepare themselves and their families for death and make important decisions about the type of treatment they wish to receive, setting their financial affairs in order, speaking with and seeing individuals that they particularly want to communicate with and so on. For some, learning the truth of their conditions and their likely time to death can be important to prepare adequately for their impending death. In order for the individual to have control, he or she must have the appropriate information. At the present time, with the majority of deaths occurring in hospitals, there is often no evidence of preparation in order to achieve the best death possible.

What is considered appropriate information varies by cultural group. For example, First Nations culture has values prohibiting direct communication involving terminal prognosis or palliative care options. Kaufert (1999) found that younger patients favoured more explicit communication about these matters than did older individuals. Such cultural attitudes make direct communication difficult. In addition, cultural attitudes can change over time. Researchers in the Netherlands (Wouters, 1990) note that the period from 1930 to 1955 was characterized by silence regarding impending death, described as "the sacred lie." By the 1955 to 1965 period, it had become more acceptable to talk about one's own and others' emotions in order to gain an acceptance of the impending death. Post-1970 is referred to as a period of secularization of the area in which emotional expression and coping strategies for dealing with death had become acceptable and considered desirable. Blackhall and associates (1995) further report that in the United States, Korean and Mexican seniors are less likely than African and European seniors (35, 48, 63, 69 percent, respectively) to believe that a patient should be told of a terminal prognosis and less likely to believe that the patient should make decisions about the use of life-supporting technologies. Korean and Mexican seniors are more likely to hold a family-centred model of medical decision making rather than one that favours patient autonomy.

Palliative Care

Because of the perception that acute care in hospitals and medical care in general are not adequately meeting the needs of dying individuals in the 21st century, that is, primarily those suffering from chronic illnesses, many advocate for an expansion of **palliative care**. Also known as **hospice care**, the first such program was established in Canada in 1974 in Montreal at the Royal Victoria Hospital under Dr. Balfour Mount. A few months later, Dr. Paul Hentleff established a similar program at St. Boniface Hospital in Winnipeg. In Quebec, the term "palliative care" was used, rather than hospice, and is a unique Canadian use of the term. The word "maison" is also used in Quebec. In the early 1980s the Palliative Care Foundation of Canada was established, closing in 1991. Later in that year, the Canadian Palliative Care Association was established. Provincial associations began first in Ontario (1982) and British Columbia (1983) and are now evident in all provinces. There are currently over 700 hospice and palliative care programs in Canada (Victoria Hospice Society, 1998).

In February 2001, the British Columbia government announced the establishment of the Palliative Care Benefits Program in order to remove financial barriers for terminally ill persons who wish to receive care at home. This program ensures the same pharmaceutical benefits, medical supplies, and equipment people would receive if they remained in hospitals. In the first nine months, 3,500 persons were enrolled, of whom the vast majority (98 percent) were cancer patients. To be eligible for this program, individuals must be in the terminal stages of a life-threatening disease or illness with a life expectancy of up to six months, be British Columbia residents, and be eligible to be covered under the provincial medical services plan.

The hospice has arisen as an alternative to institutional care. It provides care as near to home and in as home-like a setting as possible, if not in the home itself. In some instances, palliative care units or wards are established within acute care hospitals; sometimes they are free standing. Canada now has a federal minister with special responsibility for palliative care and, in June 2001, set aside $1 million to coordinate the development of a national strategy on end-of-life care, beginning with the establishment of a secretariat on palliative care. A senate subcommittee released their report on palliative care, entitled *Quality End-of-Life Care: The Right of Every Canadian*. This was a year after the formation of the Quality End-of-Life Care Coalition in 2000, at a meeting of more than 20 national stakeholder groups.

The palliative care information sheet for seniors, made available by the Division of Aging and Seniors of the Ministry of Health of the federal government, states that the goal of palliative care is to provide the best quality of life for the critically or terminally ill by ensuring their comfort and dignity. It meets not only physical needs but also psychological, social, cultural, emotional, and spiritual needs of the ill person and his or her family. Palliative care, in other words, is an idea whose time has come in Canada. The hospice movement is an effort to move away from the medicalization of death. Many of the hospices, though, are used primarily by cancer or AIDS (acquired immune deficiency syndrome) patients, denying many older individuals the specialist care offered by hospices. Many are thereby denied "a good death" by being denied control of their own dying process. Palliative care represents person-centred care, in which the dying individual develops a trusting relationship with care providers and is treated within a biographical approach, wherein her or his lived lives and present anxieties and needs are voiced.

In the United States, there is a differentiation between the terms "hospice" and "palliative care," where "hospice" is formalized with a set of practices and closely linked to federal requirements for Medicare funding. "Palliative care" is more of a descriptive term that is not linked to reimbursement or length of care. This differs from what we have in Canada. The National Hospice Organization and Accreditation Committee (1997) of the United States recommends several outcomes for hospice care. They include:

- Self-determined life closure through staff prevention of problems associated with coping, grieving, and existential results related to imminence of death
- Staff support of achievement of the highest level of consciousness possible
- Staff promotion of adaptive behaviours that are personally effective for a patient and family caregiver.

Safe and comfortable dying requires staff to appropriately treat and prevent extension of disease and/or comorbidity factors, to treat and prevent treatment side effects and distressing symptoms, to supply treatments that are consistent with the patient's and family's functional capacity, to prevent crises due to resource deficits, and to respond appropriately to financial, legal, and environmental problems that could compromise care. Effective grieving requires: the treatment and prevention of coping problems related to death; coaching patient and family through grieving; assessing and responding to incidents of anticipatory grief; preventing premature death; and identifying need for grief work—such as effecting reconciliation, assessing the potential for complicated grief, and assisting the family in integrating the memory of their loved one into their lives.

The holistic view of hospice is consistent with incorporating comfort care into this program. The focus in palliative care is on maximum comfort and not simply maximum survival. It refers to a comprehensive and interdisciplinary patient–family systematic approach to coordinated end-of-life care and services. Comfort care is often consistent with limitations on aggressive medical interventions. Aggressive medical care would include, for example, aggressive diagnostic tests and treatment of coexisting medical conditions. It can include transfer to acute care hospitals or units of hospitals and tube feeding if normal eating is not possible. Limitations to treatment that are consistent with a comfort approach include, for example, no cardiopulmonary resuscitation, no transfer to acute care for technological interventions, no aggressive treatment of intercurrent infections, and no artificial feeding. It would include medical interventions that increase comfort level.

There are criticisms of hospice care. Hospice care is not necessarily appropriate for everyone. Some individuals, for example, may not wish to forgo curative and life-sustaining treatment interventions. They may wish that everything possible, including aggressive medical treatment, be utilized in order to prolong their lives. In addition, there are still difficulties with pain management, depending on the disease one is suffering. It has been estimated that between 10 and 50 percent of patients receiving palliative care still report significant pain (Cicirelli, 2001). For others, increased dosages of pain medication can lead to decreased cognitive functioning, unconsciousness, and terminal sedation—all difficult when trying to maintain a quality of life while dying. Part of the difficulty arises from the fact that there tends to be an increase in symptoms near the end of life and increased severity of many symptoms as death nears (Miller, et al, 2001). Although higher quality of life has been shown to be related to fewer symptoms and lesser severity of symptoms at this time, there is an increasing nonresponsiveness to inform those who care for the individual of symptomatology as death nears. As many as 50 percent of patients in the two weeks prior to death and 80 percent of patients in the one week prior to death are reportedly unable to convey their symptom status.

Non-Life-Sustaining Measures, Euthanasia, Assisted Suicide

This takes us squarely to the area of non-life-sustaining measures and into the area of euthanasia and assisted suicide. There is now general consensus that "heroic," life-sustaining efforts that simply prolong the dying process are unnecessary and unacceptable. There is less consensus on active euthanasia and assisted suicide. Aggressive medical care seems to improve neither life expectancy nor quality of life. In a survey of over 2,000 Canadian adults by Singer and associates (1995), 85 percent of Canadians agreed with forgoing life-sustaining treatment in a competent individual if that individual is unlikely to recover and 35 percent if the person is likely to recover. For the individual unlikely to recover, 58 percent also approved of assisted suicide and 66 percent approved of euthanasia. Some individuals prefer a greater say in their own decision making at the end of life, whereas others prefer to delegate the decision making to physicians, to God, or to fate. In the United States, Cicirelli (1995) found that over half the seniors he studied favoured going on living, regardless of the situation; one-third favoured deferring or delegating an end-of-life decision to someone close or to a physician; and about one-tenth favoured ending life through suicide, assisted suicide, or voluntary active euthanasia. African Americans, those with less education, those with a fundamentalist church background and high religiousness, as well as those with higher self-esteem, less depression and less fear of the dying process were more likely to favour going on living, regardless of the situation. Caucasian Americans seem to be more likely than African Americans to make decisions involving limiting care and withholding treatment before death. African Americans seem more likely to want all possible care in order to prolong life.

Interestingly, in an Israeli study, Carmel and Mutrand (1999) found that over a two-year period, these preferences are largely stable among older persons. Most stable of all are those who did not want to prolong their life at baseline. There was remarkable stability in preference for life-sustaining treatments among severely ill older adults. Among a Canadian sample of seniors in a chronic care hospital, most preferred to retain some control in decision making at the end of their lives. Most wanted to make their exit quickly and painlessly with as much privacy and dignity as possible and linked euthanasia and assisted suicide with severity of illness. The more severe the illness, the more likely they were to consider euthanasia and assisted suicide acceptable (Kelner & Meslin, 1994).

The topic of euthanasia and assisted suicide is, perhaps, the most difficult. This area can include **passive euthanasia**, referring to the withholding or withdrawing of artificial life support or other medical treatment and allowing the patient to die, **physician-assisted suicide** or **active voluntary euthanasia**, wherein the physician administers a lethal dose of medication to a competent person who requests it, **involuntary euthanasia** and **nonvoluntary euthanasia**, referring to ending the life of a mentally incompetent person who is unaware of what is happening and is not able to request it. Euthanasia, furthermore, can utilize slow procedures, or it can include rapid mercy killing. Slow procedures would refer to clinical practices of treating a terminal patient that lead to a comfortable but not particularly quick death.

The extent to which seniors support euthanasia and/or assisted suicide is unclear, although a significant proportion clearly do. A survey in the United States, however, reports that only 41 percent of seniors approve of legalizing physician-assisted suicide (Seidlitz, et al. 1995). Yet, a multiracial study, including Chinese Americans, Filipino Americans, Hawaiians, Japanese Americans, and Caucasian Americans holidaying in Hawaii, found that except for Filipino Americans, 75 percent or more of each ethnic group believed that those in pain and with a terminal illness should have access to assistance with dying. Over half the respondents said that this would also be acceptable for persons with current physical disability for which they needed help with "every little thing" (Koch, et al, 1999).

In 1994, Oregon became the first state in the United States to legalize physician-assisted suicide. Mangus and colleagues (1999) surveyed medical students within Oregon State and those outside and found that 60 percent of medical students in Oregon and 60 percent of those outside favoured the legalization of physician-assisted suicide. However, Oregon students were less willing to actually write a lethal prescription themselves (52 percent of Oregon students versus 60 percent of students outside Oregon, and 44 percent of fourth-year Oregon students versus 60 percent of those outside Oregon), suggesting hesitancy to include it in one's practice. This hesitancy on the part of physicians is also reported in a study by Carver and associates (1999) that included neuro-oncologists, amylotrophic lateral sclerosis (ALS) specialists, and neurologists. They report that just over a third think it is illegal to administer analgesics in doses that risk respiratory depression to the point of death; 40 percent believe they should obtain legal counsel when considering stopping life-sustaining treatment; and 50 percent believe physician-assisted suicide should be made legal by statute for terminally ill patients.

Other research by Doukas and colleagues (1999) demonstrates how the personal values of the physician are reflected within their attitudes toward physician-assisted death. Those holding personal values promoting continued life-sustaining treatment in their own terminal care and had strong values against their own withdrawal of treatment in terminal care were more likely to be opposed to physician-assisted death. This is often a dilemma for practitioners. If they practise in an area where physician-assisted suicide is legal, they may be asked to practise against their own personally held beliefs. Even the area of the removal of life-sustaining supports is contentious. In the United States, for example, all 50 states now have laws permitting the refusal of life-support, but there seems to be a gap between physician practice and patient and family wishes. Indeed, research by Covinsky and associates (2000) notes that physician, nurse, and surrogate understanding of patient preferences when it comes to these matters is only moderately better than chance.

Advanced Directives

Given that some individuals suffer from mental impairment, including dementia, toward the end of life, the possibility of withdrawing life-sustaining treatment and of physician-assisted suicide brings us to the topic of advanced directives. Ensuring elderly individuals can make their own decisions regarding end-of-life issues does not necessarily work in instances of cognitive impairment. Often, the individual involved cannot do so. The ability to make decisions is referred to as competence or decision-making capacity. Only a court can rule that an individual is incompetent to make his or her own decisions. Courts focus on various aspects of a person's decision-making capacity, including whether the individual is able to understand information, to deliberate, and to communicate. It is not, however, clear cut, as many individuals have fluctuating competence. That is, they may be competent at some times and not at others, or in some areas and not in others. Advanced directives are for an individual to leave in case they may become unable to make their own decisions.

Both living wills and durable powers of attorney for health care are considered advanced directives. A **living will** is a document in which the individual expresses his or her treatment preferences in specific situations. A **durable power of attorney for health care** is a document in which an individual appoints a proxy decision-maker who will make their treatment decisions on their behalf when they are unable to do so. When an individual is considered incompetent and there is no advanced directive, a decision can be made using the **substituted judgment standard** in which another individual, a surrogate, is called upon to make a decision that they believe the individual would make if he or she were still capable. Alternatively, they may use a **best interests standard**, in which the substitute, the surrogate, is to decide on the basis of the well being of the individual. Often, it is a family member who is closest to the individual who is asked to be the surrogate.

The Royal Dutch Medical Association believes that in exceptional circumstances, voluntary euthanasia or physician-assisted suicide can be justified. The association names early-stage dementia, in which the patient has a clear diagnosis and a persistent and well-considered wish to die, as an exceptional circumstance. Severe dementia, in which the individual has left an advanced directive specifying life-termination should there be mental incompetence or where these wishes can be ascertained with certainty, would also receive support for euthanasia. Research in the United States (Mebane, et al, 1999) demonstrates that approximately two-thirds of all physicians support the use of advanced directives but older African American physicians are less likely to do so than younger African American or Caucasian American physicians. Caucasian American physicians are much more likely to agree that tube feeding terminally ill patients is "heroic" than is true for African American physicians. Caucasian American physicians are also much more likely to support physician-assisted suicide, for themselves personally as well as for their patients. Among Veteran's Affairs physicians in the United States, the majority believes that physicians should be responsible for initiating discussions about advanced directives and most report having done so with their older patients (Markson, et al, 1997). Advanced directives are considered important because even when family members are appointed to make decisions for seniors, research (Zweibel & Cassel, 1989) demonstrates that there is little congruence between what the family member believes the elderly person would choose and what the elderly person says they would choose.

Importantly, research (Bevans & Cole, 2001) seems to indicate that physicians are not good at perceiving patient preferences. This means advanced directives can be very important. Unfortunately, it appears that even when there are advanced directives, there is little likelihood that they will be followed. Evidence suggests that costs of end-of-life care are no different between those treated in the presence of, compared with those without, advanced directives (Lawton, 2001; Kaplan & Schneider, 2001). That is, there is little evidence to suggest that advanced directives affect either treatment provided or cost of care provided at the end of life. This is where an effective advocate can be important for the senior, someone who points out the advanced directive and monitors to ensure that the directive is followed.

Even within nursing home populations, it appears that discussions concerning advanced directives are not frequent. Indeed, Bradley and associates (1998) report that 71.5 percent of nursing home residents in their study had no discussion of future treatment preferences in their medical records. Similarly, among a study of seriously ill hospitalized patients, Heyland et al. (2000) report that only a quarter of patients had written advanced directives. However, 80 percent wanted an active role, either shared or informed, in decisions about end-of-life care. Some have reported the same black–white divide noted earlier. Hopp and Duffy (2000) report that African Americans are less likely to have advanced directives or durable power of attorney for health care and less likely to request restriction of treatment than are Caucasian Americans. However, Dupree (1998) found that African Americans did not want unconditional aggressive end-of-life treatment. Cultural differences surrounding these issues are especially important in a multicultural society, such as in Canada. The health care system, to date, has not given much attention to cultural variations in death and dying. In Japan, for example, interest in advanced directives seems to be considerably less than in North America. In Japanese culture, there is a high rate of entrusting all decisions to the family (Voltz, et al, 1998). We do not know whether Japanese Canadians feel this way or not.

Advanced directives can include preferences related to withholding life-sustaining treatments as well as requests for euthanasia and assisted suicide under some circumstances. **Aid in dying** is particularly controversial and can include both assisted suicide—as when an individual provides the means for another to end their own life, such as a physician *prescribing* a drug in a lethal dose that can be taken by the individual—and euthanasia—when the actions of an individual cause the death of another in order to relieve their suffering, such as when a physician *administers* a lethal dose of a drug to a patient. Physicians are often critical in this process because, as noted earlier, individuals tend to die in hospitals and physicians are the only individuals who can legally prescribe drugs. Assisted suicide and euthanasia, therefore, are very much medical issues as well as legal issues. It is often believed that individuals request aid in dying in order to relieve pain and discomfort and some argue that an expansion of hospice services would, in fact, take away the need for euthanasia. The argument (see, for example, Byock, 1993) is that a hospice focuses on life and the alleviation of suffering so that individuals can be confident they will not be abandoned in their dying and that the request for euthanasia would dissipate. However, in a study of over 1,000 older decedents in the United States, it was found that dissatisfaction with comfort care was not associated with requests for aid in dying and that those with hospice care were more interested in assisted suicide or euthanasia. Some suggest that one of the reasons for wishing aid in dying is a lack of hope and purpose, not physical pain (Bevans & Cole, 2001; Jacobson, et al, 1995).

Certainly, not all, or even most, individuals at the end of the life want to hasten their death, but a significant minority do. In a national study of palliative care physicians in Sweden, physicians from the Swedish Association for the Study of Pain and physicians in specialties of care of dying adult patients, more than half the physicians said that their patients had expressed a wish to die. One-third of the physicians had given analgesics or other drugs in sufficient doses to hasten a patient's death. A third had been asked for active euthanasia, and 10 percent had been asked to assist suicide. In a study of social workers in British Columbia, Ogden and Young (1998) report that over 20 percent of all social workers and nearly 40 percent of those who worked with medical employers reported having been consulted by a patient about assisted suicide or voluntary euthanasia. Data from the Netherlands reveal that among physicians attending deaths, only 2.4 percent claim that the death resulted from euthanasia and only 0.2 percent from assisted suicide in 1995, virtually no change from a similar survey in 1990. In 0.7 percent of the cases, life was ended without the patient's explicit consent (VanderMaas, et al, 1996). And an English hospital study (Seal & Addington-Hall, 1994) reports that 24 percent wished to die sooner than they did; 4 percent requested euthanasia.

The issue is not easy. Particularly given that end-of-life suffering is now largely due to chronic illnesses and the fact that many medical and technological advances have resulted in prolongation of dying, the question is often one of when to stop prolonging the dying process. Ethicists debate whether killing to relieve suffering is moral or immoral. When is the individual's right to autonomy to control his or her own destiny morally correct? Cicirelli (2001) summarizes euthanasia at the present time:

- Attitudes toward physician-assisted suicide and euthanasia are becoming more acceptable over time
- A small but significant proportion of older adults would choose this course if their quality of life were low enough

- There seems to be a preference for one of these options over suicide
- Physicians would prefer assisted suicide to euthanasia
- Fewer physicians favour **aid in dying** than is true of older adults.

Family and Friends at the End of Life

When examining end-of-life issues, the focus tends to be on the dying individual. However, many do not die alone, and most are leaving behind family and friends. Palliative care, as noted earlier, embraces both the older individual and the family as clients. Its comfort is directed toward both. Indeed, sometimes families support palliative care because they have watched a loved one suffer in the hospital, with prolongation of the dying process through technological means. Among hospitalized patients in the United States, Baker and colleagues (2000) found that 16 percent of family members of those who had died were dissatisfied with patient comfort and that 30 percent were dissatisfied with communication and decision making. Hanson and associates (1997) report, after interviewing family members, that less than 10 percent of family members wanted more or different treatment than their loved one received. For loved ones who had received hospice care, families were very satisfied (91 percent), while of those whose loved ones had died in a nursing home, only half gave very positive scores for the care received.

Although generally, families are trusted to make the right and best decisions, conflicts can and do arise between the dying individual and family members. There is not always consensus and congeniality. Family members face the death of a loved one and its accompanying bereavement and grieving. The grieving process involves not only the depth of numerous emotions, including feeling powerlessness, anxiety, depression, and immobilization, but also the challenges and opportunities of relearning one's social worlds and the relationship to self and to the deceased. Part of the grieving process is now believed to entail not necessarily letting go of the one who has died but of finding ways to maintain connections to loved ones. Memories, rituals, dreams, and thoughts can all be part of this process (Attig, 1995; Stajduhar, 1999).

One area in which wishes of the dying individual and of family members can conflict is a death at home. The senior may view staying at home as critical to maintenance of independence and of self-identity. In spite of the growing popularity of this option, it can cause great demands on family members. Stajduhar and Davies (1998) note that death at home has become a "gold standard" among palliative care practitioners. However, while it is widely believed that dying at home can increase a sense of normalcy, security, and familiarity, the situation can turn the home environment into a medicalized and institutionalized setting, disrupting the daily routine of family members.

Often, supports within community services are not available in order to assist families. Indeed, Stajduhar (2001) notes that because of the idealization of dying at home, caregivers may feel pressured into providing care at home when they do not particularly want to and when the necessary supports are not in place to permit a good death in this environment. Her findings also suggest that the wishes of the dying individual are often privileged over those of family caregivers. The fact that caregivers overlook their own needs and focus their energy and attention on the needs of the elderly individual is not new (Chappell, 1998). Importantly, the trend toward the medicalization of palliative care may be counter to some of the basic tenets of that movement. (Note the similarity to health reform and its movement that is counter to the vision of health reform.) This can increase burden on family members.

The role of non-kin, that is, of friends of the dying individual, is not well prescribed within society. Often, professionals and family members exclude (not necessarily intentionally) friends, disenfranchising them in the dying process. Indeed, friends may be seen as an intrusion into the family at this time. Family ties at the end of life are considered so strong that often individuals do not know what to do with friends, and friends do not know how to approach the family in order to see someone of value to them. We do not know the extent to which dying individuals have a preference for non-kin to be with them. Institutions often have a policy not to allow non-kin to visit those who are very ill and/or dying. Similarly, airlines tend to restrict compassionate fares only to immediate family members.

For a growing number of individuals, the end comes in a nursing home. Especially in Canada, nursing homes are a place of last abode. Few leave before they die. Nevertheless, nursing homes tend to emphasize that they are a place for living, not for dying, death, and bereavement. Moss (2001) notes that the **living-dying interval**, that is, the interval between knowledge of impending death and death itself, characterizes the nursing home environment and its exclusion from mainstream society. And while deaths occur frequently in nursing homes, the term "dying" is reserved for the very last days of life, and the ritual surrounding death tends to be invisible to nursing home residents (Marshall, 1976). Stated differently, a conspiracy of silence has been reported around death and dying in nursing homes, perhaps reflecting the staff's own discomfort and fear of their own mortality. Nursing home staff try to maintain a routine of normalcy in an environment in which death occurs regularly.

Rubinstein (2001) distinguishes between transcendence and embeddedness. **Transcendence** refers to the quality of dying that refers to its meaning in a larger context, such as spiritual or humanistic. **Embeddedness** refers to the quality of dying in terms of its meaning in the complex context of person, condition, setting, culture, social structure, and other life circumstances. He also draws the distinction between the meaning and experience of the death of a generic older person versus the death of one's close-aged kin. Without family and friends, some die alone in an institutional setting where they are only a generic older person.

Rubinstein reveals that there is among many a fear of not dying. That is, a fear of deteriorating and losing functioning, especially mental functioning.

A nursing home represents the sequestration of death and dying within modern-day society where elderly individuals in the process of dying are isolated from the rest of society. They can also experience social death, in which they are no longer active agents in other people's lives (Froggatt, 2001). And further, within the nursing home, those in their last days are further sequestered within this world. They are less likely, for example, to be brought out to public spaces to eat or watch television and are put to bed first. The author describes this sequestration in nursing homes less as a clear separation of those who are living from those who dying than as the creation of transitional states between these two conditions that could be occupied variously by residents temporarily or permanently.

At the present time, nursing homes tend not to provide hospice care, although this could change. This may partly be due to the fact that hospice has developed around the focus on treating cancer patients, whereas cancer is not a major cause of death of nursing home residents. One could think of hospice wards in nursing homes for individuals, where physicians certify that they would die within six months. In the nursing home, as in other parts of society, friends made within the residence tend not to be incorporated into the grieving process when someone dies. This tends to be reserved for family members.

Death Rituals

We all die and we need a means both to dispose of the physical remains and to cope with this important transition. Death rituals, therefore, are rites of passage that provide formal recognition of the transition from life to death. In doing so, psychologically and emotionally, they assist those left behind to accept the death of a loved one and to continue on with life without that individual. As noted in the National Advisory Committee's Guide to End-of-Life Care for Seniors (2000), funerals serve to:

- Increase the reality of death
- Provide a legitimate public occasion for expressing and validating grief
- Provide evidence for the worth of the senior who has died
- Provide social support for the survivors
- Help occupy the bereaved person's time in a difficult situation
- Provide predictability and organization in the midst of an uncontrollable situation
- Present an opportunity to reflect on one's own mortality
- May reaffirm ethnic or religious identity
- Emphasize the cohesiveness of the family or larger group beyond the loss of one of its members
- Remind survivors that structure, organization, and life go on
- Reaffirm social order

- Help children to learn about death and about the comfort, love, and support that humans can provide each other in times of crisis
- Mirror the values and expectations of a society
- Provide an opportunity to examine the nature of life within a cultural group.

Phrased slightly differently, Auger (2000) notes four functions of most funerals:

1. Provide a supportive relationship for the bereaved
2. Reinforce the reality of death
3. Acknowledge and encourage the open expression of the mourners' feelings of loss and grief and share their experiences
4. Mark a fitting conclusion to the life of the one who has died.

Most people in Canada are buried in the earth after they die. Entombment—the placing of the casket in a mausoleum above ground, arranged in rows stacked one above the other—occurs much less often. Cremation, however, is increasing in popularity. Tipper (1989) has demonstrated that cremation increased by fully 55 percent in the decade between 1977 and 1987. While cremation had been practised in Europe since 1400 B.C., Canada's first crematorium was built in Montreal in 1901. The reasons for this increase in popularity are believed to include the growing scarcity of urban space as well as the lower expense involved in cremation. Cremation costs have been estimated to be as much as 30 percent less than traditional burial services.

The funeral business has received some attention from researchers because of its role within a youth-oriented, capitalistic society. The dramaturgical aspects of the funeral industry (preparing the dead to be presentable for viewing in such a way that the horrors of mortality are tolerable) have often been highlighted. This includes, in addition, the demeanour of funeral directors when dealing with this issue with the public. Fulton and Metress (1995) have demonstrated this through the use of the language of funeral directors. For example, they favour the term "cremains" over the term "ashes"; "interment" over "burial"; "final resting place" over "graveyard" or "cemetery"; "casket" over "coffin"; "remains," "the deceased," "loved one" or "(the individual's name)" over "corpse" or "dead body"; "passing on" or "lying in repose" over "dead" or "death"; "funeral director" over "embalmer," "mortician," or "undertaker"; "preservation" or "restoration" over "embalming"; "funeral home" over "mortuary"; and "monument" over "tombstone."

In Wernick's terms (1995), funeral homes are in the business of imaging death. According to this author, they have also commodified death, turning it into a lucrative business endeavour. He points out that the North American practice of embalming and the popularity of park-like cemeteries are all attempts at making death acceptable. Death is made acceptable by removing the signs of death from the ritual. This contradiction feeds on a denial of death.

There is an increase in arranging one's own funeral, that is, bypassing the funeral director. A doctor or hospital can often provide the necessary forms and permissions. There are now, in various parts of the country, consumer-run memorial societies and funeral cooperatives, which provide simple, no-frills, and inexpensive funerals.

Funeral traditions differ both within and among groups. Subcultural groups often differ from the host society. First Nations peoples, for example, are more likely to live in rural and isolated areas and to adhere to the circle of life, wherein death is perceived as a reunion with other family members. People will relate a dream in which a mother or father or other departed family member is beckoning the elder to join them. Here, death is seen as another stage in the circle of life. On reserves, men and boys often share in the digging of graves by hand, while stories are shared about the deceased, and women provide sustenance to the workers and mourners. Among some tribes, totem poles are built to honour the dead. They draw on their visions, dreams, and spirits to help them deal with death. It is important, though, to recognize that beliefs may differ from tribe to tribe and that not all First Nations persons adhere to traditional tribal beliefs at all.

Recognizing the Importance of the End of Life

Despite the universality of death and dying, and notwithstanding funeral practices that have emerged within Canadian society, this aspect of life has not received particular attention. It is significant therefore that in the 21st century, the federal government is recognizing the importance of this area. In early 2001, the subcommittee of the standing Senate Committee on Social Affairs, Science, and Technology issued recommendations for quality end-of-life care. This subcommittee urged the development of a national strategy for end-of-life care and had among its recommendations:

- The federal government must assess the need for home-care and pharmacare for the dying, working with the provinces to develop funding for the programs. Income security and job protection for family members who care for the terminally ill should also be implemented.
- Professionals involved in end-of-life care require multidisciplinary training and education. The federal government should explore such programs with provincial governments and educational agencies.
- The federal government should have an interdepartmental approach to end-of-life care and consider the establishment of a federal, provincial, territorial strategy for this issue with appropriate funding.
- End-of-life research is needed and should be coordinated by the federal minister of health.
- The national Canadian Institutes of Health Research should focus on end-of-life issues and the National Canadian Institute for Health Information should develop indicators for quality end-of-life.

Similarly, the Canadian Palliative Care Association has identified as priority issues: the availability and access to end-of-life care, professional education, research and data collection, support to families and caregivers, and public education and awareness.

Such recognition of end-of-life issues arises from the fact that virtually all of us can now expect to live to old age and can expect to have a prolonged period of dying before actual death occurs. In the years ahead, we can expect much greater attention to this area.

CHAPTER SUMMARY

This chapter has focused on end-of-life issues, including living while dying and death itself. More than ever before, dying is a topic of old-age because so many of us now die in old age.

Key ideas to remember from this chapter include:

- Death occurs for most of us in hospital, although this is less true of those who are living in long-term care institutions prior to death.
- Given the association of prolonged chronic illness with old age, it is difficult to diagnose when one has entered the dying process as opposed to simply being ill.
- Death is no longer simply defined as the stopping of the heartbeat or the cessation of breathing. One can be brain dead.
- Dying is social, emotional, and spiritual, as well as biological. Preparation for death and the dying process can include bringing meaning to one's life. Valuation of life is a concept distinct from fear of death. One can examine trajectories of life at the end of life as well as trajectories of dying.
- A holistic model of care of the dying places focus on meaning of life and on comfort in addition to attending to the physiological needs of the individual.
- A palliative care movement has arisen because of the inappropriateness of much intensive high-tech medical care in hospitals. Hospice or palliative care is an alternative to institutional care, providing care as near to home and in as home-like a setting as possible.
- The prolongation of the dying process and appropriate care of the dying leads to issues involving euthanasia and assisted suicide. Evidence, to date, suggests that most health care workers, including physicians, do not take dying individuals' wishes into account in terms of these issues.
- Similarly, even when advanced directives are issued by individuals, current research suggests that physicians do not abide by them.
- There is little literature that focuses on understanding the experiences and needs of family and friends of the dying individual. There is some evidence that friends tend to be shut out of this experience because of cultural beliefs that family members are the only ones who should be involved at the very end, despite wishes to the contrary by friends.

- While nursing homes are seen by many in the outside world as places for the dying, within the nursing home, those closest to death are separated out so that others may attend more to immediate living.
- Funeral rituals serve many purposes for those who are left behind, including helping them to cope with the loss of a loved one, to accept the reality of the death, and to move on to a new stage in their own lives.
- Funeral practices can differ among subcultural groups.
- The need for much greater attention to quality care at the end of life is receiving recognition nationally at this time in Canada.

KEY TERMS

Brain death, **(p. 438)**

Crises of meaning, **(p. 438)**

Soul pain, **(p. 438)**

Spirituality, **(p. 438)**

Quality-adjusted life years, **(p. 438)**

Valuation of life (VOL), **(p. 439)**

Fear of death, **(p. 439)**

A good death, **(p. 440)**

Comfort, **(p. 441)**

Palliative care, **(p. 443)**

Hospice care, **(p. 443)**

Passive euthanasia, **(p. 446)**

Physician-assisted suicide, **(p. 446)**

Active voluntary euthanasia, **(p. 446)**

Involuntary euthanasia, **(p. 446)**

Nonvoluntary euthanasia, **(p. 446)**

Living will, **(p. 448)**

Durable power of attorney for health care, **(p. 448)**

Substituted judgment standard, **(p. 448)**

Best interests standard, **(p. 448)**

Aid in dying, **(p. 449)**

Living–dying interval, **(p. 452)**

Transcendence, **(p. 452)**

Embeddedness, **(p. 452)**

STUDY QUESTIONS

1. What do we mean by a "good death"? What would it look like?

2. Why has palliative care arisen, and what does it strive to offer?

3. How does support for non-life-sustaining measures, euthanasia, and assisted suicide differ between seniors and health care providers?

4. Discuss the pros and cons of advanced directives.

5. What do we know about the differential experience of friends and family of dying individuals at the end of life?

6. Why is the need for quality care at the end of life now being recognized and what issues need to be addressed?

SUGGESTED READINGS

Carmel, S. (1999). Life-sustaining treatments: What doctors do, what they want for themselves, and what elderly persons want. *Social Science and Medicine, 49*(10), 1401–1408.

Cicirelli, V.G. (1999). Personality and demographic factors in older adult's fear of death. *Gerontologist, 39*(5), 569–579.

Froggatt, K. (2001). Life and death in English nursing homes: Sequestration or transition? *Ageing and Society, 21*(3), 319–332.

Lawton, M.P., Moss, M., Hoffman, C., Grant, R., Have, T.T., & Kleban, M.H. (1999). Health, valuation of life, and the wish to live. *The Gerontologist, 39*(4), 406–416.

Stajduhar, K., & Davies, B. (1998). Death at home: Challenges for families and directions for the future. *Journal of Palliative Care, 14*(3), 8–14.

REFERENCES

Abel, E.K. (1990). Daughters caring for elderly parents. In J.F. Gubrium & A. Sankar, (Eds.). *The home care experience: Ethnography and policy*, 189-286. Newbury Park, CA: Sage Publications.

Abernethy, B., Thomas, K.T., & Thomas, J.T. (1993). Strategies for improving understanding of motor expertise [or mistakes we have made and things we have learned!] In J.I. Starkes, & F. Allard, (Eds.). *Cognitive issues in motor expertise.* North-Holland: Elsevier.

Achenbaum, W.A. (1995) *Old age in a new land.* Baltimore, MD: John Hopkins University Press.

Achenbaum, W.A. & Bengtson, V.L. (1994). Re-engaging the disengagement theory of aging: On the history and assessment of theory development in gerontology. *Gerontologist, 18*, 756-763.

Achenbaum, W.A. (1997). Critical gerontology. In A. Jamieson, S. Harper, & C. Victor, (Eds.). *Critical approaches to ageing and later life* (pp. 16-26). Buckingham, UK: Open University Press.

Administration on Aging. (1998). The National Elder Abuse Incidence Study; Final Report, September 1998. Administration of Aging and National Centre on Elder Abuse at the American Public Human Services Association.

Adult Literacy in Ontario. (1998). Ottawa, ON: Queens Printers for Ontario.

Aging: the distinction between usual and successful aging. In M.L. Howe, M.J. Stones, & C.J.Brainerd (Eds.), *Cognitive and Behavioral Performance Factors in Atypical Aging* (pp. 181-218). New York: Springer-Verlag.

Ajrouch, K.J., Antonucci, T., & Janevic, M.R. (2001). Social networks amongst blacks and whites: The interaction between race and age. *The Journals of Gerontology: Social Sciences, 56B*, S112-122.

Ajzen, I., & Fishbein, M. (1977). Attitude-behavior relations: A theoretical analysis and review of empirical research. *Psychological Bulletin, 84*, 888-918.

Allan, D.E., & Penning, M. (2001, July). *An early look at regionalization in British Columbia: Regional equity or equality?* Paper presented at the International Association of Gerontology, Vancouver, B.C.

Allard, F. (1993). Cognition, expertise, and motor performance. In J.L. Starkes, & F. Allard, (Eds.). Cognitive issues in motor expertise (pp. 17-34). Amsterdam: Elsevier Science Publishers.

Allport, G. W. (1935). Attitudes. In C. Murchison, (Ed.). Handbook of social psychology (pp. 798-844). Worcester, MA: Clark University Press.

Alwin, D. F., & Campbell, R. T. (2001). Quantitative approaches: Longitudinal methods in the study of human development and aging. In H. Binstock, & L.K. George, (Eds.). *Handbook of aging and the social sciences* (pp. 22-43). San Diego, CA: Academic Press.

Amercian Association of Retired Persons & Travelers Company Foundation (1989). *National survey of caregivers: Working caregivers report.* Washington, DC: American Association of Retired Persons, Program Department; Hartford, CT: Traveler's Companies Foundation.

American Association of Retired Persons (AARP) (1999). Great sex: Modern maturity.

American Association of Retired Persons (AARP) (2001). Public attitudes toward aging, beauty, and cosmetic surgery, http://research.aarp.org./consume/cosmetic_1.html

Andersen, K.L., Masironi, R., Rutenfranz, J., & Seliger, V. (1978). *Habitual physical activity and aging.* Copenhagen: World Health Organization.

Andersen, R., & Newman, J. F. (1973). Societal and individual health determinants of medical care utilization in the United States. *The Milbank Memorial Fund Quarterly, 51*(1), 95-124.

Anderson, J.K. (1991). Racial discourse in Canada, 1875-1980: Race, place and the power of definition. In K.J. Anderson, (Ed.). *Vancouver's China Town* (pp. 8-33). Montreal/Kingston: McGill-Queen's University Press.

Andrews, F.M. (1991). Stability and change in levels and structure of subjective well-being: USA 1972 and 1988. *Social Indicators Research, 25*, 1-30.

Andrews, G., Tennant, G., Hewson, D., & Vaillant, G. (1978). Life event stress, social support, coping style, and risk of psychological impairment. *Journal of Nervous and Mental Disease, 166*, 307-316.

Angel, R, & Tienda, M. (1982). Determinants of extended household structure: Cultural pattern or economic need? *American Journal of Sociology, 87*, 1360-1385.

Antonucci, T.C. & Akiyama, H. (1987). Examination of sex differences in social support among older men and women. *Sex Roles, 17*, 737-749.

Antonucci, T.C. (1985). Personal characteristics, social support and social behaviour. In R.H. Binstock & E. Shanas, (Eds.). *Handbook and the Social Sciences* (2nd ed.). New York, NY: Van Nostrand Reinhold.

Antonucci, T.C. (1990). Social supports and social relationships. In R.H. Binstock and L.K. George, (Eds.). *Handbook of aging and the social sciences* (3rd Ed.), New York, NY: Academic Press.

Aquino, J.A., Russell, D.W., Cutrona, C.E., & Altmaier, E.M. (1996). Employment status, social support, and life satisfaction among the elderly. *Journal of Counseling Psychology, 43*(4), 480-489.

Araujo, A.B., Durante, R., Feldman, H.A., Goldstein, I. & McKinlay, J.B. (1998). The relationship between depressive symptoms and male erectile dysfunction: Cross-sectional results from the Massachusetts Male Aging Study. *MA Psychosomatic Medicine, Cross-cultural Res, 60*(4) pp. 458-465.

Arbuckle, T.Y., Gold, D.P.; Andres, D., & Schwartzman, A. (1992). The role of psychosocial context, age and intelligence in memory performance of older men. *Psychology and Aging, 7,* 25-36.

Arbuckle, T.Y., Maag, U., Pushkar, D., & Chaikelson, J.S. (1998). Individual differences in trajectory of intellectual development over 45 years of adulthood. *Psychology and Aging, 13,* 663-675.

Armstrong, P. & Armstrong, H. (1994). *The double ghetto: Canadian women and their segregated work* (3rd Ed.). Toronto, ON: McClelland & Stewart.

Armstrong, P., & Armstrong, H. (1999). Women, privatization and health care reform: The Ontario scan. Working Paper #10 for the Health Reform Reference Group, Centres of Excellence for Women's Health Program, Women's Health Bureau. Toronto,ON: The National Network of Environments and Women's Health, York University.

Armstrong, P., Armstrong, H., & Coburn, D. (2001). Unhealthy times. Political economy perspectives on health and care in Canada. Toronto, ON: Oxford University Press.

Ashby, A. (1985). *An inquiry into the process of developing a sense of Canadian cultural identity and Canadian cultural consciousness.* Ph.D.Thesis. Toronto, ON: University of Toronto.

Association of Canadian Pension Management (ACPM) (2000). *Dependence or self-reliance: Which way for Canada's retirement income system?* Toronto, ON: ACPM.

Astrand, P-O & Rodahl, K. (1977). *Textbook of work physiology: Physiological bases of behavior* (2nd Ed.). New York, NY: McGraw-Hill.

Atchely, R.C. (1993). Critical perspectives on retirement. In T.R. Cole, W.A. Achenbaum, P.L. Jakobi & R. Kastenbaum, (Eds.). *Voices and visions of aging: Toward a critical gerontology* (pp. 3-19). New York, NY: Springer Publishing Co.

Atchley, R. (1971). Disengagement among professors. *Journal of Gerontology, 26,* 183-190.

Atchley, R. (1989). A continuity theory of normal aging. *Journal of Gerontology: Social Sciences, 52,* 183-190.

Atchley, R.C. (1976). *The sociology of retirement.* New York, NY: Wiley and Sons.

Atkinson, R.C., & Shriffrin, R.M. (1968). Human memory: A proposed system and its control processes. In K.W. Spence, & J.T. Spence, (Eds.). *The psychology of learning and motivation: Advances in research and theory,* vol. 2. New York, NY: Academic Press.

Atkinson, T. (1982). The stability and validity of quality of life measures. *Social Indicators Research, 10,* 113-132.

Attig, T. (1995). Can we talk? On the elusiveness of dialogue. *Death Studies, 19*(1), 1-19.

Auger, J.A. (2000). Social perspectives on death and dying. Halifax, NS: Fernwood Publishing.

Backett, K., Davison, C., & Mullen, K. (1994). Lay evaluation of health and healthy lifestyles: Evidence from three studies. *British Journal of General Practice, 44,* 277-280.

Backman, L. (2001). Learning and memory. In J.E. Birren, & K.W. Schaie, (Eds.). *Handbook of the psychology of aging* (5th ed). San Diego, CA: Academic Press.

Baddeley, A. (1986). Working memory. Oxford, U.K.: Oxford University Press.

Badgely, R.F. (1991). Social and economic disparities under Canadian health-care. *International Journal of Health Services, 21*(4), 659-671.

Baggs, J.G. & Schmitt, M.H. (2000). End-of-life decisions in adult intensive care: Current research base and directions for the future. *Nursing-Outlook, 48*(4), 158-164.

Bahrick, H. P., Bahrick, P. O., & Wittlinger, R. P. (1975). Fifty years of memory for names and faces: A cross-sectional approach. *Journal of Experimental Psychology: General, 104,* 54-75.

Baker, M. & Lero, D. (1996). Division of labour: Paid work and family structure. In M. Baker, (Ed.). *Families: Changing trends in Canada* (3rd Ed.). Toronto, ON: McGraw Hill Ryerson.

Baker, R., Wu, A.W., Teno, J.M., Kreling, B., Damiano, A.M., Rubin, H.R., Roach, M.J., Wenger, N.S., Phillips, R.S., & Desbiens, N.A. (2000). Family satisfaction with end-of-life care in seriously ill hospitalized adults. *Journal of the American Geriatrics Society, 48*(Suppl. 5), 61-69.

Balakrishnan, T.R., Lapierre-Adamcyk, E. & Krotki,K.J. (1993). *Family and childbearing in Canada: A demographic analysis.* Toronto, ON: University of Toronto Press.

Baltes, P.B. (1993). The aging mind: Potential and limits. *Gerontologist, 33,* 580-594.

Baltes, P.B., & Baltes, M. (1990). Psychological perspectives on successful aging: The model of selective optimization with compensation. In P.B. Baltes & M. Baltes, (Eds.) *Longitudinal research and the study of successful (optimal) aging* (pp.1-49). Cambridge, U.K.: Cambridge University Press.

Baltes, P.B., & Kliegl, R. (1992). Further testing of limits of cognitive plasticity: Negative age differences in a mnemonic skill are robust. *Developmental Psychology, 28,* 121-125.

Baltes, P.B., & Staudinger, U. (1993). The search for a psychology of wisdom. *Current Directions in Psychological Science, 2,* 75-80.

Baltes, P.B., & Schaie, K.W. (1982). The myth of the twilight years. In Steven H. Zarit, (Ed.). *Readings in aging and death: Contemporary perspectives* (2nd Ed.). New York, NY: Harper and Row.

Barer, M.L., Evans, R.G. & Hertzman C. (1995). Avalanche or glacier? Health care and the demographic rhetoric. *Canadian Journal on Aging, 14,* 193-224.

Barer, M.L., McGrail, K.M., Cardiff, K., Wood, L., & Green, C.J. (2000). *Tales from the other drug wars.* Vancouver, BC: University of British Columbia Centre for Health Services and Policy Research.

Barker, J.C. & Mitteness, L.S. (1990). Invisible caregivers in the spotlight. Non-kin caregivers of frail older adults. In J.F. Gubrium & A. Sankar, (Eds.). *The home care experience: Ethnography and policy.* Newbury Park, CA: Sage.

Barrett, R., Kazawa, C.W., McDade, T., & Armelagos, G. J. (1998). Emerging and re-emerging infectious diseases: The third epidemiologic transition. *Annual Review of Anthropology, 27*, 247-271.

Bar-Tur, L. Savaya, R. & Prager, E. (2001). Sources of meaning in life for young and old Israeli Jews and Arabs. *Journal of Aging Studies, 15*, 253-269.

Barusch, A.S. (1988). Problems and coping strategies of elderly spouse caregivers. *Gerontologist, 28*, 677-685.

Basavarajappa, (1998). *Living arrangements and residential overcrowding: The situation of older immigrants in Canada, 1991*. (Catalogue 11F0019MPE No. 115). Ottawa, ON: Family and Community Support Systems, Statistics Canada..

Bass, S.A. & Caro, F.G. (1996). Economic value of grandparent assistance. *Generations, 20,* 29-33.

Bauman, Z. (1987). *Legislators and interpreters: Modernity, post-modernity, and intellectuals*. Ithaca, NY: Cornell University Press.

Beaudry, P., & Lemieux, T. (1999). Evolution of the female labour force participation rate in Canada, 1976-1994. *Canadian Business Economics, 7*(2), 57-70.

Beaujot, R. & Bélanger, A. (2001). Perspectives on below replacement fertility in Canada: Trends, desires, and accommodations. *Discussion paper 01-6*. London, ON: University of Western Ontario, Population Studies Centre.

Beaujot, R. (1995). Family patterns at mid-life (marriage, parenting, working). In R.Beaujot, E.M. Gee, F. Rajulton & Z.R. Ravanera, *Family over the life course* (pp. 37-75). (Catalogue No. 91-643E). Ottawa, ON: Statistics Canada.

Beaujot, R. (2000). *Earning and caring in Canadian families*. Peterborough, ON: Broadview.

Beaujot, R., Gee, E.M., Rajulton, F., &. Ravanera, Z.R (1995). *Family over the life course*. (Catalogue No. 91-643E). Ottawa, ON: Statistics Canada.

Beck, S.H. (1982). Adjustment to and satisfaction with retirement. *Journal of Gerontology, 37*(5), 616-624.

Beck, U. (1992). *Risk society: Towards a new modernity*. London, U.K.: Sage Publications.

Beck, U. (1994). The reinvention of politics: Toward a theory of reflexive modernization. In U. Beck, A. Giddens & S. Lash, (Eds.). *Reflexive modernization* (pp. 1-55). Stanford, CA: Stanford University Press.

Bedard, M., Stones, M.J., Guyatt, G.H., & Hirdes, J.P. (2001). Traffic-related fatalities among older drivers and passengers: Past and future trends. *Gerontologist, 41*(6): 751-756.

Beehr, T.A., Glazer, S., Nielson, N. L., & Fanner, S.J. (2000). Work and nonwork predictors of employees' retirement age. *Journal of Vocational Behavior, 57*(2), 206-225.

Bélanger, A., Carrière, Y., & Gilbert S. (Eds.). 2000. *Report on the demographic situation in Canada, 2000*. (Catalogue No. 91-209-XPE). Ottawa, ON: Statistics Canada.

Bendick, M., Jr. (1989). Privatizing the delivery of social welfare services: An ideal to be taken seriously. In S.B. Kamerman, & A.J. Kahn, (Eds.). *Privatization and the welfare state* (pp. 97-120). Princeton, NJ: Princeton University Press.

Bengtson, V.L. & Kuypers, J. A. (1971). Generational differences and the developmental stake. *Aging and Human Development, 2,* 246-260.

Bengtson, V.L. (1985). Diversity and symbolism in grandparental roles. In V.L. Bengtson & J.F. Robertson, (Eds.). *Grandparenthood*. Newbury Park, CA: Sage.

Bengtson, V.L. (2001). Beyond the nuclear family: The increasing importance of multigenerational bonds. *Journal of Marriage and the Family, 63*, 1-16.

Bengtson, V.L., Burgess, E.O., & Parrott, T.M. (1997). Theory, explanation, and a third generation of theoretical development in social gerontology. *The Journal of Gerontology: Social Sciences, 52*, S72-S88.

Bengtson, V.L., Rice, C.J., & Johnson, M.L. (1999). Are theories of aging important? Models and explanations in gerontology at the turn of the century. In V.L. Bengtson & K.W. Shaie, (Eds.). *Handbook of theories of aging* (pp. 3-20). New York, NY: Springer.

Bengtson, V.L., Rosenthal, C. J., & Burton, L.M. (1996). Paradoxes of family and aging. In R.B. Binstock & L.K. George, (Eds.). *Handbook of aging and the social sciences* (4th ed.) (pp. 253-282). New York, NY: Academic Press.

Bergman, M., Blumenfeld, V. G., Casardo, D., Dash, B., Levitt, H., & Margulies, M.K. (1976). Age-related decrement in hearing for speech: Sampling and longitudinal studies. *Journal of Gerontology, 31*, 533-538.

Berkman, L.F. & Syme, S.L. (1979). Social networks, host resistance, and mortality: A nine-year follow-up study of Alameda County residents. *American Journal of Epidemiology, 109*(2), 186-204.

Berman, H (1994). Analyzing personal journals of later life. In J.F. Gubrium & J.A. Sankar, (Eds). *Qualitative methods in research* (pp. 211-226). Thousand Oaks, CA: Sage Publications.

Berman, L., & Sobkowska-Ashcroft, I. (1986). The old in language and literature. *Language and Communication, 6,* 139-145.

Berman, L., & Sobkowska-Ashcroft, I. (1987). Images and impressions of old age in the great works of Western literature (700 B.C.–1900 A.D.). Lewiston, NY: The Edwin Mellen Press.

Berry, J. & Kalin, R. (1990). *Some psychological and cultural implications of multiculturalism: A social cost benefit analysis from the perspectives of a larger society*. Ottawa, ON: Ecomomic Council of Canada.

Beullens, J., Marcoen, A., Jaspaert, H. & Pelmans, W. (1997). Medical students' knowledge about and attitudes towards aging and the impact of geriatric training: A review study. *Netherlands Journal of Gerontology and Geriatrics, 28*(4), 178-184.

Bevans, M., & Cole, T. (2001). Ethics and spirituality: Strangers at the end of life? In M.P. Lawton, (Ed.). *Annual review of gerontology and geriatrics: Vol. 20. Focus* on the end of life: Scientific and social issues (pp.16-38). New York: Springer Publishing Company.

Binet, A., & Simon, T. (1905). Méthodes nouvelles pour le diagnostic du niveau intellectuel des anormaux. L'Année Psychologique, 11, 191.

Binstock, R. H. (1997). The 1996 election: Older voters and implications for policies on aging. Gerontologist, 37, 15-19.

Binstock, R.H. (1994). Changing criteria in old-age programs: The introduction of economic status and need for services. The Gerontologist, 34, 726-730.

Birbili, M. (2000). Translating from one language to another. Social Research Update, 31, 1-6.

Birren, J.E. & Bengtson, V.L. (Eds.). (1988). Emergent theories of aging. New York, NY: Springer.

Bittman, M. (1999). Parenthood without penalty: Time use and public policy in Australia and Finland. Feminist Economics, 5, 27-42.

Black, C. (1995). Using existing data sets to study aging and the elderly: An introduction. Canadian Journal on Aging, 14(Suppl.), 135-150.

Black, S.A., Kyriakos, S.M., & Miller, T.Q. (1998). Correlates of depressive symptomatology among older community dwelling Mexican-Americans: The Hispanic EPSE. The Journals of Gerontology, Series B 53, S198-S208.

Blackhall, L.J., Murphy, S.T., Frank, G., & Michel, V. (1995). Ethnicity and attitudes toward patient autonomy. Journal of the American Medical Association, 274(10), 820-825.

Blakemore, K., & Boneham, M. (1994). Age, race and ethnicity: A comparative approach. Buckingham, U.K.: Open University Press.

Blando, J.A. (2001). Twice hidden: Older gay and lesbian couples, friends, and intimacy. Generations, 25, 87-89.

Blaxter, M. (1983). The causes of diseases: Women talking. Social Science and Medicine, 17, 59-69.

Blaxter, M. (1990). Health and lifestyles. London, U.K.: Tavistock/Routledge.

Blumenthal, J., Babyak, M., Moore, K.A., Craighead, W.E., Herman, S., Khatri, P., Waugh, R., Napolitano, M., Forman, L., Appelbaum, M., Doraiswamy, M., Krishman, R. (1999). Effects of exercise training on older patients with major depression. Archives of Internal Medicine, 159, 2349-2356.

Blumenthal, J.A., & Madden, D.J. (1988). Effects of aerobic exercise training, age, and physical fitness on memory-search performance. Psychology an Aging, 3, 280-285.

Blumenthal, J.A., Emery, C.F., Madden, D.J., George, L.K., Colemen, R.E., Riddle, M.W., McKee, D.C., Reasoner, J., & Williams, R.S. (1989). Cardiovascular and behavioral effects of aerobic training in healthy older men and women. Journal of Gerontology: Medical Sciences, 44, M147-M157.

Borkan, G. A., & Norris, A. H. (1980). Assessment of biological age using a profile of physical parameters. Journal of Gerontology, 35, 177-184.

Bortz, W.M. II, Wallace, D.H., & Wiley, D. (1999). Sexual function in 1,202 aging males: Differentiating aspects. Journal of Gerontology, Series A, Biological Sciences and Medical Sciences, 54(5) p M237-M241.

Bosse, R., Aldwin, C. M., Levenson, M.R., & Workman-Daniels, K. (1991). How stressful is retirement? Findings from the Normative Aging Study. Journal of Gerontology: Psychological Sciences, 46, 9-14.

Botwinick, J., West, R., & Storandt, M. (1978). Predicting death from behavioral test performance. Journal of Gerontology, 33, 755-762.

Bouchard T. J. Fr., McGue, M. Lykken D., & Tellegen, A. (1999). Intrinsic and extrinsic religiousness: Genetic and environmental influences and personality correlates. Twin Res, 2(2): 88-98.

Bouchard, T. J. & McGue, M. (1990). Genetic and rearing environmental influences on adult personality: An analysis of adopted twins reared apart. Journal of Personality, 58, 263-292.

Boyd, M. & Norris, D. (1999). The crowded nest: Young adults at home. Canadian Social Trends, Spring. (Catalogue No. 11-008). Ottawa, ON: Statistics Canada.

Boyd, M. (1991). Immigration and living arrangements: Elderly women in Canada. International Migration Review, 25, 4-7.

Boyd, M., & Vickers, M. (2000). 100 years of immigration in Canada. Canadian Social Trends, Autumn, 2-12. (Catalogue No. 11-008).

Boyd, N. (2000). The beast within: Why men are violent. Vancouver, BC: Greystone Books.

Bradley, E.H., Fried, T.R., Stanislav, V.K., & Idler, E. (2001). Quality-of-life trajectories of elders in the end of life. In M.P. Lawton (Ed.), Annual review of gerontology and geriatrics: Vol. 20. Focus on the end of life: Scientific and social issues (pp.64-96). New York, NY: Springer Publishing Company.

Bradley, E.H., Peiris, V., & Wetle, T. (1998). Discussions about end-of-life care in nursing homes. Journal of the American Geriatrics Society, 46(10), 1235-1241.

Braithwaite, V. (1998). Institutional respite care: breaking chores or breaking social bonds? Gerontologist, 38(5), 610-617.

Brecher, E.M., & Consumer Reports Book Editors (1985). Love, sex, and aging. Boston, MA: Little Brown.

Breckler, S. J. (1984a). Empirical validation of affect, behavior, and cognition as distinct components of attitude. Journal of Personality and Social Psychology, 47, 1191-1205.

Brennan, B. (1989a). Seniors as volunteers. (A profile of volunteers based on the 1987 Naitonal Survey on Volunteer Activity, Profile No. 2.) Ottawa, ON: Supply and Services Canada.

British Columbia InterMinistry Committee on elder Abuse and Continuing Care Division, Ministry of Health and Ministry Responsible for Seniors. (February 1992). Principles, procedures, and protocols for elder abuse. Victoria, BC: Ministry of Health & Ministry Responsible for Seniors.

Brody, E.M., & Schoonover, C.B. (1986). Patterns of parent-care when adult daughters work and when they do not. *The Gerontologist, 26,* 372-381.

Brody, E.M., Hoffman, C., Kleban, M.H., & Schoonover, C.B. (1989). Caregiving daughters and their local siblings: Perceptions, strains, and interactions. *The Gerontologist, 29,* 529-538.

Brown, E.R. (1979). *Rockefeller medicine men: Medicine and capitalism in America.* Berkeley, CA: University of California Press.

Browne, C. V. (1998). *Women, feminism and aging.* New York, NY: Springer Publishing Co.

Broyles, R.W., Manga, P., Binder, D.A., Angus, D.E., & Charette, A. (1983). The use of physician services under a national health insurance scheme. *Medical Care, 21,* 1037-1054.

Brunt, J.H., Chappell, N.L., Maclure, N., & Cassels, A. (1998). Assessing the effectiveness of government and industry media campaigns on seniors' perceptions of reference-based pricing policy. *The Journal of Applied Gerontology, 17*(3), 276-295.

Bryden, K. (1974). Old age pensions and policy making in Canada. Montreal, QB: McGill-Queen's University Press.

Burr, J. A., & Mutchler, J.E. (1993). Nativity, acculturation, and economic status: Explanations of Asian American living arrangements in later life. *Journal of Gerontology: Social Sciences, 48,* S55-S63.

Burr, J.A. & Mutchler, J.E. (1999). Race and ethnicity variation in norms of filial responsibility among older persons. *Journal of Marriage and the Family, 61,* 674-687.

Burton, L.M. & Bengtson, V.L. (1985). Black grandmothers: Issues of timing and continuity of roles. In V.L. Bengston & J.F. Robertson, (Eds.). *Grandparenthood* (pp. 61-77). Beverly Hills, CA: Sage.

Buss, A.H. & Plomin, R.(1984). Temperament: Early developing personality traits. Hillsdale, NJ: Erlbaun.

Butler, R. N., Lewis, M. I., & Sutherland, T. (1998). *Aging and mental health: Positive psychosocial and biomedical approaches.* Needham Heights, MA: Allyn and Bacon.

Butler, R.N. (1963). The life review: An interpretation of reminiscence in the aged. *Psychiatry, 26,* 65-76.

Butler, R.N. (1975) *Why survive? Being old in America.* New York, NY: Harper & Rowe.

Buttell, F.P. (1999). Relationship between spouse abuse and the maltreatment of dementia sufferers by their caregivers. *American Journal of Alzheimer's Disease, 14,* 230-232.

Buzzelli, S., di Francesco, L., Giaquinto, S., & Nolfe, G. (1997). Psychological and medical aspects of sexuality following stroke. *Sexuality & Disability, 15*(4) p. 261-270.

Byock, I.R. (1993). Consciously walking the fine line: Thoughts on a hospice response to assisted suicide and euthanasia. *Journal of Palliative Care, 9*(3), 25-28.

Cahill, S., South, K., & Spade, J. (2000). *Outing age: Public policy issues affecting gay, lesbian, bisexual and transgender elders.* Washington, DC: Policy Institute of the National Gay and Lesbian Task Force.

Calasanti, T. M. (1996). Incorporating diversity: Meaning, levels of research, and implications for theory. *The Gerontologist, 36*(2), 147-156.

Cameron, E., & Bernardes, J. (1998). Gender and disadvantage in health: Men's health for a change. *Sociology of Health and Illness, 20,* 673-693.

Campbell, D.T. (1963). Social attitudes and other acquired behavioral dispositions. In S. Koch, (Ed.). *Psychology: A study of a science, vol. 6,* (pp. 94-172). New York, NY: McGraw-Hill.

Campbell, D.T., & Fiske, D.W. (1959). Convergent and discriminant validation by the multitrait-multimethod matrix. *Psychological Bulletin, 56,* 81-105.

Campione, W.A. (1987). A married woman's retirement decision: A methodological Canadian study of health and aging (1994). Patterns of caring for people with dementia in Canada. *Canadian Journal of Aging, 13*(4), 470-487.

Canada. Parliament. House of Commons (1921). *House of commons debates,* (1921.3860). Ottawa, ON: Queen's Printer.

Canada's Health Promotion Survey, 1990. (1993). Technical report. T. Stephens, & D.F. Graham, (Eds.). Ottawa, ON: Health and Welfare Canada.

Canadian Heritage. (1998). Hate and bias activity in Canada. *The Evidence series: Facts about multiculturalism, 4.*

Canadian Institute for Health Information. (1998). *Provincial mini-status report: The quality of caring: Chronic care in Ontario.* Ottawa, ON: CIHI.

Canadian Medical Association. (1993). Toward a new consensus on health care financing in Canada. Discussion paper prepared by the Working Group on Health System Financing in Canada. Ottawa, ON: Canadian Medical Association.

Canadian Study of Health & Aging Working Group (1994a). The Canadian study of health and aging: Study methods and prevalence of dementia. *Canadian Medical Association Journal, 150,* 899-913.

Canadian Study of Health & Aging Working Group (1994b). The Canadian study of health and aging: Risk factors for Alzheimer's disease in Canada. *Neurology, 44,* 2073-2080.

Canadian Study on Health and Aging (1994). The Canadian study of health and aging: Study methods and prevalence of dementia. *Canadian Medical Association Journal, 150,* 899-913.

Canadian-Institute-for-Advanced-Research. (1991). *The determinants of health* (CIAR Publication No. 5).Toronto, ON: Author.

Carmel, S. (1999). Life-sustaining treatments: What doctors do, what they want for themselves and what elderly persons want. *Social Science and Medicine, 49*(10), 1401-1408.

Carmel, S., & Mutran, E.J. (1999). Stability of elderly persons' expressed preferences regarding the use of life-sustaining treatments. *Social Science and Medicine, 49*(3), 303-311.

Caro, F. G., & Bass, S.A. (1997). Receptivity to volunteering in the immediate postretirement period. *Journal of Applied Gerontology, 16* (4), 427-441.

Carver, A.C., Vickrey, B.G., Brnat, J.L., Keran, C., Ringel, S.P., & Foley, K.M. (1999). End-of-life care: A survey of US neurologists' attitudes, behavior, and knowledge. *Neurology, 53*(2), 284-293.

Casper, L.M. & Bryson, K.R. (1998). *Co-resident grandparents and their grandchildren: Grandparent maintained families.* Washington, DC: U.S. Bureau of the Census, Population Division.

Chamberlain, K. & Zika, S. (1992). Stability and change in subjective well-being over short periods of time. *Social Indicators Research, 26,* 101-117.

Chan, K. B. (1983). Coping with aging and managing self-identity: The social world of the elderly Chinese women. *Canadian Ethnic Studies, 15,* 36-50.

Chappell, N. (1995). Gerontological research in the '90s: Strengths, weaknesses and contributions to policy. *Canadian Journal on Aging, 14*(Suppl.), 23-36.

Chappell, N.L. (1992). *Social support and aging.* Toronto, ON: Butterworths.

Chappell, N.L., & Lai, D. (1998). Health care service use by Chinese seniors in British Columbia, Canada. *Journal of Cross-Cultural Gerontology, 13,* 21-37.

Chappell, N., Lai, D.C., & Gee, E. (1997). A study of the Chinese elderly in British Columbia. Ottawa, ON: National Health and Research and Development Program (NHRDP).

Chappell, N., & Lai, D.C. (2001). Social support of the elderly Chinese: Comparisons between China and Canada. In I. Chi, N. Chappell, & J. Lubben, (Eds.). *Elderly Chinese in Pacific Rim countries: Social support and integration.* Hong Kong: Hong Kong University Press.

Chappell, N., & Lai, D.C. (1998). Health care service use by Chinese seniors in British Columbia, Canada. *Journal of Cross-Cultural Gerontology, 13,* 21-37.

Chappell, N.L. & Badger, M. (1989). Social isolation and well-being. *Journal of Gerontology: Social Sciences, 44*(5), S169-S176.

Chappell, N.L. & Behie, G.E. (2000). Is there life after caregiving? A comparison of caregivers before and after the death of a loved one. Gerontological Society of America annual meetings, Washington, November.

Chappell, N.L. & Litkenhaus, R. (1995). *Informal caregivers to adults in British Columbia.* Joint Report of the Centre on Aging, University of Victoria and The Caregivers Association of British Columbia.

Chappell, N.L. & Penning, M. (1996). Behavioural problems and distress among caregivers of people with dementia. *Aging and Society, 16,* 57-73.

Chappell, N.L. & Penning, M.J. (2001). Sociology of aging in Canada: Issues for the millennium. *Canadian Journal on Aging, 20, special supplement,* 82-110.

Chappell, N.L. (1983). Informal support networks among the elderly. *Research on Aging, 5*(1), 77-99.

Chappell, N.L. (1989a). *Formal programs for informal caregivers to elders.* Report prepared for the Social Policy Directorate of the Policy Communications and Information Branch, Health and Welfare Canada.

Chappell, N.L. (1989b). Health and helping among the elderly, gender differences. *Journal of Aging and Health, 1*(1), 102-120.

Chappell, N.L. (1990a). Aging and social care (3rd Ed.). In *The handbook of aging and the social sciences* (pp. 438-454). San Diego, CA: Academic Press.

Chappell, N.L. (1990b). In-group differences among elders living with friends and family other than spouse. *Journal of Aging Studies, 5*(1), 61, 76.

Chappell, N.L. (1992). *Social support and aging.* Toronto, ON: Butterworths Canada Ltd.

Chappell, N.L. (1993a). The future of health care in Canada. *Journal of Social Policy, 22*(4), 487-505.

Chappell, N.L. (1993b). Implications of shifting health care policy for caregiving in Canada. *Journal of Aging and Social Policy, 5*(142), 39-55.

Chappell, N.L. (1998). Maintaining and enhancing independence and well-being in old age. In *Determinants of health, adults and seniors, Vol. 2* (pp.89-137). Canada Health Action: Building on the Legacy, Papers Commissioned by the National Forum on Health.

Chappell, N.L. (1999). Volunteering and healthy aging—What we know. *Volunteer Canada, Manulife Financial and Health Canada.* Victoria, BC: Author.

Chappell, N.L., & Penning, M.J. (1984). *Informal supports: Examining ethnic variations,* paper presented at the annual meeting of the Gerontological Society of America, San Antonio, Texas.

Chappell, N.L., Maclure, M., Brunt, H., Hopkinson, J., & Mullett, J. (1997). *Seniors views of medication disbursement policies: Bridging research and policy at the point of policy impact.* Special Joint Issue of the Canadian Journal of Public Policy and the Canadian Journal on Aging, Spring Supplement, 114-131.

Chappell, N.L., Reid, R.C., & Dow, E. (2001). Respite reconsidered: A typology of meanings based on the caregiver's point of view. *Journal of Aging Studies, 15* (2) 201-216.

Chard, J., & Renaud, V. (1999). Visible minorities in Toronto, Vancouver and Montreal. *Canadian Social Trends, 54,* 20-25.

Charmaz, K. (2000). Grounded theory: Objectivist and constructivist methods. In N. Denzin & Y. Lincoln, (Eds.). *Handbook of qualitative research* (2nd Ed., pp. 509-535). Thousand Oaks, CA: Sage Publications.

Charness, N. (1981). Search in chess: Age and skill differences. *Journal of Experimental Psychology: Human Perception and Performance, 7,* 467-476.

Charness, N. (1985). *Age and expertise: Responding to Talland's challenge.* Paper presented at the George A.

Talland Memorial Conference on Aging and Memory, Cape Cod, MA.

Charness, N. (1987). Component processes in bridge building and novel problem-solving tasks. *Canadian Journal of Psychology*, 41, 223-43.

Chase, W.G. & Simon, H.A. (1973). The mind's eye in chess. In W.G Chase, (Ed.). *Visual information processing*. New York, NY: Academic Press.

Che-Alford, J. & Stevenson, K. (1998). Older Canadians on the move. (Catalogue No. 11-008-XPE). *Canadian Social Trends, Spring*, 15-18. Ottawa, ON: Statistics Canada.

Chen, J., Ng, E., & Wilkins, R. (1996). The health of Canada's immigrants in 1994-95. *Health Reports*, 7(4), 33-45.

Chen, P., Ganguli, M., Mulsant, B., & DeKosky, S. (1999). The temporal relationship between depressive symptoms and dementia. *Archives of General Psychiatry*, 56, 261-266.

Chesworth, B., Curtin-Telegdi, N., Dalby, D., Hallman, K., Hirdes, J., Kirchhner, T., Poss, J., & Tjam, E. (2000). Minimum data set for home care (MDS-HC): Pilot study report. Canadian Collaborating Centre Inter-RAI.

Childs, H.W., Hayslip, B., Radika, L.M., & Reinberg, J.A. (2000). Young and middle-aged perceptions of elder abuse. *Gerontologist*, 40, 75-85.

Chipperfield, J.G., Havens, B. & Doig, W. (1997). Method and description of the aging in Manitoba project: A 20-year longitudinal study. *Canadian Journal on Aging*, 16(4), 606-625.

Chodzko-Zajko, W. J. (1994). Assessing physical performance in older adult populations. *Journal of Aging and Physical Activity*, 2, 103-104.

Chung, U. (1994). *The case for culturally sensitive health care: A comparative study of health beliefs related to culture in six north-east Calgary communities.* Executive Summary. Edmonton, AB: Alberta Community Development, Citizen and Heritage Secretariat.

Cicirelli, V.G. (1985). The role of siblings as family caregivers. In W.J. Sauer & R.T. Coward, (Eds.). *Social support networks and the care of the elderly.* New York, NY: Springer Publishing.

Cicirelli, V.G. (1995). *Personality factors related to elders' end-of-life decisions: Final report* (Study I). Lafayette, IN: Purdue University, Department of Psychological Sciences.

Cicirelli, V.G. (1999). Personality and demographic factors in older adults' fear of death. *Gerontologist*, 39(5), 569-579.

Cicirelli, V.G. (2001). Healthy elders' early decisions for end-of-life living and dying. In M.P. Lawton, (Ed.). *Annual review of gerontology and geriatrics: Vol. 20. Focus on the end of life: Scientific and social issues* (pp.163-192). New York, NY: Springer Publishing Company.

Cicirelli, V.G. (1982). Sibling influence throughout the lifespan. In M.E. Lamb & B. Sutton-Smith, (Eds.). *Sibling relationships: Their nature and significance across the lifespan.* Hillsdale, NJ: Lawrence Erlbaum.

Ciffin, S. & Martin, J. (1977). Retirement in Canada: When and why people retire. (Staff working paper SWP - 7804). Ottawa, ON: Health and Welfare Canada.

Citizenship and Immigration Canada. (1999). *Facts and figures, 1998.* (Catalogue No. MP43-333/1999E). Ottawa, ON: Minister of Public Works and Government Services Canada.

Clark, P.G. (1999). Moral economy and the social construction of the crisis of aging and health care: Differing Canadian and U.S. perspectives. In M. Minkler & C.L.Estes, (Eds.). *Critical gerontology: Perspectives from political and moral economy* (pp. 147-167). Amityville, NY: Baywood.

Clark, R.M. (1960). *Economic security for the aged in the United States and Canada. A report prepared by the Government of Canada, Vol. III.* Ottawa, ON: The Queens Printer and Controller of Stationary.

Clarke, A., & Hanson, E. (2000). Death and dying: Changing the culture of care. In A.M. Warnes, L. Warren, & M. Nolan, (Eds.). *Care services for later life —transformations and critiques* (pp. 204-218). London, U.K.: Jessica Kingsley Publishers Ltd.

Clausen, A. (1998). Life reviews and life stories. In J.Z. Giele & G.H. Elder Jr., (Eds.). *Methods of life course research: Qualitative and quantitative approaches* (pp.189-212). Thousand Oaks, CA: Sage Publications.

Clausen, J.A. (1993). *American lives: Looking back at the children of the depression.* New York, NY: Free Press.

Cliff, N. (1994). Predicting ordinal relations, British Journal of Mathematics. *Statistical Pyschology*, 47, 127-150.

Clyburn, D.L., Stones, M.J., Hadjistavropoulos, T., & Tuokko, H. (2000). Disturbing behavior in Alzheimer's disease and its relationship to caregiver distress. *Journal of Gerontology*, 55B, S2-S13.

Coale, A.J. (1956). The effects of changes in mortality and fertility on age composition. *Milbank Memorial Fund Quarterly*, 34, 79-114.

Cobb, S. (1976). Social support as a moderator of life stress. *Psychosomatic Medicine*, 38, 300-14.

Coburn D. (2001). Health, health care, and neo-liberalism. In P. Armstrong, H. Armstrong, & D. Coburn, (Eds.). *Unhealthy times. Political economy perspectives on health and care in Canada.* (pp. 45-65). Toronto, ON: Oxford University Press.

Coburn, D., Torrance, G. M., & Kaufert, J. M. (1983). Medical dominance in Canada: The rise and fall of medicine. *International Journal of Health Services*, 13, 407-432.

Cohen, M. (1988). *Women's work, markets and economic development in nineteenth-century Ontario.* Toronto, ON: University of Toronto Press.

Cohen, M.J. (1989). Employment and volunteering roles for the elderly: Characteristics, attributes, and strategies. *Journal of Leisure Research*, 21 (3) 214-227.

Cohen, S. & Hebert, T.B. (1996). Health psychology: Psychological factors and physical disease from the perspective of psychoimmunology. *Annual Review of Psychology, 47*, 113-142.

Cohen, S., & Syme, S.L. (1985). Issues in the study and application of social support. In S. Cohen, (Ed.). *Social Support and Health* (pp. 3-22), Orlando, FL: Academic Press.

Cohen, S., Tyrrell, D.A., & Smith, A.P. (1991). Psychological stress in humans and susceptibility to the common cold. *New England Journal of Medicine, 325*, 606-612.

Cohen, W. (1971). *Social security: The first thirty-five years: Papers from the 23rd Annual Conference on Aging, August 12-14, 1970*. Ann Arbor, MI: Institute of Gerontology, University of Michigan-Wayne State University.

Collings, P. (2001) "If you got everything, it's good enough": Perspectives on successful aging in a Canadian Inuit community. *Journal of Cross-Cultural Gerontology, 16*, 127-155.

Conn, D., Clarke, D., & Van Reekum, R. (2000). Depression in holocaust survivors: Profile and treatment outcomes in a geriatric day hospital program. *International Journal of Geriatric Psychiatry, 15*, 331-337.

Connidis, I.A. (2001). *Family ties and aging*. Thousand Oaks, CA: Sage.

Connidis, I.A. (1989a). Contact between siblings in later life. *Canadian Journal of Sociology, 14*, 429-442.

Connidis, I.A. (1989b). Siblings as friends in later life. *American Behavioral Scientist, 33*, 81-93.

Connidis, I.A. (1994). Growing up and old together: Some observations on families in later life. In V. Marshall & B. McPherson, (Eds.). *Aging: Canadian perspectives* (pp. 195-205). Peterborough, ON: Broadview.

Connidis, I.A. & Campbell, L.D. (1995). Closeness, confiding, and contact among siblings in middle and late adulthood. *Journal of Family Issues, 16*, 722-745.

Connidis, I.A. (1989). *Family ties and aging*. Toronto, ON: Butterworths.

Cook, P. (1994). Chronic illness beliefs and the role of social networks among Chinese, Indian, and Angloceltic Canadians. *Journal of Cross-Cultural Psychology, 25*(4), 452-465.

Cool, L.E. (1981). Ethnic identity: A source of community esteem for the elderly. *Anthropological Quarterly, 54*, 179-181.

Costa, D.L. (1999). Home of her own: Old age assistance and the living arrangements of older unmarried women. *Journal of Public Economics, 72*, 39-59.

Costa, P.T., & McRae, R.R. (1980). Still stable after all these years. In P.B Baltes, & O.G. Brim, (Eds.). *Life Span Development and Behaviour, Vol. 3*, (pp. 65-102). New York: Academic Press.

Costa, P.T., McCrae, R.R., & Zonderman, A. (1987). Environmental and dispositional influences on well-being: Longitudinal follow-up of an American national sample. *British Journal of Psychology, 78*, 299-306

Costa, P.T. Jr. & McCrae, R.R. (1980). Functional age: A conceptual and empirical critique. In S.G. Haynes, & M. Feinleib, (Eds.). *Proceedings of the Second Conference on the Epidemiology of Aging*. Bethesda, MD: National Institute on Aging.

Cottrell, L. (1942). The adjustment of the individual to his age and sex roles. *American Sociological Review, 7*, 617-620.

Council of Economic Advisors (1999). Work and retirement among the elderly. *Population and Development Review, 25*(1), 189-196.

Couper, D.P., (1994). What's wrong with this picture? Aging and education in America. *Aging Today, Sept/Oct*, 3.

Covinsky, K.E., Fuller, J.D., Yaffe, K., Johnston, C.B., Hamel, M., Lynn, J., Teno, J.M., & Phillips, R.S. (2000). Communication and decision-making in seriously ill patients: Findings of the SUPPORT project. *Journal of the American Geriatrics Society, 48*(Suppl. 5), 187-193.

Cowgill, D.O., & Holmes, L.D. (1972). *Aging and modernization*. New York, NY: Appleton Century-Crofts.

Cowgill, D.O. (1974). Aging and modernization: A revision on theory. In J.F. Gubrium, (Ed.). *Late life: Communities and environmental policy*. Springfield, IL: Thomas.

Craik, F.I.M., & Jennings, J.M. (1992). Human memory. In F.I.M. Craik & T.A. Salthouse, (Eds.). *Handbook of aging and cognition* (pp. 51-110). Hillsdale, NJ: Erlbaum.

Crawford, M.P. (1971). Retirement and disengagement. *Human Relations, 24*, 255-278.

Creswell, J. (1998). *Qualitative enquiry and research design: Choosing among five traditions*. Thousand Oaks, CA: Sage Publications.

Crimmins, E.M. (1990). Are Americans healthier as well as longer-lived? *Journal of Insurance Medicine, 22*, 89-92.

Crimmins, E.M., Reynolds, S.L., & Saito, Y. (1999). Trends in health and ability to work among the older working-age population. *Journal of Gerontology: Series B: Psychological Sciences and Social Sciences, 54B*(I), S31-S40.

Crystal, S., & Shea, D. (1990). Cumulative advantage, cumulative disadvantage, and inequality among elderly people. *The Gerontologist, 30*(4), 437-443.

Cumming, E. & Henry, W. (1961). *Growing old: The process of disengagement*. New York: Basic Books.

Cumming, E. (1963). Further thoughts on the theory of disengagement. *International Social Science Journal, 15*, 377-393.

Cutler, N.E. & Whitelaw, N.A. (2001). Results from the NCOA "Myths and Realities of Aging" Studies, *The National Council on the Aging, March 2001*.

Czaja, S.J., & J. Sharit (1998). Ability-performance relationships as a function of age and task experience for a data entry task. *Journal of Experimental Psychology: Applied, 4*, 332-351.

Dannefer, D., & Uhlenberg, P. (1999). Paths of the life course: A typology,. In V.L. Bengston, K.W. Schaie, (Eds.). *Handbook of theories on aging* (pp. 306-326). New York, NY: Springer Publishing Co.

D'Arcy, C. (1988). *Reducing inequalities in health.* Health Services and Promotion Branch Working Paper 88 - 16. Ottawa, ON: Health and Welfare Canada.

Davidson, K. (2001). Late life widowhood, selfishness and new partnership choices: A gendered perspective. *Ageing and Society, 21,* 297-317.

Davis, L., & McGadney, B.(1993). Self-care practices of black elders. In C. Barrsei, & D. Stull, (Eds.). Ethnic elderly and longterm care: Implications for ethnically sensitive services. New York, NY: Springer.

de Grace, G.R., Joshi, P., Pelltier, R., & Beaupre, C. (1994). Consequences psychologiques de la retraite en fonction du sexe et du niveau occupationel antierieur. *Canadian Journal on Aging, 13,* 149-168.

De Silva, A. (1992). *Earnings of immigrants: A comparative analysis.* Ottawa, ON: Economic Council of Canada.

De Vries J. (1995). Ethnic language maintenance and shift, 163-177. In S.S. Halli, F. Tovato, & L. Dreidger, (Eds). *Ethnic demography.* Ottawa, ON: Carleton University Press.

Dean, K. (1981). Self-care responses to illness: A selected review. *Social Science and Medicine, 151,* 673-687.

Dean, K. (1986). Self-care behavior: Implications for aging. In K. Dean, T. Hickey, & B. Holstein, (Eds.). *Self-care and health in old age.* London, U.K.: Croom Helm.

Dean, K. (1989). Self-care components of lifestyles: The importance of gender, attitudes and the social situation. *Social Science and Medicine, 29*(2), 137-152.

Deber, R., Narine, L., Baranek, P., Sharpe, N., Masnyk Duvalko, K., Zlotnik-Shaul, R., Coyte, P., Pink, G., & Williams, P. (1998). The public-private mix in health care. *Canada Health Action: Building on the Legacy*, pp. 423-546, National Forum on Health.

Dennis, W. (1996). Creative productivity between the ages of 20–80 years. *Journal of Gerontology, 21,* 1-8.

Denton, F.T. & Spencer, B.G. (1999). Population aging and its economic costs: A survey of the issues and evidence. *SEDAP Research Paper No. 1.* Hamilton, ON: McMaster University. Available at http://socserv2.mcmaster.ca/~sedap/.

Denton, F.T., Fretz, D. and Spencer, B. (Eds.) (2000). *Independence and economic security in old age.* Vancouver, BC: University of British Columbia Press.

Denton, F.T. & Spencer, B.G. (in press). Some demographic consequences of revising the definition of 'old age' to reflect future changes in life table probabilities. *Canadian Journal on Aging. [vol and pages?]*

Denton, F.T., Feaver, C.H. & Spencer, B.G. (1998). The future population of Canada, its age distribution and dependency relations. *Canadian Journal on Aging, 17,* 83-109.

Denton, M. & Walters, V. (1999). Gender differences in structural and behavioural determinants of health: An analysis of the social production of health. *Social Science and Medicine, 48,* 1221-1235.

Denton, M., Raina, P., Lian, J., Gafni, A., Joshi, A., French, S., Rosenthal, C., & Willison, D. J. (2000). Health, age and financial preparations for later life. In F.T. Denton, D. Fretz & Byron Spencer, (Eds.). *Independence and economic security in old age* (pp.136-155). Vancouver, BC: University of British Columbia Press.

Department of Finance. (2001). Tax expenditures and evaluations. (Catalogue number F1-27/2001E). Ottawa, ON: Her Majesty the Queen in Right of Canada. http://www.fin.gc.ca/

Derrida, J. (1978). *Writing and difference.* Chicago, IL: University of Chicago Press.

Desjardins, B. (1993). *Population ageing and the elderly.* (Catalogue No. 91-533E). Ottawa, ON: Statistics Canada

Diener, E., Sandvik, E., Parvot, W., & Gallagher, D. (1991) Response artifacts in the measurement of subjective well-being. *Social Indicators Research, 24,* 35-56.

Diener, E., Sandvik, E., Seidlitz, L., & Diener, M. (1993). The relationship between income and subjective well-being: Relative or absolute. *Social Indicators Research, 28,* 225-244.

Diener, E., Sandvik, E., & Parvot, W. (1991). Happiness is the frequency, not the intensity, of positive versus negative affect. In F. Strack, M. Arglye, & N. Schwarz, (Eds.). Subjective well-being: An interdisciplinary perspective (pp. 119-139). Oxford, U.K.: Pergamon Press.

Diener, E., Suh, E. M., Lucas, R. E. & Smith, H. L. (1999). Subjective well-being: Three decades of progress. *Psychological Bulletin, 125,* 276-302.

Diesfeldt, H.F.A. & Diesfeldt-Groenendijk, H. (1977). Improving cognitive performance is psychogeriatric patients: The influence of physical exercise. *Age and Aging, 6,* 58-64.

Dietz, T.L., John, R.,. & Roy, C.L. (1998). Exploring intra-ethnic diversity among four groups of Hispanic elderly: patterns and levels of service utilization. *International Journal Aging and Human Development* 46(3), 247-266.

Dobrof, R. (1987). *Ethnicity and gerontological social work.* New York, NY: Haworth Press.

Doeringer, P.B. (1990). *Economic security, labour market flexibility, and bridges to retirement. Bridge to retirement.* New York, NY: ILR Press of Cornell University.

Donahue, W., Orbach, H.L., & Pollack, O. (1960). Retirement: The emerging social pattern. In C. Tibbitts, (Ed.). *Handbook of social gerontology: Social aspects of aging.* Chicago, IL: University of Chicago Press.

Dorfman, L.T. (1995). Health conditions and perceived quality of life in retirement. *Health and Social Work, 20*(3), 192-199.

Dorfman, L.T. (2000). Still working after age 70: Older professors in academe. *Educational Gerontology, 26*(8), 695-713.

Dosa, P A. (1999). (Re) imaging aging lives: Ethnographic narratives of Muslim women in diaspora. *Journal of Cross-Sectional Gerontology, 14*, 245-272.

Doukas, D.J., Gorenflo, D.W., & Supanich, B. (1999). Primary care physician attitudes and values toward end-of-life care and physician-assisted death. *Ethics and Behavior, 9*(3), 219-230.

Dowd, J. J. (1980). *Stratification among the aged*. Monterey, CA: Brooks/Cole.

Dowd, J. J., & Bengston, V.L. (1978). Aging in minority populations : An examination of the double jeopardy hypothesis. *Journal of Gerontology, 33*, 427-436.

Dowd, J.J. (1975). Aging as exchange: A preface to theory. *Journal of Gerontology, 30*, 584-594.

Dowd, J.J. (1980). Exchange rates and old people. *Journal of Gerontology, 35*, 596-602.

Dowd, R.L., Sisson, R.P., & Kern, D.M. (1981). Socialization to violence among the aged. *Journal of Gerontology, 36*, 350-361.

Driedger, L.& Halli, S. (2000). Racial integration: Theoretical options. In L. Driedger, & S. Halli, (Eds.). *Race and racism* (pp. 55-76). Montreal, QB, and Kingston, ON: McGill-Queens University Press.

Driedger, L. & Chappell, N. (1987) *Aging and ethnicity: Toward an interface*. Toronto, ON: Butterworths.

Dulude, L. (1981). *Pension reform with women in mind*. Ottawa, ON: Canadian Advisory Council on the Status of Women.

Dumas, J. & Péron, Y. (1992). *Marriage and conjugal life in Canada*. (Catalogue No. 91-534E) Ottawa, ON: Statistics Canada.

Dunlop, B.D., Rothman, M.B., Condon, K.M., Hebert, K.S., & Martinez, I.L. (2000). Elder abuse: Risk factors and use of case data to improve policy and practice. *Journal of Elder Abuse and Neglect, 12*, 95-122.

Dunn, J., & Dyck, I. (1998). *Social determinants of health in Canada's immigration population: Results from the National Population Health Survey*. (Research on Immigration and Integration in the Metropolis Project Working Paper Series #98-20). Vancouver, BC: Research on Immigration and Integration in the Metropolis.

Dunn, K.M., Croft, P.R., & Hackett, G.I. (1999). Association of sexual problems with social, psychological, and physical problems in men and women: A cross-sectional population survey, *Journal of Epidemiology and Community Health, 53* (3) p.144-8.

Dunning, R.W. (1959). *Social and economic change among the northern Ojibwa*. Toronto, ON: University of Toronto Press.

Dupree, C.Y. (1998). The attitudes of black Americans toward advance directives. *Dissertation Abstracts International, 59*(04), 1347A.

Durin, J.V. & Passmore, R. (1967). *Energy, work and leisure*. London, U.K.: Heinemann.

Dustman, R.E., Emmerson, R.Y., & Shearer, D.E. (1990). Electrophysiology and aging: Slowing, inhibition, and aerobic fitness. In M. L. Howe, M. J. Stones, &

C. J. Brainerd, (Eds.), *Cognitive and behavorial performance factors in atypical aging* (pp. 103-149). New York, NY: Springer-Verlag.

Dustman, R.E., Emmerson, R.Y., & Shearer, D.E., (1994). Physical activity, age, and cognitive-neuropsychological function. *Journal of Aging and Physical Activity, 2*, 143-181.

Dustman, R.E., Ruhling, R.O., Russell, D.M., Shearer, D.E., Bonekat, H.W., Shigeoka, J. W., Wood, D.S., & Bradford, D.C. (1984). Aerobic exercise training and improved neuropsychological function in older individuals. *Neurobiology of Aging, 5*, 35-42.

Duxbury, L. & Higgins, C. (1994). Families in the economy. In M. Baker, (Ed.). *Canada's changing families: Challenges to public policy*. Ottawa, ON: Vanier Institute of the Family.

Dwyer, D.S., & Mitchell, O.S. (1998). Health problems as determinants of retirement: Are self-rated measures endogenous? *Journal of Health Economics, 18*(2), 173-193.

Eaves, L. J., Eysenck, H. J. & Martin, N.G. (1989). *Genes, culture, and personality: An empirical approach*. London, U.K.: Academic Press.

Eggebeen, D.J. (1992). Family structure and intergenerational exchanges. *Research on Aging, 14*, 427-447.

Ehrlich, P.D. (1968). *The population bomb*. New York, NY: Ballantine Books.

Ekerdt, D.J., Bosse, R., & Levkoff, S. (1985). Empirical test for phases of retirement: Findings from the Normative Aging Study. *Journal of Gerontology, 40*(1), 95-101.

Ekerdt, D.J., DeViney, S., & Kosloski, K. (1996). Profiling plans for retirement. *Journal of Gerontology: Series B: Psychological sciences and social sciences, 51*(3), S140.

Ekerdt, D.J., Kosloski, K. & Stanley DeViney. (2000). Normative anticipation of retirement by older workers. *Research on Aging, 22*(1), 3-22.

Elder, G.H. Jr. (1974). *Children of the great depression: Social change in life experience*. Chicago: University of Chicago Press.

Elder, G.H. Jr., & Caspi, A. (1990). Studying lives in a changing society: Sociological and personological explorations. In A.I. Rubin, R.A. Zucker, & S. Frank, (Eds.). *Studying persons and lives* (pp. 210-247). New York, NY: Springer.

Elder, G.H. Jr. (1978). Approaches to social change and the family. *American Journal of Sociology, 84*, S1-S38.

Elder, G.H. Jr. (1987). War mobilization and the life course: A cohort of World War II veterans. *Sociological Forum, 2*, 449-472.

Elder, G.H. Jr. (1992). Models of the life course. *Contemporary Sociology, 21*, 632-635.

Elder, G.H. Jr. (1994). Time, human agency, and social change. *Social Psychology Quarterly, 57*, 4-15.

Elder, G.H. Jr. (2000). The life course. In E.F. Borgatta & R.J. V. Montgomery, (Eds.). *The encyclopedia of sociology, Vol. 3* (2nd ed., pp. 939-991). New York, NY: Wiley.

Elder, G.H. Jr. (Ed.). (1985). *Life course dynamics: Trajectories and transitions, 1968-1980*. Ithaca, NY: Cornell University Press.

Elder, J.H. Jr. (1975). Age differentation and the life course. *Annual Review of Sociology, 1*, 165-190.

Elder, J.H. Jr. (1974). *Children of the great depression: Social change in life experience*. Chicago, IL: University of Chicago Press.

Employment Practices. *Ageing and Society* (UK), *18*(6), 641-658.

Employment Survey. *The Gerontologist, 29*, 382-387.

Enterline, P. E., Salter, V., McDonald, A.D., & McDonald, J.C. (1973). The distribution of medical services before and after "free" medical care: The Quebec experience. *New England Journal of Medicine, 289*, 1174-1178.

Epp, J. (1986). *Achieving health for all: A framework for health promotion*. Ottawa, ON: Health and Welfare Canada.

Epsing-Anderson, G. (1994). Welfare states and the economy. In N. J. Smelser & R. Swedberg, (Eds.). *The handbook of economic sociology* (pp. 711-732). Princeton, NJ: Princeton University Press.

Estes, C., & Associates, (2001). *Social policy and aging: A critical perspective*. Thousand Oaks, CA: Sage Publications.

Estes, C.L., Mahakian, J.L., & Weitz, T.A. (2001). A political economy critique of "productive aging". In C.L. Estes & Associates, *Social policy and aging; A critical perspective* (pp 187-199). Thousand Oaks, CA: Sage Publications.

Estes, C.L., Swan, J.H., & Gerard, L.E. (1984). Dominant and competing paradigms in gerontology: Towards a political economy on aging. In M. Minkler & C.L. Estes, (Eds). *Readings in the political economy of aging*. Farmingdale, NY: Baywood.

Estes, C.L. (1979). *The aging enterprise*. San Francisco, CA: Jossey-Bass.

Estes, C.L. (1999). Critical gerontology and the new political economy of aging. In M. Minkler & C.L. Estes, (Eds.). *Critical gerontology: Perspectives from political and moral economy* (pp. 17-35). Amityville, NY: Baywood.

Estes, C.L., & Wood, J.B. (1986). The non-profit sector and community based care for the elderly in the U.S.: A disappearing resource? *Social Science and Medicine, 23*(12), 1261-1266.

Estes, C.L., (1979). *Aging enterprise: A critical examination of social policies and services for the aged*. San Francisco, CA: Jossey-Bass.

Estes, C.L., Gerard, L.E., Zones, J.S., & Swan, J.H. (1984). *Political economy, health and aging*. Boston, MA: Little, Brown and Company.

Estes, C.L., Linkins, K.W., & Binney, E.A. (1996). The political economy of aging. In R.H. Binstock & L.K. George, (Eds.). *Handbook of aging and the social sciences* (4th Ed) (pp. 346-361). San Diego, CA: Academic Press.

Estes. C., Linkins, K.W., & Binney, E.A. (2001). Critical perspectives on aging. In C. Estes & Associates, (Eds.).

Social policy and aging; A critical perspective (pp. 23-44). Thousand Oaks, CA: Sage Publcications.

Evan, R.G., McGrail, K.M., Morgan, S.G., Barer, M.L., Hertzman, C (2001). Apocalypse No: Population aging and the future of health care systems. *Canadian Journal on Aging, 20* (suppl. 1), 160-191.

Evans, R.G. (1976). Does Canada have too many doctors? Why nobody loves an immigrant physician. *Canadian Public Policy, 2*, 47-160

Evans, R.G. (1984). Strained mercy: The economics of Canadian health care. Toronto, ON: Butterworths.

Evans, R.G., & Stoddart, G.L. (1990). Producing health, consuming health care. *Social Science & Medicine, 31*, 1347-1363.

Evans, R.G. (1990). Tension, compression, and shear: Directions, stresses, and outcomes of health care cost control. *Journal of Health Politics, Policy and Law, 15*(1), 101-128.

Evans, R.G. (1994). Health care as a threat to health: Defense, opulence, and the social environment. *Daedalus, 123*(4), 21-42.

Falcón, M., & Tucker, K.L. (2000). Prevalence and correlates of depressive symptoms among Hispanic elders in Massachusetts. *Journal of Gerontology: Social Sciences, 55B*(2), S108-S116.

Fast, J., & Da Pont, M. (1997). Changes in women's work continuity. *Canadian Social Trends, 46*(Autumn), 2-7.

Feinberg, L.F. & Kelly, K.A. (1995). A well-deserved break: Respite programs offered by California's statewide system of caregiver resource centers. *The Gerontologist, 35*(5), 701-706.

Fellegi, I.P. (1988). Can we afford an aging society? *Canadian Economic Observer*, Oct., 4.1-4.33.

Ferraro, K.F. (1997). (Ed.). *Gerontology: Perspectives and issues* (2nd Ed.). New York, NY: Springer Publishing Co.

Ferraro, K.F. (1987). Double jeopardy to health for Black older adults? *Journal of Gerontology, 43*, 528-533.

Fine, M. (1992). *Disruptive voices: The possibilities of feminist research*. Ann Arbor, MI: University of Michigan Press.

Finlayson, A. (1988). *Whose money is it anyway? The showdown on pensions*. Markham, ON: Viking.

Fischer, D.H. (1977). *Growing old in America*. New York, NY: Oxford University Press.

Fischer. L.R., Rogne, L., Eustis, N.N. (1990). Support systems for the familyless elderly: Care without commitment. In J.F. Gubrium & A. Sankar, (Eds.). *The home care experience: Ethnography and policy*. Newbury Park, CA: Sage Publications.

Fitzgerald, J.M. (1988). Vivid memories and the reminiscence phenomenon: The role of a self-narrative. *Human Development, 31*, 260-270.

Fleras, A., & Elliot, J.L. (1992). *Multiculturalism in Canada: The challenge of diversity*. Scarborough, ON: Nelson Canada.

Flippen C., & Tienda, M. (2000). Pathways to retirement: Patterns of labour force participation and retirement:

Some evidence on the role of pensions and social security in the 1970s and 1980s. *Journal of Labour Economics, 17*(4), 757-783.

Foot, D.K, & Stoffman, D. (1996). *Boom, bust and echo: How to profit from the coming demographic shift.* Toronto, ON: Macfarlane Walter and Ross.

Forbes, W.F., Jackson, J.A., & Kraus, A.S. (1987) *Institutionalization of the elderly in Canada.* Toronto, ON: Butterworths.

Ford, A.B., Haug, M.R., Roy, A.W., Jones, P.K., & Folmar, S.J. (1992). New cohorts of urban elders: Are they in trouble? *Journals of Gerontology, 47,* S297-S303.

Ford, D. & Nault, F. (1996). Changing fertility patterns, 1974 to 1994. *Health Reports, 8*(3), 39-46. (Catalogue No. 82-003). Ottawa, ON: Statistics Canada.

Fortin, P. (1996). The Canadian fiscal problem: The macro-economic connection. In L. Osberg & P. Fortin, (Eds.). *Unnecessary debts* (pp. 26-38). Toronto, ON: James Lorimer.

Foster, C. (1996). *A place called heaven: The meaning of being black in Canada.* Toronto, ON: Harper Collins Publishers Ltd.

Foucault, M. (1972). *The archaeology of knowledge.* London, U.K.: Tavistock.

Fowler, F.J., Jr. (2001). *Survey research methods* (3rd Ed.). Beverly Hills, CA: Sage.

Fox, R. (1991). Presentation to the Canadian Medical Association Conference on Challenges and Changes in the Care of the Elderly.

Fozard, J. L. (1990). Vision and hearing in aging. In J.E. Birren, & K.W. Schaie, (Eds.). *Handbook of the psychology of aging,* (3rd Ed., pp. 150-171). San Diego, CA: Academic Press.

Fozard, J.L., & Gordon-Salant, S. (2001). Sensory and perceptual changes with aging. In J.E. Virren, & K.W. Schaie, (Eds.). *Handbook of the psychology of aging* (5th Ed.). San Diego, CA: Academic Press.

Frayne, T. (1990). *The tales of an athletic supporter.* Toronto, ON: McClelland & Stewart.

Frenken, H. (1991). *Women and RRSPs. Perspectives on labour and income.* Ottawa, ON: Canada.

Frenken, H., & Standish, L. (1994). RRSP withdrawals. *Perspectives on labour and income, 6*(1), 37-40.

Frideres, J.S. (1973). Discrimination in Western Canada. *Race, 15*(2), 213-222.

Frideres, J.S. (1994). The future of our past: Native elderly in Canadian society. In *Writings in Gerontology 15,* Ottawa, ON: National Advisory Council on Aging.

Friedlander, D. & Kinov-Malul, R. (1980). Aging of populations, dependency and economic burden in developed countries. *Canadian Studies in Population, 7,* 49-55.

Friedman, L., Daly, M. P., & Lazur, A. M. (1995). Burden among white and black caregivers to elderly adults. *Journal of Gerontology: Social Sciences, 50B,* S110-S118.

Fries, J.F. (1983). Compression of morbidity. *Milbank Memorial Fund Quarterly, 61,* 397-419.

Froggatt, K. (2001). Life and death in English nursing homes: Sequestration or transition? *Ageing and Society, 21*(3), 319-332.

Fronstin, P. (1999). Retirement patterns and employee benefits: Do benefits matter? *The Gerontologist, 39*(1), 37-47.

Fulton, G., & Metress, E. (1995). *Perspectives on death and dying.* Boston, MA: Jones and Bartlett.

Fyke, K. (2001). Caring for Medicare. Sustaining a quality system. Commission on Medicare. Government of Saskatchewan.

Gairdner, W.D. (1992*). The war against the family.* Toronto, ON: Stoddart Publishing.

Galarneau, D. & Sturrock, J. (1997). Family income after separation. *Perspectives on labour and income, 9* (2), 18-28. (Catalogue No. 75-001-XPE). Ottawa: Statistics Canada.

Gall, T.L, Evans, D.R., & Howard, J. (2000). Preretirement expectations and the quality of life of male retirees in later retirement. *Canadian Journal of Behavioural Science, 32*(3), 187-197.

Gallo, J., Rabins, P., & Hopkins, J. (1999). Depression without sadness: Alternative presentations of depression in late life. *American Family Physician, 60,* 820-826.

Galton, F. (1883). *Inquiries into human faculty and its development.* New York, NY: Macmillan.

Gardyn, R. (2000). Retirement redefined. *American Demographics, 22*(11), 52-57.

Garner, J.D. (1999). *Fundamentals of feminist gerontology.* New York, NY: Haworth Press.

Gee, E.M. (1996, October). *Aging and immigration in Canada: The elderly foreign-born population.* Paper presented at the meeting of the National Symposium on Immigration and Integration. Manitoba, CA: University of Manitoba.

Gee, E.M. (1999). Ethnic identity among foreign-born Chinese Canadian elders. *Canadian Journal on Aging, 18*(4), 415-429.

Gee, E.M. (2000). Living arrangements and quality of life among Chinese Canadian elders, *Social Indicators Research, 51,* 304-329.

Gee, E.M., & Gutman, G.M. (2000). *The overselling of population aging. Apocalyptic demography, intergenerational challenges and social policy.* Don Mills, ON: Oxford University Press.

Gee, E., & Gutman, G. (1995). (Eds). *Rethinking retirement.* Vancouver, BC: Gerontology Research Centre, Simon Fraser University.

Gee, E.M. & Gutman, G.M. (Eds). (2000). *The overselling of population aging: Apocalyptic demography, intergenerational challenges, and social policy.* Toronto, ON: Oxford University Press.

Gee, E.M. & Kimball, M.M. (1987). *Women and aging.* Toronto, ON: Butterworths.

Gee, E.M. (1980). Population. In R.B. Hagedorn, (Ed.). *Sociology* (pp. 191-235). Toronto, ON: Holt, Rinehart and Winston of Canada.

Gee, E.M. (1986). The life course of Canadian women: An historical and demographic analysis. *Social Indicators Research, 18*, 263-283.

Gee, E.M. (1990). Demographic change and intergenerational relations in Canadian families: Findings and social policy implications. *Canadian Public Policy, XVI*, 191-199.

Gee, E.M. (1990). Preferred timing of women's life events: A Canadian study. *International Journal of Aging and Human Development, 34*, 281-296.

Gee, E.M. (1991). The transition to grandmotherhood: A quantitative study. *Canadian Journal on Aging, 10*, 254-270.

Gee, E.M. (1995a). Contemporary diversities. In N. Mandell & A. Duffy, (Eds.). *Canadian families: Diversity, conflict and change* (pp. 79-109). Toronto, ON: Harcourt Brace.

Gee, E.M. (1995b). Families in later life. In R.Beaujot, E.M. Gee, F. Rajulton & Z.R. Ravanera, *Family over the life course* (pp. 77-113). (Catalogue No. 91-643E). Ottawa, ON: Statistics Canada.

Gee, E.M. (1997). The living arrangements of Chinese Canadian elders: The effect of demographic, economic, and cultural variables. Paper presented at the annual meeting of the American Sociological Association, Toronto, ON, August.

Gee, E.M. (2000). Contemporary diversities. In N. Mandell & A. Duffy, (Eds.). *Canadian families: Diversity, conflict and change* (2nd Ed.) (pp. 78-111). Toronto, ON: Harcourt Canada.

Gee, E.M. (2000). Population and politics: Voodoo demography, population aging, and Canadian social policy. In E.M. Gee & G.M. Gutman, (Eds.). *The overselling of population aging: Apocalyptic demography, intergenerational challenges, and social policy* (pp. 5-25). Toronto, ON: Oxford University Press.

Gee, E.M., Mitchell, B.A., & Wister, A.V. (1995). Returning to the "parental nest": Exploring a changing Canadian life course. *Canadian Studies in Population, 22*, 121-144.

Gee, E.M., Mitchell, B.A., & Wister, A.V. (2001). Homeleaving trajectories in Canada: Exploring cultural and gendered dimensions. Paper presented at a joint session at the annual meetings of the Canadian Sociology and Anthropology Association and the Canadian Population Society, Laval University, QB, May.

Gelfand, D. (1994). *Aging and ethnicity: Knowledge and services.* New York, NY: Springer Publishing Co.

General Accounting Office. (1991). *Canadian health insurance: Lessons for the United States.* Gaithersburg, MD: U.S. General Accounting Office.

George, L.K. (1990). Social structure, social processes, and social-psychological states. In R.H. Binstock & L.K. George, (Eds.). *Aging and the social sciences* (3rd Ed., pp. 186-204). San Diego, CA: Academic Press, Inc.

George, L.K. & Gwyther, L.P. (1986). Caregiver well-being: A multidimensional examination of family caregivers of demented adults. *The Gerontologist, 26*, 253-259.

Gescheider, G.A. (1997). *Psychophysics: The fundamentals.* Mahwah, NJ: Erlbaum.

Gfellner, B.M. (1982). Case study analysis: A field placement program in the study of aging. Paper presented at the Canadian Association on Gerontology 11th Annual Scientific and Educational Meeting, Winnipeg, MB.

Giarrusso, R., Stallings, M., Bengtson, V.L., Rossi, A.S., & Marshall, V.W. (1995). "Intergenerational stake" hypothesis revisited: Parent-child differences in perceptions of relationships 20 years later. In V.L. Bengtson, K.W. Shaie, & L. Burton, (Eds.). *Adult intergenerational relations: Effects of societal change* (pp. 227-296). New York, NY: Springer.

Giddens, A. (1984). *The constitution of society: Outline of a theory of structuration.* Cambridge, U.K.: Polity Press.

Giddens, A. (1991). *Modernity and self-identity.* Cambridge, U.K.: Polity.

Giddens, A. (1994). Living in a post-traditional society. In U. Beck, A. Giddens & S. Lash, (Eds.). *Reflexive Modernization* (pp. 56-109). Stanford, CA: Stanford University Press.

Giele J.Z., & Elder Jr., G.H. (Eds.) (1998). *Methods of life course research: Qualitative and quantitative approaches.* Thousand Oaks, CA: Sage Publications.

Gilbert, S. & Bélanger, A. (2000). Impact of causes of death on life expectancy at higher ages from 1951 to 1996. In A. Bélanger, Y. Carrière, & S. Gilbert, (Eds.). *Report on the demographic situation in Canada, 2000* (pp. 137-151). (Catalogue No. 91-209-XPE). Ottawa, ON: Statistics Canada.

Gin, J., Street, D., & Arber, S. (Eds.). (2001). *Women, work and pensions: International issues and prospects.* Buckingham, U.K.: Open University Press.

Gladstone, J.W. (1989). Grandmother-grandchild contact: The mediating influence of the middle generation following marriage breakdown and remarriage. *Canadian Journal on Aging, 8*, 355-365.

Glaser, B., & Strauss, A. (1967). *The discovery of grounded theory.* Chicago, IL: Aldine.

Glazer, N., & Moynihan, D.P. (1963). *Beyond the melting pot.* Cambridge, MA: M.I.T. Press.

Globe and Mail, The. (1995). Toward a renewed pension system. March 11, D:6.

Godin, G., Jobin, J., & Bouillon, J. (1986). Assessment of leisure time exercise behavior by self-report: A concurrent validity study. *Canadian Journal of Public Health, 77*, 359-362.

Goffman, E. (1961). Asylums: Essays on the social situation of mental patients and other inmates. Garden City, NY: Anchor.

Gold, D.T. (1989). Sibling relations in old age: A typology. *International Journal of Aging and Human Development, 28*, 37-51.

Goldscheider, F.K. & Lawton, L. (1998). Family experiences and the erosion of support for intergenerational coresidence. *Journal of Marriage and the Family, 60*, 623-632.

Gordon, J., & Neal, R. (1997). Voluntary non-profit organizations: A new research agenda. *Society/Société* (Newsletter of the Canadian Sociology and Anthropology Association), *21*(1), 15-19.

Gottlieb, B.H. (1995). Impact of day programs on family caregivers of persons with dementia. Report by the Gerontology Research Centre & Psychology Department, University of Guelph, ON, February.

Government of Canada. (1970). *Income security and social services: Government of Canada working paper on the Constitution.* Ottawa, ON: Queen's Printer.

Government of Canada. (1996a). *Profiles: Hong Kong.* C&I-110-06-96 (Hong Kong).

Government of Canada. (1996b). *Profiles: People's Republic of China.* C&I-110-06-96 (China).

Gowan, M.A. (1998). Preliminary investigation of factors. Affecting appraisals of the decision to take early retirement. *Journal of Employment Counseling, 35,* 124-140.

Gower, D. (1997). Measuring the age of retirement. *Perspectives on Labour and Income, 9,* 11-17.

Graebner, W. (1980). *A history of retirement.* New Haven, CT: Yale University Press.

Graff, L.L. (1991). *Volunteer for the health of it.* Report of the findings from a health promotion grant funded by the Ontario Ministry of Health. Ottawa, ON: Volunteer Ontario Publications.

Green, K. (1985). Identification of the facets of self-health management. *Evaluation and the Health Professions, 8,* 323-338.

Grindstaff, C.F. & Trovato, F. (1990). Junior partners: Women's contribution to family income in Canada. *Social Indicators Research, 22,* 229-253.

Grindstaff, C.F. (1996). The costs of having a first child for women aged 33-38, Canada 1991. *Sex Roles, 35,* 137-151.

Groos, M.S. & Kealey, G.S. (1982). New France to the conquest, 1760. *Readings in Canadian Social History, Vol.1.* Toronto, ON: McClelland and Stewart.

Grundy, E. (1999). *Living arrangements and the health of older persons in developed countries.* New York, NY: United Nations Secretariat, Department of Social and Economic Affairs, Population Division.

Gubrium, J.F., & Holstein, J.A. (1997). *The new language of qualitative method.* New York, NY: Oxford University Press.

Gubrium, J.F., & Sankar, A. (Eds.). (1994). *Qualitative methods in research.* Thousand Oaks, CA: Sage Publications.

Guillemard, A.M. & Rein, M. (1993). Comparative patterns of retirement: Recent trends in developed societies. *Annual Review of Sociology, 19,* 469-503.

Guillemard, A.M. (1980). La Vieillesse et l'Etat. Paris: Presses Universitaires de France.

Guillemard, A.M. (2000). *Aging and the welfare state crisis.* Newark, NJ: University of Delaware Press.

Gunderson, M. (1998). Flexible retirement as an alternative to 65 and out. C.D. Howe Institute, Canada.

Gunderson, M. (1998). *Women and the Canadian labour market.* Scarborough, ON: International Thompson Publishing for Statistics Canada.

Guttman, D. (1994). *Reclaimed powers: Men and women in later life* (2nd Ed.). Evanston, IL: Northwestern University Press.

Guttman, L. (1941). The qualification of a class of attributes: A theory and method of scale construction. In P. Horst, (Ed.). *The prediction of personal adjustment* (Bulletin No. 48, pp. 319-348). New York, NY: Social Science Research Council.

Guyer, B., Freedman, M.A., Strobino, D.M., & Sondik, E.J. (2000). Annual summary of vital statistics: Trends in the health of Americans during the 20th century. *Pediatrics, 106,* 1307-1317.

Haber, C., & B. Gratton, (1994). *Old Age and the Search for Security: An American Social History.* Bloomington, IN, and Indianapolis, IN: Indiana University Press.

Habermas, J. (1972). *Knowledge and human interests.* London, U.K.: Heinemann.

Hadjistavropoulos, T. (2001). Pain research and management: Pain and aging, *Official Journal of the Canadian Pain Society, 6,* no. 3.

Hadley, M.L. (1998). Themes and challenges for future service and research. In M. Maunsell, (Ed.). *Designing meaningful new volunteer roles for retired persons.* Victoria, BC: Centre on Aging and Centre for Studies in Religion and Society, University of Victoria.

Hagestad, G.O. & Dannefer, D. (2001). Concepts and theories of aging: Beyond microfication in social science approaches. In R.H. Binstock & L.K. George, (Eds.). *Handbook of aging and the social sciences* (5th ed., pp. 3-21). San Diego, CA: Academic Press.

Hagestad, G.O. (1985). Continuity and connectedness. In V.L. Bengtson & J.F. Robertson, (Eds.). *Grandparenthood* (pp. 31-48). Beverly Hills, CA: Sage.

Hagestad, G.O. (1990). Social perspectives on the life course. In R.H. Binstock & L.K George, (Eds.). *Handbook of aging and the social sciences* (3rd ed., pp. 151-168). San Diego, CA: Academic Press.

Haldemann, V., & Lévy, R.(1995). Oecuménisme méthodologique et dialogue entre paradigms. *Canadian Journal on Aging, 14*(Suppl.), 37-51.

Haley, W.E., Roth, D.L., Coleton, M.L., Ford, G.R., & West, C.A. (1996). Appraisal, coping, social support as mediators of well-being in black and white family caregivers of patients with Alzheimer's disease. *Journal of Consulting and Clinical Psychology, 64,* 121-129.

Hall, D.R. & Zhao, J.Z. (1995). Cohabitation and divorce in Canada: Testing the selectivity hypothesis. *Journal of Marriage and the Family, 57,* 421-427.

Hall, D.R. (1996). Marriage as a pure relationship: Exploring the link between premarital cohabitation and divorce in Canada. *Journal of Comparative Family Studies, 27,* 1-12.

Hall, M., & Havens, B. (1997, April). *Aging in Manitoba study 1996: A twenty-five year longitudinal study.* Technical Report.

Hamil-Luker, J. (2001). The prospects of age war: Inequality between (and within) age groups. *Social Science Research, 30,* 386-400.

Han, Shin-Kap & Moen, S. (1999). Clocking out: Temporal patterning of retirement. *American Journal of Sociology, 105,* 191-236.

Hanawalt, B.A. (1986). The ties that bound: Peasant families in Medieval England. New York, NY: Oxford University Press.

Hanson, E.J., Danis, M., & Garrett, J. (1997). What is wrong with end-of-life care? Opinions of bereaved family members. *Journal of the American Geriatrics Society, 45*(11), 1339-1344.

Hanson, S.M. & Sauer, W.J. (1985). Children and their elderly parents. In W.J. Sauer & R.T. Coward, (Eds.). *Social support networks and the care of the elderly.* New York, NY: Springer Publications.

Hansson, R.O., DeKoekkoek, P.D., Neece, W.M., & Patterson, D.W. (1997). Successful aging at work: Annual Review, 1992-1996: The older worker and transitions to retirement. *Journal of Vocational Behaviour, 51,* 202-233.

Harada, M. (1994). Early and later life sport participation patterns among the active elderly in Japan. *Journal of Aging and Physical Activity, 2,* 105-114.

Hardy, M.A. & Quadagno, J. (1995). Satisfaction with early retirement: Making choices in the auto industry. *Journal of Gerontology: Social Sciences, 5OB,* S217-S228.

Hareven, T.K. (1992). Family and generation relations in the later years: A historical perspective. *Generations, 16,* 7-12.

Harkins, S.W., Chapman C.R., & Eisdorfer, C. (1979). Memory loss and response bias in senescence. *Journal of Gerontology, 34*(1), 66-72.

Harkins, S.W., Price, D.D., & Martelli, M. (1986). Effects of age on pain perception. *Journal of Gerontology, 41,* 58-63.

Harris, B.P. (1998). Listening to caregiving sons: Misunderstood realities. *The Gerontologist, 38*(3), 1342-1352.

Harris, D., & Guten, S. (1979). Health protective behavior: An exploratory study. *Journal of Health and Social Behavior, 20,* 17-29.

Hartley, A.A. & Hartley, J.T. (1984). Performance changes in champion swimmers aged 30-79 years. *Experimental Aging Research, 10,* 151-154.

Hasher, L., and Zacks, R.T. (1979). Automatic and effortful processes in memory. *Journal of Experimental Psychology: General, 108,* 356-388.

Hasselkus, B.R. (1988). Meaning in family caregiving: Perspectives on caregiver/professional relationships. *The Gerontologist, 28*(5), 686-691.

Havens, B. (1995). Overview of longitudinal research on aging. *Canadian Journal on Aging, 14*(Suppl.), 119-134.

Havens, B. (1997). *Annotated bibliography of papers, articles & other documents resulting from the Aging in Manitoba 1971, 1976, 1983, 1990, 1996 Cross-Sectional & Panel Studies.* Compiled by M.K. Hall.

Havens, B. (2001, November). *Healthy aging: From cell to society.* Planning workshop for the Canadian Longititudinal Study on Aging. Canadian Institute for Healthy Aging, Ottawa, ON.

Havens, B., & Chappell, N. (1983). Triple jeopardy: Age, sex and ethnicity. *Canadian Ethnic Studies, 15*(3), 119-132.

Hay, D.I. (1994). Social status and health status: Does money buy health? In B.S. Bolaria & R. Bolaria, (Eds.). *Racial minorities, medicine and health* (pp. 9-51). Nova Scotia & Saskatchewan: Fernwood Publishers and University of Saskatchewan.

Hayward, M.D., Crimmins, E.M., & Saito, Y. (1998). Cause of death and active life expectancy in the older population of the United States. *Journal of Aging and Health, 10,* 192-213.

Hayward, M.D., Freidman, S., & Chen, H. (1998). Career trajectories and older men's retirement. *The Journal of Gerontology: Series B: Psychological Sciences and Social Sciences, 53B*(2), S9l-Sl03.

Hayward, M.D., Friedman, S., & Chen, H. (1998). Career trajectories and older men's retirement. *The Journal of Gerontology, 534B*(2), S91-S103.

Hayward, M.D., Hardy, M.A., & Liu, M. (1994). Work after retirement among older men in the United States. *Social Sciences Research, 23,* 82-107.

Hazan, H. (1994). *Old age: Constructions and deconstructions.* Cambridge, U.K.: Cambridge University Press.

Heady, B & Wearing, A (1988). The sense of relative superiority—central to well-being. *Social Indicators Research, 20,* 497-517.

Health & Welfare Canada (1987). Aging: Shifting the emphasis. Working paper, Health Services and Promotion Branch, Ottawa, ON.

Health & Welfare Canada (1990). Seniors Independence Program: Today's projects enhancing the future, 1988-1989, 1989-1990 (Cat. H7430/1990E). Ottawa, ON: Supply and Services Canada.

Health Canada. (2000) http://www.hc-sc.gc.ca/seniors-aines/pubs/factoids/en/no41.htm

Health Canada. (1998a). *Reaching out: A guide to communicating with aboriginal seniors.* (Catalogue No. H88-3/20-1998E). Ottawa, ON: Minister of Public Works and Government Services, Canada.

Health Canada. (1998b). *Canada's seniors at a glance.* Ottawa, ON: Canadian Council on social Development for the Division of Aging and Seniors, Health Canada. http://www.hc-sc.gc.ca/seniors-aines/pubs/poster/seniors/page5e.htm.

Health Canada. (1999). *Canadian research on immigration health: An overview.* (Catalogue No. H21-149/1999E). Ottawa, ON: Minister of Public Works and Government Services.

Helson, R. & Wink, P. (1992). Personality change in women from the early 40s to the early 50s. *Psychology and Aging, 7*, 46-55.

Hendricks, J. (1996). The search for new solutions. *The Gerontologist, 36*, 141-144.

Hendricks, J. (1997). Bridging contested terrain: Chaos or prelude to a theory? *Canadian Journal on Aging, 16*, 197-217.

Henretta, J.C. (1992). Uniformity and diversity: Life course institutionalization and late-life work exit. *The Sociological Quarterly, 33*(2), 265-279.

Henretta, J.C., & O'Rand, A.M. (1983). Joint retirement in dual worker family. *Social Forces, 62*, 504-520.

Henretta, J.C., O'Rand, A.M., & Chan, C.G. (1993). Gender differences in employment after spouse's retirement. *Research on Aging, 15*(2), 148-169.

Heritage Canada. (1998). Hate and bias activity in Canada. *Multiculturalism*, Vol. 4, December 21. http://www.pch.gc.ca/multi/evidence/series4_e.shtml.

Heron, A. & Chown, S. (1967). *Age and function*. Boston, MA: Little Brown.

Hertzog, A.R., & Morgan, J.N. (1993). Formal volunteer work among older Americans. In S.A. Bass, F.G. Caro, and Y.P. Chen, (Eds.). *Achieving a productive aging society*. Westport, CT: Greenwood Publishing Group, Inc.

Hertzog, A.R., Kahn, R.L., Morgan, J.N., Jackson, J.S., & Antonucci, T.C. (1989). Age differences in productive activities. *Journal of Gerontology, 44* (4) 129-138.

Hertzog, C., Dixon, R.A., & Hultsch, D.F. (1990). Metamemory in adulthood: Differentiating knowledge, belief, and behavior. In T. M. Hess, (Ed.). *Aging and cognition: Knowledge organization and utilization*. Amsterdam, The Netherlands: Elsevier.

Herzog, A. R., & Kulka, R. A. (1989). Telephone and mail surveys with older populations: A methodological overview. Sampling rare population. In M. Powell Lawton, & A.R. Herzog, (Eds.). *Special research methods for gerontology* (pp. 63-90). Amityville, NY: Baywood Publishing, Inc.

Hess, B.B. & Soldo, B.J. (1985). Husband and wife networks. In W.J. Sauer & R.T. Coward, (Eds.). *Social support networks and the care of the elderly*. New York, NY: Springer Publications.

Hess, T.M., & Pullen, S.M. (1996). Memory in context. In F. Blanchard-Fields, & T.M. Hess, (Eds.). *Perspectives on cognitive change in adulthood and aging* (pp. 387-428). New York, NY: McGraw-Hill.

Heyland, D.K, Lavery, J.V., Tranmer, J.E., & Shortt, S.E.D. (2000b). The final days: An analysis of the dying experience in Ontario. *Annals of the Royal College of Physicians and Surgeons of Canada, 33*(6), 356-361.

Heyland, D.K, Tranmer, J., Feldman, & Stewart, D. (2000). End-of-life decision making in the seriously ill hospitalized patient: An organizing framework and results of a preliminary study. *Journal of Palliative Care, 16*(Suppl.), 31-39.

Heyland, D.K., Lavery, J.V., Tranmer, J.E., Shortt, S.E.D., & Taylor, S.J. (2000a). Dying in Canada: Is it an institutionalized, technologically supported experience? *Journal of Palliative Care, 16*(Suppl.), 10-16.

Hibbard, J.H. (1995) Women's employment history and their post-retirement health and resources. *Journal of Women and Aging, 7*(3), 43-54.

Hill, J.B. & Amuwo, S.A. (1998). Understanding elder abuse and neglect. In Jackson, N.A. & Oates, G.C., (Eds.), *Violence in intimate relationships: Examining sociological and psychological issues* (pp. 195-216). Boston, MA: Butterworth-Heinemann.

Hirdes, J.P., & Brown, K.S. (1994). The statistical analysis of event histories in longitudinal studies of aging. *Canadian Journal on Aging, 13*(3), 332-352.

Hirdes, J.P., & Forbes, W.F. (1993). Factors associated with the maintenance of good self-rated health. *Journal of Aging and Health, 5* (1) 101-122.

Hirdes, J.P., Fries, B.E., Morris, J.N., Steel, R.K., LaBine, S., Beaulne, P., Schalm, C., Stones, M.J., Teare, G., Smith, T., Marhaba, M., & Pérez, E. (2000). Integrated health information systems based on the RAI/MDS series of instruments. *Hospital Management Forum, 12*, 30-40.

Hirdes, J.P., Zimmerman, D.R., Hallman K.G. & Soucie, P. (1988). Use of the MDS quality indicators to assess quality of care in institutional settings. *Canadian Journal of Quality Health Care, 14*, 5-11.

Hochschild, A. (1975). Disengagement theory: A critique and proposal. *American Sociological Review, 40*, 553-569.

Holden, K.C. (1988). Poverty and living arrangements among older women: Are changes in economic well-being underestimated? *Journals of Gerontology, 43*, S22-S27.

Hollander, M., Chappell, N.L., Havens, B., & McWilliam, C. (2001). *Pilot study of the costs and outcomes of home care and residential long term care services*. Victoria, BC: Hollander Analytical Services.

Hollander, M., Chappell, N.L., Havens, B., & McWilliam, C. (2001). *Study of the costs and outcomes of home care and residential long term care services*. Victoria, BC: Hollander Analytical Services.

Hollander, M., Tessaro, T., Chappell, N.L., Havens, B., Muir, W., & Shapiro, E. (2001, March*). Evaluation of the maintenance and preventive model of home care*. Victoria, BC: Hollander Analytical Services.

Holstein, M. (1992). Productive aging: Troubling implications. In M. Minkler & C.L. Estes, (Eds.). *Critical Gerontology: Perspectives from political and moral economy* (pp 359-373). Amityville, NY: Baywood.

Homans, G.F. (1961). *Social behavior: Its elementary forms*. New York, NY: Harcourt Brace Jovanovich.

Honeyman, M. (1991). Canadian Medical Association. Challenges and changes in the care of the elderly. Ottawa, ON: CMA.

Honig, M., & Hanoch, G. (1985). Partial retirement decision of husbands and wives. Issues in the economics of aging, Chicago, IL: University of Chicago Press.

Hooyman, N. (1990). Women as caregivers of the elderly: Social implications for social welfare policy and practice. In D.E. Biegel & A. Blum, (Eds.). *Aging and caregiving—Theory, research and policy* (pp. 221-241). Newbury Park, CA: Sage Publications Inc.

Hooyman, N., & Kiyak., H.A. (1999). *Social gerontology: A multidisciplinary perspective* (5th Ed). Boston, MA: Allyn and Bacon.

Hooyman, N., Gonyea, J.G., & Montgomery, R.J.V. (1985). The impact of in-home service termination on family caregivers. *The Gerontologist, 25*, 141-145.

Hopp, F.P., & Duffy, S.A. (2000). Racial variations in end-of-life care. *Journal of the American Geriatrics Society, 48*(6), 658-663.

Horn, J.L. (1982). The theory of fluid and crystallized intelligence in relation to concepts of cognitive psychology and aging in adulthood. In F.I.M. Craik & S. Trehub, (Eds.). *Aging and cognitive processes* (Vol. 8). New York, NY: Plenum.

Hornick, J.P., McDonald, L., & Robertson, G.B. (1992). Elder abuse in Canada and the United States: Prevalence, legal and service issues. In R.D. Peters, R.J. McMahon & V.L. Quinsey, (Eds.). *Aggression and violence throughout the life span*, (pp 301-335). Newbury Park, CA.: Sage.

Horowitz, A. (1981). Sons and daughters as caregivers to older parents: Differences in role performance and consequences. Annual meeting of the Gerontological Society of America, Toronto, ON.

Horowitz, A. (1985). Family caregiving to the frail elderly. In C. Eisdorfer, (Ed.). *Annual review of gerontology and geriatrics: Vol. 5*, New York, NY: Guilford Press.

Hou, F. & Omwanda, L. (1997). A multilevel analysis of the connection between female labour force participation and divorce in Canada, 1931-1991. *International Journal of Comparative Sociology, 38*, 271-288.

House of Commons Debate (1921) Feb, 14. *House of Commons Debates of the Doninion of Canada. Fifth Session—Thirteenth Parliament*. Ottawa, ON: F.A. Ackland King's Printer.

House, J.S., & Kahn, R.L. (1985). Measures and concepts of social support. In S. Cohen & S.L. Syme, (Eds.). *Social support and health*. Orlando, FL: Academic Press.

Hovland, C.I. (1959). Reconciling conflicting results derived from experimental and survey studies of attitude change. *American Psychologist, 14*, 8-17.

Howe, M.L., & Courage, M.L. (1993). On resolving the enigma of infantile amnesia. *Psychological Bulletin, 113*, 305-326.

Hsu, H.-C., Lew-Ting, C.-Y., & Wu, S.-C. (2001). Age, period and cohort effects on the attitude toward supporting parents in Taiwan. *The Gerontologist, 41*(6), 742-750.

Hudson, M.F. (1991). Elder mistreatment: A taxonomy with definitions by Delphi. *Journal of Elder Abuse and Neglect* 3:1-20.

Hudson, M.F., & Carlson, J.R. (1999). Elder abuse: Expert and public perspectives on its meaning. *Journal of Elder Abuse and Neglect, 9*, 77-97.

Hudson, M.F., Armachain, W.D., Beasley, & C.M. Carlson J.R. (1998). Elder abuse: Two Native American views. *Gerontologist*, 38(5):538-548.

Hughes, S.L., Giobbie-Hurder, A., Weaver, F.M., Kubal, J.D., & Henderson, W. (1999) Relationship between caregiver burden and health-related quality of life. *The Gerontologist, 39*(5), 534-545.

Hultsch, D.F. (1971). Adult age differences in free classification and free recall. *Developmental Psychology, 4*, 338-342.

Hultsch, D.F., Hammer, M., & Small, B.J. (1993). Age differences in cognitive performance in later life: Relationships to self-reported health and activity life style. *Journal of Gerontology: Psychological Sciences*, 48, P1-P11.

Hultsch, D.F., Hertzog, C., Dixon, R.A., & Small, B.J. (1998). *Memory changes in the aged*. New York, NY: Cambridge University Press.

Hultsch, D.F., Hertzog, C., Small, B.J., McDonald-Miszlak, L., & Dixon, R.A. (1992).Short-term longitudinal change in cognitive performance in later life. *Psychology and Aging, 7*, 571-584.

Hultsch, D., & Dixon, R. (1984). Memory for text materials in adulthood. In P.B. Baltes, & O.G. Brim, Jr., (Eds.). *Life-span development and behavior, Vol. 6*. New York, NY: Academic Press.

Human Resources Canada. (1996). *A look at discrimination against visible minority men*. http://www.hrdc-drhc.gc.ca/arb/publications/bulletin/vol2n2/v2n2a9_e.shtml.

Human Resources Development Canada. (2001). *Annual Report of the Canada Pension Plan*. Hull, QC: Human Resources Development Canada's Income and Security Programs Communications Unit.

Human Resources Development Canada. (2000). *The ISP Stats Book 2000*. Vanier, ON.

Human Resources Development Canada. (2001). Old age security rates July-Sept. 2001. http://www.hrdc-drhc.gc.ca/isp/oas/rates_1e.shtml.

Human Resources Development Canada. (2001). *Statistical bulletin: Canada Pension Plan/Old Age Security*. Vanier, ON.

Hunter, K.I., & Linn, M.W. (1980). Psychosocial differences between elderly volunteers and non-volulnteers. *International Journal of Aging and Human Development, 12*(3), 205-213.

Hurd, M. & Macdonald, M. (2001). *Beyond coping: Widows reinventing their lives*. Halifax, NS: Pear Press.

Hurley, A.C., Volicer, L., & Mahoney, E.K. (2001). Comfort in older adults at the end of life. In M.P. Lawton, (Ed.). *Annual review of gerontology and geriatrics: Vol. 20. Focus on the end of life: Scientific and social issues* (pp.120-143). New York, NY: Springer Publishing Company.

Hutchens, R. (1999). Social security benefits and employer behaviour: Evaluating social security early retirement benefits as a form of unemployment insurance. *International Economic Review, 40*(3), 659-678.

Idler, E.L., Stanislav, V.K., & Hayes, J.C. (2001). Patterns of religious practice and belief in the last year of life. *Journal of Gerontology: Social Sciences, 56B*(6), S326-S334.

Ikels, C. (1990). Resolution of intergenerational conflict: Perspectives of elders and their family members. *Modern China, 16*(4), 379-406.

Illich, I. (1976). *Limits to medicine. Medical nemesis: The expropriation of health.* London, U.K.: Marion Boyars Publishers Ltd.

Isajiw, W. W. (1999). *Understanding diversity: Ethnicity and race in the Canadian context.* Toronto, ON: Thompson Educational Publishing Inc.

Ishii-Kuntz, M. (1997). Intergenerational relationships among Chinese, Japanese and Korean Americans. *Family Relations, 46,* 23-32.

Jacob, A.G. (1994). Social integration of Salvadoran refugees. *Journal of the National Association of Social Workers, 39*(3), 307-312.

Jacobson, S. (1995). Overselling depression to the old folks. *Atlantic Monthly, 275*(4), 46-49.

James, W. (1890). *Principles of psychology.* New York, NY: Henry Holt.

Janevic, M.R., & Connell, C.M. (2001). Racial, ethnic, and cultural differences in the dementia caregiving experience: Recent findings. *The Gerontologist, 41*(3), 334-347.

Jayachandran, J. (2000). Contributions of socioeconomic, sociopsychological and biological factors to fertility differentials in Canada. *Canadian Studies in Population, 27,* 329-354.

Jimenez, M. Changing faces of madness: Early American attitudes and treatment of the insane. Hanover and London: University Press of New England, 1987.

Johnson, C.L. & Catalano, D.H. (1981). Childless elderly and their family supports. *The Gerontologist, 21,* 610-618.

Johnson, R.W., & Neumark, D. (1997). Age discrimination, job separations, and employment status of older workers: Evidence from self-reports. *Journal of Human Resources, 32*(4), 779-811.

Joiner, T.E. Jr. (1996). A confirmatory factor-analytic investigation of the tripartite model of depression and anxiety in college students. *Cognitive Therapy and Research, 20*(5), 521-539.

Judd, C., & McClelland G. (1998). In D.T. Gilbert, S.T. Fiske, & G. Lindsey, (Eds.). *The handbook of social psychology,* New York, NY: Oxford University Press.

Judge, K., Mulligan, J. A., & Benzeval, M. (1998). Income inequality and population health. *Social Science and Medicine, 46*(4-5), 567-579.

Jutras, S. & Veilleux, F. (1991). Informal caregiving: correlates of perceived burden. *Canadian Journal on Aging, 10*(1), 40-55.

Kamo, Y., & Zhou, M. (1994). Living arrangements of elderly Chinese and Japanese in the United States. *Journal of Marriage and the Family, 56,* 544-558.

Kandrack, M.-A., Grant, K., & Segall, A. (1991). Gender differences in health related behaviour: Some unanswered questions. *Social Science and Medicine, 32,* 579-590.

Kane, R.L., Evans, J.G., MacFayden, D. (1990). *Improving the health of older people: A world view.* World Health Organization Report. Geneva: WHO.

Kaplan, R.M., & Schneider, D.L. (2001). Medical decision making toward the end of life: Ethical, economic, and health policy implications. In M.P. Lawton, (Ed.). *Annual review of gerontology and geriatrics: Vol. 20. Focus on the end of life: Scientific and social issues* (pp.39-63). New York, NY: Springer Publishing Company.

Kart, C. (1981). Experiencing symptoms: Attribution and misattribution of illness among the aged. In M. Haug, (Ed.). *Elderly patients and their doctors* (pp. 70-78). New York, NY: Springer Publishing.

Kart, C.S. & Kinney, J.M. (2001). *The realities of aging* (6th Ed.) Boston, MA: Allyn and Bacon.

Kart, C.S. & Longino, C.F. (1987). The support systems of older people: A test of the exchange paradigm. *Journal of Aging Studies,1,* 239-251.

Kasl, S.V. (1995). Strategies in research on health and aging: Looking beyond secondary data analysis. *Journal of Gerontology: Social Sciences, 50*(4), S191-S193.

Katz, M.B. (1975). *The people of Hamilton, Canada West.* Cambridge, MA.: Harvard University Press.

Katz, S. (1996). *Disciplining old age: The foundations of gerontological knowledge.* Charlottesville, VA: University Press of Virginia.

Kaufert, J.M. (1999). Aboriginal patients in Canada. *Anthropology and Medicine, 6*(3), 405-421.

Keating, N., Fast, J., Frederick, J., Cranswick, K., & Perrier, C. (1999). *Eldercare in Canada: Context, content and consequences.* (Catalogue No. 89-570-XPE). Ottawa, ON: Statistics Canada, Housing, Family and Social Statistics Division.

Keefe, J., Rosenthal, C., & Béland, F. (2000). Impact of Ethnicity on Helping Older Relatives. *Canadian Journal of Aging.* 19, 317-342.

Kelly, K. (1995). Projections of visible minority groups, 1991 to 2016. (Catalogue 11-008E). *Canadian Social Trends, Summer,* 3-8.

Kelner, M.J., Meslin, E, & Wahl, J. (1994). *Patient decision-making in critical illness: A Canadian study.* International Sociological Association, Centre for Studies on Aging, University of Toronto, ON.

Kempen, G.I.J.M., & Suurmeijer, T.P.B.M. (1990). The development of a hierarchical polychotomous ADL-IADL scale for noninstitutionalized elders. *The Gerontologist, 30,* 497-502.

Kendall, R.E. (2001). The distinction between mental and physical illness. *British Journal of Psychiatry, 178,* 490-493.

Kessler, R.C., & McLeod, J.D. (1985). Social support and mental health in community samples. In S. Cohen, & S.L. Syme, (Eds.). *Social support and health.* Orlando, FL: Academic Press.

Kiecolt, K., & Nathan, L. (1985). *Secondary analysis of survey data*. Newbury Park, CA: Sage Publications.

Kim, H-K., Hisata, M.,. Kai, I., & Lee, S. (2000). Social support exchange and quality of life among Korean elderly. *Journal of Cross-Cultural Gerontology, 15*(4), 331-347.

Kim, U. (1987). Illness behaviour patterns of Korean immigrants to Toronto: What are the hidden costs? In K.V. Uijimoto, & J. Naidoo, (Eds.). *Asian Canadians: Contemporary Issues* (pp.194-219). Guelph, ON: University of Guelph.

Kincheloe, J., & McLaren, P. (2000). Rethinking critical theory and qualitative research. In N. Denzin, & Y. Lincoln, (Eds.). *Handbook of qualitative research* (2nd ed., pp. 279-313). Thousand Oaks, CA: Sage Publications.

King, A.C., Taylor, C.B., Haskwell, W.L., & DeBusk, R.F. (1989). Influence of regular aerobic exercise on psychological health: A randomized, controlled trial of healthy middle-aged adults. *Health Psychology, 8*, 305-324.

King, A.C., Taylor, C.B., & Haskwell, W.L. (1993). Effects of differing intensities and formats of 12 months of exercise training on psychological outcomes in older adults. *Health Psychology, 12*, 292-300.

Kinsey, A.C., Pomeroy, W.B., & Martin, C. (1948). Sexual behavior in the human male. Philadelphia, PA: WB Saunders.

Kirwin, P.M. (1991). *Adult day care: The relationship of formal and informal systems of care*. New York, NY: Garland Press.

Klassen, T.R., & Gillin, C.T. (1999). The heavy hand of the law: The Canadian Supreme Court and mandatory retirement. *Canadian Journal on Aging, 18*(2), 259-275.

Kline, D.W., & Schaie, K.W. (Eds.). (1996). *Handbook of the psychology of aging* (4th Ed.) San Diego, CA: Academic Press.

Knight, B.G., Silverstein, M., McCallum, T. J., & Fox, L.S. (2000). A sociocultural stress and coping model for mental health outcomes among African American caregivers in Southern California. *Journal of Gerontology: Psychological Sciences, 55*(B), 142-150.

Knight, B.G., Lutzky, S.M., & Macofsky-Urban, F. (1993). A meta-analytic review of interventions for caregiver distress: Recommendations for future research. *The Gerontologist, 33*(2), 240-248.

Knight, C. (1999). Unpublished MA thesis, University of Waterloo.

Knox, V., Gekoski W.L.,& Kelly, L.E. (1995). The age group evaluation and description (AGED) inventory: A new instrument assessing stereotypes of and attitudes towards age groups. *Internation Journal of Aging and Human Development, 40*(1), 39-55.

Knox, V.J. & Gekoski W.L. (1989). The effect of judgement context on assessments of age groups. *Canadian Journal on Aging, 8*, 244-254.

Knox, V.J., Gekoski, W.L., & Johnson, E.A.. (1984). The relationship between contact with and perceptions of the elderly. Paper presented at the Canadian Association on Gerontology 13th Annual Scientific and Educational Meeting, Vancouver, BC.

Kobayashi, K.M. (2000). The nature of support from adult *sansei* (third generation) children to older *nisei* (second generation) parents in Japanese Canadian families. *Journal of Cross-Cultural Gerontology, 15*, 185-200.

Kobayashi, K.M. (1999*). Bunko No Tanjyo (Emergent culture: Continuity and change in older* Nisei (second generation) parent-adult Sansei (third generation) relationships in Japanese *Canadian families*. Unpublished doctoral dissertation, Simon Fraser University.

Koch, T., Braun, K.L., & Pietsch, J.H. (1999). Social necessity, individual rights, and the needs of the fragile: Euthanasia in the context of end-of-life decision making. *Journal of Ethics, Law and Aging, 5*(1), 17-28.

Kohli, M. (1988). *New patterns of transition to retirement in West Germany*. Tampa, FL: International Exchange Centre on Gerontology, University of South Florida.

Kohli, M., & Rein, M. (1991). The changing balance of work and retirement. *Time for retirement: Comparative studies of early exit from the labour force*. Cambridge, U.K.: Cambridge University Press.

Kojima, H. (1996). Determinants of attitudes toward population aging in Japan. *The Journal of Population Problems, 52*(2), 15.

Kolberg, J.E., & Esping-Andersen, G. (1991). Welfare states and employment regime. In Kolberg, J.E., (Ed.). *The welfare state as employer* (pp. 3-35). Armonk, NY: M.E. Sharpe.

Kosloski, K. & Montgomery, R.J.V. (1995). The impact of respite use on nursing home placement. *The Gerontologist, 35*(1), 67-74.

Kosloski, K., Ekerdt, D., & DeViney, S. (2001). The role of job-related rewards in retirement planning. *The Journals of Gerontology, 56*(B), 3.

Kotlikoff, L.J. (1993). *Generational accounting: Knowing who pays, and when, and what we spend*. New York, NY: Free Press.

Kovar, M.G., & LaCroix, A.Z. (1987). Aging in the eighties, ability to perform work-related activities. *National Centre for Health Statistics Advance Data, 136*, 1-12.

Kozak, J. F., Elmslie, T., & Verdun, J. (1995). Epidemiology of the abuse and neglect of seniors: A review of the national and international research literature, [journal name?] 4-3, 29-141.

Kozma, A., & Stones, M.J. (1980). The measurement of happiness: Development of the Memorial University of Newfoundland Happiness Scale (MUNSH). *Journal of Gerontology, 35*, 906-912.

Kozma, A. & Stones, M.J. (1983). Predictors of happiness. *Journal of Gerontology, 38*, 626-628.

Kozma, A. & Stones, M.J. (1987). Social desirability in measures of subjective well-being: A systematic evaluation. *Journal of Gerontology, 42*, 56-59.

Kozma, A. & Stones, M.J. (1988). Social desirability in measures of subjective well-being: Age comparisons. *Social Indicators Research, 20,* 1-14.

Kozma, A., Stones, M.J., & McNeil, K. (1991). *Subjective well-being in later life.* Toronto, ON: Butterworths.

Kozma, A., Stones, M.J., & Kazarian, S. (1985). The usefulness of the MUNSH as an index of well-being and psychopathology. *Social Indicators Research, 17,* 49-55.

Kozma, A., & Stones, M.J. (1990). Decrements in habitual and maximal performance with age. In Perlmutter, M., (Ed.). *Late life potential* (pp. 1-23). Washington D.C.: The Gerontological Society of America.

Kozma, A., Stone, S., & Stones, M.J. (2000). Stability in components and predictors of subjective well-being (SWB): Implications for subjective well-being structure. In E. Diener, (Ed.). Advances in quality of life theory and research. Dordrecht, The Netherlands: Kluwer.

Kozma, A., Stone, S., & Stones, M.J. (1997) Top-down and bottom-up approaches to subjective well-being. *Intevención Psicosocial, 21,* 77-90.

Kozma, A., Stone, S., Stones, M.J., Hannah, T.E., & McNeil, K. (1990). Long-and short-term affective states in happiness. *Social Indicators Research 22,* 119-138.

Kozma, A., Stones, M.J., & Hannah, T.E. (1991). Age, activity, and physical performance: An evaluation of performance models. *Psychology and Aging, 6,* 43-49.

Krause, N., Hertzog, A.R., & Baker, E. (1992). Providing support to others and well-being in later life. *Journals of Gerontology, 47*(5), P300-P311.

Krick, J., & Sobal, J. (1990). Relationships between health protective behaviors. *Journal of Community Health, 15,* 19-34.

Kritz, M., Gurak, D., & Chen, L. (2000). Elderly immigrants: Their composition and living arrangements. *Journal of Sociology and Social Welfare, 27*(1), 85-114.

Kronebusch, K. & Schlesinger, M. (1994). Intergenerational transfers. In V.L. Bengtson & R.A. Harooytan, (Eds.). *Intergenerational linkages: Hidden connections in American society.* New York, NY: Springer.

Kronenfeld, J., Goodyear, N., Pate, R., Blair, A., Howe, H., Parker, G., & Blair, S. (1988). The interrelationship among preventive health habits. *Health Education Research, 3,* 317-323.

Kruger, J. & Heckhausen, J. (1993). Subjective conceptions versus cross-sectional contrasts. *Journals of Gerontology, 48B*(3), P100-P108.

Kruk, E. (1995). Grandparent-grandchild contact loss: Findings from a study of "grandparent rights" members. *Canadian Journal on Aging, 14,* 737-754.

Kubler-Ross, E. (1969). *On death and dying.* New York, NY: Macmillan.

Kuhn, T. (1962). *The structure of scientific revolutions.* New York, NY: Norton.

Kuhn, T. (1970). *The structure of scientific revolutions* (2nd Ed.). Chicago, IL: University of Chicago Press.

La Riviere, J.E., & Simonson, E. (1965). The effects of age and occupation on speed of writing. *Journal of Gerontology, 20,* 415-416.

Lachman, M. (1986). Locus of control in aging research: A case for multidimensional and domain-specific assessment. *Journal of Psychology and Aging, 1,* 34-40.

Laczko, L.S. (1997). Language, region, race, gender, and income: Perceptions of inequalities in Quebec and English Canada. In A. Frizzell & J.H. Pammett, (Eds.). *Social inequality in Canada* (pp. 107-126). Ottawa, ON: Carlton University Press.

Ladson-Billings, G. (2000). Racialized discourses and ethnic epistemologies. In N. Denzin, & Y. Lincoln, (Eds.). *Handbook of qualitative research* (2nd ed., pp. 257-277). Thousand Oaks, CA: Sage Publications.

Lai, D. (2000a). Depression among the elderly Chinese in Canada. *Canadian Journal on Aging, 19*(3), 409-429.

Lai, D. (2000b). Prevalence of depression among the elderly Chinese in Canada. *Canadian Journal of Public Health, 9*(1), 64-66.

Laing, R.D.(1960). The divided self: A study of sanity and madness. London, U.K.: Tavistock.

Langer, E.J. & Rodin, J. (1976). The effects of choice and enhanced personal responsibility for the aged. *Personality and Social Psychology, 34,* 191-198.

Larsen, R. & Diener, E. (1987). Affect intensity as an individual difference characteristic: A review. *Journal of Research in Personality, 21,* 1-39.

Larson, R., Zuzanek, J., & Mannell, R. (1985). Being alone versus being with people: Disengagement in the daily experience of older adults. *Journal of Gerontology, 40,* 375-381.

Laslett, P. (1979). *The world we have lost* (2nd Ed.). London, U.K.: Methuen.

Latulippe, D., & Turner, J. (2000). Partial retirement and pension policy in industrialized countries. *International Labour Review, 139*(2), 179-195.

Lau, R., & Hartman, K. (1983). Common sense representations of common illnesses. *Health Psychology, 2,* 167-185.

Laub, J. H., & Sampson, J. (1998). Integrating qualitative and quantitative data. In J.Z. Giele, & G.H. Elder Jr., (Eds.). *Methods of life course research: Qualitative and quantitative approaches* (pp. 231-230). Thousand Oaks, CA: Sage Publications.

Lauzon, D. (1995). Worker displacement: Trends, characteristics and policy responses. Ottawa, ON: Applied Research Branch, Strategic Policy, Human Resources Development Canada (R-95-3).

Lawton, M.P., Moss, M., Kleban, M.H., Glicksman, A., & Rovine, M. (1991). A two factor model of caregiving appraisal and psychological well-being. *Journal of Gerontology: Psychological Sciences, 46,* 181-189.

Lawton, M.P. (2001). *Annual review of gerontology and geriatrics: Vol. 20. Focus on the end of life: Scientific and social issues.* New York, NY: Springer Publishing Company.

Lawton, M.P., Moss, M., Hoffman, C., Grant, R., Have, T.T., & Kleban, M.H. (1999). Health, valuation of life, and the wish to live. *The Gerontologist, 39*(4), 406-416.

LeBlanc, S., & McMullin, J.A. (1997). Falling through the cracks: Addressing the needs of individuals between employment and retirement. Canadian Public Policy-Analyse de Politique, 23(3), 289-304.

LeBourdais, C. & Marcil-Gratton, N. (1996). Family transformations across the Canadian/American border: When the laggard becomes the leader. *Journal of Comparative Family Studies, 27*, 415-436.

Lee, G.R. (1985). Theoretical perspectives on social networks. In W.J. Sauer & R.T. Coward, (Eds.). *Social support networks and the care of the elderly*. New York, NY: Springer Publishers.

Lehman, H.C. (1953). *Age and achievement*. Princeton, NJ: Princeton University Press.

Lemon, B., Bengtson, V., & Peterson, J. (1972). Activity types and life satisfaction in a retirement community. *Journal of Gerontology, 27*, 511-523.

Leung H.H., & McDonald, L., (2002). *Chinese immigrant women who care for aging parents*. Toronto, ON: Joint Centre for Excellence for Research on Immigration and Settlement.

Leventhal, L.A., & Prohaska, T.R. (1986). Age, symptom interpretation and health behavior. *Journal of the American Geriatrics Society, 34*, 185-191.

Levin, L.S., & Idler, E.L. (1983). Self-care in health. *Annual Review of Public Health, 4*, 181.

Lexchin, J. (1988). The medical profession and the pharmaceutical industry: An unhealthy alliance. *International Journal of Health Services, 18* (4), 603-616.

Lexchin, J. (1990). Prescribing by Canadian general practitioners: Review of the English language literature. *Canadian Family Physician, 36*, 465-470.

Lexchin, J. (1993). The effect of generic competition on the price of prescription drugs in the Province of Ontario. *Canadian Medical Association Journal, 148*, 35-38.

Lexchin, J. (2001). Pharmaceuticals: Politics and policy. In P. Armstrong, H. Armstrong, & D. Coburn, (Eds.). *Unhealthy times. Political economy perspectives on health and care in Canada*. (pp.31-44). Toronto, ON: Oxford University Press.

Li, P.S. (1998). The Chinese in Canada (2nd Ed). Toronto, ON: Oxford University Press.

Li, P.S. (1990). Race and ethnicity. In P.S. Li, (Ed.). *Race and ethnic relations in Canada* (pp. 3-17). Don Mills, ON: Oxford University Press.

Liang, J. & Lawrence, R. (1989). Secondary analysis of sample surveys in gerontological research. In M. Lowell Lawton & A.R. Herzog (Eds.), *Special research methods for gerontology* (pp. 31-61). Amityville, NY: Baywood Publishing, Inc.

Liang, J., Krause, N.M., & Bennett, J.M. (2001). Social exchange and well-being: Is giving better than receiving? *Psychology and Aging, 16*, 511-523.

Lichtenberg, P.A. (1997). Clinical perspectives on sexual issues in nursing homes. *Topics in Geriatric Rehabilitation, 12*(4), 1-10.

Likert, R. (1932). A technique for the measurement of attitudes. *Archives of Psychology, 140*, 5-53.

Lin, N., Simeone, R.S., Ensel, W.M., & Kuo, W. (1979). Social support, stressful life events, and illness: A model and empirical test. *Journal of Health and Social Behaviour, 20*, 108-119.

Lincoln, Y. & Guba, E. (2000). Paradigmatic controversies, contradictions, and emerging confluences. In N. Denzin & Y. Lincoln, (Eds.). *Handbook of qualitative research* (2nd ed., pp. 163-187). Thousand Oaks, CA: Sage Publications.

Lindsay, C. (1999). *A portrait of seniors in Canada*. (Catalogue No. 89-519-XPE). Ottawa, ON: Statistics Canada, Minister of Industry.

Linville, P.W., (1982). The complexity-extremity effect and age based stereotyping. *Journal of Personality and Social Psychology, 42*, 193-211.

Lithwick, M., Reis, M., Stones, M.J., Macnaughton-Osler, K., Gendron, M.J., Groves, D., & Canderan, N. (1997). Exploring definitions and developing community-based projects on the awareness and prevention of elder abuse in different cultural communities. Montreal, QB: CLSC Rene-Cassin and Foundation for Vital Aging.

Lithwick, M., Stones, M.J., & Reis, M. (1998). *Exploring definitions and developing community based projects on the awareness and prevention of senior mistreatment in ethnocultural communities*. Halifax, NS: Canadian Association on Gerontology.

Litva, A., & Eyles, J. (1994). Health or healthy: Why people are not sick in a Southern Ontarian town. *Social Science and Medicine, 39*, 1083-1091.

Litwak, E. & Longino, C.F. (1987). Migration patterns among the elderly: A developmental perspective. *The Gerontologist, 27*, 266-272.

Litwak, E. (1985). *Helping the elderly: The complementary roles of informal networks and formal systems*. New York, NY: The Guilford Press.

Litwak. E. (1960). Geographic mobility and extended family cohesion. *American Sociological Review, 25*, 385-394.

Ljunggren, G., Phillips, C.D., & Sgadari, A. (1987). Comparison of restraint use in nursing homes in eight countries. *Age and Ageing, 26*(Suppl. 2), 43-48.

Logue, B.J. (1991) Women at risk: Predictors of financial stress for retired women workers. *The Gerontologist, 31*(5), 657-665.

Lomas, J. (1990). Finding audiences, changing beliefs: The structure of research use in Canadian health policy. *Journal of Health Politics, Policy and Law, 15*, 525-542.

Longino, C.F., & Kart, C.S. (1982). Explicating activity theory: A formal replication. *Journal of Gerontology, 37*, 713-722.

Longino, C.F. Jr., & Marshall, V.W. (1990). North American research on seasonal migration. *Ageing and Society, 10*, 229-235.

Longino, C.F., Marshall, V.W., Mullins, L.C. & Tucker, R.D. (1991). On the nesting of snowbirds: A question about seasonal and permanent migrants. *Journal of Applied Gerontology, 10*, 157-168.

Longman, P. (1987). *Born to pay: The new politics of aging in America*. Boston, MA: Houghton-Mifflin.

Lopata, H.Z. (1973). *Widowhood in an American city*. Cambridge, MA: Schenkman.

Lopata, H.Z. (1975). Support systems of elderly urbanites: Chicago of the 1970s. *The Gerontologist, 15*, 35-41.

Lopata, H.Z. (1978). Contributions of extended families to the support system of metropolitan area widows: Limitations of the modified kin network. *Journal of Marriage and the Family, 40*, 355-364.

Lopata, H.Z. (1995). Feminist approaches in social gerontology. In R. Bleizner & V. Hilkevitch Bedford, (Eds.). *Handbook of aging and the family* (pp. 114-151). Westport, CT: Greenwood Press.

Lorber, J. (1993). Why women physicians will never be true equals in the American medical profession. In E. Riska & K. Wegar, (Eds.). *Gender, work and medicine. Women and the medical division of labour* (pp. 62-76). International Sociological Association: SAGE Publications, Ltd.

Lord, S.R., Clark, R.D., & Webster, I.W. (1991). Postural stability and associated physiological factors in a population of aged persons. *Journal of Gerontology: Medical Sciences, 46*, M69-M76.

Lowe, G.S. (1991). Retirement attitudes, plans and behavior. *Perspectives, Statistics Canada, Autumn*, 8-17.

Lowenthal, M.F. & Robinson, B. (1976). Social networks and isolation. In R.H. Binstock & E. Shanas, (Eds.). *Handbook of aging and the social science*, New York, NY: Van Nostrand Reinhold.

Lubben, J. and Becerra, R.M. (1987). Social support among black, Mexican, and Chinese elderly. In D. E. Gelfand, & C.M. Berresi, (Eds.). *Ethnic dimensions of aging* (Pub. 130-144). New York, NY: Springer.

Lubben, J.E., Weiler, P.G., & Chi, I. (1989). Health practices of the elderly poor. *American Journal of Public Health, 79*, 731-734.

Lubomudrov, S. (1987). Congressional perceptions of the elderly: The use of stereotypes in the legislative process. *Journal of Gerontology, 27*, 77-81.

Luchak, A.A. (1997). Retirement plans and pensions: An empirical study, *Industrial Relations, 52*, 865-886.

Lussier, G., & Wister, A.V. (1995). Study of workforce aging of the British Columbia public service, 1983-1991. *Canadian Journal of Aging, 14*(3), 480-497.

Lykken, D., & Tellegen, A. (1996). Happiness is a stochastic phenomenon. *Psychological Science, 7*,186-189.

Lynott, P.P. & Roberts, R.E.L. (1997). Developmental stake hypothesis and changing perceptions of intergenerational relations, 1971-1985. *The Gerontologist, 37*, 394-405.

Lynott, R.J. & Lynott, P.P. (1996). Tracing the course of theoretical development in the sociology of aging. *Gerontologist, 35*, 749-760.

Lyotard, J-F. (1984). *The postmodern condition*. Minneapolis, MN: University of Minnesota Press.

MacCorquodale, K., & Meehl, P.E. (1948). On a distinction between hypothetical constructs and intervening variables. *Psychological Review, 55*, 95-107.

Madden, D.J., Blumenthal, J.A., Allen, P.A., & Emery, C.F. (1989). Improving aerobic capacity in healthy older adults does not necessarily lead to improved cognitive performance. *Psychology and Aging, 4*(3), 14, 307-320.

Mallard, A.G.C., Lance, C.E., & Michalos, A.C. (1997). Culture as a moderator of overall life satisfaction-life facet satisfaction relationships. *Social Indicators Research, 40*, 259-284.

Mancini, J.A., Quinn, W., Gavigan, M.A., & Franklin, H. (1980). Social network interaction among older adults: Implications for life satisfaction. *Human Relations, 33*, 543-554.

Manga, P. (1978). *The income distribution effect of medical insurance in Ontario* (Occasional Paper No. 6). Toronto, ON: Ontario Economic Council.

Mangus, R.S., Dipiero, A., & Hawkins, C.E. (1999). Medical students' attitudes toward physician-assisted suicide. *Journal of the American Medical Association, 282*(21), 2080-2081.

Mann, P. (1991). The influence of peers and parents on youth life satisfaction in Hong Kong. *Social Indicators Research, 24*, 347-366.

Manulife Financial. (1999). *Manulife Healthstyles Study*. Toronto, ON: Market Facts of Canada Ltd.

Marcil-Gratton, N. (1998). *Growing up with mom and dad? The intricate family life courses of Canadian children*. (Catalogue No. 89-566-XIE). Ottawa, ON: Statistics Canada.

Markides, K.S. (1983). Minority aging. In M.W. Riley, B.B. Hess, & K. Bond, (Eds.). *Aging in society : Reviews of recent literature*. Hillsdale, NJ: Lawrence Erlbaum.

Markides, K.S., Liang, J., & Jackson, J.S. (1990). Race, ethnicity and aging: Conceptual and methodological issues. In R.H. Binstock, & L.K. George, (Eds.). *Handbook of Aging and the Social Sciences* (pp. 112-129, 3rd Ed). New York, NY: Academic Press.

Markides, K.S., & Black, S.A. (1996). Race, ethnicity and aging. In R.H. Binstock, & L.K. George, (Eds.). *Handbook of Aging and the Social Sciences* (4th Ed). San Diego, CA: Academic Press.

Markson, L., Clark, J., Glantz, L., Lamberton, V., Kern, D., & Stolleran, G. (1997). The doctor's role in discussing advance preferences for end-of-life care: Perceptions of physicians practicing in the VA. *Journal of the American Geriatrics Society, 45*(4), 399-406.

Marmor, T.R., & Sullivan, K. (2000). *Canada's burning! Media myths about universal health coverage*. Washington Monthly, July/August.

Marmot, M.G., Kogevinas, M., & Elston, M.A. (1987). Social economic status and disease. *Annual Review of Public Health, 8*, 111-135.

Marriott, A., Donaldson, C., Tarrier, N., & Burns, A. (2000). Effectiveness of a cognitive-behavioural family intervention in reducing the burden of care in carers of patients with Alzheimer's disease. *British Journal of Psychiatry, 176*, 557-562.

Marriott, J., & Mable, A.L. (1998). Integrated models. International trends and implications for Canada. *Canada Health Action: Building on the Legacy* (pp. 547-676). National Forum on Health.

Marshall, K. (1998). Couples working shift. *Perspectives on Labour and Income, 10*(3), 9-14.

Marshall, V.W. (1976). Organizational features of terminal status passage in residential facilities for the aged. In L.H. Lofland, (Ed.). *Toward a sociology of death and dying* (pp. 115-134). Beverly Hills, CA: Sage.

Marshall, V.W. (1995a). Next half-century of aging research and thoughts for the past. *Journal of Gerontology: Series B: Psychological Sciences and Social Sciences, 50B*(3), S131-S133.

Marshall, V.W. (1995b). Rethinking retirement: Issues for the twenty-first century. In E. Gee & G. Gutman, (Eds.). *Rethinking retirement* (pp. 31-50). Vancouver, BC: Gerontology Research Centre, Simon Fraser University.

Marshall, V.W. (1996). The state of theory in aging and the social sciences. In R.H. Binstock & L.K. George, (Eds.). *Handbook of aging and the social sciences* (4th Ed., pp. 12-30). San Diego, CA: Academic Press.

Marshall, V.W., Clarke, P.J., & Ballantyne, P.J. (2001). Instability in the retirement transition: Effects on health and well-being in a Canadian study. *Research on Aging, 23*(4).

Marshall, V.W., Longino, C.F., Jr., Tucker, R., & Mullins, L. (1989). Health care utilization of Canadian snowbirds: An example of strategic planning. *Journal of Aging and Health, 1*, 150-168.

Martel, L., & Bélanger, A. (2000). Dependence-free life expectancy in Canada. *Health Reports, 58*, 26-29. (Catalogue No. 11-008). Ottawa, ON: Statistics Canada.

Martin, H.W., Hoppe, S.K., Marshall, V.W., & Daciuk, J.F. (1992). Sociodemographic and health characteristics of anglophone Canadian and U.S. snowbirds. *Journal of Aging and Health, 4*, 500-513.

Martin, N.J., Stones, M.J., Young, J., & Bedard, M. (2000). Development of delirium: A cohort prospective study in a community hospital. *International Psychogeriatrics, 12*, 117-126.

Martin Matthews, A. (1987). Widowhood as an expectable life event. In V.W. Marshall, (Ed.). *Aging in Canada: Social perspectives* (2nd Ed., pp. 343-366). Markham,ON: Fitzhenry & Whiteside.

Martin Matthews, A. (1991). *Widowhood in later life.* Toronto, ON: Butterworths.

Martin-Matthews, A. (2000). Change and diversity in aging families and intergenerational relations. In N. Mandell & A. Duffy, (Eds.). *Canadian families: Diversity,*

conflict and change (2nd Ed, pp. 323- 360). Toronto, ON: Harcourt Canada.

Martin-Matthews, A., & Béland, F. (2001). Northern light: Reflections on Canadian gerontological research [Editorial]. *Canadian Journal of Aging, 20* (Suppl. 1), i-xvi.

Martin Matthews, A., & Brown, K.H. (1987). Retirement as a critical life event: The differential experience of women and men. *Research on Aging, 9*, 548-571.

Martin Matthews, A. & Joseph, A.E. (1994). Growing old in aging communities. In V. Marshall & B. McPherson, (Eds.), *Aging: Canadian perspectives* (pp. 20-35). Peterborough, ON: Broadview Press.

Martin Matthews, A., Tindale J.A., & Norris J.E. (1985). The facts on aging quiz: A Canadian validation and cross-cultural comparison. *Canadian Journal on Aging, 3*, 165-174.

Masters, W. & Johnson, V. (1966). Human sexual response. Boston, MA: Little Brown.

Mata, F. and Valentine, J. (1999). *Selected ethnic profiles of Canada's senior age cohorts.* Strategic research and Analysis, Multiculturalism Department of Canadian Heritage.

Matsuoka, A.K. (1993). Collecting qualitative data through interviews with ethnic older people. *Canadian Journal on Aging, 12*(2), 232.

Matthew, S.H., Delaney, P.J., & Adamek, M.E. (1989). Male kinship ties: Bonds between adult brothers. *American Behavioral Scientist, 33*, 58-69.

Matthews, B.J. (1999). The gender system and fertility: An exploration of the hidden links. *Canadian Studies in Population, 26*, 21-38.

Matthews, S. (1979). *The social world of older women: Management of identity.* Beverly Hills, CA: Sage.

Matthews, S.H. & Rosner, T.T. (1988). Shared filial responsibility: The family as the primary caregiver. *Journal of Marriage and the Family, 50*, 185-195.

Matthews, S.H. (1979). *The social world of old women: Management of self-identity.* Newbury Park, CA: Sage.

Matthews, S.H. (1986). *Friendships through the life course: Oral biographies in old age.* Newbury Park, CA: Sage Publications.

Matthias, R.E., Lubben, J.E., Atchison, K.A., & Schweitzer, S.O. (1997). Sexual activity and satisfaction among very old adults: Results from a community-dwelling Medicare population survey. *Gerontologist, 37*(1) p. 6-14.

Maule, A.J., Cliff, D.R., & Taylor, R. (1996). Early retirement decisions and how they affect later quality of life. *Ageing and Society, 16*(2), 177-204.

Maurier, W. L., & Northcott, H. C. (2000). *Aging in Ontario.* Calgary, AB: Detselig Enterprises Ltd.

McAdams, D.P., & de St. Aubin, E. (1992). A theory of generativity and its assessment through self-report, behavioral acts, and narrative themes in autobiography. *Journal of Personality and Social Psychology, 62*, 1003-1015.

McCracken, C.F.M., Boneham, M.A., Copeland, J.R.M., Williams, K.E., Wilson, K., Scott, A., McKibbin, P., & Cleave, N. (1997). Prevalence of dementia and depression among elderly people in black and ethnic minorities. *British Journal of Psychiatry, 171*, 269-273.

McCrae, R.R. (1986). Well-being scales do not measure social desirability. *Journal of Gerontology, 41*, 390-392.

McCrae, R.R., Arenberg, D., & Costa, P.T., Jr. (1987). Declines in divergent thinking with age: Cross-sectional, longitudinal, and cross-sequential analyses. *Psychology and Aging, 2*, 130-137.

McCrae, R.R., & Costa, P.T. (1990). *Personality in adulthood*. New York, NY: Guilford Press.

McDaniel, S.A. (1997) Intergenerational transfers, social solidarity, and social policy: unanswered questions and policy challenges. *Canadian Public Policy/Canadian Journal on Aging, (Joint supplementary issue)*, 1-21.

McDaniel, S. (1995). Work, retirement and women in later life. In E. Gee, & G. Gutman, (1995). (Eds). *Rethinking retirement*. Vancouver, BC: Gerontology Research Centre, Simon Fraser University.

McDaniel, S.A.(1997). Intergenerational transfers, social solidarity and social policy: Unanswered questions and policy challenges. *Canadian Journal on Aging/ Canadian Public Policy, (Suppl.)*, 1-21.

McDaniel, S.A. & Lewis, R. (1998). Did they or didn't they? Inter-generational supports in Canada's past and a case study of Brigus, Newfoundland, 1920-1949. In L. Chambers, & E-A. Montigny, (Eds.). *Family matters: Papers in post-confederation Canadian history* (pp. 475-497). Toronto, ON: Canadian Scholars Press.

McDaniel, S.A., & McKinnon, A.L. (1993). Gender differences in informal support and coping among elders: Findings from Canada's 1985 and 1990 General Social Surveys. *Journal of Women and Aging, 5*, 79-98.

McDaniel, S.A. & Tepperman, L. (2000). *Close relations*. Scarborough, ON: Prentice Hall Allyn and Bacon Canada.

McDaniel, S.A. (1986). *Canada's aging population*. Toronto, ON: Butterworths.

McDaniel, S.A. (1987). Demographic aging as a guiding paradigm in Canada's welfare state. *Canadian Public Policy, 13*, 330-336.

McDaniel, S.A. (1992). Women and family in the later years: Findings from the 1990 General Social Survey. *Canadian Woman Studies, 12*(2), 62-64.

McDaniel, S.A. (1994). *Family and friends*. (Canada Catalogue No. 11-612). Ottawa, ON: Statistics Canada.

McDaniel, S.A., & Chappell, N.L. (1999). Health care regression: Contraindications, tensions and implications for Canadian seniors. *Canadian Public Policy, 15*(1), 123-132.

McDonald, A.D., McDonald, J.C., Steinmetz, N., Enterline, P. E., & Salter, V. (1973). Physician services in Montreal before universal health insurance. *Medical Care, 11*, 269-286.

McDonald, L. & Donahue, P. (2000). Poor health and retirement income: the Canadian case. *Ageing and Society, 20*, 493-522.

McDonald, L. & Wanner, R.A. (1984). Socioeconomic determinants of early retirement in Canada. *Canadian Journal on Aging, 3*(3), 105-116.

McDonald, L. (1995) Elder abuse. In E. Birren, (Ed.). *The encyclopedia of gerontology*. Academic Press.

McDonald, L. (1997). Invisible poor: Canada's retired widows. *Canadian Journal on Aging, 16*, 553-583.

McDonald, L. (1997). The link between social research and social policy options: Reverse retirement as a case in point. *Canadian Public Policy and the Canadian Journal on Aging, (Special Edition, CPP XXIII Supplement; CJA 16th Supplement)*, 90-113.

McDonald, L., & Wanner, R. (1990). *Retirement in Canada*. Toronto, ON & Vancouver, BC: Butterworths Canada Ltd.

McDonald, L., Donahue, P., & Moore, B. (2000). Widowhood in retirement. In F.T. Denton, D. Fretz, & B. Spencer, (Eds.). *Independence and economic security in old age* (pp. 329-345). Vancouver, BC: University of British Columbia Press.

McDonald, L., Donahue, P., & Moore, B. (2000a). Retirement through unemployment: What social work needs to know. *Canadian Social Work Review,17*(1), 69-85.

McDonald, L., Donahue, P., & Moore, B. (1997). *Widowhood and retirement: Women on the margin*. Toronto, ON: Centre for Applied Social Research.

McDonald, L., Donahue, P., & Moore, B. (1997b) The economic casualties of retiring to caregiving. Toronto, ON: Centre for Applied Social Research, Faculty of Social Work, University of Toronto.

McDonald, L., George, U., Daciuk, J., Yan, M., & Rowan, H. (2001). *A study on the settlement related needs of newly arrived immigrant seniors in Ontario*. Toronto, ON: Centre for Applied Social Research, University of Toronto.

McDonald, P.L., Donahue, P., & Moore, B. (2000b). The poverty of retired widows. In F. T. Denton, D. Fretz, & B. Spencer, (Eds.). *Independence and economic security in old age* (pp. 328-345). Vancouver, BC: University of British Columbia Press.

McDonald, P.L. (1996). Transitions into retirement: A time for retirement. Toronto, ON: Centre for Applied Social Research, Faculty of Social Work, University of Toronto.

McDonald, P.L. (1997). The link between social research and social policy options: Reverse retirement as a case in point. *Canadian Public Policy/ Canadian Journal of aging, Special Joint Issue, supplement*, 90-113.

McDonald, P.L. (2000). Alarmist economics and women's pensions: A case of semanticide. In E.M. Gee, & G.M. Gutman, (Eds.). *The overselling of population aging: Apocalyptic demography and intergenerational challenges* (pp. 114-128). Toronto, ON: Oxford University Press.

McDonald, P.L., & Chen, M.Y.T. (1993). The youth freeze and the retirement bulge: Older workers and the impending labour shortage. *Journal of Canadian Studies, 28*(1), 75-101.

McDonald, P.L., & Wanner, R.A. (1990) *Retirement in Canada.* Toronto, ON: Butterworths.

McDonald, P.L., Donahue, P., & B. Moore, (1997a). *Widowhood and retirement: Women on the margin.* Toronto, ON: Centre for Applied Social Research, Faculty of Social Work, University of Toronto.

McDonald, P.L., Donahue, P., & Marshall, V. (2000). The economic consequences of early unexpected retirement. In F.T. Denton, D. Fretz, & B. Spencer, (Eds.) *Independence and economic security in old age* (pp. 267-292). Vancouver, BC: University of British Columbia Press.

McDougall, G.J. (1998). Gender differences in coping and control with memory aging. *Journal of Women & Aging, 10*(1), 21-40.

McGarry, K. & Schoeni, R.F. (2000). Social security, economic growth, and the rise in elderly widows' independence in the twentieth century. *Demography, 37,* 221-236.

McKeown, T. (1976). *The modern rise of population.* London, U.K.: Edward Arnold.

McKeown, T. (1988). *The origins of human disease.* Oxford, U.K.: Basil Blackwell.

McKeown, T., Record, R.G., & Turner, R.D. (1975). An interpretation of the decline of mortality in England and Wales during the twentieth century. *Population Studies, 29,* 391-422.

McKinlay, J.B., & McKinlay, S.M. (1977). The questionable contribution of medical measures to the decline of mortality in the United States in the twentieth century. *Health and Society,* 405-428.

McMullin, J.A., & Marshall, V.W. (2001). Ageism, age relations, and garment industry work in Montreal. *Gerontologist, 41*(1), 111-122.

McMullin, J.A. (2000). Diversity and the state of sociological aging theory. *The Gerontologist, 40*(5), S517-S530.

McNeil, J.K., Stones, M.J., Kozma, A., & Andres, D. (1994). Age differences in mood: Structure, mean level, and diurnal variation. *Canadian Journal on Aging, 31,* 201-220.

McNeil, J.K., LeBlanc, A.M., & Joyner, M. (1991).The effect of exercise on depressive symptoms in the moderately depressed elderly. *Psychol Aging, 6,* 487-488.

McNeill, W.H. (1973). *Plagues and people.* New York, NY: Doubleday.

McPherson, B.D. (1995). Aging from the historical and comparative perspective: Cultural and subcultural diversity. In R. Neugebauer-Visano, (Ed.), *Aging and inequality cultural constructions of differences* (pp. 31-67). Toronto, ON: Canadian Scholars' Press Inc.

McQuillan, K. & Belle, M. (2001). Lone-father families in Canada, 1971-1996. *Canadian Studies in Population, 28,* 67-88.

Mebane, E.W., Orman, R.F., Kroonen, L.T., & Goldstein, M.K. (1999). Influence of physician race, age, and gender on physician attitudes toward advance care directives and preferences for end-of-life decision making. *Journal of the American Geriatrics Society, 47*(5), 579-591.

Mechanic, D. (1999). Issues in promoting health. *Social Science and Medicine, 48,* 711-718.

Mendelson, M., & Divinsky, P. (2000). *Canada 2015: Globalization and the future of Canada's health and health care.* Draft Report prepared for the Future of Global and Regional Integration Project, Institute of Intergovernmental Relations. Toronto, ON: Queen's University.

Menec, V.H. & Chipperfield, J.G. (2001). A prospective analysis of the relations between self-rated health and health care use among elderly Canadians. *Canadian Journal on Aging, 20*(30), 293-306.

Merton, R.K. (1968). *Social theory and social structure.* New York, NY: Free Press.

Meston, C.M. (1997). *West Journal of Medicine, 167*(4), 285-90.

Mhatre, S.L., & Deber, R.B. (1992). From equal access to health care to equitable access to health: A review of Canadian provincial health commissions and reports. *International Journal of Health Services, 22*(4), 56-68.

Michalos, A.C., Hubley, A.M., Zumbo, B.D., & Hemingway, D. (2001). Health and other aspects of the quality of life of older people. *Social Indicators Research, 54*(3), 239-274.

Michalos, A.C. (1991). *Global report on student well-being.* New York, NY: Springer-Verlag.

Midanik, L.T., Soghikian, K., Ransom, L.J., & Tekawa, I.S. (1995). Effect of retirement on mental health and health behaviours: The Kaiser Permanente Retirement Study. *Journals of Gerontology: Series B: Psychological Sciences and Social Sciences, 50B*(1), S59-S61.

Midlarsky, E., & Kahana, E. (1994). *Altruism in later life.* Thousand Oaks, CA: Sage.

Millar, W., & Beaudet, M. (1996). Health facts from the 1994 National Population Health Survey. *Canadian Social Trends, 40,* 24-27.

Miller, B., Campbell, R.T., Davis, L., Furner, S., Giachello, A., Prohaska, T., Ksufman, J.E., Li, J. E., & Perez, C. (1996). Minority use of community long-term cares services: A comparative analysis. *Journal of Gerontology: Social Sciences, 51B,* S70-S81.

Miller, S.C., Mor, V., Gage, B., & Coppola, K. (2001). Hospice and its role in improving end-of-life care. In M.P. Lawton, (Ed.), *Annual review of gerontology and geriatrics, Vol. 20: Focus on the end of life: Scientific and social issues* (pp.193-223). New York, NY: Springer Publishing Company.

Mills, C.W. (1959). *The sociological imagination.* New York, NY: Oxford University Press.

Milne, D., Pitt, I., & Sabin, N. (1993). Evaluation of a career support scheme for elderly people: The importance of "coping". *British Journal of Social Work, 23*(2), 157-168.

Miner, S., & Montoro-Rodriguez, J. (1999). Intersections of society, family, and self among Hispanics in middle and later life. 423-552. In C.D., Ryff, & V.W. Marshall, (Eds.). *The self and society in aging processes.* New York, NY: Springer Pub. Co.

Minkler, M. & Estes, C.L. (Eds.). (1984). *Readings in the political economy of aging.* Farmingdale, NY: Baywood.

Minkler, M. (1999). Introduction. In M. Minkler & C. Estes, (Eds.), *Critical gerontology: Perspectives from political economy and moral economy* (pp. 1-13). Amityville, NY: Baywood Publishing Co.

Mitchell, B.A. & Gee, E.M. (1996). Boomerang kids and mid-life parental marital satisfaction. *Family Relations, 45,* 442-448.

Mitchell, B.A. & Gee, E.M. (1996b). Young adults returning home: Implications for social policy. In B. Galaway & J. Hudson, (Eds.). *Youth in transition to adulthood: Research and policy implications* (pp. 61-71). Toronto, ON: Thompson Educational Publishing.

Mitchell, B.A. (2000). The refilled "nest": Debunking the myth of families in crisis. In E.M. Gutman & G.M Gutman, (Eds.). *The overselling of population aging: Apocalyptic demography, intergenerational challenges, and social policy* (pp. 80-99). Toronto, ON: Oxford University Press.

Mitchell, B.A., Wister, A.V., & Gee, E.M. (2002). "There's no place like home": An analysis of young adults' mature coresidency in Canada. *International Journal of Aging and Human Development, 54,* 57-84.

Mockler, D., Riordan, J., & Murphy, M. (1998). Psychosocial factors associated with the use/non-use of mental health services by primary carers of individuals with dementia. *International Journal of Geriatric Psychiatry, 13*(5), 310-314.

Moen, P. (1996). Gender, age, and the life course. In R.H. Binstock & L.K. George, (Eds.). *Handbook of aging and the social sciences* (4th Ed, pp. 171-187). San Diego, CA: Academic Press.

Moen, P. (2000). The gendered life course. In R.H. Binstock & L.K. George (Eds.), *Handbook of Aging and the Social Sciences* (5th Ed, pp. 179-196). San Diego, CA: Academic Press.

Moen, P., Dempster-McClain, D., & Williams, R.M., Jr. (1990). Social integration and longevity: An event history analysis of women's roles and resilience. *American Sociological Review, 54,* 635-647.

Moen, P., Sweet, S., & Swisher, R. (2001). *Customizing the career clock: Retirement planning and expectations.* Bronfenbrenner Life Course Centre Working Paper #01-08. New York, NY: Cornell Employment and Family Careers Institute, Cornell University.

Moller, V. (1988). Quality of life and retirement: A case study of Zulu return migrants. *Social Indicators Research, 20,* 621-658.

Moller, V (1992). Spare time use and perceived well-being among black South African youth. *Social Indicators Research, 26,* 309-352.

Molloy, D.W., Beerschoten, D.A., Borrie, M.J., Crilly, R.G., & Cape, R.D.T. (1988). Acute effects of exercise on neuropsychological function in elderly subjects. *Journal of the American Geriatrics Society, 36,* 29-33.

Monette, M. (1996). Canada's changing retirement patterns: Findings from the General Social Survey. Ottawa, ON: Statistics Canada.

Monk, A. (1997). *Transition to retirement.* New York, NY: Springer.

Montepare, J.M., & Lachman, M.E. (1989). "You're only as old as you feel": Self-perceptions of age, fears of aging, and life satisfaction from adolescence to old age. *Psychology of Aging, 4*(1): 73-78.

Montgomery, D. (2000). Attitudes of college students toward the elderly. *Unpublished manuscript.*

Montgomery, P.R., Kirshen, A.J., & Roos, N.P. (1988). Long-term care and impending mortality influence upon place of death and hospital utilization. *Gerontologist, 28*(3), 351-354.

Montgomery, R.J.V. (1989). Investigating caregiver burden. In K.S. Markides, & C.L. Cooper (Eds.). *Aging, Stress and Health* (pp. 201-218). New York, NY: John Wiley & Sons Ltd.

Montgomery, R.J.V. (1996). Advancing caregiver research: Weight efficacy and feasibility of interventions. *Journal of Gerontology, 51B*(3), S109-S110.

Montgomery, R.J.V., Gonyea, J.G., & Hooyman, N.R. (1985). Caregiving and the experience of subjective and objective burden. *Family Relations, 34,* 19-25.

Moon, A. & Williams, O. (1993). Perceptions of elder abuse and help-seeking patterns among African-American, Caucasian American, and Korean-American elderly women. *Gerontologist 33*(3), 386-95.

Moore, E.G., & Rosenberg, M.W. (1994). Residential mobility and migration among Canada's elderly. In V. Marshall & B. McPherson, (Eds.). *Aging: Canadian perspectives* (pp. 51-69). Peterborough, ON: Broadview Press.

Moore, E.G., & Rosenberg, M. (1995). *Population health among Canada's elderly: Sociodemographic and geographic perspectives.* NHRDP.

Moore, E.G. & Rosenberg, M.W., with McGuinness, D. (1997). *Growing old in Canada: Demographic and geographic perspectives.* Toronto, ON: Statistics Canada and ITP Nelson.

Morgan, L. & Kunkel, S. (2001). *Aging: The social context* (2nd Ed.). Thousand Oaks, CA: Pine Forge Press.

Morissette, R., & Drolet, M. (2000). *Pension coverage and retirement savings of young and prime-aged workers in Canada: 1986-1997.* Ottawa, ON: Statistics Canada, Minister of Industry.

Morris, J. N., Murphy, K. & Nonemaker, S. (1995). *Long-term care facility resident assessment instrument user's manual.* Brigg Health care Products.

Morris, J.N., Chave, S.P., Adam, C., Sirey, C.F., & Epstein, L. (1956). Vigorous exercise in leisure time and the incidence of coronary heart disease. *Lancet, ii,* 569-570.

Morris, R.G., Morris, L.W., & Britton, P.G. (1988). Factors affecting the emotional wellbeing of the caregivers of dementia sufferers. *British Journal of Psychiatry, 153,* 147-156.

Morton, D., & McCallum, M.E. (1988). Superannuation to indexation: Employment pension plans. *Research Studies, 2.* Toronto, ON: Queen's Printer for Ontario.

Moss, M.S. (2001). End of life in nursing homes. In M.P. Lawton, (Ed.). *Annual review of gerontology and geriatrics: Vol. 20. Focus on the end of life: Scientific and social issues* (pp.224-258). New York, NY: Springer Publishing Company.

Moustakas, C. (1994). *Phenomenological research methods.* Thousand Oaks, CA: Sage Publications.

Mui, A.C. (1992). Caregiving strain among black and white daughter caregivers: A role theory perspective. *The Gerontologist, 32,* 203-212.

Mullan, P. (2000). *The imaginary time bomb: why an ageing population is not a social problem.* London, U.K.: IB Tauris & Co.

Mullins, L.C., & Tucker, R.D. (Eds.). (1988). *Snowbirds in the sunbelt: Old Canadians in Florida.* Tampa, FL: University of South Florida, International Exchange Center on Gerontology.

Murphy, B., & Wolfson, M. (1991). *When the baby boom grows old: Impacts on Canada's public sector.* Ottawa, ON: Statistics Canada.

Murray, C.J.L. & Lopez, A.D. (1996). *The global burden of disease: A comprehensive assessment of mortality and disability from diseases, injuries, and risk factors in 1990 and projected to 2020.* Boston, MA: Harvard School of Public Health on behalf of the World Health Organization and the World Bank

Murray, C.J.L., & Lopez, A.D. (1996). *The global burden of disease.* Geneva: World Health Organization.

Murray, I.M. (1951). Assessment of physiologic age by combination of several criteria—vision, learning, blood pressure and muscle force. *Journal of Gerontology, 6,* 120-126.

Murzello, F. (1991). Quality of life of elderly East Indian immigrants. MSW Thesis. Calgary, AB: University of Calgary.

Mussen, P., Honzik, M.P., & Eichorn, D.H. (1982). Early adult antecedents of life satisfaction at age 70. *Journal of Gerontology, 37,* 316-322.

Mustard, C.A., Derksen, S., Berthelot, J.M., Wolfson, M., & Roos, L.L. (1997). Age-specific education and income gradients in morbidity and mortality in a Canadian province. *Social Science and Medicine, 45*(3), 383-397.

Mutchler, J.E., Burr, J.A., & Rogerson, P.R. (1997). *Minority aging in a diverse society: Community, family, and individual determinants of living arrangements.* Buffalo, NY:

Research Foundation of the State University of New York State.

Mutchler. J.E., Burr, J.A., Pienta, A.M., & Massagli. M.P. (1997). Pathway to labour force exit: Work transitions and work instability. *Journal of Gerontology: Social Sciences, 52B,* S4-S12.

Myers J.K., Weissman, M.M., Tischler, G.L., Holzer, C.E. III, Leaf P.J., Orvaschel, H., Anthony J.C., Boyd, J.H., Burke, J.D. Jr, & Kramer, M. (1984). Six-month prevalence of psychiatric disorders in three communities 1980 to 1982. *Archives of General Psychiatry, 41,* 959-967.

Myers, D.G., & Diener, E. (1995). Who is happy? *Psychological Science, 6,* 10-19.

Myers, W.A. (1984). *Dynamic therapy of the older patient.* New York, NY: J. Aronson.

Myles, J. & Quadagno, J. (Eds.). (1991). *States, labour markets, and the future of old age policy* Philadelphia. PA: Temple University Press.

Myles, J. (1984). *Old age and the welfare state.* Boston, MA: Little, Brown and Company.

Myles, J. (1984). *Old age in the welfare state: The political economy of public pensions.* Boston, MA.: Little, Brown and Company.

Myles, J. (1988). Decline or impasse? The current state of the welfare state. *Studies in political economy, 26,* 73-107.

Myles, J. (1995). *The market's revenge: Old age security and social rights.* Ottawa, ON: Caledon Institute of Social Policy.

Myles, J. (2000). *The maturation of Canada's retirement income system: Income levels, income inequality and low-income among the elderly.* Ottawa, ON: Statistics Canada; and Florida State University.

Myles, J., & Street, D. (1995). Should the economic life course be redesigned? Old age security in a time of transition. *Canadian Journal on Aging, 14*(2), 335-359.

Myles, J., & Teichroew, L. (1991). The politics of dualism: Pension policy in Canada. In J. Miles & J. Quadagno, (Eds.). *States, labour markets, and the future of old-age policy* (pp. 84-104). Philadelphia, PA: Temple University Press.

Myles, J.F. (1981). Income inequality and status maintenance: Concepts methods, and measures. *Research on Aging, 3*(2), 123-141.

Myles, J.F. (1984). Old Age in the Welfare State: The political economy of public pensions. Toronto, ON: Little, Brown and Company.

Nagel, J. (1994). Constructing ethnicity: Creating and recreating ethnic identity and culture. *Social Problems, 41,* 152-176.

Najman, J. (1980). Theories of disease causation and the concept of general susceptibility. *Social Science and Medicine, 14A,* 231-237.

National Academy on an Aging Society. (1999). *Demography is not destiny.* Washington, DC: National Academy on an Aging Society.

National Advisory Committee (2000). A guide to end-of-life care for seniors. Ottawa, ON: Tri-Co Printing Inc.

National Advisory Council on Aging (NACA). (2001). *Seniors in Canada: A report card*. Ottawa, ON: Minister of Public Works and Government Services Canada.

National Advisory Council on Aging. (1994*). Marital disruption in later life*. Ottawa, ON: National Advisory Council on Aging.

National Council of Welfare. (1999). *A pension primer*. Ottawa, ON: NCW.

National Council of Welfare. (2000). *Poverty profile 1998*. Ottawa, ON: NCW.

National Forum on Health. (1997). Canada Health Action: Building on the legacy. Volume I: The Final Report of the *National Forum on Health and Volume II: Synthesis Reports and Issue Papers*. Ottawa, ON: NFH.

National Hospice Organization and Accreditation Committee. (1997). *A pathway for patients and families facing terminal disease*. Arlington, VA: Author.

National Institute on Aging. (1996). *In search of the secrets of aging*. Bethesda, MD: National Institutes of Health.

Near, J. & Rechner, P.L. (1993). Cross-cultural variations in predictors of life satisfaction: An historical view of differences among West European countries. *Social Indicators Research, 29*, 109-121.

Nelsen, N.E., & Nelsen, E.E. (1972). Passing in the age stratification system. Paper presented at the Annual Meeting of the American Sociological Association, New Orleans.

Neugarten, B.L. (1974). Age groups in American society and the rise of the young old. In F.R. Eisele, (Ed.). *Political consequences of aging* (pp. 187-198). The Annals of the American Academy of Political and Social Science.

Neupert, R.F. (1997). Demographic decomposition of household arrangements among the ethnic aged. *Australian Journal on Ageing, 16*, 213-217.

Neysmith, S. (1995). Feminist methodologies: consideration of principles and practice for research in gerontology. *Canadian Journal on Aging, 14*(Suppl. 1), 100-118.

Nkongho, N.O., & Archbold, P.G. (1995). Reasons for caregiving in African American families. *Journal of Cultural Diversity, 2*, 116-123.

Noh, S., & Avison W.R. (1996). Asian immigrants and the stress process: A study of Koreans in Canada. *Journal of Health and Social Behaviour, 37*(2),192-208.

Nolan, K.A., Trahar, M.F., Clarke, C., & Blass, J.P. (1993). Respite retreat for dementia caregivers: A demonstration. *American Journal of Alzheimer's Care and Related Disorders and Research, 8*(1), 34-38.

Norris, J.E. & Tindale, J.A. (1994). *Among generations: The cycle of adult relationships*. New York, NY: W.H. Freeman.

Northcott, H.C. (1994). Public perceptions of the population aging "crisis." *Canadian Public Policy, 20*, 66-77.

O' Hanley, S., Ward, A., Zwirren, L., McCarron, R.F., Ross, J., & Rippe, J.M. (1987). Validation of a one-mile walk test in 70-79 year olds. *Medicine and Science in Sports and Exercise, 19*, 356-362

O'Bryan, K.G. Reitz, J.G., & Kuplowska, O.M. (1976). Non-official languages: A study of Canadian multiculturalism. Ottawa, ON: Minister of Supply and Services Canada.

O'Rand, A.M., & Henretta, J.C. (1999). *Age and inequality: Diverse pathways through later life*. Boulder, CO: Westview Press.

OECD. (1998). The retirement decision in OECD countries. OECD Working papers, 6(38). Paris: OECD.

Ogden, R., & Young, M.G. (1998). Euthanasia and assisted suicide: A survey of registered social workers in British Columbia. *British Journal of Social Work, 28* (2) 161-175.

Okun, M.A. (1993). Predictors of volunteer status in a retirement community. *International Journal of Aging and Human Development, 36* (1) 57-74.

Olesen, V.L. (2000). Feminisms and qualitative research at and into the millennium. In N. Denzin & Y. Lincoln, (Eds.). *Handbook of qualitative research* (2nd Ed., pp. 215-255). Thousand Oaks, CA: Sage Publications.

Olsen, J.M., Vernon, P.A., & Harris, J.A. (2001). The heritability of attitudes: A study of twins. *The American Psychological Association*, Vol. 80, No. 6 (pp. 845-860). APA.

Olshansky, S.J. & Ault, A.B. (1986). The fourth stage of the epidemiologic transition: The age of delayed degenerative diseases. *Milbank Memorial Fund Quarterly, 64*, 355-391.

Olshansky, S.J., Carnes, B.A., Rodgers, R.G. & Smith, L. (1997). Infectious diseases—New and ancient threats to world health. *Population Bulletin 52*(2), 1-52. Washington, DC: Population Reference Bureau, Inc.

Olson, P. (1990). The Elderly in the People's Republic of China. In J. Sokolovsky, (Ed.). *The cultural context of aging: Worldwide perspectives*. New York, NY: Bergin and Garvey.

Omran, A.R. (1971). The theory of epidemiological transition. *Milbank Memorial Fund Quarterly, 49*, 509-538.

Ontario Advisory Council on Senior Citizens. (1993). *Denied too long. The needs and concerns of seniors living in First Nation communities in Ontario*. Toronto, ON: Publications Ontario.

Organization for Economic Cooperation and Development (OECD). (1998). *Social and health policies in OECD countries*. OECD Working Papers. Vol.6, No.33. Paris: OECD.

Organization for Economic Cooperation and Development. (1992). New orientations for social policy. Note by the Secretary General. Paris: Directorate for Education, Employment, Labour and Social Affairs.

Osberg, L. & Fortin, P. (1996). Credibility mountain. In L. Osberg & P. Fortin, (Eds.) *Unnecessary debts* (pp. 157-172). Toronto, ON: James Lorimer.

Osberg, L. (1993). Is it retirement or unemployment? Induced "retirement" and constrained labour supply among older workers. *Applied Economics, 25,* 505-519.

Osness, W.H. (1987). Assessment of physical function among older adults. In D. Leslie, (Ed.). *Mature stuff.* Reston, VA: American Association for Health, Physical Education, Recreation and Dance.

Pakans, A. (1989). Stepping down in former times: A comparative assessment of retirement in traditional Europe. In D.I. Kertzer & K.W. Schaie, (Eds.). *Age structuring in comparative perspective* (pp. 175-195). Hillsdale, NJ: Lawrence Erlbaum Associates.

Palameta, B. (2001). Who contributes to RRSPs? A re-examination. *Perspectives on labour and income, 13*(3). (Catalogue No. 75-001-XIE). Ottawa, ON: Statistics Canada, Minister of Industry.

Palmore, E. & Manton, K. (1974). Modernization and the status of the elderly. *Journal of Gerontology, 29,* 205-210.

Palmore, E. (1981). Social patterns in normal aging: Findings from the Duke Longitudinal Study, Durnam, NC: Duke University Press.

Palmore, E.B. (1988). The facts on aging quiz: A handbook of uses and results. New York, NY: Springer.

Palmore, E.B. (1990). Aging: Positive and negative. New York, NY: Springer

Palmore, E.B. (1971). Attitudes toward aging as shown in humor. *The Gerontologist, 11,* 181-86.

Pampel, F.C., & Hardy, M. (1994). Status maintenance and change during old age. *Social Forces, 73,* 289-314.

Pang, K.Y. (1998). Causes of dysphoric experiences among elderly Korean immigrants. *Clinical Gerontologist, 19*(4), 17-33.

Parkin, A.J., & Walter, B.M. (1992). Recollective experience, normal aging, and frontal dysfunction. *Psychology and Aging, 7,* 290-298.

Pavalko, E.K., & Elder, G.H. Jr. (1990). World War II and divorce: A life course perspective. *American Journal of Sociology, 95,* 1213-1234.

Pavalko, E.K., & Artis, J.E. (1997). Women's caregiving and paid work: Casual relationships in late life. *Journals of Gerontology Series B Psychological Sciences and Social Sciences, 52B,* (4), S170-S179.

Payne, B.J., & Strain, L.A. (1990). Family social support in later life: Ethnic group variations. *Canadian Ethnic Studies, 22*(2), 99-100.

Payne, B.K., & Berg, B.L. (1999). Perceptions of nursing home workers, police chiefs, and college students regarding crime against the elderly: An exploratory study. *American Journal of Criminal Justice, 24,* 139-149.

Pendakur, K., & Pendakur, R. (1996). *The colour of money: Earnings differentials among ethnic groups in Canada.* Ottawa, ON: Strategic Research and Analysis Publication SRA-34B, Department of Canadian Heritage.

Pendakur, R., & Hennebry, J. (1998). *Multicultural Canada: A demographic overview 1996.* Canadian Heritage Multiculturalism.

Pendry, E., Barrett, G., & Victor, C. (1999). Changes in household composition among the over sixties: A longitudinal analysis of the Health and Life Surveys. *Health and Social Care in the Community, 7,* 109-119.

Penhale, B. & Kingston, B. (1997). Elder abuse, mental health and later life: Steps towards an understanding. *Aging and Mental Health, 1,* 296-304.

Penhale, B. (1999). Bruises on the soul: Older women, domestic violence, and elder abuse. *Journal of Elder Abuse and Neglect, 11,* 1-22.

Penning, M. (1983). Multiple jeopardy: Age, sex and ethnic variations. *Canadian Ethnic Studies, 15*(3), 81-105.

Penning, M.J., & Chappell, N.L. (1993). Age-related differences. In T. Stephens & D.F. Graham, (Eds.). *Canada's Health Promotion Survey 1990: Technical report.* (Catalogue No. H39-263/2-1990E). Ottawa, ON: Minister of Supply and Services Canada.

Penning, M.J. (1995). Cognitive impairment, caregiver burden and the utilization of health services. *Journal of Aging and Health, 7*(2), 233-253.

Penning, M.J. (1998). In the middle: Parental caregiving in the context of other roles. *Journal of Gerontology: Social Sciences, 53B,* S188-S197.

Penning, M.J., Allan, D.E., & Brackley, M.E. (2001, July). *Home care and health reform: Changes in home care utilization in one Canadian province, 1990-1998.* Paper presented at the International Association of Gerontology, Vancouver, BC.

Penning, M.J., Chappell, N.L., Stephenson, P.H., Rosenblood, L., & Tuokko, H.A. (1998). *Independence among older adults with disabilities. The role of formal care services, informal caregiving and self-care.* Final Report. (NHRDP Project No. 6610-2121-602). Victoria, BC: Centre on Aging, University of Victoria, BC.

Penning, M.J., Roos, L.L., Chappell, N.L., Roos, N.P., & Lin, G. (2002, February). Health care restructuring and community-based care: A longitudinal study. CHSRF Project No. 1997-055.

Pentland, H.C. (1981). Labour and capital in Canada, 1650-1860. Toronto, ON: James Loremont.

Peracchi, F. & Welch, F. (1994). Trends in labour force transitions of older men and women. *Journal of Labour Economics, 12*(2), 210-242.

Peressini, T. & McDonald, L. (1998). An evaluation of a training program on alcoholism and older adults for health care and social service practitioners. *Journal of Gerontology and Geriatrics Education, 4(18).*

Peters, S. (1995). *Exploring Canadian values: Foundations for well-being.* Ottawa, ON: Renouf Publishing Co. Ltd.

Peterson, C., & Stunkard, A. (1989). Personal control and health promotion. *Social Science and Medicine, 28,* 819-828.

Pezzin, L.E. & Schone, B.S. (1999). Parental marital disruption and intergenerational transfers: An analysis of lone elderly parents. *Demography, 36,* 287-297.

Phillips, L.R. (2000). Domestic violence and aging women. *Geriatric Nursing, 21,*188-195.

Phillipson, C. (1982). *Capitalism and the construction of old age*. London, U.K.: Macmillan.

Phillipson, C. (1999). The social construction of retirement: Perspectives from critical theory and political economy. In M. Minkler & C.L. Estes, (Eds.). *Critical gerontology. Perspectives from political and moral economy* (pp. 315-327). Amityville, NY: Baywood Publishing Co. Inc.

Phipps, S., Burton, P., & Lethbridge, L. (2001). In and out of the labour market: Long-term economic consequences of child-related interruptions to women's paid work. *Canadian Journal of Economics, 34*, 411-429.

Phua, V.C., Kaufman, G., & Park, K.S. (2001). Strategic adjustments of elderly Asian Americans: Living arrangements and headship. *Journal of Comparative Family Studies, 32*, 263-281.

Pienta, A. (1999). Early childbearing patterns and women's labour force behaviour in later life. *Journal of Women in Aging, 11*(1), 69-84.

Pienta, A.M., Burr, J.A., & Mutchler, J.E. (1994). Women's labour force participation in later life: The effects of early work and family experiences. *Journal of Gerontology: Social Sciences, 49*, S231-S239.

Pillemer, K., & Finkelhor, D. (1988). Prevalence of elder abuse: A random sample survey. *The Gerontologist, 28*, 51-57.

Pillemer, K., & Suitor, J.J. (1990). Prevention of elder abuse. In R. Ammerman & M. Hersen, (Eds.). *Treatment of family violence: A sourcebook* (pp. 406-422). New York, NY: John Wiley and Sons.

Pillemer, K. (1986). Risk factors in elder abuse: Results from a case-control study. In K. Pillemer & R.S. Wolf, (Eds.). *Elder abuse: Conflict in the family* (pp. 239-263). Dover, MA: Auburn House.

Podnieks, E. & Baille, E. (1995). Education as the key to the prevention of elder abuse and neglect. In Maclean, M., (Ed.). *Abuse and Neglect of Older Canadians - Strategies for Change*, (pp. 81-94). Toronto, ON: Thompson Educational Publishing.

Podnieks, E. (1992a). National survey on abuse of the elderly in Canada, *Elder Abuse and Neglect, 1*, 2.

Podnieks, E. (1992b). National Survey on Abuse of the Elderly in Canada. *Journal of Elder Abuse and Neglect 4*: 5-58.

Podnieks, E., Pillemer, K., Nicholson, J.P., Shillington, T., & Frizzel, A.F. (1990). National survey on abuse of the elderly in Canada. Toronto, ON: Ryerson Polytechnical Institute.

Poland, B., Coburn, D., Robertson, A., & Eakin, J. (1998). Wealth, equity and health care: A critique of a "population health" perspective on the determinants of health. *Social Science and Medicine, 46*(7), 785-798.

Popenoe, D. (1988). *Disturbing the nest: Family change and decline in modern societies*. New York, NY: A. de Gruyter.

Population Reference Bureau. (2001). *2001 World population data sheet*. Washington, D.C.: Population Reference Bureau, Inc.

Pourat, N., Lubben, J., Wallace, S. P., & Moon, A. (1999). Predictors of use of traditional Korean healers among elderly Koreans in Los Angeles. *The Gerontologist, 39*(6), 711-719.

Prado, C.G. (1998). *Last choice: Preemptive suicide in advanced age* (2nd Ed.). Westport, CT: Greenwood Press.

Predictors of employees' retirement ages. *Journal of Vocational Behavior, 57*(2), 206-225.

Preston, S.H. (1984). Children and the elderly: Divergent paths for America's elderly. *Demography, 21*, 435-457.

Price, C. (1998). *Women and retirement: The unexplored transition*. New York, NY: Garamond Press.

Prince, M.J., & Chappell, N.L. (1994). *Voluntary action by seniors of Canada. Final Report*. Senior Independence Research Program, Human Resources Development Canada.

Proctor, W.R. & Hirdes, J.P. (2001). Pain and cognitive status among nursing home residents in Canada. *Official Journal of the Canadian Pain Society, 6*(3), 119-125.

Prohaska, T.R., Leventhal, E.A., Leventhal, H., & Keller, M.L. (1985). Health practices and illness cognition in young, middle-aged, and elderly adults. *Journal of Gerontology, 40*, 569-578.

Pruchno, R.A. (1990). Effects of help patterns on the mental health of spouse caregivers. *Research on Aging, 12*(1), 57-71.

Prus, S.G. (1999). *Income inequality as a Canadian cohort ages: An analysis of the later life course*. Paper No. 10 Social and Economic Dimensions of an Aging Population. Hamilton, ON: McMaster University.

Quadagno, J. (1982). *Aging in early industrial society*. New York, NY: Academic Press.

Quadagno, J., & Reid, J. (1999). The political economy perspective in aging. In V.L. Bengston, & K.W. Schaie, (Eds.). *Handbook of theories of aging* (pp.344-358). New York, NY: Springer Publishing Co. Inc.

Qualls, S.H. (1993). Family therapy with older adults. *Generations, 17*, 73-74.

Quick, H.E., & Moen, P.B. (1997). Gender, employment, and retirement quality: A life course approach to the differential experiences of men and women. New York, NY: Bronfenbrenner Life Course Centre, Cornell University.

Quinn, J.F. (1999). Retirement patterns and bridge jobs in the 1990s. *EBRI Issue Brief, 206*, 1-22.

Quinn, J.F., & Burkhauser, R.V., & Myers, D.L. (1990). *Passing the torch: The influence of economic incentives on work and retirement*. Kalamazoo, MI: W.E. Upjohn Institute for Employment Research.

Rachlis, M., & Kushner, C. (1989). *Second opinion: What's wrong with Canada's health care system and how to fix it*. Toronto, ON: Collins.

Rajulton, F. & Ravanera, Z.R. (1995). The family life course in twentieth century Canada: Changes, trends and interrelationships. In R.Beaujot, E.M. Gee, F. Rajulton & Z.R. Ravanera, (Eds.). *Family over the life course* (pp.

115-150). (Catalogue No. 91-643E). Ottawa, ON: Statistics Canada.

Rattenbury, C. & Stones, M.J. (1989). A controlled evaluation of reminiscence and current-topics discussion groups in a nursing home context. *The Gerontologist, 29*, 768-771.

Rein, M. (1969a). Social class and the health service. *New Society, 20*, 807.

Rein, M. (1969b). Social class and the utilization of medical care services: A study of British experience under the National Health Service. *Hospitals, 43*, 43.

Rein, M., & Turner, J. (1999). Work, family, state and market: Income packaging for older households. *International Social Security Review, 52*(3), 93-106.

Reinhardt, U.E (2001). Commentary: On the apocalypse of the retiring baby boom. *Canadian Journal on Aging, 20* (Suppl. 1), 192-204.

Reisberg, B., Ferris, S.H., & Franssen, E. (1985). An ordinal functional assessment toll for Alzheimer's type dementia. *Hospital and Community Psychiatry, 36*, 593-595.

Reisberg, B., Ferris, S.H., deLeon, & Crook, (1982). Relationships in late midlife. *The Journal of Gerontology: Series B: Psychological Sciences and Social Sciences, 52B*(4), S170-S179

Reitzes, D.C., Mutran, E.J., & Fernandez, M.E. (1996). Preretirement Influences on postretirement self-esteem. *Journal of Gerontology: Series B: Psychological Sciences* and Social sciences, *51B*(5), 8242-249.

Renaud, M., Good, D., Nadeau, L., Ritchie, J., Way-Clark, R., & Connolly, C. (1996). *Determinants of health working group synthesis report, Canada health action: Building on the legacy: Synthesis reports and issues papers, Vol. II.* Ottawa, ON: National Forum on Health.

Reno, V. (1971). *Why men stop working at or before age 65.* US department of Health, Education and welfare, Social Security Administration, Office of research and Statistics. *Research Aging, 7*, 491-515.

Retherford, R.D. (1975). *The changing sex differential in mortality.* Westport, CT.: Greenwood Press.

Richardson, C.J. (1992). The implications of separation and divorce for family structure. Report prepared for the *Review of Demography and its Social and Economic Implications*, Health and Welfare Canada.

Richardson, V., & Kilty, K.M. (1992). Retirement intentions among black professionals: implications for practice with older black adults. *The Gerontolgist, 32(1)*, 7-16.

Richardson, V., & Kilty, K.M., (1991). Adjustment to retirement: Continuity vs discontinuity. *International Journal of Aging and Human Development, 33*(2), 151-169.

Riley, M. (1987). On the significance of age in sociology. *American Sociological Review, 52*, 1-14.

Riley, M. (1998). A life course approach: Autobiographical notes. In J.Z. Giele & G.H. Elder Jr., (Eds.). *Methods of life course research: Qualitative and quantitative approaches* (pp. 28-51). Thousand Oaks, CA: Sage Publications.

Riley, M.W. & Riley, J.W. (1994). Age integration and the lives of older people. *The Gerontologist, 34*(1), 110-115.

Riley, M.W. (1971). Social gerontology and the age stratification of society. *Gerontologist, 11*, 79-87.

Riley, M.W. (1997). *Age integration: Challenge to a new institute.* Raleigh, NC: University of North Carolina, Institute on Aging.

Riley, M.W., & Riley, J.W. (1999). Sociological research on age: Legacy and challenge. *Ageing and Society, 19*, 123-132.

Riley, M.W., Foner, A. & Riley, J.W., Jr. (1999). The aging and society paradigm. In V.L. Bengtson & K.W. Shaie, (Eds.). *Handbook of theories of aging* (pp. 327-343). New York, NY: Springer.

Riley, M.W., Johnston, M., & Foner, A. (1972). *Aging and society, Vol.3: Sociology of age stratification.* New York, NY: Russell Sage Foundation.

Riska, E., & Wegar, K. (1993). *Gender, work and medicine. Women and the medical division of labour.* International Sociological Association: SAGE Publications, Ltd.

Roberto, K., & Stroes, J. (1992). Grandchildren and grandparents: Roles, influences and relationships. *International Journal of Aging and Human Development, 34*, 227-239.

Robertson, A. (2000). "I saw the Handwriting on the Wall": Shades of meaning in reasons for early retirement. *Journal of Aging Studies,14*(1), 63-79.

Roe, K.M. & Minkler, M. (1998-99). Grandparents raising grandchildren: Challenges and responses. *Generations, 22*, 25-32.

Rogers, R.G., Hummer, R.A. & Nam, C. (2000). *Living and dying in the USA.* San Diego, CA: Academic Press.

Rook, K.S. & Pietromonaco, P. (1987). Close relationships: Ties that heal or ties that bind? In W.H. Jones & D. Perlman, (Eds.). *Advances in Personal Relationships*, Greenwich, CT: JAI Press.

Roos N.P., & Roos L.L. (1994). Small area variations, practice style and quality of care. In R.G. Evans, M.L. Barer, T.R. Marmor, (Eds): Why are some people healthy and others not? The determinants of health of populations. Hawthorne, NY: Aldine de Gruyte Press.

Roos, N.P., Havens, B., & Black, C. (1993). Living longer but doing worse: Assessing health status in elderly persons at two points in time in Manitoba, Canada, 1971 and 1983. *Social Science and Medicine, 36*, 273-282.

Roots, C.R. (1998). *The sandwich generation: Adult children caring for aging parents.* New York, NY: Garland.

Rorty, R. (1991). *Objectivity, relativism, and truth.* Cambridge, U.K.: Cambridge University Press.

Rose, A. (1968). The subculture of aging: A framework for research in social gerontology. In B. L. Neugraten, (Ed.) *Middle age and Aging*, (pp. 29-34). Chicago, IL: University of Chicago Press.

Rosenau, P.M. (1992). *Post-modernism and the social sciences: Insights, inroads and intrusions.* Princeton, NJ: Princeton University Press.

Rosenbluth, G. (1996). The debt and Canada's social programs. In L. Osberg & P. Fortin, (Eds.). *Unnecessary debts* (pp. 90-111). Toronto, ON: James Lorimer.

Rosenkoetter, M.M., & Garris, J.M. (1998). Psychosocial changes following retirement. *Journal of Advanced Nursing, 27*, 966-976.

Rosenmayr, L. & Kockeis, E. (1963). Propositions for a sociological theory of aging and the family. *International Social Science Journal, 15*, 410-426.

Rosenthal, C.J. (1985). Kinkeeping in the familial division of labor. *Journal of Marriage and the Family, 47*, 965-974.

Rosenthal, C.J. (1986). Differentiation of multigenerational households. *Canadian Journal on Aging, 5*, 27-42.

Rosenthal, C.J. (1987). Aging and intergenerational relations in Canada. In V.W. Marshall, (Ed.). *Aging in Canada: Social perspectives*, (2nd Ed, pp. 311-342). Markham, ON: Fitzhenry and Whiteside.

Rosenthal, C.J. (1993). Aging in the family context: Are Jewish families different? In Brym, W. Shaffir, & W. Weinfield, (Eds.). *The Jews in Canada*, Toronto, ON: Oxford University Press.

Rosenthal, C.J.(1983). Aging, ethnicity and the family: Beyond the modernization thesis. *Canadian Ethnic Studies, 15*(3), 1-16.

Rosenthal, C.J. & Gladstone, J. (2000). *Grandparenthood in Canada*. Ottawa, ON: The Vanier Institute of the Family.

Rosenthal, C.J. (1986). Family supports in later life: Does ethnicity make a difference? *The Gerontologist, 26*(1), 19-24.

Rosenthal, C.J. (1987). The comforter: Providing personal advice and emotional support to generations in the family. *Canadian Journal on Aging, 6*, 228-239.

Rosenthal, C.J. (2000). Aging families: Have current changes and challenges been "oversold"? In E.M. & G.M. Gutman, (Eds.). *The overselling of population aging: Apocalyptic demography, intergenerational challenges, and social policy* (pp. 45-63). Toronto, ON: Oxford University Press.

Rosenthal, C.J., Martin-Matthews, A., & Matthews, S.H. (1996). Caught in the middle? Occupancy in multiple roles and help to parents in a national probability sample of Canadian adults. *Journals of Gerontology, 51B*, S274-S283.

Rosenthal, C.J., Matthews, S.H., & Marshall, V.W. (1989). Is parent care normative? The experiences of a sample of middle-aged women. *Research on Aging, 11*, 244-260.

Rothman, D.J. (1971). *The discovery of the asylum: Social order and disorder in the new republic*. Boston, MA: Little, Brown and Company.

Rowe, J.W., & Kahn, R.L. (1987). Human aging: Usual and successful. *Science, 237*, 143-149.

Rowe, J.W., & Kahn, R.L. (1997). Successful aging. *The Gerontologist, 37*(4), 433-440.

Royal Commission on Aboriginal Peoples. (1996). *Looking forward, looking back - Report of the Royal Commission on Aboriginal Peoples* (Volume 1). Ottawa, ON: Supply and Services Canada.

Rubin, A. & Babbie, E. (1997). *Research methods for social work*. Belmont, CA: Wadsworth.

Rubin, D.C. (1999). Autobiographical memory and aging: Distributions of memories across the life-span and their implications for survey research. In N. Schwarz, & D.C. Park, (Eds.). *Cognition, aging, and self-reports*, pp. 163-183). Hove, U.K.: Psychology Press/Erlbaum.

Rubinstein, R.L. (2001). The ethnography of the end of life: The nursing home and other residential settings. In M.P. Lawton, (Ed.), *Annual review of gerontology and geriatrics: Vol. 20. Focus on the end of life: Scientific and social issues* (pp. 259-272). New York, NY: Springer Publishing Company.

Rudd, M.G., Viney, L.L, & Preston, C.A. (1999). Grief experienced by spousal caregivers of dementia patients: The role of place of care of patient and gender of the caregiver. *International Journal of Aging and Human Development, 48*(3), 217-240.

Ruhm, C.J. (1990). Bridge jobs and partial retirement. *Journal of Labor Economics, 8(4)*, 482-501.

Ruhm, C.J. (1994). Bridge employment and job stopping: Evidence from the Harris/Commonwealth Fund Survey. *Journal of Aging and Social Policy, 6*(4), 73-99.

Ruth, J.E., & Birren, J.E. (1985). Creativity in adulthood and old age: Relations to intelligence, sex, and mode of testing. *International Journal of Behavioral Development, 8*, 99-109.

Rybash, J.M., Roodin, P.A., & Santrock, J.W. (1991). *Adult development and aging* (2nd Ed.). Dubuque, IA: Wm. C. Brown.

Safford, F. (1995). Aging stressors for Holocaust survivors and their families. *Journal of Gerontological Social Work, 24*(1/2), 131-153.

Salthouse, T.A. (1984). Effects of age and skill in typing. *Journal of Experimental Psychology: General, 113*, 345-371.

Salthouse, T.A. & Babcock, R.L. (1991). Decomposing adult age differences in working memory. *Developmental Psychology, 27*(5), 763-776.

Salthouse, T.A. (1991). Expertise as the circumvention of human processing limitations. In K.A. Ericsson & J. Smith, (Eds.). *Toward a general theory of expertise*, (pp.286-300). Cambridge, U.K.: Cambridge University Press.

Sato, S., Shimonaka, Y., Nakazato, K. & Kawaai, C. (1997). A life-span developmental study of age identity: Cohort and gender differences. *The Japanese Journal of Developmental Psychology, 8*(2), 88-97.

Sauer, W.J. & Coward, R.T. (1985). The role of social support networks in the care of the elderly. In W.J. Sauer, & R.T. Coward, (Eds.). *Social support networks and the care of the elderly: Theory, research, and practice*. New York, NY: Springer Publishing Co.

Schaie, K.W. (1990). The optimization of cognitive functioning in old age: Prediction based on cohort-sequential and longitudinal data. In. P. O. Baltes, & M. Baltes, (Eds.). *Longitudinal research and the study of successful (optimal) aging*, (pp.94-117). Cambridge, U.K. Cambridge University Press.

Schaie, K.W. (1996). *Intellectual development in adulthood. The Seattle longitudinal study*. New York, NY: Cambridge University Press.

Schaie, K.W., & Willis, S.L. (1993). Age difference patterns of psychometric intelligence in adulthood: Generalizability within and across ability domains. *Psychology and Aging, 8,* 44-55.

Schellenberg, G. (1994). *The road to retirement: Demographic and economic changes in the 90s*. Ottawa, ON: Canadian Council on Social Development.

Schlegel, K.L., & Shannon, S.E. (2000). Legal guidelines related to end-of-life decisions: Are nurse practitioners knowledgeable? *Journal of Gerontological Nursing, 26(9),* 14-23.

Schonfield, A.E.D., & Robertson, B.A. (1966). Memory storage and aging. *Canadian Journal of Psychology, 20,* 228-236.

Schonfield, D. (1973). Future commitments and successful aging: I. The random sample. *Journal of Gerontology, 28,* 189-196.

Schonfield, D. (1982). Who is stereotyping whom and why? *The Gerontologist, 22,* 267-272.

Schultz, K.S., Morton, K.R., & Weckerle, J.R. (1998). Influence of push and pull factors on voluntary and involuntary early retirees' retirement decision and adjustment. *Journal of Vocational Behaviour, 53,* 45-57.

Schultz, N.R., Jr., Elias, M.F., Robbins, M.A., Streeten, D.P.H., & Blakeman, N. (1986). A longitudinal comparison of hypertensive and normotensives on the Wechsler Adult Intelligence Scale: Initial findings. *Journal of Gerontology, 41,* 169-175.

Schulz, R., & Williamson, G.M. (1991). Two year longitudinal study of depression among Alzheimer's caregivers. *Psychology and Aging, 6(4),* 569-578.

Schulz, R., Beach, S., Ives, D.G., Martire, L.M., Aariyo, A.A., & Kop, W.J. (2000). Association between depression and mortality in older adults. *Archives of Internal Medicine, 160,* 1761-1768.

Schulz, R., Newsom, J.T., Fleissner, K., Decamp, A.R., & Nieboer, A.P. (1997). The effects of bereavement after family caregiving. *Aging and Mental Health, 1(3),* 269-282.

Schwandt, T. (1997). *A qualitative inquiry: A dictionary of terms*. Thousand Oaks, CA: Sage Publishing.

Schwartz, W.B. (1998). *Life without disease: The pursuit of medical utopia*. Berkeley, CA: University of California Press.

Schwartzman, A.E., Gold, D., Andres, D., Arbuckle, T.Y., & Chiakelson, J. (1987). Stability of intelligence: A forty-year follow-up. *Canadian Journal of Psychology, 41,* 244-256.

Seale, C. & Addington-Hall, J. (1994). Euthanasia: Why people want to die earlier. *Social Science and Medicine, 39,* 647-654.

Segall, A., & Chappell, N. (1991). Making sense out of sickness: Lay explanations of chronic illness among older adults. *Advances in Medical Sociology, 2,* 115-133.

Segall, A., & Chappell, N.L. (2000). *Health and health care in Canada*. Toronto, ON: Prentice Hall.

Segall, A., & Goldstein, J. (1989). Exploring the correlates of self-provided health care behaviour. *Social Science and Medicine, 29,* 153-161.

Seidlitz, L., Duberstein, P.R., Cox, C., & Conwell, Y. (1995). Attitudes of older people toward suicide and assisted suicide: An analysis of gallup poll findings. *Journal of the American Geriatrics Society, 43(9),* 993-998.

Settersten, R.A, Jr. & Hagestad, G.O. (1996). What's the latest? Cultural age deadlines for family transitions. *Gerontologist, 36,* 178-188.

Settersten, R.A. Jr. (1999). *Lives in time and place: The problems and promises of developmental science*. Amityville, NY: Baywood.

Shanahan, M.J., Elder, G.H. Jr., & Miech, R.A. (1997). History and agency in men's lives: Pathways to achievement in cohort perspective. *Sociology of Education, 70,* 54-67.

Shanas, E. (1979). Social myth as hypothesis: The case of the family relations of old people. *The Gerontologist, 19,* 3-9.

Shannon, M. & Kidd, M.P. (2001). Projecting the trend in the Canadian gender wage gap 2001-2031: Will an increase in female education acquisition and commitment be enough? *Canadian Public Policy, XXVII,* 447- 467.

Shapiro, E. (1991). *Manitoba health care studies and their policy implications*. Winnipeg, MB: Manitoba Centre for Health Policy and Evaluation, Department of Community Health Sciences, University of Manitoba.

Sharpiro, E. & Tate, R. (1988). Who is really at risk of institutionalization? *The Gerontologist, 28,* 237-245.

Sharpley, C.F., & Layton, R. (1998). Effects of age of retirement, reason for retirement, and pre-retirement training on psychological and physical health during retirement. *Australian Psychologist, 33(2),* 119-124.

Shephard, R.J. (1969). *Endurance fitness*. Toronto, ON: University of Toronto Press.

Shephard, R.J. (1978). *Physical activity and aging*. Chicago, IL:Yearbook Medical Publishers.

Shernoff, M. (1997). *Gay widowers: Life after death of a partner*. New York, NY: Haworth Press.

Shewchuk, R., Foelker, G., & Niederehe, G. (1990). Measuring locus of control in elderly persons. *International Journal of Aging and Human Development, 30,* 213-224.

Shmotkin, D (1991). The role of time orientation in life satisfaction across the life span. *Journal of Gerontology: Psychological Sciences, 46,* 243-250.

Siegel, S. (1956). *Nonparametric Statistics*. New York, NY: McGraw Hill.

Siemiatycki, J., Richardson, L., & Pless, I.B. (1980). Equality in medical care under national health insurance in Montreal. *New England Journal of Medicine, 303*, 10-14.

Simoneau, G.G., & Leibowitz, H.W. (1996). Posture, gait, and falls. In J.E. Birren, & K.W. Schaie, (Eds.), *Handbook of the psychology of aging,* (4ᵗʰ Ed.) San Diego, CA: Academic Press.

Simonton, D.K. (1990). Creativity and wisdom in aging. In. J.E. Birren, & K.W. Schaie, (Eds.). *Handbook of the psychology of aging* (3ʳᵈ Ed., pp. 320-329). San Diego, CA: Academic Press.

Simpson, I.H. (1975). Review symposium on work in America. *Sociology of Work and Occupations, 2*, 182-187.

Singer, P.A., Choudhry, S., Armstrong, J., Meslin, E.M., & Lowy, F.H. (1995). Public opinion regarding end-of-life decisions: Influence of prognosis, practice and process. *Social Science and Medicine, 41*(11), 1517-1521.

Singer, P.A., Martin, D.K., & Kelner, M. (1999). Quality end of life care: Patients' perspectives. *Journal of the American Medical Association, 28*(2), 163-168.

Singleton, R.A., Jr. & Straits, B.C. (1999). *Approaches to social research,* (3ʳᵈ Ed.). New York, NY: Oxford University Press.

Sinnott, J.D. (2000). *Growing and healing while aging: The role of spirituality in typical and complementary healing systems.* Paper presented at the Gerontological Society of America Conference, Washington, DC, November.

Sita, A., Stones, M.J., Csank, P., Knight, C., & Gauron K. [in press]. Multidimensional assessment of well-aging.

Skoog, I. (1996). Sex and Swedish 85-year-olds. *New England Journal of Medicine, 334*(17), 1140-1141.

Smith, E.L. & Gilligan, G. (1983). Physical activity prescription for the older adult. *The Physician and Sportsmedicine, 11*, 91- 101.

Smith, P. (1998). A comparative analysis of female lone parent families in Canada and the United States. In *Contributions to family demography: Essays in honour of Dr. Wayne W. McVey,* (pp. 184-204). Edmonton, AB: University of Alberta, Department of Sociology.

Snell, J. G. (1992). Maintenance agreements for the elderly: Canada, 1900-1951. *Journal of the Canadian Historical Association, 3*, 197-216.

Snell, J.G. (1996). *The citizen's wage: The state and the elderly in Canada 1900-1951, Vol. 22,* (p. 286). Toronto, ON: University of Toronto Press.

Soldo, B.J. & Hill, M.S. (1995). Family structure and transfer measures in the Health and Retirement Study. *Journal of Human Resources, 30 (Suppl.),* S108-S137.

Speare, A., & Avery, R. (1993). Who helps whom in older parent-child families? *Journals of Gerontology, 48*, S64-S73.

Spearman, C. (1927). *The abilities of man.* New York, NY: Macmillan.

Spencer, C. (1994). Abuse and Neglect of Older Adults in Institutional Settings. Ottawa: Health Canada, Health Services Directorate, Mental Health Division.

Spirduso W.W. (1995). *Physical dimensions of aging.* Champaign, IL.: Human Kinetics.

Spirduso, W.W. & Clifford, P. (1978). Neuromuscular speed and consistency of performance as a function of age, physical activity level and type of physical activity. *Journal of Gerontology, 33*, 26-30.

Spirduso, W.W. (1975). Reaction time and movement time as a function of age and physical activity level. *Journal of Gerontology, 30*, 435-440.

Spirduso, W.W. (1980). Physical fitness, aging, and psychomotor speed. *Journal of Gerontology, 35*, 850-865.

Spirduso, W.W., MacCrae, H.H., MacCrae, P.G., Prewitt, J., & Osborne, L. (1988). Exercise effects on aged motor function. *Annals of the New York Academy of Sciences, 515*, 363-375.

Spitze, G. & Logan, J. (1992). Helping as a component of parent-adult child relations. *Research on Aging, 14*, 291-312.

SPSS (1999). *SPSS 10.0 applications guide.* Chicago, IL: SPSS.

Stacey, C., Kozma, A., & Stones, M.J. (1985). Simple cognitive and performance changes resulting from improved physical fitness in persons over 50 years of age. *Canadian Journal on Aging, 4*, 67-73.

Stajduhar, K. (2001). *The idealization of dying at home: The social context of home-based palliative caregiving.* Unpublished master's thesis. Vancouver, BC: University of British Columbia.

Stajduhar, K., & Davies, B. (1998). Death at home: Challenges for families and directions for the future. *Journal of Palliative Care, 14*(3), 8-14.

Stajduhar, K., & Davies, B. (1999) Death, loss and grief. *Nursing foundations: A Canadian perspective, 2*(37), 1243-1269.

Standardized Test of Fitness. (1981). Ottawa, ON: Government of Canada (Fitness and Amateur Sport).

Standfield, J.H., II. (1994). Ethnic modeling in qualitative research. In K. Denzin & Y. Lincoln, (Eds.). *The handbook of qualitative research,* (pp. 175-188). Thousand Oaks, CA: Sage Publications.

Starr, B.D. & Weiner, M.B. (1988). The Starr-Weiner Report on sex and sexuality in the mature years. New York, NY: Stein and Day.

Statistics Canada. (1993). *1991 Census: Ethnic origin, the nation.* (Catalogue 93-315). Ottawa, ON: Ministry of Industry, Science and Technology.

Statistics Canada. (1996). *Canada's retirement income programs: A statistical overview.* (No. 74-507-XPB). Ottawa, ON: Minister of Industry.

Statistics Canada. (1998). *Income in Canada.* (No. 75-202-XIE). Ottawa, ON: Minister of Industry. http://www.statcan. ca/english//Pgdb/People/Families/famil19a.html (and famil19b.htm).

Statistics Canada. (1998). *The earnings of men and women.* (Catalogue No. 13-217-XBP). Ottawa, ON: Statistics Canada.

Statistics Canada. (1999). *A portrait of seniors in Canada,* (3rd Ed.). Ottawa, ON: Statistics Canada.

Statistics Canada. (1999). *Pension plans in Canada: Statistical highlights and key tables*. (No. 74-401-SIB). Ottawa, ON: Minister of Industry.

Statistics Canada. (1999). *Retirement savings through RPPs and RRSP*. (No. 74F0002XIB). Ottawa, ON: Minister of Industry.

Statistics Canada. (1999a). *Pension plans in Canada: Statistical highlights and key tables*. Ottawa, ON: Statistics Canada.

Statistics Canada. (1999b). *A portrait of seniors in Canada*. (No. 89-519-XPE). Ottawa, ON: Statistics Canada, Minister of Industry.

Statistics Canada. (2000). *Women in Canada: A gender-based statistical report*. (No. 89-503-XPE). Ottawa, ON: Minister of Industry (Housing, Family and Social Statistics Division).

Statistics Canada. (2001). *The assets and debts of Canadians: An overview of the results of the survey of financial security*. Ottawa, ON: Minister of Industry.

Statistics Canada. (1998a). *The Daily*, Tuesday, January 13,1998. 1996 Census: Aboriginal Data. http://www.statcan.ca/Daily/English/980113/d/980113.htm

Statistics Canada. (1998b). *The Daily*, Tuesday, February 17,1998. http://www.statcan.ca/Daily/English/980217/d980217.htm.

Statistics Canada. (1998). National Survey of Giving, Volunteering and Participating (NSGVP), (Cat. No. 11-001E). *The Daily*, 3-7, 1997..

Statistics Canada. (1999a). *Mortality—Summary list of causes, 1997*. (Catalogue No. 84F0209XPB). Ottawa, ON: Statistics Canada.

Statistics Canada. (1999c). *1996 census dictionary*. (Catalogue No. 92-351-UIE). Ottawa, ON: Statistics Canada.

Statistics Canada. (2000). *Annual demographic statistics*. (Catalogue No. 91-213). Ottawa, ON: Statistics Canada.

Statistics Canada. (2000b).*Women in Canada, 2000: A gender-based statistical report*. (Catalogue No. 89-503-XPE). Ottawa, ON: Statistics Canada

Statistics Canada. *National Population Health Survey (1994-95)*. Ottawa, ON: Statistics Canada.

Steers, W.D. (1999). Viagra - After one year. *Urology, 54*(1), 12-17.

Steffens, D.C., Skoog, I., Norton, M.C., Hart, A.D., Tschanz, J.T., Plassman, B.L., Wyse, B.W., Welsh-Bohmer, K.A. & Breitner, J.C. (2000). Prevalence of depression and its treatment in an elderly population. *Archives of General Psychiatry, 57*, 601-607.

Stephens, T. (1986). Health practices and health status: Evidence from the Canada Health Survey. *American Journal of Preventive Medicine, 2*, 209-215.

Stephens, T., Craig, C. & Ferris, B. (1986). *Adult physical activity in Canada: Findings from the Canada Fitness Survey*. *Canadian Journal of Public Health, 77*, 285-290.

Sternberg, R. J. (1984). Toward a triarchic theory of human intelligence. *Behavioral and Brain Sciences, 7*, 269-315.

Stetz, T.A., & Beehr, T.A. (2000). Organizations' environment and retirement: The relationship between women's retirement, environmental munificence, dynamism and local unemployment rate, *Journals of Gerontology: Series B Psychological Science and Social Sciences, 55B*, (4), S213-S221.

Stevens, J. C., Cruz, A., Marks, L.E., & Lakatos, S. (1998). A multimodal assessment of sensory thresholds in aging. *Journal of Gerontology: Psychological Sciences, 53B*, P263-P272.

Stewart, W.H., & Enterline, P.E. (1961). Effects of the NHS on physician utilization and health in England and Wales. *New England Journal of Medicine, 265*, 1187.

Stoller, E., Forster, L., & Portugal, S. (1993). Self-care responses to symptoms by older people: A health diary study of illness behavior. *Medical Care, 31*, 24-42.

Stoller, M.A., et al. (1994). Volunteer activity and informal assistance as investment and consumption among elderly people [Unpublished paper].

Stone, L.O. & Hubert, F. (1988). *Canada's seniors: A dynamic force*. Ottawa, ON: Statistics Canada.

Stone, L.O. & Rosenthal, C.J. (1998). How much help is exchanged in families? Towards an understanding of discrepant research findings. *SEDAP (Social and Economic Dimensions of an Aging Population) research paper no. 2*. Hamilton, ON: McMaster University.

Stone, L.O., Rosenthal, C.J., & Connidis, I.A. (1998). *Parent-child exchanges of supports and intergenerational equity*. (Catalogue No. 89-557-XPE). Ottawa, ON: Statistics Canada

Stone, R., Cafferata, G.L., & Sangl, J. (1987). Caregivers of the frail elderly: A national profile. *The Gerontologist, 27*, 616-626.

Stones, L., & Stones, M.J. (1996). *Sex may be wasted on the young*. Toronto, ON: Cactus Press.

Stones, M.J., & Dawe, D. (1993). Acute exercise facilitates semantically cued memory in nursing home residents. *Journal of American Geriatrics Society, 41*, 531-534.

Stones, M.J., Dornan, B., & Kozma, A. (1989). The prediction of mortality in elderly institution residents. *Journal of Gerontology: Social Sciences, 44*, P72-P79.

Stones, M.J. (2001). Are satisfaction surveys satisfactory for evaluating quality of care? Case Mix 2001 Conference: New frontiers in health information. Niagara Falls, ON, Canada.

Stones, M.J., & Bédard, M. [in press]. Higher thresholds for elder abuse with age and rural residence. *Canadian Journal on Aging*.

Stones, M.J., & Kozma A. (1996). Activity, exercise and behavior. In: J. Birren, & K.W. Schaie, (Eds.), *Handbook of the psychology of aging*, (5th Ed.). Orlando, FL: Academic Press.

Stones, M.J., & Kozma, A. (1980). Issues relating to the usage and conceptualization of mental health constructs employed by gerontologists. *International Journal of Aging and Human Development, 11*, 269-281.

Stones, M.J., & Kozma, A. (1982). Cross-sectional, longitudinal, and secular age trends in athletic performances. *Experimental Aging Research, 8*, 185-188.

Stones, M.J., & Kozma, A. (1984). Longitudinal trends in track and field performances. *Experimental Aging Research, 10*, 107-110.

Stones, M.J., & Kozma, A. (1986). Age trends in maximal physical performance: Comparison and evaluation of models. *Experimental Aging Research, 12*, 207-215.

Stones, M.J., & Kozma, A. (1987) Balance and age in the sighted and blind. *Archives of Physical Medicine and Rehabilitation, 66*, 85-89.

Stones, M.J., & Kozma, A. (1995). Compensation in athletic sport. In R. Dixon, & C. Bäckman, (Eds.). *Psychological compensation: Managing loses and promoting gains.* Hillsdale, NJ: Lawrence Erlbaum Ass. Inc.

Stones, M.J., & Kozma, A.(1991). A magical model of happiness. *Social Indicators Research, 25*, 31-50.

Stones, M.J., & Pittman, D. (1995). Individual differences in attitudes about elder abuse: The Elder Abuse Attitude Test. *Canadian Journal on Aging, 14*, 61-71.

Stones, M.J. (1984). Rules and tools: The meaning and measurement of elder abuse. Newfoundland: Milestones Manual.

Stones, M.J. (1995). Scope and definition of elder abuse and neglect in Canada. In Maclean, M., (Ed.). *Abuse and neglect of older Canadians - Strategies for change* (pp. 111-116). Toronto, ON: Thompson Educational Publishing.

Stones, M.J. (2000). Affect and cognition: Findings with the MDS 2.0. RAI/MDS Research and Demonstration Projects in Canada. Canadian Association on Gerontology, Edmonton, AB.

Stones, M.J. (2000). Elder abuse and medical ethics. *Medical Ethics Symposia Series, Lakehead University.*

Stones, M.J. (2001). Are satisfaction surveys satisfactory for evaluating quality of care? Case Mix 2001 Conference: New frontiers in health information. Niagara Falls, ON.

Stones, M.J. (2001). Deconstructing depression. *Gerontology, 47*(Suppl. 1), 573.

Stones, M.J., Rattenbury, C., & Kozma, A. (1995). Empirical findings on reminiscence. In BK Haight, & J Webster, (Eds.). *The art and science of reminiscing: Theory, research, methods, and applications.* Washington DC: Taylor & Francis.

Stones, M.J., & Kozma, A. (1981). Adult age trends in athletic performances. *Experimental Aging Research, 7*, 269-279.

Stones, M.J., & Kozma, A. (1988). Physical activity, age, and cognitive/motor performance. In M.L. Howe & C.J. Brainerd, (Eds.). *Cognitive development in adulthood: Progress in cognitive development research,* (pp. 273-321). New York, NY: Springer Verlag.

Stones, M.J., & Kozma, A., (1986) "Happy are they who are happy...". A test between two causal models of relationships between happiness and its correlates. *Experimental Aging Research, 12*, 23-29.

Stones, M.J., Dornan, B., & Kozma, A. (1989). The prediction of mortality in elderly institution residents. *Journal of Gerontology, 1989, 44*, 72-79.

Stones, M.J., Farrell, J., & Taylor, J. (2001). Age differences in sports performance. In N. Smelser & P.B. Baltes, (Eds). *International encyclopedia of the social and behavioral sciences.* Amsterdam, The Netherlands: Elsevier.

Stones, M.J., Hadjistravopoulos, T., Tuokko, H., & Kozma, A. (1995) Happiness has traitlike and statelike properties: A reply to Veenhoven. *Social Indicators Research. 36*, 129-144.

Stones, M.J., Kozma, A., Hirdes, J., Gold, D., Arbuckle, T., & Kolopack, P. (1995). Short happiness and affect research protocol. *Social Indicators Research, 37*, 75-91.

Stones, M. J., Kozma, A., & Hannah, T.E. (1990). Measurement of individual differences in aging: The distinction between usual and successful aging. In Howe, M.L., Stones, M.J., & Brainerd, C.J., (Eds.), *Cognitive and behavioral performance factors in atypical aging.* NY: Springer-Verlag.

Stones, M.J., & Kozma, A., (Eds.). Multidimensional assessment of the elderly via a microcomputer: The SENOTS program and battery. *Psychology and Aging, 4*, 113-118.

Stones, M.J., & Kozma, A. (1994). The relationships of affect intensity to happiness. *Social Indicators Research, 31*, 159-174.

Strachen, J., Johansen, H., Nair, C., & Nardundkar, M. (1990). Canadian suicide mortality rates: First generation immigrants versus Canadian born. *Health Reports, 2*(4), 327-341.

Strain, L.A. & Chappell, N.L. (1982). Confidantes: Do they make a difference in quality of life? *Research on Aging, 4*(4), 479-502.

Strain, L.A., & Chappell, N.L. (1984). *Social support among elderly Canadian natives: A comparison with elderly non-natives.* Paper presented at the annual meeting of the Canadian Association on Gerontology Vancouver, BC.

Strong-Boag, V.J. (1993). *The new day recalled: Lives of girls and women in English Canada 1919-1939.* Mississauga, ON: Copp Clark Pitman.

Struthers, J. (1992). Regulating the elderly: Old age pensions and the formation of a pension bureaucracy in Ontario, 1929-1945. *Journal of the Canadian Historical Association.* 235-255.

Stull, D.E., Kosloski, K., & Kercher, K. (1994). Caregiver burden and generic well-being: Opposite sides of the same coin? *The Gerontologist, 34*(1), 88-94.

Sugimen, P, and Nishio, H.K. (1983). Socialization and cultural duality among Japanese Canadians, *Canadian Ethnic Studies, 15*(3), 17-35.

Sullivan, M.J., & Scattolon, Y. (1995). Health policy planning: A look at consumer involvement in Nova Scotia. *Canadian Journal of Public Health, 86*(5), 317-320.

Sunter, D. (2001). Demography and the labour market. *Perspectives on labour and income,* (pp. 28-39).

(Catalogue No. 75-001 - XPE). Ottawa, ON: Statistics Canada.

Suwal, J. & Trovato, F. (1998). Canadian aboriginal fertility. *Canadian Studies in Population, 25,* 69-86.

Syme, S.L. (1994). The social environment and health. *DAEDALUS, Journal of the American Academy of Arts and Sciences, 123*(4), 79-86.

Szasz, T. (1961). *The myth of mental illness: Foundations of a theory of personal conduct.* New York, NY: Hoeber-Harper.

Szinovacz, M. & DeViney, S. (1999). The retiree identity: Gender and race differences. *Journal of Gerontology: Social Sciences, 54B,* S207-S218.

Szinovacz, M. (1997). Adult children taking parents into their homes: Effects of childhood living arrangements. *Journal of Marriage and the Family, 59,* 700-717.

Szinovacz, M.E., & DeViney, S. (2000). Martial characteristics and retirement decisions. *Research on Aging, 22*(5), 470-498.

Talbott, M.M. (1998). Older widows' attitudes towards men and remarriage. *Journal of Aging Studies, 12,* 429-449.

Tamblyn, R, & Perreault, R. (2000). Prescription drug use and seniors. *Canadian Journal on Aging, 19*(Suppl.1), 143-175.

Taylor, F. (1947). *Scientific Management.* New York, NY: Harper.

Taylor, M.A., & Shore, L.M. (1995). Predictors of planned retirement age: An application of Beehr's model. *Psychology and Aging, 10*(1), 76-83.

Tebb, S.S. (1995). Aid to empowerment: A caregiver well-being scale. *Health and Social Work, 20*(2), 87-92.

Tedlock, B. (2000). Ethnography and ethnographic representation. In N. Denzin & Y. Lincoln, (Eds.). *Handbook of qualitative research* (2nd Ed., pp. 455-486). Thousand Oaks, CA: Sage Publications.

Tennstedt, S., & Chang, B.H. (1998). The relative contribution of ethnicity versus socioeconomic status in explaining differences in disability and receipt of informal care. *Journal of Gerontology, 53B*(2), S61-S70.

Tennstedt, S.L., McKinlay, J.B., & Sullivan, L.M. (1989). Informal care for frail elders: The role of secondary caregivers. *The Gerontologist, 29,* 677-683.

Teno, J.M., McNiff, K., & Lynn, J. (2001). Measuring quality of medical care for dying persons and their families: Preliminary suggestions for accountability. In M.P. Lawton, (Ed.). *Annual review of gerontology and geriatrics: Vol. 20. Focus on the end of life: Scientific and social issues,* (pp.97-119). New York, NY: Springer Publishing Company.

The Globe. (1905). Link took chloroform. March,.2, p. 7.

Theriault, J. (1994). Retirement as a psychosocial transition: Process of adaptation to change. *International Journal of Aging and Human Development, 38,* 153-170.

Thomas, K., & Wister, A. (1984). Living arrangements of older women: The ethnic dimensions. *Journal of Marriage and the Family, 46,* 301-311.

Thomas, P.D., Garry, P.J., Goodwin, J.M., & Goodwin, J.S. (1985). Social bonds in a healthy elderly sample: Characteristics and associated variables. *Social Science and Medicine, 20,* 365-369.

Thorson, J.A. (2000). *Aging in a changing society* (2nd Ed.). Philadelphia, PA: Taylor & Francis.

Thurstone, L.L. (1938). *Primary mental abilities.* Chicago, IL: University of Chicago Press.

Thurstone, LL. (1928). Attitudes can be measured. *American Journal of Sociology, 33,* 529-554.

Tierny, W.G. (2000). Undaunted courage: Life history and postmodern challenge. In N. Denzin & Y. Lincoln, (Eds.). *Handbook of qualitative research* (2nd Ed., pp. 537-553). Thousand Oaks, CA: Sage Publications.

Tinetti, M.E., (1986). Performance-oriented assessment of mobility problems in elderly patients. *Journal of the American Geriatrics Society, 34,* 119-126.

Tipper, S. (1989). Cremation is an opportunity for funeral directors. *Canadian Funeral News, August,* 10-11.

Tompa, E. (1999). *Transition to retirement: Determinants of age of social security take up.* Paper No. 6, Social and Economic Dimensions of an Aging Population, McMaster University.

Torczyner, J.L. (1997). *Diversity, mobility and change: The dynamics of black communities in Canada.* McGill Consortium for Ethnicity and Strategic Planning. Ottawa, ON: Multiculturalism Branch, Department of Canadian Heritage.

Torrance, G.W., Zhang, Y., Feeny, D., & Boyle, M.H. (1992). Multi-attribute preference functions for a comprehensive health status classification system. [Unpublished]. Hamilton, ON: Centre for Health Economics and Policy Analysis, McMaster University.

Townsend, P. (1962). *The last refuge.* In US Department of Health and Social Services (1999). *Mental health: A report of the Surgeon General.* Rockville, MD: US Public Health Service.

Townsend, P. (1981). The structured dependency of the elderly: A creation of social policy in the twentieth century. *Ageing and society, 1*(1), 5-28.

Townson, M. (2000). *Reducing poverty among older women: The potential of retirement incomes policies.* Ottawa, ON: Status of Women Canada.

Tranoy, K.E. (1996). Vital needs, human rights, health care law. *Medical Law, 15*(2), 183-188.

Troyer, W.C. Jr., Eisdorfer, C., Bogdonoff, M.D., Wilkie, F. (1967). Experimental stress and learning in the aged. *Journal of Abnormal Psychology, 72*(1), 65-70.

Tucker, R.D., Marshall, V.W., Longino, C.F. Jr., & Mullins, L.C. (1988). Older Anglophone Canadian snowbirds in Florida: A descriptive profile. *Canadian Journal on Aging, 7,* 218-232.

Tulving, E. (1993). Varieties of consciousness and levels of awareness in memory. In A. Baddeley & L. Weiskrantz, (Eds.). *Attention: Selection, awareness, and control. A tribute to Donald Broadbent*, (pp. 283-299). London, U.K.: Oxford University Press.

Tulving, E., Hayman, C.A.G., & MacDonald, C.A. (1991). Long-lasting priming in amnesia: A case experiment.

Journal of Experimental Psychology: Learning, Memory, and Cognition, 17, 595-617.

U.S. Department of Health and Social Services. (1999). *Mental health: A report of the Surgeon General.*

Uhlenberg, P. & Miner, S. (1996). Life course and aging: A cohort perspective. In R.H. Binstock & L.K. George, (Eds.), *Handbook of aging and the social sciences* (4th Ed., pp. 208-228). San Diego, CA: Academic Press.

Uhlenberg, P. (1993). Demographic change and kin relationships in later life. In G. Maddox & M.P. Lawton, (Eds.). *Annual review of gerontology and geriatrics, Vol. 13* (pp. 219-238). New York, NY: Springer.

Ujimoto, K. (1985). Organizational activities, cultural factors, and well-being of aged Japanese Canadians. In D.E. Gelfand, & C.M. Barresi, (Eds.). *Ethnic dimensions of aging,* (pp. 145-160). New York, NY: Springer Publishing.

Ujimoto, K. (1995). Ethnic dimension of aging in Canada. In R. Neugebauer-Visano, (Ed.). *Aging and inequality: Cultural constructions of differences,* (pp. 3-29). Toronto, ON: Canadian Scholars' Press Inc.

Ujimoto, K.V., Nishio, H.K., Wong, P.T.P., & Lam. L. (1995). Cultural factors affecting self assessment of health satisfaction of Asian Canadian elderly. In R. Neugebauer-Visano, (Ed.), *Aging and inequality: Cultural constructions of differences* (pp. 131-141). Toronto, ON: Canadian Scholars' Press Inc.

United Nations Secretariat. (1988). Sex differentials in life expectancy and mortality in developed countries: An analysis by age groups and causes of death from recent and historical Data. *Population Bulletin of the United Nations, 25*, 65-106.

United Nations. (2000). *World population prospects: The 1998 revision. Volume III: Analytical report.* New York, NY: United Nations.

Vallee, R. (1998). *Caregiving across cultures.* Washington, DC: Taylor and Francis.

van den Hoonaard, D.K. (2001). *The widowed self: The older woman's journey through widowhood.* Waterloo, ON: Wilfred Laurier Press.

van der Suiijs, H.A. (1972). A standardized analysis of daily energy expenditure and patterns of physical activity. In J.M. Dirken, (Ed.). *Functional age of industrial workers.* The Netherlands: Walters-Noordhalt.

Van Maanen, H. (1991). Canadian Medical Association. *Challenges and changes in the care of the elderly.* Ottawa, ON: CMA.

Van Ranst, N., Verschuerenm K., & Marcoen, A. (1995). The meaning of grandparents as viewed by adolescent grandchildren: An empirical study in Belgium. *International Journal of Aging and Human Development, 41*, 311-324.

Vanderburgh, R. (1995). Modernization and aging in the Anicinabe context. In R. Neugebauer-Visano, (Ed.). *Aging and inequality: Cultural constructions of differences,* (pp. 101-113). Toronto, ON: Canadian Scholars' Press Inc.

VanderMaas, P.J., vanderWal, G., Haverkate, I., deGraaff, C.L.M., Kester, J.G.C., Onwuteaka-Philipson, B.D., vanderHeide, A., Bosma, J.M., & Willems, D.L. (1996). Euthanasia, physician-assisted suicide, and other medical practices involving the end of life in the Netherlands. *New England Journal of Medicine, 335*(22), 1699-1705.

Veenhoven, R (1994). Is happiness a trait? Tests of the theory that a better society does not make people any happier. *Social Indicators Research, 33*, 101-160.

Veevers, J.E. (1984). Age-discrepant marriages: Cross-national comparisons of Canadian-American trends. *Social Biology, 31*, 18-27.

Veevers, J.E., Gee, E.M., & Wister, A.V. (1996). Homeleaving age norms - conflict or consensus? *International Journal of Aging and Human Development, 43*, 1-19.

Verbrugge, L.M. (1984). A longer life but worsening health? Trends in health and mortality of middle-aged and older persons. *Milbank Memorial Fund Quarterly, 62*, 475-519.

Verbrugge, L.M. (1979). Marital status and health. *Journal of Marriage and the Family, 41*, 267-285.

Victor, C.R. (1994). *Old age in modern society.* London, U.K.: Chapman & Hall.

Victoria Hospice Society. (1998). *Medical care of the dying* (3rd Ed.). Victoria, BC: Victoria Hospice Society.

Voltz, R., Akabayashi, A., Reese, C., Ohi, G., & Sass, H.M. (1998). End of life decisions and advance directives in palliative care: A cross-cultural survey of patients and health-care professionals. *Journal of Pain and Symptom Management, 16*(3), 153-162.

Waldron, I. (1985). What do we know about causes of sex differences in mortality? A review of the literature. *Population Bulletin of the United Nations, 18*, 59-76.

Waldron, I. (1998). Sex differences in infant and early childhood mortality: Major causes of death and possible biological causes. In *Too young to die: Genes or gender?* New York, NY: United Nations.

Walford, R.L. (1983). *Maximum life span.* New York, NY: Norton.

Walker, A. (1981). Towards a Political economy of Old Age, *Ageing and Society, 1*(1), 73-94.

Walker, A. (Ed.) (1996). *The new generational contract: Intergenerational relations, old age, and welfare.* London, U.K.: UCL Press.

Walker, B.L., Osgood, N.J., Richardson, J.P., & Ephross, P.H. (1998). Staff and elderly knowledge and attitudes toward elderly sexuality. *Educational Gerontology, 24*(5), 471-489.

Walker, K.N., McBride, A., & Vachon, M.L.S. (1977). Social support networks and the crisis of bereavement. *Social Science and Medicine, 11*, 35-41.

Wallace, J.B. (1994). Life stories. In J.F. Gubrium & J.A. Sankar, (Eds). *Qualitative methods in research,* (pp. 137-154). Thousand Oaks, CA: Sage Publications.

Wallace, W. (1971). *The logic of science in sociology*. Chicago, IL: Aldine-Atherton.

Waller, N.G., Kojetin, B.A., Bouchard, T. J. Jr., Lykken, D.T., & Tellegen, A. (1990). Genetic and environmental influences on religious interests, attitudes, and values: A study of twins reared apart and together. *Psychological Science*, 1, 138-142.

Wanner, R. A., & McDonald, L. (1989). Ethnic diversity and patterns of retirement. In J. Frideres, (Ed.). *Multiculturalism and intergroup relations*. New York, NY: Greenwood Press.

Ward. R.L. (1979). The never married in later life. *Journal of Gerontology*, 34, 861-869.

Warren, R., Gartstein, V., Kligman, A.M., Montagna, W., Allendorg, R.A. & Ridder, G.M. (1991). Age, sunlight, and facial skin: A histologic and quantitative study. *Journal of the American Academy of Dermatology*, 25, 751-760.

Watson, D., Clark, L.A., Weber, K., & Assenheimer, J.S. (1995). Testing a tripartite model: II. Exploring the symptom structure of anxiety and depression in student, adult and patient samples. *Journal of Abnormal Psychology*, 104(1), 15-25.

WAVA (1994). Age grading tables. World Association of Veteran Athletes.

Webster, I.W., & Logie, A.R. (1976). A relationship between functional age and health status in female subjects. *Journal of Gerontology*, 31, 546-550.

Webster, P.S. & Herzog, R.A. (1995). Effects of parental divorce and memories of family problems on relationships between adult children and their parents. *Journals of Gerontology*, 50B, S24-34.

Wechsler, D. (1958). *The measurement and appraisal of adult intelligence*. Baltimore, MD: Williams & Wilkins.

Wechsler, D. (1972). "Hold" and "Don't Hold" tests. In S.M. Chown, (Ed.). *Human aging*. New York, NY: Penguin.

Weigel, R.H., & Newman, L.S. (1976). Increasing attitude-behavior correspondence by broadening the scope of the behavioral measure. *Journal of Personality and Social Psychology*, 33, 793-802.

Weissman, M.M., Bland, R.C., Canino, G.J., Faravelli, C., Greenwald, S., Hwu, H.G., Joyce, P.R., Karam, E.G., Lee, C.K., Lellouch, J., L'epine, J.P., Newman, S.C., Rubio-Stipec,M., Wells, J.E., Wickramaratne, P.J., Wittchen, H., & Yeh, E.K. (1996). Cross-national epidemiology of major depression and bipolar disorder. *Journal of the American Medical Association*, 276, 24-31.

Wells, D. (1997). A critical ethnography of the process of discharge decision-making for elderly patients. *Canadian Journal on Aging*, 16(4), 682-699.

Wernick, A. (1995). Selling funerals, imaging death. In M. Featherstone & A. Wernick, (Eds.). *Images of aging*, (pp. 280-293). London, U.K.: Routledge.

Wheeler, J.A., Gorey, K.M., & Greenblatt, B. (1998). Beneficial effects of volunteering for older volunteers and the people they serve: A meta-analysis.

International Journal of Aging and Human Development, 47, (1) 69-79.

White, H., McConnell, E., Clipp, E., Bynum, L., Teague, C., Navas, L., Craven, S. & Halbrecht, H. (1999). Surfing the net life: A review of the literature and a pilot study of computer use and quality of life. *Journal of Applied Gerontology*, 18(3), 358-378.

Whitfield, K., & Baker-Thomas, T. (1999). Individual differences in aging minorities. *International Journal Aging and Human Development*, 48(1), 73-79.

Whitford, G.S. (1997). Realities and hopes for older gay males. *Journal of Gay and Lesbian Social Services*, 6(1), 79-95.

Wicker, A.W. (1969). Attitude versus actions: The relationship of verbal and overt behavioral responses to attitude objects. *Journal of Social Issues*, 25(4), 41-78.

Wiehe, V.R. (1998). Elder abuse. In V.R. Wiehe, (Ed.). *Understanding family violence: Treating and preventing partner, child, sibling, and elder abuse*, (pp. 127-165). Thousand Oaks, CA: Sage.

Wierzbicki, M. (1986). Similarity of monozygotic and dizygotic twins in level and lability of subclinically depressed mood. *Journal of Clinical Psychology*, 42, 577-585.

Wiley, D., & Bortz, W.M. II, (1996). Sexuality and aging - Usual and successful. *Journals of Gerontology: Series A: Biological and Medical Sciences*, 51A(3), M142-M146.

Wilkins, R., Adams, O., & Brancker, A. (1991). Changes in mortality by income in urban Canada from 1971 to 1986. *Health Reports*, 1, 137-174.

Wilkinson, R.G. (1994). The epidemiological transition: From material scarcity to social disadvantage? *DAEDALUS, Journal of the American Academy of Arts and Sciences*, 123(4), 61-77.

Wilkinson, R.G. (1996). *Unhealthy societies: The afflictions of inequality*. New York, NY: Routledge.

Williams, A.P., Deber, R., Baranek, P., & Gildiner, A. (2001). From Medicare to home care: Globalization, state retrenchment, and the profitization of Canada's healthcare system. In P. Armstrong, H. Armstrong, & D. Coburn, (Eds.).*Unhealthy times. Political economy perspectives on health and care in Canada*, (pp.7-30). Toronto, ON: Oxford University Press.

Williams, D.R., & Wilson, C.M. (2001). Race, ethnicity and aging. In R.H. Binstock, & L.K. George, (Eds.). *Handbook of aging and the social sciences*, (5th Ed., pp. 160-178). New York, NY: Academic Press.

Williamson, J.B. & Watts-Roy, D.M. (1999). Framing the generational equity debate. In J.B. Williamson, D.M. Watts-Roy, & E.R. Kingson, (Eds.). *The generational equity debate*, (pp. 3-37). New York, NY: Columbia University Press.

Wilmoth, J.M. (2001). Living arrangements among older immigrants in the United States. *The Gerontologist*, 41, 228-238.

Winsborough, H., Bumpass, L., & Aquilino, W. (1991). The death of parents and the transitions to old age.

National Survey of Family and Households working paper no. 39. Madison, WI: University of Wisconsin.

Wise, D. (1993). *Firms, pension policy and early retirement. Age, work, and social security,* New York, NY: St. Martin's Press.

Wister, A., & Moore, C. (1998). First Nations elders in Canada: Issues, problems, successes in health care policy. In A.V. Wister, & G.M. Gutman, (Eds.). *Health systems and aging in selected Pacific Rim countries: Cultural diversity and change,* (pp.103-124). Vancouver, BC: Gerontology Research Centre, Simon Fraser University.

Wolf, D.A. (1990). Household patterns of older women. *Research on Aging, 12,* 463-486.

Wolf, D.A. & Soldo, B.J. (1988). Household composition choices of older unmarried women. *Demography, 25,* 387-403.

Wolf, D.A. (1995). Changes in the living arrangements of older women: An international comparison. *The Gerontologist, 35,* 724-731.

Wolf, R.S. (1999). Factors affecting elder abuse reporting to a state protective services program. *Gerontologist, 39,* 222-228.

Wolfson, M., Rowe, G., Gentleman, J.F., & Tomiak, M. (1993). Career earnings and death: A longitudinal analysis of older Canadian men. *Journal of Gerontology, 48*(4), 167-179.

Wong, P.T., & Reker, G.T. (1985). Stress, coping and well-being in Anglo and Chinese elderly. *Canadian Journal on Aging, 4,* 29-37.

Wood, J.B., & Wan, T. (1993). Ethnicity and minority issues in family caregiving to rural black elders. In C. Barresi, & D. Stull, (Eds.). *Ethnic elderly and longterm care.* New York, NY: Springer.

Woodbury, R.G. (1999). Early retirement in the United States. *Statistical Bulletin, 80*(3), 2-7.

World Health Organization. (1948). *Official records of the World Health Organization,* Number 2 : WHO Interim Commission, United Nations.

Wortman, C.B. & Conway, T.L. (1985). The role of social support in adaptation and recovery from physical illness. In S. Cohen & S.L. Syme, (Eds.). *Social Support and Health,* Orlando, FL: Academic Press.

Wotherspoon, T. (1994). *Colonization, self-determination and the health of Canada's First Nations peoples, Racial minorities medicine and health,* (pp. 247-268). Halifax, NS: Fernwood.

Wouters, C. (1990). Changing regimes of power and emotions at the end of life: The Netherlands 1930-1990. *The Netherlands Journal of Social Sciences, 26*(2), 151-167.

Wright, R.O. (1997). *Life and death in the United States.* Jefferson, NC: McFarland & Company.

Wu, Z. (1995). Remarriage after widowhood: A marital history study of older Canadians. *Canadian Journal on Aging, 14,* 719-736.

Wu, Z. (2000). *Cohabitation: An alternative form of family living.* Toronto, ON: Oxford University Press.

Wu. Z. & Wang, H. (1998). Third birth intentions and uncertainty in Canada. *Social Biology, 45,* 96-112.

Yaffe, K., Blackwell, T., Gore, R., Sands, L., Reus, V., & Browner, W. (1999). Depressive symptoms and cognitive decline in nondemented elderly women. *Archives of General Psychiatry, 56,* 425-431.

Yates, M.E., Tennstedt, S., & Chang, B.-H. (1999). Contributors to and mediators of psychological well-being for informal caregivers. *Journal of Gerontology: Psychological Sciences, 54B*(1), P12-P22.

Young, C.M. (1991). Changes in the demographic behaviour of migrants in Australia and the transition between generations. *Population Studies, 45,* 67-89.

Young, F.W., & Glasgow, N. (1998). Voluntary social participation and health. *Research on Aging, 20* (3) 339-362.

Yu, E.S. & Zhang, M.Y. (1987). Translation of instruments procedures, issues and dilemmas. In W.T. Liu, (Ed.). *A decade review of mental health research, training, and services,* (pp. 101-107). Pacific / Asian American Mental Research Centre.

Zal, H.M. (1992). *The sandwich generation: Caught between growing children and aging parents.* New York, NY: Insight Books.

Zanna, M.P., & Rempel, J.K. (1988). Attitudes: A new look at an old concept. In D. Bar-Tal & A.W. Kruglanski, (Eds.). *The social psychology of knowledge,* (pp.315-334). Cambridge, U.K.: Cambridge University Press.

Zarit, S.H. & Zarit, J.M. (1983). *The burden interview.* Los Angeles, CA: Ethel Percy Andrus Gerontology Centre.

Zenchuk, J. (1989). *We, the volunteers: From the volunteers' perspective.* (A profile of volunteers based on the 1987 National Survey on Volunteer Activity, Profile No. 31.) Ottawa, ON: Supply and Services.

Zimmerman, L., Mitchell, B., Wister, A., & Gutman, G. (2000). Unanticipated consequences: A comparison of expected and actual retirement timing among older women. *Journal of Women and Aging, 12,* (1-2), 109-128.

Zisook, S. & Shuchter, S.R. (1991). Depression through the first year after the death of a spouse. *American Journal of Psychology, 148,* 1346-1352.

Zong, L., & Li, P.S. (1994). *Different cultures or unequal life chances: A comparative analysis of race and health, Racial minorities medicine and health,* (pp. 113-126). Halifax, NS: Fernwood.

Zweibel, N.R., & Cassel, C.K. (1989). Treatment choices at the end of life: A comparison of decisions by older patients and their physician-selected proxies. *Gerontologist, 29*(5), 615-621.

INDEX